THE **BCOM** SOLUTION

Print + Online

BCOM⁸ delivers all the key terms and core concepts for the **Business Communication** course.

BCOM Online provides the complete narrative from the printed text with additional interactive media and the unique functionality of **StudyBits**—all available on nearly any device!

What is a StudyBit™? Created through a deep investigation of students' challenges and workflows, the StudyBit™ functionality of **BCOM Online** enables students of different generations and learning styles to study more effectively by allowing them to learn their way. Here's how they work:

WEAK

FAIR

STRONG

UNASSIGNED

COLLECT WHAT'S IMPORTANT
Create StudyBits as you highlight text, images or take notes!

RATE AND ORGANIZE STUDYBITS
Rate your understanding and use the color-coding to quickly organize your study time and personalize your flashcards and quizzes.

StudyBit™

TRACK/MONITOR PROGRESS
Use Concept Tracker to decide how you'll spend study time and study YOUR way!

85%

PERSONALIZE QUIZZES
Filter by your StudyBits to personalize quizzes or just take chapter quizzes off-the-shelf.

○ CORRECT

○ INCORRECT

○ INCORRECT

○ INCORRECT

BCOM8

Carol Lehman, Debbie DuFrene, Robyn Walker

Vice President, General Manager, 4LTR Press: Neil Marquardt

Product Director, 4LTR Press: Steven E. Joos

Product Manager: Laura Redden

Content/Media Developer: Patricia Hempel

Product Assistant: Lauren Dame

Marketing Manager: Jeff Tousignant

Marketing Coordinator: Casey Binder

Content Project Manager: Darrell E. Frye

Manufacturing Planner: Ron Montgomery

Production Service: Integra Software Services Pvt. Ltd.

Sr. Art Director: Bethany Casey

Internal Design: Lou Ann Thesing / Thesing Design

Cover Design: Curio Press, LLC/ Lisa Kuhn

Cover Image: Computer and tablet illustration: ©iStockphoto.com/ furtaev

Title Page Images: Jozsef Bagota/Shutterstock.com

Back Cover Images: Smart Phone illustration: ©iStockphoto.com/ dashadima

Intellectual Property Analyst: Diane Garrity

Intellectual Property Project Manager: Betsy Hathaway

Internal Ads:

Computer and tablet illustration: ©iStockphoto.com/ furtaev

Smart Phone illustration: ©iStockphoto.com/ dashadima

Last ad: Shutterstock.com/ Rawpixel.com

For product information and technology assistance, contact us at
Cengage Learning Customer & Sales Support, 1-800-354-9706

For permission to use material from this text or product,
submit all requests online at **www.cengage.com/permissions**
Further permissions questions can be e-mailed to
permissionrequest@cengage.com

Library of Congress Control Number: 2015958835

Student Edition ISBN: 978-1-305-66085-4

Student Edition with Online ISBN: 978-1-305-66086-1

Cengage Learning
20 Channel Center Street
Boston, MA 02210
USA

Cengage Learning is a leading provider of customized learning solutions with employees residing in nearly 40 different countries and sales in more than 125 countries around the world. Find your local representative at:
www.cengage.com

Cengage Learning products are represented in Canada by Nelson Education, Ltd.

To learn more about Cengage Learning Solutions, visit
www.cengage.com

Purchase any of our products at your local college store or at our preferred online store **www.cengagebrain.com**

Printed in the United States of America
Print Number: 01   Print Year: 2016

LEHMAN / DUFRENE

BCOM⁸

BRIEF CONTENTS

CONTENTS

PART 3
COMMUNICATION THROUGH VOICE AND DIGITAL MESSAGES 72

POST
SHARE
CONNECT

MAIL

☑ COMMUNICATION

Rawpixel/Shutterstock.com

5 Communicating Electronically 72

6 Delivering Good- and Neutral-News Messages 86

7 Delivering Bad-News Messages 106

PART 4

COMMUNICATION THROUGH REPORTS AND BUSINESS PRESENTATIONS 146

ra2studio/Shutterstock.com

PART 5
COMMUNICATION FOR EMPLOYMENT 224

Production Perig/Shutterstock.com

13 Preparing Résumés and Application Messages 224

14 Interviewing for a Job and Preparing Employment Messages 256

1 Establishing a Framework for Business Communication

Rawpixel/Shutterstock

LEARNING OBJECTIVES

After studying this chapter, you will be able to…

1-1 Define communication and describe the value of communication in business.

1-2 Explain the communication process model and the ultimate objective of the communication process.

1-3 Discuss how information flows in an organization.

1-4 Explain how legal and ethical constraints, diversity challenges, changing technology, and team environment act as contextual forces that influence the process of business communication.

After finishing this chapter, go to **PAGE 19** for **STUDY TOOLS.**

1-1 VALUE OF COMMUNICATION

We communicate to satisfy needs in both our work and private lives. Each of us wants to be heard, appreciated, and wanted. We also want to accomplish tasks and achieve goals. Generally people communicate for three basic purposes: to inform, to persuade, and to entertain. However, in the professional workplace some of these purposes have greater importance. Informing and persuading are common purposes of communication in the workplace; entertainment is less so. In addition, establishing and maintaining our credibility and positive relationships with others are also important purposes in an organizational setting.

What is communication? Communication is the process of exchanging and interpreting information and meaning between or among individuals through a system of symbols, signs, and behavior. In ideal situations, the goal is to reach mutual understanding. Studies indicate that managers typically spend 60% to 80% of their time involved in communication. In your career activities, you will communicate in a wide variety of ways, including

- listening and contributing to decision making and problem solving while attending meetings;
- writing various types of messages to inform and persuade others about your ideas and the services and products your organization provides;
- presenting information and persuasive messages to large and small groups in face-to-face and virtual environments;
- explaining and clarifying management procedures and work assignments;
- coordinating the work of various employees, departments, and other work groups;
- evaluating and counseling employees;
- promoting the company's products, services, and image using a variety of channels in various contexts.

> Abilities in writing and speaking are major determinants of career success.

1-2 THE COMMUNICATION PROCESS

Effective business communication is essential to success in today's work environments. Recent surveys of executives demonstrate that abilities in writing and speaking are major determinants of career success in many fields.[1] Although essential to personal and professional success, effective business communication does not occur automatically. Your own experiences likely have taught you that a message is not interpreted correctly just because you transmitted it. An effective communicator anticipates possible breakdowns in the communication process—the unlimited ways the message can be misunderstood. This mind-set provides the concentration to plan and design the initial message effectively and to be prepared to intervene at the appropriate time to ensure that the message received is on target.

Consider the transactional process model of communication presented in Figure 1.1. These seemingly simple steps actually represent a very complex process.

A number of communication process models exist. The transactional model is useful, though, because it illustrates the complexity of the communication process and reveals some of the challenges to effective

FIGURE 1.1 THE TRANSACTIONAL PROCESS MODEL OF COMMUNICATION

Cengage Learning

Interruptions or distractions can create barriers to understanding.

communication that might emerge in a communication encounter.

According to the transactional process model, two parties involved in a communication encounter are potentially both communicating at the same time, particularly if the encounter is face-to-face. That's because in face-to-face communication situations, parties to the encounter are continuously interpreting each other's nonverbal signals. Some scholars say more than 90% of the information in a face-to-face encounter may be sent nonverbally. But even in a cellphone conversation, silences and tone of voice may be interpreted in various ways. Even a written message may provide information about the writer that he or she did not intend to convey.

In an ideal communication situation, one party would be able to encode his or her message in such a way that the receiving party would understand it exactly as intended. However, this goal can be challenging for a variety of reasons, or what are called **interferences** or *barriers* to effective communication. For example,

- differences in educational level, experience, culture, and other characteristics of the sender and the receiver increase the complexity of encoding and decoding a message;
- physical interferences in the channel, including a noisy environment, interruptions, and uncomfortable surroundings, can occur;
- mental distractions, such as being

preoccupied with other matters and developing a response, rather than listening, create barriers to understanding.

Because of these barriers and because both parties to a communication encounter may be sending information both orally and nonverbally simultaneously, it can be very challenging to ensure that the information is received as intended. For this reason, it is particularly important to check for understanding rather than assume that it has taken place, particularly when communicating important messages to audiences that are less familiar to us.

You can surely compile a list of other barriers that affect your ability to communicate with friends, instructors, coworkers, supervisors, and others. By being aware of them, you can concentrate on removing these interferences.

1-3 COMMUNICATING WITHIN ORGANIZATIONS

To be successful, organizations must create an environment that energizes and encourages employees to accomplish tasks by promoting genuine openness and effective communication.

Organizational communication is communication that occurs with an organizational context. Regardless of your career or level within an organization, your ability to communicate will affect not only the success of the organization but also your personal success and advancement within that organization.

1-3a Communication Flow in Organizations

Communication occurs in a variety of ways within an organization. Some communication flows are planned and structured; others are not. Some communication flows can be formally depicted, whereas some defy description.

FORMAL AND INFORMAL COMMUNICATION NETWORKS

Communication within an organization involves both formal and informal networks.

- **Formal communication network.** This channel is typified by the formal organization chart, which is created by management to define individual and group relationships and to specify lines of responsibility. Essentially, the formal system is

interferences also called *barriers*; numerous factors that hinder the communication process

organizational communication the movement of information within the company structure

formal communication network a network of communication flow typified by the formal organization chart; dictated by the technical, political, and economic environment of the organization dictated by the managerial, technical, cultural, and structural environment of the organization. Within this system, people are required to behave and to communicate in certain ways simply to get work done.

- **Informal communication network.** This network, which is commonly called "the grapevine," continuously develops as people interact within the formal system to accommodate their social and psychological needs. Because the informal network undergoes continual changes and does not parallel the organizational chart, it cannot be depicted accurately by any graphic means.

The Formal Communication Network When employees rely almost entirely on the formal communication system as a guide to behavior, the system might be identified as a *bureaucracy*. Procedures manuals, job descriptions, organization charts, and other written materials dictate the required behavior. Communication channels are followed strictly, and red tape is abundant. Procedures are generally followed exactly; terms such as *rules* and *policies* serve as sufficient reasons for actions. Even the most formal organizations, however, cannot function long before an informal communication system emerges. As people operate within the organized system, they interact on a person-to-person basis and create an environment conducive to meeting their personal emotions, prejudices, likes, and dislikes.

In a workplace, employees are generally expected to satisfy a formal system of arriving at work on time, fulfilling their job duties, working well with others, and addressing their supervisor's requests. However, some employees may not openly accept these expectations and may arrive at work late and spend an undue amount of time "around the water cooler." If these informal practices become more widely spread, the purposes of the group may move from a focus on completing tasks to that of socializing with others or speculating about organizational events or activities. Obviously, the informal system benefits people because it meets their needs, but it also may affect the overall communication of the group in important ways.

The Informal Communication Network As people talk casually during breaks, text one another, or chat online, the focus usually shifts from topic to topic. One of the usual topics is work—job, company, supervisor, fellow employees. Even though the formal system includes definite communication channels, the grapevine tends to develop and operate within all organizations. Consider these points related to the accuracy and value of grapevine communication:

The office grapevine carries informal messages.

- As a communication network, the grapevine has a reputation for being speedy but inaccurate. In the absence of alarms, the grapevine might be the most effective way to let occupants know that the building is on fire. It certainly beats sending an email.

- Although the grapevine often is thought of as a channel for inaccurate communication, in reality it is no more or less accurate than other channels. Even formal communication can become inaccurate and filtered as it passes from level to level in the organizational hierarchy.

- The inaccuracy of the grapevine has more to do with the message input than with the output. For example, the grapevine is noted as a carrier of rumors, primarily because it carries informal messages. If the input is a rumor, and nothing more, the output obviously will be inaccurate. But the output might be an accurate description of the original rumor.

- In a business office, news about promotions, personnel changes, company policy changes, and annual salary adjustments often is communicated through the grapevine long before being conveyed through formal channels. The process works similarly in colleges, where information about instructors typically is not officially published but is known by students, often through word-of-mouth. How best to prepare for examinations, instructor attitudes on attendance and homework, and even faculty personnel changes are messages that travel over the grapevine.

- A misconception about the grapevine is that the message passes from person to person until it finally reaches a person who can't pass it on—the

informal communication network a network of communication flow that continuously develops as people interact within the formal system to accommodate their social and psychological needs end of the line. Actually, the grapevine works as a network channel. Typically, one person tells two or three others, who each tell two or three others, who each tell two or three others, and so on. Thus, the message might spread to a huge number of people in a short time, especially now that the grapevine includes digital forms of communication, such as social networking sites and Twitter.

- The grapevine has no single, consistent source. Messages might originate anywhere and follow various routes.

Due at least in part to widespread downsizing and corporate scandals during the last few years, employees in many organizations are demanding that they be better informed. Some companies have implemented new formal ways, such as newsletters and intranets, as well as informal ways, including blogs and Twitter, for sharing information with their internal constituents. Company openness with employees about management decisions and financial issues means conveying more information through the formal system rather than risking its miscommunication through informal channels. Online eyewear retailer Warby Parker, for example, grew from a small start-up to a 300-employee company in just three years. In order to keep the lines of communication open, the company has an "Ask Anything" segment of its weekly meetings, in which employees can ask anything. The Warby Parker Wiki enables employees to add notes from meetings, key lessons from the past or present, or team updates. The transparent company culture extends to each of its employees submitting weekly "happiness ratings" (on a 0 to 10 scale) and participating in quarterly, one-on-one, "360 reviews" in which brutal honesty is encouraged.[2]

An informal communication network will emerge from even the most carefully designed formal system. Managers who ignore this fact are attempting to manage blindfolded. Instead of denying or condemning the grapevine, the effective manager will learn to use the informal communication network. The grapevine, for instance, can be useful in counteracting rumors and false information.

downward communication a type of communication that flows from supervisor to employee, from policy makers to operating personnel, or from top to bottom on the organization chart

upward communication a type of communication that is generally a response to requests from supervisors

DIRECTIONS OF COMMUNICATION FLOW

The direction in which communication flows in an organization can be downward, upward, or horizontal, as shown in Figure 1-2. Because these three terms are used frequently in communication discussions, they deserve clarification. Although the concept of flow seems simple, direction has meaning for those participating in the organizational communication process.

Downward Communication The communication that flows from supervisor to employee, from policy makers to operating personnel, or from top to bottom on the organization chart is called **downward communication**. A simple policy statement from the top of the organization might grow into a formal plan for operation at lower levels. Teaching people how to perform their specific tasks is an element of downward communication. Another element is orientation to a company's rules, practices, procedures, history, and goals. Employees learn about the quality of their job performance through downward communication.

Downward communication normally involves both written and spoken methods and makes use of the following assumptions:

DOWNWARD COMMUNICATION

▸ People at high levels in the organization usually have greater knowledge of the organization's mission and goals than do people at lower levels.

▸ Both spoken and written messages tend to become larger as they move downward through organizational levels. This expansion results from attempts to prevent distortion and is more noticeable in written messages.

▸ Spoken messages are subject to greater changes in meaning than are written messages.

When a supervisor sends a message to a subordinate employee who then asks a question or nods in agreement, the employee has given signs of feedback. Feedback can flow both downward and upward in organizational communication through traditional as well as informal channels.

Upward Communication The information that flows from the front lines of an organization to the top is **upward communication**. When management requests information from lower organizational levels, the resulting information becomes feedback to that request. Employees talk to supervisors about themselves, their fellow employees, their work and methods of doing it, customer needs and perceptions, and their own perceptions of the organization. These comments are commonly feedback to the downward flow transmitted in

FIGURE 1.2 FLOW OF INFORMATION WITHIN AN ORGANIZATION

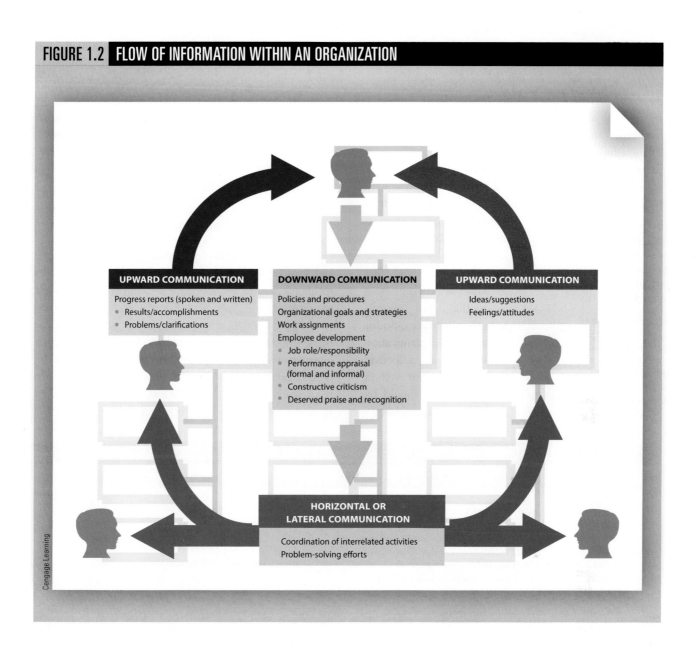

UPWARD COMMUNICATION

Progress reports (spoken and written)
- Results/accomplishments
- Problems/clarifications

DOWNWARD COMMUNICATION

Policies and procedures
Organizational goals and strategies
Work assignments
Employee development
- Job role/responsibility
- Performance appraisal (formal and informal)
- Constructive criticism
- Deserved praise and recognition

UPWARD COMMUNICATION

Ideas/suggestions
Feelings/attitudes

HORIZONTAL OR LATERAL COMMUNICATION

Coordination of interrelated activities
Problem-solving efforts

Cengage Learning

UPWARD COMMUNICATION

▶ Upward communication is primarily feedback to requests and actions of supervisors.

▶ Upward communication can be misleading because lower-level employees often tell their superiors what they think their superiors want to hear. Therefore, their messages might contradict their true observations and perceptions.

▶ Upward communication frequently involves risk to an employee and is dependent on trust in the supervisor.

▶ Employees will reject superficial attempts by management to obtain feedback.

both spoken and written forms by group meetings, emails, procedures or operations manuals, company news releases, the company intranet, and the grapevine.

Although necessary and valuable, upward communication involves risks. The following factors are important to consider when upward communication is involved:

When effectively used, upward communication keeps management informed about the feelings of lower-level employees, taps the expertise of employees, helps management identify both difficult and potentially promotable employees, and paves the way for even more effective downward communication. Upward communication is key to keeping employees engaged and informed and is especially critical in tapping the power of younger employees who expect to collaborate rather than to be supervised.[3]

Horizontal Communication Horizontal, or lateral, **communication** describes interactions between organizational units on the same hierarchical level. These interactions reveal one of the major shortcomings of organizational charts: they do not recognize the role of horizontal communication when they depict authority relationships by placing one box higher than another and define role functions by placing titles in those boxes. Yet management should realize that horizontal communication is the primary means of achieving coordination in a functional organizational structure. Units coordinate their activities to accomplish task goals just as adjacent workers in a production line coordinate their activities. So for horizontal communication to be maximally effective, the people in any system or organization should be available to one another.

horizontal (or lateral) communication
interactions between organizational units on the same hierarchical level

internal messages
messages intended for recipients within the organization

external messages
messages directed to recipients outside the organization

Many companies realize that the traditional hierarchy organized around functional units is inadequate for competing in increasingly competitive global markets. They value work teams that integrate work-flow processes rather than specialists in a single function or product. Such work teams can break down communication barriers between isolated functional departments, and communication patterns take on varying forms to accommodate team activities.

1-3b Levels of Communication

Communication can involve sending messages to both large and small audiences. **Internal messages** are intended for recipients within the organization. **External messages** are directed to recipients outside the organization. When considering the intended audience, communication can be described as taking place on five levels: intrapersonal, interpersonal, group, organizational, and public. Figure 1.3 depicts the five audience levels. An effective communicator has a clearly defined purpose for each message and selected strategies for targeting his or her intended audience.

FIGURE 1.3 — LEVELS OF COMMUNICATION

COMMUNICATION LEVELS	EXAMPLES
INTRAPERSONAL • Communication within oneself • Not considered by some to be true communication as it does not involve a separate sender and receiver	*Individual considers how others respond to his or her verbal and/or nonverbal communication.*
INTERPERSONAL • Communication between two people • Task goal to accomplish work confronting them • Maintenance goal to feel better about themselves and each other because of their interaction	*Supervisor and subordinate, two coworkers*
GROUP • Communication among more than two people • Goal of achieving greater output than individual efforts could produce	*Work group, project team, department meeting*
ORGANIZATIONAL • Groups combined in such a way that large tasks may be accomplished • Goal of providing adequate structure for groups to achieve their purposes	*Company, organization*
PUBLIC • The organization reaching out to its public to achieve its goals • Goal of reaching many with the same message	*Media advertisement, website communication, annual report*

Cengage Learning

CONTEXTUAL FORCES INFLUENCING BUSINESS COMMUNICATION

All communication occurs within a **context**, which is the situation or setting. Context can influence the content, the quality, and the effectiveness of a communication event. The effective communicator will recognize the importance of context, identify the contextual elements that will influence communication, and adjust messages in response. Four important contextual forces influence the communication process today and help determine and define the nature of the communication that should occur, as shown in Figure 1.4. These forces are legal and ethical constraints, diversity challenges, changing technology, and team environment.

1-4a Legal and Ethical Constraints

Legal and ethical constraints act as contextual or environmental forces on communication because they set boundaries in which communication rightfully occurs. International, federal, state, and local laws affect the way that various business activities are conducted. For instance, laws specify that certain information must be stated in messages that reply to credit applications and those dealing with the collection of outstanding debts. Furthermore, one's own ethical standards will often influence what a person is willing to say in a message. For example, a system of ethics built on honesty might require that the message provide full disclosure rather than a shrouding of the truth. Legal responsibilities, then, are the starting point for appropriate business communication. One's ethical belief system, or personal sense of

right and wrong behavior, provides further boundaries for professional activity.

The press is full of examples of unethical conduct in business and political communities, but unethical behavior is not relegated to the papers—it has far-reaching consequences. Those affected by decisions, the **stakeholders**, can include people inside and outside the organization. Employees and stockholders are obvious losers when a company fails. Competitors in the same industry also suffer because their strategies are based on what they perceive about their competition. Beyond that, financial markets as a whole suffer due to erosion of public confidence.

Business leaders, government officials, and citizens frequently express concern about the apparent erosion of ethical values in society. Even for those who want to do the right thing, matters of ethics are seldom clear-cut decisions of right versus wrong, and they often contain ambiguous

> **context** a situation or setting in which communication occurs
>
> **stakeholders** people inside and outside the organization who are affected by decisions

---

FIGURE 1.4 FACTORS INFLUENCING BUSINESS COMMUNICATION

LEGAL AND ETHICAL CONSTRAINTS	CHANGING TECHNOLOGY	DIVERSITY CHALLENGES	TEAM ENVIRONMENT
• International Laws	• Accuracy and Security Issues	• Cultural Differences	• Trust
• Domestic Laws	• Telecommunications	• Language Barriers	• Team Roles
• Codes of Ethics	• Software Applications	• Gender Issues	• Shared Goals and Expectations
• Stakeholder Interests	• "High-Touch" Issues	• Education Levels	• Synergy
• Ethical Frameworks	• Telecommuting	• Age Factors	• Group Reward
• Personal Values	• Databases	• Nonverbal Differences	• Distributed Leadership

Cengage Learning

elements. In addition, the pressure appears to be felt most strongly by lower-level managers, often recent business school graduates who are the least experienced at doing their jobs.

THE FOUNDATION FOR LEGAL AND ETHICAL BEHAVIOR

Although ethics is a common point of discussion, many find defining ethics challenging. Most people immediately associate ethics with standards and rules of conduct, morals, right and wrong, values, and honesty. Dr. Albert Schweitzer defined *ethics* as "the name we give to our concern for good behavior. We feel an obligation to consider not only our own personal well-being, but also that of others and of human society as a whole."[4] In other words, **ethics** refers to the principles of right and wrong that guide you in making decisions that consider the impact of your actions on others as well as yourself.

Although the recorded accounts of legal and ethical misconduct would seem to indicate that businesses are dishonest and unscrupulous, keep in mind that millions of business transactions are made daily on the basis of honesty and concern for others. Why should a business make ethical decisions? What difference will it make? Johan Karlstrom, global chief executive officer of construction giant Skanska, gave a powerful reply to these questions:

> When you understand that profits and a strong values base go together then you have a company that employees are so proud of. We want our team to feel that they're doing something that has a higher meaning, that they feel like "I'm part of something bigger, part of a bigger puzzle driving society in a positive direction."[5]

CAUSES OF ILLEGAL AND UNETHICAL BEHAVIOR

Understanding the major causes of illegal and unethical behavior in the workplace will help you become sensitive to signals of escalating pressure to compromise your values. Unethical corporate behavior can have a number of causes:

- **Excessive emphasis on profits.** Business managers are often judged and paid on their ability to increase business profits. This emphasis on profits might send a message that the end justifies the means.

- **Misplaced corporate loyalty.** A misplaced sense of corporate loyalty might cause an employee to do what seems to be in the best interest of the company, even if the act is illegal or unethical.

- **Obsession with personal advancement.** Employees who wish to outperform their peers or are working for the next promotion might feel that they cannot afford to fail. They might do whatever it takes to achieve the objectives assigned to them.

- **Expectation of not getting caught.** Thinking that the end justifies the means, employees often believe illegal or unethical activity will never be discovered. Unfortunately, a great deal of improper behavior escapes detection in the business world. Believing no one will ever find out, employees are tempted to lie, steal, and perform other illegal acts.

- **Unethical tone set by top management.** If top managers are not perceived as highly ethical, lower-level managers might be less ethical as a result. Employees have little incentive to act legally and ethically if their superiors do not set an example and encourage and reward such behavior. The saying "The speed of the leader is the speed of the pack" illustrates the importance of leading by example.

- **Uncertainty about whether an action is wrong.** Many times, company personnel are placed in situations in which the line between right and wrong is not clearly defined. When caught in this gray area, the perplexed employee asks, "How far is too far?"

- **Unwillingness to take a stand for what is right.** Often employees know what is right or wrong but are not willing to take the risk of challenging a wrong action. They might lack the confidence or skill needed to confront others with sensitive legal or ethical issues. They might remain silent and then justify their unwillingness to act.

FRAMEWORK FOR ANALYZING ETHICAL DILEMMAS

Determining whether an action is ethical can be difficult. Learning to analyze a dilemma from both legal and ethical perspectives will help you find a solution that conforms to your own personal values. Figure 1.5 shows the four conclusions you might reach when considering the advisability of a particular behavior.

Dimension 1: Behavior that is illegal and unethical

When considering some actions, you will reach the conclusion that they are both illegal and unethical. The law specifically outlines the "black" area—those alternatives that are clearly wrong—and your employer will expect you to become an expert in the laws that affect your particular area. When you encounter an unfamiliar area, you must investigate any possible legal implications. Obviously,

ethics the principles of right and wrong that guide one in making decisions that consider the impact of one's actions on others as well as on the decision maker

FIGURE 1.5 | FOUR DIMENSIONS OF BUSINESS BEHAVIOR

DIMENSION 1 Behavior that is illegal and unethical	**DIMENSION 2** Behavior that is illegal yet ethical
DIMENSION 3 Behavior that is legal yet unethical	**DIMENSION 4** Behavior that is both legal and ethical

Cengage Learning

obeying the law is in the best interest of all concerned: you as an individual, your company, and society. Contractual agreements between two parties also offer guidance for legal decision making. Frequently, your own individual sense of right and wrong will also confirm that the illegal action is wrong for you personally. In such situations, decisions about appropriate behavior are obvious.

Dimension 2: Behavior that is illegal yet ethical Occasionally, a businessperson will decide that even though a specific action is illegal, there is a justifiable reason to break the law. A case in point is a law passed in Vermont that makes it illegal for a pharmaceutical company to give any gift valued at more than $25 to doctors or their personnel.[6] Those supporting the law charge

ETHICAL DILEMMAS ...

Identifying ethical issues in typical workplace situations can be difficult, and coworkers and superiors might apply pressure for seemingly logical reasons. To illustrate, examine each of the following workplace situations for a possible ethical dilemma:

▶ In order to achieve profit expectations, a stockbroker hides the financial risk of an investment product from potential clients.

▶ To prevent an adverse effect on stock prices, corporate officers deliberately withhold information concerning a possible corporate takeover.

▶ To protect the organization, management decides not to publicize a design flaw in an automobile that could lead to possible injury and even death to consumers, because the announcement might result in legal action.

▶ A supervisor takes advantage of his position and threatens an employee with dismissal if she does not acquiesce to his inappropriate requests and language use.

▶ Angry because of an unfavorable performance appraisal of a colleague, an employee leaks confidential information to the colleague that creates distrust among others in the department and results in a lawsuit.

Your fundamental morals and values provide the foundation for making ethical decisions. However, as the previous examples imply, even seemingly minor concessions in day-to-day decisions can gradually weaken an individual's ethical foundation.

that the giving of freebies drives up medical costs by encouraging doctors to prescribe new, more expensive brand-name drugs. The law's opponents contend that the gifts do not influence doctors and are merely educational tools for new products. Although a pharmaceutical firm and its employees might see nothing wrong with providing gifts worth in excess of $25, they would be well advised to consider the penalty of $10,000 per violation before acting on their personal ethics. A better course of action would be to act within the law, possibly while lobbying for a change in the law.

Dimension 3: Behavior that is legal yet unethical If you determine that a behavior is legal and complies with relevant contractual agreements and company policy, your next step is to consult your company's or profession's *code of ethics*. This written document summarizes the company's or profession's *standards of ethical conduct*. Some companies refer to this document as a *credo*. If the behavior does not violate the code of ethics, then put it to the test of your own personal integrity. You may at times reject a legal action because it does not "feel right." Most Americans were appalled to learn that the marketing of sub-prime loans packaged as reputable securities has been blamed for causing the "Great Recession." Although they might have acted legally, their profiting at the expense of company employees, stockholders, and the public hardly seemed ethical. You might be faced with situations in which you reject a behavior that is legal because you would not be proud to have your family and community know that you engaged in it.

Dimension 4: Behavior that is both legal and ethical Decisions in this dimension are easy to make. Such actions comply with the law, company policies, and your professional and personal codes of ethics.

The Pagano Model offers a straightforward method for determining whether a proposed action is advisable.[7] For this system to work, you must answer the following six questions honestly:

1. Is the proposed action legal? (This is the core starting point.)
2. What are the benefits and costs to the people involved?
3. Would you want this action to be a universal standard, appropriate for everyone?
4. Does the action pass the light-of-day test? That is, if your action appeared on television or others learned about it, would you be proud?
5. Does the action pass the Golden Rule test? That is, would you want the same to happen to you?
6. Does the action pass the ventilation test? Ask the opinion of a wise friend with no investment in the outcome. Does this friend believe the action is ethical?

1-4b Diversity Challenges

Diversity in the workplace is another force influencing communication. Differences between the sender and the receiver in areas such as culture, age, gender, and education require sensitivity on the part of both parties so that the intended message is the one that is received.

Understanding how to communicate effectively with people from other cultures has become more integral to the work environment as many US companies are increasingly conducting business with international companies or becoming multinational. Even *when* a person can communicate, it may differ in other countries. For example, France's administrative court recently ruled that tech workers' right to health and rest was not sufficiently protected by existing laws. What this means is that a tech worker in France can choose to not check his work email during his legally mandated rest period and not face retribution.[8] For Americans, who may dare not even think of "unplugging," cultural differences might require adjustments to communication expectations.

When addressing cultural differences, successful communication must often span barriers of language and differing worldviews resulting from societal and religious beliefs and practices. When a person fails to consider these factors, communication suffers, and the result is often embarrassing and potentially costly. To be successful on an international scale, managers need to be aware of cultural differences and be willing to work to ensure that effective communication occurs despite these barriers.

Cultural blunders aren't limited to international communication situations, however. In April 2014, the magazine *Marie Claire* tweeted a

©Philip Date/Shutterstock.com

photo of American television personality Kendall Jenner wearing cornrows with the message "Kendall Jenner takes bold braids to a new epic level." Twitter followers interpreted the message to insinuate that Jenner had invented the braided hairstyle, and a flurry of responses ensued reminding the magazine that African Americans and others have worn the hairstyle for centuries.[9] This example shows how much "homework" is involved in maintaining good relations with customers or clients from other cultures, and the danger of instantaneous messaging. The potential barrier of language is obvious in international situations; however, successful communicators know that much more is involved when interacting across cultures, genders, ages, abilities, and other differences, regardless of national boundaries.

COMMUNICATION OPPORTUNITIES AND CHALLENGES IN DIVERSITY

As world markets continue to expand, US employees at home and abroad will be doing business with more people from other countries. You might find yourself working abroad for a large American company, an international company with a plant in the United States, or a company with an ethnically diverse workforce. Regardless of the workplace, your **diversity skills**—that is, your ability to communicate effectively with both men and women of all ages, cultures, and minority groups—will affect your success in today's culturally diverse global economy.

Workplace diversity can lead to misunderstandings and miscommunications, but it also poses opportunities to improve both workers and organizations. Employees must be prepared to communicate effectively with workers of different nationalities, genders, races, ages, abilities, and other characteristics.

Being a part of a diverse workforce will require you to communicate with *everyone* and to support colleagues in reaching their fullest potential and contributing to the company's goals. To lessen miscommunication, which inevitably occurs, increasing numbers of companies have undertaken *diversity initiatives* and are providing diversity training seminars to help workers understand and appreciate gender and age differences and the cultures of coworkers.

CULTURE AND COMMUNICATION

The way messages are decoded and encoded is not just a function of the experiences, beliefs, and assumptions of the person sending or receiving those messages but also is shaped by the society in which he or she lives.

People learn patterns of behavior from their culture. The *culture* of a people is the product of their living experiences within their own society. Culture could be described as "the way of life" of a people and includes a vast array of behaviors and beliefs. These patterns affect how people perceive the world, what they value, and how they act. Differing patterns can also create barriers to communication.

BARRIERS TO INTERCULTURAL COMMUNICATION

Because cultures give different definitions of such basics of interaction as values and norms, people raised in two different cultures can clash in various ways.

- **Ethnocentrism.** Problems occur between people of different cultures primarily because people tend to assume that their own cultural norms are the right way to do things. They wrongly believe that the specific patterns of behavior desired in their own cultures are universally valued. This belief, known as **ethnocentrism**, is certainly natural; but learning about other cultures and developing sensitivity will help minimize ethnocentric reactions when dealing with other cultures.

- **Stereotypes.** We often form a mental picture of the main characteristics of another group, creating preformed ideas of what people in this group are like. These pictures, called **stereotypes**, influence the way we interact with members of the other group. When we observe a behavior that conforms to the stereotype, the validity of the preconceived notion is reinforced. We often view the other person as a representative of a class of people rather than as an individual. People of all cultures have stereotypes about other cultural groups they have encountered. These stereotypes can interfere with communication when people interact on the basis of the imagined representative and not the real individual.

- **Interpretation of time.** The study of how a culture perceives time and its use is called **chronemics.** In the United States, we have a saying that "time is money." Canadians, like some northern Europeans who are also concerned about punctuality, make appointments, keep them, and complete them, and waste no time in the process. In some other cultures, time is the cheapest

diversity skills the ability to communicate effectively with both men and women of all ages, cultures, and minority groups

ethnocentrism the assumption that one's own cultural norms are the right way to do things

stereotypes mental pictures that one group forms of the main characteristics of another group, creating preformed ideas of what people in this group are like

chronemics the study of how a culture perceives time and its use

Although Americans and some Europeans believe "time is money," other cultures are less concerned about economy of time. Above, the Prague Orloj astronomical clock, installed in 1410, is the oldest still-working clock in the world.

cultural meanings—the familiar North American symbol for "okay" means zero in France, money in Japan, and an expression of vulgarity in Brazil. Similarly, eye contact, posture, and facial expressions carry different meanings throughout the world.

- **Translation limitations.** Words in one language do not always have an equivalent meaning in other languages, and the concepts the words describe are often different as well. Translators can be helpful, but keep in mind that a translator is working with a second language and must listen to one language, mentally cast the words into another language, and then speak them. This process is difficult and opens the possibility that the translator will fall victim to one or more cultural barriers. Even if you cannot speak or write another language fluently, people from other cultures will appreciate simple efforts to learn a few common phrases.

commodity and an inexhaustible resource; time represents a person's span on Earth, which is only part of eternity. To these cultures, engaging in long, casual conversations prior to serious discussions or negotiations is time well spent in establishing and nurturing relationships. On the other hand, the time-efficient American businessperson is likely to fret about wasting precious time.

- **Personal space requirements.** Space operates as a language just as time does. The study of cultural space requirements is known as **proxemics**. In all cultures, the distance between people functions in communication as "personal space" or "personal territory." In the United States, for example, for intimate conversations with close friends and relatives, individuals are willing to stay within about a foot and a half of each other; for casual conversations, up to two or three feet; for job interviews and personal business, four to twelve feet; and for public occasions, more than twelve feet. However, in many cultures outside the United States, closer personal contact is accepted, or greater distance might be the norm.

- **Body language.** The study of body language is known as **kinesics**. Body language is not universal, but instead is learned from one's culture. Even the most basic gestures have varying

proxemics the study of cultural space requirements

kinesics the study of body language, which is not universal, but instead is learned from one's culture

DEVELOPING CULTURAL INTELLIGENCE

One way to improve your ability to communicate with those from other cultures is to develop your *cultural intelligence*. Cultural intelligence can be defined as "a person's capability to adapt as he or she interacts with others from different cultural regions."[10] There are three elements of cultural intelligence:

- Cognitive knowledge: The possession of a wide-ranging information base about a variety of people and their cultural customs.
- Motivation: Healthy self-efficacy, persistence, goals, value questioning, and integration.
- Behavioral adaptability: The capacity to interact in a wide range of situations, environments, and diverse groups.

The Global Literacy Competence (GLC) Model offers a road map to begin to conceptualize the stages of cultural intelligence development (see Figures 1.6 and 1.7). The GLC assumes that ascending to a higher level of global functioning is not only possible but is required for excellence in a cross-cultural environment. To do so requires a commitment to personal growth, openness, and continuous learning about other cultures and customs.

1-4c Changing Technology

Electronic tools create opportunities that range from new kinds of communications to improved quality of the messages themselves. Electronic tools, such as

FIGURE 1.6 GLOBAL LEADERSHIP COMPETENCY MODEL

Cengage Learning

Source: C. O. Chin, J. Gu, and S. Tubbs. (2001). Developing global leadership competencies. *Journal of Leadership Studies*, 7(4): 20–35.

iStockphoto.com/IS_ImageSource

It's critical in business to develop a cultural intelligence.

the Internet, intranets, document production software, multimedia presentations, web publishing tools, and email, can help people in various ways, such as by (1) collecting and analyzing data, (2) shaping messages to be clearer and more effective, and (3) communicating quickly and efficiently with others in geographically dispersed locations.

Using various communication technologies, individuals can often work in their homes or other remote locations and send and receive work from the company office electronically. **Telecommuting** (also referred to as *teleworking*) offers various advantages, including reduced travel time and increased work flexibility. Laptops and smartphones provide computing power and connectivity for professionals wherever they are. Although the public Internet is accessible to everyone and offers a wide array of information, organizations are establishing intranets, which can be understood as a private analog of the Internet or as a private extension of the Internet confined to a particular organization. An intranet is a computer network that uses Internet Protocol technology to share information, operational systems, or computing services within an organization. Increasingly, intranets are being used to deliver tools, for example, collaboration (to facilitate working in groups and teleconferencing) or sophisticated corporate directories, sales and

telecommuting also called *teleworking*; working at home or other remote locations and sending and receiving work from the company office electronically

FIGURE 1.7 | LEVELS OF GLOBAL COMMUNICATION COMPETENCE

LEVEL	DESCRIPTION
Awareness	This is the novice stage; with exposure come vague impressions. They are brief sensations of which people are barely conscious. At this level, there is little or no sense-making, but a dawning awareness of something different and possibly interesting, strange, frightening, or annoying.
Understanding	At this stage individuals begin to exhibit some conscious effort to learn why people are the way they are and why people do what they do. They display interest in those who are different from themselves. Sanchez et al. (2000) refer to this as the "transition stage." This is a stage whereby the individual collects information through reading, observation, and real experiences as well as by asking questions to learn more about the new cultural phenomenon.
Appreciation	Individuals begin to take a "leap of faith" and experience a genuine tolerance of different points of view. Through understanding the basic differences as well as areas where one thinks, acts, and reacts similarly, a positive feeling towards the "new" cultural phenomenon begins to form. Individuals not only put up with the "new" culture but also display a genuine appreciation of and, in some cases, preference for certain aspects of the "new" culture.
Acceptance	In this stage, the possibility of interaction between cultures increases appreciably. People are more sophisticated both in terms of recognizing commonalities and in terms of effectively dealing with differences. At this stage, there is the willingness to acquire new patterns of behavior and attitudes. This is a departure from the ethnocentric notion that "my way is the best way and the only way."
Internalization	At this stage, the individual goes beyond making sense of information and actually embarks on a deliberate internalization process, with profound positive feelings for the once unknown cultural phenomenon. At this stage, there is a clear sense of self-understanding leading to readiness to act and interact with the locals/nationals in a natural, appropriate, and culturally effective manner.
Adaptation	Cultural competence becomes a way of life. It is internalized, to the degree that it is out of one's consciousness, thus becomes effortless and second nature. Individuals at this level display and possess (1) The capacity for gathering knowledge about different cultures, (2) drive or motivation, and (3) behavioral adaptability—the capacity to act effectively based upon their knowledge and motivation.

Source: C. O. Chin, J. Gu, and S. Tubbs. (2001). Developing global leadership competencies. *Journal of Leadership Studies*, 7(4): 20–35.

customer relationship management tools, and project management, to advance productivity.

Intranets are also being used as corporate culture-change platforms. For example, large numbers of employees discussing key issues in an intranet forum application could lead to new ideas in management, productivity, quality, and other corporate issues. When part of an intranet is made accessible to customers and others outside the business, that segment becomes part of an extranet, or a network between organizations.

A related development is the growing use of **social media** in organizations. Social media is "a group of Internet-based applications that build on the ideological and technological

social media a group of Internet-based applications that allow the creation and exchange of user-generated content

foundations of Web 2.0, and that allow the creation and exchange of user-generated content." Social media depends on mobile and Web-based technologies to create highly interactive platforms through which individuals and communities share, co-create, discuss, and modify user-generated content. It introduces substantial and pervasive changes to communication between organizations, communities, and individuals. In a business context, social media provides opportunities to engage in marketing research, communication, sales promotions/discounts, and relationship development/loyalty programs.

Although many benefits are provided through the use of technology in organizations, challenges or risks also must be recognized. Knowing how to "tunnel" through the vast amounts of irrelevant information available on the "digital highway" to find what you want can be overwhelming. The experience can also be expensive in terms of human time spent and charges incurred for online time. Locating information from electronic sources requires that you know the search procedures and methods for constructing an effective search strategy. There are also possible legal liabilities that can arise from improper use of technological resources.

Effective use of various communication technologies helps ensure timely, targeted messages and responses and helps build interpersonal relationships. This responsiveness leads to positive interactions with colleagues and strong customer commitment.

1-4d Team Environment

As firms around the world face problems of decreasing productivity, faltering product quality, and worker dissatisfaction, work teams are seen as a way to help firms remain globally competitive. Decentralized decision making enables teams of people to communicate in a peer-to-peer fashion, rather than following traditional lines of authority, and new technologies give employees the ability to communicate easily and openly with one another and with those outside the firm.

Although worker involvement in the management process has long been the hallmark of Japanese business, many businesses in the United States and elsewhere are empowering self-directed work teams to accomplish various assignments.[12] The list of companies using self-directed work teams is diverse, including Hunt-Wesson, Federal Express, Kraft Foods, Inc., Hewlett-Packard, Southwest Airlines, Toyota, Motorola, General Electric, and Corning.

WORK TEAM DEFINED

The terms *team, work team, group, work group, cross-functional team,* and *self-directed team* are often used interchangeably.[13] Whatever the title, a **team** is a small number of people with complementary skills who work together for a common purpose. Team members set their own goals, in cooperation with management, and plan how to achieve those goals and how their work is to be accomplished. The central organizing element of a team is that it has a common purpose and measurable goals for which the team can be held accountable, independent of its individual members. Employees in a self-directed work team handle a wide array of functions and work with a minimum of direct supervision.[14]

Some major strengths of teams are as follows:[15]

- Teams make workers happier by causing them to feel that they are shaping their own jobs.

- Teams increase efficiency by eliminating layers of managers whose job was once to pass orders downward.

- Teams enable a company to draw on the skills and imagination of a whole workforce.

A key element in team success is the concept of **synergy**, defined as a situation in which the whole is greater than the sum of the parts. Teams provide a depth of expertise that is unavailable at the individual level. Teams open lines of communication that then lead to increased

team a small number of people with complementary skills who work together for a common purpose

synergy a situation in which the whole is greater than the sum of the parts

To improve group communication, time needs to be set aside to assess the quality of interaction. Questions to pose about the group process might include the following:

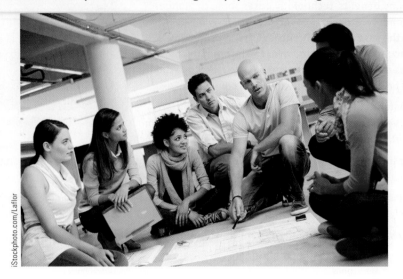

Is the group dealing with conflict in a positive way?

What in the group process is going well?

What roles are members playing? For instance, is one person dominating while others contribute little or nothing?

What are our common goals?

What about the group process could be improved?

iStockphoto.com/Laflor

interaction among employees and between employees and management. The result is that teams help companies reach their goals of delivering higher-quality products and services faster and with more cost-effectiveness.

COMMUNICATION DIFFERENCES IN WORK TEAMS

In the past, most businesses were operated in a hierarchical fashion, with most decisions made at the top and communication following a top-down/bottom-up pattern. Communication patterns are different in successful team environments as compared with traditional organizational structures:

- Trust building is the primary factor that changes the organization's communication patterns.
- Open meetings are an important method for enhancing communication, as they educate employees about the business while building bridges of understanding and trust.
- Shared leadership, which involves more direct and effective communication between management and its internal customers, is common.
- Listening, problem solving, conflict resolution, negotiation, and consensus become important factors in group communication.
- Information flows vertically up to management and down to workers, as well as horizontally among team members, other teams, and supervisors.

Communication is perhaps the single most important aspect of successful teamwork. Open lines of communication increase interaction between employees

and management. All affected parties should be kept informed as projects progress.

MAXIMIZING WORK TEAM EFFECTIVENESS

Grouping employees into a team structure does not mean that they will automatically function as a team. A group must go through a developmental process to begin to function as a team. Members need training in such areas as problem solving, goal setting, and conflict resolution. Teams must be encouraged to establish the "three Rs"—roles, rules, and relationships.[16]

The self-directed work team can become the basic organizational building block to best ensure success in dynamic global competition. Skills for successful participation in team environments are somewhat different from those necessary for success in old-style organizations. Today successful business communicators and team members must possess the ability to

- give and take constructive criticism, actively listen, clearly impart one's views to others, and provide meaningful feedback;
- break down emotional barriers, such as insecurity or condescension;
- promote team functioning by removing process barriers, such as rigid policies and procedures;
- understand the feelings and needs of coworkers so members feel comfortable stating their opinions and discussing the strengths and weaknesses of the team;
- overcome cultural barriers, such as stereotyped roles and responsibilities, that can separate workers from management;[17]

FIGURE 1.8 CHARACTERISTICS OF DEFENSIVE AND SUPPORTIVE COMMUNICATION CLIMATES

DEFENSIVE

1. Evaluation. To pass judgment on another.

2. Control. To try to do something to another; to try to change behavior or attitudes of others.

3. Strategy. To manipulate another, to engage in multiple or ambiguous motivations.

4. Neutrality. To express a lack of concern for the other; the clinical, person-as-object-of-study attitude.

5. Superiority. To communicate that you are superior in position, wealth, intelligence, and so on, to arouse feelings of inadequacy in others.

6. Certainty. To seem to know the answers and be dogmatic wanting to win an argument rather than solve a problem; seeing one's ideas as truths to be defended.

SUPPORTIVE

1. Description. Nonjudgmental. To ask questions, present feelings, refrain from asking the other to change his or her behavior.

2. Problem orientation. To convey a desire to collaborate in solving a mutual problem or defining it; to allow the other to set his or her goals.

3. Spontaneity. To express naturalness, free of deception; straightforwardness; uncomplicated motives.

4. Empathy. To respect the other person and show it; to identify with his or her problems; to share his or her feelings.

5. Equality. To be willing to enter into participative planning with mutual trust and respect; to attach little importance to differences of worth, status, and so on.

6. Provisionalism. To be willing to experiment with your own behavior; to investigate issues rather than taking sides; to solve problems, not debate.

Source: Jack Gibb. (1961). Defensive communication, *Journal of Communication*, 11: 141–48.

- **apply leadership skills in a dynamic group setting that results in team success. In dynamic team leadership, referred to as *distributed leadership*, the role of leader can alternate among members, and more than one leadership style can be active at any given time.**[18]

Gender, cultural, and age differences among members of a team can present barriers to team communication. Knowing what behaviors can limit the group process is imperative to maximizing results. Team members might need awareness training to assist in recognizing behaviors that may hinder team performance and in overcoming barriers that can limit the effectiveness of their communication.

VIRTUAL TEAMS

The convergence of the last three developments—globalization and increased reliance on technology and teams—has resulted in the increased use of a special kind of team—the virtual team. A virtual team is defined as "a group of geographically, organizationally and/or time dispersed workers brought together by information and telecommunication technologies to accomplish one or more organizational tasks."[19] Members of virtual teams communicate electronically and may never meet face-to-face.

As with most technology-enabled developments, both advantages and disadvantages can result from virtual team use. Advantages include increased productivity, extended market opportunities, and improved knowledge transfer among employees across an organization.

Common disadvantages include reduced communication effectiveness caused by more limited access to various communication media, poor leadership, and incompetent team members. These disadvantages can be overcome through effective virtual team training, proper goal setting, team building, and successful coordination.

STUDY TOOLS 1

LOCATED AT BACK OF THE TEXTBOOK
☐ Tear-Out Chapter Review Card

LOCATED AT WWW.CENGAGEBRAIN.COM
☐ Review Key Term flashcards and create your own cards

☐ Track your knowledge and understanding of key concepts in business communication

☐ Complete practice and graded quizzes to prepare for tests

☐ Complete interactive content within BCOM8 Online

☐ View the chapter highlight boxes for BCOM8 Online

2

Focusing on Interpersonal and Group Communication

Rawpixel/Shutterstock.com

LEARNING OBJECTIVES

After studying this chapter, you should be able to ...

2-1 Explain how behavioral theories about human needs, trust and disclosure, and motivation relate to business communication.

2-2 Describe the role of nonverbal messages in communication.

2-3 Identify aspects of effective listening.

2-4 Identify factors affecting group and team communication.

2-5 Discuss aspects of effective meeting management.

After finishing this chapter, go to **PAGE 35** for **STUDY TOOLS.**

2-1 BEHAVIORAL THEORIES THAT IMPACT COMMUNICATION

Interpersonal intelligence pertains to the ability to read, empathize with, and understand others.[1] People with interpersonal intelligence are good with people and thrive in social interaction. Rather than being a quality that some are born with and others are not, interpersonal intelligence can be improved by broadening your understanding of human behavior and motivation and by practicing certain behaviors when in interpersonal situations. Knowledge from the fields of sociology and psychology is helpful to understanding human needs and providing you with valuable insights about how to achieve effective communication in the workplace.

2-1a Recognizing Human Needs

Psychologist Abraham Maslow developed the concept of a hierarchy of needs through which people progress. In our society, most people have reasonably satisfied their two lower-level needs: (1) physiological needs (food and basic provision) and (2) security and safety needs (shelter and protection from the elements and physical danger). Beyond these two basic need levels, people progress to satisfy the three upper-level needs: (3) social needs for love, acceptance, and belonging; (4) ego or esteem needs to be heard, appreciated, and wanted; and (5) self-actualizing needs, including the need to achieve one's fullest potential through professional, philanthropic, political, educational, and artistic channels.

As people satisfy needs at one level, they move on to the next. The levels that have been satisfied still are present, but their importance diminishes. Effective communicators are able to identify and appeal to need levels in various individuals or groups. Advertising is designed to appeal to need levels. Luxury car and dream vacation ads appeal to ego needs; teeth whitening and anti-aging product messages appeal to social needs; and identity theft, health and fitness, and environmentally friendly commercials appeal to security and safety needs. Efforts to help employees satisfy their needs are essential, since a satisfied worker is generally more productive than a dissatisfied one. In communication activities, a sender's message is more likely to appeal to the receiver if the receiver's need is accurately identified and addressed.

> Effective communicators are able to identify and appeal to need levels in various persons or groups.

2-1b Stroking

People engage in communication with others in the hope that the outcome might lead to mutual trust, mutual pleasure, and psychological well-being. The communication exchange is a means of sharing information about things, ideas, tasks, and selves.

Each communication interaction, whether casual or formal, provides an emotional **stroke** that can have either a positive or a negative effect on your feelings about yourself and others. Getting a pat on the back from the supervisor, receiving a congratulatory phone call or text message, and being listened to by another person are examples of everyday positive strokes. Negative strokes might include receiving a hurtful comment, being avoided or left out of conversation, and receiving a reprimand from a superior. By paying attention to the importance of strokes, managers can greatly improve communication and people's feelings about their work.

2-1c Exploring the Johari Window

As relationships develop, the people involved continue to learn about each other and themselves, as shown by the Johari Window in Figure 2.1. Area I, the free or open area, represents what we know about ourselves and what others know about us. Area II, the blind area, designates those things others know about us but that we don't know about ourselves. For example, you are the only person who can't see your physical self as it really is. Things we know about ourselves but that others don't know about us occupy the hidden or secret area III. Area IV includes the unknown: things we don't know about ourselves and others don't know about us, such as our ability to handle emergency situations if we've never been faced with them.

Each of the window areas can vary in size according to the degree to which we learn about ourselves and are willing

interpersonal intelligence the ability to read, empathize, and understand others

stroke emotional response one gets in a communication interaction that has either a positive or negative effect on feelings about oneself and others

FIGURE 2.1 **THE JOHARI WINDOW**

KNOWN TO SELF

NOT KNOWN TO SELF

KNOWN TO OTHERS

I
Free or Open Area

II
Blind Area

NOT KNOWN TO OTHERS

III
Hidden Area

IV
Unknown Area

© Cengage Learning

parents, deeper, personal feelings are entrusted to each other.

The idea that trust and openness lead to better communication between two people also applies to groups. Managers engaged in *organizational development* (OD) are concerned with developing successful organizations by building effective small groups. They believe small-group effectiveness evolves mostly from a high level of mutual trust among group members. The aim of OD is to open emotional as well as task-oriented communication. To accomplish this aim, groups often become involved in encounter sessions designed to enlarge the open areas of the Johari Window.[2]

2-1d Contrasting Management Styles

Douglas McGregor, a management theorist, attempted to distinguish between the older, traditional view that workers are concerned only about satisfying lower-level needs and the more contemporary view that productivity can be enhanced by assisting workers in satisfying higher-level needs. Under the older view, management exercised strong control, emphasized the job to the exclusion of concern for the individual, and sought to motivate solely through external incentives—a job and a paycheck. McGregor labeled this management style Theory X. Under the contemporary style, Theory Y, management strives to balance control and individual freedom. By treating the individual as a mature person, management lessens the need for external motivation; treated as adults, people will act as adults.

The situational leadership model developed by Paul Hersey and Kenneth Blanchard does not prescribe a single leadership style, but advocates that what is appropriate in each case depends on the follower (subordinate) and the task to be performed. **Directive behavior** is characterized by the leader's giving detailed rules and instructions and monitoring closely that they are followed. The leader decides what is to be done and how. In contrast, **supportive behavior** is characterized by the leader's listening, communicating, recognizing, and encouraging. Different degrees

to disclose things about ourselves to others. Reciprocal sharing occurs when people develop *trust* in each other. When a confidant demonstrates that he or she can be trusted, trust is reinforced and leads to an expansion of the open area of the Johari Window. Usually we are willing to tell people about various things that aren't truly personal. But we share personal thoughts, ambitions, and inner feelings only with selected others—those whom we have learned to trust. The relationships existing between supervisor and employee, doctor and patient, and lawyer and client are those of trust, but only in specific areas. In more intimate relationships with significant others, siblings, and

directive behavior
characterized by leaders who give detailed rules and instructions and monitor closely that they are followed

supportive behavior
characterized by leaders who listen, communicate, recognize, and encourage their followers

of directive and supportive behavior can be desirable, given the situation.[3] Combining the ideas of Maslow and McGregor with those of Hersey and Blanchard leads to the conclusion that "the right job for the person" is a better philosophy than "the right person for the job."

The **Total Quality Management** movement focuses on creating a more responsible role for the worker in an organization. In a Total Quality Management environment, decision-making power is distributed to the people closest to the problem, who usually have the best information sources and solutions. Each employee, from the president to the custodian, is expected to solve problems, participate in team-building efforts, and expand the scope of his or her role in the organization. The goal of employee empowerment is to build a work environment in which all employees take pride in their work accomplishments and begin motivating themselves from within rather than through traditional extrinsic incentives.[4] Managers of many companies understand that empowering employees to initiate continuous improvements is critical for survival. Only companies producing quality products and services will survive in today's world market.

Leadership studies have taken a new turn in recent years with the emergence of the social constructionist view of leadership. A social constructionist view sees leadership differently than the psychological approach of the management discipline. A social constructionist view sees leadership as a co-constructed reality that emerges from the interaction of social actors. What this means is that certain leadership behaviors are acceptable to group members while others are not. Because of this, a person may position him- or herself as a leader, but others may not perceive these communication behaviors as corresponding with their perception of a leader.

From this perspective, the leader of a group may not be the formally appointed manager or in certain situations, as discussed in Chapter 1, leadership may be distributed among team members. The value of this approach to leadership is its focus on the importance of communication practices in creating leadership.

NONVERBAL COMMUNICATION

Managers use verbal and nonverbal messages to communicate ideas to employees. *Verbal* means "through the use of words," either written or spoken. *Nonverbal* means "without the use of words." Although major attention in communication study is given to verbal messages, studies show that nonverbal elements can account for more than 90% of the total meaning of a message.[5] Nonverbal communication includes *metacommunication* and *kinesic messages*.

2-2a Metacommunication

A **metacommunication** is a message that, although *not* expressed in words, accompanies a message that *is* expressed in words. For example, "Don't be late for work" communicates caution; yet the sentence might imply (but not express in words) such additional ideas as "You are frequently late, and I'm warning you," or "I doubt your dependability." "Your solution is perfect" might also convey a metacommunication such as "You are efficient," or "I certainly like your work." Whether you are speaking or writing, you can be confident that those who receive your messages will

> **Total Quality Management** focuses on creating a more responsible role for the worker in an organization by distributing decision-making power to the people closest to the problem, empowering employees to initiate continuous improvements

> **metacommunication** a nonverbal message that, although not expressed in words, accompanies a message that is expressed in words

wavebreakmedia/Shutterstock.com

be sensitive to the messages expressed in words and to the accompanying messages that are present but not expressed in words.

2-2b Kinesic Messages

People constantly send meaning through kinesic communication, an idea expressed through nonverbal behavior. In other words, receivers gain additional meaning from what they see and hear—the visual and the vocal:

- **Visual kinesic communication**—gestures, winks, smiles, frowns, sighs, attire, grooming, and all kinds of body movements.
- **Vocal kinesic communication**—intonation, projection, and resonance of the voice.

Following are some examples of kinesic messages and the meanings they can convey.

Action	Possible Kinesic Message
A wink or light chuckle follows a statement.	"Don't believe what I just said."
A manager is habitually late for staff meetings and with email replies.	"My time is more important than yours. You can wait for me." Alternately, the action might be ordinary for a manager not born in the United States.
A group leader sits at a position other than at the head of the table.	"I want to demonstrate my equality with other members."
An employee wears clothing that reveals tattoos, which violates the company's dress code.	"Rules are for other people; I can do what I want." Alternately, "I do not understand the expectations."
A job applicant submits a résumé containing errors.	"My language skills are deficient." Alternately, "I didn't care to do my best."

2-2c Understanding Nonverbal Messages

Metacommunications and kinesic messages have characteristics that all communicators should take into account.

visual kinesic communication gestures, winks, smiles, frowns, sighs, attire, grooming, and all kinds of body movements

vocal kinesic communication intonation, projection, and resonance of the voice

- **Nonverbal messages cannot be avoided.** Both written and spoken words convey ideas in addition to the ideas contained in the words used. All actions—and even the lack of action—have meaning to those who observe them.

- **Nonverbal messages can have different meanings for different people.** If a team member smiles after making a statement, one member might conclude that the speaker was trying to be funny; another might conclude that the speaker was pleased about having made such a great contribution; another might see the smile as indicating friendliness.

- **Nonverbal messages vary between and within cultures.** Not only do nonverbal messages have different meanings from culture to culture, but men and women from the same culture typically exhibit different body language. As a rule, US men make less body contact with other men than do women with women. Acceptable male body language might include a handshake or a pat on the back, whereas women are afforded more flexibility in making body contact with each other.

- **Nonverbal messages can be intentional or unintentional.** "You are right about that" can be intended to mean "I agree with you" or "You are right on *this* issue, but you have been wrong on all others discussed."

- **Nonverbal messages can contradict the accompanying verbal message and affect whether your message is understood or believed.** The adage "actions speak louder than words" reveals much about how people perceive messages. Picture a person who says, "I'm happy to be here," but looks at the floor, talks in a weak and halting voice, and clasps his hands timidly in front of his body. Because his verbal and nonverbal messages are contradictory, his audience might not trust his words. Similarly, consider the negative effect of a sloppy personal appearance by a job candidate.

- **Nonverbal messages can receive more attention than verbal messages.** If a supervisor repeatedly glances at his smartphone for text messages or rhythmically taps a pen while making a statement, the words might not register in the employee's mind. An error in basic grammar might receive more attention than the idea that is being transmitted.

- **Nonverbal messages provide clues about the sender's background, attitudes, and motives.** For example, excessive use of big words might suggest that a person reads widely or has an above-average education. It might also suggest a need for social recognition or insecurity about his or her social background.

- **Nonverbal messages are influenced by the circumstances surrounding the communication.** Assume that two men, Ganesh and Jacob, are friends at work. When they are together on the job, Ganesh sometimes puts his hand on Jacob's shoulder. To

Jacob, the act could mean nothing more than "We are close friends." But suppose Ganesh is a member of a committee that subsequently denies a promotion for Jacob. Afterward, the same act could mean "We are still friends," but it could also cause resentment. Because of the circumstances, the same act could now mean something such as "Watch the hand that pats; it can also stab."

- **Nonverbal messages can be beneficial or harmful.** Words or actions can be accompanied by nonverbal messages that help or hurt the sender's purpose. Metacommunications and kinesic communications can convey such messages as "I am competent and considerate of others," or they can convey the opposite. They cannot be eliminated, but you can make them work for you instead of against you by recognizing their value and becoming more aware of them.

Marcin Balcerzak/Shutterstock.com

2-3 LISTENING AS A COMMUNICATION SKILL

Despite the fact that many professionals believe incorrectly that business communication is about presentation and not interaction, most employees spend a major part of their day listening to others. In fact, listening is our most used communication skill. In the corporate world, managers may devote more than 60% of their workday to listening to others.[6] Chief executives may spend as much as 75% of their communicating time listening.[7] Listening to supervisors, employees, customers, and colleagues commonly consumes more of employees' time than reading, writing, and speaking combined.

With smartphones, tablets, and 24/7 access to information, it is harder than ever to pay attention to something without a screen, let alone be an effective listener. But although people may be glued to their device of choice, listening is even more crucial to effective communication, and real knowledge. Learning not only happens by reading, researching or through today's favorite shiny object—Big Data. True learning comes from *sharing* ideas through conversation, which involves being fully engaged in listening, in business, and in life. Only then can ideas evolve, leaders lead, and teams flourish. Strategist Peter Senge emphasizes the value of developing "learning organizations" to deal with the rapid changes of a globalized world, and listening to others is a critical component of such an organization.[8]

EFFECTIVE LISTENING HABITS PAY OFF IN SEVERAL WAYS

- ▶ Good listeners are liked by others because they satisfy the basic human needs of being heard and being wanted.

- ▶ People who listen well are able to separate fact from fiction, cope effectively with false persuasion, and avoid having others use them for personal gain.

- ▶ Effective listening leads to sensitivity and tolerance toward key individuals who are critical to the organization's success, such as employees, customers, and suppliers.

- ▶ Effective listeners are engaged and constantly learning—gaining knowledge and skills that lead to increased creativity, job performance, advancement, and satisfaction.

- ▶ Job satisfaction increases when people know what is going on, when they are heard, and when they participate in the mutual trust that develops from good communication.

Listening depends on your abilities to receive and decode both verbal and nonverbal messages. The best-devised messages and sophisticated communication systems will not work unless people on the receiving end of spoken messages actually listen.

2-3a Listening for a Specific Purpose

Individuals satisfy a variety of purposes through listening: (1) interacting socially, (2) receiving information, (3) solving problems, and (4) sharing feelings with others.

Each activity may call for a different style of listening or for a combination of styles.

- **Casual listening.** Listening for pleasure, recreation, amusement, and relaxation is casual listening. Some people listen to music all day long for relaxation and to mask unwanted sounds during daily routines, work periods, and daily commutes. Aspects of casual listening are as follows:
  - It provides relaxing breaks from more serious tasks and supports our emotional health.
  - It illustrates that people are selective listeners. You listen to what you want to hear. In a crowded room in which everyone seems to be talking, you can block out all the noise and engage in the conversation you are having with someone.
  - It doesn't require much emotional or physical effort.

- **Listening for information.** Listening for information involves the search for data or material. In a lecture class, for example, the instructor usually has a strategy for guiding the class to desired goals. The instructor will probably stress several major points and use supporting evidence to prove or to reinforce them. When engaged in this type of listening, you could become so focused on recording every detail that you take copious notes with no organization. When listening for information:
  - Use an outlining process to help you capture main ideas and supporting sub-points in a logical way.
  - Watch the speaker as you listen to him or her, because most speakers exhibit a set of mannerisms composed of gestures and vocal inflections to indicate the degree of importance or seriousness that they attach to portions of their presentations.

- **Intensive listening.** When you listen to obtain information, solve problems, or persuade or dissuade (as in arguments), you are engaged in intensive listening. Intensive listening involves greater use of your analytical ability to proceed through problem-solving steps. When listening intensively:
  - Become a good summarizer.
  - Trace the development of the discussion, and then move from there to your own analysis.

- **Empathetic listening.** *Empathy* occurs when a person attempts to share another's feelings or emotions. Counselors attempt to use empathetic listening in dealing with their clients, and good friends listen empathetically to each other. Empathy is a valuable trait developed by people skilled in interpersonal relations. When you take the time to listen to another, the courtesy is usually returned. When listening empathetically:
  - Avoid preoccupation with your own problems. Talking too much and giving strong nonverbal signals of disinterest destroy others' desire to talk.
  - Remember that total empathy can never be achieved simply because no two people are exactly alike. The more similar our experiences, however, the better the opportunity to put ourselves in the other person's shoes. Listening with empathy involves some genuine tact along with other good listening habits.

You might have to combine listening intensively and listening empathetically in some situations. Performance appraisal interviews, disciplinary conferences, and other sensitive discussions between supervisors and employees require listening intensively for accurate understanding of the message and listening for feelings, preconceived points of view, and background.

2-3b Bad Listening Habits

Most of us have developed bad listening habits in one or more of the following areas:

- **Faking attention.** Have you ever been introduced to someone only to realize 30 seconds later that you missed the name? We can look directly at a person, nod, smile, and *pretend* to be listening.
- **Allowing disruptions.** We welcome disruptions of almost any sort when we are engaged in somewhat difficult listening. The next time someone enters your classroom or meeting room, notice how almost everyone in the room turns away from the speaker and the topic to observe the latecomer.
- **Over-listening.** When we attempt to record many details in writing or in memory, we can *over-listen* and miss the speaker's major points.
- **Stereotyping.** We make spontaneous judgments about others based on such issues as appearances, mannerisms, dress, and speech delivery. If a speaker doesn't meet our standards in these areas, we simply turn off our listening and assume the speaker can't have much to say.
- **Dismissing subjects as uninteresting.** People tend to use disinterest as a rationale for not listening. Unfortunately, the decision is usually made before

casual listening listening for pleasure, recreation, amusement, and relaxation

listening for information listening that involves the search for data or material

intensive listening listening to obtain information, solve problems, or persuade or dissuade

empathetic listening listening to others in an attempt to share their feelings or emotions

2-4a Increasing Focus on Groups

In recent years, developments among US businesses have shifted attention away from the employment of traditional organizational subunits as the only mechanisms for achieving organizational goals and toward the increased use of groups.

- **Flat organizational structures.** Many businesses today have downsized and eliminated layers of management. Companies implementing Total Quality Management programs are reorganizing to distribute the decision-making power throughout the organization. The trend is to eliminate functional or departmental boundaries. Instead, work is reorganized in cross-disciplinary teams that perform broad core processes (e.g., product development and sales generation) and not narrow tasks (e.g., forecasting market demand for a particular product).

the topic is ever introduced. A good way to lose an instructor's respect when you have to miss class is to ask, "Are we going to do anything important in class today?"

- **Failing to observe nonverbal aids.** To listen effectively, you must observe the speaker. Facial expressions and body motions always accompany speech and contribute much to messages.

Many bad listening habits develop simply because the speed of spoken messages is far slower than our ability to receive and process them. Normal speaking speeds are between 100 and 150 words a minute. The human ear can actually distinguish words in speech in excess of 500 words a minute, and many people read at speeds well beyond 500 words a minute. Finally, our minds process thoughts at thousands of words a minute.

A second reason for poor listening habits is that it takes effort to listen as opposed to simply hearing. We need to take steps to concentrate on what we are hearing to eliminate distractions, and to take notes, and engage in active listening techniques as described in the box found on page 28.

In a flat organizational structure, communicating across the organization chart (among the cross-disciplinary teams) becomes more important than communicating up and down in a top-heavy hierarchy. An individual can take on an expanded **role** as important tasks are assumed. This role can

> **role** tasks employees assume that can involve power and authority that surpass their formal position on the organization chart

Although much research has been conducted in the area of group size, no optimal number of members has been identified. Groups of five to seven members are thought to be best for decision-making and problem-solving tasks. An odd number of members is often preferred because decisions are possible without tie votes.

2-4 GROUP COMMUNICATION

Although much of your spoken communication in business will occur in one-to-one relationships, another frequent spoken-communication activity will likely occur when you participate in groups, committees, and teams.

involve power and authority that surpass the individual's **status**, or formal position in the organizational chart. Much of the communication involves face-to-face meetings with team members rather than numerous, time-consuming "handoffs" as the product moves methodically from one department to another. Companies such as IKEA, the Swedish furniture manufacturer and retailer, are using flat organizational structures within stores to build an employee attitude of job involvement and ownership.

- **Heightened focus on cooperation.** Competition has been a characteristic way of life in US companies. Organizations and individuals compete for a greater share of scarce resources, for a limited number of positions at the top of organizations, and for esteem in their professions. Such competition is a healthy sign of the human desire to succeed, and in terms of economic behavior, competition is fundamental to the private enterprise system. At the same time, when excessive competition replaces the cooperation necessary for success, communication can be diminished, if not eliminated.

status one's formal position in the organizational chart

Just as you want to look good in the eyes of your coworkers and supervisors, units within organizations want to look good to one another. This attitude can cause behavior to take the competitive form, a "win/lose" philosophy. When excessive competition has a negative influence on the performance of the organization, everyone loses.

Although competition is appropriate and desirable in many situations, many companies have taken steps through open communication and information and reward systems to reduce competition and to increase cooperation. Cooperation is more likely when the competitors (individuals or groups within an organization) have an understanding of and appreciation for others' importance and functions. This cooperative spirit is characterized as a "win/win" philosophy. One person's success is not achieved at the expense or exclusion of another. Groups identify a solution that everyone finds satisfactory and is committed to achieving. Reaching this

SUGGESTIONS FOR EFFECTIVE LISTENING

You can enhance the effectiveness of your face-to-face listening by following these suggestions:

▶ **Minimize environmental and mental distractions.** Take time to listen. Move to a quiet area where you are not distracted by noise or other conversation. Avoid becoming so preoccupied with what you will say next that you fail to listen.

▶ **Get in touch with the speaker.** Maintain an open mind while attempting to understand the speaker's background, prejudices, and points of view. Listen for emotionally charged words and watch for body language, gestures, facial expressions, and eye movements as clues to the speaker's underlying feelings.

▶ **Use your knowledge of speakers to your advantage.** Some people seem to run on and on with details before making the point. With this kind of speaker, you must anticipate the major point, but not pay much attention to details. Other speakers give conclusions first and perhaps omit support for them. In this case, you must ask questions to obtain further information.

▶ **Let the speaker know you are actively involved.** Show genuine interest by remaining physically and mentally involved. Provide nonverbal feedback by maintaining eye contact and smiling or nodding at statements with which you agree. Signal that you understand with such verbal messages as "I see," "go on," "I agree."

▶ **Do not interrupt the speaker.** Try to understand the speaker's full meaning, and wait patiently for an indication of when you should enter the conversation.

▶ **Ask reflective questions that assess understanding.** Simply restate in your own words what you think the other person has said. This paraphrasing will reinforce what you have heard and allow the speaker to correct any misunderstanding or add clarification.

▶ **Use probing prompts to direct the speaker.** Use probing statements or questions to help the speaker define the issue more concretely and specifically.

▶ **Use lag time wisely.** Listening carefully should be your primary focus; however, you can think ahead at times as well. Making written or mental notes allows you to provide useful feedback when the opportunity arises. If you cannot take notes during the conversation, record important points as soon as possible so you can summarize the speaker's key points.

mutual understanding requires a high degree of trust and effective interpersonal skills, particularly empathetic and intensive listening skills, and the willingness to communicate long enough to agree on an action plan acceptable to everyone (see Figure 2.2 for a discussion of interpersonal style).

2-4b Characteristics of Effective Groups

Groups form for synergistic effects. Through pooling their efforts, members can achieve more collectively than they could individually. At the same time, the social nature of groups contributes to the individual as well. Although communication in small groups leads to decisions that are generally superior to individual decisions, the group process can motivate members, improve thinking, and assist attitude change.

As you consider the following factors of group communication, try to visualize their relationship to the groups to which you have belonged, such as in school, religious organizations, athletics, and social activities.

- **Common goals.** In effective groups, participants share a common goal, interest, or benefit. This focus on goals allows members to overcome individual differences of opinion and to negotiate acceptable solutions.

- **Role perception.** People who are invited to join groups have perceptions of how the group should operate and what it should achieve. In addition, each member has a self-concept that dictates how he or she will behave. Those known to be aggressive will attempt to be confrontational and forceful; those who like to be known as moderates will behave in moderate ways by settling arguments rather than initiating them. In successful groups, members play a variety of necessary roles and seek to eliminate nonproductive ones.

- **Longevity.** Groups formed for short-term tasks, such as arranging a dinner and program, will spend more time on the task than on maintenance. However, groups formed for long-term assignments, such as an accounting team auditing a major corporation, may devote much effort to maintenance goals. Maintenance includes division of duties, scheduling, recordkeeping, reporting, and assessing progress.

- **Size.** The smaller the group, the more its members have the opportunity to communicate with each

FIGURE 2.2 FOUR INTERPERSONAL COMMUNICATION STYLES

Aggressive	Verbally attacking someone else, being controlling, provoking, and maybe even physically intimidating or violent.
	Example: "What is wrong with you? All you ever think about is yourself!"
Passive-Aggressive	Retaliating in an indirect manner rather than expressing negative feelings, such as anger, directly. This type of behavior may cause confusion because the person on the receiving end may feel "stung" but can't be sure how or why.
	Example: An employee who is angry about his low salary may make negative comments on Twitter about the company rather than discuss the issue with his supervisor.
Passive	Withdrawing in an attempt to avoid confrontation. Passive people let others think for them, make decisions for them, and tell them what to do.
	Example: An employee feels a colleague is treating her poorly. She feels resentful but doesn't express it because she believes her colleague will not listen to her concerns anyway. She is likely to feel down, perhaps even depressed, and avoids interacting with her colleague.
Assertive	Knowing what you feel and what you want. This behavior involves expressing feelings and needs directly and honestly without violating the rights of others. Assertive people accept responsibility for their feelings and actions.
	Example: "I was angry when you didn't show up for our meeting. I know that your time is as valuable to you as my time is to me. I would appreciate it if in the future you would call me if you know you can't make an appointment or if you are going to be late."

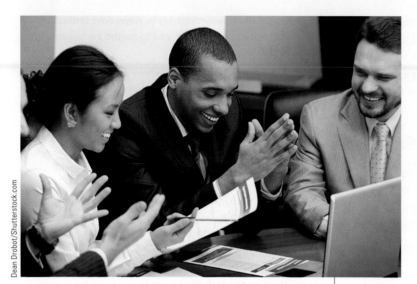
Dean Drobot/Shutterstock.com

substantially, but they still have an important part to play. The ability of a group leader to work toward task goals while contributing to the development of group and individual goals is often critical to group success. Leadership activities may be shared among several participants, and leadership may also be rotated, formally or informally. As part of the group, the leader can affect the establishment of norms by determining who can speak and when, encouraging contribution, and providing motivation for effective group activity.[9]

2-4c Group Roles

Groups are made up of members who play a variety of roles, both positive and negative. Negative roles detract from the group's purposes and include those in the list below.

NEGATIVE GROUP ROLES

▶ **Isolator**—one who is physically present but fails to participate

▶ **Dominator**—one who speaks too often and too long

▶ **Free rider**—one who does not do his or her fair share of the work

▶ **Detractor**—one who constantly criticizes and complains

▶ **Digresser**—one who deviates from the group's purpose

▶ **Airhead**—one who is never prepared

▶ **Socializer**—one who pursues only the social aspect of the group

A list of positive group roles can be found below.

POSITIVE GROUP ROLES

▶ **Facilitator** (also known as *gatekeeper*)—one who makes sure everyone gets to talk and be heard

▶ **Harmonizer**—one who keeps tensions low

▶ **Record keeper**—one who maintains records of events and activities and informs members

▶ **Reporter**—one who assumes responsibility for preparing materials for submission

▶ **Leader**—one who assumes a directive role

other. Large groups often inhibit communication because the opportunity to speak and interact is limited. However, when broad input is desired, large groups can be good if steps are taken to ensure that there is effective communication. Interestingly, large groups generally divide into smaller groups for maintenance purposes, even when the large group is task oriented.

- **Status.** Some group members will appear to have higher ranking than others. Consider a group in which the chief executive of the organization is a member. When the chief executive speaks, members agree. When members speak, they tend to direct their remarks to the one with high status—the chief executive. People are inclined to communicate with peers as their equals, but they tend to speak upward to their supervisor and downward to lower-level employees. In general, groups require balance in status and expertise.

- **Group norms.** A **norm** is a standard or average behavior. All groups possess norms. An instructor's behavior helps establish classroom norms. If some students are allowed to arrive late for class, others will begin to arrive late. If some are allowed to talk during lectures, the norm will be for students to talk. People conform to norms because conformity is easy and nonconformity is difficult and uncomfortable. Conformity leads to acceptance by other group members and creates communication opportunities.

- **Leadership.** The performance of groups depends on several factors, but none is more important than leadership. Some hold the mistaken view that leaders are not necessary when an organization moves to a group concept. The role of leaders changes

norm a standard or average behavior

In healthy groups, members may fulfill multiple roles, which rotate as the need arises. Negative roles are extinguished as the group communicates openly about its goals, strategies, and expectations. The opinions and viewpoints of all members are encouraged and expected.

2-4d From Groups to Teams

Some use the terms *group* and *team* interchangeably; others distinguish between them. The major distinction between a group and a team is in members' attitudes and level of commitment. A team is typified by a clear identity and a high level of commitment on the part of members. A variety of strategies has been used for organizing workers into teams:

- A **task force** is generally given a single goal and a limited time to achieve it.

- A **quality assurance team**, or *quality circle*, focuses on product or service quality, and projects can be either short or long term.

- A **cross-functional team** brings together employees from various departments to solve a variety of problems such as productivity issues, contract estimations and planning, and multidepartment difficulties.

- A **product development team** concentrates on innovation and the development cycle of new products, and is usually cross-functional in nature.

Whereas chain of command is still at work in formal organizational relationships and responsibilities, team structures unite people from varying portions of the organization. Work teams are typically given the authority to act on their conclusions, although the level of authority varies, depending on the organization and the purpose of the team. Typically, the group supervisor retains some responsibilities, some decisions are made completely by the team, and the rest are made jointly.

Merely placing workers into a group does not make them a functional team. A group must go through a developmental process to begin to function as a team. The four stages of team development include:

1. **Forming**—becoming acquainted with each other and the assigned task

2. **Storming**—dealing with conflicting personalities, goals, and ideas

3. **Norming**—developing strategies and activities that promote goal achievement

4. **Performing**—reaching the optimal performance level

For a variety of reasons, teams are often unable to advance through all four stages of development. Even long-term teams might never reach the optimal performing stage, settling instead for the acceptable performance of the norming stage. Studies indicate that virtual teams require additional attention to the planning and use of technology as well as to members' attitudes and knowledge of such technology. See Figure 2.3 for a discussion of the stages of virtual team formation.

Research into what makes workplace teams effective indicates that training is beneficial for participants in such areas as problem solving, goal setting, conflict resolution, risk taking, active listening, and recognizing the interests and achievements of others. Participants need to be able to satisfy one another's basic needs for belonging, personal recognition, and support. Team members at the performing stage of team development exhibit the following behaviors:[10]

- **Commitment.** They are focused on the mission, values, goals, and expectations of the team and the organization.

- **Cooperation.** They have a shared sense of purpose, mutual gain, and teamwork.

- **Communication.** They know that information must flow smoothly between top management and workers. Team members are willing to face confrontation and unpleasantness when necessary.

- **Contribution.** All members share their different backgrounds, skills, and abilities with the team.

Teams have existed for hundreds of years throughout many countries and cultures. Teams are more flexible than larger organizational groupings because they can be assembled, deployed, refocused, and disbanded more quickly, usually in ways that enhance rather than disrupt more permanent structures and processes. Organizational

task force a team of workers that is generally given a single goal and a limited time to achieve it

quality assurance team a team that focuses on product or service quality; projects can be either short or long term

cross-functional team a team that brings together employees from various departments to solve a variety of problems

product development team usually cross-functional in nature; a group of employees who concentrate on innovation and the development cycle of new products

forming stage one of team development, in which team members become acquainted with each other and the assigned task

storming stage two of team development, in which team members deal with conflicting personalities, goals, and ideas

norming stage three of team development, in which team members develop strategies and activities that promote goal achievement

performing stage four of team development, in which team members reach the optimal performance level

FIGURE 2.3 STAGES OF VIRTUAL TEAM FORMATION

Forming	Members begin to develop codes of virtual conduct, to review software and hardware requirements, and to raise and answer questions about how they will use technology to accomplish the group's goals. Some groups arrange a face-to-face meeting before going online, especially when members do not know each other and the project or work is complex and requires a high degree of interaction.
Storming	Members must deal with the added complication imposed by the virtual environment. In addition to expressing opinions and debating substantive issues, the group may encounter technical problems and different levels in member expertise. For example, what should the group do if technical systems are not compatible or if some members are technically unskilled or apprehensive about using advanced technology? Virtual groups must solve technical problems if they hope to address task-related issues and move beyond this stage.
Norming	Virtual groups define members' roles, resolve conflicts, solve most technical problems, and accept the group's norms for interaction. They will be ready to focus on the task. They will also resolve issues related to differences in time, distance, technology, member cultures, and organizational environments.
Performing	Members engage in ongoing virtual interaction and encourage equal participation by all members. They have overcome or adjusted to technical roadblocks and have become comfortable with the virtual media used by the group.
Adjourning	A group may rely on virtual communication to blunt the separation anxiety that comes with the adjourning stage. If a group has matured and performed well, its members will be reluctant to give up relationships with colleagues. Even if a virtual group no longer operates in an official capacity, members may continue to use technological media to consult and interact with one another.

Source: I. N. Engleberg and D. R. Wynn. (2012). *Working in Groups: Communication Principles and Strategies*, 6th ed. Pearson.

changes are often necessary, however, because support must be in place for performance evaluation, recognition, communication, and training systems. Strategies for bringing about needed change might include arranging site visits to similar organizations that already have teams, bringing in a successful team to speak to the organization, and bringing in consultants to discuss the team development process.

 ## 2-5 MEETING MANAGEMENT

Meetings are essential for communication in organizations. They present opportunities to acquire and disseminate valuable information, develop skills, and make favorable impressions on colleagues, supervisors, and subordinates. US businesses spend more money on conducting meetings than do businesses in any other country in the world, and they also spend more time in meetings than do people of other countries.[11] International meetings are imperative for solid business reasons but are facing greater planning scrutiny because of tightening travel budgets and a recovering global economy.

Workers frequently have negative attitudes toward meetings because they are perceived as a waste of time. Studies support this opinion, revealing that as much as one-third of the time spent in meetings is unproductive. Negative attitudes toward meetings can be changed when meetings are conducted properly, giving attention to correct procedures and behavior. Successful meetings don't just happen; rather, they occur by design. Careful planning and attention to specific guidelines can help ensure the success of your meetings, whether they are conducted in a face-to-face format or electronically.

2-5a Face-to-Face Meetings

Face-to-face meetings continue to be the most-used meeting format in most organizations. They offer distinct advantages and are appropriate in the following situations:[12]

- **When you need the richest nonverbal cues, including body, voice, proximity, and touch**

Face-to-face meetings continue to be a frequently used format in most organizations.

- When the issues are especially sensitive
- When the participants don't know one another
- When establishing group rapport and relationships is crucial
- When the participants can be in the same place at the same time

Face-to-face meetings can be enhanced with the use of various media tools such as flip charts, handouts, and electronic slide decks. Although face-to-face meetings provide a rich nonverbal context and direct human contact, they also have certain limitations. In addition to the obvious logistical issues of schedules and distance, face-to-face meetings may be dominated by overly vocal, quick-to-speak, and high-status members.

2-5b Electronic Meetings

Electronic meetings allow companies to reduce travel budgets, save professional time, and minimize the environmental impact caused by travel. A variety of technologies is available to facilitate electronic meetings. Participants may communicate with one another through telephones, computers, or video broadcast equipment using groupware or meeting management software applications. Electronic meetings

offer certain advantages. They facilitate geographically dispersed groups because they provide the choice of meeting at different places/same time, different places/different times, same place/same time, or same place/different times. Electronic meetings also speed up meeting follow-up activities because decisions and action items can be recorded electronically. Electronic meetings also have certain limitations:[13]

- They cannot replace face-to-face contact, especially when group efforts are just beginning and when groups are trying to build group values, trust, and emotional ties.

- They can make it harder to reach consensus, because more ideas are generated and because it might be harder to interpret the strength of other members' commitment to their proposals.

- The success of same-time meetings is dependent on all participants having excellent keyboarding skills to engage in rapid-fire, in-depth discussion. This limitation might be overcome as the use of voice input systems becomes more prevalent.

2-5c Suggestions for Effective Meetings

Whether you engage in face-to-face or electronic meetings, observing the following guidelines can help ensure that your meetings are productive:

- **Identify the purpose of the meeting.** Meetings typically have various purposes: to inform, to gather information, to make decisions. Consider whether sending an email would be a better option as a channel choice.

FIGURE 2.4 FORMAL GENERIC AGENDA FOR MEETINGS

Agenda for [name of group] Meeting
Prepared on [date agenda created]
By [name of author of agenda]

Attendees: [those invited to attend, often in alphabetical order]
Date and time of meeting:
Location of meeting:
Subject: [major issues to be discussed or purpose of meeting]
Agenda items:

1. Call to order
2. Routine business [procedural or administrative matters]   (10–15 minutes)
   a. Approval of agenda for this meeting
   b. Reading and approval of minutes of last meeting
   c. Committee reports
3. Old business [unfinished matters from previous meeting]   (15–20 minutes)
   a. Discussion of issue(s) carried over from previous meeting
   b. Issue(s) arising from decision(s) made at previous meeting
4. New business   (20–25 minutes)
   a. Most important issue
   b. Next most important issue
   c. Other issues in decreasing order of importance
   d. Business from the floor not included on the agenda
      [only as time permits; otherwise, these issues should be
      addressed in the next meeting]
5. Adjournment

Cengage Learning

- **Limit meeting length and frequency.** Any meeting held for longer than an hour or more frequently than once a month should be scrutinized. Ask yourself whether the meeting is necessary. Perhaps the purpose can be achieved in another way, such as email, instant messaging, or telephone.

- **Make satisfactory arrangements.** Select a date and time convenient for the majority of expected participants. For face-to-face meetings, plan the meeting site with consideration for appropriate seating for attendees, media equipment, temperature and lighting, and necessary supplies. For electronic meetings, check hardware and software and connectivity components.

- **Distribute the agenda well in advance.** The **agenda** is a meeting outline that includes important information: date, beginning and ending times, place, topics to be discussed, and responsibilities of those involved. Having the agenda prior to the meeting allows participants to know what is expected of them. A sample agenda template is provided in Figure 2.4.

- **Encourage participation.** Although it is certainly easier for one person to make decisions, the quality of the decision making is often improved by involving the team. Rational decision making may begin with **brainstorming**, the generation of many ideas from among team members. Brainstormed ideas can then be discussed and ranked, followed by some form of voting.

- **Maintain order.** An organized democratic process ensures that the will of the majority prevails; the minority is heard; and group goals are achieved as expeditiously as possible. Proper parliamentary procedure may be followed in formal meetings, as outlined in sources such as *Robert's Rules of Order* and *Jones' Parliamentary Procedure at a Glance*. For less formal meetings, the use of parliamentary procedure may not be necessary to ensure effective contribution by attendees.

agenda a meeting outline that includes important information (e.g., date, beginning and ending times, place, topics to be discussed, and responsibilities of those involved)

brainstorming the generation of many ideas from among team members

- **Manage conflict.** In an autocratic organization, conflict might be avoided because employees are conditioned to be submissive. Such an environment, however, leads to smoldering resentment. On the other hand, conflict is a normal part of any team effort and can lead to creative discussion and superior outcomes. Maintaining focus on issues and not personalities helps ensure that conflict is productive rather than destructive.
- **Seek consensus.** Although unanimous agreement on decisions is an optimal outcome, total agreement cannot always be achieved. **Consensus** represents the collective opinion of the group or the informal rule that all team members can live with at least 70% of what is agreed upon.
- **Prepare thorough minutes.** Minutes provide a concise record of meeting actions, ensure the tracking and follow-up of issues from previous meetings, and assist in the implementation of previously reached decisions.

In addition to these general rules for meetings, preparing for and holding virtual meetings include some extra considerations. First, it is important that participants are knowledgeable about the use of the meeting technology, so training may be required. At the beginning of the meeting, individuals should introduce themselves, particularly if a meeting tool is being used that does not provide visual access to attendees. For clarity, questions and comments should be directed to specific individuals. It is also important that noise is reduced to ensure clear reception, so smartphones and pagers should be turned off, and side conversations should be avoided. For videoconferences, participants need to be aware of their nonverbal behaviors to avoid distracting or disconcerting practices, such as tapping a pen or reviewing text messages. Because you are on camera, it is important to maintain eye contact by looking at the camera.

Meetings are an important management tool and are useful for idea exchange. They also provide opportunities for you, as a meeting participant, to enhance your credibility and communicate impressions of power, competence, and status. Knowing how to present yourself and your ideas and exhibiting knowledge about correct meeting management will assist you in your career advancement.

consensus represents the collective opinion of the group or the informal rule that all team members can live with at least 70% of what is agreed upon

STUDY TOOLS 2

LOCATED AT BACK OF THE TEXTBOOK
☐ Tear-Out Chapter Review Card

LOCATED AT WWW.CENGAGEBRAIN.COM
☐ Review Key Term flashcards and create your own cards

☐ Track your knowledge and understanding of key concepts in business communication

☐ Complete practice and graded quizzes to prepare for tests

☐ Complete interactive content within BCOM8 Online

☐ View the chapter highlight boxes for BCOM8 Online

3 Planning and Decision Making

LEARNING OBJECTIVES

After studying this chapter, you will be able to …

3-1 Consider contextual forces that may affect whether, how, to whom, and when a message is sent.

3-2 Identify the purpose of the message and the appropriate channel and medium.

3-3 Develop clear perceptions of the audience to enhance the impact and persuasiveness of the message, improve goodwill, and establish and maintain the credibility of the communicator.

3-4 Apply tactics for adapting messages to the audience, including those for communicating ethically and responsibly.

3-5 Recognize the importance of organization when planning the first draft.

After finishing this chapter, go to **PAGE 49** for **STUDY TOOLS**.

In a report titled "Writing: A Ticket to Work ... or a Ticket Out," the National Commission on Writing reported that two-thirds of salaried employees in large companies have some writing responsibilities, and getting hired and promoted in many industries requires strong writing abilities. Although writing is important in most managerial-level jobs, the Commission also concluded that one-third of employees in corporate America write poorly. Knowing that effective communication is tied to the corporate bottom line and many employees can't write well, businesses are investing $3.1 billion annually to train employees to write.[1] Remedies are needed to prevent confusion, waste, errors, lost productivity, and a damaged corporate image—all caused by employees, customers, and clients muddling their way through unreadable messages.

As a capable communicator, you can immediately add value to your organization and positively set yourself apart from your peers who are struggling to articulate ideas in writing and in presentations. Communication that commands attention and can be understood easily is essential for survival during the information explosion we are experiencing today. On the job, you will be expected to process volumes of available information and shape useful messages that respond to the needs of customers or clients, coworkers and supervisors, and other key business partners. Additionally, increased use of electronic communication (email, texts, instant messages, blogs, wikis, videoconferences, etc.) will require you to be technologically savvy and capable of adapting the rules of good communication to the demands of emerging technology.

How can you learn to plan and prepare powerful business messages? The systematic analysis process outlined in Figure 3.1 will help you develop messages that save you and your organization valuable time and resources and portray you as a capable, energetic professional.

> Increased use of technological communication will require you to be technologically savvy...

A thorough analysis of the audience and your specific communication assignment will empower you to create a first draft efficiently and to revise and proofread your message for accuracy, conciseness, and appropriate tone.

 3-1

STEP 1: CONSIDER THE APPLICABLE CONTEXTUAL FORCES

Chapter 1 discussed four contextual forces that may affect whether, how, to whom, and when a message is sent. These were legal and ethical constraints, diversity challenges, changing technology, and team environment. In addition to these four forces, communication patterns within an organization are a contextual force that should also be considered when planning a message. The organizational culture as well as the four dimensions of context may influence how, whether, to whom, and when a message is sent. These two issues are discussed in the sections that follow.

3-1a Organizational Culture

Organizational culture can be variously defined depending on the theoretical assumptions of the definer. One perspective of culture is that it is "a pattern of shared basic assumptions that the group learned as it solved its problems of external adaptation and

> **organizational culture**
> a pattern of shared basic assumptions that the group learned as it solved its problems of external adaptation and internal integration and which has worked well enough to be taught to new members as the correct way to perceive, think, and feel in relation to these problems

FIGURE 3.1	**PROCESS FOR PLANNING AND PREPARING SPOKEN AND WRITTEN MESSAGES**

STEP 1	STEP 2	STEP 3	STEP 4	STEP 5	STEP° 6
Consider the applicable contextual forces	Determine the purpose and select an appropriate channel and medium	Envision the audience	Adapt the message to the audience's needs and concerns	Organize the message	Prepare the first draft

°You will focus on the planning process (Steps 1–5) in this chapter; you will learn to prepare the message in Chapter 4 (Step 6).

© Cengage Learning

internal integration and which has worked well enough to be taught to new members as the correct way to perceive, think, and feel in relation to these problems."[2] This view assumes that culture exists outside of the participants and their communication patterns. Another perspective of organizational culture is that it is created and reproduced through the communication practices of its participants, with an expansive view of what constitutes communication: symbols, artifacts such as company logos and accepted employee dress, and structural elements such as office layout and design. Regardless of the perspective applied to defining the phenomenon, an organization's culture determines what it can and cannot do, and to the extent of individual members' socialization into that culture, it determines what they can and cannot do. This is true of actions, behaviors, communicative practices, and use and inclusion of accepted artifacts.

In other words, organizational culture affects the type, amount, and quality of communication that is generally accepted within an organization (and vice versa in the latter definition of corporate culture). The culture of a business provides part of the *context* for interpreting the meaning of everyday organizational life, as well as determining what are considered appropriate messages, the proper or expected ways to convey them, and to whom.

For example, Mindvalley, a progressive personal development company based in Malaysia, has declared "Love Week" to honor the values of Valentine's Day. During this annual one-week event in February, each employee is assigned a Secret Angel who anonymously performs acts of caring and kindness for him or her. Studies show that employees are more engaged and productive when they are happy and when their interactions with colleagues are positive. The event has been so powerful that Mindvalley is globally encouraging and inspiring other companies to try it as well.[3]

Compare these values with the type of culture that you might find in an investment banking firm in which competition, individualism, and the drive for profits and bonuses would likely be key elements, and it should be easy to see how culture might affect how communication occurs and what is expected and accepted within an organization in terms of behaviors.

Theorists have constructed a variety of models to try to capture the essence of corporate culture, a discussion of which goes beyond the scope of this text. But one simple model based on the Competing Values Framework distinguishes four culture types, which are summarized here to illustrate the differences that might emerge in corporate cultures:

- **Clan culture (internal focus and flexible)**—A friendly workplace where leaders act like father figures.

- **Adhocracy culture (external focus and flexible)**—A dynamic workplace with leaders who stimulate innovation.

- **Market culture (external focus and controlled)**—A competitive workplace where leaders are hard drivers.

- **Hierarchy culture (internal focus and controlled)**—A structured and formalized workplace where leaders act like coordinators or administrators.

Generally speaking, the culture of business can be characterized as typically having a bias toward action, a demand for confidence, and a results orientation. The culture of business can be seen in everyday office interactions. Being knowledgeable about an organization's culture can help you gauge the type and quality of communication that takes place, as well as whether you are a good match with an organization. For example, does the organization have an "open door" policy, or are you expected to obey the hierarchical order of management when communicating concerns? Does the office have an open floor plan, or do employees have private offices? Do people wear T-shirts and shorts or suits to work every day? The first situation in each of these cases probably signals that the culture is less formal in terms of its expectations and communication patterns, whereas the second situation may indicate a culture that is more formal in terms of its expectations regarding punctuality and communication choices and behaviors.

3-1b Dimensions of Context

In addition to the other elements of context discussed in previous chapters and sections, there are several dimensions to context, including the physical, social, chronological, and cultural. The *physical* context or setting can influence the content and quality of interaction. For example, if you were to ask your boss for a raise, the effect of the setting might dramatically affect your chances for success. How might the following settings affect the success of such an interaction, how it might

Grasko/Shutterstock.com

Contextual forces may affect how a message is sent.

take place, or whether it should take place: In the boss's office? At a company picnic? Over lunch at a restaurant? In your work area with others observing?

The *social context* refers to the nature of the relationship between the communicators, as well as who is present. In the same situation mentioned above, imagine how the relationship between your manager and yourself might affect your request for a raise, depending on the various scenarios that follow:

- You and the manager have been friends for several years, as opposed to a situation in which you and your manager have no personal relationship.

- You are the same age as your manager, *or* she or he is 15 years older (or younger) than you.

- You and the manager have gotten along well in the past, compared to a situation in which you and the manager have been involved in an ongoing personal conflict.

The *chronological context* refers to the ways time influences interactions. For example, how might the time of day affect the quality of an interaction? How might the communicator's personal preferences regarding time affect communication and its success? Is it a busy time of year for employees and managers? Has there just been a major layoff, downsizing, or profit loss? In this last case, you might want to put off your request for a raise until conditions improve.

The *cultural context* includes both the organizational culture as well as the cultural backgrounds of the people with whom you may be communicating. A person's cultural influences also can affect the kind and

quality of communication that takes place, and they can help determine approaches that will be more effective. For example, young people have different expectations than seniors; Hispanics have different expectations than Asians; Californians have different expectations than people from the Midwest or East Coast; and men may communicate differently than women.

Environmental factors may also affect what should be communicated and how. For example, if the economy is doing poorly, then some messages may be inappropriate or may have little chance for success. If you work in a highly litigious environment or one that is strongly regulated, then constraints may exist for what you can communicate and how. Larger social, political, or historical events may affect whether certain messages are appropriate or have a chance of success. As mentioned earlier, in an economic downturn, it may be difficult, depending on the industry, to be successful at negotiating a pay raise, because the employer may feel that employees should feel lucky to simply have a job during difficult times.

As this discussion shows, context is a complex, multidimensional force that should be considered when planning a message and determines whether it should be sent, when it should be sent, to whom, and how.

3-2 STEP 2: DETERMINE THE PURPOSE, AND SELECT AN APPROPRIATE CHANNEL AND MEDIUM

To speak or write effectively, you must think through what you are trying to say and understand it thoroughly before you begin. Ask yourself why you are preparing the message and what you hope to accomplish. Is the purpose to get information, to answer a question, to accept an offer, to deny a request, or to seek support for a product or idea? Condense the answers into a brief sentence that outlines the purpose for writing or the central idea of your message. You will use the central idea to organize your message to achieve the results you desire.

The major purpose of many business messages is to have the receiver understand logical information. Informative messages are used to convey the vast amounts of information needed to complete the day-to-day operations of the business—explain instructions to employees, announce meetings and procedures, acknowledge orders, accept contracts for services, and so forth. Some messages are intended to persuade—to influence or change the attitudes or actions of the receiver. These messages include promoting a product or service and seeking support for ideas and worthy causes presented to supervisors, employees, stockholders, customers or clients, and others. Additional purposes include establishing a good relationship with your audience, which is discussed later in this chapter, and establishing and maintaining your own credibility as a professional, both of which can help increase persuasiveness. You will learn to prepare messages that are for each of these purposes later in this text. In addition to identifying the purposes of the message, it is also important to decide which channel and medium would be most effective and appropriate.

3-2a Selecting the Channel and Medium

Broadly speaking, four channels of communication exist: visual, written, oral, and nonverbal. However, these broad categories can be broken down further. For example, written communication can be disseminated using a variety of media or forms, including memos, letters, emails, instant or text messaging, faxes, press releases, company websites, blogs, blog applications, wikis, and reports. Oral communication can also use various media or forms such as face-to-face or interpersonal, telephone, voice messages, teleconferences and videoconferences, speeches, meetings, and podcasts. Typically, nonverbal communication supplements oral forms, but it shouldn't be underestimated because most communication in face-to-face situations is often nonverbal. Similarly, visual communication supplements both written and oral forms of communication in the form of slide presentations, diagrams, photographs, charts, tables, video, and artwork.

Channel choice might be influenced or informed by earlier steps in the planning process. For instance, the contextual forces may affect how a message is sent. If the organization typically conveys most routine messages using email, for instance, this may be the most obvious choice. The purpose of communication might affect channel choice as well. In a situation in which the purpose is primarily to establish a relationship or convey goodwill, a face-to-face meeting might be the best choice to achieve this goal. Audience analysis might yield information that indicates it prefers a particular medium of communication such as email or phone discussions.

Common channel choice considerations include the following:

- **Richness versus leanness.** Some channels of communication provide more information than others. Generally, the richest channels of communication provide nonverbal information in addition to that provided in written or oral form. For this reason, the richest channel of communication is face-to-face, or interpersonal. Face-to-face communication provides participants a rich source of information, including vocal cues, facial expressions, bodily movement, bodily appearance, the use of space, the use of time, touching, and clothing and other artifacts. In addition, face-to-face communication provides opportunities to facilitate feedback and establish a personal focus. These aspects also contribute to the richness of interpersonal communication as a channel of communication.

- **Need for interpretation.** Some channels of communication are more ambiguous or leave more room for interpretation of the message being sent than others. Nonverbal communication may be the most ambiguous channel of communication because it requires the audience to interpret almost the entirety of the message. Nonverbal communication is difficult to interpret for a variety of reasons, mainly because it is not generally considered a coded language. Because of this, one nonverbal code may communicate a variety of meanings. Similarly, nonverbal communication can be difficult to interpret because a variety of codes may communicate the same meaning. A third issue that may affect a person's ability to interpret nonverbal codes accurately is intentionality. Some nonverbal codes are sent intentionally, and others unintentionally.

- **Speed of establishing contact.** Another important consideration, particularly in the business world, is the time it will take for a message to be delivered. For this reason, electronic forms of communication have become popular. Using the telephone, writing an email or text message, using blogs and blog applications (such as Twitter) or other social media such as Facebook or LinkedIn, posting to wikis, Skyping, using virtual team applications, or sending a fax are nearly instantaneous channels of communication. In contrast, sending a written message or package by mail may take days.

- **Time required for feedback.** Just as we may need to contact someone immediately, we may also need a response from that person just as rapidly. The most rapid forms of communication, as explained above, are generally electronic. However, depending on the person with whom you are communicating, his or her personality, and your relationship, communicating with a person via an electronic channel does not guarantee prompt feedback. In other words, corporate cultures and individual people may have preferences for specific communication channels or mediums and differing communication practices.

- **Cost.** Many channels of communication are relatively inexpensive for business users. Mail, email, text messages, telephones, faxes, wikis, blogs and blog applications, social media, videoconferencing and teleconferencing tools, and Skype are generally considered inexpensive forms of communication. These tools have made it much less expensive for stakeholders both inside and outside organizations to communicate with each other, regardless of their location. Still, there are times when it may be appropriate to choose the greater expense of arranging a face-to-face meeting, such as when introducing members of a virtual team who will be working on an important project for some time or interviewing job applicants for key positions.

- **Amount of information conveyed.** The best channel for conveying large amounts of information is generally a written one. One reason is that most of us are generally poor listeners. Studies indicate that we retain only 10% or so of what we hear. Therefore, if you want people to have the opportunity to process and remember the information you have to deliver, particularly if the message is long or complex, then it is generally best delivered using a written channel rather than an oral one.

- **Need for a permanent record.** Businesspeople are often involved in situations where they must keep records of what occurred during various work activities throughout the day or week. These situations include the need to record what occurred at a department meeting, an employee's work history, the findings of an audit of a client's financial records, and an employee's travel expenses. Most legal documents, including contracts, use the written channel of communication for this reason: the need to maintain a record. Email messages and other electronic forums such as websites, social networking sites, and blogs, if stored and backed up properly, can also serve as a record.

- **Control over the message.** Written channels of communication also are often the best choice when you wish to maintain greater control of the message that you send. The reason? If information is presented orally and interpersonally, you have a greater chance of persons who disagree with you speaking out and potentially derailing or confusing the message. That is why many negative messages, such as informing a job applicant that he or she was not selected, are sent using a written channel of communication.

Gemenacom/Shutterstock.com

Figure 3.2 provides a summary of the proper use of differing media within an organizational context.

3-3 STEP 3: ENVISION THE AUDIENCE

Perception is the part of the communication process that involves how we look at others and the world around us. It's a natural tendency to perceive situations from our own limited viewpoint. We use the context of the situation and our five senses to absorb and interpret the information bombarding us in unique ways.

Individual differences in perception account for the varied and sometimes conflicting reports given by eyewitnesses to the same accident. Our senses can be tricked when there is a difference in what we expect and what really is happening. For example, consider how your *perception* affects your ability to accurately or completely interpret an optical illusion.

Perception of reality is also limited by previous experiences and our attitudes toward the sender of the message. We support ideas that are in line with our own and decide whether to focus on the positive or the negative of a situation. We may simply refuse to hear a message that doesn't fit into our view of the world.

Much of the confusion in communication is caused by differences in the sender's and receiver's perceptions. For example, a manager's brief email requesting a status report on a task may come across as curt to the employees. Perceptions vary between individuals with similar backgrounds, and even more so when people from different cultures, generations, and genders communicate.

Overcoming perceptual barriers is difficult but essential if you are to craft messages that meet the needs and concerns of your audience. To help you envision the audience, first focus on relevant information you know about the receiver. The more familiar you are with the receiver, the easier this task will be. When communicating with an individual, you immediately recall a clear picture of the receiver—his or her physical appearance, background (education, occupation, religion, culture),

FIGURE 3.2 USE OF COMMUNICATION MEDIA

MEDIUM	BEST USES
Memo	• Simple, routine messages • Confirming policies • Distributing to a large, internal audience • Providing information when a response isn't required
Letter	• Communicating with an external audience • Conveying formality • Providing a written record • Writing a complaint • Communicating condolences or thanks
Email	• Sending brief, impersonal, or routine messages • Providing a hard copy
Fax	• Sending a visual display of information • Communicating general information about a company and its products or services
Web page	• Sharing information with large audiences in an economical fashion • Inspiring and motivating others • Demonstrating products or training

MEDIUM	BEST USES
Oral presentation	• Introducing a persuasive message or following up on one when goodwill and credibility are especially important • Delivering bad news to a large audience when goodwill and credibility are especially important
Face-to-face	• Communicating confidential information • Negotiating • Promoting or firing an employee • Communicating personal warmth or care • Reading nonverbal communication cues
Telephone	• Providing quick feedback or response • Sending confidential information • Discussing bad news • Confirming
Voice mail	• Informing when feedback isn't needed • Confirming • Sending a simple message
Video conferencing	• Making a personal connection with a large audience • Economical and efficient • Training

© Cengage Learning

values, opinions, preferences, and so on. Most importantly, your knowledge of the receiver's reaction in similar, previous experiences will aid you in anticipating how this receiver is likely to react in the current situation. Consider the following audience characteristics:

- **Age.** A message answering an elementary-school student's request for information from your company would not be worded the same as a message answering a similar request from an adult.

- **Economic level.** A solicitation for a business donation for a charity project written to a small business owner would likely differ from one written to a representative of a major corporation.

- **Educational/occupational background.** The technical jargon and acronyms used in a financial proposal sent to bank loan officers may be inappropriate in a proposal sent to a group of private investors.

- **Needs and concerns of the audience.** Just as successful sales personnel begin by identifying the needs of the prospective buyer, an effective manager attempts to understand the receiver's frame of reference as a basis for organizing the message and developing the content.

- **Culture.** The vast cultural differences between people (e.g., language, expressions, customs, values, and religion) increase the complexity of the communication process as was discussed in Chapter 1. An email containing typical American expressions (e.g., "The estimate is in the ballpark," and "Our new sales director really knows all the ropes.") would likely confuse a manager from a different culture. Differences in values influence communication styles and message patterns. For example, Japanese readers value the beauty and flow of words and prefer an indirect writing

Perceptions can vary between people of different cultures, genders, backgrounds, and generations.

Ollyy/Shutterstock.com

approach, unlike Americans who prefer clarity and conciseness.[4]

- **Rapport.** A sensitive message prepared for a long-time client may differ significantly from a message prepared for a newly acquired client. Emails discussing expectations for completing an assignment may be briefer and more direct when sent to an employee with whom you share a strong business relationship built on mutual trust. The rapport created by previous dealings with the recipient aids understanding in a current situation.

- **Expectations.** Because accountants, lawyers, and other professionals are expected to meet high standards, a message from one of them containing errors in grammar or spelling would likely cause a receiver to question the credibility of the source.

You may find that envisioning an audience you know well is often such an automatic action that you may not even recognize that you are doing it. On the other hand, envisioning those you do not know well requires additional effort. In these cases, simply assume an empathetic attitude toward the receiver to assist you in identifying his or her frame of reference (knowledge, feelings, and emotions). In other words, project mentally how you believe you would

FIGURE 3.3 CULTURAL DIMENSIONS IDENTIFIED BY THE GLOBE STUDIES

Uncertainty Avoidance	The extent to which a cultural group relies on established social norms, rituals, and procedures to avoid uncertainty.
Power Distance	The degree to which members of a cultural group expect and agree that power should be shared unequally.
Institutional Collectivism	The degree to which a cultural group encourages institutional or societal collective action. It is concerned with whether cultures identify with broader societal interests rather than with individual goals.
In-Group Collectivism	The degree to which people express pride, loyalty, and cohesiveness in their groups or families.
Gender Egalitarianism	The degree to which a cultural group minimizes gender role differences and promotes gender equality.
Assertiveness	The degree to which people in a culture are determined, assertive, confrontational, and aggressive in their social relationships.
Future Orientation	The extent to which people engage in future-oriented behaviors such as planning, investing, and delaying gratification.
Performance Orientation	The extent to which a cultural group encourages and rewards its members for improved performance and excellence.
Humane Orientation	The degree to which a culture encourages and rewards people for being fair, altruistic, generous, and caring to others.

Source: R. J. House, P. J. Hanges, M. Javidan, P. W. Dorfman, V. & Gupta (Eds.) (2004). *Culture, Leadership, and Organizations: The GLOBE Study of 62 Societies.* Thousand Oaks, CA: Sage Publications.

feel or react in a similar situation and use that information to communicate understanding back to the person.

Consider the use (or lack) of empathy in the following workplace examples:

Sample Message

Example 1: A US manager's instructions to a new employee from an Asian culture: Trying to manufacture a product with a zero failure rate would be a **train wreck**. We have to **strike the right balance** between customer safety and cost efficiency. We cannot be **held hostage** by threats of class action lawsuits. Do you understand?

Example 2: An excerpt from a message sent to M. Bobby Christiansen, who happens to be female:

Ms. Christiansen

The wireless iPod kit that you expressed an interest in is now available at your local car dealer. This innovative Bluetooth technology can be demonstrated at your convenience. Please call your local sales representative to schedule an appointment.

Problem Analysis

- The use of expressions peculiar to US environment can confuse and intimidate.

- This open-ended question at the end disregards the importance of saving face to a person of Asian culture. Cultural influences may prevent employee from asking questions that might indicate lack of understanding.

- Misspelling receiver's name and misinterpreting gender shows disrespect for receiver.

- Omission of contact information reduces writer's credibility and shows lack of genuine concern for sender's needs.

- Overlooking mechanical errors implies incompetence or carelessness.

Taking the time and effort to obtain a strong mental picture of your audience through firsthand knowledge or your empathetic attitude *before* you write will enhance your message in the following ways:

1. **Establishes rapport and credibility needed to build long-lasting personal and business relationships.** Your audience will appreciate your attempt to connect and understand their feelings. A likely outcome is mutual trust, which can greatly improve communication and people's feelings about you, your ideas, and themselves (as shown in the discussion of the Johari Window in Chapter 2).

2. **Permits you to address the audience's needs and concerns.** Such knowledge allows you to select relevant content and to communicate in a suitable style.

3. **Simplifies the task of organizing your message.** From your knowledge of yourself and from your experiences with others, you can reasonably predict receivers' reactions to various types of messages. To illustrate, ask yourself these questions:

   ° Would I react favorably to a message saying my request is being granted or that a new client is genuinely pleased with a job I'd just completed?

   ° Would I experience a feeling of disappointment when I learn that my request has been refused or that my promised pay raise is being postponed?

   ° Would I need compelling arguments to convince me to purchase a new product or support a new company policy?

Now, reread the questions as though you were the message recipient. Because you know *your* answers, you can predict *others'* answers with some degree of accuracy.

Such predictions are possible because of commonality in human behavior.

Your commitment to identifying the needs and concerns of your audience before you communicate is invaluable in today's workplace. Organizations must focus on providing quality customer service and developing work environments supportive of talented, diverse workers. Alienating valuable customers and talented employees as a result of poor audience analysis is not an option in today's competitive environment.

 3-4

STEP 4: ADAPT THE MESSAGE TO THE AUDIENCE'S NEEDS AND CONCERNS

After you have envisioned your audience, you are ready to adapt your message to fit the specific needs of your audience. Adaptations include focusing on the audience's point of view; communicating ethically and responsibly; building and protecting goodwill; using simple, contemporary language; writing concisely; and projecting a positive, tactful tone.

3-4a Focus on the Audience's Point of View

Ideas are more interesting and appealing if they are expressed from the audience's viewpoint. Developing a "you attitude" rather than a "me attitude" involves thinking in terms of the other person's interests and trying to see a problem from the other's point of view. A letter, memo, email, or phone call reflecting a "you attitude" sends a direct signal of sincere concern for the receiver's needs and interest.

HOW TO CULTIVATE A "YOU ATTITUDE"

To cultivate a "you attitude," concentrate on the following questions:

▶ Does the message address the receiver's major needs and concerns?

▶ Would the receiver feel this message is receiver-centered? Is the receiver kept clearly in the picture?

▶ Will the receiver perceive the ideas to be fair, logical, and ethical?

▶ Are ideas expressed clearly and concisely (to avoid lost time, money, and possible embarrassment caused when messages are misunderstood)?

▶ Does the message promote positive business relationships—even when the message is negative? For example, are *please, thank you*, and other courtesies used when appropriate?

▶ Are ideas stated tactfully and positively and in a manner that preserves the receiver's self-worth and cultivates future business?

▶ Is the message sent promptly and through the preferred channel to indicate courtesy?

▶ Does the message reflect the high standards of a business professional: accurate and appealing document design, quality printing, and absence of misspellings and grammatical errors?

The use of the word *you* (appropriately used) conveys to receivers a feeling that messages are specifically for them. However, if the first-person pronoun *I* is used frequently, especially as the subject, the sender may impress others as being self-centered—always talking about self. Compare the following examples of sender-centered and receiver-centered statements:

"I"—or Sender-Centered	"You"—or Receiver-Centered
I wanted to congratulate you on your recent promotion.	Congratulations on your promotion to sales manager!
We are changing our operating hours and dates.	You will find the new hours and days of operation below.

Compliments (words of deserved praise) are another effective way of increasing an audience's receptiveness to ideas that follow. Give sincere compliments judiciously as they can do more harm than good if paid at the wrong time, in the wrong setting, in the presence of the wrong people, or for the wrong reasons. Likewise, avoid flattery (words of undeserved praise). Although the recipient may accept your flattery as a sincere compliment, it is more likely that the recipient will interpret your undeserved praise as an attempt to gain favor or special attention. Suspicion of your motive makes effective communication less likely.

3-4b Communicate Ethically and Responsibly

The familiar directive "With power comes responsibility" applies to your use of communication skills. Because business communication often affects the lives of many, you must accept responsibility for using it to uphold your own personal values and your company's standards of ethical conduct. Before speaking or writing, use the following guidelines to help you communicate ethically and responsibly.

● **Is the information stated as truthfully, honestly, and fairly as possible?** Good communicators recognize that ensuring a free flow of essential information is in the interest of the public and the organization. Living Essentials, the distributor of 5-Hour Energy, a high-selling energy drink, was asked by the National Advertising Division, an advertising watchdog group, to drop its "no crash" claim. A clinical trial run by the company five years earlier showed that the product resulted in a "moderately severe crash" in nearly 25% of users.[5] Similarly, McDonald's and one of its franchise owners agreed to pay $700,000 to members of the Muslim community to settle allegations a Detroit-area restaurant falsely advertised its food as being prepared according to Islamic dietary law.[6] As these examples indicate, dishonesty can cost organizations money, as well as incur damage to their reputation.

At the personal level, honor, honesty, and credibility can help build strong, long-lasting relationships that contribute to the long-term success of your company. Sending complete, accurate, and timely information, regardless of whether it supports your interests, will help you build credibility.

● **Does the message embellish or exaggerate the facts?** Legal guidelines related to advertising provide clear guidance for avoiding *fraud*, the misrepresentation of products or services; however, overzealous sales representatives or imaginative

How truthful, honest, and fair is the information being presented?

- **Are the ideas expressed clearly and understandably?** If a message is to be seen as honest, you must be reasonably confident that the receiver can understand it. Ethical communicators select words that convey the exact meaning intended and that are within the reader's vocabulary.

- **Is your viewpoint supported with objective facts?** Are facts accurately documented to allow the reader to judge the credibility of the source and to give credit where credit is due? Can opinions be clearly distinguished from facts? Have you evaluated honestly any real or perceived conflict of interest that could prevent you from preparing an unbiased message?

- **Are ideas stated with tact and consideration that preserve the receiver's self-worth?** The metaphor "An arrow, once it is shot, cannot be recalled" describes the irrevocable damage caused by cruel or unkind words.[9] Ego-destroying criticism, excessive anger, sarcasm, hurtful nicknames, betrayed secrets, rumors, and malicious gossip pose serious ethical problems in the workplace because they can ruin reputations, humiliate, and damage a person's self-worth. Serious legal issues arise when negative statements are false, constituting defamation. Written defamatory remarks are referred to as **libel**, and similar spoken remarks are referred to as **slander**. If you choose to make negative statements about a person, be sure the facts in question are supported. Additionally, you'll hone your abilities to convey negative information and to handle sensitive situations in a constructive, timely manner rather than ignoring them until they are out of control. For considerate, fair, and civilized use of words, follow this simple rule: Communicate with and about others with the same kindness and fairness that you wish others to use when communicating with and about you.

- **Are graphics carefully designed to avoid distorting facts and relationships?** Communicating ethically involves reporting data as clearly and accurately as possible. Misleading graphics result either from the developers' deliberate attempt to confuse the audience or from their lack of expertise in constructing ethical graphics.

writers can use language skillfully to create less than accurate perceptions in the minds of receivers. As the previous examples illustrate, businesses have learned the hard way that overstating the capabilities of a product or service (promising more than can be delivered) is not good for business in the long run. In 2014, Vibram, the company behind FiveFingers shoes, settled a $3.75 million class-action lawsuit over false claims that its running shoe provided health benefits. The thin-soled, flexible shoes, which cost about $100 a pair, were advertised as mimicking the experience of running in bare feet, and thus improving foot health, an unsupported claim the company falsely advertised.[7]

Although surveys indicate many job seekers believe companies expect résumé padding, companies repeatedly report that this perception is not true. Yahoo CEO Scott Thompson was asked to step down after Yahoo shareholder and hedge fund manager Daniel S. Loeb exposed him for misreporting his degrees on his résumé. Thompson graduated from Stonehill College in Massachusetts with a degree in accounting—but he also claimed he had a degree in computer science. It turned out, though, that the college didn't offer that degree until several years after Thompson claimed he earned his.[8]

Skill in communicating persuasively will be important throughout your profession. The techniques you will read about in this text, such as those related to writing a winning résumé and application message, will be helpful as you begin your career; however, these techniques should *not* be used if your motive is to exploit your audience.

libel written defamatory remarks

slander spoken defamatory remarks

 3-5 ## STEP 5: ORGANIZE THE MESSAGE

After you have identified the specific ways you must adapt the message to your particular audience, you are ready to organize your message. In a discussion of communication, the word *organize* means "the act of dividing a topic into parts and arranging them in an appropriate sequence." Before undertaking this process, you must be convinced that the message is the right message—that it is complete, accurate, fair, reasonable, ethical, and logical. If it doesn't meet these standards, it should not be sent. Good organization and good writing or speaking cannot be expected to compensate for a bad decision.

If you organize and write simultaneously, the task seems hopelessly complicated. Writing is much easier if questions about the organization of the message are answered first: What is the purpose of the message? What is the receiver's likely reaction? Should the message begin with the main point? Once these decisions have been made, you can concentrate on expressing ideas effectively.

3-5a Outline to Benefit the Sender and the Audience

When a topic is divided into parts, some parts will be recognized as central ideas and the others as minor ideas (details). The process of identifying these ideas and arranging them in the right sequence is known as **outlining**. Outlining *before* communicating complex messages provides numerous benefits:

- **Encourages accuracy and brevity.** Outlining reduces the chance of leaving out an essential idea or including an unessential idea.

- **Permits concentration on one phase at a time.** Having focused separately on (a) the ideas that need to be included, (b) the distinction between major and minor ideas, and (c) the sequence of ideas, total concentration can now be focused on the next challenge—expressing.

- **Saves time in structuring ideas.** With questions about which ideas to include and their proper sequence already answered, little time is lost in moving from one point to the next.

- **Provides a psychological lift.** The feeling of success gained in preparing the outline increases confidence that the next step—writing or speaking—will be successful, too.

- **Facilitates emphasis and de-emphasis.** Although each sentence makes its contribution to the

message, some sentences need to stand out more vividly in the receiver's mind than others. An effective outline ensures that important points will appear in emphatic positions.

The preceding benefits derived from outlining are sender oriented. Because a message has been well outlined, receivers benefit, too:

- **The message is more concise and accurate.**

- **Relationships between ideas are easier to distinguish and remember.**

- **Reactions to the message and its sender are more likely to be positive.**

Tomasz Trojanowski/Shutterstock.com

A receiver's reaction to a message is strongly influenced by the sequence in which ideas are presented. A beginning sentence or an ending sentence is in an emphatic position.

3-5b Sequence Ideas to Achieve Desired Goals

When planning your communication, you should strive for an outline that will serve you in much the same way a blueprint serves a builder or an itinerary serves a traveler. Organizing your message first will ensure that your ideas are presented clearly and logically and all

> **outlining** the process of identifying central ideas and details and arranging them in the right sequence; should be completed prior to writing

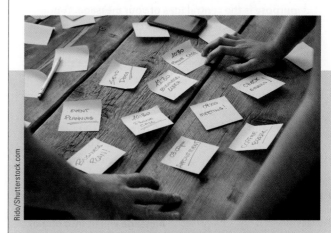

Rido/Shutterstock.com

Organizing your message first will ensure that your ideas are presented clearly and logically.

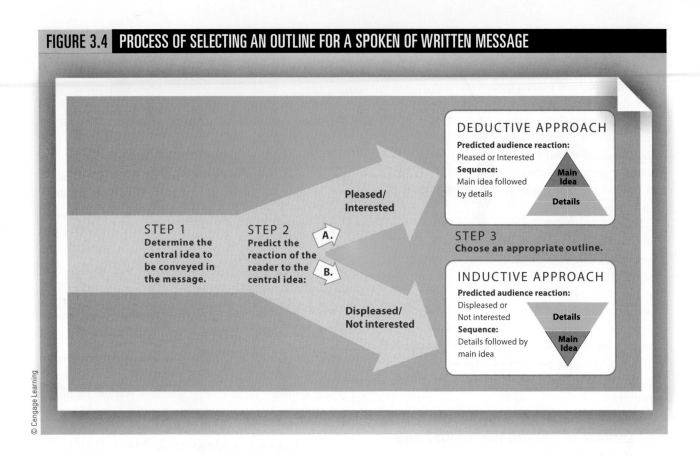

© Cengage Learning

vital components are included. To facilitate your determining an appropriate sequence for a business document or presentation, follow the three-step process illustrated in Figure 3.4. This process involves answering the following questions in this order:

1. **What is the central idea of the message?** Think about the *reason* you are writing or speaking—the first step in the communication process. What is your purpose—to extend a job offer, decline an invitation, or seek support for an innovative project? The purpose is the central idea of your message. You might think of it as a message condensed in one brief statement.

2. **What is the most likely audience reaction to the message?** Ask, "If I were the one receiving the message I am preparing to send, what would *my* reaction be?" Because you would react with pleasure to good news and displeasure to bad news, you can reasonably assume a receiver's reaction would be similar. By considering anticipated audience reaction, you build goodwill with the receiver. Almost every message will fit into one of four categories of anticipated audience reaction, as shown in Figure 3.4: pleasure, displeasure, interest but neither pleasure nor displeasure, or no interest.

3. **In view of the predicted audience reaction, should the central idea be listed first in the outline or should it be listed as one of the last items?** When a message begins with the major idea, the sequence of ideas is called **deductive**. When a message withholds the major idea until accompanying details and explanations have been presented, the sequence is called **inductive**.

Consider the audience to determine whether to use the inductive or deductive sequence. If an audience might be antagonized by the main idea in a deductive message, lead up to the main idea by making the message inductive. If a sender wants to encourage audience involvement (to generate some concern about where the details are leading), use the inductive approach. Inductive organization can be especially effective if the main idea confirms the conclusion the audience has drawn from the preceding details—a cause is worthy of support, a job applicant should be interviewed, a product/service should be selected, and so on. As you learn in later chapters about writing letters, memos, and email messages and about planning spoken communications, you will comprehend the benefits of using the appropriate outline for each receiver reaction:

deductive a message in which the major idea precedes the details

inductive a message in which the major idea follows the details

▶ Ten years ago, PepsiCo's food division began a quest to make its Lay's potato chips more appealing to local tastes in Russia. It wasn't easy. Russians still like packaged versions of a Soviet-era snack—stale bread slathered in oil and baked to a crisp.

▶ To get a better sense of what Russians like, employees traveled around the country to visit people in their homes and talk about what they eat day-to-day. That was a big task. Russia has nine time zones and spans 7,000 miles, with eating habits that vary by region.

▶ The findings were invaluable for PepsiCo executives. In the eastern part of Russia, PepsiCo found that fish is a big part of the diet. So it introduced "Crab" chips. It's now the third most popular flavor in the country.

▶ A "Red Caviar" flavor does best in Moscow, where caviar is particularly popular. "Pickled Cucumber," which piggybacks off of a traditional appetizer throughout Russia, was introduced and is already the fourth most popular flavor. Other favorites include "Onion," "Bacon", and "Sour Cream and Herbs," which is a bit sweeter than the American version.

▶ The chip translations are paying off; sales of Lay's have more than doubled. As for the classic Lay's—an American favorite—Russians still aren't biting. "They find it a very boring flavor," said Marc Schroeder, head of PepsiCo's food division in Russia.[10]

Dmitrydesign/Shutterstock.com

Deductive Order (main idea first)	Inductive Order (details first)
When the message *will* please the audience	When the message will *displease* the audience
When the message is *routine* (will not please nor displease)	When the audience *might* not be *interested* (will need to be persuaded)

The same organizational patterns are recommended for written and spoken communication.

These patterns are applicable in email messages, blogs, letters, memos, and reports.

For determining the sequence of minor ideas that accompany the major idea, the following bases for idea sequence are common:

- **Time.** When writing a report or email message about a series of events or a process, paragraphs proceed from the first step through the last step.

- **Space.** If a report is about geographic areas, ideas can proceed from one area to the next until all areas have been discussed.

- **Familiarity.** If a topic is complicated, the presentation can begin with a known or easy-to-understand point and proceed to progressively more difficult points.

- **Importance.** In analytical reports in which major decision-making factors are presented, the factors can be presented in order of most important to least important, or vice versa.

- **Value.** If a presentation involves major factors with monetary values, paragraphs can proceed from those with greatest values to those with least values, or vice versa.

STUDY TOOLS 3

LOCATED AT BACK OF THE TEXTBOOK
☐ Tear-Out Chapter Review Card

LOCATED AT WWW.CENGAGEBRAIN.COM
☐ Review Key Term flashcards and create your own cards

☐ Track your knowledge and understanding of key concepts in business communication

☐ Complete practice and graded quizzes to prepare for tests

☐ Complete interactive content within BCOM8 Online

☐ View the chapter highlight boxes for BCOM8 Online

4 Preparing Written Messages

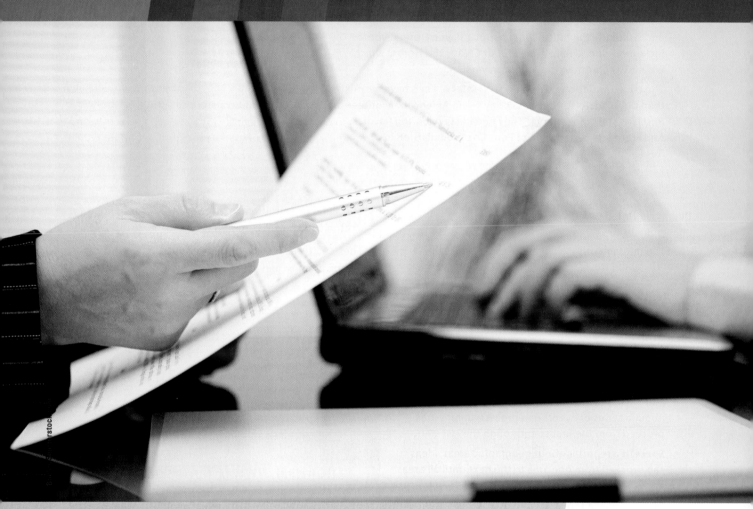

LEARNING OBJECTIVES

After studying this chapter, you will be able to …

4-1 Apply techniques for developing effective sentences and unified and coherent paragraphs.

4-2 Prepare visually appealing documents that grab the reader's attention and increase comprehension.

4-3 Identify factors affecting readability, and revise messages to improve readability.

4-4 Revise and proofread a message for content, organization, style, and tone; and mechanics, format, and layout.

After finishing this chapter, go to **PAGE 70** for **STUDY TOOLS**.

In Chapter 3, you learned about the importance of following a systematic process to develop business messages. The applications in Chapter 3 guided you in developing a clear, logical plan for your message that focuses on the needs of the receiver (Steps 1–5). Effectively capturing your ideas for various business communication situations involves skillful use of language and careful attention to accuracy and readability issues—the remaining two steps in this important process are shown in Figure 4.1.

> Business communicators normally use active voice more than passive voice...

Concentrating on getting your ideas down as quickly as you can is an efficient approach to writing. During this process, remember that you are preparing a draft and not the final copy. If you are composing at the computer, you can quickly and easily revise your draft throughout the writing process. This seamless approach to writing allows you to continue to improve your working draft until the moment you are ready to submit the final copy. Numerous electronic writing tools are available, and technology will continue to unfold to enhance the writing process.

4-1 EFFECTIVE SENTENCES AND COHERENT PARAGRAPHS

STEP 6: PREPARE THE FIRST DRAFT

Once you have determined whether the message should be presented deductively (main idea first) or inductively (explanation and details first) and have planned the logical sequence of minor points, you are ready to begin composing the message.

Normally, writing rapidly (with intent to rewrite certain portions, if necessary) is better than slow, deliberate writing (with intent to avoid any need for rewriting portions). The latter approach can be frustrating and can reduce the quality of the finished work. Time is wasted in thinking of one way to express an idea, discarding it either before or after it is written, waiting for new inspiration, and rereading preceding sentences.

4-1a Craft Powerful Sentences

Well-developed sentences help the receiver to understand the message clearly and to react favorably to the writer or speaker. In this section, you will learn about predominant use of active voice and emphasis of important points, which affect the clarity and goodwill of your message.

RELY ON ACTIVE VOICE

Business communicators normally use active voice more heavily than passive voice because active voice conveys ideas more vividly. In sentences in which the subject is the *doer* of action, the verbs are called *active*. In sentences in which the subject is the *receiver* of action, the verbs are called *passive*. Review the differences in the impact of **passive voice** and **active voice**:

> **passive voice** when the subject of a sentence is the receiver of an action
>
> **active voice** when the subject of a sentence is the doer of an action

FIGURE 4.1 PROCESS FOR PLANNING AND PREPARING SPOKEN AND WRITTEN MESSAGES

STEP 1	STEP 2	STEP 3	STEP 4	STEP 5	STEP* 6	STEP* 7
Consider the applicable contextual forces	Determine the purpose, and select an appropriate channel and medium	Envision the audience	Adapt the message to the audience's needs and concerns	Organize the message	Prepare the first draft	Revise and proofread for accuracy and desired impact

*You will focus on the planning process (Steps 1–5) in Chapter 3; you will learn to prepare the message (Steps 6–7) in this chapter.

© Cengage Learning

Rvisoft/Shutterstock.com

EMPHASIZE IMPORTANT IDEAS

A landscape artist wants some features in a picture to stand out boldly and others to get little attention. A musician sounds some notes loudly and others softly. Likewise, a writer or speaker wants some ideas to be *emphasized* and others to be *de-emphasized.* Normally, pleasant and important ideas should be emphasized; unpleasant and insignificant ideas should be de-emphasized. Emphasis techniques include sentence structure, repetition, words that label, position, and space and format.

SENTENCE STRUCTURE

For emphasis, place an idea in a simple sentence. The simple sentence in the following example has one independent clause. Because no other idea competes with it for attention, this idea is emphasized.

Passive Voice	Active Voice
Reports are transferred electronically from remote locations to the corporate office.	Our sales reps transfer reports from remote locations to the corporate office.

The active sentence invites the receiver to see the sales reps as actively engaged in setting expectations, whereas the passive sentence draws attention to reports. Using active voice makes the subject the actor, which places greater emphasis on his or her concerns. In the passive sentence, the receiver becomes aware that soft drink refills are an issue, but it does not reveal who is concerned.

Even when a passive sentence contains additional words to reveal the doer, the imagery is less distinct than it would be if the sentence were active: *Free refills of soft drinks are expected by our customer base and shouldn't be the focus of cutbacks. Free refills* gets the most attention because it is the subject. The sentence seems to let the audience know the *result* of the action before revealing the doer; therefore, the sentence is less emphatic.

Although active voice conveys ideas more vividly, passive voice is useful for the following purposes:

- **Concealing the doer.** ("Shortages in inventory have been found," rather than employees are the cause of inventory shortages.)
- **Placing more emphasis on *what* was done and who or what it was *done to* than on *who* did it.** ("The reports have been compiled by our sales representatives.")
- **Subordinating an unpleasant thought or avoiding finger-pointing.** ("The printer on the second floor is not working properly," rather than "Lucy apparently fouled up the printer on the second floor.")

Simple Sentence Is More Emphatic	Compound Sentence Is Less Emphatic
Travis accepted a position in marketing.	Travis accepted a position in marketing, but he would have preferred a job in finance.

For emphasis, place an idea in an independent clause; for de-emphasis, place an idea in a dependent clause. In the following compound sentence, the idea of finance work is in an independent clause. Because an independent clause makes sense if the rest of the sentence is omitted, an independent clause is more emphatic than a dependent clause. In the complex sentence, the idea of finance work is in a dependent clause. Compared with the independent clause that follows ("Travis accepted a position ..."), the idea in the dependent clause is de-emphasized.

Compound Sentence Is More Emphatic	Complex Sentence Is Less Emphatic
Travis accepted a position in marketing, but he would have preferred a job in finance.	Although he would have preferred a job in finance, Travis accepted a position in marketing.

REPETITION

To emphasize a word, let it appear more than once in a sentence. For example, a clever advertisement by Office-Max used the word *stuff* repeatedly to describe generically several types of office-supply needs ranging from paper clips to color copies, and then ended succinctly with "OfficeMax … for your office stuff." Likewise, in the following example, "successful" receives more emphasis when the word is repeated.

Less Emphatic	More Emphatic
The meeting was successful because . . .	The meeting was successful; the success was attributed to . . .

WORDS THAT LABEL

For emphasis or de-emphasis, use words that label ideas as significant or insignificant. Note the labeling words used in the following examples to emphasize or de-emphasize an idea:

> *But most important of all …*
> *A less significant aspect was …*

POSITION

To emphasize a word or an idea, position it first or last in a sentence, clause, paragraph, or presentation. Note that the additional emphasis placed on the words "success" or "failure" (or its equivalent) in the examples in the right column, because these phrases appear early or late in their clauses.

Less Emphatic	More Emphatic
Our efforts ensured the <u>success</u> of the project; without them, <u>failure</u> would have been the result.	<u>Success</u> resulted from our efforts; <u>failure</u> would have resulted without them.
The project was <u>successful</u> because of our efforts; without them, <u>failure</u> would have been the result.	<u>Success</u> resulted; without our efforts, <u>failure</u> would have been the outcome.

In paragraphs, the first and last words are in particularly emphatic positions. An idea that deserves emphasis can be placed in either position, but an idea that does not deserve emphasis can be placed in the middle of a long paragraph. The word *I*, which is frequently overused in messages, is especially noticeable if it appears as the first word. *I* is more noticeable if it appears as the first word in *every* paragraph. Avoid using the word *However* as the first word in a paragraph if the preceding paragraph is neutral or positive. These words imply that the next idea will be negative. Unless the purpose is to place emphasis on negatives, such words as *denied*, *rejected*, and *disappointed* should not appear as the last words in a paragraph.

Likewise, the central idea of a written or spoken report appears in the introduction (the beginning) and the conclusion (the end). Good transition sentences synthesize ideas at the end of each major division.

SPACE AND FORMAT

The various divisions of a report or spoken presentation are not expected to be of equal length, but an extraordinary amount of space devoted to a topic attaches special significance to that topic. Similarly, a topic that receives an especially small amount of space is de-emphasized. The manner in which information is physically arranged affects the emphasis it receives and consequently the overall impact of the message.

4-1b Develop Coherent Paragraphs

Well-constructed sentences are combined into paragraphs that discuss a portion of the topic being covered. To write effective paragraphs, you must learn to (a) develop deductive or inductive paragraphs consistently, (b) link ideas to achieve coherence, (c) keep paragraphs unified, and (d) vary sentence and paragraph length.

POSITION THE TOPIC SENTENCE APPROPRIATELY

Typically, paragraphs contain one sentence that identifies the portion of the topic being discussed and presents the central idea. That sentence is commonly called a **topic sentence**. For example, consider operating instructions prepared for company-owned GPS navigation systems. The overall topic is how to get satisfactory performance from the device. One portion of that topic is setup; another portion (paragraph) discusses operation, and so forth. Within each paragraph, one sentence serves a special function. Sentences that list the steps can appear as one paragraph, perhaps with steps numbered as follows:

> *To set up the system, take the following steps:*

1. Connect …

2. Go to menu settings to …

In this illustration, the paragraphs are **deductive**; that is, the topic sentence *precedes* details. When topic sentences *follow* details, the paragraphs are **inductive**. As discussed previously, the receiver's likely reaction to the main idea (pleased, displeased, interested, not interested) aids in selecting the appropriate sequence.

When the subject matter is complicated and the details are numerous,

topic sentence a sentence that identifies the portion of the topic being discussed and presents the central idea of the paragraph

deductive paragraph a paragraph in which the topic sentence precedes the details

inductive paragraph a paragraph in which the topic sentence follows the details paragraphs sometimes begin with a main idea, follow with details, and end with a summarizing sentence. But the main idea might not be in the first sentence; the idea could need a preliminary statement. Receivers appreciate consistency in the placement of topic sentences. Once they catch on to the writer's or speaker's pattern, they know where to look for main ideas.

These suggestions seldom apply to the first and last sentences of letters, memos, and email messages. Such sentences frequently appear as single-sentence paragraphs. But for reports and long paragraphs of letters, strive for paragraphs that are consistently deductive or inductive. Regardless of which is selected, topic sentences are clearly linked with details that precede or follow.

LINK IDEAS TO ACHIEVE COHERENCE

Careful writers use coherence techniques to keep receivers from experiencing abrupt changes in thought. Although the word **coherence** is used sometimes to mean "clarity" or "understandability," it is used throughout this text to mean "cohesion." If writing or speaking is coherent, the sentences stick together; each sentence is in some way linked to the preceding sentences. Avoid abrupt changes in thought, and link each sentence to a preceding sentence.

The following techniques for linking sentences are common:

1. **Repeat a word that was used in the preceding sentence.** The second sentence in the following example is an obvious continuation of the idea presented in the preceding sentence.

   … to take responsibility for the decision. This responsibility can be shared …

2. **Use a pronoun that represents a noun used in the preceding sentence.** Because *"it"* means *"responsibility,"* the second sentence below is linked directly with the first.

   … to take this responsibility. It can be shared …

3. **Use connecting words.** Examples include *however, therefore, yet, nevertheless, consequently, also,* and *in addition. "However"* implies "We're continuing with the same topic, just moving into a different phase." Remember, though, that good techniques can be overused. Unnecessary

Tanewpix/Shutterstock.com

connectors are space consuming and distracting. Usually they can be spotted (and crossed out) in proofreading.

… to take this responsibility. However, few are willing to …

Just as sentences within a paragraph must link, paragraphs within a document must also link. Unless a writer or speaker is careful, the move from one major topic to the next will seem abrupt. A good transition sentence can bridge the gap between the two topics by summing up the preceding topic and leading a receiver to expect the next topic:

Once the new accounting system is put into place, training employees in its operation is vital.

This sentence could serve as a transition between the "Installation" and "Training" division headings. Because a transition sentence comes at the end of one segment and before the next, it emphasizes the central idea of the preceding segment and confirms the relationship of the two segments. Although transition sentences are helpful if properly used, they can be overused. For most reports, transition sentences before major headings are

coherence cohesion, so that each sentence in some way is linked to the preceding sentences sufficient. Normally, transition sentences before subheadings are unnecessary.

KEEP PARAGRAPHS UNIFIED

Receivers expect the first paragraph of a message to introduce a topic, additional paragraphs to discuss it, and a final paragraph to tie all of the paragraphs together. The middle paragraphs should be arranged in a systematic sequence, and the end must be linked easily to some word or idea presented in the beginning. The effect of a message that is *not* unified is like that of an incomplete circle or a picture with one element obviously missing.

- **A unified email message, letter, memo, or report covers its topic adequately but does not include extraneous material. The document should have a beginning sentence appropriate for the expected receiver reaction, paragraphs that present the bulk of the message, and an ending sentence that is an appropriate closing for the message presented.**

- **A unified report or presentation begins with an introduction that identifies the topic, reveals the thesis, and previews upcoming points. The introduction often includes some background, sources of information, and the method of treating data. Between the beginning and the ending, a unified report should have paragraphs arranged in a systematic sequence. A summary or conclusion brings all major points together.**

VARY SENTENCE AND PARAGRAPH LENGTH

Sentences of short or average length are easy to read and preferred for communicating clearly. However, keeping *all* sentences short is undesirable because the message might sound monotonous, unrealistic, or elementary. A 2-word sentence is acceptable; so is a 60-word sentence—if it is clear. Just as sentences should vary in length, they should also vary in structure. Some complex or compound sentences should be included with simple sentences.

Variety is just as desirable in paragraph length as it is in sentence length. A paragraph can be from one line in

---

FIGURE 4.2 CONTRAST THE READABILITY AND APPEAL OF BULKY (LEFT) VERSUS BROKEN (RIGHT) TEXT

OLD MESSAGE

To: All employees

From: Gina Park [gina.park@xyzco.com]

Subject: Travel card changes

Everyone,

For those of you who hold or wish to have a company credit card for travel purposes, we will be switching from Mastercard to Visa in 30 days. You can sign up for the new card online. Please just access Human Resources' web page at www.xyzco.com/human resources and click on the link "Travel Card Application." Fill out the form that appears and submit it. You will receive a confirmation message if your submission was successful. In about two weeks, Human Resources will notify you via email when your card is available for pick up.

If you currently have a Mastercard, you should return it to Human Resources by March 30. If you have questions about this change, please contact me at gina.park@xyzco.com.

NEW MESSAGE

To: All employees

From: Gina Park [gina.park@xyzco.com]

Subject: Travel card changes

Everyone,

For those of you who hold or wish to have a company credit card for travel purposes, we will be switching from Mastercard to Visa in 30 days.

You can sign up for the new card online. Please just access Human Resources' web page at www.xyzco.com/human resources and click on the link "Travel Card Application." Fill out the form that appears and submit it. You will receive a confirmation message if your submission was successful. In about two weeks, Human Resources will notify you via email when your card is available for pick up.

If you currently have a Mastercard, you should return it to Human Resources by March 30.

If you have questions about this change, please contact me at gina.park@xyzco.com.

length to a dozen lines or more. However, just as with sentence length, average paragraph length also should be kept short, as appropriate to the document type:

- **Paragraphs in letters, memos, and email messages are typically shorter than paragraphs in business reports.**

- **First and last paragraphs are normally short (one to four lines), and other paragraphs are normally no longer than *six lines*. A short first paragraph is more inviting to read than a long first paragraph, and a short last paragraph enables a writer to emphasize parting thoughts.**

- **The space between paragraphs is a welcome resting spot. Long paragraphs are difficult to read and make a message appear uninviting. Paragraph length will vary depending on the complexity of the subject matter. However, as a general rule paragraphs should be no longer than *eight to ten lines*. This length usually allows enough space to include a topic sentence and three or four supporting statements. If the topic cannot be discussed in this space, divide the topic into additional paragraphs.**

To observe the effect large sections of unbroken text have on the overall appeal of a document, examine the memos in Figure 4.2. Without question, the memo with the short, easy-to-read paragraphs is more inviting than the memo with one bulky paragraph.

Although variety is a desirable quality, it should not be achieved at the expense of consistency. Using *I* in one part of a message and then without explanation switching to *we* is inadvisable. Using the past tense in one sentence and the present tense in another sentence creates variety at the expense of consistency—unless the shift is required to indicate actual changes in time. Unnecessary changes from active to passive voice and from third to first person are also discouraged.

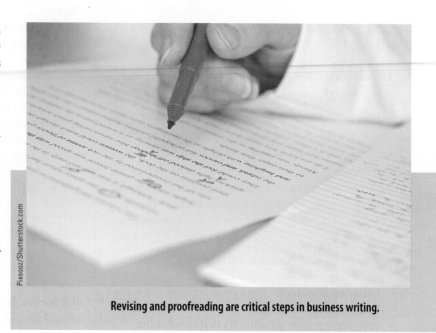

Pxsooz/Shutterstock.com

Revising and proofreading are critical steps in business writing.

4-2a Cultivate a Frame of Mind for Effective Revising and Proofreading

The following suggestions will guide your efforts to develop business documents that achieve the purpose for which they are intended.

- **Attempt to see things from your audience's perspective rather than from your own.** Being empathetic with your audience isn't as simple as it seems, particularly when dealing with today's diverse workforce. Erase the mind-set, "I know what *I* need to say and how *I* want to say it." Instead, ask, "How would my audience react to this message? Is this message worded so that my audience can easily understand it? Does it convey a tone that will build goodwill?"

- **Revise your documents until you cannot see any additional ways to improve them.** Resist the temptation to think of your first draft as your last draft. Instead, look for ways to improve, and be willing to incorporate valid suggestions once you have completed a draft. Experienced writers believe that there is no such thing as good writing, but there is such a thing as good rewriting. Author Dorothy Parker, who wrote for *Vanity Fair* and *Esquire*, once said, "I can't write five words but that I change seven."[1] Skilled speech writers might rewrite a script 15 or 20 times. Writers in public relations firms revise brochures and advertising copy until perhaps only a comma in the final draft is recognizable from the first draft. Even simple email messages require revision for clarity and mechanical errors, with extra passes needed depending on the number of recipients and the context of the message. Regardless of

REVISE TO GRAB YOUR AUDIENCE'S ATTENTION

Professional writers often recognize that the real work of writing occurs during the revision process. It is this step, however, that is often overlooked or given short shrift by those who do not write for a living. Revising and proofreading effectively, therefore, require a change in mind-set.

the message type, your careful revising will aid you in creating accurate, readable documents that produce results.

- **Be willing to allow others to make suggestions for improving your writing.** Because most of us consider our writing personal, we often feel reluctant to share it with others and can be easily offended if they suggest changes. This syndrome, called *writer's pride of ownership*, can prevent us from seeking needed assistance from experienced writers—a proven method of improving communication skills. On the job, especially in today's electronic workplace, your writing will be showcased to your supervisor, clients/customers, members of a collaborative writing team, and more. You have nothing to lose but much to gain by allowing others to critique your writing. This commitment is especially important considering the mistake hardest to detect is your own. However, you have the ultimate responsibility for your document; don't simply trust that someone else will catch and correct your errors.

The ability you've gained in following a systematic process for developing effective business messages will prove valuable as you direct your energies to developing effective messages as a member of a team. Refer to the "Check Your Communication" checklist on the Chapter 4 Review Card to review the guidelines for preparing and proofreading a rough draft.

The speed and convenience of today's electronic communication have caused many communicators to confuse informality with sloppiness. Sloppy messages contain misspellings, grammatical errors, unappealing and incorrect formats, and confusing content—all of which create a negative impression of the writer and the company and affect the receiver's ability to understand the message. Some experts believe the increased use of email is leading to bosses becoming ruder. To combat against the harsh tone that often sets in when managers must respond to 300 to 500 emails weekly, Unilever is providing writing training and urging staff to think before they press the send button.[2]

As the sender, you are responsible for evaluating the effectiveness of each message you prepare. You must not use informality as an excuse to be sloppy. Instead, take one consultant's advice: "You can still be informal and not be sloppy. You can be informal and correct."[3] Take a good hard look at the messages you prepare. Commit to adjusting your message to the audience, designing appealing documents that are easily read, and following a systematic proofreading process to ensure error-free messages. This effort could save you from being embarrassed or jeopardizing your credibility.

4-2b Apply Visual Enhancements to Improve Readability

The vast amount of information created in today's competitive global market poses a challenge to you as a business writer. You must learn to create visually appealing documents that entice the audience to read rather than discard your message. Additionally, an effective design will enable you to highlight important information for maximum attention and to transition a receiver smoothly through sections of a long, complex document. These design techniques can be applied easily using word-processing software. However, add visual enhancements only when they aid in comprehension. Overuse will cause your document to appear cluttered and will defeat your purpose of creating an appealing, easy-to-read document.

ENUMERATIONS

To emphasize units in a series, place a number, letter, or bullet before each element. Words preceded by numbers, bullets, or letters attract the receiver's special attention and are easier to locate when the page is reviewed.

Original	Highlighted
The department problems have been identified as tardiness, absenteeism, and low productivity.	The department problems have been identified as • Tardiness • Absenteeism • Low productivity

ENUMERATED OR BULLETED LISTS

Writers often want to save space; however, cluttered text is unappealing and difficult to read. *Chunking*—a desktop publishing term—is an answer to the problem. Chunking involves breaking down information into easily digestible pieces. It's the communication equivalent of Butterfinger BBs rather than the whole candy bar. The added white space divides the information into blocks, makes the page look more organized, and increases retention by 50%.[4]

Enumerated or bulleted lists can be used to chunk and add even greater visual impact to items in a series. Items appear on separate lines with numerals, letters, or various types of bullets (•, ◊, □, ✓, and so on) at the beginning. Multiple-line items often are separated by a blank line. This design creates more white space, which isolates the items from other text and demands attention. Bullets are typically preferred over numerals unless the sequence of the items in the series is critical (e.g., steps in a procedure that must be completed in the correct order). In the following excerpt from a long analytical report, the four supporting reasons for a conclusion are highlighted in a bulleted list:

Original	Highlighted
Although there are some disadvantages that should not be overlooked, virtual teams provide many benefits, including cost savings from reduced travel, convenient access to team members, time savings and greater productivity, and the potential for greater creativity and better solutions.	Although there are some disadvantages that should not be overlooked, virtual teams provide many benefits, including these: • Cost savings from reduced travel • Convenient access to team members • Time savings and greater productivity • Potential for greater creativity and better solutions

HEADINGS

Headings are signposts that direct the receiver from one section of the document to another. Studies have shown that readers find documents with headings easier to grasp and that they are more motivated to pay attention to the text, even in a short document such as a half-page warranty.[5] You'll find that organizing the content of various types of documents with logical, well-written headings will make the documents more readable and appealing. Follow these general guidelines for writing effective headings:

- **Compose brief headings that make a connection with the receiver, giving clear cues as to the usefulness of the information (e.g., "How Do I Apply?"). Consider using questions rather than noun phrases to let readers know they are reading the information they need (i.e., choose "Who Is Eligible to Apply?" rather than "Eligible Loan Participants").[6] Consider talking headings that reveal the conclusions reached in the following discussion, rather than general topic headings. For example, "Costs Are Prohibitive" is more emphatic than "Cost Factors."**

- **Strive for parallel structure of readings within a section. For example, mixing descriptive phrases with questions requires additional mental effort and distracts readers who expect parallel writing.**

- **Follow a hierarchy, with major headings receiving more attention than minor headings or paragraph headings. To draw more attention to a major heading, center it and use a heavier, larger typestyle or brighter text color.**

TABLES AND GRAPHS

Tables and graphs are used to simplify and clarify information and to add variety to long sections of dense text. The clearly labeled rows and columns in a table organize large amounts of specific numeric data and facilitate analysis. Graphics such as pie, line, and bar charts visually depict relationships within the data. They provide quick estimates rather than specific information.

LINES AND BORDERS

Horizontal and vertical lines can be added to partition text or to focus attention on a specific line or lines. For example, a thin line followed by a thick line effectively separates the identification and qualifications sections of a résumé. Placing a border around a paragraph or section of text sets that information apart and adding shading inside the box adds greater impact. For example, a pull-quote format might spotlight a testimonial from a satisfied customer in a sales letter, important dates to remember in a memorandum, or a section of a document that must be completed and returned.

RELEVANT IMAGES

A variety of interesting shapes can be used to highlight information and add appeal. Examples include creating a rectangular call-out box highlighting a key idea, with an arrow pointing to a specific number in a table; surrounding a title with a shaded oval for added impact; and using built-in designs to illustrate a process, cycle, hierarchy, or other relationship. Clip art or photos can also be added to reinforce an idea and add visual appeal. The following example from the Plain Language website shows how visual communication can convey important safety information more effectively than words can.

Sergey Nivens/Shutterstock.com

Before

This is a multipurpose passenger vehicle which will handle and maneuver differently from an ordinary passenger car, in driving conditions which may occur on streets and highways and off road. As with other vehicles of this type, if you make sharp turns or abrupt maneuvers, the vehicle may roll over or may go out of control and crash. You should read driving guidelines and instructions in the Owner's Manual, and WEAR YOUR SEAT BELTS AT ALL TIMES.

 WARNING: HIGHER ROLLOVER RISK

Avoid Abrupt Maneuvers and Excessive Speed.

Always Buckle Up.

See Owner's Manual For Further Information.

Battling to manage an avalanche of information, the recipients of your messages will appreciate your extra effort to create an easy-to-read, appealing document. These fundamental techniques will be invaluable as you enhance printed documents, such as letters, memos, reports, agendas, handouts, and minutes for meetings.

4-2c Improve Readability

Although sentences are arranged in a logical sequence and are written coherently, the receiver might find reading the sentences difficult. Several programs have been developed to measure the reading difficulty of your writing. Electronic tools aid you in making computations and identifying changes that will improve readability.

The grammar and style checker feature of leading word-processing software calculates readability measures to aid you in writing for quick and easy reading and listening. The Fog Index, a popular readability index developed by Robert Gunning, and the Flesch–Kincaid Grade Level calculator available in Microsoft Word consider the length of sentences and the difficulty of words, to produce the approximate grade level at which a person must read in order to understand the material. For example, a grade level of 10 indicates a person needs to be able to read at the tenth-grade level to understand the material. Fortunately, you don't have to calculate readability manually, but understanding the manual calculation of the Fog index will illustrate clearly how sentence length and difficulty of words

affect readability calculations and will guide you in adapting messages.

Trying to write at the exact grade level of the receiver is not advised. You may not know the exact grade level, and even those who have earned advanced degrees appreciate writing they can read and understand quickly and easily. Also, writing a passage with a readability index appropriate for the audience does not guarantee the message will be understood. Despite simple language and short sentences, the message can be distorted by imprecise words, biased language, jargon, and translations that ignore cultural interpretations, to name just a few. The value of calculating a readability measure lies in the feedback you gain about average length of sentences and the difficulty of the words. Revise and recalculate the readability index, and continue revising until you feel the reading level is appropriate for the intended audience.

The grammar and style feature in word-processing programs also locates grammatical errors, including misspellings and common usage errors, such as the use of fragments, run-on sentences, subject–verb disagreement, passive voice, double words, and split infinitives. Because it can only guess at the structure of a sentence and then apply a rigid set of rules, a grammar and style checker, such as a spell checker, must be used cautiously. It is not a reliable substitute for a human editor who has an effective writing style and is familiar with the rules the software displays. Allow the software to flag misspellings and writing errors as you write; then, accept or reject the suggested changes based on your knowledge of effective writing, and use the readability

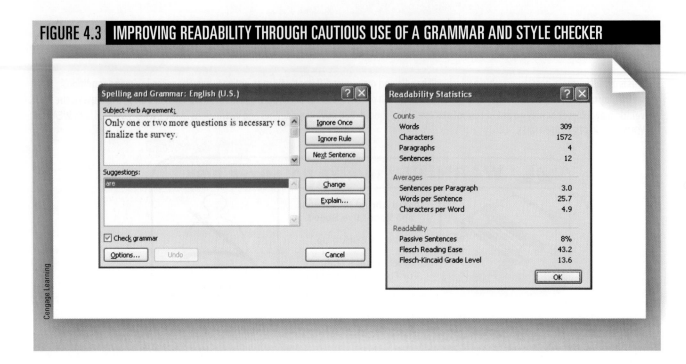

Cengage Learning

measures to adjust your writing levels appropriately, as shown in Figure 4.3.

4-3 IMPROVE READABILITY

STEP 7: REVISE FOR STYLE AND TONE

4-3a Eliminate Outdated Expressions

Using outdated expressions will give your message a dull, stuffy, unnatural tone. Instead, substitute fresh, original expressions that reflect today's language patterns.

Outdated Expressions	Improvement
<u>As per your request</u>, the report has been submitted to the client.	<u>As you requested</u>, the report has been submitted to the client.
<u>Enclosed please find</u> a copy of my transcript.	The <u>enclosed</u> transcript should answer your questions.
<u>Very truly yours</u> (used as the complimentary close in a letter)	Sincerely

clichés overused expressions that can cause their users to be perceived as unoriginal, unimaginative, lazy, and perhaps even disrespectful

4-3b Curb Clichés

Clichés, or overused expressions, are common in our everyday conversations and in business messages. These handy verbal shortcuts are convenient, quick, easy to use, and often include simple metaphors and analogies that effectively communicate the most basic idea or emotion or the most complex business concept. However, writers and speakers who routinely use stale clichés may be perceived as unoriginal, unimaginative, lazy, and perhaps even disrespectful. Less frequently used words capture the receiver's attention because they are original, fresh, and interesting.

Clichés present another serious problem. Consider the scenario of shoppers standing in line at a discount store with the cashier saying to each, "Thanks for shopping with us today. Please come again." Because the last shopper has heard the words several times already, he or she may not consider the statement genuine. The cashier has used an expression that can be stated without thinking and possibly without meaning. A worn expression can convey messages such as "You

D. Pimborough/Shutterstock.com

are not special," or "For you, I won't bother to think. The phrases I use in talking with others are surely good enough for you." Original expressions convey sincerity and build strong human relations.

Cliché	Improvement
Pushed (or stretched) the envelope	Took a risk or considered a new option
Skin in the game	Committed to the project
Cover all the bases	Get agreement/input from everyone
That sucks!	That's unacceptable/needs improvement

4-3c Eliminate Profanity

Increasing tolerance of profanity is an issue of concern to society as a whole and also for employers and employees as they communicate at work. You must consider the potential business liabilities and legal implications resulting from the use of profanity that may offend others or create a hostile work environment. Recognize that minimizing or eliminating profanity is another important way you must adapt your language for communicating effectively and fostering human relations in a professional setting.

4-3d Use Simple, Informal Words

Business writers prefer simple, informal words that are readily understood and less distracting than more difficult, formal words. If a receiver questions the sender's motive for using formal words, the impact of the message may be diminished. Likewise, the impact would be diminished if the receiver questioned a sender's use of simple, informal words. That distraction is unlikely, however, if the message contains good ideas that are well organized and well supported. Under these conditions, simple words enable a receiver to understand the message clearly and quickly.

To illustrate, consider the unnecessary complexity of a notice that appeared on a corporate bulletin board: "Employees impacted by the strike are encouraged to utilize the hotline number to arrange for alternative transportation to work. Should you encounter difficulties in arranging for alternative transportation to work, please contact your immediate supervisor." A simple, easy-to-read revision would be, "If you can't get to work, call the hotline or your supervisor." For further illustration, note the added clarity of the following words:

Formal Words	Informal Words
terminate	end
procure	get

Formal Words	Informal Words
remunerate	pay
corroborate	support

Using words that have more than two or three syllables when they are appropriate is acceptable. However, you should avoid regular use of a long, infrequently used word when a simpler, more common word conveys the same idea. Professionals in some fields often use specialized terminology, referred to as **jargon**, when communicating with colleagues in the same field. In this case, the audience is likely to understand the words, and using the jargon saves time. However, when communicating with people outside the field, professionals should select simple, common words to convey messages. Using clear, jargon-free language that can be readily understood by non-native recipients and easily translated is especially important in international communication.

You should build your vocabulary so that you can use just the right word for expressing an idea and can understand what others have said. Just remember the purpose of business messages is not to advertise a knowledge of infrequently used words, but to transmit a clear and tactful message. For the informal communication practiced in business, use simple words instead of more complicated words that have the same meaning.

4-3e Communicate Concisely

Concise communication includes all relevant details in the fewest possible words. Abraham Lincoln's two-minute Gettysburg Address is a premier example of concise communication. Mark Twain alluded to the skill needed to write concisely when he said, "I would have written a shorter book if I had had time."

Some executives have reported that they read memos that are two paragraphs long but may only skim or discard longer ones. Yet it's clear that this survival technique can lead to a vital message being discarded or misread. Concise writing is essential for workers struggling to handle an avalanche of information that often is read on the run on their smartphone. Concise messages save time and money for both the sender and the receiver, as the receiver's

jargon specialized terminology that professionals in some fields use when communicating with colleagues in the same field

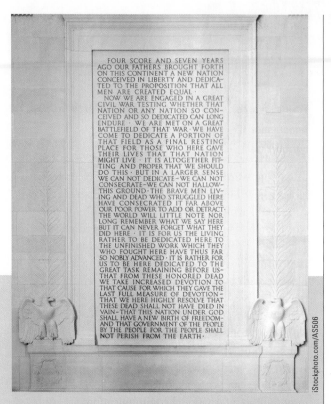

Abraham Lincoln's two-minute Gettysburg Address is a classic example of concise communication.

attention is directed toward the important details and is not distracted by excessive words and details.

The following techniques will produce concise messages:

- **Eliminate redundancies.** A **redundancy** is a phrase in which one word unnecessarily repeats an idea contained in an accompanying word. "Absolutely necessary" and "negative misfortune" are redundant because both words have the same meaning; only "necessary" and "misfortune" are needed. A few of the many redundancies in business writing are shown in the following list. Be conscious of redundancies in your speech and writing patterns.

Redundancies to Avoid

Needless repetition:	advance forward, it goes without saying, best ever, cash money, important essentials, each and every, dollar amount, pick and choose, past experience

> **redundancy** a phrase in which one word unnecessarily repeats an idea contained in an accompanying word (e.g., "exactly identical")

Redundancies to Avoid

Unneeded modifiers:	new innovations, personal friend, actual experience, brief summary, complete stop, collaborate together, disappear from sight, honest truth, trickle down, month of May, personal opinion, red in color, severe crisis, currently available
Repeated acronyms:	ATM machine, PIN number, SAT tests, SIC code

Redundancy is not to be confused with repetition used for emphasis. In a sentence or paragraph, you may need to use a certain word again. When repetition serves a specific purpose, it is not an error. Redundancy serves no purpose and *is* an error.

- **Use active voice to reduce the number of words.** Passive voice typically adds unnecessary words, such as prepositional phrases. Compare the sentence length in each of these examples:

Passive Voice	Active Voice
Work schedules will be updated by department supervisors.	Department supervisors will update work schedules.
The project planning department will be transferred to the third floor next month by a moving company.	Next month, movers will transfer the project planning department to the third floor.

- **Review the main purpose of your writing, and identify relevant details needed for the receiver to understand and take necessary action.** More information is not necessarily better information. You may be so involved and perhaps so enthusiastic about your message that you believe the receiver needs to know everything that you know. Or perhaps you just need to devote more time to audience analysis and empathy.

- **Eliminate clichés that are often wordy and not necessary to understand the message.** For example, "Thank you for your letter," "I am writing to," "May I take this opportunity," "It has come to my attention," and "We wish to inform you" only delay the major purpose of the message.

- **Do not restate ideas that are sufficiently implied.** Notice how the following sentences are improved when ideas are implied. The revised sentences are concise, yet the meaning is not affected.

Wordy	Concise
John prepared PowerPoint slides and practiced his presentation.	John prepared for his presentation.
The manager reviewed team reports and revised the project schedule.	The manager revised the project schedule.

- **Shorten sentences by using suffixes or prefixes, making changes in word form, or substituting precise words for phrases.** In the following examples, the expressions in the right column provide useful techniques for saving space and being concise. However, the examples in the left column are not grammatically incorrect. Sometimes their use provides just the right emphasis.

Wordy	Concise
She completed her work in a competent manner.	She was a competent worker.
His style of writing was quite florid.	He had a florid writing style.
He believes the new policy guidelines to be of little value.	He believes the new policy guidelines are valueless.
Sales staff with high energy levels …	Energetic sales staff …
… arranged in chronological order.	… arranged chronologically …

- **Use a compound adjective.** By using the compound adjective, you can reduce the number of words required to express your ideas and thus save the reader a little time.

Wordy	Concise
The corporation values employees who speak well.	The corporation values well-spoken employees.
Karen Lewis, who is well liked by her colleagues, will take …	Well-liked Karen Lewis will take …
The intranet will be down for two days for routine upgrades on July 23 and 24.	The two-day intranet upgrade will occur on July 23 and 24.

4-3f Project a Positive, Tactful Tone

Being adept at communicating negative information will give you the confidence you need to handle sensitive situations in a constructive manner, resulting in a positive **tone**. The following suggestions reduce the sting of an unpleasant thought:

- **State ideas using positive language.** Rely mainly on positive words—words that speak of what can be done instead of what cannot be done, of the pleasant instead of the unpleasant. In each of the following pairs, both sentences are sufficiently clear, but the positive words in the improved sentences make the message more diplomatic and promote positive human relations.

Negative Tone	Positive Tone
You forgot to fill in the last column of the annual budget report.	Please fill in the last column of the annual budget report.
We cannot complete your order without your email address.	Please supply your email address so that we can complete your order.
You failed to submit your expense report by the monthly deadline.	Please submit your expense report by the next monthly deadline.

- **Avoid using second person when stating negative ideas.** Use second person for presenting pleasant ideas; use third person for presenting unpleasant ideas. Note the following examples:

Pleasant Idea (Second Person Preferred)	
You delivered a compelling presentation.	*The person will appreciate the emphasis placed on his or her excellent performance.*

Unpleasant Idea (Third Person Preferred)	
The supply order was incorrectly filled out.	*"You filled out the supply order incorrectly" directs undiplomatic attention to the person who made the error.*

- **Use passive voice to convey negative ideas.** Presenting an unpleasant thought emphatically (as active verbs do) makes human relations difficult. Compare the tone of the following negative thoughts written in active and passive voices:

> **tone** the way a statement sounds; it conveys the writer's or speaker's attitude toward the message and the receiver

Active Voice	Passive Voice (Preferred for Negative Ideas)
Juanita did not complete the order form correctly.	The order needed revision.
Shelly missed the deadline for proposal submission by a week.	The proposal was submitted a week after deadline.

- Positive words are normally preferred, but sometimes the addition of negative words can sharpen a contrast (and thus increase clarity):

Please complete the online order form; phone and email requests will take longer to process. Original copies are to be submitted to the certification board; photocopies will not be accepted.

Because the subject of each active sentence is the doer, the sentences are emphatic. As the idea is negative, Shelly probably would appreciate being taken out of the picture. The passive voice sentences place more emphasis on the job than on who failed to complete it. They retain the essential ideas, but the ideas seem less irritating. For negative ideas, use passive voice.

- **Use active voice to promote positive ideas.** Just as emphasis on negatives hinders human relations, emphasis on positives promotes human relations. Which sentence makes the positive idea more vivid?

Passive Voice	Active Voice (Preferred for Positive Ideas)
The proposal was submitted before the deadline.	Shelly submitted the proposal before the deadline.

Because "Shelly" is the subject of the active voice sentence, the receiver can easily envision the action. Shelly is recognized for meeting the deadline in this sentence. In the passive message, the fact that the deadline was met receives emphasis.

- **Use the subjunctive mood.** Sometimes the tone of a message can be improved by switching to the subjunctive mood. **Subjunctive sentences** speak of a wish, necessity, doubt, or condition contrary to fact and use such conditional expressions as *I wish, as if, could, would*, and *might*. In the following examples, the sentence in the right column conveys a negative

subjunctive sentences
sentences that speak of a wish, necessity, doubt, or condition contrary to fact and employ such conditional expressions as *I wish, as if, could, would,* and *might*

Dirk Ercken/Shutterstock.com

idea in positive language, which is more diplomatic than negative language.

Negative Tone	Subjunctive Mood Conveys Positive Tone
I can't complete the report.	When the information is made available, I can complete the report.
I <u>cannot</u> attend the planning meeting.	I <u>could</u> attend the planning meeting if the date were changed to next week.
I <u>don't believe</u> his statements about the product's efficiency.	I <u>wish</u> I <u>could</u> believe his statements about the product's efficiency.

Sentences in subjunctive mood often include a reason that makes the negative idea seem less objectionable and thus improves the tone. Tone is important, but clarity is even more important. The revised sentence in each of the preceding pairs sufficiently *implies* the unpleasant idea without stating it directly. If for any reason a writer or speaker suspects the implication is not sufficiently strong, a direct statement in negative terms is preferable.

- **Include a pleasant statement in the same sentence.** A pleasant idea is included in the following examples to improve the tone:

Negative Tone	Positive Tone
Your ability to meet deadlines is satisfactory.	Although your ability to meet deadlines was satisfactory, <u>your work to motivate your team was excellent</u>.

Negative Tone	Positive Tone
Increased health-care costs have <u>decreased funds</u> available for salary adjustments.	Increased health-care costs have decreased funds available for salary adjustments, but we hope a shorter workweek <u>will offset</u> employee expectations.

4-3g Use Euphemisms Cautiously

A **euphemism** is a kind word substituted for one that may offend or suggest something unpleasant. For example, the idea of picking up neighborhood garbage does not sound especially inviting. Someone who does such work is often referred to as a *sanitation worker.* This term has a more pleasant connotation than *garbage collector.*

Choose the euphemistic terms rather than the negative terms shown in the following examples:

Negative Tone	Euphemistic Tone
aged or elderly	senior citizen
dying	fading away/near the end
used or secondhand	pre-owned
prison	correctional facility
disabled or handicapped	physically challenged/ differently abled
patient management	care coordination/ supportive services

Generally, you can recognize such expressions for what they are—unpleasant ideas presented with a little sugarcoating. Knowing the sender was simply trying to be polite and positive, receivers are more likely to react favorably. You should avoid, however, euphemisms that excessively sugarcoat and those that suggest subtle sarcasm. For example, to refer to a janitor as a *maintenance engineer* is to risk conveying a negative metacommunication, such as "This person does not hold a very respectable position, but I did the best I could to make it sound good." To the receiver (and to the janitor), just plain *janitor* would sound better.

You will also want to avoid **doublespeak**, also known as *doubletalk* or *corporate speak*. Such terms refer to euphemisms that deliberately mislead, hide, or evade the truth. This distortion of the truth is often found in military, political, and corporate language. A loss of credibility may result when a police officer refers to *nontraditional organized crime* rather than *gang activity*. Another example would be a politician who talks of an *enhanced interrogation technique*

rather than *torture,* or *collateral damage* or *friendly fire* rather than civilians killed accidentally by the military's own weapons. Companies use doublespeak when they make *workforce reductions* or offer workers a *career opportunity adjustment* or *voluntary termination*. One company called the permanent shutdown of a steel plant an *indefinite idling* in an attempt to avoid paying severance or pension benefits to the displaced workers.

Despite your training in writing, you may fall into the trap of mirroring the writing of people above you on the career ladder who prefer writing in doublespeak. They often choose doublespeak over clear, concise writing because of the misguided belief that doublespeak makes them sound informed and professional. Such vagueness protects them when they're unsure how their messages will be received and makes writing easy once they learn the code. Instead of falling into doublespeak, learn to develop clear, concise messages that clarify ideas and provide direction to recipients, regardless of their culture, while enhancing your credibility as an honest communicator. A CEO of a writing training company has another interesting angle on clear writing. He contends, "Articulation of thought is an element of intelligence, and you can increase your intelligence through writing." Working to articulate ideas clearly and logically through writing makes people smarter! That is a motivating reason for perfecting writing (and speaking) skills in our professional and personal lives.

4-3h Avoid Condescending or Demeaning Expressions

Condescending words seem to imply that the communicator is temporarily coming down from a level of superiority to join the receiver on a level of inferiority. Such words damage efforts to build and protect **goodwill**. Note how the reminders of inequality in the following examples hamper communication:

A demeaning expression (sometimes called a *dysphemism*) makes an idea seem negative or disrespectful. Avoid demeaning expressions because they divert attention from the real message to emotional issues that have little to do with the message.

euphemism a kind word substituted for one that may offend or suggest something unpleasant

doublespeak also called doubletalk or corporate speak; euphemisms that deliberately mislead, hide, or evade the truth

goodwill an attitude of kindness or friendliness that results in a good relationship

Many examples can be taken as contempt for an occupation or a specific job or position (*bean counters* for accountants, *ambulance chasers* for lawyers, *spin doctors* for politicians or public relations directors, and *shrinks* for psychiatrists). Like words that attack races or nationalities, words that ridicule occupations work against a communicator's purpose.

Many demeaning expressions are common across regions, ages, and perhaps even cultures. Some demeaning expressions belong to a particular company. For example, *turtles* was coined in one firm to mock first-year employees for their slow work pace. President Obama quickly recognized and apologized for his late-night talk show quip that equated his bowling skills to those of athletes with disabilities. Seeing the president's gaffe as a "teachable moment" for the country, Special Olympics Chairman Tim Shriver emphasized that "words hurt and words do matter and these words that in some respect can be seen as humiliating … do cause pain."[7] Effective communicators choose respectful expressions that build and protect goodwill.

4-3i **Use Connotative Tone Cautiously**

Human relations can suffer when connotative words are inadvertently or intentionally used instead of denotative words. The **denotative meaning** of a word is the literal meaning that most people assign to it. The **connotative meaning** is the literal meaning plus an extra message that reveals the speaker's or writer's qualitative judgment, as shown in this example:

Connotative Meaning with Negative Implication	Denotative Meaning (Preferred)
Please don't hassle the customer service representatives with too frequent questions.	Please don't question the customer service representatives too frequently.

The connotative meaning of *hassle* carries an additional message that the writer has a bias against asking questions. The connotation may needlessly introduce thoughts about whether asking questions is beneficial and may distract the receiver from paying sufficient attention to the statements that follow. Connotations, like metacommunications discussed in Chapter 2, involve messages that are implied. In the preceding example, the connotation seems to be more harmful than helpful.

At times, however, connotations can be helpful, as seen in the following examples:

Connotative Meaning with Positive Meaning (Preferred)	Denotative Meaning
Our corporate think tank has developed an outstanding production process.	Research and Development has developed an outstanding production process.
Rita is a real spark plug when it comes to sales.	Rita's drive and enthusiasm make her successful at sales.

In crafting business messages, rely mainly on denotative or connotative words that will be interpreted in a positive manner. To be sure that your connotative words are understood and will generate goodwill, consider your audience, the context, and the timing of the message.

- **Connotative words may be more easily misinterpreted than denotative words.** Because of differences in peoples' perceptions based on their life experiences, words that are perceived positively by one person may be perceived negatively by another. In some cases, receivers may simply not understand the connotative words. Damaged human relations occur when managers repeatedly convey connotative messages without considering whether employees can interpret the meanings as they are intended.

- **The appropriateness of connotations varies with the audience to which they are addressed and the context in which they appear.** For example, referring to a car as a *foreign job* or *sweet* might be received differently by teenagers than by senior citizens. Such expressions are less appropriate in a research report than in a blog or popular magazine.

4-3j **Use Specific Language Appropriately**

To help the receiver understand your message easily, select words that paint intense, colorful word pictures. Creating clear mental images adds energy and imagination to your message, thus increasing its overall impact.

denotative meaning the literal meaning of a word that most people assign to it

connotative meaning the literal meaning of a word plus an extra message that reveals the speaker's or writer's qualitative judgment

General	Specific (Preferred)
The <u>public outcry</u> was huge.	<u>More than 3 million emails were received</u> from the public.
Please get back to me soon about your proposal changes.	Please supply me with the changes to the proposal by <u>this Friday at noon</u>.
Sam is a great manager.	Sara shines as a manager because of her <u>ability to stay on task and yet make people feel supported</u>.

Sometimes, using general statements can be useful in building and protecting goodwill. General words keep negative ideas from receiving more emphasis than they deserve. In addition, senders who don't have specific information, or for some reason don't want to divulge it, use general words.

General (Preferred)	Specific
Three customers complained about their <u>service</u>.	Three customers complained because their <u>food order was incomplete and the food was delivered cold</u>.
I look forward to <u>working with you again</u>.	I look forward to <u>working with you again because of your easygoing manner and attention to details</u>.

4-3k Use Bias-Free Language

Being responsive to individual differences requires you to make a conscious effort to use bias-free (nondiscrimatory) language. Using language that does not exclude, stereotype, or offend others permits them to focus on your message rather than to question your sensitivity. Goodwill can be damaged when biased statements are made related to gender, race or ethnicity, religion, age, or disability. The following guidelines will help you avoid bias:

1. **Avoid referring to men and women in stereotyped roles and occupations.** The use of *he* to refer to anyone in a group was once standard and accepted; however, this usage is considered insensitive and, to some, offensive. Therefore, do not use the pronoun *he* when referring to a person in a group that may include women or the pronoun *she* to refer to

a group that may include men. Otherwise, you may unintentionally communicate an insensitive message that only women or only men can perform certain tasks or serve in certain professions. Follow these four approaches to avoid gender bias:

Guideline	Gender-Biased	Improved
Avoid using a pronoun	Each employee must complete <u>his</u> vacation request form.	Employees must complete a vacation request form.
Repeat the noun	Expect promptness from your guide. Ask <u>him</u> to …	Expect promptness from your <u>guide</u>. Ask the <u>guide</u> to …
Use a plural noun	Each employee should update and confirm his contact information.	Employees should update and confirm their contact information.
Use pronouns from both genders (when necessary, but not repeatedly)	Please page a doctor. <u>He</u> should respond …	Please page a doctor. <u>He or she</u> should respond …

2. **Use occupational titles that reflect genuine sensitivity to gender.** Note the gender-free titles that can be easily substituted to avoid bias:

Gender-Biased	Gender-Free
Salesman	Salesperson
Chairman	Chair

3. **Avoid designating an occupation by gender.** For example, omit "woman" in "A woman doctor has initiated this research." The doctor's profession, not the gender, is the point of the message. Similarly, avoid using the *-ess* ending to differentiate genders in an occupation:

Gender-Biased	Gender-Free
waiter or waitress	server
Hostess	host

thodonal88/Shutterstock.com

4. **Avoid using expressions that may be perceived to be gender-biased.** Avoid commonly used expressions in which "man" represents all humanity, such as "To go where no man has gone before," and stereotypical characteristics, such as "man hours," "man-made goods," and "work of four strong men." Note the

improvements made in the following examples by eliminating the potentially offensive words.

Gender-Biased	Improved
Our energy products will benefit <u>all of mankind</u>.	Our energy products will benefit <u>humanity</u>.
Laurence is the best <u>man for</u> the job.	Laurence is the best <u>person</u> for the job.

5. **Avoid racial or ethnic bias.** Include racial or ethnic identification only when relevant, and avoid referring to these groups in stereotypical ways.

Racially or Ethnically Biased	Improved
The salespeople ran around like a bunch of wild <u>Indians</u>.	The salespeople were extremely busy on the floor today.
Please give your form to Sheila, the Asian woman.	Please give the form to Sheila, the woman at that desk.
The articulate <u>African American</u> engineer overseeing the product redesign plans suggested …	The engineer overseeing the product redesign plans suggested …

6. **Avoid age bias.** Include age only when relevant, and avoid demeaning expressions related to age.

Age-Biased	Improved
George is <u>the older gentleman</u> who works downstairs.	George works downstairs in the office on the right.

7. **Avoid disability bias.** When communicating about people with disabilities, use people-first language. That is, refer to the person first and the disability second so that focus is appropriately placed on the person's ability rather than on the disability. Also avoid words with negative or judgmental connotations, such as *handicap*, *unfortunate*, *afflicted*, and *victim*. When describing people without disabilities, use the word *typical* rather than *normal*; otherwise, you may inadvertently imply that people with disabilities are abnormal. Consider these more sensitive revisions:

Insensitive	Sensitive (People-First)
<u>Blind</u> employees receive …	Employees with <u>vision impairments</u> receive …
The elevator is for the exclusive use of <u>handicapped</u> employees and should not be used by <u>normal</u> employees.	The elevator is for the exclusive use of employees <u>with disabilities</u>.

4-4 PROOFREAD AND REVISE

Errors in writing and mechanics may seem isolated, but the truth is, proofreading *is* important. You don't have to look far to see silly typos or obvious instances of writers relying only on the computer spell checker. The classifieds in a small-town newspaper advertised "fully fascinated and spade damnation puppies." The advertisement was for fully vaccinated and spayed Dalmatian puppies. These errors clearly illustrate how spell check can fail, but goofs such as this one are not limited to small-town newspapers.

It was not a spelling error, but a simple transposition in a telephone number, that created an unbelievably embarrassing situation for a telecommunications giant. AT&T customers calling to redeem points earned in a True Rewards program were connected to pay-by-the-minute erotic phone entertainment.[8] Mistakes ranging from printing ordinary typos to running entirely erroneous ads forced newspapers to refund $10.6 million to dissatisfied advertisers and to print $10.5 million in free, make-good ads. The University of California at San Diego inadvertently sent an acceptance email message to all 28,000 students it had rejected, raising their hopes only to dash them when the mistake was discovered and corrected.[9] Each of these actual mistakes illustrates that inattention to proofreading can be potentially embarrassing and incredibly expensive.

Following systematic revision procedures will help you produce error-free documents that reflect positively on the company and you. Using the procedures that follow, you will see that effective proofreading must be done several times, each time for a specific purpose.

Follow these simple procedures to produce a finished product that is free of errors in content, organization, and style; mechanics; and format and layout:

1. **Use the spell checker to locate simple keying errors and repeated words.** When the software cannot guess the correct spelling based on your incorrect attempt, you will need to consult a dictionary, other printed source, or online reference.

2. **Proofread the document onscreen, concentrating first on errors in content, organization, and style.** To locate errors, ask the following questions:

   ○ **Content.** Is the information complete? Have I included all the details the receiver needs to understand the message and to take necessary action? Is the information accurate? Have I

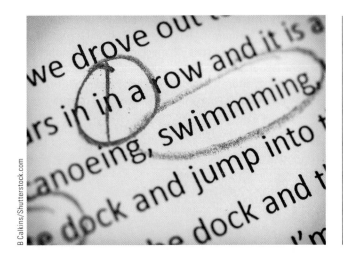

checked the accuracy of any calculations, dates, names, addresses, and numbers? Have words been omitted?

○ **Organization.** Is the main idea presented appropriately, based on the receiver's likely reaction (deductive or inductive organization)? Are supporting ideas presented in a logical order?

○ **Style.** Is the message clear? Will the receiver interpret the information correctly? Is the message concise and written at an appropriate level for the receiver? Does the message reflect a considerate, caring attitude and focus primarily on the receiver's needs? Does the message treat the receiver honestly and ethically?

FIGURE 4.4 ROUGH DRAFT OF A LETTER (EXCERPT)

September 8, 2016a
FAX Transmission

Conrad Harris, Owner
Xcess
2054 Pioneer Square
Portland, OR ~~Oregon~~ 85301

Dear Mr. Haris:
Congratulations on the recent opening of your innovative chocolate and wine bar! We are excited to learn of your interest in the Trayne commercial oven line and believe you will find a model that meets your exact needs.

Available with radiant, direct-fired convection and hybrid radiant/convection heating, Trayne ovens are highly energy efficient owing to both heating system design and their low surface area to volume ratio. Fully automated, they incorporate a user-friendly touch-screen interface, plus full-length viewing doors for visual inspection of the bake at every level and easy access for cleaning and maintenance.

Trayne ovens provide enormous advantages over conventional oven technologies, including

- Iimproved product quality and consistency.; The ultra-compact design is based on a transport technology where pans are conveyed horizontally through the oven via a vertical 'S' configuration.
- R~reduced footprint. Typically one-tenth the footprint of an equivalent tunnel oven, Trayne ovens offer a crucial advantage in environments where production floor space is at a premium ~~and~~.
- Ssuperior flexibility. Trayne ovens offer superior flexibility, allowing product changes by simply changing pans; and ~~ancillary~~ additional tooling.

Mr. Harris, were eager to schedule your visit to our nearby showroom to introduce our product line. At your convenience, please review the enclosed brochures and I will call you next week to schedule an appointment.

● Adds mailing notation.

● Uses two-letter abbreviation.

● Corrects spelling of name.

● Adds smooth transition to next paragraph.

● Bullet list for emphasis and conciseness.

● Eliminates unnecessary comma.
● Replace with simple word for clarity.

● Errors Undetectable by Spell-Check
Check correctness of word substitutions: "to" for "too" and "your" for "you."

● Correct proofreading error.

3. **Proofread a second time, concentrating on mechanical errors.** You are searching for potentially damaging errors that the spell checker cannot detect. These problem areas include:

   ◦ **Grammar, capitalization, punctuation, number usage, and abbreviations.** Review the grammatical principles presented in the appendix if necessary.

   ◦ **Word substitutions.** Check the proper use of words such as *your* and *you* and words that sound alike (*there, they're,* or *their*; *affect* or *effect*).

   ◦ **Parts of the document other than the body. Proofread the entire document.** Errors often appear in the opening and closing sections of documents because writers typically begin proofreading at the first paragraph.

4. **Display the document in print preview mode, and edit for format and layout.** Follow these steps to be certain the document adheres to appropriate business formats and is visually appealing:

   ◦ **Format according to a conventional format.** Compare your document to the conventional business formats shown on your Style and Formatting cards, and make any revisions. Are all standard parts of the document included and presented in an acceptable format? Are all necessary special parts (e.g., attention line, enclosure) included? Does the message begin on the correct line? Should the right margin be justified or jagged?

   ◦ Be sure numbered items are in the correct order. Inserting and deleting text might have changed the order of these items.

   ◦ Evaluate the visual impact of the document. Could you increase the readability of long, uninterrupted blocks of text by using enumerated or indented lists, headings, or graphic borders or lines? Would adding images or varying print styles add visual appeal? View Web documents on several different browsers to ensure readability and appeal.

   ◦ Be certain the document is signed or initialed (depending on the document). Ensure that email messages are addressed to the appropriate person or persons.

5. **Print a draft copy and proofread a third time if the document is nonroutine and complex.** Read from *right to left* to reduce your reading speed, allowing you to concentrate deliberately on each word. If a document is extremely important, you might consider reading the document aloud, spelling names and noting capitalization and punctuation, while another person verifies the copy.

6. **Print written documents on high-quality paper.** The message in Figure 4.4 has been revised for (1) content, organization, and style; (2) mechanics; and (3) format and layout. Study the revisions made using the track-changes feature in word-processing software. The commentary makes it easy to see how revising this draft improved the document's quality.

To Recap:

☑ Use the spell checker to locate simple keying errors and repeated words.

☑ Proofread once, concentrating on errors in content, organization, and style.

☑ Proofread a second time, concentrating on mechanical errors.

☑ Edit for format and layout.

☑ Print a draft copy of the document.

☑ Proofread a third time if the document is nonroutine and complex.

☑ For documents to be delivered on paper, print on high-quality paper.

STUDY TOOLS 4

LOCATED AT BACK OF THE TEXTBOOK

☐ Tear-Out Chapter Review Card

LOCATED AT WWW.CENGAGEBRAIN.COM

☐ Review Key Term flashcards and create your own cards

☐ Track your knowledge and understanding of key concepts in business communication

☐ Complete practice and graded quizzes to prepare for tests

☐ Complete interactive content within BCOM8 Online

☐ View the chapter highlight boxes for BCOM8 Online

5 Communicating Electronically

POST
SHARE
CONNECT

RACK ID.
FIND

MAIL

☑ COMMUNICATION

SEND

RawPixel/Shutterstock.com

LEARNING OBJECTIVES

5-1 Discuss the effective use of email, instant messaging, and text messaging in business communication.

5-2 Explain principles for writing effectively for the Web.

5-3 Discuss the effective use of voice and wireless technologies in business communication.

5-4 Consider legal and ethical implications associated with the use of communication technology.

After finishing this chapter, go to **PAGE 85** for **STUDY TOOLS**.

5-1 APPROPRIATE USE OF TECHNOLOGY

Technology offers numerous advantages, but a technological channel is not always the communication method of choice. Before sending a message, be certain the selected channel of communication is appropriate by considering the message's purpose, confidentiality issues, and human relations factors.

5-1a Determine the Purpose of the Message

If a message is straightforward and informative, chances are a technological option might be appropriate. Although the use of instantaneous and efficient communication methods is quite compelling, keep in mind that written communication, printed or online, cannot replace the personal interaction so essential in today's team-based work environments. Employees that are floors apart or in different offices or time zones benefit from email and Web communications, but two people sitting side by side or on the same floor shouldn't have to communicate solely by electronic means.

A second question when selecting among communication options is whether a permanent record of the message is needed or if a more temporary form such as a phone call or instant message would suffice.

5-1b Determine Whether the Information Is Personal or Confidential

As a general guideline, keep personal correspondence off-line if you don't want it to come back and haunt you. The content of an email message could have embarrassing consequences since such documents often become a part of public records, and wireless communications might be unexpectedly intercepted. Your company technically "owns" your electronic communications and thus can monitor them to determine legitimate business use or potential abuse. Undeliverable email messages are delivered to a mail administrator, and many networks routinely store backups of all email messages that pass through them.

Even deleted messages can be "resurrected" with little effort, as several public figures discovered when investigators retrieved archived email as evidence in court cases. For sensitive situations, a face-to-face encounter is often preferred.

Before sending a message, be certain the selected channel of communication is appropriate.

5-1c Decide Whether Positive Human Relations Are Sacrificed

Be wary of using an electronic communication tool as an avoidance mechanism. Remember, too, that some people do not regularly check their email or voice mail, and some have unreliable systems that are slow or prone to losing messages. Some news will be received better in person than through an electronic format that might be interpreted as cold and impersonal.

Additionally, some people, especially those of certain cultures, prefer a personal meeting even if you perceive that an electronic exchange of information would be a more efficient use of everyone's time. Choose the communication channel carefully to fit both your purpose and the preference of the receiver.

5-2 ELECTRONIC MAIL COMMUNICATION

As you read in Chapter 1, the continuous evolution of technology has expanded communication options. Email, instant messaging, Web communications, and voice and wireless technologies are important tools for accomplishing company goals. In fact, email has overtaken the telephone in terms of the most common workplace communication tool.[1] The ability to use email communications effectively is essential to success in virtually every career.

5-2a Advantages of Email

Electronic mail, or email, offers numerous advantages. Its ready availability, convenience, and ease of use have resulted in its skyrocketing popularity. The advantages of email are numerous:

- **It facilitates the fast, convenient flow of information among users at various locations and time zones.** Mail service is often too slow for communicating timely information, and the telephone system is inconvenient and costly when communicating with people located in several locations and time zones. For these reasons, email is especially effective when sending a single message to several recipients and when needing to communicate 24 hours a day, 365 days a year.

- **It increases efficiency.** Email reduces "telephone tag" and unnecessary telephone interruptions caused when delivering messages that are unlikely to require a verbal response.

- **It reduces costs.** Sending email messages represents a substantial savings to companies in long-distance telephone costs and postal mail-outs.

- **It reduces paper waste.** Often an electronic message can be read and immediately discarded without the need for a printed copy.

5-2b Guidelines for Preparing Email Messages

Following these guidelines will enable you to use email efficiently and effectively when communicating with both valued coworkers and outside parties:

- **Send to single or multiple addressees.** The same message can be sent to one or many recipients simultaneously. Sending an email message to multiple recipients routinely involves keying the email address of each recipient into a distribution list and selecting the distribution list as the recipient.

- **Provide a useful subject line.** A descriptive subject line assists the receiver's understanding of the message and is helpful for future reference to it. Additionally, a well-written subject line in an email message will help the receiver sort through an overloaded mailbox and read messages in priority order. When writing a subject line, think of the five Ws—Who, What, When, Where, and Why—to give you some clues for wording. For instance, "Budget Committee Meeting on Thursday" is a more meaningful subject line than "Meeting."

- **Restate the subject in the body of the message.** The body of the message should be a complete thought and should not rely on the subject line for elaboration. A good opening sentence might be a repetition of most of the subject line. Even if the reader skipped the subject line, the message would still be clear, logical, and complete.

- **Focus on a single topic directed toward the receiver's needs.** An email message is generally limited to one idea rather than addressing several issues. If you address more than one topic in a single email message, chances are the recipient will forget to respond to all points discussed. Discussing one topic allows you to write a descriptive subject line, and the receiver can file the single subject message in a separate mailbox if desired. If you must send a lengthy email, preview the topics to be covered in the introduction, and then divide the message into logical sections for easy comprehension.

- **Sequence your ideas based on anticipated reader reaction.** As you learned previously, ideas should be organized deductively when a message contains good news or neutral information. Inductive organization is recommended when the message contains bad news or is intended to persuade. Email messages should be organized according to the sequence of ideas—for example, time order, order of importance, or geography. As a general rule, present the information in the order it is likely to be needed. For example, describe the nature and purpose of an upcoming meeting before giving the specifics (date, place, time).

- **Make careful use of jargon, technical words, and shortened terms.** The use of jargon and technical terms is more common in email messages than in business letters. Such shortcuts save time with audiences who will understand the intent. In practicing empathy, however, consider whether the receiver will likely understand the terms used.

- **Use graphic highlighting to add emphasis.** Enumerated or bulleted lists, tables, graphs, pictures, or other images can be either integrated into the content of the email or attached as supporting material.

- **Revise your email before sending.** Even the average email requires at least one pass to ensure that the intended message is clear, concise, and error-free. The number of passes increases depending on the number of people receiving the email and the complexity of the message. Revising for brevity and conciseness is a primary goal for messages that are often read on the run and on mobile devices. Keep to one screen, eliminate redundancies, and tighten wording. Avoid off-topic material that detracts from the email's single subject, as well as clever or amusing statements that are funny only to the writer.[2] Direct, concise messages sometimes sound impersonal and curt if not revised for goodwill. Question whether a phone call would be more appropriate for the message; a businesslike, yet conversational tone might sound less aggressive or demanding. Revise emails to achieve a similar tone.[3] Use the email spell checker and then proofread onscreen for content and grammatical errors.

5-2c Effective Use of Email

The email message in Figure 5.1 illustrates guidelines for using professional email. The sender begins the email message by announcing the topic of enhanced shipping services. The paragraphs that follow include timely instructions to find more detailed pickup and delivery times as well as how to schedule service.

FIGURE 5.1 | GOOD EXAMPLE OF AN EMAIL MESSAGE

New Message

To: Freda Ruiz [fruiz@happy!.com]

From: Martin Curtin [mcurtin@speedxpress.com]

Subject: Enhanced delivery service

Hi, Freda,

SpeedXPress has resumed its regular pickup and delivery schedule for freight packages. You can now take advantage of more frequent pickup and delivery times to ensure faster service to your customers. For schedule details, please go to our company website, www.speedxpress.com.

To schedule a pickup, please use the same website. We are able to provide same-day service for last-minute shipments. You may also call our automated scheduling system at 1-888-422-7533.

We look forward to providing you the fastest delivery services in the New York area.

Regards,
Martin Curtin, Operations

- Provides subject line that is meaningful to reader and writer.
- Includes salutation and closing to personalize message.
- Conveys short, concise message limited to one idea and one screen.

Cengage Learning

Although email offers various advantages in speed and convenience, problems arise when it is managed inappropriately. Learning fundamental **netiquette**, the buzzword for proper behavior on the Internet, will ensure your online success. The following guidelines will assist you in using email effectively:

- **Check mail promptly.** Generally, a response to email is expected within 24 hours. Ignoring messages from coworkers can erode efforts to create an open, honest, and cooperative work environment. On the other hand, responding every second could indicate that you are paying more attention to your email than your job.

- **Do not contribute to email overload.** To avoid clogging the system with unnecessary messages, follow these simple guidelines:
  - Be certain individuals need a copy of the email, and forward an email from another person only with the original writer's permission.
  - Never address an email requesting general action to more than one person if you want to receive an individual response. Sharing responsibility will lead to no one taking responsibility.
  - Avoid sending formatted documents. Messages with varying fonts, special print features (bold, italics, etc.), and images take longer to download, require more storage space, and could be unreadable on some computers. In addition, enhancing routine email messages does not support the goals of competitive organizations, and employees and clients or customers might resent such frivolous use of time.
  - Edit the original message when you reply to email if the entire body of the original message is not needed for context. Instead, you can cut and paste pertinent sections within a reply that you believe will help the recipient understand your reply. You can also key brief comments in all caps below the original section.
  - Follow company policy for personal use of email. Obtain a private email account if you are job hunting or sending many private messages to friends and relatives.

- **Use email selectively.** Send short, direct messages for routine matters that need not be handled immediately (scheduling meetings,

netiquette the buzzword for proper behavior on the Internet

Feng Yu/Shutterstock.com

©Arek Malang/Shutterstock.com

giving your supervisor quick updates, or addressing other uncomplicated issues).

- **Do not send messages when you are angry.** Email containing sensitive, highly emotional messages could be easily misinterpreted because of the absence of nonverbal communication (facial expressions, voice tone, and body language). Sending a *flame*, the online term used to describe a heated, sarcastic, sometimes abusive message or posting, might prompt a receiver to send a retaliatory response. Email messages written in anger and filled with emotion and sarcasm could result in embarrassment or even end up as evidence in litigation. Because of the potential damage to relationships and legal liability, read email messages carefully before sending them. Unless a response is urgent, store a heated message for an hour until you have cooled off and thought about the issue clearly and rationally. When you *must* respond immediately, you might acknowledge that your response is emotional and has not been thoroughly considered. Give this warning by using words such as "I need to vent my frustration for a few paragraphs" or "flame on—I'm writing in anger."[4]

- **Exercise caution against email viruses and hoaxes.** An ounce of prevention can avert the problems caused by deadly *viruses* that destroy data files or annoying messages that simply waste your time while they are executing. Install an *antivirus software program* that will scan your hard drive each time you start the computer or access external devices, and keep backups of important files. Be suspicious of email messages that contain attachments if they are from people you don't know. Email text is usually safe to open, but the attachment could contain an executable file that can affect your computer's operations. **Social networking sites** such as Facebook and MySpace are also common sources of viruses and spyware.

social networking sites
websites that provide virtual communities in which people with shared interests can communicate

- Additionally, be wary of *computer hoaxes*—email messages that incite panic, typically related to risks of computer viruses or deadly threats, and urge you to forward them to as many people as possible. Forwarding a hoax can be embarrassing and causes inefficiency by overloading email boxes and flooding computer security personnel with inquiries from alarmed recipients of your message. Investigate the possible hoax by visiting websites such as the following that post virus alerts and hoax information and provide tips for identifying a potential hoax:

  ○ Urban legends: www.urbanlegends.com

  ○ Snopes: www.snopes.com

  ○ Truth or Fiction: www.truthorfiction.com

If a bogus message is forwarded to you, reply to the person politely that the message is a hoax. This action allows you to help stop the spread of the malicious message and will educate one more person about the evils of hoaxes.

- **Develop an effective system for handling email.** Some simple organization will allow you to make better use of your email capability:

  ○ Set up separate accounts for receiving messages that require your direct attention.

  ○ Keep your email inbox clean by reading an email and taking action immediately. Delete messages you are not using and those not likely to be considered relevant for legal purposes.

  ○ Move saved messages into a limited number of email folders for quick retrieval. The email search feature is also useful for identifying saved messages quickly. If you receive many messages, consider setting up your account to sort and prioritize messages, send form letters as replies to messages received with a particular subject line, automatically forward specified email, and sound an alarm when you receive a message from a particular person.

5-2d Instant and Text Messaging

Business use of **instant messaging (IM)** has phenomenal growth. Analysts estimate that in 90% of companies, some employees use IM, whether to close a sale, collaborate with a colleague, or just trade pleasantries with a colleague.[5] This real-time email technology allows the sender to know when someone is available to respond immediately.

The best known IM programs are free and require no special hardware and little training. With some programs, users can exchange graphics and audio and video clips. To use instant messaging, you maintain a list of people with whom you want to interact. You can send messages to any or all of the people on your list as long as the people are online. Sending a message opens up a window in which you and your contact can key messages that you both can see immediately. Figure 5.2 illustrates a sample IM conversation that occurred to arrange for last-minute project changes.

Many of the guidelines that apply to the use of email for business purposes also apply to instant messaging. With IM, however, spelling and grammar matter less when trading messages at high speed. IM users often use shorthand for common words and phrases. IM and telephone communication also share common challenges: being sure that the sender is who he or she claims to be and that the conversation is free from eavesdropping.

Some managers worry that employees will spend too much work time using IM to chat with buddies inside and outside the company. They also emphasize that IM is not the right tool for every business purpose. Employees should still rely on email when they need a record and use the telephone for a personal touch.

5-2e Text Messaging

Text messaging has grown in popularity as cellphones and other handheld devices with text capability have proliferated. Messages can be sent from one cellphone to another, a cellphone to a computer, or computer to computer. **Text messaging** on a cellphone or personal digital assistant is a refinement of computer instant

instant messaging (IM) a real-time email technology that blends email with conversation; sender and receiver who are online at the same time can type messages that both see immediately

text messaging messages that can be sent from one cellphone to another, a cellphone to a computer, or computer to computer; a refinement of computer instant messaging

---

FIGURE 5.2 GOOD EXAMPLE OF AN INSTANT MESSAGE

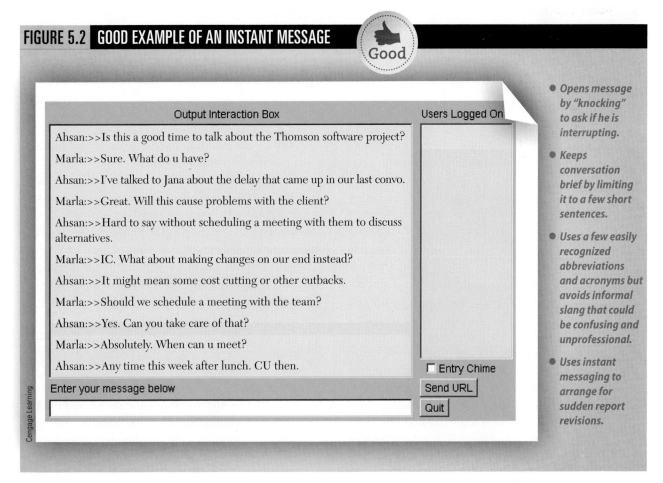

Good

Output Interaction Box

Ahsan:>>Is this a good time to talk about the Thomson software project?

Marla:>>Sure. What do u have?

Ahsan:>>I've talked to Jana about the delay that came up in our last convo.

Marla:>>Great. Will this cause problems with the client?

Ahsan:>>Hard to say without scheduling a meeting with them to discuss alternatives.

Marla:>>IC. What about making changes on our end instead?

Ahsan:>>It might mean some cost cutting or other cutbacks.

Marla:>>Should we schedule a meeting with the team?

Ahsan:>>Yes. Can you take care of that?

Marla:>>Absolutely. When can u meet?

Ahsan:>>Any time this week after lunch. CU then.

Users Logged On

Enter your message below

☐ Entry Chime

Send URL

Quit

- *Opens message by "knocking" to ask if he is interrupting.*
- *Keeps conversation brief by limiting it to a few short sentences.*
- *Uses a few easily recognized abbreviations and acronyms but avoids informal slang that could be confusing and unprofessional.*
- *Uses instant messaging to arrange for sudden report revisions.*

Cengage Learning

FIGURE 5.3 LEVELS OF FORMALITY REQUIRED BY VARIOUS TECHNOLOGIES

Cengage Learning

messaging. The typical cellphone screen can accommodate no more than 160 characters, and because the keypad is far less versatile, text messaging puts an even greater premium on conciseness. An entire code book of acronyms and abbreviations has emerged, ranging from CWOT (complete waste of time) to DLTBBB (don't let the bed bugs bite). The use of emoticons has also advanced far beyond the traditional smiley face and includes drooling (:-)…) and secrecy (:X). Inventive and young users frequently insert their own style, substituting "z" for "s," or "d" for "th." Shortened lingo or text gets right to the point. For instance, a sender might send the following message that can be easily deciphered by most: "Pk u up @730." Cellphone programs are also available to assist in efficiency when texting. T9 (text on nine keys) and similar programs use predictive text to finish words after the first few characters are keyed. T9 can be "trained" to recognize new vocabulary.[6]

Texting is a viable alternative to phone calls for those with hearing impairments. Economic and cultural factors have also driven the advancement of text messaging in some parts of the world where voice conversations are more expensive than texting and short conversations are considered impolite. Some of the most avid users of text messaging are clustered in Southeast Asia. The Chinese language is particularly well suited to text messaging because in Mandarin the names of the numbers are also close to the sounds of certain words.[7] Japanese commuters use their cellphones to text silently, as talking on the phones on the train would be impolite. In the United States, teenagers have popularized texting and carry the habit into places of work. Both abroad and at home, text messaging can be used as an avoidance mechanism that preserves the feeling of communication without the burden for actual intimacy or substance. Most text messages are superficial greetings and are often sent when the two parties are within speaking distance of each other. Like a wave or nod, they are meant to merely establish connection without getting specific.

Although text messaging is generally considered a social communication tool, it is finding more use for business. Text messages can be sent or retrieved in situations when a ringing phone would be inappropriate, such as during meetings. With research showing that many more text messages are opened than are email messages, advertisers are using text messages to send their marketing messages.[8] Refer to Figure 5.3, which compares the completeness and relative formality of an email message to the informal nature of the instant message and the abbreviated style of the text message. Each medium requires its own appropriate writing style to maximize effectiveness and social expectations.

5-2f Electronic Messages and the Law

US courts have established the right of companies to monitor the electronic mail of an employee because they own the facilities and intend them to be used for job-related communication only. On the other hand, employees typically expect that their email messages will be kept private. To protect themselves against liability imposed by the Electronic Communications Privacy Act (ECPA), employers simply provide a legitimate business reason for the monitoring (e.g., preventing computer crime, retrieving lost messages, and regulating employee morale) and obtain written consent to intercept email or at least notify employees. Employees who use the system

You are responsible for the content of any electronic message you send, which could have legal ramifications.

after the notification may have given implied consent to the monitoring.[9]

The legal status of text messaging has been murkier. A 2008 court ruling made a distinction between electronic communications employers store on their servers and communication that is contracted out to third parties. Employers must have either a warrant or the employee's permission to view messages stored by someone other than the employer. Employers who intend to monitor electronic communications must be specific in their written employee policy statements that they intend to access text messages sent with company-issued devices.[10]

Remember that you are responsible for the content of any electronic message you send. Because electronic messages move so quickly between people and often become very informal and conversational, individuals might not realize (or might forget) their responsibility. If a person denies commitments made via an electronic message, someone involved can produce a copy of the message as verification.

Electronic communicators must abide by copyright laws. Be certain to give credit for quoted material, and seek permission to use copyrighted text or graphics from printed or electronic sources. Unless you inform the reader that editing has occurred, do not alter a message you are forwarding or reposting, and be sure to ask permission before forwarding it.

Federal and state bills related to employee privacy are frequently introduced for legislative consideration. Although litigation related to present privacy issues is underway, the development of law is lagging far behind technology; nevertheless, employers can expect changes in the laws as technology continues to develop. Electronic messages have often become the prosecutor's star witness, the corporate equivalent of DNA evidence, as it and other forms of electronic communication are subject to subpoena in litigation. Referring to this issue, former New York Attorney General Eliot Spitzer had this to say: "Never write when you can talk. Never talk when you can nod. And never put anything in an email [that you don't want on the front page of the newspaper]."[11] Several perils of "evidence" mail that companies must address are illustrated in these cases:

- **Including inappropriate content in an email can humiliate and lead to indictment. Detroit Mayor Kwame Kilpatrick and his chief of staff were charged in a 12-count indictment including perjury and obstruction of justice when text messages exchanged between the two were revealed. The pair's secret love affair played out in the messages was also disclosed to a shocked public.[12] The press dubbed the resulting disastrous professional result as "death by Blackberry."

- Failing to preserve or destroying email messages in violation of securities rules is a sure path to destruction. Deleting Enron scandal-related messages led to Arthur Andersen's criminal conviction and eventually to Enron's implosion.

- Inability to locate emails and other relevant documents demanded by the courts is unacceptable and considered negligence by the courts. Penalties have included monetary fines, assessment of court costs or attorney's fees, and dismissal of the case in favor of the opposing side.[13]

On the other hand, evidence mail can protect a company from lawsuits. A company being sued by a female employee because a male executive had allegedly sexually abused her retrieved a trail of emails with lurid attachments sent by the female employee to the male executive named in the case.[14]

To avoid the legal perils of electronic communications, employees must be taught not to write loose, potentially rude, and overly casual messages; to avoid carelessly deleting messages; and to take the time to identify and organize relevant messages for quick retrieval.

5-3 WEB PAGE COMMUNICATION AND SOCIAL MEDIA

Most organizations now have their own websites to accomplish a number of activities, such as updating employees and customers about organizational changes; selling products and services; advertising employment opportunities; and creating a first point of contact for customers through order entry, customer service systems, and online call centers. Although effective web page development is a highly specialized activity, understanding the process will be useful to any business communicator. Organizations can use the Web not only to communicate with customers and clients but also to interact with business associates.

Designing web pages that are accessible by the millions of people with permanent or temporary disabilities, including visual impairments, is good for business.[15] Research by the 2004 Disability Rights Commission has found that the websites that were most accessible for users with disabilities were also easier for people without disabilities to operate, with some online tasks performed 35% faster on the more accessible sites.[16] US businesses have legal requirements for online content to be available

TIP SHEET

The following tips will help you compose appropriate Web content:[17]

▶ Be brief. A good rule is to reduce the wording of any print document by 50% when you put it on the Web.

▶ Keep it simple. Use short words that allow for fast reading by people of various educational backgrounds. Use mixed case because all caps are slower to read.

▶ Consider appropriate jargon. If all of your site users share a common professional language, use it. Otherwise, keep to concise yet effective word choices.

bleakstar/Shutterstock.com

▶ Use eye-catching headlines. They catch interest, ask a question, present the unusual, or pose a conflict.

▶ Break longer documents into smaller chunks. Provide ways to easily move through the document and return to the beginning.

▶ Use attention-getting devices judiciously. Bolding, font changes, color, and graphics do attract attention but can be overdone, causing important ideas to be lost.

▶ Avoid placing critical information in graphic form only. Many users are averse to slow-loading graphics and skip over them.

to everyone under equal opportunity and antidiscrimination laws. The National Federation of the Blind filed a class action suit against Target Corporation because the online store offered values that could not be accessed by screen reader software.[18] The Web Content Accessibility Guidelines provided by The World Wide Web Consortiums (W3C) at **www.w3.org** are helpful resources for ensuring Web accessibility. The same group has also developed Mobile Web Accessibility Guidelines for making websites usable from mobile devices.

5-3a Writing for a Website

Many of the same standard rules for writing apply, whether writing for the Web or print. However, some important differences exist between readers of paper material and Web users:[19]

- **Web users do not want to read. They skim, browse, and hop from one highlighted area to another trying to zero in on the word or phrase that relates to their search.**

- **English-speaking readers typically start scanning at the top left side of the main content area. Their attention moves from top to bottom and left to right. Given this pattern, placing frequently accessed items close to the top of the content area is important. Information should follow the pyramid style of writing common in newspaper writing: the main idea or conclusion is presented first, and subsequent sections and pages expand upon it.**

- **Users can more quickly scan items in columns rather than rows, especially if they are categorized, grouped, and have headings. You can have more lists on the Web than in a typical print document.**

- **Users refer infrequently to directions. It is unlikely they will read little notes, sidebars, and help files, so directions must appear in simple, numbered steps.**

- **In recognition of these Web user characteristics, writers should tailor their styles accordingly.**

Effective Web writing involves moving beyond the paper mode into the Web mode of thinking. Understanding the distinctive expectations of Web readers will allow you to structure your ideas effectively and efficiently.

5-3b Social Media

Web 2.0, which encourages online interaction, made it possible for people to participate on the Web. Unlike web pages, which are not generally interactive, social media enables people to connect online and have a conversation. Web 2.0 technologies include blogs, wikis, video, and social networking sites that enable users to generate their own content.

More and more organizations are using social media tools to communicate with customers. Seventy-nine percent of the Fortune Global 100 companies use at least one of four social platforms—Facebook, videos, Twitter, and blogs—for this purpose.[20] As with company websites, most employees are not responsible for posting to their organization's social media platforms, but as with web pages, employees should understand the process and expectations for doing so.

WRITING FOR WEBLOGS

A **weblog**, or **blog**, is a type of online journal typically authored by an individual and does not allow visitors to change the original posted material, but only to add comments. Some of the millions of blogs now populating the Web are online scrapbooks for pasting links, information, and quotes. Some resemble personal diaries, often illustrated with digital snapshots. Others serve as digital soapboxes, providing a platform for airing opinions and commentary about the world at large or on a special topic of interest. Users (known as bloggers) add entries (referred to as posts) using a simple online form in their browsers, and the weblog publishing software takes care of formatting the page layout and creating archive pages.[21]

> **weblog (or blog)** a type of online journal, typically authored by an individual, that does not allow visitors to change the original material posted, but only to add comments

Blogs differ from websites in that blogs are dynamic, with rapidly changing content that does not require authorization to post. The creator of the message does not have to be familiar with special coding and uploads a message simply by clicking the "Publish" button.[22] Blogging allows average citizens to become publishers. Bloggers, however, should write each post with the realization that it is publicly available.

Blog formats have been adapted for business uses, including commercial publishing, marketing, and as a knowledge management tool. Blogs can store knowledge in searchable archives for future use. This function can be helpful, for example, for service teams as they search past communications to troubleshoot current problems. Many companies, such as Microsoft, Sun Microsystems, and General Motors, encourage blogging among employees.[23] An effective corporate blog begins with a clear goal, such as winning business or building customer loyalty, and then provides relevant, frequently updated information for the target audience to return to regularly. Like other effective Web communications, blogs must be promoted creatively to attract avid readers.[24]

Internal blogs can be established that are not published to anyone outside the company. They present similar legal issues to those surrounding email and instant messaging. One of the most important considerations is whether posts are truly anonymous. The potential for anonymous speech creates an atmosphere that can encourage irresponsible behavior, such as harassment, defamation, and gossip. To reduce this problem, IT professionals can configure internal blogs so that all users can be identified, at least by the company.[25]

WRITING WIKIS

Although a traditional website's content is usually controlled by the sponsoring individual or agency, a wiki is a collaborative website that hosts the collective work of many authors. Similar to a blog in structure and logic, a wiki allows anyone to edit, delete, or modify content, even the work of previous authors. Although allowing everyday users to create and edit a website encourages cooperative use of electronic information, the content posted at such sites should not be considered authoritative. When wiki writing, avoid the first-person blogging style and conform to the tone and flow of the existing article. Wikis are not typically the place for personal opinion and analysis. Instead, present factual information in clear, concise, and neutral language.[26]

Many businesses make use of wikis to encourage free flow of ideas within the organization. Content in a wiki can be updated in real time, without any real administrative effort, and without the need for deliberate

SOCIAL APPS FOR WORK

Boxcar is a social media app that lets you have one central location for all of your social connection apps. It has notifications from your email, Twitter, Facebook, and Google accounts as well as any RSS feeds that you follow. The iPhone will give you a push notification every time you get a direct message, are mentioned in a tweet, get new followers or friends, or when your preferred websites add new content. For example, software programmers can hook up Boxcar and Github if they need to make sure their team is committing code or they want to monitor commits to open source projects. With a hookup, they can get notifications whenever a commit is made.

distribution. Contributors simply visit and update a common website. Wikis facilitate the exchange of information within and between teams. They allow maintenance of a series of unique documents with evolving content. Placing a document in a wiki does not necessarily make it editable by everyone with access to the wiki. For example, the marketing department can make a PowerPoint slide deck available to the sales team or the company at large without letting them change or overwrite it. Most companies implement their wikis behind a firewall to limit participation to their internal user base.[27]

SOCIAL NETWORKING

Social networking sites are for communities of people who share common interests or activities. Common social networking sites include Facebook, LinkedIn, Twitter, and YouTube. Early on, social networking sites were used largely for making personal connections, but more and more, companies are using them to interact with customers. Companies such as Dell and Southwest Airlines employ "communities and conversation teams" or a "social media team" who track comments posted on sites such Twitter, YouTube, Flickr, and Facebook, verify facts, and respond quickly to any customer complaint appearing in cyberspace. In addition to being an early warning system, these online conversations are sources of feedback on customer needs and pain points that lead to innovation in products and services.[28]

CONSIDERATIONS FOR SOCIAL MEDIA USE

As use of social media platforms becomes more common in organizational settings, more companies are creating policies to ensure that employees use them responsibly. Harvard University, Intel Corp., and medical and religious organizations all have policies for use of social media. Typically, these policies address three broad areas: communicating honestly and ethically, protecting the corporation's proprietary information and employee privacy, and maintaining the employee's credibility and the organization's reputation.

- **Communicate honestly and ethically.** When using social media platforms, writers should be transparent about who they are, who they work for, their role, and whether they have a vested interest in an issue. Contributors should write about their area of expertise. For example, a marketing specialist should not contribute information about human resources practices.

- **Protect the company's proprietary and employees' private information.** This should be obvious. Sharing proprietary information can cost an organization thousands or millions of dollars. Sharing private employee information can expose the writer and the company to legal damages and may endanger or harm individuals if personal addresses or information that enables identity theft is publicized.

- **Protect yours as well as the company's reputation.** When communicating on social media sites, the writer should be concerned about projecting a professional persona for him or herself and a reputable image of the company. Making negative statements about competitors, supervisors, colleagues, or company policies may expose the contributor to disciplinary measures or the company to legal threats or bad publicity.

5-4 VOICE AND WIRELESS COMMUNICATION

Not so long ago, voice communication referred strictly to communication over phone lines, and using the telephone effectively is still an important skill in any profession. Although the traditional telephone still plays an important role in business activity, voice communication extends to voice mail systems and cellphone usage. Both voice and data can be transmitted now using wireless communication systems.

5-4a Voice Mail Communication

Voice mail technology allows flexibility in staying in touch without the aid of a computer and reduces telephone tag. Just as email communication can be enhanced by adhering to some basic principles, voice mail communication can be more effective by following recommended guidelines:[29]

- **Update your greeting often to reflect your schedule and leave special announcements.**

- **Leave your email address, fax number, or mailing address on your greeting if this information might be helpful to your callers.**

- **Encourage callers to leave detailed messages. If you need certain standard information from callers, use your greeting to prompt them for it. Such information often eliminates the need to call back.**

- **Instruct callers on how to review their message or be transferred to an operator.**

- **Check your voice mail regularly, and return all voice messages within 24 hours.**

iStockphoto.com/Erik Khalitov

When leaving a message, you can improve your communication by following these tips:[30]

- **Speak slowly and clearly, and repeat your name and phone number at the beginning and end of the message.**

- **Spell your name for the recipient, who might need the correct spelling.**

- **Leave a detailed message, not just your name and number, to avoid prolonged phone tag.**

- **Keep your message brief, typically 60 seconds or less.**

- **Ensure that your message will be understandable. Don't call from places with distracting background noise or an inadequate signal connection.**

The sound of your voice makes a lasting impression on the many people who listen to your greeting or the messages you leave. To ensure that the impression you leave is a professional one, review your voice greeting before you save it. Rerecord to eliminate verbal viruses ("um," "uh," stumbles), flat or monotone voice, and garbled or rushed messages that are difficult to understand. Consider scripting the message to avoid long, rambling messages. As you are recording, stand, smile, and visualize the person receiving the message; you'll hear the added energy, enthusiasm, and warmth in your voice.[31]

Remember that the voice mail message you leave should be seen as permanent. In some systems the digital files are backed up and stored for possible retrieval by managers or other company personnel. A voice mail message can also be used as evidence in a lawsuit or other legal proceeding.[32]

5-4b Cellphone Communication

Cellphone use has significantly enhanced the ability to communicate when away from the office. It has also been shown to dramatically improve performance among salespersons by improving their outreach to clients.[33] Unfortunately, the increasing functionality and ease of use of cellphones have led to their misuse, in many cases. To address this, some employers are developing policies for proper cellphone use. According to a recent poll, almost 7 out of 10 Americans say they observe poor cellphone etiquette at least once every day.[34] Cellphone abuse in the workplace causes annoyance and intrusion that leads to ineffectiveness and can endanger employee safety. Your attention to a few commonsense guidelines will help ensure that you are not seen as a discourteous cellphone user.[35]

- **Be aware of company cellphone policies and obey them.** Some companies do not allow cellphone use for personal reasons during work hours. Most companies have policies prohibiting the harassment of others, and today's smartphones make it easy to send thoughtless messages using various media instantaneously. Not only might these messages damage the sender, but they may also reflect poorly on the employer if posted to Twitter or some other public social medium.

- **Observe wireless-free quiet zones.** This obviously includes theaters, performances, and religious services, but can also include meetings, restaurants, hospitals, and other public places. Exercise judgment about silencing your ringer, switching to vibrate mode, or turning off your phone. To increase the effectiveness of meetings, cellphone policies in some businesses ask that employees leave their cellphones at their desks; vibrating mode is acceptable for an anticipated emergency. To encourage proper cellphone etiquette, one business requires managers to deposit a designated amount of money in a jar should their cellphones ring during a meeting; monies collected are donated to a charity.

- **Respect others in crowded places and be wary of publicizing company information.** Speak in low conversational tones, and consider the content of your conversation. You should use good judgment in determining when and where to discuss proprietary company information or client data. Divulging such information in public places might enable its abuse by others.

- **Think safety.** Some states and municipalities have banned the use of cellphones while driving. Others

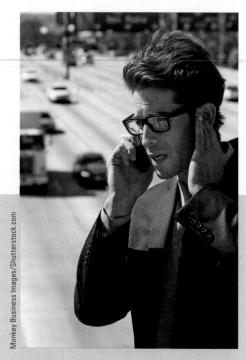

Be cognizant of time and place when discussing business on a cellphone.

allow the use of hands-free devices only. Even if not illegal, cellphone usage increases the risk of accident by distracting the driver. Some companies are implementing cellphone policies that prohibit operators of company-owned vehicles from using cellphones or other communication devices while driving in order to minimize risks to their employees and liability resulting from accidents.

Cellphone users should remember that the technology is not secure. Perhaps you have overheard another party's phone conversation when using your cellphone. The radio frequencies that transmit the voice signals can be picked up by other equipment. For this reason, information that is confidential or sensitive should be shared using an alternate communication channel.

5-5 TECHNOLOGY AND THE FUTURE

With the many communication innovations that have occurred in the last 20 years, one can only wonder what the next 20 years will hold. Whatever the breakthroughs, wireless technology will figure strongly in the changes. Wireless communication has freed us from the necessity of being literally plugged in while enabling us to communicate voice and high-speed data transmission virtually anytime, anywhere.

Wireless technology drives many of the significant changes that are affecting today's businesses. Smartphones offer advanced capabilities, such as the continuing development of innovative phone apps (shorthand for phone applications) that customize smartphone capabilities to fit users' needs. Security will continue to be a challenging consideration as workers use their phones to hold and transmit confidential information.[36]

The mobility provided by wireless technology, though, wouldn't be possible without the corresponding development of smaller, faster, and smarter computer chips. Computer chips will likely continue to get smaller, enabling us to carry the technology of a laptop on our wrist.

Voice input and output technology offers the ability to communicate through a computer system without a keyboard. Although such technology has been around for more than two decades, newer systems have more powerful processors, are smaller in size, and better tolerate variances in speakers' accents and inflections without sacrificing speed and accuracy.

As more and more information is stored in the "cloud," threats to its security will likely continue to grow. (Cloud storage is a model of networked enterprise storage where data is stored in virtualized pools of storage that are generally hosted by third-party providers.) The *New York Times* cataloged a list of recent app and cloud-based breaches, including Chinese hackers obtaining access to hundreds of US government accounts on Google's Gmail and a loss of data from a large number of Dropbox customers. More recently, Evernote said user names, email addresses, and encrypted passwords had been stolen in an attack, requiring the passwords of more than 50 million accounts to be reset.[37] As incidents of cyber attacks grow, billions of dollars are stolen, and billions of people are placed at risk each year. Organizations and their employees will need to spend more time and resources ensuring the safety of company knowledge, and customer and employees' private information.

The convergence of these developments will increase the speed of making and conveying key business decisions, resulting in greater revenues and profitability. However, being able to make decisions quickly does not ensure that they will be the right decisions. As in the past, workers will need to have correct and timely information for making decisions, and then use that information ethically. An additional challenge will be balancing electronic communication capabilities with the need for human interaction.

McCarony/Shutterstock.com

TO RECAP—EFFECTIVE USE OF EMAIL

- ☑ Check email promptly.
- ☑ Do not contribute to email overload.
- ☑ Use email selectively.
- ☑ Do not send messages when you are angry.
- ☑ Exercise caution against email viruses and hoaxes.
- ☑ Develop an effective system for handling email.

STUDY TOOLS 5

LOCATED AT BACK OF THE TEXTBOOK

- ☐ Tear-Out Chapter Review Card

LOCATED AT WWW.CENGAGEBRAIN.COM

- ☐ Review Key Term flashcards and create your own cards
- ☐ Track your knowledge and understanding of key concepts in business communication
- ☐ Complete practice and graded quizzes to prepare for tests
- ☐ Complete interactive content within BCOM8 Online
- ☐ View the chapter highlight boxes for BCOM8 Online

TO RECAP—EMAIL ADVANTAGES

- ☑ Allows communication 24 hours a day, 365 days a year
- ☑ Reduces telephone interruptions by delivering messages that are unlikely to require a verbal response
- ☑ Saves companies the costs of long-distance telephone bills and postal mail-outs
- ☑ Reduces the need to print messages

6

Delivering Good- and Neutral-News Messages

Andor Bujdoso/Shutterstock.com

LEARNING OBJECTIVES

After studying this chapter, you will be able to ...

6-1 Describe the deductive outline for good and neutral news and its adaptations for specific situations and for international audiences.

6-2 Prepare messages that convey good news, including thank-you and appreciation messages.

6-3 Write messages presenting routine claims and requests, and favorable responses to them.

6-4 Write messages acknowledging customer orders, providing credit information, and extending credit.

6-5 Prepare procedural messages that ensure clear and consistent application.

After finishing this chapter, go to **PAGE 104** for **STUDY TOOLS**.

DEDUCTIVE ORGANIZATIONAL PATTERN

You read in Chapter 4 that you can organize business messages either *deductively* or *inductively* depending on your prediction of the audience's reaction to your main idea. Learning to organize business messages according to the appropriate outline will improve your chances of preparing a document that elicits the response or action you desire.

In this chapter, you will learn to compose messages that convey ideas that you're audience likely will find either *pleasing* or *neutral*. Messages that convey pleasant information are referred to as **good-news messages**. Messages that are of interest to your audience but are not likely to generate an emotional reaction are referred to as **neutral-news messages**. The strategies discussed for structuring good- and neutral-news messages generally can be applied to North American audiences. Because message expectations and social conventions differ from culture to culture, the effective writer will adapt as necessary when writing for various audiences. People in organizations use a number of channels to communicate with internal and external audiences. When sending a message that is positive or neutral, you have numerous choices, as shown in Figure 6.1. Depending on the message, audience, and constraints of time and location, the best channel might be spoken or electronic. In addition to the electronic and verbal tools presented in Chapter 5 (email, instant messaging, Web communications, and phone), companies also use written documents such as memorandums and letters to communicate information.

The principles for preparing memorandums (commonly referred to as *memos*) are similar to those you've already applied when composing email messages, as both are channels for sharing information of a somewhat informal nature. Memos provide a more formal means of sharing information with people inside an organization. Letters are a more formal method of conveying information to external audiences such as customers, clients, business partners, or suppliers. Regardless of whether the audience is an internal or external one, communication should be carefully structured to achieve the desired purpose.

Good-news or neutral-news messages follow a **deductive** or **direct sequence**—the message begins with the main idea. To present good news and neutral information deductively, begin with the major idea, followed by supporting details, as depicted in Figure 6.1. In both outlines, the third point (closing thought) might be omitted without seriously impairing effectiveness; however, including it unifies the message and avoids abruptness.

The deductive pattern has several advantages:

- **The first sentence is easy to write. After it is written, the details follow easily.**
- **The first sentence gets the attention it deserves in this emphatic position.**
- **Encountering good news in the first sentence puts your audience in a pleasant frame of mind, so it is more receptive to the details that follow.**
- **The arrangement might save your audience some time. Once it understands the important idea, it can move rapidly through the supporting details.**

As you study sample deductive messages in this chapter, note the *poor example* notations that clearly mark the examples

> Whether the audience is internal or external, communication should be structured to achieve the desired purpose.

good-news messages messages that convey pleasant information

neutral-news messages messages that are of interest to the reader but are not likely to generate an emotional reaction

deductive (or direct) sequence when the message begins with the main idea followed by supporting details

NOBODY TURNED UP TO THE 'EFFECTIVE COMMUNICATIONS' SEMINAR ...THEY DIDN'T GET OUR MEMO!

FRAN

Fran/Cartoon Stock

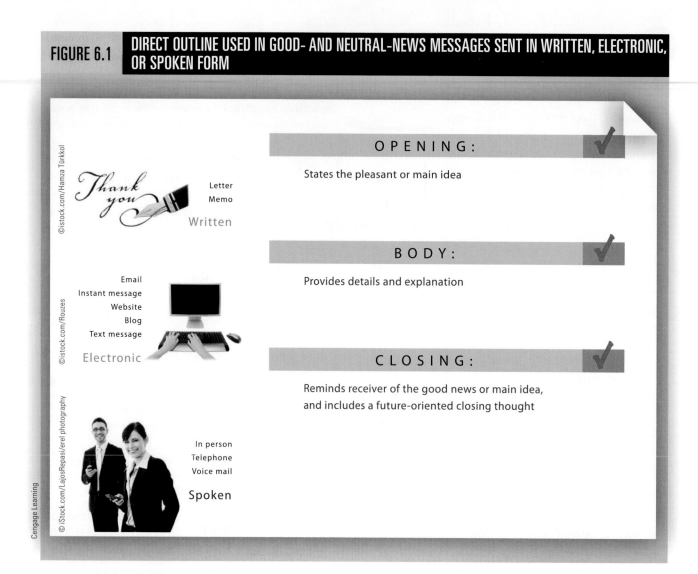

Letter
Memo
Written

Email
Instant message
Website
Blog
Text message
Electronic

In person
Telephone
Voice mail
Spoken

OPENING:
States the pleasant or main idea

BODY:
Provides details and explanation

CLOSING:
Reminds receiver of the good news or main idea, and includes a future-oriented closing thought

©istock.com/Hamza Türkkol

©istock.com/Rouzes

© iStock.com/LajosRepasi/erel photography

Cengage Learning

of ineffective writing. Detailed comments highlight important writing strategies that have been applied or violated. While gaining experience in developing effective messages, you will also learn to recognize standard business formats. Fully formatted messages are shown as printed documents (letters on company letterhead or paper memos) or as electronic formats (email messages or online input screens).

6-2 GOOD-NEWS MESSAGES

Messages delivering good news are organized using a direct approach, as illustrated in Figure 6.1. For illustration, you'll study examples of messages that convey positive news as well as thank-you and appreciation messages that generate goodwill.

6-2a Positive News

The memo sent to all employees in Figure 6.2 begins directly with the main idea: a new flex-time workplace policy for employees. The discussion that follows includes a brief review of the policy and ends positively by encouraging employees to seek additional information from the company website or contact the recipient's supervisor.

6-2b Thank-You and Appreciation Messages

Empathetic managers take advantage of occasions to write goodwill messages that build strong, lasting relationships with employees, clients, customers, and various other groups. People are usually not reluctant to say, "Thank you," "What a great performance," "You have

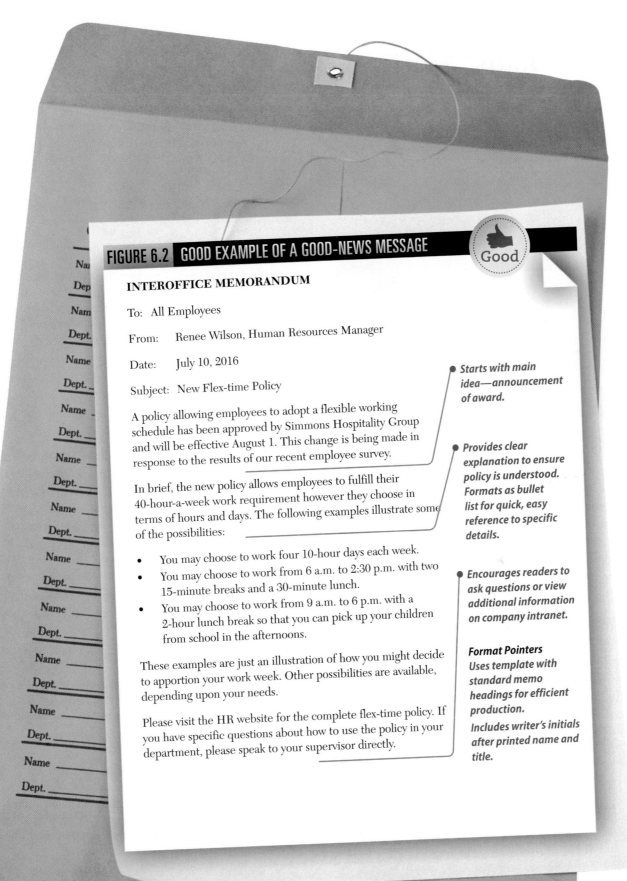

FIGURE 6.2 · GOOD EXAMPLE OF A GOOD-NEWS MESSAGE

Good

INTEROFFICE MEMORANDUM

To: All Employees

From: Renee Wilson, Human Resources Manager

Date: July 10, 2016

Subject: New Flex-time Policy

A policy allowing employees to adopt a flexible working schedule has been approved by Simmons Hospitality Group and will be effective August 1. This change is being made in response to the results of our recent employee survey.

In brief, the new policy allows employees to fulfill their 40-hour-a-week work requirement however they choose in terms of hours and days. The following examples illustrate some of the possibilities:

- You may choose to work four 10-hour days each week.
- You may choose to work from 6 a.m. to 2:30 p.m. with two 15-minute breaks and a 30-minute lunch.
- You may choose to work from 9 a.m. to 6 p.m. with a 2-hour lunch break so that you can pick up your children from school in the afternoons.

These examples are just an illustration of how you might decide to apportion your work week. Other possibilities are available, depending upon your needs.

Please visit the HR website for the complete flex-time policy. If you have specific questions about how to use the policy in your department, please speak to your supervisor directly.

Starts with main idea—announcement of award.

Provides clear explanation to ensure policy is understood. Formats as bullet list for quick, easy reference to specific details.

Encourages readers to ask questions or view additional information on company intranet.

Format Pointers
Uses template with standard memo headings for efficient production.
Includes writer's initials after printed name and title.

Thank You!

Written appreciation messages are meaningful.

a business situation, the message might be printed on company letterhead. Your message should be written deductively and reflect your sincere feelings of gratitude. The thank-you messages shown on this page (1) identify the circumstances for which the writer is grateful and (2) provide specific reasons the action is appreciated.

TO EXTEND THANKS FOR HOSPITALITY

Thank you for opening your home for our annual barbecue. Your beautiful garden and inviting pool made the event one of our best summer parties yet. I enjoyed meeting your lovely family and especially wanted to thank your husband for grilling all those delicious burgers and brats. Thanks again for your generosity in sharing your home and family with your colleagues.

APPRECIATION MESSAGES

You will write appreciation messages to recognize, reward, and encourage the receiver; however, you will also gain satisfaction from commending a deserving person. Such positive thinking can be a favorable influence on your own attitude and performance. In appropriate situations, you might wish to address an appreciation message to an individual's supervisor and send a copy of the document to the individual to share the positive comments. In any case, an appreciation message should be sent to commend deserving people and not for possible self-gain.

For full potential value, follow these guidelines for appreciation messages:

- **Send in a timely manner.** Sending an appreciation message within a few days of the circumstance will emphasize your genuineness. The receiver might question the sincerity of appreciation messages that are sent long overdue.

- **Avoid exaggerated language that is hardly believable.** You might believe the exaggerated statements to be true, but the recipient might find them unbelievable and insincere. Strong language with unsupported statements raises questions about your motive for the message.

- **Make specific comments about outstanding qualities or performance.** Compared to Figure 6.3, the following message might lack the impact of one that contains more detail and is written with more

certainly helped me," and so on. Despite good intentions, however, often people don't get around to sending thank-you and appreciation messages. Because of their rarity, written appreciation messages are especially meaningful—even treasured.

TO EXPRESS THANKS FOR A GIFT

Thank you for the gift certificate to Bath Bubbles Boutique. You know how much I like to relax in a hot, aromatic bath after a stressful day at work! I was happy to fill in for you during the hiring meeting, since our input is so important to our team. I hope your sister's wedding was a success.

THANK-YOU MESSAGES

After receiving a gift, being a guest, attending an interview, or benefiting in various other ways, a thoughtful person will take the time to send a written thank-you message. A simple handwritten note or email is sufficient for some social situations. However, when written from a professional office to respond to

FIGURE 6.3 **GOOD EXAMPLE OF AN APPRECIATION MESSAGE**

Good

New Message

To: Laura Snell [laura.snell@snellconsulting.com]
From: Maxwell Robinson [mrobinson@firewall.com]
Subject: Appreciation for Leadership Workshop

Laura,

Completing the Shared Leadership course at your training facility was an eye-opening and motivational experience for our management group.

Your course was particularly helpful in illustrating for our employees the importance of building a leadership skills based upon effective communication and workplace behaviors to enhance team performance. Understanding the importance of working as a team rather than as a group of individuals was particularly eye opening.

One manager said the course led him to the epiphany that leading was primarily relational rather than transactional. Thanks for helping us see a new path to growth.

Sincerely,
Maxwell Robinson
Chief, Organizational Development
Firewall Software, Inc.
509-269-4100, Fax: 509-269-4103
mrobinson@firewall.com

• *Extends appreciation for company's providing quality opportunities for leadership development.*

• *Provides specific example without exaggerating or using overly strong language or insincere statements.*

• *Reciprocates goodwill.*

Format Pointers
Uses short lines, mixed case; omits special formatting such as emoticons and email abbreviations for improved readability.

Cengage Learning

---

care. Although the sender cared enough to say thank you, the message could have been given to any speaker, even if the sender had slept through the entire workshop. Similarly, a note merely closed with "sincerely" does not necessarily make the ideas seem sincere. Including specific remarks about understanding and applying the speaker's main points makes the message meaningful and sincere.

Original: Your workshop on using the new database software program was very much appreciated. I'm sure it will help staff tremendously. Thanks.

Improved: Your workshop on the use of our new database software program has enabled staff to apply its broad array of features much more quickly.

SINCERE APOLOGY

Gajus/Shutterstock.com

One of the most important takeaways from the workshop was the emphasis you placed on creating and communicating clear procedures for work processes. Based upon your suggestions, our team created a draft of these guidelines during our first meeting. Thank you for the suggestions that have put my colleagues and me on the path to becoming a more effective virtual team.

The appreciation message in Figure 6.3 sent from an organizational development officer to consultant conveys sincere appreciation for the positive results of a workshop. The net effects of this message are positive: the sender feels good for having passed on a deserved compliment, and the receiver is encouraged by the recipient's recognition of the value of her organization's work.

An apology is written much like an appreciation message. A sincere written apology is needed to preserve relationships when regrettable situations occur. Though difficult to prepare, a well-written apology will usually be received favorably.

6-3 ROUTINE CLAIMS

A **claim** is a request for an adjustment. When business communicators ask for something to which they think they are entitled (such as a refund, replacement, exchange, or payment for damages), the message is called a *claim message*.

6-3a Claim Message

Requests for adjustments can be divided into two groups: **routine claims** and **persuasive claims**. Persuasive claims, which are discussed in Chapter 8, assume that a request will be granted only after explanations and persuasive arguments have been presented. Routine claims (possibly because of guarantees, warranties, or other contractual conditions) assume that a request will be granted quickly and willingly, without persuasion. Because you expect routine claims to be granted willingly, a forceful, accusatory tone is inappropriate.

When the claim is routine, the direct approach shown in Figure 6.1 is appropriate. Let's consider the situation referred to in Figures 6.4 and 6.5. Surely, the computer company intended its laptop computers to be fully functioning. Because the damage is obvious, the computer company can be expected to correct the

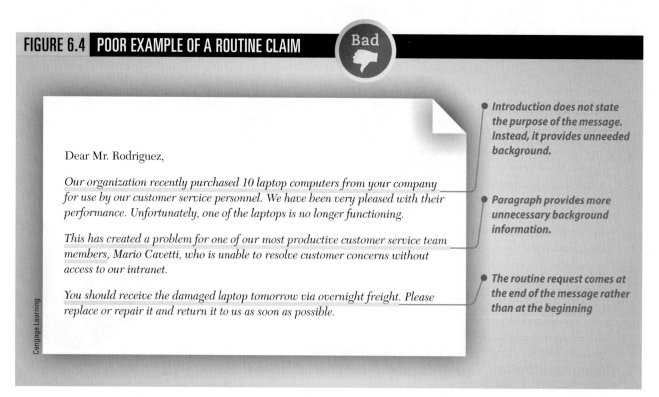

FIGURE 6.4 POOR EXAMPLE OF A ROUTINE CLAIM Bad

Dear Mr. Rodriguez,

Our organization recently purchased 10 laptop computers from your company for use by our customer service personnel. We have been very pleased with their performance. Unfortunately, one of the laptops is no longer functioning.

This has created a problem for one of our most productive customer service team members, Mario Cavetti, who is unable to resolve customer concerns without access to our intranet.

You should receive the damaged laptop tomorrow via overnight freight. Please replace or repair it and return it to us as soon as possible.

- Introduction does not state the purpose of the message. Instead, it provides unneeded background.

- Paragraph provides more unnecessary background information.

- The routine request comes at the end of the message rather than at the beginning

Cengage Learning

FIGURE 6.5 GOOD EXAMPLE OF A ROUTINE CLAIM

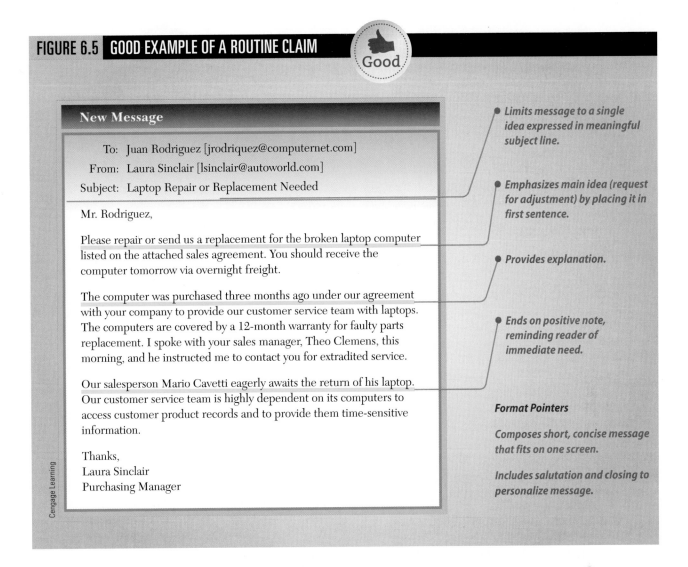

New Message

To: Juan Rodriguez [jrodriquez@computernet.com]

From: Laura Sinclair [lsinclair@autoworld.com]

Subject: Laptop Repair or Replacement Needed

Mr. Rodriguez,

Please repair or send us a replacement for the broken laptop computer listed on the attached sales agreement. You should receive the computer tomorrow via overnight freight.

The computer was purchased three months ago under our agreement with your company to provide our customer service team with laptops. The computers are covered by a 12-month warranty for faulty parts replacement. I spoke with your sales manager, Theo Clemens, this morning, and he instructed me to contact you for extradited service.

Our salesperson Mario Cavetti eagerly awaits the return of his laptop. Our customer service team is highly dependent on its computers to access customer product records and to provide them time-sensitive information.

Thanks,
Laura Sinclair
Purchasing Manager

- Limits message to a single idea expressed in meaningful subject line.

- Emphasizes main idea (request for adjustment) by placing it in first sentence.

- Provides explanation.

- Ends on positive note, reminding reader of immediate need.

Format Pointers

Composes short, concise message that fits on one screen.

Includes salutation and closing to personalize message.

Cengage Learning

---

problem without persuasion. Thus the manager can ask for an adjustment before providing an explanation, as shown in Figure 6.5. Beginning with the request for an adjustment gives it the emphasis it deserves. Note, however, that the message in Figure 6.4 is written inappropriately using an indirect approach—the details are presented before the main idea, and ends abruptly.

6-3b Favorable Response to a Claim Message

Businesses *want* their customers to communicate when merchandise or service is not satisfactory. They want to learn of ways in which goods and services can be improved, and they want their customers to receive value for the money they spend. With considerable confidence, they can assume that writers of claim messages think their claims are valid. By responding fairly

to legitimate requests in **adjustment messages**, businesses can gain a reputation for standing behind their goods and services. A loyal customer is likely to become even more loyal after a business has demonstrated its integrity.

Ordinarily, a response to a written message is also a written message. Sometimes people communicate to confirm ideas they have already discussed on the phone. When the response to a claim is favorable, present ideas in the direct sequence. Although the word *grant* is acceptable when talking about claims, its use in adjustment messages is discouraged. An expression such as "Your claim is being granted" unnecessarily implies that you are in a position of power.

Because the subject of an adjustment is related to the goods or services

adjustment messages
messages that are fair responses by businesses to legitimate requests in claim messages by customers

FIGURE 6.6 | POOR EXAMPLE OF A POSITIVE RESPONSE TO A ROUTINE CLAIM — Bad

Thank you for your letter of January 21. It has been referred to me for reply.

We have received the laptop of which you wrote and have identified a faulty battery as the cause of the computer malfunction.

We will replace the battery and return it to you soon.

We apologize for any inconvenience.

- **This introduction states the obvious and does not address reader concerns.**
- **Paragraph is too descriptive of the writer's experience.**
- **Ending is too generic to effectively promote.**

Cengage Learning

---

provided, the message can include a brief sales idea. With only a little extra space, the message can include resale or sales promotional material. **Resale** refers to a discussion of goods or services already bought. It reminds customers and clients that they made a good choice in selecting a company with which to do business, or it reminds them of the good qualities of their purchase. **Sales promotional material** refers to statements made about related merchandise or service. For example, a message about a company's recently purchased office furniture might also mention available office equipment. Mentioning the office equipment is using sales promotional material. Subtle sales messages that are included in adjustments have a good chance of being read, whereas direct sales messages might not be read at all.

Consider the ineffective response in Figure 6.6 to Laura Sinclair's claim letter and the message it sends about the company's commitment. Now notice the deductive outline and the explanation

resale a discussion of goods or services already bought

sales promotional material statements made about related merchandise or service

routine requests messages that assume that a request will be granted quickly and willingly, without persuasion

persuasive requests messages that assume that a requested action will be taken after persuasive arguments are presented

in the revision in Figure 6.7. Because the writer knows that Laura Sinclair will be pleased the laptop has been repaired and shipped, the good news appears in the first sentence. The details and closing sentence follow naturally and show a desire to correct the problem.

6-4 ROUTINE REQUESTS

Like claims, requests are divided into two groups: **routine requests** and **persuasive requests**. Persuasive requests, which are discussed in Chapter 8, assume that action will be taken after persuasive arguments are presented. Routine requests and favorable responses to them follow the deductive sequence.

6-4a Requests for Information

Requests for information about people, prices, products, and services are common. Because these requests from customers and clients are door openers for future business, businesses accept them optimistically. At the same time, they arrive at an opinion about the sender based on the quality of the message. Follow the points in the deductive outline for preparing effective requests you are confident will be fulfilled.

The message in Figure 6.8 does not follow the deductive outline that is appropriate for a routine

Good

New Message

To: Laura Sinclair [lsinclair@autoworld.com]

From: Juan Rodriguez [jrodriguez@computernet.com]

Subject: Repaired Laptop Delivered Tomorrow

Ms. Sinclair,

The repaired laptop has been shipped to you via overnight freight. You should receive it tomorrow.

The battery has been replaced, and we have conducted a systems test to ensure that all of the computer components are in working order.

We pride ourselves on our timely service response. Please do not hesitate to contact us with any concerns regarding your laptop orders or their performance.

Sincerely,

Juan Rodriguez
Manager, Customer Service

- Begins with good news (main idea) with assurance of desired action.

- Presents explanation and assurance of a process for quality control.

- Attempts to regain possible lost goodwill by offering personalized assistance.

Cengage Learning

FIGURE 6.8   POOR EXAMPLE OF A ROUTINE REQUEST

Bad

Subject: Need information

Our company is doing a periodic review of computer service providers to ensure that we are contracted with the company who provides the best quality service for the most competitive price. Based on a review of your website, it appears that your organization provides the type of service we need. Obviously, a website is a limited source of information, so I am uncertain as to whether your organization will be able to accommodate our needs.

Our organization has 500 networked desktops and 100 printers that need to be maintained and upgraded as needed. In addition, computer service personnel would be expected to provide technical support to our computer users. Does your company provide resources to support these needs?

I look forward to receiving your reply as quickly as possible.

- The subject line could be more informational.

- The introduction could more clearly state the purpose of the message.

- The writer's needs could be stated more clearly and systematically.

- The generic close fails to build goodwill or a sense of urgency.

Cengage Learning

request. The request is too vague and the sales manager receiving the message is not provided with enough useful information.

Note that the revision in Figure 6.9 starts with a direct request for specific information. Then as much detail as necessary is presented to enable the receiver to answer specifically. The revision ends confidently with appreciation for the action requested. The email message is short, but because it conveys enough information and has a tone of politeness, it is effective.

FIGURE 6.9 GOOD EXAMPLE OF A ROUTINE REQUEST

Good

New Message

To:	Don Pearson [dpearson@globaltech.com]
From:	Lana Taylor [ltaylor@worldwide.com]
Subject:	Information Needed for Review of IT Providers

Mr. Pearson,

The helpful information on your website describing the services your organization provides to medium-sized organizations such as ours encouraged me to contact you for more information. Our organization is undertaking a periodic review of IT services providers to ensure that we are receiving quality service at a competitive price. To assist us in this review, please provide the following information:

- Can your organization provide maintenance and upgrading services for 500 networked desk-top computers and 100 networked printers? If so, what is your rate for providing these services?

- Can your organization provide technical support to our 500 computer users? If so, what is your rate for providing these services?

- What other types of service or support does your organization provide? Are these services included as part of a package or can they be added on?

The information you provide could help us to determine whether you are the IT services provider that will best meet our service and support needs. At any time that you would like to contact me directly, please call (307) 213-6770.

Thanks,

Lana Taylor, Operations Manager
Worldwide Consumer Products, Inc.
307-213-6770, Fax: 307-213-6775
ltaylor@worldwide.com

States request clearly.

Asks specific questions with necessary explanation; uses list for emphasis.

Expresses appreciation and alludes to benefits for quick action.

Opens door for personal dialogue by providing telephone number.

Format Pointers

Provides salutation appropriate for company.

Includes a complete signature block below writer's name for complete reference.

6-4b Favorable Response to a Routine Request

Vinne/Shutterstock.com

The message in Figure 6.10 on page 97 responds favorably but with little enthusiasm to an online request for detailed information related to IT services provided by Global Tech. With a little planning and consideration for the needs outlined in the request, the message in Figure 6.11 on page 98 could have been written just as quickly. Note the specific answers to questions prepared in the convenient Q&A format and the helpful, sincere tone.

6-4c Positive Response to a Favor Request

Occasionally, as a business professional, you will be asked for special favors. You might receive invitations to speak at various civic or education events, spearhead fund-raising and other service projects, or offer your expertise in other ways. If you say "Yes," you might as well say it enthusiastically. Sending an unplanned, stereotyped acceptance suggests that the contribution will be similar.

If you find yourself responding to invitations frequently, you can draft a form message that you'll revise for each invitation you receive. Go to www.cengagebrain.com to view a television production manager's gracious acceptance of an invitation to emcee an awards program for a civic group. This well-written acceptance illustrates how form messages can be effectively individualized to enable businesses to communicate quickly and efficiently.

6-4d Form Messages for Routine Responses

Form messages are a fast and efficient way of transmitting frequently recurring messages to which receiver reaction is likely favorable or neutral. Inputting the

---

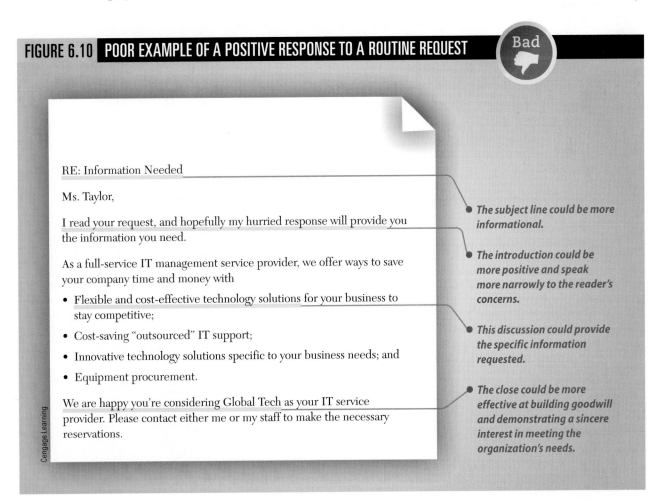

FIGURE 6.10 — POOR EXAMPLE OF A POSITIVE RESPONSE TO A ROUTINE REQUEST — Bad

RE: Information Needed

Ms. Taylor,

I read your request, and hopefully my hurried response will provide you the information you need.

As a full-service IT management service provider, we offer ways to save your company time and money with

- Flexible and cost-effective technology solutions for your business to stay competitive;
- Cost-saving "outsourced" IT support;
- Innovative technology solutions specific to your business needs; and
- Equipment procurement.

We are happy you're considering Global Tech as your IT service provider. Please contact either me or my staff to make the necessary reservations.

- *The subject line could be more informational.*
- *The introduction could be more positive and speak more narrowly to the reader's concerns.*
- *This discussion could provide the specific information requested.*
- *The close could be more effective at building goodwill and demonstrating a sincere interest in meeting the organization's needs.*

Cengage Learning

FIGURE 6.11 GOOD EXAMPLE OF A POSITIVE RESPONSE TO A ROUTINE REQUEST

Good

New Message

To: Lana Taylor [ltaylor@worldwide.com]

From: Don Pearson [dpearson@globaltech.com]

Subject: Providing your IT management service needs

Global Tech is the ideal provider for your information technology management needs. My staff and I can assist you with maintaining and upgrading your current computer network, providing technical support to your employees, and other support services, all at prices that are competitive.

As a full-service IT management service provider, we offer ways to save your company time and money by being able to

- Set up an infrastructure that works for your staff, ultimately allowing it to use the new technologies that will increase its work output, productivity and company-wide communication.

- Provide a talented staff of experts ready to help, over the phone or online. The resources that we provide will allow your business to get access to specialized expertise at a fraction of the cost of in-house development and maintenance.

- Provide a planned approach to systems maintenance, data backup, disaster recovery, and system security to significantly reduce downtime in the future while keeping your business running smoothly and reliably for your employees on a day-to-day basis.

- Purchase equipment at lower costs due to economies of scale and to provide the best solutions for your needs due to our deep knowledge of products, machines and software.

With technology changing rapidly, it's critical to have a trusted and experienced resource on your side to provide you with the latest in technical capabilities. We keep our staff trained and up-to-date with the changing world of technology so you don't have to.

Whether it's updating your business with the right equipment to get to the next level or implementing a streamlined technical solution to maximize workflow optimization or a combination thereof, we employ our knowledge of more than 18 years of information technology experience to get you there.

As your technology provider, we instill our values into every interaction with every client so you can expect to be treated with professionalism and respect.

In order to provide you an accurate cost estimate for our services, one of our service managers will need to visit your organization to gather specific information about your current setup and assess your future needs. May I call you next Monday to schedule a site visit?

Regards,
Don Pearson
President
Global Tech, Inc.

Cengage Learning

Revises subject line after clicking "Reply" to communicate enthusiasm for providing exceptional personalized service.

Highlights specific answers to recipient's questions using an articulate, concise writing style.

Shows sincere interest in request and person.

Addresses audience's concerns using an articulate, concise writing style.

Provides more useful information that communicates genuine interest in person and expertise in area of information technology.

Format Pointers

Uses bullet list format to enhance readability.

customer's name, address, and other variables (information that differs for each receiver) personalizes each message to meet the needs of its receiver. Companies might use form paragraphs that have been saved as template documents. When composing a document, select the appropriate paragraph according to your receiver's request. After assembling the selected files on the computer screen, input the particular information for the situation (e.g., name and address), and print a copy of the personalized message on letterhead to send to the receiver.

Form letters have earned a negative connotation because of their tendency to be impersonal. Many people simply refuse to read such letters for that reason. Personalizing a form letter can circumvent this problem.

6-5 ROUTINE MESSAGES ABOUT ORDERS AND CREDIT

Routine messages, such as customer order acknowledgments, are written deductively. Normally, credit information is requested and transmitted electronically from the national credit reporting agencies to companies requesting credit references. However, when companies choose to request information directly from other businesses, individual credit requests and responses must be written.

6-5a Acknowledging Customer Orders

When customers place orders for merchandise, they expect to get exactly what they ordered as quickly as possible. Most orders can be acknowledged by shipping the order; no message is necessary. For an initial order and for an order that cannot be filled quickly and precisely, companies typically send an **acknowledgment message**, a document that indicates the order has been received and is being processed. Typically, acknowledgment messages are preprinted letters or copies of the sales order. An immediate email message acknowledges a new customer and assures quality service, as shown in Figure 6.12 on page 100. Individualized letters are not cost effective and will not reach the customer in a timely manner. Although the form message is impersonal, customers appreciate the order acknowledgment and information as to when the order will arrive.

TO MAKE A FORM LETTER MORE PERSONAL ...

▸ **Add more variables to the standard text to tailor the message to the individual.**

▸ **Use personalized envelopes instead of mass-produced mailing labels.**

▸ **Be sure to spell names correctly.**

▸ **Produce a higher-quality document by using a good grade of paper and a high-quality printer.**

Yuri Arcurs/Shutterstock.com

TWEETING THE CUSTOMER WELL

▸ **Email links, chat rooms, and bulletin boards on corporate websites foster dialogue that leads to strong relationships. Today, an increasing number of businesspeople are participating in social exchange networking and blogging services, such as Twitter (www.twitter.com), to provide updates to customers.**

▸ **"Tweet" postings must be brief; messages cannot exceed 140 characters.[1] Such forced brevity might be one reason for the service's popularity. If customers are invited to talk, companies must be prepared to respond with timely, effective—even if brief—messages.**

rvlsoft/Shutterstock.com

Nonroutine orders, such as initial orders, custom orders, and delayed orders, require individualized acknowledgment messages. When well-written, these messages not only

acknowledgment message a document that indicates an order has been received and is being processed

FIGURE 6.12 **GOOD EXAMPLE OF AN ONLINE ORDER CONFIRMATION** Good

New Message

To: David Thomas [david.thomas@gmail.com]

From: Magdalena Fritti [mfritti@fredericks.com]

Subject: Frederick's Insurance welcomes David as a new customer!

• *Provides warm, personal subject line.*

Hi, David,

Welcome to Frederick's Insurance! I'm excited to see that you have enrolled as a new customer.

• *Welcomes new customer.*

You will be contacted soon by your personal customer service representative Lauren Bacon. Lauren has been with the company for ten years, is well versed in our product line, and receives top rankings in customer service.

• *Assures quality service by indicating customer service representative's knowledge and achievements.*

You can be assured that Lauren will help you identify the financial products that suit you and your family's needs. She will keep in touch regarding your family's changing needs and will inform you about beneficial changes to your financial planning.

I have complete confidence in the care you will receive from Lauren, but if for any reason you aren't completely satisfied or have other concerns, please let me know right away.

• *Provides phone number and email address to reinforce commitment to customer service.*

You can reach me at 213-561-8300, extension 201, or you can email me at mfritti@fredericks.com.

Thank you for trusting in us for your insurance needs.

Best regards,

Magdalena Fritti
Customer Service Manager
Frederick's Insurance Corp.

P.S. Be sure to watch your mailbox for our Welcome to Frederick's package sent to new customers. You will receive coupons for discounts at several retail and restaurant outlets in your area as a sign of our appreciation for your business.

Cengage Learning

acknowledge the order but also create customer goodwill and encourage the customer to place additional orders.

6-5b Providing Credit Information

Replies to requests for credit information are usually simple—just fill in the blanks and return the document. If the request does not include a form, follow a deductive plan in writing the reply: the major idea first, followed by supporting details.

When providing credit information, you have an ethical and legal obligation to yourself, the credit applicant, and the business from which credit is requested. You must be able to document any statement you make to defend yourself against a defamation charge. Thus, good advice is to stick with facts; omit any opinions. "I'm sure he will pay promptly" is an opinion that should be omitted, but include the documentable fact that "His payments are always prompt." Can you safely say a customer is a good credit risk when all you know is that the customer had a good credit record when purchasing from you?

6-5c Extending Credit

A timely response is preferable for any business document, but it is especially important when communicating about credit. The Equal Credit Opportunity Act (ECOA) requires that a credit applicant be notified of the credit decision within 30 days of receipt of the request or application. The party granting the credit must also disclose the terms of the credit agreement, such as the address for sending or making payments, due dates for payments, and the interest rate charged.

When extending credit, follow these guidelines as you write deductively:

1. **Open by extending credit and acknowledging shipment of an order.** Because of its importance, the credit aspect is emphasized more than the acknowledgment of the order. In other cases (in which the order is for cash or the credit terms are already clearly understood), the primary purpose of writing might be to acknowledge an order.

2. **Indicate the basis for the decision to extend credit and explain the credit terms.** Indicating that you are extending credit on the basis of an applicant's prompt paying habits with present creditors might encourage this new customer to continue these habits with you.

3. **Present credit policies.** Explain policies (e.g., credit terms, authorized discounts, payment dates). Include any legally required disclosure documents.

4. **Communicate a genuine desire to build a strong business relationship.** Include resale, sales promotional material, and comments that remind the customer of the benefits of doing business with you and encourage additional orders.

The letter in Figure 6.13 was written to a retailer; however, the same principles apply when writing to a consumer. Each message should be addressed in terms of individual interests. Dealers are concerned about markup, marketability, and display; consumers are concerned about price, appearance, and durability. Individual consumers might require a more detailed explanation of credit terms.

Companies receive so many requests for credit that the costs of individualized letters are prohibitive; therefore, most favorable replies to credit requests are form letters. To personalize the letter, however, the writer should merge the customer's name, address, amount of loan, and terms into the computer file containing the form letter information. Typically, form messages read something like this:

DEAR [TITLE] [LAST NAME]:

 Trueman's Electronics is pleased to extend credit privileges to you. Initially, you may purchase up to [CREDIT LIMIT] worth of merchandise. Our credit terms are [TERMS]. We welcome you as a credit customer at Trueman's Electronics and look forward to serving your needs for the latest electronics devices designed and manufactured by the world's top companies.

Although such form messages are effective for informing the customer that credit is being extended, they do little to build goodwill and promote future sales. Managers can personalize form messages that recipients do not perceive as canned responses.

6-6 PROCEDURAL MESSAGES

Memos or email messages are the most frequently used methods of communicating standard operating procedures and other instructions, changes related to personnel or the organization, and other internal matters for which a written record is needed.

Instructions to employees must be conveyed clearly and accurately to facilitate the day-to-day operations of business and to prevent negative feelings that occur when mistakes are made and work must be redone. Managers must take special care in writing standard operating procedures to ensure that all employees complete the procedures accurately and consistently.

Before writing instructions, walk through each step to understand it and to locate potential trouble spots. Then attempt to determine how much employees already know about the process and to anticipate any questions or problems. Then as you write

FIGURE 6.13 | GOOD EXAMPLE OF A LETTER EXTENDING CREDIT

Good

Global Home
123 Pike Avenue
Seattle, WA 89001

January 24, 2016

Frank Benjamin
Purchasing Department
World Interiors, Inc.
123 Colville Avenue
Salt Lake City, UT 84001

Dear Mr. Benjamin:

Welcome to the most unique designs in home furnishings available in the U.S. Our expert buyers tour every region of the world to find the most innovative designs in furnishings for every room in the house.

Because of your favorable current credit rating, we are pleased to provide you with a $15,000 credit line subject to our standard 2/10, n/30 terms. By paying your invoice within ten days, you can save 2 percent on your purchases.

You can use our convenient online ordering system to search our extensive line of home furnishings and to place your orders. If you need additional assistance, please call our 24-hour service line, where you will be assisted with our number one rated customer service personnel.

The most innovative home furnishings are now available to you and your customers, so please take some time to familiarize yourself with our extensive line.

Sincerely,

Candice Clark

Candice Clark
Credit Manager

Cengage Learning

- *Implies credit extension.*

- *Recognizes dealer for earning credit privilege and gives reason for credit extension.*

- *Includes credit terms and encourages taking advantage of discount.*

- *Presents reseller a reminder of product benefits and encourages future business.*

- *Includes sales promotion; assumes satisfaction with initial order and looks confidently for future business.*

Legal and Ethical Considerations
Provides answer to request for credit within required time frame (30 days from receipt of request) and mentions terms of credit that will be provided, as required by law.

Uses letter channel rather than email to communicate a contractual message.

instructions that require more than a few simple steps, follow these guidelines:

1. **Begin each step with an action statement to create a vivid picture of the employee completing the task.** Using an action verb and the understood subject *you* is more vivid than a sentence written in the passive voice. For example, a loan officer attempting to learn new procedures for evaluating new venture loans can more easily understand "*identify* assets available

to collateralize the loan" than "assets available to collateralize the loan should be identified."

2. **Itemize each step on a separate line to add emphasis and to simplify reading.** Number each step to indicate that the procedures should be completed in a particular order. If the order of steps is not important, use bullets rather than numbers.

3. **Consider preparing a flow chart depicting the procedures.** The cost and effort involved in creating

FIGURE 6.14 GOOD EXAMPLE OF A PROCEDURAL EMAIL WITH AN ATTACHMENT

Good

To: All Employees
From: Edward Lawson [elawson@officetemps.com]
Subject: New Procedures for Requesting Technology Services

Attachment: Computer_Service_Request_Procedures.docx

Hi all,

The number of computer service requests has increased proportionately with the growth of our organization. In order to continue to provide you timely responses to your requests, additional technicians have been hired and a new service reporting system put in place, beginning September 1.

To report a computer problem or to request technology services, please follow the procedure provided in the attached file. (This file can also be found on the company intranet under "Technology Resources.") You can complete these procedures at any computer, including your home machine.

Thanks,
Edward Lawson
Information Technology Manager

- *Includes attached file of document requiring involved formatting.*
- *Introduces main idea.*
- *Explains new procedures outlined in attached file.*

Procedures for Requesting Technology Services

1. Access http://www.officetemps.com/it and click the Technology Services link.

2. Provide the information requested in the form. Be certain to complete the required items denoted with asterisks.

3. Check your email for the response to your request, which typically will arrive within 48 hours.

4. Complete normal shutdown when leaving your computer station or other device. Service work will be completed after hours; technicians will start your device using their personal login procedures.

5. Check your email for a service completion notification. Please contact us if the work was not completed to your satisfaction. Our email is itservices@officetemps.com. A coordinator will contact you within 24 hours.

Dated 02/22/2016

- *Provides descriptive title that clearly identifies procedures.*
- *Enumerates to direct attention to each step and emphasize need for sequence.*
- *Begins each item with action verb to help employees visualize completing procedures.*
- *Includes date of last revision to ensure currency.*

Cengage Learning

a sophisticated flow chart might be merited for extremely important and complex procedures. For example, take a look at the flow chart in Figure 10.7, which simplifies the steps involved in processing a telephone order in an effort to minimize errors.

4. **Complete the procedure by following your instructions step-by-step.** Correct any errors you locate.

5. **Ask a colleague or employee to walk through the procedures.** This walk-through will allow you to identify ambiguous statements, omissions of relevant information, and other sources of potential problems.

Consider the seemingly simple task of requesting technology assistance. The IT manager might respond to such a request, "No need for written instructions; just request technology help any way you wish." Ambiguous verbal instructions (reported in haste) could lead to confusion about technology assistance and bad feelings about the efficiency of the process. The clear, consistent procedure in Figure 6.14 was prepared after the manager anticipated employee issues in requesting technology services. The policy is sent as an email attachment and posted to the company intranet for easy reference.

© Tom Wang/Shutterstock.com

BCOM
ONLINE

STUDY YOUR WAY
WITH STUDYBITS!

WEAK

FAIR

STRONG

UNASSIGNED

Rate and Organize StudyBits

Collect What's Important

Create Flashcards From Your StudyBits

Track/Monitor Your Progress

85%

CORRECT

INCORRECT

INCORRECT

INCORRECT

Personalize Your Quizzes

4LTR PRESS

Access BCOM ONLINE at www.cengagebrain.com

7 Delivering Bad-News Messages

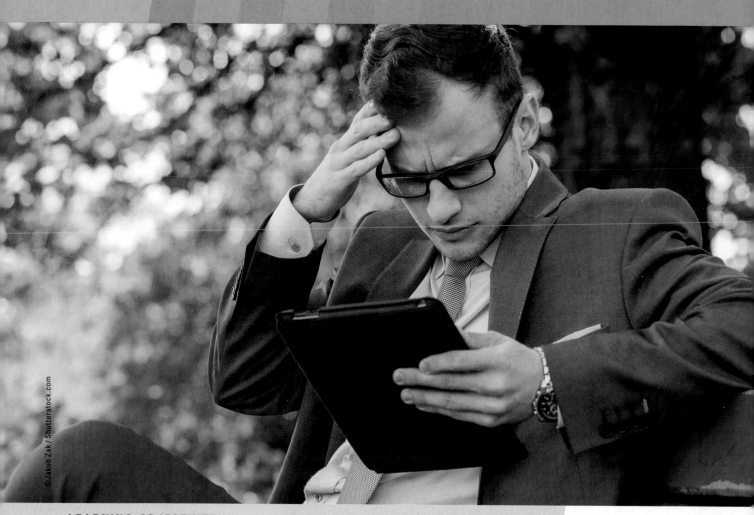

©Jakub Zak / Shutterstock.com

LEARNING OBJECTIVES

After studying this chapter, you will be able to …

7-1 Explain the steps in the inductive outline, and understand its use for specific situations.

7-2 Discuss strategies for developing the five components of a bad-news message.

7-3 Prepare messages refusing requests and claims.

7-4 Prepare messages handling problems with customers' orders and denying credit.

7-5 Prepare messages providing constructive criticism.

7-6 Prepare messages communicating negative organizational news.

7-7 Prepare messages responding to crises.

After finishing this chapter, go to **PAGE 126** for **STUDY TOOLS**.

7-1 CHOOSING AN APPROPRIATE CHANNEL AND ORGANIZATIONAL PATTERN

An organization's ability to handle difficult situations with tact and empathy powerfully influences the perceptions of employees, local citizens, and the public at large. As a skilled communicator, you will attempt to deliver bad news in such a way that the recipient supports the decision and is willing to continue a positive relationship. To accomplish these goals, allow empathy for your audience to direct your choice of an appropriate channel and an outline for presenting a logical discussion of the facts and the unpleasant idea. Use tactful and effective language to aid you in developing a clear, yet sensitive, message.

7-1a Channel Choice and Commitment to Tact

Personal delivery has been the preferred medium for delivering bad news because it signals the importance of the news and shows empathy for the recipient. Face-to-face delivery also provides the benefit of nonverbal communication and immediate feedback, which minimizes the misinterpretation of these highly sensitive messages. Personal delivery, however, carries a level of discomfort and the potential for escalation of emotion. A voice on the telephone triggers the same discomfort as a face-to-face meeting, and the increased difficulty of interpreting the intensity of nonverbal cues over the telephone only adds to the natural discomfort associated with delivering negative information.

You must be cautious when you deliver bad news electronically, whether by email or electronic postings. While you might feel more comfortable avoiding the discomfort of facing the recipient, the impersonal nature of the computer might lead to careless writing that is tactless and lacking in empathy, and perhaps even defamatory. Stay focused and follow the same communication strategies you would apply if you were speaking face-to-face or writing a more formal message. Regardless of the medium, your objective is to help your audience understand and accept your message, and this requires empathy and tact.

"You're fired" became a familiar phrase immortalized by Donald Trump on the hit show *The Apprentice*.

> If the bad news is presented in the first sentence, the reaction is likely to be negative.

Though such bluntness might work on television, it is rarely recommended in actual work situations. Tactlessness can have serious effects when your personal response fails to soothe negative feelings and ensure a harmonious relationship with a customer, client, or employee. You might find it difficult to show tact when you doubt the legitimacy of a request or simply don't have the time to prepare an effective bad-news message. When this conflict exists, you must remember that your message delivered on behalf of the company is a direct reflection on the company's image.

7-1b Use of the Inductive Approach to Build Goodwill

Just as good news is accompanied by details, bad news is accompanied by supporting reasons and explanations. If the bad news is presented in the first sentence, the reaction is likely to be negative: "They never gave me a fair chance," "That's unfair," "This just can't be." Having made a value judgment on reading the first sentence, receivers are naturally reluctant to change their minds before the last sentence—even though the intervening sentences present a valid basis for doing so. Once disappointed by the idea contained in the first sentence, receivers are tempted to concentrate on *refuting* (instead of *understanding*) supporting details.

From the communicator's point of view, details that support a refusal are very important. If the supporting details are understood and believed, the message might be readily accepted and good business relationships preserved. Because the reasons behind the bad news are so important, the communicator needs to organize the message in such a way as to emphasize the reasons.

The chances of getting your audience to understand the reasons are much better *before* the bad news is presented than *after* the bad news is presented. If the bad news precedes the reasons, the message might be discarded before this important portion is even read, or the disappointment experienced when reading the bad news might interfere with your audience's ability to comprehend or accept the supporting explanation.

The five-step outline shown in Figure 7.1 simplifies the process of organizing bad-news messages. These five steps are applied in messages illustrated in this chapter.

FIGURE 7.1 | INDUCTIVE OUTLINE USED IN BAD-NEWS MESSAGES

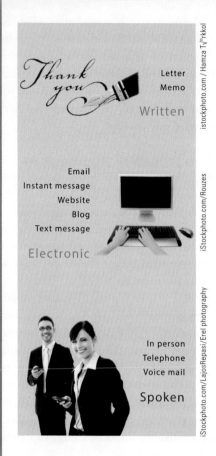

OPENING:

1. Begins with neutral idea that leads to refusal or bad news

BODY:

2. Presents facts, analysis, and reasons for refusal or bad news

3. States bad news using positive tone and de-emphasis techniques

4. Includes counterproposal or "silver lining" idea when possible or appropriate

CLOSING:

5. Closes with ideas that shift focus away from refusal or bad news, and indicates continuing relationship with receiver

Although the outline has five points, a bad-news message may or may not have five paragraphs. More than one paragraph might be necessary for conveying supporting reasons. In the illustrations in this chapter, note that the first and final paragraphs are seldom longer than two sentences. In fact, one-sentence paragraphs at the message's beginning look inviting to read.

You might speculate that your audience might become impatient when a message is inductive. Concise, well-written explanations are not likely to make a reader impatient. They relate to the audience's problem, present information not already known, and help your audience understand. However, if a receiver becomes impatient while reading a well-written explanation, that impatience is less damaging to understanding than would be the anger or disgust that often results from encountering bad news in the first sentence.

THE INDUCTIVE SEQUENCE OF IDEAS HAS THE FOLLOWING ADVANTAGES:

▸ **Sufficient identification of the subject of the message without first turning off the audience.**

▸ **Presentation of the reasons *before* the refusal, where they are more likely to be understood and will receive appropriate attention.**

▸ **Avoidance of a negative reaction. By the time the reasons are read, they seem sensible, and the refusal is foreseen. Because it is expected, the statement of refusal does not come as a shock.**

▸ **De-emphasis of the refusal by closing on a neutral or pleasant note. By showing a willingness to cooperate in some way, the sender conveys a desire to be helpful.**

7-1c Exceptions to the Inductive Approach

Normally, the writer's purpose is to convey a clear message and retain the recipient's goodwill; thus, the inductive outline is appropriate. In the rare circumstances in which a choice must be made between clarity and goodwill, clarity is the better choice. When the deductive approach will serve a communicator's purpose better, it should be used. For example, if you submit a clear and tactful refusal and your audience submits a second request, a deductive presentation might be justified in the second refusal. Apparently, the refusal needs the emphasis provided by a deductive outline.

In most situations, the preceding circumstances do not exist. When they do, a sender's goals might be accomplished by stating bad news in the first sentence.

7-2 DEVELOPING A BAD-NEWS MESSAGE

Developing a bad-news message following the inductive outline is challenging. The following suggestions will aid you in writing the (1) introductory paragraph, (2) explanation, (3) bad-news statement, (4) counterproposal or "silver lining" idea, and (5) closing paragraph.

7-2a Writing the Introductory Paragraph

The introductory paragraph in the bad-news message should accomplish the following objectives: (1) provide a buffer to cushion the bad news that will follow, (2) let the audience know what the message is about without stating the obvious, and (3) serve as a transition into the discussion of reasons without revealing the bad news or leading the audience to expect good news. If these objectives can be accomplished in one sentence, that sentence can be the first paragraph.

Here are several ideas that can be incorporated into effective beginning paragraphs:

- **Compliment.** A message denying a customer's request could begin by recognizing the customer's promptness in making payments.

- **Point of agreement.** A sentence that reveals agreement with a statement made in the message could get the message off to a positive discussion of other points.

- **Good news.** When a message contains a request that must be refused and another that is being answered favorably, beginning with the favorable answer can be effective.

- **Resale.** A claim refusal could begin with some favorable statement about the product.

- **Review.** Refusal of a current request could be introduced by referring to the initial transaction or by reviewing certain circumstances that preceded the transaction.

- **Gratitude.** In spite of the unjustified request, the audience might have done or said something for which you are grateful. An expression of gratitude could be used as a positive beginning.

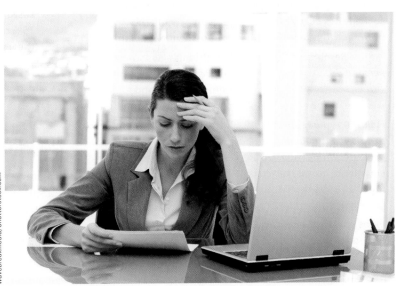

wavebreakmedia/Shutterstock.com

▶ **Empty acknowledgments of the obvious.** *"I am writing in response to your letter requesting …"* or *"Your message of the 14th has been given to me for reply"* wastes space to present points of no value. Beginning with *I* signals the message might be writer-centered.

▶ **Tipping off the bad news too early.** *"Although the refund requested in your letter of May 1 cannot be approved …"* might cause an immediate emotional reaction resulting in the message being discarded or interfering with understanding the explanations that follow.

The neutral statement *"Your request for an adjustment has been considered. However, …"* does not reveal whether the answer is "Yes" or "No," but the use of "however" signals that the answer is "No" before the reasons are presented. Such a beginning has about the same effect as an outright "No."

▶ **Starting too positively so as to build false hopes.** Empathetic statements such as *"I can understand how you felt when you were asked to pay an extra $54"* might lead the audience to expect good news. When a preceding statement has implied that an affirmative decision will follow, a negative decision is all the more disappointing.

7-2b Presenting the Facts, Analysis, and Reasons

The reasons section of the bad-news message is extremely important because people who are refused want to know why. If a message is based on a sound decision, and if it has been well written, recipients will understand and accept the reasons and the forthcoming refusal statement as valid.

To accomplish this goal, begin with a well-written first paragraph that transitions the reader smoothly into the reasons section. Then develop the reasons section following these guidelines:

- **Provide a smooth transition from the opening paragraph to the explanation.** The buffer should help set the stage for a logical movement into the discussion of the reasons.

- **Include a concise discussion of one or more reasons that are logical to the reader.** Read the section aloud to identify flaws in logic or the need for additional explanation.

- **Show audience benefit and/or consideration.** Emphasize how your audience will benefit from the decision. Avoid insincere, empty statements such as "To improve our service to you, …"

- **Avoid using "company policy" as the reason.** Disclose the reason behind the policy, which likely will include benefits to the reader. For example, a customer is more likely to understand and accept a 15% restocking fee if the policy is not presented as the "reason" for the refusal.

The principles for developing the reasons section are illustrated in Figure 7.2, a letter written by an attorney refusing a request to represent a client.

7-2c Writing the Bad-News Statement

A paragraph that presents the reasoning behind a refusal at least partially conveys the refusal before it is stated directly or indirectly. Yet one sentence needs to convey (directly or by implication) the conclusion to which the preceding details have been leading. A refusal (bad news) needs to be clear; however, you can subordinate the refusal so that the reasons get the

STUDY THE FOLLOWING EXAMPLES THAT USE TRANSITION STATEMENTS TO ACHIEVE A COHERENT OPENING:

Your employment application package has been reviewed by Human Resources.	Reveals the topic as a reply to a recipient's employment application.
Human Resources personnel …	Uses "Human Resources personnel" to transition from first to second paragraph.
Following your request for permission to submit a proposal to continue subsidizing employees' access to exercise facilities, we reviewed recent records of attendance.	Reveals subject of message as reply to employee's request.
In the past two years, attendance …	Uses "recent" and "attendance" to tie second paragraph to first.

FIGURE 7.2 | DEVELOPING THE COMPONENTS OF A BAD-NEWS MESSAGE

Audited financial statements will improve your ability to negotiate contracts with suppliers, banks, and customers, as well as provide your stockholders with confidence regarding their investment. For these reasons, the auditor you select must be capable of providing quality audit services.

Reveals subject of message and transitions into reasons.

To eliminate the appearance of a conflict of interest, Rule 101 of the AICPA Code of Professional Conduct requires auditors to be independent of their clients. One of our audit partners, Ryan Bass, is a significant stockholder in the First National Bank, which currently has loaned a large amount of money to your company. Because of this indirect financial interest, we recommend that you seek another firm to perform the 2010 financial statement audit.

Supports refusal with logical reasoning.

States refusal positively and clearly using complex sentence and positive language.

Because the independence rule applies only to audits of financial statements, we are available to provide other professional services. Our tax accountants are ready to assist you in finding methods to reduce your income tax liability. Please call me at 501-555-1245 to discuss these services.

Cengage Learning

deserved emphasis. The following techniques will help you achieve this goal.

- **Position the bad-news statement strategically.** Using the inductive outline positions the bad-news statement in a less important position—sandwiched between an opening buffer statement and a positive closing. Additionally, the refusal statement should be included in the same paragraph as the reasons, since placing it in a paragraph by itself would give too much emphasis to the bad news. When the preceding explanation is tactful and relevant, resentment over the bad news is minimized. Positioning the bad-news statement in the dependent clause of a complex sentence will also cushion the bad news. This technique places the bad news in a less visible, less emphatic position. In the sentence, *"Although the company's current financial condition prevents us from providing raises this year, we hope to make up for the freeze when conditions improve,"* the emphasis is directed toward a promise of raises at another time.

- **Use passive voice, general terms, and abstract nouns.** Review the *emphasis techniques* that you studied in Chapter 3 as you consider methods for presenting bad news with human relations in mind.

- **Use positive language to accentuate the positive.** Simply focus on the good instead of the bad, the pleasant instead of the unpleasant, or what can be done instead of what cannot be done. Compared with a negative idea presented in negative terms, a negative idea presented in positive terms is more likely to be accepted. When you are tempted to use the following terms, search instead for words or ideas that sound more positive:

Words That Evoke Negative Feelings

complaint   incompetent   misled   regrettable
error   inexcusable   mistake   unfortunate
failure   lied   neglect   wrong

Words That Evoke Positive Feelings

accurate   concise   enthusiasm   productive
approval   durable   generous   recommendation
assist   energetic   gratitude   respect

- **Imply the refusal when the audience can understand the message without a definite statement of the bad news.** By *implying* the "No" answer, the response has the following positive characteristics: (1) it uses positive language, (2) it conveys reasons or at least a positive attitude, and (3) it seems more respectful. For example, during the noon hour one employee says to another, "Will you go with me to see this afternoon's baseball game?" "No, I won't," communicates a negative response, but it seems unnecessarily direct and harsh. The same message (invitation is rejected) can be clearly stated in an *indirect* way (by implication) by saying "I must get my work done," or even, "I'm a football fan." Note the positive tone of the following implied refusals:

Implied Refusal	Underlying Message
I wish I could.	• Other responsibilities prohibit, but recipient would like to accept.
Had you selected our newest calling plan, you could have reduced your monthly rates by 10% or more.	• States a condition under which answer would have been "Yes" instead of "No." Note use of subjunctive words "had" and "could."
By accepting the new terms, Southern Wood Products would have doubled its energy costs.	• States the obviously unacceptable results of complying with request.

7-2d Offering a Counterproposal or "Silver Lining" Idea

Following negative news with an alternative action, referred to as a **counterproposal**, will assist in preserving a relationship with the reader. Because it states what you *can* do, including a counterproposal might eliminate the need to state the refusal directly. The counterproposal can follow a refusal stated in a tactful, sensitive manner. When global Internet services and media company AOL was faced with laying off 2,000 workers, the silver lining offered was a generous severance package and aid in transitioning to other job opportunities.[1]

While the counterproposal might represent a tangible benefit, at times it is more intangible in nature. For instance, in a letter that informs a job applicant that he or she was not selected to fill the position, the counterproposal might be an offer to reconsider the applicant's résumé when other appropriate positions become available. Any counterproposal must, of course, be reasonable. For instance, when informing a customer of an inability

counterproposal in a bad-news message, an alternative to the action requested that follows the negative news and can assist in preserving future relationships with the audience

Offering a counterproposal or "silver lining" idea can assist in preserving a relationship with the receiver of bad news.

to meet a promised delivery deadline, an unreasonable counterproposal would be to offer the merchandise at no charge. A reasonable counterproposal might be to include some additional items at no charge or to offer a discount certificate good on the customer's next order.

When no reasonable counterproposal is apparent, the sender might be able to offer a silver lining thought that turns the discussion back into the positive direction. For instance, a statement to tenants announcing an increase in rent might be followed by a description of improved lighting that will be installed in the parking lot of the apartment complex. When offering a counterproposal or silver lining statement, care must be taken to ensure that the idea does not seem superficial or minimize the recipient's situation.

7-2e Closing Positively

After presenting valid reasons and a tactful refusal followed with a counterproposal or silver lining statement, a closing paragraph should demonstrate empathy without further reference to the bad news. A pleasant closing paragraph should close with an empathetic tone and achieve the following goals:

- **De-emphasize the unpleasant part of the message.** End on a positive note that takes the emphasis away from the bad news previously presented. A statement of refusal (or bad news) in the last sentence

▶ **Trite statements that might seem shallow and superficial.** The well-worn statement "Thank you for your interest" is often used thoughtlessly. It might seem shallow and superficial. "When we can be of further help, please do not hesitate to call or write" is also well worn and negative. *Further help* might seem especially inappropriate to someone who has just read a denial.

▶ **Statements that could undermine the validity of your refusal.** The statement "We trust this explanation is satisfactory" or "We hope you will understand our position" could be taken as a confession of doubt about the validity of the decision. Use of position seems to heighten controversy; positions are expected to be defended. Saying "We are sorry to disappoint you" risks a negative reply: "If it made you feel so bad, why did you do it?" It can also be interpreted as an apology for the action taken. If a decision merits an apology, its validity might be questionable.

▶ **Statements that encourage future controversy.** Statements such as "If you have questions, please do not hesitate to let us know" could also be perceived as doubt and possibly communicate a willingness to change the decision. If the decision is firm, including this type of closing could result in your having to communicate the negative message a second time.

or paragraph would place too much emphasis on it. Preferably, *reasons* (instead of bad news) should remain uppermost in the audience's mind. Placing bad news last would make the ending seem cold and abrupt. When no reasonable counterproposal is apparent, the sender might be able to offer a silver lining thought that turns the discussion back into the positive direction.

- **Add a unifying quality to the message.** Make your final sentence an *appropriate* closing that brings a unifying quality to the whole message. Repetition of a word or reference to some positive idea that appears early in the message serves this purpose well. Avoid restatement of the refusal or direct reference to it. This paragraph is usually shorter than the preceding explanatory paragraphs, often one or two sentences.

- **Include a positive, forward-looking idea.** This idea might include a reference to some pleasant aspect of the preceding discussion or a future aspect of the business relationship, resale or sales promotion, or an offer to help in some way. Consider the following closures that apply these suggestions:

Reference to some pleasant aspect of the preceding discussion:

"Your decision to refinance your mortgage last year was a wise choice." Home mortgage and other provisions had been mentioned in the early part of a letter to a client who was refused a double-indemnity settlement.

Use of resale or sales promotional material:

"Selecting our new hybrid Breeze with its 50-miles-per-gallon fuel usage was a wise decision with today's gas prices." A reminder that the hybrid has superior gas mileage will assist in regaining goodwill after a customer's request for free repair has been refused.

An expression of willingness to assist in some other way:

Specifically, you might offer an alternative solution to the audience's problem or useful information that could not be presented logically with the bad news. *"Our representative will show you some samples during next week's sales call."* The samples are being proposed as a possible solution to the reader's problem.

Note the closing paragraph in Figure 7.2 is a positive, forward-looking statement that includes promotion of other services the attorney might provide.

REFUSING A REQUEST

It's a good idea to use the inductive approach (reasons before refusal) for refusing requests for a favor, an action, or even a donation. Present clear, understandable reasons in a way that minimizes the audience's disappointment.

You can examine a company's refusal to lend an organization an executive in Figure 7.3 on page 114. This *response* to prior correspondence uses the same principles of sequence and style that are recommended for messages that *initiate* communication about unpleasant topics. The same principles apply whether the communication is a spoken message, letter, memo, or email message.

Companies have learned that building employee relationships is just as important as developing customer goodwill. Refusing employees' requests requires sensitivity and complete, honest explanations, qualities not included in the bad email in Figure 7.4 on page 115.

The manager's hasty and vague response to a valued employee's request to create an exercise facility uses a direct, blunt approach. In the revision illustrated in Figure 7.5 (on page 116), the manager takes the time to prepare a response that reflects detailed explanation supporting the refusal and genuine respect for the employee.

FIGURE 7.3 GOOD EXAMPLE OF A REFUSAL FOR A FAVOR

Good

2700 Rosehill Way• Canton, OH 02139-2700
• Phone 617 555-8700 • 617 555-7961

October 12, 2016

Debra Jones, President
American Rivers Project
385 Quail Run Avenue
Jackson Hole, WY 83331

Dear Samuel:

You are commended for your commitment to restore the renowned fly-fishing stream, Feather Creek, to its original crystalline flow. In a decade in which nationwide, water quality is suffering from agricultural and urban run-off, once-pristine streams deserve to be maintained and preserved.

Reaching this goal depends on directors to the board who can commit the necessary time and energy. The communication skills and connection to the community you described demand a director with significant organizational experience. During the last year, Snow Queen Resort has reduced its management team to balance lowered revenues from tourism. With reduced employees comes greater demands on remaining personnel, so we hesitate to recommend someone from our management team to serve on your board.

Ronald Crimmons has recently retired and has been an active environmental voice in the community. If you might benefit from his knowledge and insight, please call him at 888-2351.

Sincerely,
Nancy
Nancy Johns
Manager of Operations

• *Introduces subject without revealing whether answer will be "Yes" or "No."*

• *Gives reasons that will seem logical to reader.*

• *Subordinates refusal by placing it in dependent clause of complex sentence. Alludes to help in another form.*

• *Closes positively with counterproposal. Conveys genuineness by summarizing executive's responsibilities and providing telephone number.*

Format Pointer
Signs first name only because writer knows receiver well.

Cengage Learning

STUDY THE TECHNIQUES USED TO CUSHION THIS BAD-NEWS STATEMENT:

Although Richardson Contracting was selected as the building contractor, expertise with environmentally friendly construction techniques was considered a plus for S and S Builders.

▶ **States what was done rather than what was not done.**

▶ **Includes a positive idea ("expertise with environmentally friendly construction techniques") to accentuate a positive aspect and cushion the bad news.**

▶ **Uses passive voice ("Richardson Contracting was selected") to depersonalize the message.**

▶ **Places the bad news in the dependent clause of a complex sentence ("although Richardson Contracting was selected"). The positive idea in the independent clause ("expertise with environmentally friendly construction techniques") will receive more attention.**

7-4 DENYING A CLAIM

Companies face a challenging task of refusing claims from customers while maintaining goodwill and building customer loyalty. Claim refusals are necessary when a warranty does not apply or has expired or a customer has misused the product. Companies must also write refusals when customers ask for something that a company simply can't do. For example, many retailers charge customers a $25–$40 fee on returned checks. A retailer who receives a customer's request to waive the charge must refuse because the claim is inconsistent with the retailer's policies and objectives.

FIGURE 7.4 POOR EXAMPLE OF A REFUSAL TO AN EMPLOYEE'S REQUEST

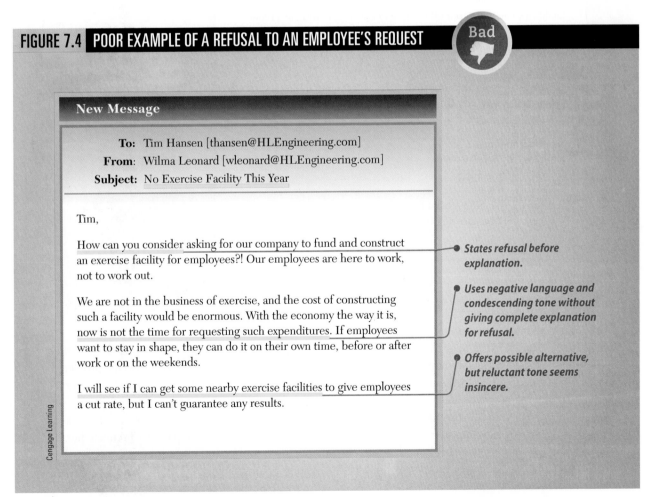

New Message

To: Tim Hansen [thansen@HLEngineering.com]
From: Wilma Leonard [wleonard@HLEngineering.com]
Subject: No Exercise Facility This Year

Tim,

How can you consider asking for our company to fund and construct an exercise facility for employees?! Our employees are here to work, not to work out.

● *States refusal before explanation.*

We are not in the business of exercise, and the cost of constructing such a facility would be enormous. With the economy the way it is, now is not the time for requesting such expenditures. If employees want to stay in shape, they can do it on their own time, before or after work or on the weekends.

● *Uses negative language and condescending tone without giving complete explanation for refusal.*

I will see if I can get some nearby exercise facilities to give employees a cut rate, but I can't guarantee any results.

● *Offers possible alternative, but reluctant tone seems insincere.*

Cengage Learning

FIGURE 7.5 GOOD EXAMPLE OF A REFUSAL TO AN EMPLOYEE'S REQUEST

Good

New Message

To: Tim Hansen [thansen@HLEngineering.com]
From: Wilma Leonard [wleonard@HLEngineering.com]
Subject: Request for Employee Exercise Facility

Hi, Tim,

Because we want you to work at the highest level possible, your suggestion to construct an employee exercise facility on site has been carefully considered. Taking a break from work to exercise is an excellent way to energize employees and to ensure a healthy workforce.

Constructing an employee exercise facility on site would be a time-consuming and expensive project because of architectural, labor and building material costs. Construction of the 1,000-square-foot facility and fitting it with the required exercise equipment would cost nearly $200,000.

In response to your idea, I am checking with existing exercise facilities located near our offices to see if we might arrange a reduced membership fee for employees. The company might also be able to subsidize a portion of the fee with the savings in reduced sick time you mentioned.

Tim, I will get back to you as soon as I have gathered information about the costs of membership at local facilities.

Regards,
Wilma Leonard
Human Resources Manager
HL Engineering, Inc.
Tampa, FL 90349
509-823-4211, Fax 509-823-4200
wleonard@HLEngineering.com

Cushions bad news with sincere compliment for suggestion.

Transitions to reasons and provides complete explanation for refusal.

Restates reason to justify refusal.

Includes logical alternative and closes with positive look toward future expansion.

Format Pointers
Sends message by email—medium preferred by recipient.

Includes .sig file to identify writer and provide contact information.

Cengage Learning

The inductive approach is helpful in communicating this disappointing news to customers. Presenting the explanation for the refusal first leads customers through the reasoning behind the decision and helps them *understand* the claim is unjustified by the time the refusal is presented. Tone is especially important when denying claims. Present the reasons objectively and positively without casting blame or judgment on the customer for the problem. Avoid lecturing a customer on the actions he or she should have taken to avoid the problem. Finally, close the message with resale or sales promotional material that indicates you expect future business. Although disappointed with your decision, customers continue doing business with companies who make fair, objective decisions and communicate the reasons for those decisions in a positive, respectful manner.

Assume a manufacturer of LED screens received the following email from a customer:

New Message

To: Gala Foster [gfoster@blueice.com]
From: Lisa Thompson [lthompson@skiskatesurf.com]
Subject: Refund error

Please issue a credit to my account for $254. Although you accepted the four pairs of skis I returned, you only credited my account for $1,569.75. Because I could find no explanation for the discrepancy, I assume an error has been made.

The company's return policy allows customers to return unsold merchandise at the end of the holiday season, subject to a 15% restocking charge. The return policy is printed clearly on the inside cover of its catalog and in bold print at the bottom of both the printed and Internet order forms. Telephone operators explain the restocking charge to customers placing orders via the company's toll-free number.

The customer's inquiry shows a lack of understanding of the return policy. Although a frustrated company representative might question why the customer can't read the return policy, the response must be more tactful than that illustrated in Figure 7.6. The example in Figure 7.7 reveals the subject of the message in the first sentence and leads into a discussion of the reasons. Reasons for the restocking fee, including benefits to the customer, precede the refusal. The tone is positive and respectful. The refusal statement uses several de-emphasis techniques to cushion its impact, and the final sentence turns the discussion away from the refusal with reference to future business with the customer.

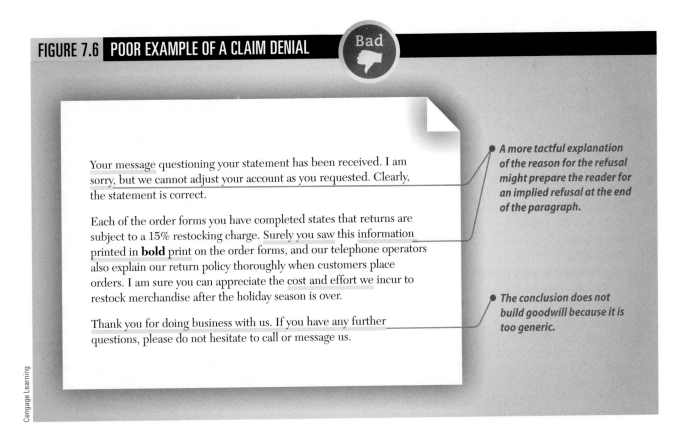

FIGURE 7.6 | POOR EXAMPLE OF A CLAIM DENIAL

Your message questioning your statement has been received. I am sorry, but we cannot adjust your account as you requested. Clearly, the statement is correct.

Each of the order forms you have completed states that returns are subject to a 15% restocking charge. Surely you saw this information printed in **bold** print on the order forms, and our telephone operators also explain our return policy thoroughly when customers place orders. I am sure you can appreciate the cost and effort we incur to restock merchandise after the holiday season is over.

Thank you for doing business with us. If you have any further questions, please do not hesitate to call or message us.

A more tactful explanation of the reason for the refusal might prepare the reader for an implied refusal at the end of the paragraph.

The conclusion does not build goodwill because it is too generic.

FIGURE 7.7 | **GOOD EXAMPLE OF A CLAIM DENIAL**

Good

HUNTINGTON SURF & SPORTS

1905 BEACH BOULEVARD
HUNTINGTON BEACH, CA 97501-7313

TELEPHONE: 800-555-6000
FAX: 800-555-0583

January 24, 2016

Lisa Thompson
Ski, Skate, and Surf
1905 South Pacific Street
San Pedro, CA 97501-7313

Dear Ms. Thompson:

Restocking of Returned Merchandise

The Blue Ice skis you stocked this past season are skillfully crafted and made from the most innovative materials available. Maintaining a wide selection of quality skiing products is an excellent strategy for developing customer loyalty and maximizing your sales.

Our refund policies provide you the opportunity to keep a fully stocked inventory at the lowest possible cost. You receive full refunds for merchandise returned within 10 days of receipt. For unsold merchandise returned after the primary selling season, a modest 15% restocking fee is charged to cover our costs of holding this merchandise until next season. The credit applied to your account for $1,569.75 covers merchandise you returned at the end of December.

While relaxing from another great skiing season, take a look at our new Blue Ice skis and other items available in the enclosed catalog for the 2015 season. You can save 10% by ordering premium ski products before September 10.

Sincerely,

Gala Foster

Gala Foster
Credit Manager
Enclosure: Catalog

Cengage Learning

Legal and Ethical Consideration
Avoids corrective language that might insult, belittle, or offend.

• *Uses subject line that identifies subject without revealing refusal.*

• *Uses resale to cushion bad news and lead into explanation.*

• *Presents clear explanation of reasons behind policy with emphasis on ways reader benefits.*

• *Implies refusal by stating amount credited to account.*

• *Shifts emphasis away from refusal by presenting silver lining sales promotion for next season's merchandise.*

• *Specifies enclosure to emphasize importance of exact items.*

7-5 DENYING CREDIT

Once you have evaluated a request for credit and have decided "No" is the better answer, your primary writing challenge is to refuse credit so tactfully that you keep the business relationship on a cash basis. When requests for credit are accompanied with an order, your credit refusals might serve as order acknowledgments. Of course, every business message is directly or indirectly a sales message. Prospective customers will be disappointed when they cannot buy on a credit basis. However, if you keep them sold on your goods and services, they might prefer to buy from you on a cash basis instead of seeking credit privileges elsewhere.

When the credit investigation shows that applicants are poor credit risks, too many credit writers no longer regard them as possible customers. They write to them in a cold, matter-of-fact manner. They do not consider that such applicants might still be interested in doing business on a cash basis and might qualify for credit later.

In credit denials, as in other types of refusals, the major portion of the message should be an explanation for the denial. You cannot expect your audience to agree that your "No" answer is the right answer unless you give the reasons behind it.

Both writers and readers benefit from the explanation of the reasons behind the denial. For writers, the explanation helps to establish fair-mindedness; it shows that the decision was not arbitrary. For readers, the explanation not only presents the truth to which they are entitled, it also has guidance value. From it they learn to adjust habits and, as a result, qualify for credit purchases later.

Because of the legal implications involved in denying credit, legal counsel should review your credit denial messages to ensure that they comply with laws related to fair credit practices. For example, the Equal Credit Opportunity Act (ECOA) requires that the credit applicant be notified of the credit decision within 30 calendar days following application. Applicants who are denied credit must be informed of the reasons for the refusal. If the decision was based on information obtained from a consumer reporting agency (as opposed to financial statements or other information provided by the applicant), the credit denial must include the name, address, and telephone number of the agency. It must also remind applicants that the **Fair Credit Reporting Act** provides them the right to know the nature of the information in their credit file. In addition, credit denials must include a standard statement that the ECOA prohibits creditors from discriminating against credit applicants on the basis of a number of protected characteristics (race, color, religion, national origin, sex, marital status, and age).

To avoid litigation, some companies choose to omit the explanation from the credit denial letter and invite the applicant to call or come in to discuss the reasons. Alternately, they might suggest that the audience obtain further information from the credit reporting agency whose name, address, and telephone number are provided.

7-6 DELIVERING CONSTRUCTIVE CRITICISM

A person who has had a bad experience as a result of another person's conduct might be reluctant to write or speak about that experience. However, because one person took the time to communicate, many could benefit. Although not always easy or pleasant, communicating about negatives can be thought of as a social responsibility. For example, a person who returns from a long stay at a major hotel might, upon returning home, write a letter or email message to the management commending certain employees. If the stay was not pleasant and weaknesses in hotel operation were detected, a tactful message pointing out the negatives would probably be appreciated. Future guests could benefit from the effort of that one person.

Before communicating about the problem, an individual should recognize the following risks: being

iStockphoto.com/DNY59

Fair Credit Reporting Act federal law that provides consumers the right to know the nature of the information in their credit file and gives them other protections when they apply for and are denied credit stereotyped as a complainer, being associated with negative thoughts and perceived in negative terms, and appearing to challenge management's decisions concerning hotel operations. Yet such risks might be worth taking because of the benefits:

- **The communicator gets a feeling of having exercised a responsibility.**
- **Management learns of changes that need to be made.**
- **The hotel staff about whom the message is written modifies techniques and is thus more successful.**
- **Other guests will have more enjoyable stays in the hotel.**

In the decision to communicate about negatives, the primary consideration is intent. If the intent is to hurt or to get even, the message should not be sent. Including false information would be *unethical* and *illegal.* To avoid litigation charges and to respond ethically, include only specific facts you can verify, and avoid evaluative words that present opinions about the person's character or ability. For example, instead of presenting facts, the message in Figure 7.8 judges the staff member sent to perform auditing services at a client's office. Overall, the message is short, general, and negative. By comparison, the revision in Figure 7.9 on page 121 has positive intent, is factual, uses positive language, and leaves judgment to the recipient.

7-7 COMMUNICATING NEGATIVE ORGANIZATIONAL NEWS

Being able to initiate messages that convey bad news about an organization is as important as responding "No" to messages from customers/clients and others outside the company. Employees and the public are seeking, and expecting, *honest* answers from management about situations adversely affecting the company—slumping profits, massive layoffs, bankruptcy, a variety of major changes in the organization, and negative publicity that affects the overall health of the business and retirement plans, to name a few.

Managers who can communicate negative information in a sensitive, honest, and timely way can calm fears and doubts and build positive employee and public relations. Effective managers recognize that employee morale, as well as public goodwill, is fragile—easily damaged and difficult to repair. If handled well, these bad-news messages related to the organization can be opportunities to treat employees, customers, and the general public with respect, thus building unity and trust.

Strong internal communication is a key to involving employees in corporate strategies and building an important sense of community. Transparency can have a positive effect on an organization's culture. According

FIGURE 7.8 **POOR EXAMPLE OF A CONSTRUCTIVE CRITICISM** Bad

Sara French, an account auditor in your firm, is not working out well on our audit. She is constantly accepting cellphone calls, even while in meetings with our employees. The constant distraction of her phone conversation, sometimes highly personal, has our employees complaining that she is preoccupied with non-business matters. She has even asked our employees to repeat conversations that she missed while on her cellphone.

This information should be placed in a second paragraph that describes specific behaviors in order to maintain neutrality.

Although extensive knowledge of auditing procedures is important, French's lack of respect for others far outweighs her professional expertise. I seriously hope French is able to take steps to correct the situation.

The close would better maintain goodwill if it were more positive in tone and content.

Cengage Learning

FIGURE 7.9 **GOOD EXAMPLE OF A CONSTRUCTIVE CRITICISM**

Good

OSI
Office Systems Incorporated
2500 lincoln Green Road/Austin,
TX 78710-2500 / Phone: 512-555-9000 / Fax: 512-555-6573.

May 2, 2016

Charles Smithers
Delon and Smithers Associates
3504 Oak Street
Seattle, WA 80340

Dear Mr. Smithers:

Your auditing team has been working with us on site for about 10 days, with excellent results. Early in the audit, Sara French, one of your auditors, identified several key problems with our accounting procedures that we will address.

While working with our staff, Sara's attention is constantly diverted from conversations by her receipt of cellphone calls. Although she rarely stops the meeting, the constant distraction of her conversation—sometimes personal in nature—has caused some of our employees to comment that she is preoccupied with non-business matters.

Our managers cited several occasions when Sara had to ask them to repeat a conversation that occurred while she was on the phone. Sara is obviously quite good at her job; her expertise in accounting procedures explains why she is a member of your respected team. Please convey my concerns to Sara confidentially so that the rest of her time in our office will go smoothly for her and for us.

Sincerely,

Dana Simmons
Chief Financial Officer

Cengage Learning

- **Introduces discussion of audit work underway.**

- **Conveys fair-mindedness and establishes credibility by acknowledging good as well as bad points.**

- **Presents verifiable statements without labeling them in negative, judgmental terms.**

- **Ends on pleasant note that seeks to add credibility to preceding negatives.**

Legal and Ethical Considerations

- **Conveys positive intent to help—not to hurt or get even.**

- **Avoids potential litigation charges by including specific, verifiable facts and avoiding evaluative, judgmental statements.**

- **Uses "confidential" as safeguard; information is intended for professional use only, not designed to hurt or to be thought of as gossip.**

Format Pointer

- **Uses letter channel rather than email to communicate a sensitive message.**

---

to a recent workplace survey, open, honest communication between corporate leaders and employees can lead to a more productive and ethical workplace. According to Deloitte Chairperson Sharon Allen, motivating communication patterns are "increasingly critical to retaining talent and preserving the health of today's organizations."[2]

Obviously, business and competitive reasons prevent a company from always being completely transparent with its staff, but every attempt should be made to do so when possible. The best companies use a variety of communication tools that promote an open exchange of honest, candid communication and welcome input from employees. Newsletters, email updates, town hall or focus meetings, videoconferencing, phone calls, and discussion boards drive home relevant messages and allow employees to pose questions to management. This quality two-way communication involves employees in corporate strategies; employees who are aware of company goals and potential problems feel connected and accountable. Informed employees are also better prepared for bad news when it must be shared.

7-7a Breaking Bad News

Assuming this long-term commitment to keep employees informed, the following suggestions provide guidance in breaking bad news to employees and the public:[3]

- **Convey the bad news as soon as possible.** Timeliness will minimize damage caused by rumors and will give employees the concern and respect they deserve. Nestlé Purina and others in the pet food industry acted early and effectively to recall potentially deadly pet food tainted with wheat gluten from China and to assure pet owners that steps were in place to ensure healthy ingredients would be used in the future.[4]

- **Give a complete, rational explanation of the problem.** Be candid about what is happening, why, and its effect on employees, customers, and the public. Provide enough detail to establish your credibility and provide context so your audience can understand the situation. Stressing positive aspects will provide needed balance and avoid sugarcoating or minimizing the severity of the news to the point that the message is misunderstood. Bridgestone, makers of Firestone tires, was criticized for botching its recovery efforts from claims of accidents being caused by faulty tires when it initially attempted to blame Ford for the problems instead of taking responsibility and seeking corrective actions.[5]

- **Show empathy.** There is really no good way to break bad news, such as the announcement of layoffs or closures, to employees. The economic downturn and job insecurity has resulted in increased stress for many employees, which raises the potential for workplace aggression. However, methods that reflect respect and proper timing reduce the likelihood of an emotional boil over.[6]

- **Respond to the feelings.** Allow people adequate time to react to the bad news. Listen attentively for understanding and then address the concerns, issues, and potential problems presented.

- **Follow-up.** Let people know what will happen next—what is expected of employees or customers, and what the company will do and when. Plan to repeat your explanations and assurances that you are available to respond to concerns in several communications that extend over a given time.

Consider the company president who emailed employees about a relocation of the

There is really no good way to break bad news, such as the announcement of layoffs or closures, to employees, but methods that reflect respect and proper timing reduce the likelihood of emotional scenes in the workplace.

company's manufacturing facility (Figure 7.10). The president should not be surprised to learn that employees are resisting the relocation; some perceive the company to be an enemy uprooting families from their homes simply for financial gain. In the revision (Figure 7.11), the president anticipates the employees' natural resistance to this stunning announcement and crafts a sensitive message.

A printed memo is a more effective channel for communicating this sensitive and official information than the efficient, yet informal, email message. The revision indicates that the company's internal communications (newsletters and intranet) have been used to prepare the employees for this negative announcement. Thus, the official memo is no surprise; nor is the company's commitment to listen to the employees' concerns and to provide up-to-date information as it develops.

7-7b Responding to Crisis Situations

Crises can occur in any organization, disrupting business activity and posing significant political, legal, financial, or governmental impacts. Crisis situations can result from various events, including accidents, weather-related disasters, equipment failures, procedural errors, and deliberate maliciousness. When crises occur, the communication that is offered can either help ease situations or worsen

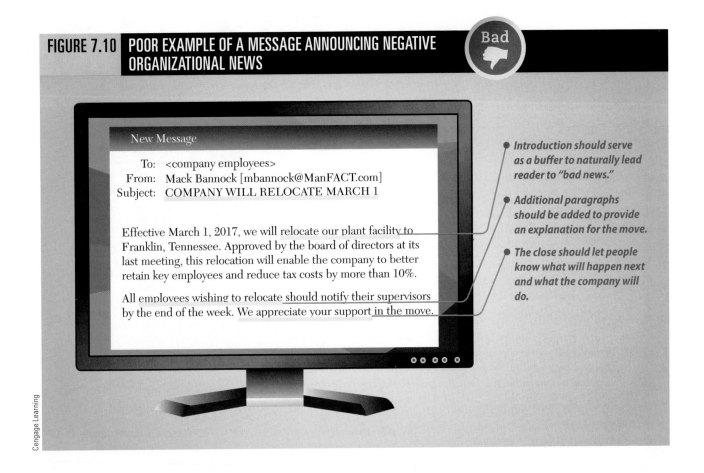

New Message

To: <company employees>
From: Mack Bannock [mbannock@ManFACT.com]
Subject: COMPANY WILL RELOCATE MARCH 1

Effective March 1, 2017, we will relocate our plant facility to Franklin, Tennessee. Approved by the board of directors at its last meeting, this relocation will enable the company to better retain key employees and reduce tax costs by more than 10%.

All employees wishing to relocate should notify their supervisors by the end of the week. We appreciate your support in the move.

Introduction should serve as a buffer to naturally lead reader to "bad news."

Additional paragraphs should be added to provide an explanation for the move.

The close should let people know what will happen next and what the company will do.

Cengage Learning

them. Rather than waiting for a crisis to occur, an organization should examine its state of preparedness and have a carefully considered plan of action that includes the following steps:

- **Anticipate potential crises in terms of areas of vulnerability and what could happen.**

RESPONSE IN A CRISIS

In responding to a crisis, the message conveyed is extremely important in reassuring employees and business partners and in shaping public opinion. These guidelines can help ensure an effective message:

▶ Determine what your message is, and prepare a checklist of what it should contain before writing.

▶ Keep the message simple, and arrange it in logical sections.

▶ Include verbiage that demonstrates your concern, compassion, and control.

▶ Prepare separate messages for internal and external audiences, including the appropriate level of detail.

- **Establish emergency procedures, including an alternate command center and chain of command.** Ensure that more than one employee is media trained and able to respond appropriately if needed.

- **Identify who will need to be contacted, and plan for multiple means of disseminating information.** Cellphones and text messaging have proven themselves valuable when other contact means might not work, but keep in mind that telecommunication circuits can be overloaded in mass disaster situations, necessitating multiple means for sharing news.

- **Ensure current contact information is available for employees, media, and other pertinent parties.**

- **Maintain an up-to-date fact sheet about the company, its products/services, locations, and operations.**

While crises can seldom be predicted, an organization can position itself to respond to them appropriately when they do occur by preparing for crises before they occur.

Adequate pre-crisis planning is necessary for a rapid, effective crisis response, the second stage of crisis management. A key task during crisis response is to identify the type of crisis in order to better develop communication messages. Three broad types of crises exist: victim,

INTEROFFICE MEMORANDUM

TO: All Employees

FROM: Mack Bannock, President

DATE: January 4, 2016

SUBJECT: Proposed Plan for Managing Future Growth

Our company has weathered the recent recession by taking advantage of international business opportunities in Southeast Asia. Our location in Southern California has provided us a well-educated and skilled workforce to produce the innovation needed in today's automobile market.

However, the rise in cost-of-living due to high taxes, comparatively high housing costs, and relatively higher costs for food and utilities has made it more difficult to retain top employees. The cost of living in Southern California is 15% higher than in many other parts of the country. The school system in Los Angeles is one of the poorest in the country in terms of graduation rates from high school. Similarly, L.A. ranks at the top of the list in terms of time spent commuting on overcrowded freeways.

Housing prices, although dramatically lower than they were several years ago, are still well above the national average, particularly in safe neighborhoods with good schools. All of these issues make it much more difficult to retain skilled employees who have the option to move to other parts of the country without these challenges. In fact, three of our top engineers have left in the past year, citing the high cost of living and poor school system as their reasons.

While relocating could provide a long-term economic benefit to the company in terms of tax savings, moving out of Los Angeles could enhance the quality of life for all of us. Consequently, we have been working with state and local governments in other parts of the country to find an area with lower cost of living, good neighborhoods and schools, and a skilled labor force. This search has led us to identify Franklin, Tennessee, a thriving suburb located approximately 18 miles south of Nashville, as our new plant location.

Your supervisor will explain the logistics of the relocation at your next team meeting. In the meantime, please visit the Franklin link on the company intranet to read more about what Tennessee can offer us and our families. Check back for updates on the FAQ page designed to provide responses to your concerns. Now let us work together for a smooth transition to Franklin.

Uses subject line to introduce topic but does not reveal bad news.

Uses buffer to introduce topic familiar to employees through previous communication and leads into reasons.

Provides rational explanation including benefits.

Presents bad news while reminding receiver of benefits.

Follows up by assuring continued exchange of timely information through discussions and web pages.

Ends with positive appeal for unity.

Legal and Ethical Consideration
Uses memo channel rather than email for conveying sensitive message.

Cengage Learning

FIGURE 7.12 COMPONENTS OF CRISIS COMMUNICATION RESPONSES

Concern	Express concern for all affected by the crisis.
Corrective Actions	Describe specific steps the organization is taking to correct the problem.
Instructions	Tell those affected what to do to stay informed and to protect themselves.
Excuse	Deny intent to harm, or point out inability to control events.
Justification	Minimize the perceived damage of the crisis.
Compensation	Offer money or gifts to victims.
Apology	Take full responsibility for the crisis.

Cengage Learning

Sources: W. T. Coombs (2007). Protecting organization reputations during a crisis: The development and application of situational crisis communication theory. *Corporate Reputation Review 10* (3), 163–176; W.T. Coombs (2004). Impact of past crisis on current crisis communications: Insights from situational crisis communication theory. *Journal of Business Communication 41* (3), 265–289; W. T. Coombs & S. J. Holladay (2002). Helping crisis managers protect reputational assets: Initial tests of the situational crisis communication theory. *Management Communication Quarterly 16* (2), 165–186.

accident, and preventable crises.[7] In a victim crisis, the organization is viewed as a victim of the event. This type includes natural disasters, workplace violence, product tampering, and rumors. In an accident crisis, the event is considered unintentional or uncontrollable by the organization and include accidents or harm from technical errors or equipment failure. In a preventable crisis, the event is considered purposeful and includes accidents or harm caused by human error as well as organizational misdeeds such as fraud.[8]

After identifying the type of crisis, you can select the appropriate components of an effective crisis message, as depicted in Figures 7-12 and 7-13.

Figure 7.14 provides an example of an effective response to an accident crisis. It includes the appropriate crisis communication components of showing concern, explaining corrective actions, providing instructions, and giving a brief justification.

During a crisis, the organization should monitor the situation carefully and provide quick and accurate communication to all stakeholders through all available communication channels. After the crisis has passed—the post-crisis stage of crisis management—the organization should carefully plan and create a consistent stream of messages to help repair any damage to its reputation sustained by the crisis.

FIGURE 7.13 TYPES OF CRISES AND APPROPRIATE MESSAGE COMPONENTS

Type of Crisis	Concern	Corrective Actions	Instructions	Excuse/ Justification	Compensation/ Apology
Victim	X	X	X		
Accident	X	X	X	X	
Preventable	X	X	X	X	X

Cengage Learning

Sources: W. T. Coombs (2007). Protecting organization reputations during a crisis: The development and application of situational crisis communication theory. *Corporate Reputation Review 10* (3), 163–176; W.T. Coombs (2004). Impact of past crisis on current crisis communications: Insights from situational crisis communication theory. *Journal of Business Communication 41* (3), 265–289; W. T. Coombs & S. J. Holladay (2002). Helping crisis managers protect reputational assets: Initial tests of the situational crisis communication theory. *Management Communication Quarterly 16* (2), 165–186.

FIGURE 7.14 **EXAMPLE OF CORPORATE WEB SITE POST FOR A VICTIM CRISIS**

At 4:30 p.m. this afternoon (March 12), EastAir Flight EA3201 was involved in an incident upon landing at Los Angeles International Airport. All passengers and crew have been deplaned from the aircraft, and 23 passengers and crew who sustained non-life-threatening injuries have been transported to local hospitals for observation and treatment.

Shows concern.

EastAir personnel are currently on site providing assistance to passengers, and additional EastAir teams are on their way to provide additional support. This assistance will include:

1. Providing accommodations for passengers and families until transportation to their final destination can be arranged.
2. Arranging for transportation to final destinations of passengers and families.
3. Providing access to counseling services of passengers and families as needed.

Explains corrective action.

No further details are available at this time; however, EastAir will provide regular updates on Twitter and on its website at EastAir.com as information becomes known. Family members who seek information about passengers on Flight EA3201 may telephone EastAir at 1-800-912-7099.

Provides instructions.

EastAir will be cooperating fully with authorities in their investigation.

"We at EastAir are greatly relieved that no one was critically injured," said Clyde Gotham, Executive Vice President and Chief Operating Officer of EastAir. "Yet we fully appreciate this has been a very unsettling experience for our customers and their families, as well as our employees, and we are focused on caring for all those affected. We will also fully cooperate with the Transportation Safety Board as it begins an investigation to determine the cause."

Provides brief justification.

Flight EA3201 was carrying 133 passengers and five crew members at the time of the incident.

Cengage Learning

STUDY TOOLS 7

LOCATED AT BACK OF THE TEXTBOOK
☐ Tear-Out Chapter Review Card

LOCATED AT WWW.CENGAGEBRAIN.COM
☐ Review Key Term flashcards and create your own cards

☐ Track your knowledge and understanding of key concepts in business communication
☐ Complete practice and graded quizzes to prepare for tests
☐ Complete interactive content within BCOM8 Online
☐ View the chapter highlight boxes for BCOM8 Online

BCOM
ONLINE
PREPARE FOR TESTS ON THE STUDYBOARD!

○ CORRECT

○ INCORRECT

○ INCORRECT

○ INCORRECT

Personalize Quizzes from Your StudyBits

Take Practice Quizzes by Chapter

CHAPTER QUIZZES

▶ Chapter 1

Chapter 2

Chapter 3

Chapter 4

4LTR PRESS

Access BCOM ONLINE at www.cengagebrain.com

8 Delivering Persuasive Messages

LEARNING OBJECTIVES

After studying this chapter, you should be able to …

8-1 Develop effective outlines and appeals for messages that persuade.

8-2 Write effective sales messages.

8-3 Write effective persuasive requests (making a claim or asking for a favor or information) and persuasion within an organization.

After finishing this chapter, go to **PAGE 145** for **STUDY TOOLS.**

PERSUASION STRATEGIES

Businesspeople regularly seek to persuade others. **Persuasion** is the ability to influence others to accept your point of view. It is not an attempt to trap someone into taking action favorable to the communicator. Instead, it is an honest, organized presentation of information on which a person can choose to act. Professionals in all fields benefit from well-prepared communications that persuade others to accept their ideas or buy their products, services, or ideas.

How do you learn to persuade others through spoken and written communication? Have you ever made a persuasive request, written employment documents or an essay for college entry or a scholarship, or given a campaign speech? If so, you already have experience with this type of communication. While the persuasive concepts discussed in this chapter are directed primarily at written communication, they can also be applied in many spoken communication situations.

For persuasion to be effective, you must understand your product, service, or idea; know your audience; anticipate the arguments that might come from the audience; and have a rational and logical response to those arguments. Remember, persuasion need not be a hard sell; it can simply be a way of getting a client or your supervisor to say yes. Although much of this chapter concentrates on selling products and services, similar principles apply to selling an idea, your organization, and your own abilities.

> Persuasion can simply be a way of getting a client or supervisor to say yes.

8-1a Plan Before You Write

Success in writing is directly related to success in preliminary thinking. If the right questions have been asked and answered, the composing will be easier and the message will be more persuasive. Specifically, you need information about (1) your product, service, or idea; (2) your audience; and (3) the desired action.

KNOW THE PRODUCT, SERVICE, OR IDEA

You cannot be satisfied with knowing the product, service, or idea in a general way; you need details. Get your information by (1) reading available literature; (2) using the product and watching others use it; (3) comparing the product, service, or idea with others; (4) conducting tests and experiments; and (5) soliciting reports from users.

Before you write, you need concrete answers to such questions as these:

- **What will the product, service, or idea do for the reader(s)?**
- **What are its superior features (e.g., design and workmanship or audience benefit)?**
- **How is the product or service different from its competition?**
  - **How is the proposed idea superior to other viable alternatives?**
  - **What is the cost to the receiver?**

Similar questions must be answered about other viable alternatives or competing products. Of particular importance is the question, "What is the major difference?" People are inclined to choose an item (or alternative) that has some distinct advantage. For example, some people might choose a particular car model because of its style and available options; still others might choose the model because of its safety record.

KNOW THE AUDIENCE

Who are the people to whom the persuasive message is directed? What are their wants and needs? Is a persuasive message to be written and addressed to an individual or to a group? If it is addressed to a group, what characteristics do the members have in common? What are their common goals, their occupational levels, and their educational status? To what extent have their needs and wants been satisfied? How might cultural differences affect your message?

Recall the discussion of Maslow's hierarchy of needs in Chapter 2. Some people might respond favorably to appeals to physiological, security, and safety needs (to save time and money, to be comfortable, to be healthy, or to avoid danger). People with such needs would be impressed with a discussion of the benefits of convenience, durability, efficiency, or serviceability. Others might respond favorably to appeals to their social, ego, and self-actualizing needs (to be loved, entertained, remembered, popular, praised, appreciated, or respected). Consider the varying appeals used in a memo to employees and to

persuasion the ability of a sender to influence others to accept his or her point of view supervisors seeking support of teleworking. The memo to employees would appeal to the need for greater flexibility and reduced stress. Appeals directed at supervisors would focus on increased productivity and morale, reduced costs for office space, and compliance with the Clean Air Act, a federal law requiring companies to reduce air pollution and traffic congestion.

IDENTIFY THE DESIRED ACTION

What do you want the reader to do? Complete an online order and make a payment? Receive a demonstration version for trial? Return a card requesting a representative to call? Email for more information? Approve a request? Accept a significant change in service, style, and procedures? Whatever the desired action, you need to have a clear definition of it before composing your message.

8-1b Use the Inductive Approach

More than 100 years ago, Sherwin Cody summarized the persuasive process into four basic steps called **AIDA**.[1] The steps have been varied somewhat and have had different labels, but the fundamentals remain relatively unchanged. The persuasive approach illustrated in Figure 8.1 is inductive. The main idea, which is the request for action, appears in the *last* paragraph after presenting the details—convincing reasons for the audience to comply with the request.

Each step is essential, but the steps do not necessarily require equal amounts of space. Good persuasive messages do not require separate sentences and paragraphs for each phase of the outline. The message *could* gain the reader's attention and interest in the same sentence, and creating desire *could* require many paragraphs.

nasirkhan/Shutterstock.com

AIDA the four basic steps of the persuasive process, including gaining attention, generating interest, creating desire, and motivating action

central selling point the primary appeal on which a persuasive message focuses

8-1c Apply Sound Writing Principles

The principles of unity, coherence, and emphasis are just as important in persuasive messages as in other messages. In addition, the following principles seem to be especially helpful in preparing persuasive messages:

- **Keep paragraphs short.** The spaces between paragraphs show the dividing place between ideas, improve appearance, and provide convenient resting places for the eyes. Hold the first and last paragraph to three or fewer lines; a one-line paragraph (even a very short line) is acceptable. You can even use paragraphs less than one sentence long by putting four or five words on the first line and completing the sentence in a new paragraph. Be careful to include key attention-getting words that either introduce the product, service, or idea or lead to its introduction.

- **Use concrete nouns and active verbs.** Concrete nouns and active verbs help readers see the product, service, or idea and its benefits more vividly than do abstract nouns and passive verbs.

- **Use specific language.** General words won't mean much unless they are well supported with specifics. Specific language is space consuming (saying that something is "great" requires fewer words than telling what makes it so); therefore, persuasive messages are usually longer than other messages. Still, persuasive messages need to be concise; they should say what needs to be said without wasting words.

- **Let readers have the spotlight.** If readers are made the subject of some of the sentences, if they can visualize themselves with the product in their hands, or if they can get the feel of using it for enjoyment or to solve problems, the chances of creating a desire are increased.

- **Stress a central selling point or appeal.** A thorough analysis ordinarily will reveal some feature that is unique or some benefit that is not provided by other viable alternatives—the **central selling point.** This point of difference can be developed into a theme that is woven throughout the entire message. Or, instead of using a point of difference as a central selling point, a writer could choose to stress a major satisfaction to be gained from using the item or doing as asked. A central selling point (theme) should be introduced early and reinforced throughout the remainder of the message.

ATTENTION:

Get the receiver's attention

 INTEREST:

Introduce the product, service, or idea and arouse interest in it

DESIRE:

Create desire by presenting convincing evidence of the value of the product, service, or idea

 ACTION:

Encourage action

Cengage Learning

8-2 SALES MESSAGES

The four-point persuasive outline is appropriate for an *unsolicited sales message*—a letter, memo, or email message written to someone who has not requested it. A *solicited sales message* has been requested by a potential buyer or supporter; that is, the message is prepared to answer this interested person's questions.

A person requesting sales information has given some attention to the product, service, or idea already; therefore, an attention-getting sentence is hardly essential. However,

Lvelin Radkov/Shutterstock.com

such a sentence is needed when the audience is not known to have expressed an interest previously. The very first sentence, then, is deliberately designed to make a reader put aside other thoughts and concentrate on the rest of the message.

8-2a Gain Attention

Various techniques have been successful in convincing readers to consider an unsolicited sales message. Regardless of the technique used, the attention-getter should achieve several important objectives: introduce a relationship, focus on a central selling feature, and use an original approach.

SOME COMMONLY USED ATTENTION-GETTING DEVICES INCLUDE:

▶ **A personal experience:** When a doctor gives you instructions, how often have you thought, "I wish you had time to explain" or "I wish I knew more about medical matters"?

▶ **A solution to a problem (outstanding feature/benefit):** Imagine creating a customized multimedia presentation that …

▶ **A startling announcement:** More teens die as a result of suicide each month than die in auto accidents in the same time period.

▶ **A what-if opening:** What if I told you there is a savings plan that will enable you to retire three years earlier?

▶ **A question:** Why should you invest in a company that has lost money for six straight years?

▶ **A story:** Here's a typical day in the life of a manager who uses an iPad.

▶ **A proverb or quote from a famous person:** Vince Lombardi, one of the most successful coaches in the history of football, once said, "If winning isn't everything, why do they keep score?" At Winning Edge, we specialize in making you the winner you were born to be.

▶ **A split sentence:** Sandy beaches, turquoise water, and warm breezes … it's all awaiting you on your Mesa cruise.

▶ **An analogy:** Like a good neighbor, State Farm is there.

Other attention-getters include a gift, an offer, a bargain, or a comment on an enclosed product sample.

INTRODUCE A RELATIONSHIP BETWEEN THE AUDIENCE AND THE PRODUCT, SERVICE, OR IDEA

Remaining sentences grow naturally from this beginning sentence. If readers do not see the relationship between the first sentence and the sales appeal, they could react negatively to the whole message—they might think they have been tricked into reading it. For example, consider the following poor attention-getter:

> **Would you like to be the chief executive officer of one of America's largest companies? As CEO of Graham Enterprises, you can launch new products, invest in developing countries, or arrange billion-dollar buyouts. Graham Enterprises is one of several companies at your command in the new computer software game developed by Creative Diversions Software.**

The beginning sentence of the preceding ineffective example is emphatic because it is a short question. However, it suggests the message will be about obtaining a top management position, which it is not. All three sentences combined suggest high pressure. The computer software game has relevant virtues, and one of them could have been emphasized by placing it in the first sentence.

8-2b Focus on a Central Selling Feature

Almost every product, service, or idea will in some respects be superior to its competition. If not, such factors as favorable price, fast delivery, or superior service can be used as the primary appeal. This central selling point must be emphasized, and one of the most effective ways to emphasize a point is by position in the message. An outstanding feature mentioned in the middle of a message might go unnoticed, but it will stand out if mentioned in the first sentence. Note how the following opening sentence introduces the central selling feature and leads naturally into the sentences that follow:

> **Like running through a sprinkler on a warm summer day, our latest iced coffee creation combines hot and cold in a way that's totally invigorating. The heat comes from the warm cinnamon notes you taste on first sip, followed by a sweet orange finish. Our classic Orange Spice iced coffee is there to refresh you all the while. Jump in!**

8-2c Use an Original Approach

To get the reader's attention and interest, you must offer something new and fresh. Thus, choose an anecdote likely unfamiliar to your audience or use a unique combination of words to describe how a product, service, or idea can solve the reader's problem:

 The nine-year-old boy rushes to the store's toy department, unaware that his parents are far behind him in housewares. Surrounded by the latest action figures, electronic games, and cartoon DVDs, he hardly knows where to start in his search for the perfect gifts to include on his holiday wish list. For the next hour, his parents indulge his enthusiasm as he tries out every displayed product.

In many ways, Adobe Photoshop Elements is like that toy department. The new Photoshop offers a plethora of powerful, useful features that will hold your attention for hours on end.

8-2d Generate Interest by Introducing the Product, Service, or Idea

A persuasive message is certainly off to a good start if the first sentences cause the reader to think, "Here's a solution to one of my problems," "Here's something I need," or "Here's something I want." You can lead the reader to such a thought by introducing the product, service, or idea in the very first sentence. If you do, you can succeed in both getting attention and creating interest in one sentence. An effective introduction of the product, service, or idea is cohesive and action centered, and continues to stress a central selling point.

BE COHESIVE

If the attention-getter does not introduce the product, service, or idea, it should lead naturally to the introduction. In the following example, note the abrupt change in thought and the lack of connection between the attention-getter in the first sentence and the idea presented in the second sentence:

 Employees appreciate a company that provides a safe work environment.

The Adcock Human Resources Association has been conducting a survey for the last six months. Their primary aim is to improve the safety of office work environments.

The last words of the first sentence, "safe work environment," are related to "safety of office work environments"—the last words of the last sentence. No word or phrase in the first sentence connects the words of the second sentence, which creates an abrupt, confusing change in thought. In the following revision, the second sentence is tied to the first by the word *that's. Safety* in the second sentence refers to *protection* in the third. The LogicTech low-radiation monitor is introduced as a means of providing a safe work environment. Additionally, notice that the attention-getter leads smoothly to the discussion of the survey results.

 Employees appreciate a company that provides a safe work environment.

That's one thing the Tucker Human Resources Association learned from its six-month survey of the safety of the office work environment. For added protection from radiation emissions, more companies are purchasing LogicTech's low-radiation computer monitors ...

BE ACTION ORIENTED

To introduce your offering in an interesting way, you must place the product, service, or idea in your audience's hands and talk about using it or benefiting from accepting your idea. Your audience will get a clearer picture when reading about something happening than when reading a product description. Also, the picture becomes all the more vivid when the reader is in the spotlight. In a sense, you do not sell products, services, or ideas; instead, you sell the pleasure people derive from their use. Logically, then, you have to focus more on that use than on the offering itself. If you put readers to work using your product, service, or idea to solve problems, they will be the subject of most of your sentences.

Some product description is necessary and natural. In the following example, the writer focuses on the product and creates an uninteresting, still picture:

> ✗ The Elise CR is a stripped-back racer that doesn't just deliver on the road. Eibach anti-roll bar and springs plus Bilstein sports dampers mean the Elise CR provides fingertip responsiveness on the racetrack, too.

In the revision, a person is the subject of the message and is enjoying the benefits of the sports car.

> ✓ Channel your inner Kimi Räikkönen in this stripped-back racer worthy of the best Formula One tracks in the world. The Elise CR is an uncompromised sports machine that doesn't just deliver on the road. Eibach anti-roll bar and springs plus Bilstein sports dampers mean the Elise CR provides fingertip responsiveness on the racetrack, too. Handling is assisted further with the latest Lotus Dynamic Performance Management (DPM) system, and selectable Sport setting, giving the driver ultimate power and control.[2]

In a sense, you do not sell products, services, or ideas; instead, you sell the pleasure people derive from their use.

STRESS A CENTRAL SELLING POINT

If the attention-getter does not introduce a distinctive feature, it should lead to it. Note below how the attention-getter introduces the distinctive selling feature (app availability) and how the following sentences keep the audience's eyes focused on that feature:

> ✓ With more than 375,000 apps made just for iPad, there's almost no end to what you can do. These aren't merely scaled-up versions of phone apps that lack features designed for a larger screen. They're powerful apps tailor-made to take full advantage of everything iPad has to offer. And because iPad and iPad mini are so thoughtfully designed, virtually every app works on both devices.
>
> With iPad, all that content is available from one source: Apple. The iTunes Store is the world's largest and most trusted entertainment store. Other mobile platforms have a myriad of fragmented store options, resulting in availability issues, developer frustration, and security risks.[3]

By stressing one main point, you do not limit the message to that point. For example, although app availability is being stressed, other features are also mentioned.

8-2e Create Desire by Providing Convincing Evidence

After you have made an interesting introduction to your product, service, or idea, present enough supporting evidence to satisfy your audience's needs. Keep one or two main features uppermost in the reader's mind, and include evidence that supports these features. For example, using fuel economy as an outstanding selling feature of hybrid cars, while presenting abundant evidence about performance, would be inconsistent.

PRESENT AND INTERPRET FACTUAL EVIDENCE

Few people will believe general statements without having supporting factual evidence. Saying a certain method is efficient is not enough. You must say how it is efficient and present some data to illustrate this. Saying a piece of furniture is durable is not enough. Durability exists in varying degrees. You must present information that shows what makes it durable and also define how durable. Durability can be established, for example, by presenting information about the manufacturing process, the quality of the raw materials, or the skill of the workers:

✓ **If you're looking for plush comfort, then look no further than Ashley's DuraPella® upholstery collection. DuraPella® is a high-tech fabric that is a breakthrough in comfort and durability. DuraPella® consists of 100% MicroDenier Polyester Suede, which gives you the subtle look and elegant feel of suede, yet is durable and stain-resistant ... the best of both worlds! Everyday spills like coffee, wine, and even ballpoint pen are cleaned easily and effectively with a mixture of low pH balance liquid soap and water. You can enjoy luxury in everyday living with DuraPella®.**

Presenting research evidence (hard facts and figures) to support your statements is another way to increase your chances of convincing your audience. Presenting results of a research study takes space but makes the message much more convincing than general remarks about superior durability and appearance.

Evidence must not only *be* authentic; it must *sound* authentic, too. Talking about pages treated with special protectants to retard aging and machine-sewn construction suggests the sender is well informed, which increases audience confidence. Facts and figures are even more impressive if they reflect comparative advantage, as illustrated in the following example:

✓ **With thousands of new viruses created every day, relying on traditional security updates isn't enough anymore. Unlike the competition, exclusive McAfee Total Protection™ technology instantly analyzes and blocks new and emerging threats in milliseconds, so there's virtually no gap in your protection. McAfee is 99.9% effective in detecting malware, the best rating among competitors.⁴**

Naturally, your audience will be less familiar with the product, service, or idea and its uses than you will be. Not only do you have an obligation to give information, you should interpret it if necessary and point out how the information will benefit the audience. Notice how the following example clearly interprets *why* an induction cooktop is superior to electric or gas cooktops. The interpretation makes the evidence understandable and thus convincing.

Cold Statement Without Interpretation	Specific, Interpreted Fact
Cooking with an induction cooktop is the latest in technology for a restaurant environment or for just the average household.	Induction cooking is an entirely new way of cooking. Forget about red-hot electric coils or open gas flames. An induction cooktop converts your cookware into the heating element by using a magnetic field to energize the atoms in the cookware. Your food cooks faster, using less energy, while providing you with instantaneous temperature control.

The previous example uses a valuable interpretative technique—the comparison. You can often make a point more convincing by comparing something unfamiliar with something familiar. Most people are familiar with electric coils and gas flames, so they can now visualize how the cookware becomes the heating element. Comparison can also be used to interpret prices. Advertisers frequently compare the cost of sponsoring a child in a third-world country to the price of a fast-food lunch. An insurance representative might write this sentence: *The monthly premium for $300,000 of term life insurance is $18, the mere cost of two movie tickets.*

Do not go overboard and bore or frustrate your audience with an abundance of facts or technical data. Never make your reader feel ignorant by trying to impress him or her with facts and figures he or she might not understand.

BE OBJECTIVE

Use language people will believe. Specific, concrete language makes your message sound authentic. Excessive superlatives, exaggerations, flowery statements, unsupported claims, and incomplete comparisons all make your message sound like high-pressure sales talk. Just one such sentence can destroy confidence in the whole message. Examine the statements in the following paragraphs to see whether they give convincing evidence. Would they make a reader want to buy? Or do they merely remind the audience of someone's desire to sell?

This antibiotic is the best on the market today. It represents the very latest in biochemical research. Identifying the best-selling antibiotic requires gathering information about all antibiotics marketed and then choosing the one with superior characteristics. You know the sender is likely to have a bias in favor of the particular drug being sold. However, you do not know whether the sender actually spent time researching other antibiotics or whether he or she would know how to evaluate this information. You certainly do not know whether the sender knows enough about biochemical research to say truthfully what the very best and latest is.

Similarly, avoid preposterous statements (*Gardeners are turning handsprings in their excitement over our new weed killer!*) or subjective claims (*Stretch out on one of our memory foam mattresses. It's like floating on a gentle dream cloud on a warm, sunny afternoon. Ah, what soothing relaxation!*). Even though some people might be persuaded by such writing, many will see it as absurd.

Note the incomplete comparison in the following example: *SunBlock provides you better protection from the sun's dangerous ultraviolet rays.* Is SunBlock being compared with *all* other sunscreens, *most* other sunscreens, *one* unnamed brand, or others? Unless an additional sentence identifies the other elements in the comparison, you do not know. Too often, the writer of such a sentence hopes the reader will assume the comparison is with *all* others. Written with that intent, the incomplete comparison is *unethical*. Likewise, statements of certainty are often inaccurate or misleading.

Alexskopje/Shutterstock.com

INCLUDE TESTIMONIALS, GUARANTEES, AND ENCLOSURES

One way to convince prospective customers that they will like your product, service, or idea is to give them concrete evidence that other people like it. Tell what others have said (with permission, of course) about the usefulness of your offering. Guarantees and free trials convey both negative and positive connotations. By revealing willingness to refund money or exchange an unsatisfactory unit, a writer confesses a negative: the purchase could be regretted or refused. However, the positive connotations are stronger than the negatives: the seller has a definite plan for ensuring that buyers get value for money spent. In addition, the seller conveys willingness for the buyer to check a product, service, or idea personally and compare it with others. The seller also implies confidence that a free trial will result in a purchase and that the product will meet standards set in the guarantee. A long or complex guarantee can be included in an enclosure or attachment.

A message should persuade the audience to read an enclosure, attachment, or file link that includes more detailed information. Thus, refer to the added material late in the message after the major portion of the evidence has been given. An enclosure or link is best referred to in a sentence that is not a cliché ("Enclosed you will find," or "We have enclosed a brochure") and says something else:

The enclosed annual report will help you understand the types of information provided to small- and medium-sized companies by Lincoln Business Data, Inc.

Click here to view the huge assortment of clearance-priced items and other end-of-season specials.

SUBORDINATE THE PRICE

Logically, price should be introduced late in the message—after most of the advantages have been discussed. Use the following techniques to overcome people's natural resistance to price:

- **Introduce price only after creating a desire for the product, service, or idea and its virtues.** Let readers see the relationship of features and benefits to the price.

- **Use figures to illustrate that the price is reasonable or that the reader can save money.** Example: Purigard saves the average pool owner about $50 in chemicals each month; thus, the $200 unit pays for itself in a single swim season.

- **State price in terms of small units.** Thirty dollars a month seems like less than $360 a year.

- **Invite comparison of like products, services, or ideas with similar features.**

- **Consider mentioning price in a complex or compound sentence that relates or summarizes the virtues of the product, service, or idea.** Example: For just $79 a year, Amazon Prime brings you access to Instant Videos and Kindle Books as well as free two-day shipping on selected products.

8-2f Motivate Action

For proper clarity and emphasis, the last paragraph should be relatively short. Yet it must accomplish four important tasks: define the specific action wanted, present it as easy to take, encourage quick action, and ask confidently.

MAKE THE ACTION CLEAR AND SIMPLE TO COMPLETE

Define the desired action in specific terms that are easy to complete. For example, you might ask the reader to complete an order blank and return it with payment, place a phone call, or order online. General instructions such as "Let us hear from you," "Take action on the matter," and "Make a response" are ineffective. Make action simple to encourage the audience to act immediately. Instead of asking readers to fill in their names and addresses on order forms or return cards and envelopes, do that work for them. Otherwise, they might see the task as difficult or time consuming and decide to procrastinate.

RESTATE THE REWARD FOR TAKING ACTION (CENTRAL SELLING POINT)

The central selling point should be introduced early in the message, interwoven throughout the evidence section, and included in the last paragraph as an emphatic, final reminder of the reason for taking action.

PROVIDE AN INCENTIVE FOR QUICK ACTION

If the reader waits to take action on your proposal, the persuasive evidence will be harder to remember, and the audience will be less likely to act. Therefore, you prefer the audience to act quickly. Reference to the central selling point (assuming it has been well received) helps stimulate action. Commonly used appeals for getting quick action are to encourage customers to buy while prices are in effect, while supplies last, when a rebate is being offered, when it is a particular holiday, or when they will receive benefits.

ASK CONFIDENTLY FOR ACTION

If you have a good product, service, or idea and have presented evidence effectively, you have a right to feel confident. Demonstrate your confidence when requesting action: "To save time in organizing appointments and tasks, complete and return…." Avoid statements suggesting lack of confidence, such as "If you want to save time in organizing appointments and tasks, complete and return….," "If you agree…," and "I hope you will…."

Figures 8.2 (on page 138) and 8-3 (on page 139) illustrate poor and good *unsolicited sales messages* for a service. Figure 8.4 (on page 140) presents an unsolicited sales message promoting a product. The same principles apply in writing a *solicited sales message*, with one exception: because the solicited sales message is a response to a request for information, an attention-getter is not essential. Typically, sales messages are longer than messages that present routine information or convey good news. Specific details (essential in prompting action) require space.

More and more organizations are using email as a means to persuade existing and potential customers to buy their products. Although email marketing is a relatively new field, marketers are learning how to use email effectively with various audiences.

To gain desired attention from customers, email messages must be carefully timed to arrive when they will gain the most attention. Over-messaging can be annoying, and under-messaging can cause the company to miss potential sales. The subject line is of utmost importance, as it must catch the attention of the reader and create a desire to learn more.

OBSERVE HOW THE FOLLOWING CLOSING PARAGRAPH ACCOMPLISHES THE FOUR IMPORTANT TASKS OF AN EFFECTIVE SALES MESSAGE:

- refers to the central selling point,
- makes a specific action easy,
- provides an incentive for quick action, and
- asks confidently for action.

Simply dial 1-800-555-8341. Then input the five-digit number printed in the top right corner of the attached card. Your name and address will be entered automatically into our system, a speedy way to get your productivity software to you within five working days along with a bill for payment. When you order by August 12, you will also receive a free subscription to Time Resource Magazine. TMC's new productivity software is as easy to use as it is to order!

FIGURE 8.2 **POOR EXAMPLE OF A SALES MESSAGE PROMOTING A SERVICE**   Bad

Dear Ms. Chen:

We have all the capabilities of a full-service communication consultant, including strategy assessment and program planning, implementation, and assessment. We also offer unique services that can truly incorporate your corporate communication strategy among all key stakeholders.

We believe that an integrated communication strategy, one that includes both internal and external stakeholders, is a central need of most organizations today. Most organizations have piecemeal strategies aimed at individual stakeholders and controlled by various departments. Such an approach fails to communicate the overall strategy and brand of the organization in a consistent, coherent manner and may result in confusion about who or what the organization is, severely inhibiting its ability to compete in today's global marketplace. Let our team help you create and communicate your message—whether it's driving sales, bringing people together for important causes, or reputation management. There couldn't be a more critical time to plan an integrated corporate communication strategy with the fierce competition most organizations face today.

Our billing hours are in line with the industry. At just $300 per hour, our team of consultants can help you to maximize your marketing strategies to attract and retain valuable customers and increase employee morale.

If you contact us before March 1, you will also receive a free assessment of your current marketing program from our proprietary MarkETit analysis tool. Please call me at 509-788-1302 to make an appointment with a consultant today.

- **Introduction might better engage the reader by addressing his or her needs in a more personal way.**

- **The language is a bit overblown and vague in terms of concrete actions or results. This approach may damage the writer's credibility in the area of trust.**

- **This paragraph adds little in terms of concrete actions or results.**

- **The cost of the consultant might put off the reader before he or she has a chance to be persuaded by concrete results or actions.**

- **The close might be considered too direct for a "cold-call" message.**

Cengage Learning

8-3 PERSUASIVE REQUESTS

The preceding discussion of sales messages assumed the product, service, or cause was sufficiently worthy to reward the audience for taking action. The discussion of persuasive requests assumes requests are reasonable—that compliance is justified when the request is for an adjustment and that compliance will (in some way) be rewarded when the request is for a favor.

Common types of persuasive requests are claim requests and messages that ask for special favors and information. Although their purpose is to get favorable action, the messages invite action only after attempting to create a desire to take action and providing a logical argument to overcome any anticipated resistance.

8-3a Making a Claim

Claim messages are often routine because the basis for the claim is a guarantee or some other assurance that an adjustment will be made without need of persuasion.

FIGURE 8.3 | GOOD EXAMPLE OF A SALES MESSAGE PROMOTING A SERVICE

Good

Strategic Solutions, Inc.
Full-service Communication Consulting
4208 Olympic Boulevard
Springfield, IL 62702
509-788-1302

January 21, 2016

Suzi Chen, Vice President, Corporate Communication
Finest Pharmaceuticals, Inc.
2010 Emerald Boulevard
Detroit, MI 50089

Dear Ms. Chen:

Are you looking for help to develop your organization's communication strategy? . . . enhancing employee communication? . . . improving communication with external stakeholders? Then you need the services of the full-time communication strategy implementation firm COMMStar, Inc. to develop an integrated communication plan that ensures your organization's success.

With COMMStar's full-service capabilities, you will receive support in all of the following areas:

- **Strategy assessment and identification.** Using our tested data collection techniques, we will assess how well your current communication strategy is working among major stakeholders and identify areas that need development or improvement.

- **Communication planning.** Based on our assessment of your current communication strategy, we will create an integrated plan to help you more effectively communicate your company's mission and brand to both internal and external organizational constituents.

- **Strategy implementation.** Our team of experts will ensure that the integrated communication strategy is implemented properly by holding orientation and training sessions for key players among internal and external constituents.

- **Strategy evaluation.** After the plan has been implemented, our team of experts will evaluate its success and prepare a report that identifies areas where additional work is needed and proposes continuing improvements in those areas that have reached strategic goals.

Visit www.commstar.com today and check out the list of consulting services we provide and read real-life stories from past clients about how we enhanced their communication strategy. If you contact us before March 1, you will also receive a free assessment of your current marketing program from our proprietary MarkETit analysis tool. Our team is ready to assist you in improving the impact of your communication strategy today. Please call me at 509-788-1302 to make an appointment with a consultant.

Sincerely,

Frank Foxworthy
Frank Foxworthy
Engagement Director

Enclosure

Uses a series of phrases rather than complete sentences to gain attention. Introduces needs familiar to a marketing director.

Presents "everything-in-one-place" service as solution to problem and reinforces central selling point.

Uses easy-to-read bulleted list to present evidence that reflects understanding receiver's desired needs.

Keeps focus on receiver by use of second person, active-voice sentences.

States specific action with reward. Makes action easy and provides incentive for quick response.

Cengage Learning

FIGURE 8.4 GOOD EXAMPLE OF A SALES MESSAGE PROMOTING A PRODUCT

Good

New Message

To: Joshua Ingraham [jingraham@hotmail.com]
From: Janelle Woods [jwoods@newvision.com]
Subject: End Lifetime of Reliance on Glasses or Contacts

Joshua,

Do you ever imagine being able to see the alarm clock when you wake each morning? No more hassle of daily contact maintenance? Perhaps you have imagined playing your favorite sport with complete peripheral vision—no fogging or slipping glasses. Millions of people across the world have chosen LASIK, a laser vision correction procedure, as an alternative to glasses and contact lenses. They now are enjoying the freedom that you might have only imagined.

The New Vision Optical Center is eager to inform patients who are potential candidates for laser vision correction of the benefits of this remarkable new procedure. Take a moment to visit our website at www.newvision/optical.com to see skilled surgeons use an excimer laser to correct the shape of the cornea with absolutely no pain to the patient. Many of your questions will be answered by reading about the vision improvements you can realistically expect, testimonials of our many satisfied patients, and the experience of our five resident surgeons.

You are also invited to attend a special laser seminar held at our clinic on January 18 at 7 p.m. that will feature a live laser vision correction procedure followed by a question/ answer period led by our laser correction experts. You'll have an opportunity to enter your name in a drawing for a free laser vision correction procedure to be presented at the close of the seminar.

Would you like to join the millions of people who have chosen LASIK vision correction and end a lifetime of reliance on glasses and contacts in a blink of an eye? Get started today by calling our clinic to register for the laser seminar or to schedule a personal consultation to determine whether you are a candidate for this life-changing procedure. Learn for yourself whether LASIK vision correction could do for you what it has done for so many.

Cordially,

Janelle Woods, Office Manager

- Sends customized email message to customers who may be interested in product.

- Gains attention by introducing familiar annoyances. Presents improved skin appearance as central selling point.

- Introduces product as potential solution to reader's skin concerns.

- Builds interest by offering an invitation to see the product demonstrated.

- Requests specific action and associates it with central selling point.

Legal and Ethical Consideration
- *Abides by requirements under the Federal Trade Commission Act regarding false and deceptive advertising.*

Cengage Learning

However, when an immediate remedy is doubtful, persuasion is necessary. In a typical large business, customer service representatives handle claims.

Often, any reasonable claim will be adjusted to the customer's satisfaction. Therefore, venting strong displeasure in the claim message will likely alienate the claims adjuster—the one person whose cooperation is needed. Remember, adjusters might have had little or

nothing to do with the manufacture and sale of the product or direct delivery of the service. They did not create the need for the claim.

Companies should welcome claims. Only a small percentage of claims are from unethical individuals; the great bulk is from people who believe they have a legitimate complaint. Research indicates that only 4% of customers complain, so for every complaint received, many

FIGURE 8.5 POOR EXAMPLE OF A PERSUASIVE CLAIM — Bad

We just reviewed the initial architectural design and drawings for the design of our building facade and find them totally unacceptable. It must be redone to our specifications.

We made it clear that the design needs to transition smoothly from the existing traditional design of the building to the more modern façade. Instead, the planned façade looks tacked on.

Call us immediately to discuss the changes that you need to make to meet our expectations.

- Introduction is too direct. May damage goodwill.
- The tone is too negative to be persuasive and fails to provide a clear and persuasive reason for requested change.
- Close is too demanding to maintain goodwill.

Cengage Learning

more customers have been satisfied. Complaints help companies identify problem areas and correct them. Another advantage that companies derive from the claim process is that when complaints are handled appropriately, complainers can become very loyal customers.[5] Thus, the way a complaint is handled determines, to a large extent, the goodwill toward the company.

Like sales messages, persuasive claims should use an inductive sequence. Unlike routine claim messages, persuasive claims do not begin by asking for an adjustment.

The poor example shown in Figure 8.5 could be improved by (1) writing inductively (to reduce the chance of a negative reaction in the first sentence), and (2) stressing an appeal throughout the message (to emphasize an incentive for taking favorable action). In a persuasive claim, an appeal serves the same purpose that a central selling feature does in a sales message. Both serve as a theme; both remind the reader of a benefit gained from doing as asked. Note the application of these techniques in the revision in Figure 8.6.

Knowledge of effective claim writing should never be used as a means of taking advantage of someone. Hiding an unjustifiable claim under a cloak of untrue statements is difficult and strictly unethical. Adjusters typically are fair-minded people who will give the benefit of the doubt, but they will not satisfy an unhappy customer simply to avoid a problem.

8-3b Asking a Favor

Occasionally, everyone has to ask someone else for a special favor—action for which there is little reward, time, or inclination. For example, suppose a professional association wants to host its annual fund-raiser dinner at an exclusive country club. The program chair of the association must write the club's general manager requesting permission to use the facility. Will a deductive message be successful?

When a deductive approach is used in a persuasive situation, chances of getting cooperation are minimal. For example, what might be a probable reaction to the following beginning sentence? *Please send me, without charge, your $450 interactive video training game on workplace safety.*

If the first sentence gets a negative reaction, a decision to refuse might be made instantly. Having thought "No," the reader might not read the rest of the message or might hold stubbornly to that decision in spite of a well-written persuasive argument that follows the opening sentence. Note that the letter in Figure 8.7 asks the favor before presenting any benefit for doing so. The letter illustrated in Figure 8.8 (on page 143) uses an inductive approach and applies the principles discussed earlier. As this message shows, if the preceding paragraphs adequately emphasize a reader's reward for complying, the final paragraph need not shout loudly for action.

8-3c Requesting Information

Requests for information are common in business. Information for research reports frequently is obtained by questionnaire, and the reliability of results is strongly influenced by the percentage of return. If a message inviting respondents to complete a questionnaire is written carelessly, the number of responses might be insufficient.

FIGURE 8.6   GOOD EXAMPLE OF A PERSUASIVE CLAIM

Anderson Volk
Simplicity Restaurant
3443 Fruit Arbor Street
Boise, ID 82009
May 2, 2016

Donna Hopkins, Partner
Hopkins and Lowe Architects.
234 27th Avenue
Salt Lake City, UT 83201

Dear Donna:

When Simplicity Restaurant negotiated with your firm to design our new building façade, we were impressed with your previous track record of success. Especially impressive was the building you designed for AppWorks Technologies here in Boise with its simplicity of structure and abundant use of glass to bring in natural lighting and provide access to its park-like surroundings.

In our meeting with your architects, we discussed a façade design that incorporated some of these features but relates harmoniously with the existing building. However, after viewing the initial plan and drawings for the facade, we were disappointed with the planned transition from the more traditional design of the existing building with that to the more modern façade.

With Hopkins and Lowe's reputation for innovative architectural designs, we are confident that the plans can be redrawn to better meet our expectations. We are happy to meet with you again if you would like more specific suggestions regarding changes. Please call me at 330-662-4434 if a meeting would be helpful in this regard.

Sincerely,

Anderson Volk
Anderson Volk, Owner

- **Seeks attention by giving sincere compliment that reveals subject of message.**

- **Continues central appeal— commitment to creative production—while providing needed details.**

- **Presents reasoning that leads to request and subtle reminder of central appeal.**

- *Connects specific request with firm's commitment to develop a creative production.*

Legal and Ethical Consideration
- *Uses letter rather than less formal email format to add formality to contractual agreement.*

Cengage Learning

The most serious weakness is asking for action too quickly and providing no incentive for action. Sometimes the reward for taking action is small and indirect, but the message needs to make these benefits evident.

8-3d **Persuading Within an Organization**

The majority of memos are of a routine nature and essential for the day-to-day operation of the business. For example, giving instructions for performing work assignments, scheduling meetings, and providing project progress reports. In many organizations, such matters are handled through the use of email rather than paper memos. These routine messages, as well as messages conveying good news, are written deductively. However, some circumstances require that a supervisor write a persuasive message that motivates employees to accept a change in their jobs that might have a negative effect on the employees or generate resistance (e.g., a job transfer, change in work procedures, software upgrade).

For example, imagine that Pub on the Green restaurant was faced with the challenge of communicating

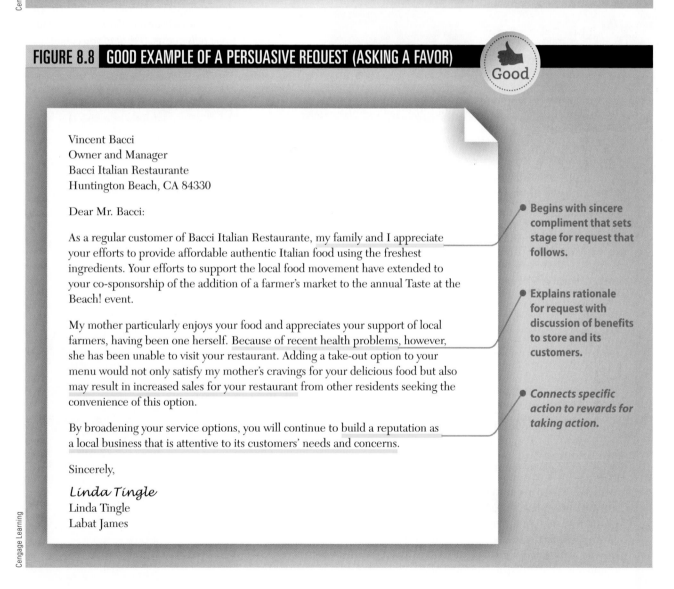

FIGURE 8.7 | POOR EXAMPLE OF A PERSUASIVE REQUEST (ASKING A FAVOR) — Bad

Your restaurant does not offer a take-out option. My mother is unable to visit your restaurant due to health problems.

Would you consider providing this option so that people such as my mom could enjoy your food?

- Does not use an inductive approach to set a more positive tone. Fails to provide good reasons to comply with the request.

- Close does little to build goodwill or encourage compliance.

FIGURE 8.8 | GOOD EXAMPLE OF A PERSUASIVE REQUEST (ASKING A FAVOR) — Good

Vincent Bacci
Owner and Manager
Bacci Italian Restaurante
Huntington Beach, CA 84330

Dear Mr. Bacci:

As a regular customer of Bacci Italian Restaurante, my family and I appreciate your efforts to provide affordable authentic Italian food using the freshest ingredients. Your efforts to support the local food movement have extended to your co-sponsorship of the addition of a farmer's market to the annual Taste at the Beach! event.

My mother particularly enjoys your food and appreciates your support of local farmers, having been one herself. Because of recent health problems, however, she has been unable to visit your restaurant. Adding a take-out option to your menu would not only satisfy my mother's cravings for your delicious food but also may result in increased sales for your restaurant from other residents seeking the convenience of this option.

By broadening your service options, you will continue to build a reputation as a local business that is attentive to its customers' needs and concerns.

Sincerely,

Linda Tingle
Linda Tingle
Labat James

- Begins with sincere compliment that sets stage for request that follows.

- Explains rationale for request with discussion of benefits to store and its customers.

- *Connects specific action to rewards for taking action.*

to its employees a significant change in service and style, which included new uniforms. Rather than coercing or demanding that employees accept the change, a letter from the president could emphasize reasons the changes were being made (benefits to guests, the company, and the employees) and the employee's important role in implementing the changes. Using a lighthearted, entertaining approach, the message could include (a) a visual model of the fresh, crisp, and professional look the company

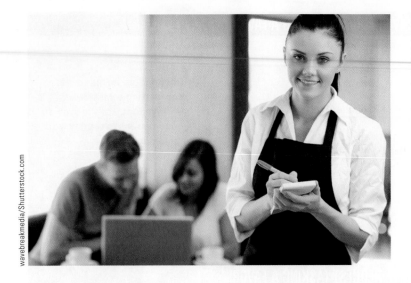

expected with the uniform change and (b) helpful information on ways to achieve this look. The following excerpt shows how a "you" orientation and "style flashes" could be interwoven into the letter:

- ***Make sure your hair is neatly tied back.*** *Messy hair is a problem for guests—they don't want it getting it into their food. You might even get a better tip.*
- ***Don't wear a lot of bling.*** *Guests may think you don't need as large a tip.*
- ***Remember to smile.*** *Your smile is the first sign to guests that their Pub on the Green experience will be a memorable one. Your smile tells guests, "I'm glad you came!"*

FIGURE 8.9 GOOD EXAMPLE OF A PERSUASIVE MESSAGE

To: Jee Kim [jkim@smithassociates.com]
From: Larita Brown [lbrown@smithassociates.com]
Subject: Wellness Program

During our leadership meeting last month, HR Director Cathryn Willis noted a significant uptick in employee sick-day requests over the past year. A discussion followed about the cost of sick-days to the company. As you recall, I offered to do some research on how other firms of our size have responded to this issue.

My research has found that on-site exercise programs have resulted in notable decreases in sick-pay requests. Obviously, we don't have space for such a program, but an alternative would be to provide an incentive for employees to exercise at the Buff workout facility located just a block from our offices.

In my research I found that a number of organizations offer employees incentives for their active involvement in exercise programs. These incentives include free movie tickets, dinners, coffee mugs, T-shirts, etc. I am proposing that we provide such incentives by using the savings we should achieve through decreased sick time.

I have approached the management of Buff, and it is willing to offer our employees a discounted membership if we can guarantee a 50% sign-up rate.

With our goals of decreasing sick-leave requests, would you allow me to test the exercise incentive program in the sales department during May? Employees participating in the program would be asked to sign up for the program and to turn in a stamped card from Buff, indicating the number of times they have used the facility during the month. At the end of the pilot program, I will compile a report of the results, thereby allowing us to consider whether to expand the program to all departments.

- Opens with reference to meeting discussion and company goal.
- Presents a solution to the identified problem.
- Builds interest by mentioning benefits of the program.
- *Reduces potential resistance by tracking use and reporting results.*
- *Alludes to benefits and closes with specific action to be taken.*

Deductive sequence (main idea first) works well for routine messages and good-news messages.

Inductive sequence (details first) works well if the reader needs to be persuaded.

But don't just take our word for it. A recent Bay College study found that smiling reflects an awareness of other people and their needs. That's probably why a "winning smile" is so charming!

The detailed language leaves no doubt in an employee's mind as to what management considers clean, crisp, and professional. However, by continually emphasizing the benefits employees gain from the change, management garners support for the high standards being imposed.

Similarly, employees must often make persuasive requests of their supervisors. For example, they might recommend a change in procedure, acquisition of equipment or software, or attendance at a professional development program. They might justify a promotion or job reclassification or recommendation for policy changes, and so on. Persuasive memos and email messages are longer than most routine messages because of the extra space needed for developing an appeal and providing convincing evidence.

When preparing to write the memo in Figure 8.9, a manager recognizes that implementation costs could affect the president's reaction to her proposal to implement a wellness program. Anticipating resistance, the manager writes inductively and builds a logical, compelling argument for her proposal.

STUDY TOOLS 8

LOCATED AT BACK OF THE TEXTBOOK
☐ Tear-Out Chapter Review Card

LOCATED AT WWW.CENGAGEBRAIN.COM
☐ Review Key Term flashcards and create your own cards

☐ Track your knowledge and understanding of key concepts in business communication

☐ Complete practice and graded quizzes to prepare for tests

☐ Complete interactive content within BCOM8 Online

☐ View the chapter highlight boxes for BCOM8 Online

9 Understanding the Report Process and Research Methods

ra2studio/Shutterstock.com

LEARNING OBJECTIVES

After studying this chapter, you should be able to …

9-1 Identify the characteristics of a report and the various classifications of business reports.

9-2 Apply steps in the problem-solving process and methods for solving a problem.

9-3 Use appropriate printed, electronic, and primary sources of information.

9-4 Demonstrate appropriate methods of collecting, organizing, and referencing information.

9-5 Explain techniques for the logical analysis and interpretation of data.

After finishing this chapter, go to **PAGE 164** for **STUDY TOOLS.**

CHARACTERISTICS OF REPORTS

"Hi, Kate. This is Lewis in sales. Do you know whether the latest sales figures report is ready? My supervisor wants me to review it in preparation for next week's presentation."

"Hi, Lewis. Yes, I just finished a draft of the report yesterday. I will email it to you right now. If there are any changes, I will let you know."

This brief exchange illustrates a simple reporting task. A question has been posed; the answer given (along with supporting information) satisfies the reporting requirement. Although Kate might never have studied report preparation, she did an excellent job; so Lewis can prepare to report the sales figures. Kate's spoken report is a simple illustration of the four main characteristics of reports:

> Because reports contribute to decision making and problem solving, they should be as objective as possible.

- **Reports typically travel upward in an organization because they usually are requested by a higher authority.** In most cases, people would not generate reports unless requested to do so.

- **Reports are logically organized.** In Kate's case, she answered Lewis's question first and then supported the answer with evidence to justify it. Through your study of message organization, you learned the difference between deductive and inductive organization. Kate's report was deductively organized. If Kate had given the supporting evidence first and followed that with the answer that she would meet the deadline, the organization of her reply would have been inductive and would still have been logical.

- **Reports are objective.** Because reports contribute to decision making and problem solving, they should be as objective as possible. When nonobjective (subjective) material is included, the report writer should make that known.

- **Reports are generally prepared for a limited audience.** This characteristic is particularly true of reports traveling within an organization and means that reports, like letters, memos, and emails, should be prepared with the receivers' needs in mind.

9-1a Types of Reports

Based on the four characteristics, a workable definition of a *report* is an orderly, objective message used to convey information from one organizational area to another

or from one organization to another to assist in decision making or problem solving. Reports have been classified in numerous ways by management and by report-preparation authorities. The form, direction, functional use, and content of the report are used as bases for classification. However, a single report might fit several classifications. The following brief review of classification illustrates the scope of reporting and establishes a basis for studying reports.

- **Formal or informal reports.** The formal/informal classification is particularly helpful because it applies to all reports. A **formal report** is carefully structured; it is logically organized and objective, contains much detail, and is written in a style that tends to eliminate such elements as personal pronouns. An **informal report** is usually a short message written in natural or personal language. An internal memo generally can be described as an informal report. All reports can be placed on a continuum of formality, as shown in Figure 9.1. The distinction among the degrees of formality of various reports is explained more fully in Chapter 11.

- **Short or long reports.** Reports can be classified generally as short or long. A one-page memo is obviously short, and a report of 20 pages is obviously long. What about in-between lengths? One important distinction generally holds true: as it becomes longer, a report takes on more characteristics of formal reports. Thus, the classifications of formal/informal and short/long are closely related.

- **Informational or analytical reports.** An **informational report** carries objective information from one area of an organization to another. An **analytical report** presents suggested solutions to problems. Company annual reports, monthly financial statements, reports of sales volume, and reports of employee or personnel absenteeism and turnover are informational reports. Reports of scientific research, real estate appraisal reports, and feasibility reports by consulting firms are analytical reports.

formal report carefully structured report that is logically organized and objective, contains much detail, and is written in a style that tends to eliminate such elements as personal pronouns

informal report usually a short message written in natural or personal language

informational report a report that carries objective information from one area of an organization to another

analytical report a report that presents suggested solutions to problems

FIGURE 9.1   REPORT FORMALITY CONTINUUM

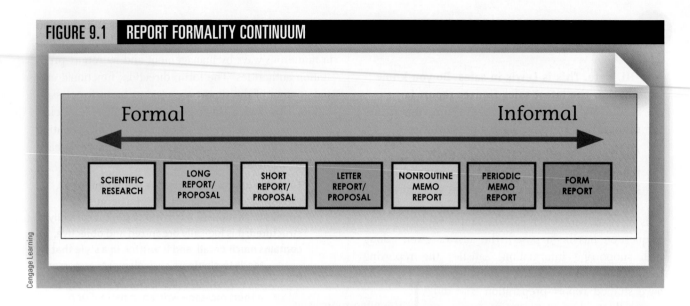

Formal   Informal

| SCIENTIFIC RESEARCH | LONG REPORT/ PROPOSAL | SHORT REPORT/ PROPOSAL | LETTER REPORT/ PROPOSAL | NONROUTINE MEMO REPORT | PERIODIC MEMO REPORT | FORM REPORT |

- **Vertical or lateral reports.** The vertical/lateral classification refers to the directions in which reports travel. Although most reports travel upward in organizations, many travel downward. Both represent vertical reports and are often referred to as *upward-directed* and *downward-directed* reports. The main function of **vertical reports** is to contribute to management *control*, as shown in Figure 9.2. **Lateral reports**, on the other hand, assist in *coordination* in the organization. A report traveling between units on the same organizational level, as between the production department and the finance department, is lateral.

FIGURE 9.2   THE GENERAL UPWARD FLOW OF REPORTS

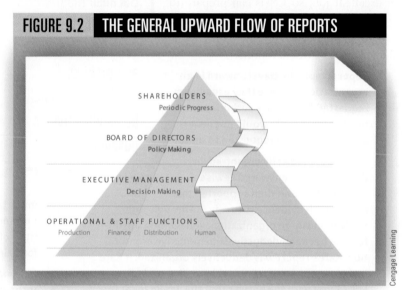

SHAREHOLDERS
Periodic Progress

BOARD OF DIRECTORS
Policy Making

EXECUTIVE MANAGEMENT
Decision Making

OPERATIONAL & STAFF FUNCTIONS
Production   Finance   Distribution   Human

vertical report a report that can be upward- or downward-directed

lateral report a report that travels between units on the same organizational level

internal report a report that travels within an organization, such as a production or sales report

external report a report prepared for distribution outside an organization

periodic report a report that is issued on regularly scheduled dates

functional report a report that serves a specified purpose within a company

- **Internal or external reports.** An **internal report**, such as a production or sales report, travels within an organization. An **external report**, such as a company's annual report to stockholders, is prepared for distribution outside an organization.

- **Periodic reports.** **Periodic reports** are issued on regularly scheduled dates. They are generally directed upward and serve management control purposes. Daily, weekly, monthly, quarterly, semiannual, and annual time periods are typical for periodic reports. Preprinted forms and computer-generated data contribute to uniformity of periodic reports.

- **Functional reports.** A **functional report** serves a specified purpose within a company. The functional classification includes accounting reports, marketing reports, financial reports, personnel reports, and a variety of other reports that take their functional designation from their ultimate use. For example, a justification of the need for additional personnel or for new equipment is described as a *justification report* in the functional classification.

9-1b Proposals

A **proposal** is a written description of how one organization can meet the needs of another; for example, by providing products or services or solving problems. Businesses issue *calls for bids* that present the specifications for major purchases of goods and certain services. Most governmental and nonprofit agencies issue *requests for proposals*, or RFPs. Potential suppliers prepare proposal reports telling how they can meet that need. Those preparing the proposal create a convincing document that will lead to obtaining a contract.

In our information-intensive society, proposal preparation is a major activity for many firms. In fact, some companies hire consultants or designate employees to specialize in proposal writing. Chapter 11 presents proposal preparation in considerable detail.

As you review these report classifications, you will very likely decide—correctly—that almost all reports could be included in these categories. A report may be formal or informal, short or long, informational or analytical, vertically or laterally directed, internal or external, periodic or non-periodic, functionally labeled, a proposal, or some other combination of these classifications. These report categories are in common use and provide necessary terminology for the study and production of reports.

9-2 BASIS FOR REPORTS: THE PROBLEM-SOLVING PROCESS

The upward flow of reports provides management with data that someone might use to make a decision. The purpose is to use the data to solve a problem. Some problems are recurring and call for a steady flow of information; other problems might be unique and call for information on a one-time basis. A problem is the basis for a report. The following steps are used for finding a solution:

1. **Recognize and define the problem.**
2. **Select a method of solution.**
3. **Collect and organize the data and document the sources.**
4. **Arrive at an answer.**

Only after all four steps have been completed is a report written for presentation. Reports represent an attempt to communicate how a problem was solved. These problem-solving steps are completed *before* the report is written in final form.

9-2a Recognizing and Defining the Problem

Problem-solving research cannot begin until the researchers define the problem. Frequently, those requesting a report will attempt to provide a suitable definition. Nevertheless, researchers should attempt to state the problem clearly and precisely to ensure they are on the right track.

USING PROBLEM STATEMENTS, STATEMENTS OF PURPOSE, AND HYPOTHESES

The **problem statement**, or statement of the problem, is the particular problem that is to be solved by the research. The **statement of purpose** is the goal of the study and includes the aims or objectives the researcher hopes to accomplish. Research studies often have both a problem statement and a statement of purpose. For example, a real estate appraiser accepts a client's request to appraise a building to determine its market value. The problem is to arrive at a fair market value for the property. The purpose of the appraisal, however, might be to establish a value for a mortgage loan, to determine the feasibility of adding to the structure, or to assess the financial possibility of demolishing the structure and erecting something else. Thus, the purpose might have much to do with determining what elements to consider in arriving at an answer. In other words, unless you know *why* something is wanted, you might have difficulty knowing *what* is wanted. Once you arrive at the answers to the *what* and *why* questions, you will be on your way to solving the problem.

A **hypothesis** is a statement to be proved or disproved through research. For example, a study of skilled manufacturing employees under varying conditions might be made to determine

proposal a written description of how one organization can meet the needs of another

problem statement the particular problem that is to be solved by the research

statement of purpose the goal of the study; includes the aims or objectives the researcher hopes to accomplish

hypothesis a statement to be proved or disproved through research

Hypotheses are statements that may be proved or disproved through research.

desirable limits. The *scope* of the report helps to establish boundaries in which the report will be researched and prepared. Assume, for instance, that you want to study salaries of computer technicians. Imagine the enormity of such a task. Millions of people are employed in computer jobs. Perhaps a thousand or so different types of jobs fall into this classification. Use the *what, why, when, where,* and *who* questions to reduce such a problem to reasonable proportions.

whether production would increase if each employee were part of a team, as opposed to being a single unit in a production line. For this problem, the hypothesis could be formulated in this way:

> **Hypothesis:** Productivity will increase when skilled manufacturing employees function as members of production teams rather than as single units in a production line.

Because the hypothesis tends to be stated in a way that favors one possibility or is prejudiced toward a particular answer, many researchers prefer to state hypotheses in the null form. The *null hypothesis* states that no relationship or difference will be found in the factors being studied, which tends to remove the element of prejudice toward a certain answer. The null hypothesis for the previous example could be written as follows:

> **Null hypothesis:** No significant difference will be found in productivity between workers organized as teams and workers as individual production line units.

Using the problem/purpose approach, the hypothesis approach, or both, is a choice of the researcher. In many ways, the purpose of a study is determined by the intended use of its results.

LIMITING THE SCOPE OF THE PROBLEM

A major shortcoming that often occurs in research planning is the failure to establish or to recognize

LIMITS YOU MIGHT SET AS THE HUMAN RESOURCES MANAGER OF A COMPUTER COMPANY:

What:	A study of salaries of technical support personnel
Why:	To determine whether salaries in our firm are competitive and consistent
When:	Current
Where:	United States
Who:	Technical support personnel at a computer company

Now you can phrase the problem this way:

Statement of purpose: *The purpose of this study is to survey salaries of technical support personnel at computer companies working in the United States to determine whether our salaries are competitive and consistent.*

Note that this process of reducing the problem to a workable size has also established some firm limits to the research. You have limited the problem to website functionality, the particular area, and a certain group of users. Note, too, how important the *why* was in helping to establish the limits. Limiting the problem is "zeroing in on the problem."

In some reports, it is desirable to differentiate between the boundaries that were placed on the project outside the control of the researchers and those that were chosen by the researchers. Boundaries imposed outside the control of the researchers are called *limitations*; they might include the assignment of the topic, allotted budget, and time for completion of the report. These boundaries affect what and how the topic can be researched. Boundaries chosen by the researchers to make the project more manageable are called *delimitations*; they might include the sources and methods chosen for research.

DEFINING TERMS CLEARLY

Words often have more than one meaning, and technical or special-use words might occur in the report that are not widely used or understood. Such terms would require a definition for the reader's understanding of the information presented. In the previously used example concerning the study of computer technicians' salaries, a comparison of one bank's salaries with those paid by others would be meaningful only if the information gathered from other banks relates to identical jobs. A job description defining the duties performed by a computer technician, for example, would help ensure that all banks would be talking about the same job tasks regardless of the job title. In addition, the term *salary* requires definition. Is it hourly, weekly, monthly, or yearly? Are benefits included?

DOCUMENTING PROCEDURES

The procedures or steps a writer takes in preparing a report are often recorded as a part of the written report. This **procedures** section, or **methodology**, adds credibility to the research process and also enables subsequent researchers to repeat, or replicate, the study in another setting or at a later time. Reports that study the same factors in different time frames are called **longitudinal studies**.

The procedures section of a report records the major steps taken in the research, and possibly the reasons for their inclusion. It might, for instance, tell the types of printed and electronic sources that were consulted and the groups of people interviewed and how they were selected. Steps in the procedures section are typically listed in chronological order so that the reader has an overall understanding of the timetable that existed for the project.

9-3 SELECTING A METHOD OF GATHERING INFORMATION

After defining the problem, the researcher will plan how to arrive at a solution. The research methods you use to collect necessary information can be secondary, primary, or both.

Kheng Guan Toh/Shutterstock.com

9-3a Secondary Research

Secondary research provides information that has already been created by others. Researchers save time and effort by not duplicating research that has already been undertaken. They can access this information easily through the aid of electronic databases and bibliographic indexes. Suppose that a marketing manager has been asked to investigate the feasibility of implementing a strategic information system. The manager knows other companies are using this technology. By engaging in secondary research, the manager can determine the boundaries of knowledge before proceeding into the unknown.

Certain truths have been established and treated as principles reported in textbooks and other publications. However, because knowledge is constantly expanding, the researcher knows that new information is available. The job, then, is to canvass the literature of the field and attempt to redefine the boundaries of knowledge.

procedures (or methodology) the steps a writer takes in preparing a report; often recorded as a part of the written report

longitudinal studies reports that study the same factors in different time frames

secondary research provides information that has already been reported by others

SECONDARY RESEARCH ACCOMPLISHES THE FOLLOWING OBJECTIVES:

▸ **Establishes a point of departure for further research**

▸ **Avoids needless duplication of costly research efforts**

▸ **Reveals areas of needed research**

▸ **Makes a real contribution to a body of knowledge**

Secondary research can be gathered by means of traditional printed sources or by using electronic tools.

PRINTED SOURCES

Major categories of printed sources are books, periodicals, and government documents. Books are typically cataloged in libraries by call number, with larger libraries using the Library of Congress classification system. Traditional card catalogs in libraries have been replaced by online catalogs, which allow the user to locate desired books by author, title, subject, or keyword. A wide assortment of reference books is typically available for use within libraries; these include dictionaries, encyclopedias, yearbooks, and almanacs. Some of these volumes contain general information on a wide array of topics, whereas others are designed for a specific field of study.

Periodicals, referred to as *serials* by librarians, include various types of publications that are released on a periodic basis. Newspapers, magazines, and journals are all types of periodicals. Newspapers, which are usually published daily, are a good initial source for investigation because they give condensed coverage of timely topics. Magazines might be published weekly, monthly, bimonthly, or in some other interval. They are typically written for a general readership, providing expanded coverage in an easy-to-read format. Journals, on the other hand, are written for more specialized audiences, are peer reviewed, and are more research oriented and thus more credible. Journal articles share the results of research studies and provide data that support their findings. They also provide bibliographies or citation lists that can be used to locate related materials. Articles on specific topics can be located using both printed and online indexes. A partial list of these sources is shown in Figure 9.3.

FIGURE 9.3   USEFUL REFERENCE SOURCES

Printed Indexes

Business Periodicals Index
Education Index
The New York Times Index
Readers' Guide to Periodical Literature
Social Science and Humanities Index
The Wall Street Journal Index

Electronic Databases

ABI/INFORM
Academic Search Elite
Business & Company Resource Center
Business Dateline
Business Source Premier
DIALOG Information Services
ERIC
First Search
FSI Online
General BusinessFile
LexisNexis Academic Universe
Periodical Abstracts
ProQuest
Westlaw

Biography

Who's Who in America
Similar directories for specific geographic areas, industries, and professions

General Facts and Statistics

Statistical Abstract of the United States
Bureau of the Census publications
Dictionaries (general and discipline specific)
Encyclopedia (*Americana* or *Britannica*)
Fortune Directories of U.S. Corporations
World Atlas
LexisNexis Statistics
Almanacs

Report Style and Formation

American Psychological Association. (2010).
   *Publication Manual of the American Psychological
   Association* (6th ed.). Washington, DC: Author.
   [www.apastyle.org]

Gibaldi, J. (2009). *MLA Handbook for Writers of
   Researcher Papers* (7th ed.). New York: Modern
   Language Association.
   [www.mla.org/style_faq]

Cengage Learning

ELECTRONIC SOURCES

The availability of computer-assisted data searches has simplified the time-consuming task of searching through indexes, card catalogs, and other sources. Weekly and monthly updates keep electronic databases current, and they are easy to use. Databases such as LexisNexis Academic Universe have full-text retrieval capability, meaning you can retrieve the entire article for reviewing and printing. Other databases offer only some articles in full text, with citations or abstracts provided for others. Note the list of electronic databases for business users listed in Figure 9.3.

The Internet and its subset, the World Wide Web, have made thousands of reference sources available in a matter of seconds. However, the vastness of this resource can be overwhelming to the novice researcher. The following tips will help make your Internet search more productive:

- **Choose your search engine or database appropriately.** A *search engine* is a cataloged database of websites that allows you to search specific topics. Several popular search engines exist, including Yahoo!, Ask, AOL, and MyWebSearch. Megasearch engines such as Google and Bing, which index billions of web pages, search through a number of other engines to produce "hits."[1] (A *hit* is a located website that contains the word or words specified in the search.) You want to obtain a sufficient number of hits, but not thousands. Although the variety of these larger engines is greater, they pose more difficulty in narrowing a search.

Electronic databases provide access to articles from newspapers, magazines, journals, and other types of publications. The database provider might charge a subscription fee or a document delivery fee to access articles. These types of databases are not accessible by a search engine and are often described as the *hidden Internet.* Many libraries provide access to these databases. Some databases are suited for topic searches of general interest; others are geared toward specialized fields. A topic search will produce a listing of references and article abstracts, or even full-text articles in some cases. Databases available through your library might include Business Source Premier (an offering of EBSCO), Academic Search Elite, LexisNexis Academic Universe, ABI Inform First Search, Business and Company Resource Center, General BusinessFile, and others.

- **Structure searches from broad to specific.** Use words for your topic that are descriptive and do not have multiple meanings. Once sites have been located for your general topic, you can use *Boolean logic* to narrow the selection. Boolean operands (*and, or, not*) serve to limit the identified sites. The following example shows how these delimiters can assist you in locating precisely what you want:

  ○ Using the key phrase *workplace productivity* will produce all sites that have either of the key words in the title or descriptors.

  ○ Placing "and" between key words will produce hits that have both words.

  ○ Keying *workplace productivity not United States* will eliminate hits that refer to the United States.

- **Use quotation marks when literal topics are desired.** Putting quotation marks around your topic words can drastically affect the number of hits. The quotation marks cause the search engine to look for the designated words as a phrase, thus producing only those sites that have the phrase present. Without the quotation marks, the search engine will treat the words individually and produce many more hits, most of which might not be useful. For instance, if you are looking for sites related to "international communication," placing quotation marks around the desired phrase would eliminate the sites that deal with international topics that are not communication oriented.

- **Look for web pages that have collections of links to other related topics.** Clicking on these hyperlinks will allow you to maximize your time investment in the data-gathering phase of your research.

- **Be adaptable to the various access format requirements.** Each search engine and database has its own particular format and instructions for use. The method for specifying and narrowing your search will vary.

Anaken2012/Shutterstock.com

9-3b Primary Research

After reviewing the secondary data, you might need to collect primary data to solve your problem. **Primary research** relies on firsthand data, such as responses from pertinent individuals or observations of people or phenomena related to your study. Recognized methods to obtain original information are observational studies, experimental research, and normative surveys.

Observational studies are those in which the researcher observes and statistically analyzes certain phenomena to assist in establishing new principles or discoveries. For example, market analysts observe buying habits of certain income groups to determine the most desirable markets. Internal auditors analyze expected patterns in expense reimbursement amounts to identify potential fraud activity. Developing an objective system for quantifying observations is necessary to collect valid data. For example, to gain insight into the effect of a comprehensive ethics program, a researcher might record the number of incidents of ethical misconduct reported or the number of calls made to an ethics helpline designed to provide advice about proper conduct. Observational studies typically involve no contact with the human subjects under study.

Experimental research typically involves the study of two or more samples that have exactly the same components before a variable is added to one of the samples. Any differences observed are viewed as due to the variable. Like scientists, businesses use experimental research to solve various problems. For example, a company conducts new employee training with all new hires. Two training methods are presently used: new hires in one regional office receive their training in a traditional classroom setting with other new employees, while employees at the other regional office take a web-based training class. Management wants to determine whether one method is superior to the other in terms of learning success. During the period of the study, learning differences in the two study groups are noted. Because the training method is assumed to be the only significant variable, any difference is attributed to its influence. Experimental research involves very careful recordkeeping and can require informed consent from participants who are subjected to experimental methods.

Normative survey research is undertaken to determine the status of something at a specific time. Survey instruments such as questionnaires, opinion surveys, checklists, and interviews are used to obtain information from participants. Election opinion polls represent one type of normative survey research. The term *normative* is used to qualify surveys because surveys reveal "norms" or "standards" existing at the time of the survey. A poll taken two months before an election might have little similarity to one taken the week preceding the election.

Surveys can help verify the accuracy of existing norms. The U.S. Census is conducted every decade to establish an actual population figure, and each person is supposedly counted. In effect, the census tests the accuracy of prediction techniques used to estimate population during the years between censuses. A survey of what employees consider a fair benefits package would be effective only for the date of the survey. People retire, move, and change their minds often. These human traits make survey research of opinions somewhat tentative. Yet surveys remain a valuable tool for gathering information on which to base decisions and policies.

Researchers normally cannot survey everyone, particularly if the population is large and the research budget is limited. **Sampling** is a survey technique that eliminates the need for questioning 100% of the population. Sampling is based on the principle that a sufficiently large number drawn at random from a population will be representative of the total population. That is, the sample will possess the same characteristics in the same proportions as the total population. For example, a company collecting market research data before introducing a new low-fat food product would survey a small number of people. The data are considered *representative* if the sample of people surveyed has the same percentage of ages, genders, purchasing power, and so on as the anticipated target market.

As a researcher, you must be cautious about drawing conclusions from a sample and generalizing them to a population that might not be represented by the sample. For example, early-morning shoppers might differ from afternoon or evening shoppers; young adults might differ from senior citizens; male shoppers might differ from female shoppers. A good researcher defines the

---

primary research data collected for the first time, usually for a specific purpose

observational studies studies in which the researcher observes and statistically analyzes certain phenomena in order to assist in establishing new principles or discoveries

experimental research the study of two samples that have exactly the same components before a variable is added to one of the samples

normative survey research research to determine the status of something at a specific time

sampling a survey technique that eliminates the need for questioning 100% of the population

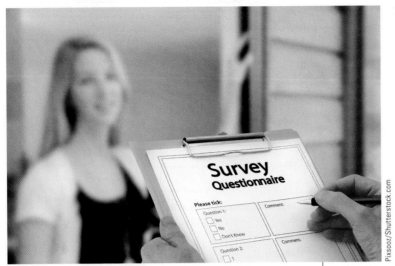

Responses to surveys often represent only a small percentage of the total mailings. In some cases, a return of 3% to 5% is considered adequate and is planned for by researchers. In other cases, such as employee surveys or questionnaires, a return of considerably more than half the mailings might be a planned result. Selecting an appropriate data collection method and developing a sound survey instrument are crucial elements of an effective research study.

9-4 COLLECTING AND ORGANIZING THE DATA

population as distinctly as possible and uses a sampling technique to ensure that the sample is representative.

Whether a survey involves personal interviewing or the distribution of items such as checklists or questionnaires, some principles of procedure and planning are common to both methods. These principles assure the researcher that the data gathered will be both valid (i.e., it will measure what the researcher intended to measure) and reliable (i.e., it will measure data accurately).

- **Validity** refers to the degree to which the data measure what you intend to measure. It generally results from careful planning of the questionnaire or interview questions or items. Cautious wording, preliminary testing of items to detect misunderstandings, and some statistical techniques are helpful in determining whether the responses to the items are valid. A *pilot test* of the instrument is often conducted prior to the full-scale survey so that a smaller number of participants can test the instrument, which can then be revised prior to wide-scale administration.

- **Reliability** refers to the level of consistency or stability over time or over independent samples; that is, reliable data are reasonably accurate or repeatable. Reliability results from asking a large enough sample of people so that the researcher is reasonably confident the results would be the same even if more people were asked to respond or if a different sample were chosen from the same population. For example, if you were to ask 10 people to react to a questionnaire item, the results might vary considerably. If you were to add 90 more people to the sample, the results might tend to reach a point of stability where more responses would not change the results. Reliability would then be reasonably established.

Collecting the right data and ensuring that they are recorded appropriately is paramount to the success of a business report. Various techniques can assist in this process when collecting both secondary and primary research.

9-4a Collecting Secondary Data

When beginning to collect secondary data, beware of collecting too much information—one of the major deterrents to good report writing. Although you want to be thorough, you do not want to collect and record such a large amount of information that you will hardly know where to begin your analysis.

The availability of computer-assisted data searches has simplified the time-consuming task of searching through indexes, card catalogs, and other sources. For example, suppose you select an online database such as Business Source Premier or an Internet search engine such as Google to research the role of microblogging in the workplace. By inputting the key term *instant message* in an online database, you receive the screen output in Figure 9.4. The screen output contains information that will facilitate your research.

First, you can quickly evaluate the relevance of references by reading each article's title and abstract, if available, to determine appropriateness to your topic. Retrieved full-text articles can be read and analyzed for useful information, saved, and printed for later use. Be sure to

validity the degree to which the data measure what the researcher intends to measure

reliability the level of consistency or stability over time or over independent samples

FIGURE 9.4 A SAMPLE COMPUTER DATA SEARCH USING AN ONLINE DATABASE

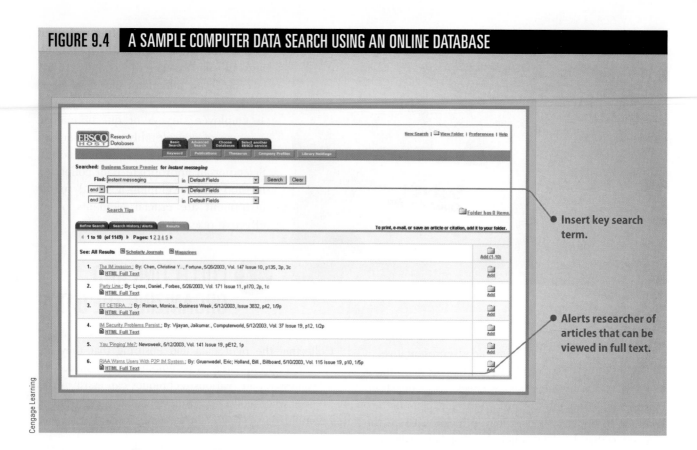

Insert key search term.

Alerts researcher of articles that can be viewed in full text.

Cengage Learning

record a full bibliographic citation for each reference you obtain, to avoid the need to relocate the online source or revisit the library to find it again.

After you have located relevant sources, you can take notes using various methods. When your aim is to *learn*, the following technique for taking notes is effective: (1) read an article rapidly and put it aside, (2) *from memory*, list main and supporting points, and (3) review the article to see whether all significant points have been included.

Rapid reading forces concentration, builds a strong understanding of the topic, and reveals

plagiarism the presentation of someone else's ideas or words as your own

relationships between ideas. Traditionally, researchers read the article and immediately wrote notes on cards. Currently, researchers typically prefer copying and pasting relevant information into a word-processing file or highlighting important points on a photocopy or printout of the article; then, from the selected passages, they compose notes at the keyboard.

You can use two kinds of note-taking: direct quotation or paraphrase. The *direct quotation method* involves citing the exact words from a source. This method is useful when the exact words have specific impact or expert appeal. The *paraphrase method* involves summarizing information in your own words without changing the

Plagiarism is the presentation of someone else's ideas or words as your own. To safeguard your reputation against plagiarism charges, be certain to give credit where credit is due. Specifically, provide a citation for each (1) direct quotation and (2) passage from someone else's work that you stated in your own words rather than using the author's words—the words are your own, but the idea is not.

To attribute information to another source, develop complete, accurate citations and a reference page according to some recognized referencing method.

© iStock.com/Merce Bellera

author's intended meaning. Put direct quotes in quotation marks, and indicate the page numbers, if available.

9-4b Collecting Data Through Surveys

The method of distribution and the makeup of the questionnaire are critical factors in successful survey research.

SELECTING A DATA COLLECTION METHOD

Selecting an appropriate data collection method is crucial to effective research. Researchers must consider various factors when selecting an appropriate method for collecting data, as illustrated in Figure 9.5.

| FIGURE 9.5 | SELECTING AN APPROPRIATE DATA-COLLECTION METHOD |

METHOD	ADVANTAGES	LIMITATIONS
Online surveys	• Are relatively inexpensive to administer • Can reach a wide number of people who complete the survey at their convenience • Allow anonymity, which may produce more honest responses • Remove difference-in-status barriers	• May yield a low response rate • Are not useful for obtaining detailed information
Telephone surveys	• Provide inexpensive and rapid data collection • Allow personal contact between interviewer and respondent for clarification or follow-up questions	• Must be relatively short to minimize perceived intrusion and to increase typical small return rate • May exclude respondents with unlisted numbers and those without telephones
Personal interviews	• Are useful to obtain in-depth answers and explore sensitive topics • Allow personal contact between interviewer and respondent for clarification and follow-up questions	• Are time-consuming and resource intensive • Require proper interviewer • Vary in value, depending on quality and consistency of interviewer
Email polling	• Is inexpensive • Provides for easy response • Yields quick results that can be updated electronically as responses are received	• Is limited to respondents with computer access

Mama_mia/Shutterstock.com
Freer/Shutterstock.com
Iakov Filimonov/Shutterstock.com
Steamroller blues/Shutterstock.com

Cengage Learning

DEVELOPING AN EFFECTIVE SURVEY INSTRUMENT

No matter which survey technique or combination of techniques is used, the way in which the survey instrument is designed and written has much to do with the validity and reliability of results, response rate, and quality of information received.

The construction of the survey instrument—usually a questionnaire or interview guide—is critical to obtaining reliable and valid data. Before developing items for a questionnaire or opinion survey, a researcher should visualize the ways responses will be compiled and included in a final report. Here are some suggestions for developing an effective questionnaire:

- **Provide brief, easy-to-follow directions.** Explain the purpose of the study in a cover letter or in a brief statement at the top of the questionnaire so that the respondents understand your intent. Although a screening question might be needed to determine whether the respondent is qualified to answer a set of questions, minimize confusing "skip-and-jump" instructions such as the following:

If you answered Yes to item 4, skip directly to item 7; if you answered No, explain your reason in items 5 and 6.

With the availability of online survey technology, you can automate whether and how respondents are advanced to the next question based on answers to screening questions.

- **Arrange the items in a logical sequence.** If possible, the sequence should proceed from easy to difficult items; simple, nonthreatening items involve respondents and encourage them to finish. You might group related items such as demographic questions or those that use the same response options (multiple choice, rating scales, open-ended questions).

- **Create an appealing, easy-to-comprehend design.** Use typefaces, bold, underline, and italics to emphasize important ideas. Use text boxes and graphic lines to partition text so that the reader can identify and move through sections quickly.

- **Use short items that ask for a single answer to one idea.** Include only the questions needed to meet the objectives of your study, because long questionnaires affect the return rate negatively.

- **Design questions that are easy to answer and to tabulate.** Participants might not take the time to answer numerous open-ended questions that require essay-style answers. When open-ended questions are included, provide enough space for respondents to answer adequately.

- **Strive to write clear questions that all respondents will interpret in the same way.** Avoid words with imprecise meanings (e.g., *several, usually*) and specialized terms and difficult words that respondents might not understand. Use accurate translations for each concept presented if other cultures are involved. Provide examples for items that might be difficult to understand.

- **Ask for information that can be recalled readily.** Asking for "old" information might not result in sound data.

- **Provide all possible answer choices on multiple-choice items.** Add an "undecided" or "other" category so that respondents are not forced to choose a nonapplicable response.

- **Ask for factual information whenever possible.** Opinions might be needed in certain studies, but opinions might change daily. As a general rule, the smaller the sample, the less reliable are any conclusions based on opinions.

- **Decide on an optimal number of choices to place on a ranking scale.** Ranking scales, also called Likert scales, allow participants to indicate their opinion on a numbered continuum. When deciding the numbers to place on the scale, consider the tendency of some groups to choose the noncommittal midpoint in a scale with an odd number of response choices (for instance, choosing 3 on a scale from 1 to 5).

- **Avoid questions that might be threatening or awkward to the respondent.** For sensitive issues, such as age and income, allow respondents to select among ranges if possible. Ensure that ranges do not overlap, and provide for all possible selections.

- **Consider the advisability of prompting a forced answer.** A forced-answer question can be used to determine which single factor is most critical to a respondent, as shown in the following examples:

Of the locations listed, which is the most convenient for your use?

Do you agree to the terms of use provided in the attached document?

❏ *Yes* ❏ *No*

When using forced-choice items, avoid "leading questions" that cause people to answer in a way that is not their true opinion or situation. The following item is an example of such a question:

 Would you participate in unethical acts, such as insider trading, if this potential were provided?

❑ *Yes*   ❑ *No*

Various types of items can be used in questionnaire design, depending on your purpose and the characteristics of your participants. Figure 9.6 illustrates the principles of effective questionnaire design.

A final step in questionnaire design is to test the instrument by asking others to complete and critique the questionnaire. For surveys of major importance, researchers typically conduct a pilot study, disseminating the questionnaire to a small group of the population involved. This process allows them to correct problems in clarity and design, and typically leads to better response and quality of answers. A pilot study might uncover factors affecting your results, which you can address in the final research design and before conducting the actual survey.

Researchers must select from among the several formats available the one best suited to the situation. Criteria for selecting one alternative over the others might include the following: Which format leaves the least chance for misinterpretation? Which format provides information in the way it can best be used? Can it be tabulated easily? Can it be cross-referenced to other items in the survey instrument?

9-4c **Avoiding Data-Gathering Errors**

If acceptable data-gathering techniques have been used, data will measure what they are intended to measure (have validity) and will measure it accurately (have reliability). Hopefully, a carefully designed research process will yield useful data for analysis.

SOME COMMON ERRORS AT THE DATA-GATHERING STAGE:

▸ Using samples which are too small

▸ Using samples which are not representative

▸ Using poorly constructed data-gathering instruments

▸ Using information from biased sources

▸ Failing to gather enough information to cover all important aspects of a problem

▸ Gathering too much information

9-4d **Documenting Sources of Information**

A crucial part of ethical, honest research writing is documenting or referencing sources fairly and accurately. Although time consuming and tedious, careful attention to documentation marks you as a respected, highly professional researcher.

An important first step is to pledge that you will not, for any reason, present someone else's ideas as your own. Then develop a systematic checklist for avoiding plagiarism. Carelessly forgetting to enclose someone else's words within quotation marks or failing to paraphrase another's words can cause others to question your ethical conduct. When you feel that the tedious work required to document sources fairly and accurately is not worth the time invested, remind yourself of the following reasons for documentation:

- **Citations give credit where it is due—to the one who created the material.** People who document demonstrate high standards of ethical conduct and responsibility in scholarship. Those exhibiting this professional behavior will gain the well-deserved trust and respect of peers and superiors.

- **Documentation protects writers against plagiarism charges.** Plagiarism occurs when someone steals material from another and claims it as his or her own writing. Besides suffering embarrassment, the plagiarist might be assessed fines, penalties, or professional sanctions.

- **Documentation supports your statements.** If recognized authorities have said the same thing, your work takes

FOLLOW THESE GENERAL SUGGESTIONS FOR PREPARING ACCURATE DOCUMENTATION:

▸ **Decide which authoritative style manual to follow for preparing in-text parenthetical citations or footnotes (endnotes) and the bibliography (references).** Some companies and most journals require writers to prepare reports or manuscripts following a particular style manual. Once you are certain you have selected the appropriate manual, follow it precisely as you prepare the documentation and produce the report.

▸ **Be consistent.** If you are carefully following a format, you shouldn't have a problem with consistency. For example, one style manual might require an author's initials in place of the first name in a bibliography; another manual requires the full name. The placement of commas and periods and other information varies among manuals. Consult the manual, apply the rules methodically, and proofread carefully to ensure accuracy and consistency.

FIGURE 9.6 | EXAMPLE OF AN EFFECTIVE QUESTIONNAIRE

1. **Rank the following job factors in the order of their importance to you. Add other factors important to you in the space provided.**

		1	2	3	4	5	6	7
a.	Wages	○	○	○	○	○	○	○
b.	Health and retirement benefits	○	○	○	○	○	○	○
c.	Job security	○	○	○	○	○	○	○
d.	Ability to maintain balance between work and family life	○	○	○	○	○	○	○
e.	Creativity and challenge of work assignment	○	○	○	○	○	○	○
f.	Perceived prestige of work	○	○	○	○	○	○	○
g.		○	○	○	○	○	○	○
h.		○	○	○	○	○	○	○

2. **Which of the following is the single job satisfaction factor that you feel needs more attention in our company? (Please select only one.)**

   ○ Wages
   ○ Health and retirement benefits
   ○ Job security
   ○ Ability to maintain balance between work and family life
   ○ Creativity and challenge of work assignment
   ○ Perceived prestige of work
   ○ Other (specify) [▼]

3. **How would you rate your overall job satisfaction?**

Very unsatisfied	Unsatisfied	Somewhat unsatisfied	Somewhat satisfied	Satisfied	Very satisfied
1	2	3	4	5	6
○	○	○	○	○	○

4. **How would you rate your overall job satisfaction 12 months ago?**

Very unsatisfied	Unsatisfied	Somewhat unsatisfied	Somewhat satisfied	Satisfied	Very satisfied
1	2	3	4	5	6
○	○	○	○	○	○

5. **Indicate your age group:**

   ○ 20–29
   ○ 30–39
   ○ 40–49
   ○ 50–59
   ○ 60–69
   ○ 70 years and over

6. **Indicate your time with the company:**

   ○ Less than 1 year
   ○ 1–3 years
   ○ 4–6 years
   ○ 7–10 years
   ○ Over 10 years

7. **What could the company do to enhance your satisfaction as a company employee?**

   [   ]

   Thanks for your participation. Click to submit your questionnaire.

   [Submit]

- *Uses variety of items to elicit different types of responses.*
- *Uses clear, concise language to minimize confusion.*
- *Provides clear instructions for answering each item.*
- *Provides additional lines to allow for individual opinions.*
- *Provides even number of rating choices to eliminate "fence" responses.*
- *Asks for easily recalled information.*
- *Provides non-overlapping categories of response and open-ended final category.*

Format Pointers

Provides adequate space for answering open-ended item.

Keeps length as short as possible while meeting survey objectives.

Includes instructions for submitting completed questionnaire.

on credibility; you have put yourself in good company.

- **Documentation can aid future researchers pursuing similar material.** Documentation must be complete and accurate so that the researcher can locate the source.

Many style guides are available to advise writers how to organize, document, and produce reports and manuscripts. Figure 9.3 includes two of the most popular authoritative style manuals. The *Publication Manual of the American Psychological Association* has become the most-used guide in the social and "soft" sciences and in many scholarly journals. The *MLA Handbook for Writers of Research Papers* is another authoritative source used in the humanities.

CITATIONS

Two major types of citations are used to document a report: source notes and explanatory notes. Depending on the authoritative style manual used, these notes might be positioned in parentheses within the report, at the bottom of the page, or at the end of the report.

- **Source notes.** These citations acknowledge the contributions of others. They might refer readers to sources of quotations, paraphrased portions of someone else's words or ideas, and quantitative data used in the report. Source notes must include complete and accurate information so that the reader can locate the original source if desired.

- **Explanatory notes.** These citations are used for several purposes: (1) to comment on a source or to provide information that does not fit easily in the text, (2) to support a statistical table, or (3) to refer the reader to another section of the report. The following sample footnote describes the mathematics involved in preparing a table:

  *The weighted opinion was derived by assigning responses from high to low as 5, 4, 3, 2, 1; totaling all respondents; and dividing by the number of respondents.

  In this case, the asterisk (*) was used, rather than a number, to identify the explanatory footnote both in

the text and in the citation. This method is often used when only one or two footnotes are included in the report. If two footnotes appear on the same page, two asterisks (**) or numbers or letters are used to distinguish the second from the first. An explanatory note that supports a graphic or a source note that provides the reference from which data were taken appears immediately below the graphic.

REFERENCING METHODS

Various reference methods are available for the format and content of source notes: in-text parenthetical citations, footnotes, and endnotes. Note the major differences among the methods in the following discussion.

- **In-text parenthetical citations.** The *APA Publication Manual*, *MLA Handbook*, and some other documentation references eliminate the need for separate footnotes or endnotes. Instead, an in-text citation, which contains abbreviated information within parentheses, directs the reader to a list of sources at the end of a report. This list contains all publication information on every source cited. It is arranged alphabetically by the author's last name or, if no author is provided, by the first word of the article title.

- **Footnote citation method.** Placing citations at the bottom of the page on which they are cited is the footnote citation. The reader can conveniently refer to the source if the documentation is positioned at the bottom of the page. Alternatively, a list of footnotes can be included in an endnotes page at the end of the document in the order they appeared. Footnotes and endnotes are not used in APA and MLA referencing, as these styles permit the use of in-text citations only.

- **References (APA) or Works Cited (MLA).** The APA and MLA styles use different terms to distinguish between these types of lists. This document is an alphabetized list of the sources used in preparing a report. Each entry contains the publication information necessary for locating the source. In addition, the bibliographic entries give evidence of the nature of sources the author consulted. The term *bibliography* (literally "description of books") is sometimes used to refer to this list. A researcher often uses sources that provide information but do not result in citations. To acknowledge that you might have consulted these works and to provide the reader with a comprehensive reading list, you might include them in the list of sources.

yurchello108/Shutterstock.com

9-5 ARRIVING AT AN ANSWER

Even the most intelligent person cannot be expected to draw sound conclusions from faulty information. Sound conclusions can be drawn only when information has been properly organized, collected, and interpreted.

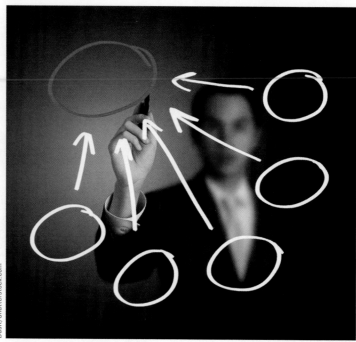

Dusit/Shutterstock.com

9-5a Analyzing the Data

Follow a step-by-step approach to the solution of your research problem. Plan your study and follow the plan. Question every step for its contribution to the objective, and keep a record of actions. In a formal research study, the researcher is expected to make a complete report. Another qualified person should be able to make the same study, use the same steps, and arrive at the same conclusion.

Suppose you have conducted a survey and collected several hundred replies to a 30-item questionnaire. Appropriate statistical analysis must be applied to interpret survey results. Statistical analysis is a complex task, involving specialized understanding that is gained through appropriate training, but some of the common terms are identified here. *Tabulation* techniques should be used to reduce quantitative data such as numerous answers to questionnaire items. For instance, you might want to tabulate the number of males and females participating in the study, along with the appropriate percentages for each gender.

For many kinds of studies, *measures of central tendency* might help in describing distributions of quantitative data. The *range* assists the researcher in understanding the distribution of the scores. The *mean*, *median*, and *mode* are descriptions of the average value of the distribution.

Other statistical techniques may be used. For example, *correlation analysis* might be used to determine whether a relationship existed between how respondents answered one item and how they answered another. Were males, for example, more likely to have chosen a certain answer to another item on the survey than were females?

The report process is one of reducing the information collected to a size that can be handled conveniently in a written message, as shown in Figure 9.7. Visualize the report process as taking place in a huge funnel.

At the top of the funnel, pour in all the original information. Then through a process of compression within the funnel, take these steps:

1. **Evaluate the information for its usefulness.**

2. **Reduce the useful information through organization of notes and data analysis.**

3. **Combine like information into understandable forms through the use of tables, charts, graphs, and summaries (see Chapter 10).**

4. **Report in written form the information that remains (see Chapter 11).**

9-5b Interpreting the Data

Your ethical principles affect the validity of your interpretations. Through all steps in the research process, you must attempt to maintain the integrity of the research. Strive to remain objective, design and conduct an unbiased study, and resist any pressure to slant research to support a particular viewpoint.

Some common errors that seriously hinder the interpretation of data include the following:

- **Trying, consciously or unconsciously, to make results conform to a prediction or desire.** Seeing predictions come true might be pleasing, but objectivity is much more important. Facts should determine conclusions.

FIGURE 9.7 THE REPORT PROCESS

RESEARCH

Primary
· Surveys
· Observations
· Experiments

Secondary
· Review of printed and online sources
· Company records

CONDENSATION

Compile using notes, cards, or word-processing program
· Direct quotations
· Paraphrased citations

COMBINATION

· Charts
· Tables
· Graphs
· Summaries

ASSIMILATION

Analysis
· Findings
· Conclusions
· Recommendations

CONCLUSIONS

WRITING

· Finished report

Cengage Learning

- **Hoping for spectacular results.** An attempt to astonish supervisors by preparing a report with revolutionary conclusions can have a negative effect on accuracy.

- **Attempting to compare when commonality is absent.** Results obtained from one study might not always apply to other situations. Similarly, research with a certain population might not be consistent when the same research is conducted with another population.

- **Assuming a cause–effect relationship when one does not exist.** A company president might have been in office one year, and sales might have doubled. However, sales might have doubled in spite of the president rather than because of the president.

LEARN THE TERMS WHEN DOING RESEARCH

Keep in mind the differences in meaning of some common research terms as you analyze your material and attempt to seek meaning from it. Most research reports include all three of the following items or sections:

Finding: A specific, measurable fact from a research study

Conclusion: Summation of major facts and evidence derived from findings

Recommendation: A suggested action based on your research

Consider the following examples of conclusions and recommendations generated by analyzing research findings:

Example 1

Finding: Fully 90% of managers responded that poor writing skills are the biggest communication problem in the workplace today.

Conclusion: Greater emphasis on the development of good writing skills is needed at all levels of education.

Recommendation: Schools need to ensure that more time is spent on writing instruction to ensure that employees have the requisite skills for the workplace.

Example 2

Finding: Only 20% of online customers rated our system as "Excellent," while nearly 40% checked "Needs Improvement."

Conclusion: Our online ordering system needs improvement.

Recommendation: Designers in charge of the online ordering system need to use the findings from our recent customer survey to improve the quality of the system.

- **Failing to consider important factors.** For example, although Eastman Kodak developed the digital camera in 1975, it didn't invest in the technology for fear it would undercut sales of its film business. Only when film's popularity began to wane in the mid-1990s in favor of digital photography did the company push into the digital market. But competitors entered the market faster, and Kodak was never able to fully capitalize on the product it invented.[2]

- **Basing a conclusion on lack of evidence.** "We have had no complaints about our present policy" does not mean that the policy is appropriate. Conversely, lack of evidence that a proposed project will succeed does not necessarily mean that it will fail.

- **Assuming constancy of human behavior.** A survey conducted in March indicating 60% of the public favors one political party over the other might not have the same results if conducted in November. Because some people paid their bills late last year does not mean a company should refuse to sell to them next year, because reasons for slow payment might have been eliminated.

If you avoid common data-collection errors, you are more likely to collect valid and reliable data and reach sound conclusions. However, if you interpret valid and reliable data incorrectly, your conclusions will still *not* be sound.

STUDY TOOLS 9

LOCATED AT BACK OF THE TEXTBOOK
- [ ] Tear-Out Chapter Review Card

LOCATED AT WWW.CENGAGEBRAIN.COM
- [ ] Review Key Term flashcards and create your own cards
- [ ] Track your knowledge and understanding of key concepts in business communication
- [ ] Complete practice and graded quizzes to prepare for tests
- [ ] Complete interactive content within BCOM8 Online
- [ ] View the chapter highlight boxes for BCOM8 Online

BCOM
ONLINE
REVIEW FLASHCARDS ANYTIME, ANYWHERE!

Create Flashcards from Your StudyBits

Review Key Term Flashcards Already Loaded on the StudyBoard

10 Managing Data and Using Graphics

LEARNING OBJECTIVES

After studying this chapter, you will be able to…

10-1 Communicate quantitative information effectively.

10-2 Apply principles of effectiveness and ethical responsibilities in the construction of graphic aids.

10-3 Select and design appropriate and meaningful graphics.

10-4 Integrate graphics within documents.

After finishing this chapter, go to **PAGE 177** for **STUDY TOOLS.**

10-1 COMMUNICATING QUANTITATIVE INFORMATION

Before you can interpret quantitative data, the elements must be classified, summarized, and condensed into a manageable size. This condensed information is meaningful and can be used to answer your research questions. For example, assume that you have been given 400 completed questionnaires from a study of your current clients' future travel destinations. This large accumulation of data is overwhelming until you tabulate the responses for each questionnaire item by manually inputting or compiling responses received through an online survey or optically scanning the responses into a computer. Then, you can apply appropriate statistical analysis techniques to the tabulated data.

The computer generates a report of the total responses for each possible answer to each item. For example, the tabulation of responses from each client about his or her future travel destinations might appear like this:

Hawaii	329
Caribbean	278
Alaska	218
Europe	185
Mexico	120

The breakdown reduces 400 responses to a manageable set of information. The tabulation shows only five items, each with a specific number of responses from the total of 400 questionnaires. Because people tend to make comparisons during analysis, the totals are helpful. People generally want to know proportions or ratios, and these are best presented as percentage parts of the total.

Future Travel Destinations	Number	Percentage
Hawaii	329	82
Caribbean	278	69.5
Alaska	218	54.5
Europe	185	46.25
Mexico	120	30

Now analyzing the data becomes relatively easy. Of the survey participants, 82% selected Hawaii, while only 30% selected Mexico. Other observations, depending on how exactly you intend to interpret percentages, could be that more than half selected Alaska.

> Because people tend to make comparisons during analysis, the totals are helpful.

Combining data in two categories allows you to summarize that all respondents intend to take a tropical island vacation in the future.

When tabulating research results of people's opinions, likes, preferences, and other subjective items, rounding off statistics to fractions helps paint a clear picture for readers. In actuality, if the same group of people were asked this question again a day or two later, a few probably would have changed their minds. For example, a participant who had not indicated a desire to travel to Europe may have attended a travel show that increased her interest in doing so. The next day, the respondent might indicate a desire to travel to Europe in the future.

Fractions, ratios, and percentages are examples of **common language**. In effect, common language reduces difficult figures to the "common denominators" of language and ideas. Although "218 of 400 expect to travel to Alaska in the future" is somewhat easy to understand, "54.4% prefer . . ." is even easier, and "one out of two indicate a preference for traveling to Alaska" is even more understandable.

Common language also involves the use of indicators other than actual count or quantity. The Dow Jones Industrial Average provides a measure of stock market performance and is certainly easier to understand than the complete New York Stock Exchange figures. Similarly, oil is counted in barrels rather than in the quart or gallon sizes purchased by consumers. Because of inflation, dollars are not accurate items to use as comparisons from one year to another in certain areas. For example, automobile manufacturers use "automobile units" to represent production changes in the industry. The important thing for the report writer to remember is that reports are communication media, and everything possible should be done to make sure communication occurs effectively.

10-2 USING GRAPHICS

Imagine trying to put in composition style all the information available in a financial statement. Several hundred pages might be necessary to explain material that could otherwise be contained in three or four pages of balance sheets and income statements. Even then, the reader would no doubt be thoroughly

> **common language** reduces difficult figures to the common denominators of language and ideas

confused! To protect readers from being overwhelmed or simply bored with data, report writers can design visually appealing graphics that are appropriate for the data being presented. Data reported in a table, graph, or picture will make your written analysis clearer to the reader.

The term **graphics** is used in this chapter to refer to all types of illustrations used in written and spoken reports. The most commonly used graphics are tables, bar charts, line charts, pie charts, pictograms, maps, flowcharts, diagrams, and photographs.

Roger Asbury/Shutterstock.com

10-2a Effective and Ethical Use of Graphics

The use of graphics with a written discussion serves three purposes: to clarify, to simplify, or to reinforce data. As you read this chapter, ask yourself if the discussion would be effective if the accompanying graphic figures were not included. Use the following questions to help you determine whether using a graphic element is appropriate and effective in a written or spoken report.

graphics all types of illustrations used in written and spoken reports

- **Is a graphic needed to clarify, reinforce, or emphasize a particular idea?** Or can the material be covered adequately in words rather than in visual ways? To maintain a reasonable balance between words and graphics, save graphics for data that are difficult to communicate in words alone.

- **Does the graphic presentation contribute to the overall understanding of the idea under discussion?** Will the written or spoken text add meaning to the graphic display?

- **Is the graphic easily understood?** Does the graphic emphasize the key idea and spur the reader to think intelligently about this information? Follow these important design principles:

  - **Avoid *chartjunk*.** This term, coined by design expert Edward Tufte, describes decorative distractions that bury relevant data.[2] Extreme use of color, complicated symbols and art techniques,

---

and unusual combinations of typefaces reduce the impact of the material presented.

- **Develop a consistent design for graphics.** Arbitrary changes in the design of graphics (e.g., use of colors, typefaces, three-dimensional, or flat designs) within a written or spoken report can be confusing as the receiver expects consistency in elements within a single report.

- **Write meaningful titles that reinforce the point you are making.** For example, a receiver can interpret data faster when graphics use a talking title; that is, a title that interprets the data. Consider the usefulness of the following graphic titles for a customer service manager browsing through survey results in preparation for a meeting with top management:

Descriptive Title: *White-Cell Counts During April*

Talking Title: *White-Cell Count Has Fallen Throughout April*

The talking title saves the manager time in understanding the data and also ensures the accuracy of his interpretation, his recommendations, and the content of his presentation. Similarly, poor business decisions can be averted if graphic titles reveal key information. You will learn more about the appropriate use of descriptive and talking headings as you study the preparation of informational and analytical reports in Chapter 11.

- **Is the graphic honest?** Visual data can be distorted easily, leading the reader to form incorrect opinions about the data.

- **Can a graphic used in a presentation be seen by the entire audience?** Electronic presentations, flip charts, whiteboards, and overhead transparencies are the visual means most often used to accompany presentations.

The key to preparing effective graphics is selecting an appropriate graphic for the data and developing a clean, simple design that allows the reader or audience to quickly extract the needed information and meaning.

> We remember more of what we both see and hear than of what we receive through only one sensory channel. When text and graphics are combined, retention goes up an average of 42%.[3]

10-3   TYPES OF GRAPHIC AIDS

Using powerful software programs, managers can perform data management functions discussed in this chapter to produce highly professional graphics. The information can be reproduced in a variety of ways for integrating into reports and for supporting highly effective presentations.

Selecting the graphic type that will depict data in the most effective manner is the first decision you must make. After identifying the idea you want your receiver to understand, you can choose to use a table, bar chart, line chart, pie chart, flowchart, organization chart, photographs, models, and so on. Use Figure 10.1 on the next page to help you choose the graphic type that matches the objective you hope to achieve.

Figures 10.2 through 10.7 on the following pages illustrate a variety of graphics commonly used in reports. The figures show acceptable variations in graphic design, including placement

Ra2studio/Shutterstock.com

Graphic Type	Objective	Graphic Type	Objective
Table	To show exact figures	Gantt chart	To track progress toward completing a project
Bar chart	To compare one quantity with another	Map	To show geographic relationships
Line chart	To illustrate changes in quantities over time	Flowchart	To illustrate a process or procedure
Pie chart	To show how the parts of a whole are distributed	Photograph	To provide a realistic view of a specific item or place

Note: Data presented in charts are fictional and for demonstration only.

Niels Poulsen simi1/Alamy

Cengage Learning

of the caption (figure number and title), inclusion or exclusion of grid lines, proper labeling of the axes, proper referencing of the source of data, and other features. When designing graphics, adhere to the requirements in your company policy manual or the style manual you are instructed to follow. Then be certain that you design graphics for a particular document or presentation consistently. When preparing a graphic for a slide show or mounted chart, remove the figure number and include the title only.

10-3a Tables

A **table** presents data in columns and rows, which aid in clarifying large quantities of data in a small

space. Proper labeling techniques make the content clear. Guidelines for preparing an effective table follow and are illustrated in Figure 10.2:

- **Number tables and all other graphics consecutively throughout the report.** This practice enables you to refer to "Figure 1" rather than to "the following table" or "the figure on the following page."

- **Give each table a title that is complete enough to clarify what is included without forcing the reader to review the table.** Table titles can be quite long as they can contain sources of data, numbers included in the table, and the subject, as shown in Figure 10.2. Titles should be written in either all capitals or upper and lowercase letters. Titles that extend beyond one line should be arranged on the page so that they are balanced.

- **Label columns of data clearly enough to identify the items.** Usually, column headings are short

table a graphic that presents data in columns and rows, which aid in clarifying large quantities of data in a small space

Cengage Learning

FIGURE 10.2 EFFECTIVE TABLE LAYOUT, IDENTIFYING INFORMATION, LABELS, AND SOURCE

Travel Destinations	Percentage		
	2014	2015	2016
Hawaii	90	87	82
Caribbean	53	59	69.5
Alaska	65	60	54.5
Europe	23	33	46.25
Mexico	12	17	30

and easily arranged. If, however, they happen to be lengthy, use some ingenuity in planning the arrangement.

- **Indent the second line of a label for the rows (horizontal items) two or three spaces.** Labels that are subdivisions of more comprehensive labels should be indented, as should summary labels such as "total."

- **Place a superscript symbol beside an entry that requires additional explanation, and include the explanatory note beneath the visual.**

- **Document the source of the data presented in a visual by adding a source note beneath the visual.** If more than one source was used to prepare a visual, use superscripts beside the various information references and provide the sources beneath the figure.

10-3b Bar Charts

A **bar chart** is an effective graphic for comparing quantities (see Figure 10.3 on page 172). The length of the bars, horizontal or vertical, indicates quantity. Vertical bars, as shown Figure 10.3a, are most commonly used. Because of the lengthy labels in Figure 10.3b, horizontal bars are ideal. Variations of the simple bar chart make it useful for a variety of purposes:

- **Grouped bar charts** (also called *clustered bar charts*) are useful for comparing more than one quantity.

- **Segmented bar charts** (also called *subdivided, stacked bar,* or *100% bar charts*) show how components contribute to a total figure. The segments in Figure 10.3c illustrate the composition of minerals in three samples.

- **Pictograms** use pictures or symbols to illustrate objects, concepts, or numerical values. A simple use of a pictogram is a picture of an envelope used to represent an email message. Pictograms are common in everyday life, such as on signs in public places or roads, whereas the term *icon* is specific to interfaces on computers or other electronic devices. An image of a computer is used in Figure 10.3d to show computer sales in a company's first quarter.

- The **Gantt chart**, another variation of the bar chart, is useful for tracking progress toward completing a series of events over time. The Gantt chart in Figure 10.3e shows the time spent on various activities necessary to complete a project. This version of the Gantt chart not only schedules the important activities required to complete this research but also plots the *actual* progress of each activity along with the *planned* progress. Simple Gantt charts can be created using a spreadsheet program such as Microsoft Excel.

In addition to the suggestions for developing tables, here are further suggestions related to constructing bar charts:

- **Avoid visual distortion that could exaggerate the data.** Begin the quantitative axis at zero; divide the bars into equal increments; and use bars of equal width.

- **Position chronologically or in some other logical order.**

- **Use color to convey meaning.** For example, use variations in color to distinguish among the bars when the bars represent different data. Avoid large surfaces of bright colors that may be tiring to the audience and detract from the data.

bar chart a graphic used to compare quantities

grouped bar chart a graphic used for comparing more than one quantity (set of data) at each point along the y-axis (vertical) or x-axis (horizontal); also called a *clustered bar chart*

segmented bar chart a graphic used to show how different facts (components) contribute to a total; also called a *subdivided, stacked bar,* or *100% bar chart*

pictogram a graphic that uses pictures or symbols to illustrate objects, concepts, or numerical relationships

Gantt chart a specific type of bar chart that is useful for tracking progress toward completing a series of events over time

FIGURE 10.3 · VARIETY OF BAR CHART FORMATS

(a) Vertical bar chart

(b) Horizontal bar chart

(c) Segmented bar chart

(d) Pictograph

(e) Gantt chart

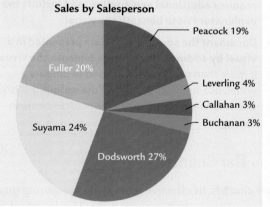

(f) Pie chart

Note: Data presented in charts are fictional and for demonstration only.

Cengage Learning

- **Avoid fancy formatting such as 3D that makes values more difficult to distinguish.**
- **Keep the labeling simple to reduce clutter and increase readability.** Exclude nonessential information such as data labels, gridlines, and explanatory notes if the meaning is understood. To determine labeling needs, consider the audience's use of the data. Omit actual amounts if a visual estimate is adequate for understanding the relationships presented in the chart. Include the data values above the bars or as a data table for an audience who expects specific data.

10-3c Line Charts

A **line chart** depicts changes in quantitative data over time and illustrates trends. The line chart shown in Figure 10.4 shows a company's stock price fluctuations over a six-hour period. When constructing line charts, keep these general guidelines in mind:

- **Use the vertical axis for amount and the horizontal axis for time.**
- **Begin the vertical axis at zero.**
- **Divide the vertical and horizontal scales into equal increments.** The vertical or quantity increments, however, need not be the same as the horizontal or time increments so that the line or lines drawn will have reasonable slopes. Unrealistic scales might produce startling slopes that could mislead readers.

An **area chart**, also called a *cumulative line chart* or a *surface chart*, is similar to a segmented bar chart because it shows how different factors contribute to a total. An area chart is especially useful when you want to illustrate changes in components over time. For example, the area chart in Figure 10.5 illustrates a company's sales in three regions during one fiscal year. A reader can easily recognize the sales figures by region and how each compares.

10-3d Pie Charts

Pie charts, like segmented charts and area charts, show how the parts of a whole are distributed. Pie charts are effective for showing percentages (parts of a whole), but they are ineffective in showing quantitative totals or comparisons. Bars are used for those purposes. The pie chart in Figure 10.3f shows the percentage of total sales contributed by salesperson for an organization.

FIGURE 10.4 LINE CHART

28.7
28.6
28.5
28.4
28.3

10 am   12 pm   2 pm   4 pm

Stock price, May 23, 2016

Cengage Learning

line chart a graphic that depicts changes in quantitative data over time and illustrates trends

area chart a graphic that shows how different factors contribute to a total; also referred to as a *cumulative line chart* or *surface chart*

pie chart a graphic that shows how the parts of a whole are distributed

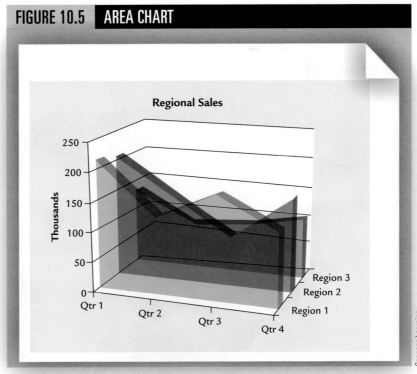

FIGURE 10.5 AREA CHART

Regional Sales

250
200
150
100
50
0

Thousands

Qtr 1   Qtr 2   Qtr 3   Qtr 4

Region 3
Region 2
Region 1

Cengage Learning

Here are some general guidelines for constructing pie charts:

- **Position the largest slice or the slice to be emphasized at the 12 o'clock position.** Working clockwise, place the other slices in descending order of size or some other logical order of presentation.

- **Label each slice and include information about the quantitative size (percentage, dollars, etc.) of each slice.** If you are unable to attractively place the appropriate labeling information beside each slice, use a legend to identify each slice.

- **Draw attention to one or more slices for desired emphasis.** Special effects include exploding the slice(s) to be emphasized (i.e., removing it from immediate contact with the pie) or displaying or printing only the slice(s) to be emphasized.

- **Avoid using 3D-type formatting that makes values more difficult to distinguish.**

Your software may limit your ability to follow rules explicitly, and the nature of the data or the presentation may require slight deviations. For example, if you intend to explode the largest pie slice, placing it in the 12 o'clock position may not be desirable because the slice is likely to intrude into the space occupied by a title positioned above the graphic.

map a graphic that shows geographic relationships

flowchart a step-by-step diagram of a procedure or a graphic depiction of a system or organization

10-3e Maps

A **map** shows geographic relationships. This graphic type is especially useful when a receiver may not be familiar with the geography discussed in a report. The map shown in Figure 10.6 shows the population of China by city. The map gives the information visually and thus eliminates the difficulty of explaining the information in words. In addition to being less confusing, a map is more concise and interesting than a written message.

10-3f Flowcharts

A **flowchart** is a step-by-step diagram of a procedure or a graphic depiction of a system or organization. A variety of problems can be resolved by using flowcharts to support written analyses. For example, most companies have procedure manuals to instruct employees in certain work tasks. Including a flowchart with written instructions minimizes the chance of errors. The flowchart in Figure 10.7 illustrates the steps in a simple writing process. Presenting this information graphically makes it much easier to understand than a written explanation of the process.

Organization charts, discussed in Chapter 1, are widely used to provide a picture of the authority structure and relationships within an organization. They provide employees with an idea of what their organization looks like in terms of the flow of authority and responsibility. When businesses change (because of new employees or reorganization of units and responsibilities), organization charts must be revised. Revisions to organizational charts are simple when prepared using word-processing or graphics software.

10-3g Other Graphics

Other graphics, such as architectural plans, photographs, cartoons, blueprints, and lists of various kinds, may be included in reports. The availability of graphics and sophisticated drawing software facilitate inclusion of these more complex visuals in reports and spoken presentations. Photographs are used frequently in annual reports to help the general audience understand complex

FIGURE 10.6   **MAP CONVEYING STATISTICAL DATA**

China Population
Source: PopulationLabs.com. Retrieved from http://www.populationlabs.com/China_Population.asp

concepts and to make the documents more appealing to read. Frequently, you must include some graphic material in a report that would make the narrative discussion otherwise unwieldy. In this case, the material might be placed in an appendix and only referred to in the report.

10-4   INCLUDING GRAPHICS IN TEXT

Text and graphics are partners in the communication process. If graphics appear before readers have been informed, they will begin to study the graphics and draw their own inferences and conclusions. For this reason, always introduce a graphic in the text immediately before the graphic appears. A graphic that follows an introduction and brief explanation will supplement what has been said in the report.

Additional interpretation and needed analysis should follow the graphic.

10-4a   Positioning Graphics in Text

Ideally, a graphic should be integrated within the text material immediately after its introduction. A graphic that will not fit on the page where it is introduced should appear at the top of the following page. The previous page is filled with text that would have ideally followed the graphic. In this chapter, figures are placed as closely as possible to their introductions in accordance with these suggestions. However, in some cases, several figures may be introduced on one page, making perfect placement difficult and sometimes impossible.

When interpreting and analyzing the graphic, avoid a mere restatement of what the graphic obviously

The pattern for incorporating graphics in text is (1) introduce, (2) show, and (3) interpret and analyze. The following range of examples, from poor to best, explain how to introduce graphic and tabular material.

		Example	Rationale
✗	**Poor:**	Figure 1 shows preferences for shopping locations.	Poor because it tells the reader nothing more than would the title of the figure.
✓	**Acceptable:**	About two-thirds of the consumers preferred to shop in suburban areas rather than in the city (see Figure 1).	Acceptable because it interprets the data, but it places the figure reference in parentheses rather than integrating it into the sentence.
✓⁺	**Better:**	As shown in Figure 1, about two-thirds of the consumers preferred to shop in suburban areas rather than in the city.	Better than the previous examples but puts reference to the figure at the beginning, thus detracting from the interpretation of the data.
✓⁺⁺	**Best:**	About two-thirds of the consumers preferred to shop in suburban areas rather than in the city, as shown in Figure 1.	Best for introducing figures because it talks about the graphic and also includes introductory phrasing, but only after stressing the main point.

shows. Instead, emphasize the main point you are making. Contrast the boring style of the following discussion of graphic data with the improved revision: the following discussion of graphic data with the improved revision:

Obvious Restatement of Data:	When asked to identify the causes of ineffective meetings, 10% of employees blamed poor communication skills, 8% cited egocentric behavior by attendees, 7% attributed nonparticipation, and 6.5% said the discussion became sidetracked.

Emphasis on Main Point:	The most cited reason for ineffective meetings is poor communication skills, while issues related to poor interpersonal communication skills were also blamed.

Your analysis may include summary statements about the data, compare information in the figure to information obtained from other sources, or extend the shown data into reasonably supported speculative outcomes. Strive to transition naturally from the discussion of the graphic into the next point you wish to make.

FIGURE 10.7 — FLOWCHART SIMPLIFYING UNDERSTANDING OF TASKS

Select Communication Media → Complete Team Charter → Identify Project Scope and Approach → Complete First Progress report → Submit Final Report

Cengage Learning

CONSISTENCY COUNTS

Throughout the discussion of tables and graphs, the term *graphics* has been used to include all illustrations. Although your report may include tables, graphs, maps, and even photographs, you will find organizing easier and writing about the illustrations more effective if you label each item as a "Figure" followed by a number; then number the items consecutively.

Some report writers prefer to label tables consecutively as "Table 1," and so on, and graphs and charts consecutively in another sequence as "Graph 1," and so on. When this dual numbering system is used, readers of the report may become confused if they come upon a sentence that reads, "Evidence presented in Tables 3 and 4 and Graph 2 supports..." Both writers and readers appreciate the single numbering system, which makes the sentence read, "Evidence presented in Figures 3, 4, and 5 supports..."

Khapaev Vladimir/Shutterstock.com

STUDY TOOLS 10

LOCATED AT BACK OF THE TEXTBOOK
☐ Tear-Out Chapter Review Card

LOCATED AT WWW.CENGAGEBRAIN.COM
☐ Review Key Term flashcards and create your own cards

☐ Track your knowledge and understanding of key concepts in business communication

☐ Complete practice and graded quizzes to prepare for tests

☐ Complete interactive content within BCOM8 Online

☐ View the chapter highlight boxes for BCOM8 Online

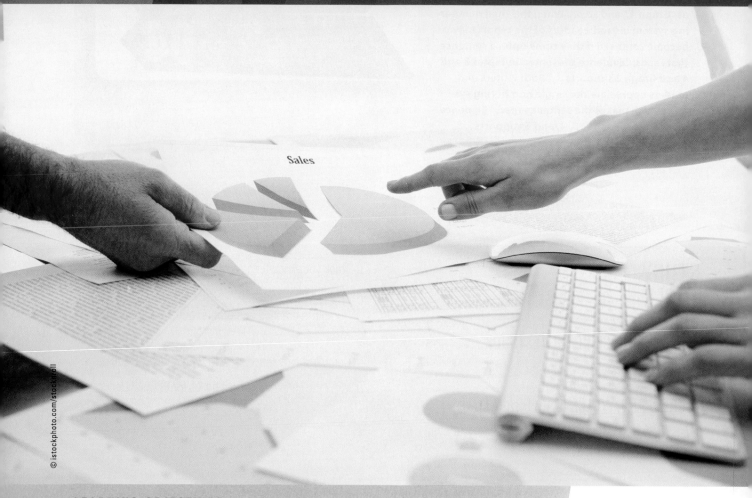

11 Organizing and Preparing Reports and Proposals

© istockphoto.com/stockdroll

LEARNING OBJECTIVES

After studying this chapter, you should be able to …

11-1 Identify the parts of a formal report and the contribution each part makes to the report's overall effectiveness.

11-2 Organize report findings.

11-3 Prepare effective formal reports using an acceptable format and writing style.

11-4 Prepare effective short reports in memorandum, email, and letter formats.

11-5 Prepare effective proposals for a variety of purposes.

After finishing this chapter, go to **PAGE 198** for **STUDY TOOLS**.

11-1 PARTS OF A FORMAL REPORT

Reports serve a variety of purposes; the type of report you prepare depends on the subject matter, the purpose of the report, and the readers' needs. The differences between a formal report and an informal report lie in the format and possibly in the writing style. At the short, informal end of the report continuum described in Chapter 9, a report could look exactly like a brief memorandum. At the long, formal extreme of the continuum, the report might include most or all of the parts shown in Figure 11.1 on page 180.

A business report rarely contains all of the parts shown but may include any combination of them. The preliminary parts and addenda are organizational items that support the body of a report. The body contains the report of the research and covers the four steps in the research process. The organization of the body of a report leads to the construction of the contents page.

Because individuals usually write to affect or influence others favorably, they often add report parts as the number of pages increases. When a report exceeds one or two pages, you might add a cover or title page. When the body of a report exceeds four or five pages, you might even add a finishing touch by placing the report in a binder or binding it in a professional manner. Reports frequently take on the characteristics of the formal end of the continuum simply by reason of length. First, note how the preliminary parts and addenda items shown in Figure 11.2 on page 181 increase in number as the report increases in length. Second, notice the order in which report parts appear in a complete report and the distribution of reports in print and electronic forms.

Memo and letter reports are often one page in length, but they can be expanded into several pages. As depicted, long reports may include some special pages that do not appear in short reports. The format you select—long or short, formal or informal—may help determine the supporting preliminary and addenda items to include.

To understand how each part of a formal report contributes to reader comprehension and ease of access to the information in the report, study the following explanations of each part shown in Figure 11.1. The three basic sections—preliminary parts, report text, and addenda—are combined to prepare a complete formal report.

11-1a Preliminary Parts of a Report

Preliminary parts are included to add formality to a report, emphasize report content, and aid the reader in locating information in the report quickly and in understanding the report more easily. These parts might include a half-title page, title page, authorization, transmittal, table of contents, table of figures, and executive summary. The most frequently used preliminary parts are described here.

TITLE PAGE

The title page includes the title, author, date, and often the name of the person or organization who requested the report. A title page is often added when opting for a formal report format rather than a memorandum or letter arrangement.

The selected title should be descriptive and comprehensive; its words should reflect the content of the report. Avoid short, vague titles or excessively long titles. Instead, use concise wording to identify the topic adequately. For example, a title such as "Marketing Survey: Internet Providers" leaves the reader confused when the title could have been "Internet Provider Preferences of Residents of St. Louis." To give some clues for writing a descriptive title, think of the "Five W's": *Who, What, When, Where,* and *Why.* Avoid such phrases as "A Study of ... ," "A Critical Analysis of ... ," or "A Review of ... ."

Follow company procedures or a style manual to place the title attractively on the page. Arrange the title consistently on the half-title page, title page, and the first page of a report.

> Avoid short, vague titles or excessively long titles.

WHO?
WHERE?
WHEN?
WHAT?
WHY?

McCarony/Shutterstock.com

TABLE OF CONTENTS

The table of contents provides the reader with an analytical overview of the

preliminary parts report sections included to add formality to a report, emphasize report content, and aid the reader in locating information in the report quickly and in understanding the report more easily

FIGURE 11.1   PARTS OF A FORMAL REPORT: PRELIMINARY PARTS, REPORT TEXT, AND ADDENDA

PRELIMINARY PARTS

Half-title page (Title Fly)
Contains report title; adds formality.

Title page
Includes title, author, and date; adds formality.

Authorization
Provides written authorization to complete report.

Transmittal
Presents report to reader and summarizes main points or analysis.

Table of contents
Provides overview of report and order in which information will be presented; contains headings and page numbers.

Table of figures
Includes number, title, and page number of tables and graphics.

Executive summary
Summarizes essential elements in report.

REPORT TEXT

Introduction
Orients reader to topic and previews major divisions.

Body
Presents information collected.

Analysis
Reviews main points presented in body and may include conclusions and recommendations.

ADDENDA

References
Includes alphabetical list of sources used in preparing report.

Appendix
Contains supplementary information that supports report, but placing this information in report would make report bulky and unmanageable.

Index
Includes alphabetical guide to subjects in report.

Cengage Learning

---

report and the order in which information is presented. Thus, this preliminary part aids the reader in understanding the report and in locating a specific section of it. The list includes the name and location (beginning page number) of every report part except those that precede the contents page. Include the list of figures and the transmittal, executive summary, report headings, references, appendixes and index. Placing spaced periods (leaders) between the report part and the page numbers helps lead the reader's eyes to the appropriate page number.

Word-processing software simplifies the time-consuming, tedious task of preparing many of the preliminary and addenda report parts, including the table of contents. Because the software can generate these parts automatically, report writers can make last-minute changes to a report with updated preliminary and addenda parts.

executive summary short summary of the essential elements in an entire report; also called an *abstract, overview,* or *précis*

TABLE OF FIGURES

To aid the reader in locating a specific graphic in a report with many graphics, the writer might include a list of figures separate from the contents. The list should include a reference to each figure that appears in the report, identified by both figure number and name, along with the page number on which the figure occurs. The contents and the figures can be combined on one page if both lists are brief. Word-processing software can be used to automatically generate the list of figures.

EXECUTIVE SUMMARY

The **executive summary** (also called the *abstract, overview,* or *précis*) summarizes the essential elements in an entire report. This overview simplifies the reader's understanding of a long report and is positioned before the first page of the report.

Typically, an executive summary is included to assist the reader in understanding a long, complex report. Because of the increased volume of information that managers must review, some managers require an executive summary regardless of the length and complexity of a report. The executive summary presents the report in miniature: the introduction, body, and summary as well as any conclusions and recommendations. Thus, an executive summary should (1) introduce

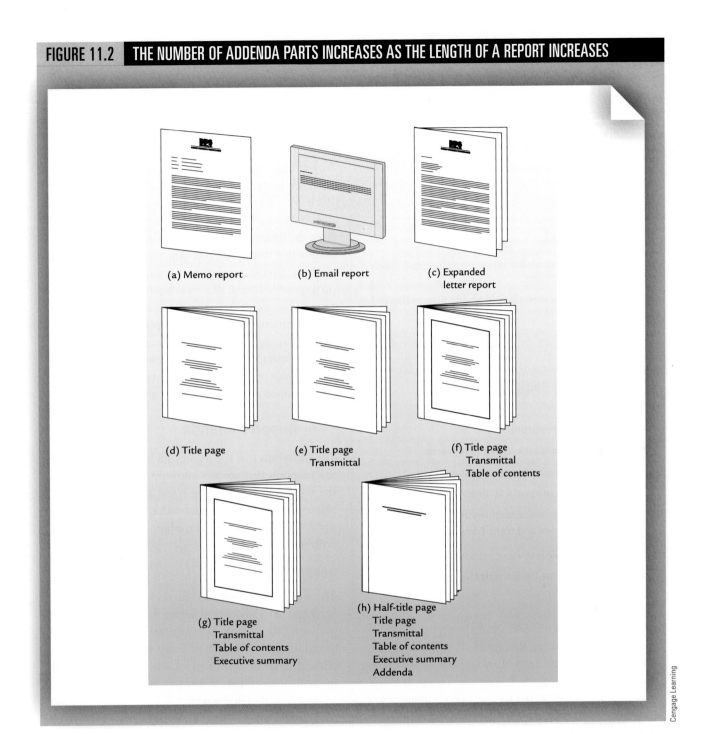

(a) Memo report

(b) Email report

(c) Expanded
letter report

(d) Title page

(e) Title page
Transmittal

(f) Title page
Transmittal
Table of contents

(g) Title page
Transmittal
Table of contents
Executive summary

(h) Half-title page
Title page
Transmittal
Table of contents
Executive summary
Addenda

Cengage Learning

briefly the report and preview the major divisions, (2) summarize the major sections of the report, and (3) summarize the report summary and any conclusions and recommendations. Pay special attention to topic sentences and to concluding sentences in paragraphs or within sections of reports. This technique helps you write concise executive summaries based on major ideas and reduces the use of supporting details and background information.

To assist them in staying up-to-date professionally, busy executives frequently request assistants to prepare executive summaries of articles they do not have time to read and conferences and meetings they cannot attend. Many practitioner journals include an executive summary (abstract) of each article. The executive summary provides the gist of the article and alerts the executive to articles that should be read in detail. The executive summary is prepared with the needs of specific executive readers in mind. For instance, a technically oriented executive may require more detail, whereas a strategist may require more analysis. An executive summary should "boil down" a report to its barest essentials without making the overview meaningless. Top executives should be able to glean enough information and understanding to feel confident making a decision.

Preliminary pages are numbered with small Roman numerals (i, ii, iii, etc.). Figure 11.1 provides more information about the purpose of each preliminary part.

11-1b Report Text

The report itself contains the introduction, body, summary, and any conclusions and recommendations. Report pages are numbered with Arabic numerals (1, 2, 3, etc.).

INTRODUCTION

The introduction orients the reader to the problem. It may include the following information:

- **What the topic is**
- **Why it is being reported on**
- **The scope and limitations of the research**
- **Where the information came from**
- **An explanation of special terminology**
- **A preview of the major sections of the report to provide coherence and transitions:**
  - **How the topic is divided into parts**
  - **The order in which the parts will be presented**

BODY

The body, often called the heart of the report, presents the information collected and relates it to the problem. To increase readability and coherence, this section contains numerous headings to denote the various divisions within a report. Refer to the section titled "Organization of Formal Reports" in this chapter for an in-depth discussion of preparing the body.

ANALYSIS

A good report ends with an analysis of what the reported information means or how it should be acted upon. An informational report ends with a brief summary that adds unity to a report by reviewing the main points presented in the body. A summary includes only material that is discussed in a report. Introducing a new idea in the summary may suggest that the study was not completed adequately or that the writer did not plan the report well before beginning to write.

An **analytical report** is designed to solve a specific problem or answer research questions. It will end with an "analysis," which may include a summary of the major research findings, particularly if the report is lengthy. Reviewing the major findings prepares the reader for the conclusions, which are inferences the writer draws from the findings. If required by the person/organization authorizing the report, recommendations follow the conclusions. Recommendations present the writer's opinion on a possible course of action based on the conclusions. Review the examples of findings, conclusions, and recommendations presented in Chapter 9.

For a long report, the writer may place the summary, the conclusions, and the recommendations in three separate sections or in one section referred to as *analysis*. For shorter reports, all three sections are often combined.

11-1c Report Addenda

The **addenda** to a report may include materials used in the research that are not appropriate to be included in the report itself. The three basic addenda parts are the references, appendixes, and index. Addenda parts continue with the same page numbering system used in the body of the report.

REFERENCES

The references (also called *works cited* or *bibliography*) section is an alphabetical listing of the sources used in preparing the report. Because the writer may be influenced by any information consulted, some reference manuals require all sources consulted to be included in the reference list. When the reference list includes sources not cited in the report, it is referred to as a *bibliography* or a list of *works consulted*. If a report includes endnotes rather than in-text parenthetical citations (author and date within the text), the endnotes precede the references. Using word-processing software to create footnotes and endnotes reduces much of the effort of preparing accurate documentation.

APPENDIX

An appendix contains supplementary information that supports the report but is not appropriate for inclusion in the report itself. This information may include questionnaires and accompanying transmittal letters, summary tabulations, verbatim comments from respondents, complex

---

analytical report a type of report designed to solve a specific problem or answer research questions

addenda may include all materials used in the research but not appropriate to be included in the report itself mathematical computations and formulas, legal documents, and a variety of items the writer presents to support the body of the report and the quality of the research. Placing supplementary material in an appendix helps prevent the report body from becoming excessively long.

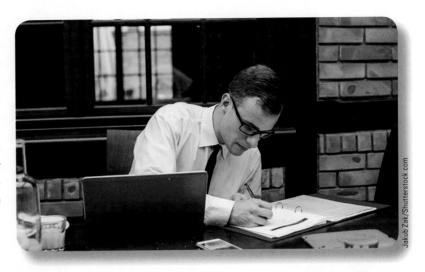

Jakub Zak/Shutterstock.com

If the report contains more than one appendix, label each with a capital letter and a title. For example, the two appendices (or appendixes) in a report could be identified as follows:

Appendix A: Employee Benefits Survey

Appendix B: Results of Employee Benefits Survey

Each item included in the appendix must be mentioned in the report. A reference within the report to the two appendixes mentioned in the previous example might appear as follows:

The survey (Appendix A) was distributed to employees on May 4, 2015. The tabulated results (Appendix B) were delivered to management on June 1.

INDEX

The index is an alphabetical guide to the subject matter in a report. The subject and each page number on which the subject appears are listed. Word-processing software can generate the index automatically. Each time a new draft is prepared, a new index with revised terms and correct page numbers can be generated quickly and easily.

11-2 ORGANIZATION OF FORMAL REPORTS

The authors of certain types of publications known as tabloids typically have no valid documentation to support their claims, so they make up their own support. Hopefully, absolutely no one believes them. The purpose of such publications is to entertain, not to inform. The writer of a bona fide report, however, must do a much more convincing and thorough job of reporting.

11-2a Writing Convincing and Effective Reports

As discussed in Chapter 9, reports often require you to conduct research to find quotes, statistics, or ideas from others to back up the ideas presented. This support from outside sources serves to bolster the research as well as your credibility. Doing research and taking notes, however, are only parts of the process of putting together a well-documented, acceptable report. Careful organization and formatting ensure that the reader will understand and comprehend the information presented. Although many companies have their own style manuals that give examples of acceptable formats for reports, this section presents some general organization guidelines.

OUTLINING AND SEQUENCING

The content outline serves as a framework on which to build the report. In the development of the outline, the writer identifies the major and minor points that are to be covered and organizes them into a logical sequence. Outlining is an essential prerequisite to writing the report. The outline is a planning document and is thus subject to modification as the writer develops the report.

Developing an outline requires the writer to think about the information to be presented and how it can best be organized for the clear understanding of the reader. Assume, for instance, your firm must decide whether to develop their own wellness program or contract with an outside provider. You need to research the steps and costs associated with developing your own program and compare them to the cost and benefits of a packaged service. Your analysis, along with your reasons and recommendations, will be delivered in a **justification report**.

> **justification report** a report that outlines comparative information clearly to the reader; used commonly when comparing items for purchase

The Annual Report: Of all the documents corporations publish, none receives as much attention as the annual report. Offering a valuable glimpse into the workings and financial performance of companies, these annual scorecards guide investors' decisions.

In addition to projecting profitability, many U.S. firms see the annual reports as a vehicle for illuminating prevailing management philosophy, projecting corporate charisma, and humanizing themselves to the public.

You gather all available information about wellness programs and wellness program providers and compare the two against a list of criteria created by management. Your final selection is to contract with a program provider. Why did you select it? What criteria served as decision guides? When you write the report, you will have to tell the reader—the one who will pay for the provider—how the selection was made so that he or she is "sold" on your conclusion.

If you organize your report so that you tell the reader everything about the two options—in-house program versus outside provider—each in a separate section, the reader may have trouble making comparisons. Your content outline might look like this:

I.   Introduction
     A. The Problem
     B. The Method Used
II. In-House Program
III. Outside Provider
IV. Conclusion

Note that this outline devotes two Roman numeral sections to the findings, one to the introduction that presents

> A final caution: Beware of over-dividing the sections. Too many divisions might make the report appear disorganized and choppy. On the other hand, too few divisions might cloud understanding for the reader.

the problem and the method, and one to the conclusion. This division is appropriate because the most space must be devoted to the findings. However, the reader may have difficulty comparing the two options because the information is in two different places. Would discussing the differences in the options in the same section of the report be better? Would costs be compared more easily if they were all in the same section? Most reports should be divided into sections that reflect the criteria used rather than into sections devoted to the alternatives compared.

If you selected your service based on cost, quality, services available, and time to implement, these criteria rather than the wellness options themselves might serve as divisions of the findings. Then, your content outline would appear this way:

I.   Introduction
     A. The Problem
     B. The Methods Used
II. Product Comparison
     A. Outside Provider Is Least Expensive
     B. Outside Provider Is Higher Quality
     C. Outside Provider Offers More Services
     D. Outside Provider Offers Faster Implementation
III.   Conclusion: Outside Provider Is the Best Choice

The outline now has three major sections, with the product comparison consisting of four subsections. When the report is prepared in this way, the features of each wellness approach (the evaluation criteria) are compared in the same section, and the reader is led logically to the conclusion.

Note the headings used in Sections II and III. These are called *talking headings* because they talk about the content of the section and even give a conclusion about the section. Adding page numbers after each outline item will convert the outline into a contents page. Interestingly, the headings justify the selection of an outside provider. As a result, a knowledgeable reader who has confidence in the researcher might be satisfied by reading only the content headings.

In addition to organizing findings for analytical reports by criteria, report writers can also use other organizational plans. When a report is informational and not analytical, you should use the most logical organization. A report on sales might be divided by geographic sales region, by product groups sold, by price range, or by time periods. A report on the development of a product might use chronological order. By visualizing the whole report first, you can then divide it into its major components and perhaps divide the major components into their parts.

When developing content outlines, some report writers believe that readers expect the beginning of the body to be an introduction, so they begin the outline with the first heading related to findings. In our example then, Section I would be "Product Comparison." Additionally, when they reach the contents page, writers may eliminate the Roman numeral or other outline symbols.

The research process consists of inductively arranged steps as shown in Figure 11.3: (1) Problem, (2) Method, (3) Findings, and (4) Conclusion. Note how the four steps of research have been developed through headings in the Roman numeral outline and in a contents page for a report. When the report is organized in the same order, its users must read through the body to learn about the conclusions—generally the most important part of the report to users. To make the reader's job easier, report writers may organize the report deductively, with the conclusions at the beginning. This sequence is usually achieved by placing a synopsis or summary at the beginning:

I. Conclusion Reported in the Synopsis
II. Body of the Report
   A. Problem
   B. Method
   C. Findings
III. Conclusion

This arrangement permits the reader to get the primary message early and then to look for support in the body of the report. The deductive arrangement contributes to the repetitious nature of reports, but it also facilitates understanding.

FIGURE 11.3 THE BASIC OUTLINE EXPANDS INTO A CONTENTS PAGE

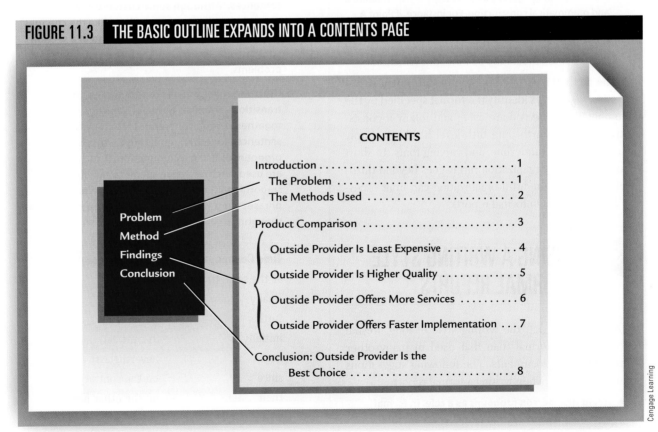

CONTENTS

Introduction 1
  The Problem 1
  The Methods Used 2

Product Comparison 3
    Outside Provider Is Least Expensive 4
    Outside Provider Is Higher Quality 5
    Outside Provider Offers More Services 6
    Outside Provider Offers Faster Implementation . . . 7

Conclusion: Outside Provider Is the
    Best Choice 8

Problem
Method
Findings
Conclusion

Cengage Learning

USING HEADINGS EFFECTIVELY

Headings are signposts informing readers about what text is ahead. Headings take their positions from their relative importance in a complete outline. For example, in a Roman numeral outline, "I" is a first-level heading, "A" is a second-level heading, and "1" is a third-level heading:

I. First-Level Heading
   A. Second-Level Heading
   B. Second-Level Heading
      1. Third-Level Heading
      2. Third-Level Heading
II. First-Level Heading

Two important points about the use of headings also relate to outlines:

- **Because second-level headings are subdivisions of first-level headings, you should have at least two subdivisions (A and B).** Otherwise, the first-level heading cannot be divided—something divides into at least two parts, or it is not divisible. Thus, in an outline, you must have a "B" subsection if you have an "A" subsection following a Roman numeral, or you should have no subsections. The same logic applies to the use of third-level headings following second-level headings.

- **All headings of the same level must be treated consistently.** Consistent elements include the physical position on the page, appearance (type style, underline), and grammatical construction. For instance, if Point A is worded as a noun phrase, Point B should be worded in the same manner. Or if Point I is a complete sentence, Points II and III should also be worded as sentences.

The method illustrated in Figure 11.3 is typical, but not universal. Always identify the format specified by the documentation style you are using and follow it consistently. Develop fourth- and fifth-level headings simply by using boldface, underline, and varying fonts. In short reports, however, organization rarely goes beyond third-level headings; thoughtful organization can limit excessive heading levels in formal reports.

11-3 CHOOSING A WRITING STYLE FOR FORMAL REPORTS

As you might expect, the writing style of long, formal reports is more formal than that used in many other routine business documents. The following suggestions should be applied when writing a formal report:

- **Avoid first-person pronouns as a rule.** In formal reports, the use of *I* is generally unacceptable.

Because of the objective nature of research, the fewer personal references you use, the better. However, in some organizations the first person is acceptable. Certainly, writing is easier when you can use yourself as the subject of sentences.

- **Use active voice.** "Acceptance was received from the seller" might not be as effective as "The seller accepted the offer." Subjects that can be visualized are advantageous, but you should also attempt to use the things most important to the report as subjects. If "acceptance" were more important than "buyer," the writer should stay with the first version.

- **Use tense consistently.** Because you are writing about past actions, much of your report writing is in the past tense. However, when you call the reader's attention to the content of a graphic, remember that the graphic *shows* in the present tense, and use the future-tense verb if you want to mention that the study *will convince* the reader.

- **Avoid placing two headings consecutively without any intervening text.** For example, always write something following a first-level heading and before the initial second-level heading.

- **Use transition sentences to link sections of a report.** Because you are writing a report in parts, show the connection between those parts by using transition sentences. "Although some customers may like the new sales program, many will not like the changes" may be a sentence written at the end of a section stressing advantages and before a section stressing problems.

- **Use a variety of coherence techniques.** Just as transition sentences bind portions of a report together, certain coherence techniques bind sentences together: repeating a word, using a pronoun, or using a conjunction. If such devices are used, each sentence seems to be joined smoothly to the next. The following words and phrases keep you from making abrupt changes in thought:

Time Connectors	Contrast Connectors
at the same time	although
finally	despite
further	however
initially	in contrast
next	nevertheless
since	on the contrary
then	on the other hand
while	yet

Similarity Connectors	Cause-and-Effect Connectors
for instance/example	alternately
in the same way	because
just as	but
likewise	consequently
similarly	hence
thus	therefore

Other ways to improve transition include the following:

- **Use tabulations and enumerations.** When you have a series of items, bullet them or give each a number and list them consecutively. This list of writing suggestions is easier to understand because it contains bulleted items.

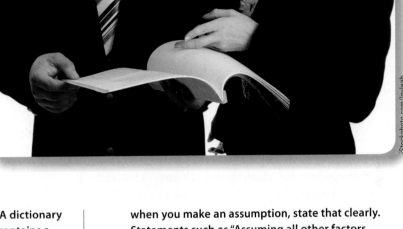

- **Define terms carefully.** When terms are not widely understood or have specific meanings in the study, define them. Definitions should be written in the term-family-differentiation sequence: "A dictionary (*term*) is a reference book (*family*) that contains a list of all words in a language (*point of difference*)." "A sophomore is a college student in the second year."

- **Check for variety.** In your first-draft stage, most of your attention should be directed toward presenting the right ideas and support. When reviewing the rough draft, you may discover certain portions with a monotonous sameness in sentence length or construction. Changes and improvements in writing style at this stage are easy and well worth the effort.

11-3a Enhancing Credibility

Readers are more likely to accept your research as valid and reliable if you have designed the research effectively and collected, interpreted, and presented the data in an objective, unbiased manner. The following writing suggestions will enhance your credibility as a researcher:

- **Avoid emotional terms.** "The program was fantastic" doesn't convince anyone. However, "The program saw an increase of 18% over that of the previous year" does convince.

- **Identify assumptions.** Assumptions are things or conditions that are taken for granted. However,

when you make an assumption, state that clearly. Statements such as "Assuming all other factors remain the same …" inform the reader of important assumptions.

- **Label opinions.** Facts are preferred over opinion, but sometimes the opinion of a recognized professional is the closest thing to fact. "In the opinion of legal counsel …" lends conviction to the statement that follows and lends credence to the integrity of the writer.

- **Use documentation.** Citations and references (works cited) are evidence of the writer's scholarship and honesty. These methods acknowledge the use of secondary material in the research.

11-4 SHORT REPORTS

Short reports incorporate many of the same organizational strategies as long reports. However, most **short reports** include only the minimum supporting materials to achieve effective communication. Short reports focus on the body—problem,

> **short reports** reports that include only the minimum supporting materials to achieve effective communication

method, findings, and conclusion. In addition, short reports might incorporate any of the following features:

- **Personal writing style using first or second person**

- **Contractions when they contribute to a natural style**

- **Graphics to reinforce the written text**

- **Headings and subheadings to partition portions of the body and to reflect organization**

- **Memorandum, email, and letter formats when appropriate**

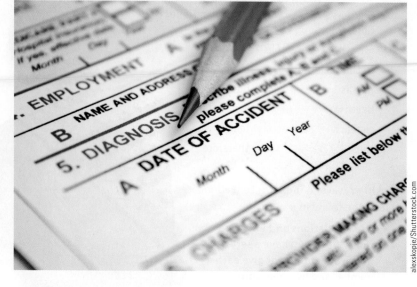

alexskopje/Shutterstock.com

11-4a Memorandum, Email, and Letter Reports

Short reports are often written in memorandum, email, or letter format. The memorandum report is directed to an organizational insider, as are most email reports. The letter report is directed to a reader outside the organization. Short reports to internal and external readers are illustrated in Figures 11.4 and 11.5. The commentary in the right column will help you understand how effective writing principles are applied.

The memo report in Figure 11.4 communicates a weekly report of sales computer products. The periodic report is formatted as a memorandum because it is prepared for personnel within the organization and is a brief, informal report. An outside auditing firm presents an audit of a company's software licensing in the short report in Figure 11.5. A concise, professional email will serve as a transmittal for this one-page report sent to the client as an email attachment.

The report in Figure 11.6 on pages 191–193 is written deductively. Recommendations for software training of employees are described in an expanded letter report written by a consultant to a client (external audience). The consultant briefly describes the procedure used to analyze the problem, presents the findings in a logical sequence, and provides specific recommendations.

11-4b Form Reports

Form reports meet the demand for numerous, repetitive reports. College registration forms, applications for credit, airline tickets, and bank checks are examples of simple form reports. Form reports have the following benefits:

- **When designed properly, form reports increase clerical accuracy by providing designated places for specific items.**

- **Forms save time by telling the preparer where to put each item and by preprinting common elements to eliminate the need for narrative writing.**

- **In addition to their advantages of accuracy and saving time, forms make tabulation of data relatively simple. The value of the form is uniformity.**

Most form reports, such as a bank teller's cash sheet, are informational. At the end of the teller's work period, cash is counted and totals are entered in designated blanks. Cash reports from all tellers are then totaled to arrive at period totals and perhaps to be verified by computer records.

In addition to their informational purpose, form reports assist in analytical work. A residential appraisal report assists real estate appraisers in analyzing real property. With this information, the appraiser is able to determine the market value of a specific piece of property.

Many form reports are computer generated. For example, an automated hospital admission process expedites the repetitive patient reports that must be created. The admission clerk inputs the patient information using the carefully designed input screen. If the patient has been admitted previously, the patient's name, address, and telephone number are displayed automatically for the clerk to verify. When the clerk inputs the patient's date of birth, the computer

form reports reports that meet the demand for numerous, repetitive reports; include college registration forms, applications for credit, airline tickets, and bank checks

FIGURE 11.4   SHORT, PERIODIC REPORT IN MEMORANDUM FORMAT

TO: Samuel Ledbetter, President
FROM: Darlene Wang, Sales Manager
DATE: April 1, 2016
SUBJECT: Monthly Sales Report, Computer Department

Sales for the month remained at about the same level as previous months this year at $319,600. Sales figures for the month by item are as follows:

Item	Quantity Sold	Total Revenue from Sales ($)
Laptops	91	63,700
Desktops	25	15,000
Tablets	162	64,800
Notebooks	103	61,800
Monitors	34	6,800

In terms of our marketing efforts, we sent email alerts to our previous customers, notifying them of our monthly specials on computer products. These specials were also highlighted on our web and Facebook pages. As such, we incurred no costs for advertising other than the time incurred by our web page manager to design these messages.

We continue to employ two full-time salespeople on the floor and two part-time salespersons to cover the weekend shift. Current staffing levels are sufficient for the current sales volume.

Like other "brick-and-mortar" retail outlets, we continue to feel increased competition from online competitors. As such, we need to increase our online presence to more effectively compete head-to-head with these operations and/or strategize ways of drawing more customers to our store who complete sales transactions, if company goals include growing sales of computer products.

The attached document provides a more detailed breakdown of product sales by model and maker. This data will be used to determine our product promotions for next month. We continue to work with our suppliers on pricing strategies to maintain our competitiveness with online rivals.

Attachment

Includes headings to serve formal report functions of transmittal and title page.

Uses deductive approach to present periodic report requested by management on weekly basis.

Uses table to highlight standard information; allows for easy update when preparing subsequent report.

Attaches information page that would be appendix item in a formal report.

Format Pointer
Uses memorandum format for brief periodic report prepared for personnel within company.

Cengage Learning

---

calculates the patient's age, eliminating the need to ask a potentially sensitive question and ensuring accuracy when patients cannot remember their ages. All data are stored in a computer file and retrieved as needed to generate numerous reports required during a patient's stay, such as the admissions summary sheet, admissions report, pharmacy profile, and even the addressograph used to stamp each page of the patient's record and the identification arm band.

Using the computer to prepare each report in the previous example leads to higher efficiency levels and minimizes errors because recurring data are entered

FIGURE 11.5   AUDIT REPORT IN SHORT REPORT FORMAT

Computer Software Audit for XYZ Company

The personal computer software audit for XYZ Company has been completed according to the procedures recommended by Software Publishers Association. These procedures and our findings are summarized below.

PROCEDURES

Specific procedures involved

- Reviewing the software policy of the organization and its implementation and control.

- Reviewing the organization's inventory of software resources, including a list of all personal computers by location and serial number.

- Using Visual Audit X4 to obtain a list of all the software on the hard disk of each computer.

- Matching purchase documentation with the software inventory record we had established. This procedure included reviewing software purchase records, such as invoices, purchase orders, check registers, canceled checks, manuals, installation media, license agreements, and registration cards.

FINDINGS

In the area of software policy and controls, we found that the organization owns a total of 432 copies of 11 applications from seven vendors. No record of registration with the publisher was available for 81 of the programs owned. In addition, we identified 65 copies of software programs for which no corresponding purchase records existed. These copies appear to be illegal. Of the 113 personal computers, we found 14 machines with software that had been brought from home by employees. A summary of the software license violations identified follows:

Identified Software License Violations

Total Copies	Total Copies Found	Legal Copies Found	Copies in Violation
Microsoft Office	110	100	10
Windows 10	115	75	40
Norton Virus	90	75	15

We have deleted all copies in excess of the number of legal copies, and you are now in full compliance with applicable software licenses. We have also ordered legal software to replace the necessary software that was deleted.

CONCLUSIONS AND RECOMMENDATIONS

Although some departments had little or no illegal software, others had significant violations. Therefore, the following recommendations are made:

1. Institute a one-hour training program on the legal use of software, and require it for all employees. Repeat it weekly over the next few months to permit all employees to attend. Additionally, require all new employees to participate in the program within two weeks of their start date.

2. Implement stricter software inventory controls, including semi-annual spot audits.

Thank you for the opportunity to be of assistance to you with your software compliance needs.

Format Pointers
Uses short format for report prepared by outside consultant.

Uses email channel to transmit formatted document as attachment for quick, convenient delivery.

Cengage Learning

FIGURE 11.6 **SHORT REPORT IN EXPANDED LETTER FORMAT, PAGE 1**

January 23, 2016

Ms. Jenny Franklin, President
PharmaTech, Inc.
1660 Main Street
Kansas City, MO 77539

Dear Ms. Franklin:

RECOMMENDATIONS FOR IMPLEMENTING CULTURALLY
DIVERSE VIRTUAL TEAMS

Thank you for allowing us to assist you in outlining a plan for successful
implementation of culturally diverse virtual teams for PharmaTech, Inc.
This trend is gaining wide support throughout the business community
as more companies go international and as budgets for employee travel
shrink.

Procedures

In preparing this report, a variety of resources were consulted, including
paper and online resources. Additionally, interviews were conducted with
20 businesspeople from a variety of organizations in Missouri that have
utilized culturally diverse virtual teams. Their perceptions, along with
published research, led to the recommendations in this report. Published
resources, as well as firsthand interviews, generally support the use of
well-managed culturally diverse virtual teams.

Findings

Research revealed useful information concerning the unique challenges
faced by cross-cultural virtual teams.

Challenges Faced by Culturally Diverse Virtual Teams

Virtual teams have various challenges, even when their membership
is homogeneous. Virtual teams can lack cohesion; members may feel
isolated; and coordination of work is more challenging. Special leadership
skills are required to manage the challenges of virtual teams. An effective
team leader must be able to skillfully leverage team talent, include all
members, provide the team with necessary information, promote trust,
encourage healthy discussions, and help manage conflict. Unless teams can
effectively deal with interpersonal communication challenges, members
quickly face burnout. Research indicates that virtual team performance
typically peaks and then declines after the first year.

Ms. Jenny Franklin

(continued on next page)

Cengage Learning

FIGURE 11.6   SHORT REPORT IN EXPANDED LETTER FORMAT, PAGE 2

January 23, 2016

Culturally heterogeneous groups have the potential for greater conflict than do groups in which members are culturally similar. Obviously, a certain degree of fluency in the common language used by the team is a requisite to effective communication. Beyond the basic language consideration, team members must recognize other challenges of cultural diversity and adapt their behavior accordingly. Recognition of cultural patterns and expectations and adaptations to spoken and written messages can improve culturally diverse team interactions.

Recommendations for Effective Culturally Diverse Virtual Teams

Culturally diverse virtual teams do have a greater potential for conflict than do teams that are homogeneous and are able to meet face to face. Although variations in beliefs, behaviors, and expectations occur within all cultural groups, certain generalities about a person based on his or her cultural group can be useful for others seeking better understanding. Given little or no other information about an individual's values and behaviors, culture provides a foundation for judgment.

Experiences in cross-cultural interactions do serve to improve one's agilities to adapt in such situations. One advantage gained through experience is the overcoming of cultural stereotypes that often stand in the way of effective communication. Cross-cultural experience also leads to the establishment of norms that support interaction among individuals and to the development of mutual consideration for people. Several studies have established that individuals who learn a foreign language also gain appropriate culturally determined behavior and are thus better able to adapt to specific characteristics of the other culture.

Some individuals are better suited than are others for membership in culturally diverse teams because of their temperament and experiences. In addition to possessing strong technical skills, qualities that are important to successful membership in cross-cultural virtual teams include the following:

- Flexibility and adaptability
- Strong interpersonal skills
- Ability to think both globally and locally
- Linguistic skills
- Listening (interpretive) skills
- Initiative
- Enthusiasm
- Consensus-building skills
- Patience and empathy
- Nonjudgmental attitude

Ms. Jenny Franklin

(continued on next page)

Cengage Learning

FIGURE 11.6 **SHORT REPORT IN EXPANDED LETTER FORMAT, PAGE 3**

January 23, 2016

A primary goal of culturally diverse teams should be to harmonize differences between cultures so that normal business activity can occur. Some suggestions for building harmony include the following:

- Provide cross-cultural training to increase ability to identify and cope with potential conflicts.

- Select a skillful leader who can perceive and facilitate handling of potential cultural misunderstandings.

- Strive for transparency in all stages of activity, which aids in the development of trust.

- Set a clear, specific agenda with no surprises that could be seen as hidden agendas.

- Encourage the use of questions to solicit input and check for understanding.

Success in culturally diverse virtual teams is largely dependent on the formation of a group culture that supersedes the individual cultural norms of the various members.

Summary

In the global business environment, the success of many organizations depends on the effective functioning of cross-cultural virtual teams, and individuals possessing the specific skill set to be successful in these teams are highly marketable to a wide variety of organizations. Obviously, teams cannot pay constant attention to cross-cultural differences. However, virtual teams whose members recognize, respect, and respond to cultural expectations for behavior enhance their prospects for achieving high levels of performance. Education about other cultures and experience in cross-cultural exchange will serve to strengthen team members' ability to interact effectively in cross-cultural virtual teams.

Thank you for the opportunity to provide this information concerning cross-cultural virtual team development. Please let us know how we can assist you further with this project or with other related matters.

Sincerely,

Patrick Laurence
Patrick Laurence, Consultant

Format Pointers

- *Letterhead and letter address function as title page and transmittal.*

- *Uses deductive approach to present main idea to president.*

- *Provides research methods to add credibility.*

- *Uses centered heading to denote major division of body.*

- *Uses transition sentence to move reader smoothly to minor section.*

- *Uses bulleted list to emphasize important information.*

Cengage Learning

only once. Preparing error-free form reports is a critical public relations tool because even minor clerical errors may cause patients or customers to question the organization's ability to deliver quality service. The "Check Your Communication" section on the Chapter 11 Review Card provides a comprehensive checklist for use in preparing effective reports.

11-5 PROPOSALS

Managers prepare **internal proposals** to justify or recommend purchases or changes in the company; for instance, installing a new

internal proposals
proposals used by managers to justify or recommend purchases or changes in the company

computer system, introducing telecommuting or other flexible work schedules, or reorganizing the company into work groups. An **external proposal**, as described in Chapter 9, is a written description of how one organization can meet the needs of another by, for example, providing products or services. Written to generate business, external proposals are a critical part of the successful operation of many companies.

Proposals may be solicited or unsolicited. **Solicited proposals** are invited and initiated when a potential customer or client submits exact specifications or needs in a bid request or a request for proposal, commonly referred to as an *RFP*. Governmental agencies such as the Department of Education solicit proposals and place orders and contracts based on the most desirable proposal. The bid request or RFP describes a problem to be solved and invites respondents to describe their proposed solutions.

An **unsolicited proposal** is prepared by an individual or firm who sees a problem to be solved and submits a solution. For example, a business consultant is a regular customer of a family-owned retail store. On numerous occasions she has attempted to purchase an item that was out of stock. Recognizing that stock shortages decrease sales and profits, she prepares a proposal to assist the business in designing a computerized perpetual inventory with an automatic reordering system. For the business to accept the proposal, the consultant must convince the business that the resulting increase in sales and profits will more than offset the cost of the computer system and the consulting fee.

11-5a Proposal Structure

A proposal includes (1) details about the manner in which the problem will be solved and (2) the price to be charged or costs to be incurred. Often the proposal is a lengthy report designed to "sell" the prospective buyer on the ability of the bidder to perform. However, a simple price quotation also constitutes a proposal in response to a request for a price quotation.

The format of a proposal depends on the length of the proposal and the intended audience:

Format	Proposal Length and Intended Audience
Memo or email report	Short; remains within the organization
Letter report	Short; travels outside the organization
Formal report	Long; remains within the organization or travels outside the organization

Most work resulting from proposals is covered by a working agreement or contract to avoid discrepancies in the intents of the parties. In some cases, for example, users of outside consultants insist that each consultant be covered by a sizable general personal liability insurance policy that also insures the company. Many large firms and governmental organizations use highly structured procedures to ensure understanding of contract terms.

The following general parts, or variations of them, might appear as headings in a proposal: (1) Problem or Purpose, (2) Scope, (3) Methods or Procedures, (4) Materials and Equipment, (5) Qualifications, (6) Follow-Up and/or Evaluation, (7) Budget or Costs, (8) Summary, and (9) Addenda. In addition to these parts, a proposal might include preliminary report parts such as the title page, transmittal message, and contents, as well as addenda parts such as references, appendix, and index.

PROBLEM AND/OR PURPOSE

Problem and purpose are often used as interchangeable terms in reports. Here is the introductory purpose statement, called "Project Description," in a proposal by a firm to construct a commercial building:

> *Project Description: You will be offered complete 3D architectural design from our architects for residential homes, business offices, housing complexes, and commercial buildings. The process starts with discussing the concepts, designs, and purposes of the building and extends to assessing the personality or lifestyle of the client to determine exactly what you want. Design scope is unlimited. Depending on what you want, we design comprehensive land and space planning, including building placement and irrigation and drainage design as well as the design of retaining walls, patios, driveways, lighting, pedestrian access, pools, courts, and other features.*

Note how the heading "Project Description" has been used in place of "Purpose." In the following opening statement, "Problem" is used as the heading:

> *Problem: Determining how well employees meet organizational goals and identifying the appropriate rewards can be challenging. This report will examine the benefits*

external proposal a proposal written to generate business; one organization describes how it can meet the needs of another by, for example, providing a product or service

solicited proposals proposals generated when a potential buyer submits exact specifications or needs in a bid request

unsolicited proposal a proposal prepared by an individual or firm who sees a problem to be solved and proposes a solution *of using our human resources software system to track and measure employees' behaviors and outcomes to ensure your organization is on the path of success.*

The purpose of the proposal may be listed as a separate heading (in addition to "Problem") when the proposal intends to include objectives of a measurable nature. When you list objectives such as "To reduce overall expenses for compensation management by 10%," attempt to list measurable and attainable objectives, and list only enough to accomplish the purpose of selling your proposal. Many proposals are rejected simply because writers promise more than they can actually deliver.

SCOPE

When determining the scope of your proposal, you can place limits on what you propose to do or on what the material or equipment you sell can accomplish. The term *scope* need not necessarily be the only heading for this section. "Areas Served," "Limitations to the Study," and "Where (*specify topic*) Can Be Used" are examples of headings that describe the scope of a proposal. Here is a "Scope" section from a consulting firm's proposal to conduct a marketing study.

Tang Yan Song/Shutterstock.com

> **What the Study Will Cover:** *To assist Ginger Sensations in formulating a marketing strategy, Thomsen Consulting will provide an analysis of all competitors in the natural ingredient body moisturizer business, including their sales, target market, and promotion and distribution methods. In addition, Thomsen will provide an analysis of the market potential for Ginger Sensations' unique product given the competition, product trends, and the target market for the product. Finally, Thomsen will provide recommendations for distribution, promotion, and placement of Ginger Sensations' line of moisturizing products based on its analysis.*

Another statement of scope might be as follows:

> **Scope:** *This report will examine employment trends for the past five years for the information technology (IT) specialists in the United States and Canada and will use that data to provide recommendations to Western Data Systems to help it plan future staffing strategies.*

METHODS AND/OR PROCEDURES

The method(s) used to solve the problem or to conduct the business of the proposal should be spelled out in detail. In this section, simply think through all the steps necessary to meet the terms of the proposal, and write them in sequence. When feasible, you should include a time schedule for implementation of the project.

MATERIALS AND EQUIPMENT

For large proposals, such as construction or research and development, indicate the nature and quantities of materials and equipment to be used. In some cases, several departments will contribute to this section. When materials and equipment constitute a major portion of the total cost, include prices. Much litigation arises when clients are charged for "cost overruns." When contracts are made on the basis of "cost plus XX%," the major costs of materials, equipment, and labor/personnel must be thoroughly described and documented.

QUALIFICATIONS

Assuming your proposal is acceptable in terms of services to be performed or products to be supplied, your proposal must convince the potential buyer that you have the expertise to deliver what you have described and that you are a credible individual or company. Therefore, devote a section to presenting the specific qualifications and special expertise of the personnel involved in the proposal.

You may include past records of the bidder and the recommendations of its past customers, and the proposed cost. Note how the brief biography of the principal member in the following excerpt from a proposal contributes to the credibility of the proposer: *Sofia Tranti, Senior Editor at Social Media Management and best-selling author of* Marketing your Business on Social Media, *is an award-winning businesswoman and writer. Her book has been featured in* Fortune *and* Forbes *and been the number-one-ranked business writing skills book on Amazon for over a year. Brenda holds a B.A. in English from New York University and an M.A. in Professional Writing from Yale University. She and her highly trained team leverage their combined 20 years of experience in social media management to design the marketing platform that best meets each client's unique needs.*

In another related section, the proposal might mention other work performed:

> **Major Clients:** *Palace Shopping Plaza, Duluth, Minnesota; eLearning Inc., Lansing, Michigan; Surf, Skate,*

and Ski, Chicago, IL; Minnesota State Teachers' Association, Minneapolis, Minnesota; and CompuTation Software, Corp., Dayton, Ohio. Personal references are available on request.

FOLLOW-UP AND/OR EVALUATION

Although your entire proposal is devoted to convincing the reader of its merit, clients are frequently concerned about what will happen when the proposed work or service is completed. Will you return to make certain your work is satisfactory? Can you adjust your method of research as times change?

If you propose to conduct a study, do not promise more than you can deliver. Not all funded research proves to be successful. If you propose to prepare a study in your firm's area of expertise, you may be more confident. A public accounting firm's proposal to audit a company's records need not be modest. The accountant follows certain audit functions that are prescribed by the profession. However, a proposal that involves providing psychological services probably warrants a thoughtful follow-up program to evaluate the service.

BUDGET OR COSTS

The budget or costs of the program should be detailed when materials, equipment, outside help, consultants, salaries, and travel are to be included. A simple proposal for service by one person might consist of a statement such as "15 hours at $200/hour, totaling $3,000, plus mileage and expenses estimated at $550." Present the budget or costs section after the main body of the proposal.

SUMMARY

You might conclude the proposal with a summary. This summary may also be used as the initial section of the proposal if deductive sequence is desired.

ADDENDA

When supporting material is necessary to the proposal but would make it too bulky or detract from it, include the material as addenda items. A bibliography and an appendix are examples of addenda items. References used should appear in the bibliography or as footnotes. Maps, questionnaires, letters of recommendation, and similar materials are suitable addenda items.

A short, informal proposal that includes several of the parts previously discussed is shown in Figure 11.7. This proposal consists of three major divisions: "Purpose," "Proposed Course

of Instruction," and "Cost." The "Proposed Course of Instruction" section is divided into five minor divisions to facilitate understanding. Wanting to increase the chances of securing the contract, the writer made sure the proposal was highly professional and had the impact needed to get the reader's attention. To add to the overall effectiveness of the proposal, the writer incorporated appealing, but not distracting, page design features. Printing the proposal with a laser printer using fonts of varying sizes and styles resulted in a professional appearance and an appealing document. The reader's positive impression of the high standards exhibited in this proposal is likely to influence his or her confidence in the writer's ability to implement the training program.

11-5b Proposal Preparation

Writers have much flexibility in preparing proposals. When they find a particular pattern that seems to be successful, they no doubt will adopt it as their basic plan. The ultimate test of a proposal is its effectiveness in achieving its purpose. The task is to assemble the parts of a proposal in a way that persuades the reader to accept it.

As with most report writing, first prepare the pieces of information that you will assemble later as the "whole" report. Determine the parts to include; select one part that will be easy to prepare; prepare that part; and then go on to another. When you have completed the parts, you can arrange them in whatever order you like, incorporate the transitional items necessary to create coherence, and then put the proposal in finished form. Allow adequate time after completing the research and writing for proofreading and editing. Figures should be checked carefully for accuracy, because underreporting costs can lead to

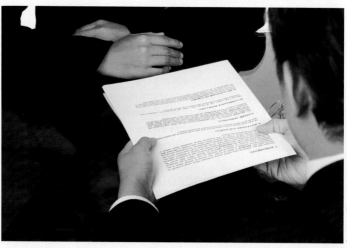

OtnaYdur/Shutterstock.com

FIGURE 11.7 **SHORT PROPOSAL, PAGE 1**

**PROPOSAL FOR STAFF DEVELOPMENT SEMINAR:
PROMOTING PRODUCTIVE CULTURALLY DIVERSE VIRTUAL
TEAMS**

for PharmaTech, Inc.
by Patrick Laurence, Communications Consultant
March 14, 2016

Purpose

After careful study, the management of PharmaTech has implemented cross-cultural virtual teams with members representing the eight international locations. The proposed training course is designed to help participants understand the purposes of the decision and ensure needed education in the functioning of culturally diverse virtual teams.

Proposed Course of Instruction

The training course will be delivered by Clarence Mason, a dynamic associate with more than 10 years of business experience in cultural training and instruction. Because behavior in culturally diverse virtual teams is a reflection of one's personality and cultural understanding, the program will actively involve participants and facilitate personal application of the new strategy.

Teaching/Learning Methods

This activity-oriented training program will involve response to videos, role playing, and case discussion. The trainer will act as a facilitator to assist each participant in assessing cultural behaviors and expectations and planning effective strategies for improving overall effectiveness.

Program Content

The following topics constitute the content core of the program:

- History and background of culturally diverse teams
- Challenges faced by culturally diverse virtual teams
- Issues culturally diverse virtual teams face in the stages of development
- Strategies for participating in culturally diverse virtual teams

Learning Materials

The following materials will be provided to facilitate learning:

- Copies of current published articles on the importance and function of culturally diverse virtual teams
- Consultant-development workbook for each participant

(*continued on next page*)

Cengage Learning

a financial loss if the proposal is accepted, and over reporting costs may lead to refusal of the proposal. If you fail to allow sufficient time for proposal completion, you may miss the required deadline for proposal submission.

If you become part of a collaborative writing team producing a proposal of major size, you will probably be responsible for writing only a small portion of the total proposal. For example, a proposal team of 16 executives, managers, and engineers might be required to prepare

FIGURE 11.7 **SHORT PROPOSAL, PAGE 2**

PharmaTech, Inc. March 14, 2016

Length of Course

As requested by management, this course will consist of three two-hour sessions; each session will be held on a selected day of the week for three consecutive weeks.

Number of Participants

The seminar will serve all 67 PharmaTech employees involved in culturally diverse virtual team activity.

Cost

All teaching-learning materials will be provided by the consulting firm and will include workbooks, videos, and video camera and recorder. Exact cost figures are as follows:

Workbooks and other materials for 67 participants	$ 835.00
Equipment lease fees	100.00
Professional fees (6 hours' instruction @ $250/hour)	1,500.00
Travel/meals	75.00
Total	$2,510.00

- Describes problem and presents proposed plan as solution to problem.
- Uses headings to aid reader in understanding proposal's organization. Boldface font adds emphasis.
- Divides "Scope of Services" into three minor divisions for easier comprehension.
- Uses bulleted lists to highlight services provided.
- Includes informational header to identify second page and client.
- Provides enclosure that itemizes costs so reader understands exactly how figure was calculated. Disclosing detailed breakdown gives reader confidence that cost is accurate.

Format Pointer
Incorporates page design features to enhance appeal and readability (e.g., headings styles including color; crisp, open fonts and wide line-spacing for easy onscreen reading or print copy; bulleted lists; and appealing table).

Cengage Learning

an 87-page proposal presenting a supplier's plan to supply parts to a military aircraft manufacturer. After the group brainstorms and plans the proposal, a project director delegates responsibility for the research and origination of particular sections of the proposal. Finally, one person compiles all the sections, creates many of the preliminary and addenda parts, and produces and distributes the final product.

STUDY TOOLS 11

LOCATED AT BACK OF THE TEXTBOOK
☐ Tear-Out Chapter Review Card

LOCATED AT WWW.CENGAGEBRAIN.COM
☐ Review Key Term flashcards and create your own cards

☐ Track your knowledge and understanding of key concepts in business communication

☐ Complete practice and graded quizzes to prepare for tests

☐ Complete interactive content within BCOM8 Online

☐ View the chapter highlight boxes for BCOM8 Online

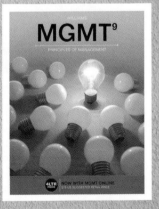

12 Designing and Delivering Business Presentations

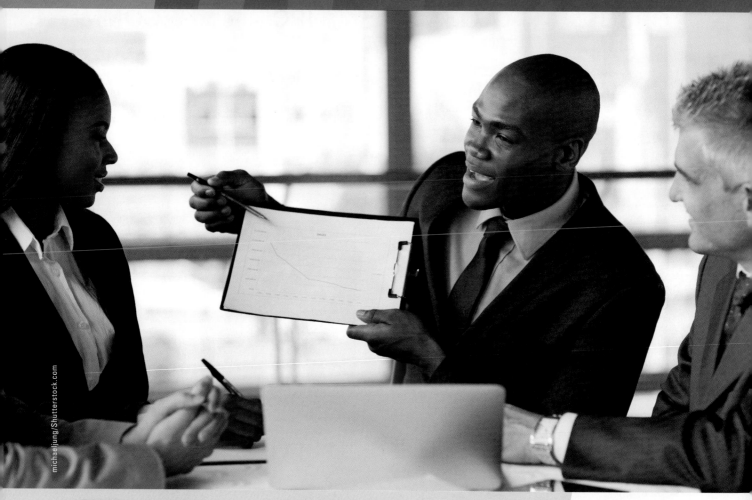

michaeljung/Shutterstock.com

LEARNING OBJECTIVES

After studying this chapter, you should be able to …

12-1 Plan a business presentation that accomplishes the speaker's goals and meets the audience's needs.

12-2 Organize and develop the three parts of an effective presentation.

12-3 Select, design, and use presentation visuals effectively.

12-4 Deliver speeches with increasing confidence.

12-5 Discuss strategies for presenting in alternate delivery situations such as culturally diverse audiences, teams, and distance presentations.

After finishing this chapter, go to **PAGE 222** for **STUDY TOOLS**.

12-1 PLANNING AN EFFECTIVE BUSINESS PRESENTATION

The simplicity of writing email and talking on the phone has deterred many workers from learning to communicate in front of people with authority and authenticity.[1] Being a skilled business communicator requires skill in both writing and speaking. A business presentation is an important means of exchanging information for decision making and policy development; relating the benefits of the services offered; and sharing our goals, values, and vision. Because multiple people receive the message at the same time and are able to provide immediate feedback for clarification, presentations can significantly reduce message distortion and misunderstanding.

Many of the presentations you give will be formal, with sufficient time allowed for planning and developing elaborate visual support. You might present information and recommendations to external audiences such as customers and clients whom you've never met or to an internal audience made up of coworkers and managers you know well. You can also expect to present some less formal presentations, often referred to as **oral briefings**. An oral briefing might entail a short update on a current project requested during a meeting without advance notice or a brief explanation in the hallway when your supervisor walks past. Sales representatives give oral briefings daily as they present short, informal pitches for new products and services.

Regardless of the formality of the presentation, the time given to prepare, the nature of the audience (friends or strangers), or the media used (live, distant, Web, or DVD delivery on demand), your success depends on your ability to think on your feet and speak confidently as you address audience needs. Understanding the purpose you hope to achieve through your presentation and conceptualizing your audience will enable you to organize the content in a way the audience can understand *and* accept.

As with written messages, presentations should be well planned. The steps in the process for planning, preparing, and rehearsing presentations are shown in Figure 12.1.

12-1a Identify Your Purpose and Consider the Channel

Determining what you want to accomplish during a presentation is a fundamental principle of planning an effective presentation. Some speech coaches recommend completing the following vital sentence to lay the foundation for a successful presentation: "At the end of my presentation, the audience will _____." In his book *Do's and Taboos of Public Speaking*, Roger E. Axtell provides two excellent mechanisms for condensing your presentation into a brief, achievable purpose that will direct you in identifying and supporting the major points:[2]

- Ask yourself, "What is my message?" Then, develop a phrase, a single thought, or a conclusion you want the

> A business presentation is an important means of exchanging information for decision making and policy development.

oral briefings informal presentations prepared and presented with little time for planning and developing

---

FIGURE 12.1 PROCESS FOR PLANNING, PREPARING, AND REHEARSING PRESENTATIONS

STEP 1	STEP 2	STEP 3	STEP 4	STEP 5	STEP 6	STEP 7
Consider the applicable contextual forces.	Determine the purpose and consider channel constraints and benefits.	Envision the audience.	Adapt the message to the audience's needs and concerns.	Organize the message.	Prepare visual aids.	Rehearse delivery.

Cengage Learning

audience to take with them from the presentation. This elementary statement will likely be the final sentence in your presentation—the basic message you want the audience to remember.

- Imagine a member of your audience has been asked to summarize your message. Ideally, you want to hear him or her describe your central purpose.

If your purpose for presenting is primarily informative and you plan to provide a good deal of information and details, you might wish to select a two-channel approach to message delivery. In other words, you might find it more appropriate to deliver the bulk of the information via email or informal report, and then follow up with a presentation to answer questions or emphasize key points to ensure accuracy of message reception. That is because, although a useful medium because of the opportunity to establish rapport and receive and provide feedback, a presentation is one of the most misused communication channels. That's because presentations are often used to deliver large amounts of detailed information and may succeed only in boring the audience. The challenge of keeping an audience's attention for an extended period of time becomes obvious when we consider that the average attention span in 2013 was eight seconds,[3] and most educators and psychologists agree that attention spans have been decreasing over the past decade with the increase in external stimulation. Because of this single challenge, the decision to communicate with a presentation deserves due consideration and, if selected, generally requires substantial planning so as to be effective and enhance rather than detract from the presenter's credibility.

For this reason, it is important to emphasize when to choose an oral presentation as the method of message delivery. Presentations are good for the following situations:

- **Inspiring and motivating others.** If the presenter is able to bring enthusiasm and energy and an inspirational message to the situation, then oral message delivery is highly appropriate.

- **Demonstrations of products or for training purposes.** Oral presentations work well when audience members are able to view how a product works and better understand its functions. They are also useful for training purposes, particularly, if the audience is able to apply the presented material through practice or use as part of the presentation.

- **To introduce a complex persuasive written message (generally a report or a proposal).** This helps increase audience interest by emphasizing the key benefits of the proposal in an engaging manner and allows the presenter to answer audience questions.

- **As a follow-up to a complex persuasive written message (generally a report or a proposal).** The personal presence of an advocate can help establish goodwill and credibility and move the persuasive process forward. In these cases, the oral message should generally emphasize the benefits of the proposal and answer audience questions.

- **To deliver bad news to a large audience.** In some circumstances, the personal presence of an organizational representative helps to establish or maintain goodwill and credibility and, by extension, the image and reputation of the firm.

Once the decision has been made that a presentation is the best medium for message delivery, then the preparer needs to do additional planning by analyzing her audience and considering the context of the presentation.

12-1b Know Your Audience and Consider the Context

A common mistake for many presenters is to presume they know the audience without attempting to find out about it. If you expect to get results, you must commit the time to know your audience and focus your presentation on it—from planning your speech to practicing its delivery.

As a general rule, audiences *do* want to be in tune with a speaker. Yet people listen to speeches about things of interest to them. "What's in it for me?" is the question most listeners ask. A speech about climate change to a farm group should address the farmers' problems, for example, and not focus on theories of global warming. Additionally, different strategies are needed for audiences who think and make decisions differently. For instance, different strategies are needed for making a successful presentation to sell software to a group of lawyers than to a group of doctors. Lawyers typically think quickly and are argumentative and decisive, whereas doctors are often cautious, skeptical, and don't make quick purchasing decisions.[4]

To deliver a presentation that focuses on the wants and expectations of an audience, you must determine who it is, what motivates it, how members think, and how members make decisions. Helpful information you can obtain about most audiences includes ages, genders, occupations, educational levels, attitudes, values, broad and specific interests, and needs. In addition, you should also consider certain things about the occasion and location. Patriotic speeches to a group of military veterans will differ from speeches to a group of new recruits, just as Fourth of July speeches will differ from Veterans Day speeches. Seek answers to the following questions when you discuss your speaking engagement with someone representing the group or audience:

1. **Who is the audience and who requested the presentation?** General characteristics of the audience should be considered, as well as the extent of their knowledge and experience with the topic, attitude toward the topic and you as a credible speaker, anticipated response to the use of electronic media, and required or volunteer attendance.

2. **Why is this topic important to the audience?** What will the audience do with the information presented? How will the information benefit audience members?

3. **What** environmental factors affect the presentation?

   ◦ How many will be in the audience?

   ◦ Will I be the only speaker? If not, where does my presentation fit in the program? What time of day?

   ◦ How much time will I be permitted? Minimum? Maximum?

   ◦ What are the seating arrangements? How far will the audience be from the speaker? Will a microphone or other equipment be available?

   ◦ What are my technical requirements and will they be met at the presentation location?

   ◦ Will I have time to test my media before the presentation? If not, how can I ensure that my presentation will go off without any problems or snags?

Answers to these questions reveal whether the speaking environment will be intimate or remote, whether the audience is likely to be receptive and alert or nonreceptive and tired, and whether you will need to use additional motivational or persuasive techniques.

12-2 ORGANIZING THE CONTENT

With an understanding of the purpose of your business presentation—why you are giving it and what you hope to achieve—the constraints and benefits of the oral medium, and a conception of the size, interest, and background of the audience, you are prepared to outline your presentation and identify appropriate content.

The biggest mistake that presenters often make is not clearly understanding that oral presentations as a medium of communication are quite different from written messages in terms of the kind of information they are useful for conveying. In other words, the biggest mistake that presenters make is treating a presentation as if it were a written document or formal report. The written channel and the oral channel are generally good for communicating different kinds of information and for achieving quite different goals. Even if a presentation is based on written material, the presenter should start planning as if he or she was developing an entirely new message because of this fact. If this isn't understood from the beginning, an oral presentation is likely to fall flat—and the presenter with it. What this means is that rather than writing a script or working from a report, a presenter should begin with an outline of the presentation contents.

First introduced by famous speech trainer Dale Carnegie and still recommended by speech experts today, the simple but effective basic presentation structure includes an introduction, the body, and a closing.

12-2a Introduction

What you say at the beginning sets the stage for your entire presentation and initiates your rapport with the audience. However, inexperienced speakers often settle for unoriginal and overused introductions that reduce the audience's desire to listen, such as "My name is…, and my topic is…" or "It is a pleasure…"; or negative statements, such as apologies for lack of preparation, boring delivery, or late arrival. An effective introduction accomplishes the following goals:

- **Captures attention and involves the audience.** Choose an attention-getter that is relevant to the subject and appropriate for the situation.

To involve the audience directly, ask for a show of hands in response to a direct question; allow the audience time to think about the answer to a rhetorical question; or explain why the information is important and how it will benefit the listeners. Consider the following examples.

ATTENTION-GETTING TECHNIQUES MIGHT INCLUDE:

▶ A shocking statement or startling statistic

▶ A quotation by an expert or well-known person

▶ A rhetorical or open-ended question that generates discussion from the audience

▶ An appropriate joke or humor

▶ A demonstration or dramatic presentation aid

▶ An anecdote or timely story from a business periodical

▶ A personal reference, a compliment to the audience, or a reference to the occasion of the presentation

An alcohol awareness speech to young people might begin with a true story:

> **"My son was a straight 'A' student who had just been accepted by Harvard. But his dream of becoming a psychologist ended the night he drove his car into a tree, after a party with friends, and suffered serious brain trauma."**

A report presenting a plan for restructuring could introduce the subject and set the stage for the findings (inductive sequence) or the recommendation (deductive sequence).

Inductive: "When the company experienced a dramatic downturn in stock values, a management team immediately began to put together a plan to cut costs and improve productivity."

Deductive: "By reducing levels of management and cutting red tape, we can decrease costs and improve productivity, ensuring future growth of our company."

- **Establishes rapport.** Initiate rapport with the listeners; convince them that you are concerned that they benefit from the presentation and that you are qualified

to speak on the topic. You might share a personal story that relates to the topic but reveals something about yourself, or discuss your background or a specific experience with the topic being discussed.

- **Presents the purpose statement and previews the points that will be developed.** To maintain the interest you have captured, present your purpose statement directly so that the audience is certain to hear it. Use original statements and avoid clichés such as "My topic today is …" or "I'd like to talk with you about …"

> **"The acquisition and construction cost of all three sites were comparable. The decision to locate the new distribution facility in Cincinnati, Ohio, is based on the quality of living, transportation accessibility, and an adequate work force."**

Next, preview the major points you will discuss in the order you will discuss them. For example, you might say, "First, I'll discuss … , then … , and finally … ."

Revealing the presentation plan will help the audience understand how the parts of the body are tied together to support the purpose statement, thus increasing their understanding. For a long, complex presentation, you might display a presentation visual that lists the points in the order they will be covered. As you begin each major point, display a slide that contains that point and perhaps a related image. These section slides partition your presentation just as headings do in a written report, and thus move the listener more easily from one major point to the next.

12-2b Body

In a typical presentation of 15–20 minutes, limit your presentation to only a few major subpoints (typically three to five) that support or flesh out your primary theme or topic in order to avoid overwhelming and boring your audience. Making every statement in a presentation into a major point—something to be remembered—is impossible, unless the presentation lasts only 2 or 3 minutes.

Once you have selected your major subpoints, locate your supporting material. You can use several techniques to ensure the audience understands your point and to reinforce it:

- **Provide support in a form that is easy to understand.** Three techniques will assist you in accomplishing this goal:

  1. **Use simple vocabulary and short sentences that the listener can understand easily and that sound conversational and interesting.** Spoken communication is more difficult to process than written communication; therefore, complex, varied vocabulary and long sentences often included in written documents are not effective in a presentation.

  2. **Avoid jargon or technical terms that the listeners might not understand.** Instead, use plain English that the audience can easily comprehend. Make your speech more interesting and memorable by using word pictures to make your points. Matt Hughes, a speech consultant, provides this example: "If your message is a warning of difficulties ahead, you might say: 'We're climbing a hill that's getting steeper, and there are rocks and potholes in the road.'"[5]

  3. **Use a familiar frame of reference.** Drawing analogies between new ideas and familiar ones is another technique for generating understanding. For example, noting that the U.S. blog-reading audience is already one-half the size of the newspaper-reading population helps clarify an abstract or complex concept. Saying that "info dumping" is the verbal equivalent of email spam explains well the expected consequences of overloading an audience with too many details.[6]

- **Provide relevant statistics.** Provide statistics or other quantitative measures to lend authority and credibility to your points. A word of warning: Do not overwhelm your audience with excessive statistics. Instead, round off numbers and use broad terms or word pictures that the listener can remember. Instead of "68.2%" say "more than two-thirds"; instead of "112% rise in production" say "our output more than doubled."

- **Use quotes from prominent people.** Comments made by other authorities are helpful in establishing credibility.

- **Use interesting anecdotes.** Audiences like and remember anecdotes or interesting stories that tie into the presentation and make strong emotional connections. In her book *Whoever Tells the Best Story Wins*, Annette Simmons stresses that when telling stories, the storyteller allows the audience to feel his or her presence and reveals a trace of humanity, which is vital for developing understanding, influence, and strong relationships with the audience. She encourages leaders to craft personal stories into specific, intentional messages that communicate values, vision, and important lessons.[7] Although communicating their values leaders communicate the values they expect from employees. As with jokes, be sure you can get straight to the point of a story.

- **Use jokes and humor appropriately.** A joke or humor can create a special bond between you and the audience, ease your approach to sensitive subjects, disarm a nonreceptive audience, or make your message easier to understand and remember. Plan your joke carefully so that you can (1) get the point across as quickly as possible, (2) deliver it in a conversational manner with interesting inflections and effective body movements, and (3) deliver the punch line effectively. If you cannot tell a joke well, use humor instead—amusing things that happened to you or someone you know, one-liners, or humorous quotations that relate to your presentation. Refrain from any humor that reflects negatively on race, color, religion, gender, age, culture, or other personal areas of sensitivity.

- **Use presentation visuals.** Presentation visuals, such as handouts, presentation software, and demonstrations, enhance the effectiveness of the presentation. Develop presentation visuals that will enable your audience to see, hear, and even experience your presentation.

- **Encourage audience involvement.** Skilled presenters involve their audiences through techniques such as asking reflective questioning, role-playing, directing audience-centered activities, and incorporating current events or periodicals that tie directly to the message. One communications coach's advice for getting

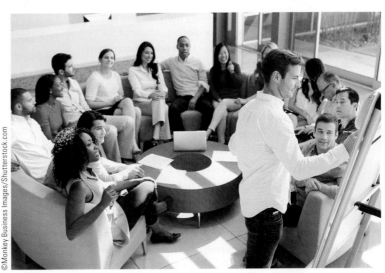

©Monkey Business Images/Shutterstock.com

an audience "to sit up and listen" is to make the presentation contemporary by working Twitter, texting, video, and other technologies into the speech.[8]

12-2c Closing

The closing provides unity to your presentation by "telling the audience what you have already told them." The conclusion should be "your best line, your most dramatic point, your most profound thought, your most memorable bit of information, or your best anecdote."[9] Because listeners tend to remember what they hear last, use these final words strategically. Develop a closing that supports and refocuses the audience's attention on your purpose statement.

- **Commit the time and energy needed to develop a creative, memorable conclusion.** An audience is not impressed with endings such as "That's all I have" or "That's it." Useful concluding techniques include summarizing the main points that have been made in the presentation and using anecdotes, humor, and illustrations. When closing an analytical presentation, state your conclusion and support it with the highlights from your supporting evidence: "In summary, you should select our communication training program because it offers … ." In a persuasive presentation, the closing is often an urgent plea for the members of the audience to take some action or to look on the subject from a new point of view.

- **Tie the closing to the introduction to strengthen the unity of the presentation.** For example, you might answer the rhetorical question you asked in the opening, refer to and build on an anecdote included in the introduction, and so on. A unifying close to a speech to motivate women business owners might be, "Life is too short to spend it doing other people's work and paying the price with unhappiness. With appropriate planning, you can spend your days as I do, making a life you love."

- **Use transition words that clearly indicate you are moving from the body to the closing.** Attempt to develop original words rather than rely on standard statements such as "In closing" or "In conclusion."

- **Practice your closing until you can deliver it without stumbling.** Use your voice and gestures to communicate this important idea clearly, emphatically, and sincerely rather than fade out at the end as inexperienced speakers often do.

- **Smile and stand back to accept the audience's applause.** A solid closing does not require a "thank you"; instead, wait confidently for the audience's spontaneous applause to thank you for a worthwhile presentation. Appear eager to begin a question-and-answer period or walk with assurance to your seat.

12-3 DESIGNING COMPELLING PRESENTATION VISUALS

Speakers who use presentation visuals are considered better prepared and more interesting, and achieve their goals more often than speakers who do not use visuals. Presentation visuals support and clarify a speaker's ideas and help the audience visualize the message. A speaker using presentation visuals reaches the receiver with double impact—through the eyes and the ears—and achieves the results quoted in an ancient Chinese proverb: "Tell me, I'll forget. Show me, I'll remember. But involve me and I'll understand." Research studies confirm that using visuals enhances a presentation.

The effective use of presentation visuals provides several advantages:[10]

- clarifies and emphasizes important points

- increases retention from 14% to 38%

- reduces the time required to present a concept

- results in a speaker achieving goals 34% more often than when presentation visuals are not used

- increases occurrence of group consensus by 21% when presentation visuals are used in a meeting

12-3a Design of Presentation Visuals

PowerPoint still remains the standard presentation software used in most organizational settings, even though its use has given rise to such sayings as "Death by Power-Point" and "PowerPoint poisoning." The problem is that too many presenters approach a presentation as if they were reading a document to their audience rather than delivering an interesting and inspiring message. The result is "docu-points," or presentations composed of too many text slides that are overly complex, difficult to understand, and boring. One example is an "electability" PowerPoint slideshow sent by the 2008 Hillary Clinton Campaign to all House Democrats that contained nine slides, 275 words, one table, three bar charts, and two pie charts. Such "docu-points" are usually less effective than a concise, well-designed handout or summary report.[11]

Even though PowerPoint remains a standard in many professional environments, other presentation software packages are available. Flash is one of the best presentation software tools on the market because of its animation effects and ability to import video. Unfortunately, it also takes a high degree of proficiency to use. Prezi is another popular software tool that is available online and provides a very different experience than PowerPoint in

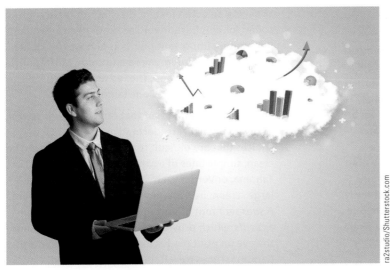

that it is nonlinear and more interactive and dynamic. Apple users can use Apple Keynote. Other presentation tools include Google Docs and SlideRocket.

Regardless of the software package you choose, your goal is to create an appealing, easy-to-read visual aid that supports and enhances your main points without overwhelming the audience. Presentation visuals should possess the same degree of professionalism as your delivery and personal appearance. You can create dynamic and useful presentation visuals, including slides, handouts, and notes pages, by following these simple guidelines:

- **Limit the number of visual aids used in a single presentation.** Although audiences value being able to "see" your points, they also welcome the variety provided by listening and the break from concentrating on visuals. Design compelling visuals that direct the audience's attention to major points and clarify or illustrate complex information. Use precise, vivid language that will involve the audience and enrich your message and delivery style.

- **Limit slide content to key ideas presented in as few words as possible or, better yet, visually.** Well-organized, crisp slide content enhances the audience's ability to grasp the speaker's meaning and find immediate value in the information. Good content also leads to an extemporaneous delivery rather than a speaker's monotonous reading of scripted slides. Short text lines are also easier for the eye to follow and open up the slide with appealing white space. Whenever possible, present complex information using graphic aids, such as tables, charts, or diagrams.

- **Develop only one major idea using targeted keywords the audience can scan quickly, understand, and remember.** Full sentences can be used for a direct quotation; otherwise, less is more. William Earnest, author of *Save Our Slides*, offers a cure for verbalitis: "PowerPoint is not a word processor"—it

is a visual medium in which fewer words are always more.[12]

  ○ Keep type sizes large enough to read when projected and to discourage crowding slides with text. Strive for these font sizes: slide titles, 44 points; main bullets, 32 points; sub-bullets, 24 points. Do not use text smaller than 18 points, as it is unreadable when projected.

  ○ Limit slide titles and headings to four words and follow the 7 × 7 rule, which limits text to 7 lines per slide and 7 words per line. Eliminate articles (*a*, *an*, *the*), understood pronouns/possessives (*we*, *you*, *your*), simple verbs and infinitive beginnings (*are*, *to*), and repetitive phrasing.[13]

  ○ If you must use text, develop powerful bulleted lists that are easy to follow and remember. For easy recall, limit the list to three to five main bullets, but absolutely no more than seven. To eliminate confusion and rereading, use bulleted lists that are grammatically parallel. One item appearing out of place weakens the emphasis given to each item and can distract audience attention from the message. Be certain each major point relates to the key concept presented in the slide title and each subpoint relates to its major point. Unless sequence is important, use bullets as they add less clutter and are easier to follow than numbers.

- **Choose an effective template and powerful images to reinforce ideas, illustrate complex ideas, and enliven boring content.** Images and shapes are more visually appealing and memorable than words, and they enable audiences to grasp information more easily. Today's audiences expect media-rich, dynamic visuals, not a speaker's dense crutch notes displayed on screen. Although photographs and clip art available in your presentation software gallery are acceptable, avoid images that are overused, outdated, grainy, and convey an unprofessional tone. Instead search for or create high-quality, professional images that convey the desired message and can project onscreen without distortion.

- **Choose an effective color scheme.** The colors you choose and the way you combine them determine the overall effectiveness of your presentation and add a personal touch to your work. Follow these simple rules to plan a nondistracting, complementary color scheme that has unity with the template graphics:

- **Limit colors to no more than three colors on a slide, to avoid an overwhelming feel.**

- **Begin by selecting a background color that conveys the appropriate formality and tone.** Choose cool colors (blue and green) in muted shades for formal presentations; choose warm colors (red, orange, and yellow) or brighter shades of cool colors for a less formal and perhaps trendy look. Think carefully about whether your color selection has a natural association with your topic or organization. For example, a presentation on environmentally friendly policies might incorporate colors naturally associated with nature and cleanliness (earth tones, white and blue); a presentation to Pepsi-Cola likely would be designed around the company colors of red, white, and blue.

- **Choose complementary foreground (text) colors that have high contrast to the background to ensure readability.** To ensure high contrast, choose either dark text on a light background or light text on a dark background. For example, the often-used color scheme of yellow slide title text and white bulleted list with a blue background is a good choice because the colors are complementary and have high contrast. Choose a slightly brighter color for the slide title that distinguishes it from the color chosen for the bullet list.

Black text against a white background has the greatest contrast. A blue background with yellow text contrasts well, but a light blue background with white text would be difficult to read because of low contrast. Evaluate the readability of the following contrast variations:

High-contrast options:	Dark text on a light background	Light text on dark background

Poor contrast options:	White text on a light blue background	Bright text on a bright background

Because the lower resolution of projectors can wash out colors and make them less vibrant than what is seen on a printed page or computer screen, choose options with very high—not minimally high—contrast. Project your presentation ahead of time in the room where you are to present so you can assess the color scheme. You can also double-check for readability and typographical errors at the same time.

- **Choose the accent colors that complement the color scheme.** Accent colors are used in small doses to draw attention to key elements: bullet markers; bars/slices in graphs, backgrounds (fills) of shapes

and lines, selected text; or drawings that are color coded for emphasis. Avoid red and green when differentiating important points as almost 10% of the population is color impaired and cannot distinguish between red and green. The red and green bars in a graph would be seen as one large area.

- **Choose an appealing font that can be read on-screen easily.** Avoid delicate, decorative, or condensed choices that are difficult to read when projected. The clean, simple lines of a sans serif font, such as Calibri, Tahoma, or Verdana, are ideal for projecting on a large screen, newspaper headline, sign, or billboard. A *sans serif* font has no short cross-strokes, known as *serifs*, which provide extra detail that helps guide the eye on print media. Examples of serif fonts are Cambria, Times New Roman, and Garamond.

- **Follow these keyboarding rules for easy reading.** Use capital letters sparingly as they are difficult to read from a distance. Capitalize the first letter of important words in slide titles (initial caps) and the first letter of the first word and proper nouns in a bulleted list (sentence case). Omit hard-to-see punctuation at the end of bulleted lists and elsewhere, and avoid abbreviations and hyphenations that might cause confusion.

- **Reflect legal and ethical responsibility in the design of presentation visuals.** Like the graphics you developed in Chapter 10, presentation visuals should be uncluttered, easily understood, and should depict information honestly.

- **Proofread the visual carefully following the same systematic procedures used for printed letters and reports and electronic communication.** Misspellings in visuals are embarrassing and diminish your credibility. Double-check to be certain that names of people, companies, and products are spelled correctly.

Figure 12.2 offers a review of slide design guidelines. The poor example (left) relies on text to convey the message, whereas the good example (right) illustrates the point.

12-3b Design Tips for Audience Handouts and Notes Pages

Audience handouts should add value for individual audience members; otherwise, the information can better be conveyed in a projected format for group benefit. An effective handout can help audience members remember your message, serve as a reference for later consideration or action, and encourage involvement when space is provided for note taking or response. You can prepare useful presenter notes on small index cards or on pages generated by electronic presentation software.

FIGURE 12.2 DESIGNING COMPELLING SLIDES

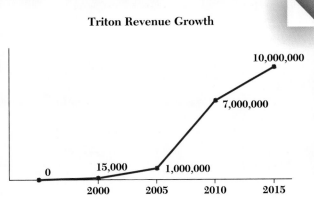

Triton Enterprises

- Founded in 1999
- 1,239 employees
- Annual gross sales of $1 million plus

Triton Revenue Growth

The revised slide

- Uses a simple but appealing template with high-quality, relevant image that is large enough for audience to see and has not been overused.
- Uses high-contrast background and sans serif fonts to assure legibility. Color choices are complementary and convey a professional tone.
- Provides a graphic (line chart) that conveys main idea instantly: Company's growth and success.
- Proofreads carefully to avoid misspellings that damage credibility.

Cengage Learning

12-4 REFINING YOUR DELIVERY

After you have organized your message, you must identify the appropriate delivery method, refine your vocal qualities, and practice your delivery.

12-4a Delivery Method

Four presentation methods can be used: memorized, scripted, impromptu, and extemporaneous. Impromptu and extemporaneous styles are generally more useful for business presentations.

Memorized presentations are written out ahead of time, memorized, and recited verbatim. Memorization has the greatest limitations of the speech styles. Speakers are almost totally unable to react to feedback, and the speaker who forgets a point and develops a mental block might lose the entire speech. Memorized speeches tend to sound monotonous, restrict natural body gestures and motions, and lack conviction. For short religious or fraternal rites, however, the memorized presentation is often impressive.

Manuscript, or *scripted*, **presentations** involve writing the speech word for word and reading it to the audience. For complex material and technical conference presentations, manuscript presentations ensure content coverage. Additionally, this style protects speakers against being misquoted (when accuracy is absolutely critical) and fits into exact time constraints, as in television or radio presentations. Speeches are sometimes read when time does not permit adequate preparation or when several different presentations are given in one day (e.g., the speaking demands of the president of the United States and other top-level executives). Manuscript presentations limit speaker–audience rapport, particularly when speakers keep their eyes and heads buried in their manuscripts. Teleprompters that project the manuscript out of view of the audience allow the speaker to appear to be speaking extemporaneously.

memorized presentation
a presentation in which a speaker writes out a speech, commits it to memory, and recites it verbatim

manuscript presentation
a presentation in which a speaker writes out the entire speech and reads it to the audience; also called a *scripted presentation*

tmcphotos/Shutterstock.com

Impromptu presentations are frightening to many people because the speaker is called on without prior notice. Experienced speakers can easily analyze the request, organize supporting points from memory, and present a simple, logical response. In many cases, businesspeople can anticipate a request and be prepared to discuss a particular idea when requested (e.g., status report on an area of control at a team meeting). Because professionals are expected to present ideas and data spontaneously on demand, businesspeople must develop the ability to deliver impromptu presentations.

Extemporaneous presentations are planned, prepared, and rehearsed, but not written in detail. Brief notes prompt the speaker on the next point, but the words are chosen spontaneously as the speaker interacts with the audience and identifies this audience's specific needs. Extemporaneous presentations include natural body gestures, sound conversational, and can be delivered with conviction because the speaker is speaking "with" the listeners and not "to" them. The audience appreciates a warm, genuine communicator and will forgive an occasional stumble or groping for a word that occurs with an extemporaneous presentation.

12-4b **Vocal Qualities**

The sound of your voice is a powerful instrument used to deliver your message and to project your professional image. To maximize your vocal strengths, focus on three important qualities of speech: phonation, articulation, and pronunciation.

Phonation involves both the production and the variation of the speaker's vocal tone. You project your voice and convey feelings—even thoughts—by varying your vocal tones. Important factors of phonation are pitch, volume, and rate. These factors permit us to recognize other people's voices over the phone.

- **Pitch.** The highness or lowness of the voice is called pitch. Pleasant voices have medium or low pitch; however, a varied pitch pattern is desirable. The pitch of the voice rises and falls to reflect emotions; for example, fear and anger are reflected in a higher pitch; sadness, in a lower pitch. Lower pitches for both men and women are perceived as sounding more authoritative; higher pitches indicate less confidence and suggest pleading or whining. Techniques discussed later in this section can help you lower the pitch of your voice.

- **Volume.** The loudness of tones is referred to as volume. Generally, good voices are easily heard by everyone in the audience but are not too loud. Use variety to hold the audience's attention, emphasize words or ideas, and create a desired atmosphere (energetic, excited tone versus a dull, boring one).

- **Rate.** The speed at which words are spoken is called rate. Never speak so quickly that the audience cannot understand your message or so slowly that they are distracted or irritated. Vary the rate with the demands of the situation. For example, speak at a slower rate when presenting a complex concept or emphasizing an important idea. Pause to add emphasis to a key point or to transition to another major section of the presentation. Speak at a faster rate when presenting less important information or when reviewing.

An inherent problem related to speaking rate is verbal fillers—also called non-words. Verbal fillers, such as *uhhh*, *ahhh*, *ummm*, and *errr*, are irritating to the audience and destroy your effectiveness. Many speakers fill space with their own verbal fillers; these include *you know*, *I mean*, *basically*, *like I said*, *okay*, and *as a matter of fact*. Because of the conversational style of impromptu and extemporaneous presentations, a speaker will naturally struggle for a word or idea from time to time. Become aware of verbal fillers you frequently use by critiquing a recording of yourself and then focus on replacing fillers with a three- to five-second pause. This brief gap between thoughts gives you an opportunity

impromptu presentation a presentation in which a speaker is called on without prior notice

extemporaneous presentation a presentation in which a speaker plans, prepares, and rehearses but does not write everything down; brief notes prompt the speaker, but the exact words are chosen spontaneously as the speaker interacts with the audience and identifies its specific needs

phonation the production and variation of a speaker's vocal tone to think about what you want to say next and time for your audience to absorb your idea. Presenting an idea (sound bite) and then pausing briefly is an effective way to influence your audience positively. The listener will not notice the slight delay, and the absence of meaningless words will make you appear more confident and polished. Also avoid annoying speech habits, such as clearing your throat or coughing, that shift the audience's attention from the speech to the speaker.

The following activities will help you achieve good vocal qualities:

- **Breathe properly and relax.** Nervousness affects normal breathing patterns and is reflected in vocal tone and pitch. The better prepared you are, the better your phonation will be. Although relaxing might seem difficult to practice before a speech, a few deep breaths, just as swimmers take before diving, can help.

- **Listen to yourself.** A recording of your voice reveals much about pitch, intensity, and duration. Most people are amazed to find their voices are not quite what they had expected. "I never dreamed I sounded that bad" is a common reaction. Nasal twangs usually result from a failure to speak from the diaphragm, which involves taking in and letting out air through the larynx, where the vocal cords operate. High pitch can occur from the same cause, or it can be a product of speaking too fast or experiencing stage fright.

- **Develop flexibility.** A good speaking voice is somewhat musical, with words and sounds similar to notes in a musical scale. Read each of the following sentences aloud, and emphasize the *italicized* word in each. Even though the sentences are identical, emphasizing different words changes the meaning.

I am happy you are here.	*Maybe I'm the only happy one.*
I *am* happy you are here.	*I really am.*
I am *happy* you are here.	*Happy best describes my feeling.*
I am happy *you* are here.	*Yes, you especially.*
I am happy you *are* here.	*You may not be happy, but I am.*
I am happy you are *here.*	*Here and not somewhere else.*

Articulation involves smooth, fluent, and pleasant speech. It results from the way in which a speaker produces and joins sounds. Faulty articulation is often caused by not carefully forming individual sounds. Common examples include:

SFerdon/Shutterstock.com

- **Dropping word endings**— saying *workin'* for *working*

- **Running words together**— saying *kinda* for *kind of*, *gonna* for *going to*

- **Imprecise enunciation**—saying *dis* for *this*, *wid* for *with*, *dem* for *them*, *pin* for *pen*, or *pitcher* for *picture*

These examples should not be confused with *dialect*, which people informally call an *accent*. A dialect is a variation in pronunciation, usually of vowels, from one part of the country to another. Actually, everyone speaks a dialect; speech experts can often identify, even pinpoint, the section of the country from where a speaker comes. In the United States, common dialects are New England, New York, Southern, Texan, Midwestern, and so forth. Within each of these, minor dialects often arise regionally or from immigrant influence. The simple fact is that when people interact, they influence each other even down to speech sounds. Many prominent speakers have developed a rather universal dialect, known as Standard American Speech or American Broadcast English that seems to be effective no matter who the audience is. This model for professional language is widely used by newscasters and announcers and is easily understood by those who speak English as a second language because they likely listened to this speech pattern on television as they learned the language.

You can improve the clarity of your voice, reduce strain and voice distortion, and increase your expressiveness by following these guidelines:

- **Stand up straight with your shoulders back, and breathe from your diaphragm rather than your chest.** If you are breathing correctly, you can then use your mouth and teeth to form sounds precisely. For example, vowels are always sounded with the mouth open and the tongue clear of the palate. Consonants are responsible primarily for the distinctness of speech and are formed by an interference with or stoppage of outgoing breath.

- **Focus on completing the endings of all words, not running words together, and**

articulation smooth, fluent, and pleasant speech

enunciating words correctly. To identify recurring enunciation errors, listen to a recording and seek feedback from others.

- **Obtain formal training to improve your speech.** Pursue a self-study program by purchasing recordings that help you reduce your dialect and move more closely to a universal dialect. You can also enroll in a diction course to improve your speech patterns or arrange for private lessons from a voice coach.

Pronunciation involves using principles of phonetics to create accurate sounds, rhythm, stress, and intonation. People might articulate perfectly but still mispronounce words. A dictionary provides the best source to review pronunciation. Two pronunciations are often given for a word, the first one being the desired pronunciation and the second an acceptable variation. An American adopting a pronunciation commonly used in England, such as *shedule* for *schedule* or *a-gane* for *again*, could be seen negatively. In some cases, leeway exists in pronunciation. The first choice for pronouncing *data* is to pronounce the first *a* long, as in *date*; but common usage is fast making pronunciation of the short *a* sound, as in *cat*, acceptable. Likewise, the preferred pronunciation of *often* is with a silent *t*. Good speakers use proper pronunciation and refer to the dictionary frequently in both pronunciation and vocabulary development.

When your voice qualities combine to make your messages pleasingly receptive, your primary concerns revolve around developing an effective delivery style.

12-4c Delivery Style

Speaking effectively is both an art and a skill. Careful planning and practice are essential for increasing speaking effectiveness.

BEFORE THE PRESENTATION

Follow these guidelines when preparing for your presentation:

- **Prepare thoroughly.** You can expect a degree of nervousness as you anticipate speaking before a group. This natural tension is constructive because it increases your concentration and your energy and enhances your performance. However, even those seasoned to the spotlight can experience a debilitating case of the jitters. In spring 2013, New Kids on the Block singer Jonathan Knight walked offstage in the middle of a concert in New York, prompting him to tweet apologies about his anxiety.[14] Being well prepared is the surest way to control speech anxiety. Develop an outline for your presentation that supports your purpose and addresses the needs of your audience, and take advantage of every opportunity to gain speaking experience.

- **Prepare effective presentation support tools.** Follow the guidelines presented in the preceding section to select and design visuals, handouts, and notes pages appropriate for your audience and purpose. Additionally, develop a contingency plan in the event of technical difficulties with computer equipment, such as hard copies of the slides or a backup computer preloaded and ready. Arrive early so you can troubleshoot unexpected technological glitches. Despite your degree of planning, however, technical problems might occur during your presentation. Remain calm and correct them as quickly and professionally as you can. Take heart in the fact that Bill Gates's computer once crashed when he introduced a new version of Windows!

- **Practice, but do not rehearse.** Your goal is to become familiar with the key phrases on your note cards so that you can deliver the presentation naturally as if you are talking with the audience—not reciting the presentation or acting out a role. Avoid over practicing, which can make your presentation sound mechanical and limit your ability to respond to the audience.

- **Practice the entire presentation.** This practice will allow you to identify (1) flaws in organization or unity, (2) long, complex sentences or ineffective expressions, and (3) "verbal potholes." Verbal potholes include word combinations that could cause you to stumble, words you have trouble pronouncing ("irrelevant" or "statistics"), and words that accentuate your dialect ("get" can sound like "git" regardless of the intention of a Southern speaker).

- **Spend additional time practicing the introduction and conclusion.** You will want to deliver these important parts with finesse while making a confident connection with the audience. A good closing leaves the audience in a good mood and can help overcome some possible weaknesses during the speech. Depending on the techniques used, consider memorizing significant brief statements to ensure their accuracy and impact (e.g., direct quotation, exact statistic).

- **Practice displaying presentation visuals so that your delivery appears effortless and seamless.** Your goal is to make the technology virtually transparent, positioned in the background to support *you* as the primary focus of the presentation. First, be sure you know basic commands for advancing through your presentation without displaying distracting menus. Develop skill in returning to a specific slide in the event of a computer glitch or an audience question.

pronunciation using principles of phonetics to create accurate sounds, rhythm, stress, and intonation

- **Seek feedback on your performance to help you to polish your delivery and improve organization.** Critique your own performance by practicing in front of a mirror and evaluating a recording of your presentation. If possible, present to a small audience ahead of time for feedback and to minimize anxiety when presenting to the real audience.

- **Request a lectern to hold your notes and to steady a shaky hand, at least until you gain some confidence and experience.** Keep in mind, though, that weaning yourself from the lectern will eliminate a physical barrier between you and the audience. Without the lectern, you will speak more naturally. If you are using a microphone, ask for a portable microphone so that you can move freely.

- **Request a proper introduction if the audience knows little about you.** An effective introduction will establish your credibility as a speaker on the subject and will make the audience eager to hear you. You can prepare your own introduction as professional speakers do, or you can provide concise, targeted information that answers these three questions: (1) Why is the subject relevant? (2) Who is the speaker? and (3) What credentials qualify the speaker to talk about the subject? Talk with the person introducing you to verify any information, especially the pronunciation of your name, and to review the format of the presentation (time limit, question-and-answer period, etc.). Be certain to thank the person who made the introduction as you begin your presentation. "Thank you for your kind introduction, Ms. Garcia" is adequate. Then follow with your own introduction to your presentation topic.

- **Dress appropriately to create a strong professional image and to bolster your self-confidence.** An audience's initial impression of your personal appearance, your clothing and grooming, affects their ability to accept you as a credible speaker. Because first impressions are difficult to overcome, take time to groom yourself immaculately and to select clothing that is appropriate for the speaking occasion and consistent with the audience's expectations.

- **Arrive early to become familiar with the setup of the room and to check the equipment.** Check the location of your chair, the lectern, the projection screen, light switches, and electrical outlets. Check the microphone and Internet connection and ensure that all equipment is in the appropriate place and working properly. Project your electronic

iStockphoto.com/Alxpin

presentation so you can adjust the color scheme to ensure maximum readability. Finally, identify the technician who will be responsible for resolving any technical problems that might occur during the presentation.

DURING THE PRESENTATION

The following are things you can do during your presentation to increase your effectiveness as a speaker:

- **Communicate confidence, warmth, and enthusiasm for the presentation and the time spent with the audience.** "Your listeners won't care how much you know until they know how much you care" is pertinent advice.[15]

  - **Exhibit a confident appearance with alert posture.** Stand tall with your shoulders back and your stomach tucked in. Stand in the "ready position"—no slouching, hunching over the lectern, or rocking. Keep weight forward with knees slightly flexed so you are ready to move easily rather than rooted rigidly in one spot, hiding behind the lectern.

  - **Smile genuinely throughout the presentation.** Pause as you take your place behind the lectern, and smile before you speak the first word. Smile as you finish your presentation and wait for the applause.

  - **Maintain steady eye contact with the audience in random places throughout the room.** Stay with one person approximately three to five seconds—long enough to finish a complete thought or sentence to convince the listener you are communicating individually with him or her. If the audience is large, select a few friendly faces and concentrate on speaking to them rather than to a sea of nondescript faces.

  - **Refine gestures to portray a relaxed, approachable appearance.** Vary hand motions to emphasize important points; otherwise, let hands fall naturally to your side. Practice using only one hand to make points unless you specifically need two hands, such as when drawing a figure or showing dimensions or location. Eliminate any nervous gestures that can distract the audience (e.g., clenching your hands in front of or behind your body, steepling your hands, placing your hands in your pockets, jingling keys or change, or playing with a ring or pen).

  - **Move from behind the lectern and toward the audience to reduce the barrier created between you and the audience.** You can stand to one side

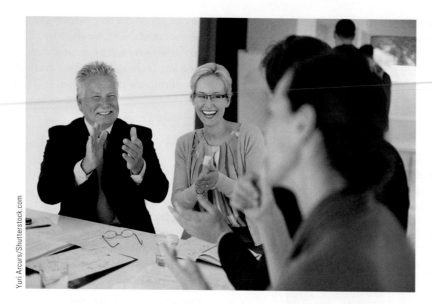

later in the presentation, say, "I believe the next slide will clarify that point; if not, we will come back to it." If the question can be answered quickly, you should do so while indicating that it will also be covered more later. Anticipate and prepare for questions that might be raised. You can generate presentation visuals pertaining to certain anticipated questions and display them only if the question is posed. An audience will appreciate your thorough and complete explanation and your ability to adjust your presentation to their needs—this strategy is much more professional than stumbling through an explanation or delaying the answer until the information is available. Speakers giving electronic presentations have ready access to enormous amounts of information that can be displayed instantly for audience discussion. Hyperlinks created within a presentation file will move a speaker instantaneously to a specific slide, another file, or an embedded music or video file.

and casually present a relaxed pose beside the lectern. However, avoid methodically walking without a purpose.

- **Exercise strong vocal qualities.** Review the guidelines provided for using your voice to project confidence and credibility.

- **Watch your audience.** They will tell you how you are doing and whether you should shorten your speech. Be attentive to negative feedback in the form of talking, coughing, moving chairs, and other signs of discomfort.

- **Use your visuals effectively.** Many speakers will go to a great deal of effort to prepare good presentation visuals—and then not use them effectively. Inexperienced speakers often ignore the visual altogether or fall into the habit of simply nodding their heads toward the visual. Neither of these techniques is adequate for involving the audience with the visual. In fact, if the material is complex, the speaker is likely to lose the audience completely.

  - **Step to one side of the visual so the audience can see it.** Use a pointer if necessary. Direct your remarks to the audience, so that you can maintain eye contact and resist the temptation to look over your shoulder or turn your back to read the information from the screen behind you.

  - **Paraphrase the visual rather than reading it line for line.** To increase the quality of your delivery, develop a workable method of recording what you plan to say about each graphic.

- **Handle questions from the audience during the presentation.** Questions often disrupt carefully laid plans. At the same time, questions provide feedback, clarify points, and ensure understanding. When people ask questions that will be answered

- **Keep within the time limit.** Be prepared to complete the presentation within the allotted time. In many organizations, speakers have one or more rehearsals before delivering reports to a group such as a board of directors. These rehearsals, or dry runs, are made before other executives, and are critiqued, timed, revised, and rehearsed again. Presentation software makes rehearsing your timing as simple as clicking a button and advancing through the slides as you practice. By evaluating the total presentation time and the time spent on each slide, you can modify the presentation and rehearse it again until the presentation fits the time slot.

AFTER THE PRESENTATION

How you handle the time following a presentation is as important as preparing for the presentation itself:

- **Be prepared for a question-and-answer period.** Encourage the audience to ask questions, recognizing an opportunity to ensure that your presentation meets audience needs. Paraphrasing the question allows you time to reflect on what was asked, ensures that everyone heard the question, and assures the questioner that he or she was understood. You can ask the questioner if your answer was adequate. Be courteous even to hostile questioners so you will maintain the respect of your audience. Stay in control of the time by announcing that you have time for one or two more questions, and then invite individual questions when the presentation is over.

- **Distribute handouts.** Distribute the handout when it is needed rather than at the beginning of the presentation. Otherwise, the audience might read the handout while you are explaining background information needed to understand the written ideas. If you expect the audience to take notes directly on the handout or if the audience will need to refer to the handout immediately, distribute the handout at the beginning of the presentation or before it begins. To keep control of the audience's attention, be sure listeners know when they should be looking at the handout or listening to you. If the handout is intended as resource material only, post the handout to a web page or place it on a table at the back of the room and at the front for those who come by to talk with you after the presentation.

12-5 ADAPTING TO ALTERNATE DELIVERY SITUATIONS

As you've learned, presenting a dynamic presentation that focuses on the audience's needs and expectations is the fundamental principle in presenting effectively. Along with the solid foundation you've set for spoken communication, you'll also need to adapt your presentation style to the ever-changing business environment and the special needs of culturally diverse audiences. Delivering team presentations and presenting in distance formats are other common situations you'll need to master.

12-5a Culturally Diverse Audiences

When speaking to a culturally diverse audience, you will want to be as natural as possible while adjusting your message for important cultural variations. Using empathy, you can effectively focus on the listener as an individual rather than a stereotype of a specific culture. Be open and willing to learn, and you will reap the benefits of communicating effectively with people who possess a variety of strengths and creative abilities. Additionally, follow these suggestions for presenting to people from outside your own culture:

- **Speak simply.** Use simple English and short sentences. Avoid acronyms and expressions that can be confusing to non-native English speakers—namely slang, jargon, figurative expressions, and sports analogies.

- **Avoid words that trigger negative emotional responses such as anger, fear, or suspicion.** Such "red flag" words vary among cultures; thus, try to anticipate audience reaction and choose your words carefully.

- **Enunciate each word precisely and speak somewhat slowly.** Clear, articulate speech is especially important when the audience is not familiar with various dialects and vocabulary. Avoid the temptation to speak in a loud voice, a habit considered rude in any culture and especially annoying to the Japanese, who perceive the normal tone of North Americans as too loud.

- **Be extremely cautious in the use of humor and jokes.** Cultures that prefer more formality might think you are not serious about your purpose or find your humor and jokes inappropriate. Asians, for instance, do not appreciate jokes about family members and the elderly.

- **Learn the culture's preferences for a direct or indirect presentation.** Although North Americans tend to prefer directness, with the main idea presented first, people from many cultures, such as Japanese, Latin American, and Arabic, consider a straightforward approach tactless and rude.

- **Adapt to subtle differences in nonverbal communication.** The direct eye contact expected by most North Americans is not typical of Asian listeners, who often keep their eyes lowered and avoid eye contact to show respect. Arab audiences might stare into your eyes in an attempt to "see into the window of the soul." Cultures also vary on personal space and degree of physical contact (slap on the back or arm around the other as signs of friendship).

- **Adapt your dress and presentation style to fit the formality of the culture.** Some cultures prefer a higher degree of formality than the casual style of

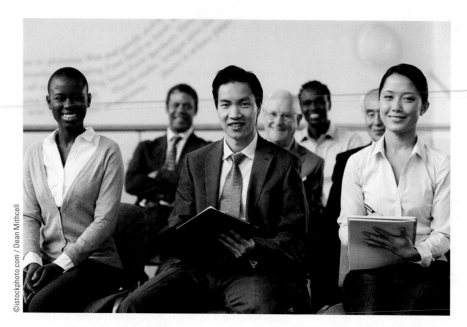
©istockphoto.com / Dean Mithcell

idea. In fact, some Japanese have asked how North Americans can think and talk at the same time. Understanding patterns of silence can help you feel more comfortable during these seemingly endless moments and less compelled to fill the gaps with unnecessary words or to make concessions before the other side has a chance to reply.

Other significant points of difference between cultures are the varying rules of business etiquette. Should you use the traditional American handshake or some other symbol of greeting? Is using the person's given name acceptable? What formal titles should be used with a surname? Can you introduce yourself, or must you have someone else who knows the other person introduce you? Are business cards critical, and what rules should you follow when presenting a business card? Should you have business cards that are printed in two languages?

Gift giving can be another confusing issue. When you believe a gift should be presented to your event host, investigate the appropriateness of gift giving, types of gifts considered appropriate or absolutely inappropriate, and colors of wrapping to be avoided in the speaker's culture. Liquor, for example, is an inappropriate gift in Arab countries.

Gaining competence in matters of etiquette will enable you to make a positive initial impression and concentrate on the presentation rather than agonizing over an awkward, embarrassing slip in protocol. Your audience will appreciate your willingness to learn and value their customs. Being sensitive to cultural issues and persistent in learning specific differences in customs and practices can minimize confusion and unnecessary embarrassment.

12-5b **Team Presentations**

Because much of the work in business today is done in teams, many presentations are planned and delivered by teams of presenters. Well-conducted team presentations give an organization an opportunity to showcase its brightest talent while capitalizing on each person's unique presentation skills. Email, collaborative software, and other technologies make it easy to develop, edit, review, and deliver impressive team presentations.

North Americans. To accommodate, dress conservatively; strive to connect with the audience in a formal, reserved manner; and use highly professional visuals rather than jotting ideas on a flip chart.

- **Seek feedback to determine whether the audience is understanding your message.** Observe listeners carefully for signs of misunderstanding, restating ideas as necessary. Consider allowing time for questions after short segments of your presentation. Avoid asking "Is that clear?" or "Do you understand?" as these statements might elicit a "Yes" answer if the person perceives saying "No" to be a sign of incompetence.

Potential frustrations can also occur when presentations or meetings bring together North Americans, who see "time as money," with people of cultures who are not time conscious and who believe that personal relationships are the basis of business dealings (e.g., Asian, Latin American). When communicating with cultures that are not time driven, be patient with what you might consider time-consuming formalities and courtesies and lengthy decision-making styles when you would rather get right down to business or move to the next point. Recognize that the presentation might not begin on time or stay on a precise schedule. Allow additional time at the beginning of the presentation to establish rapport and credibility with the audience, and perhaps provide brief discussion periods devoted to building relationships during the presentation.

Be patient and attentive during long periods of silence; in many cultures people are inclined to stay silent unless they have something significant to say or if they are considering (not necessarily rejecting) an

The potential payoff of many team presentations is quite high—perhaps a $200,000 contract or a million-dollar account. Yet, according to experts, team presentations fail primarily because presenters don't devote enough time and resources to develop and rehearse them.[16] Resist the sure-to-fail strategy of "winging" a team presentation rather than taking the time to do it correctly. Instead, adapt the skills you already possess in planning and delivering an individual presentation to ensure a successful team presentation. Follow these guidelines as you plan and prepare your team presentation:

- **Select a winning team.** Begin by choosing a leader who is well liked and respected by the team, is knowledgeable of the project, is well organized, and will follow through. Likewise, the leader should be committed to leading the team in the development of a cohesive strategy for the presentation as well as the delegation of specific responsibilities to individual members. Frank Carillo, president of Executive Communications Group, warns team presenters that a frequent problem with "divvying up" work into pieces is that the "pieces don't fit together well when they come back."[17] The core team members, along with management, should choose a balanced mix of individuals who each have something important to contribute to the team. Use these questions to guide team selection: What are this member's complementary strengths and style (e.g., technical expertise, personality traits, and presentation skills)? Can this member meet the expectations of the audience (e.g., a numbers person, technical person, person with an existing relationship with the audience)? Is this member willing to support the team strategy and commit to the schedule?[18]

- **Agree on the purpose and schedule.** The team as a whole should plan the presentation using the same process used for an individual presentation.

A member of a winning team will have:
☞ Complementary strengths/style
☞ Ability to meet expectations
☞ Willingness to support team strategy
☞ Willingness to commit to schedule

Andresr/Shutterstock.com

Agreeing on the purpose to be achieved and selecting content that focuses on a specific audience will prevent the challenges caused by an individual's submitting off-target material. The quality of the presentation deteriorates when material must be redone hurriedly in the final days before the deadline or when unacceptable material is included just because the team worked so hard on it. Mapping out a complete presentation strategy can also minimize bickering among team members because of uneven workloads or unfavorable work assignments.

The team will also need to agree on a standard design for presentation visuals to ensure consistency in the visuals prepared by individual presenters. Assign a person to merge the various files, to edit for consistency in design elements and the use of jargon and specialized terminology, and to proofread carefully for grammatical accuracy.

Developing a rehearsal schedule ensures adequate time for preparation and practice. Many experts recommend five practice sessions to produce team presentations that are delivered with a unified look. Planning time in the schedule to present before a review team is especially useful for obtaining feedback on team continuity and adjustments needed to balance major discrepancies in the delivery styles of individual presenters.

- **Practice ahead of time.** The team must be well prepared, which will require several rehearsals. Each member must know what others will say to avoid repetition and to fit the time slot. The team must also work out logistical details such as where people will stand, who will run the slides, and when handouts will be distributed. A great deal of the rehearsal time for a team presentation should be spent planning and rehearsing appropriate verbal and physical transitions between team members. The transitions serve to introduce each part of the presentation and make the whole presentation cohesive. This continuity makes the team look polished and conveys team commitment.

Follow these suggestions for delivering seamless, impressive team presentations:

- **Decide who will open and conclude the presentation.** The team member who knows the audience and has established rapport is a logical choice for these two critical sections of a presentation. If no one knows the audience, select the member with the strongest presentation skills and personality traits for connecting well with strangers. This person will introduce all team members and give a brief description of the roles they will play in the presentation.

- **Build natural bridges between segments of the presentation and presenters.** A lead presenter must build a bridge from the points that have been made that will launch the following presenter smoothly into what he or she will discuss. If a lead presenter forgets to make the connection to the next section clear, the next person must summarize what's been said and then preview his or her section. These transitions might seem repetitive to a team that has been working extensively with the material; however, audiences require clear guideposts through longer team presentations. Also, courtesies such as maintaining eye contact, thanking the previous speaker, and clearing the presentation area for the next speaker communicate an important message that the presenters are in sync and work well together.

- **Deliver as a team.** You must present a unified look and communicate to the audience that you care about the team. Spend your time on the "sideline" paying close attention to the current presenter, monitoring the audience for feedback, and being ready to assist the presenter with equipment malfunctions, handouts, and so on. Avoid side conversations and reading notes, yawning, or coughing. To keep an audience engaged in a team presentation, Frank Carillo recommends that team members not presenting should focus on the presenter at least two-thirds of the time. "It may be the 27th time you've heard it, but for that audience it's the first time. Keep it fresh for the listeners."[19]

- **Field questions as a team.** Decide in advance who will field questions to avoid awkward stares and silence that erode the audience's confidence in your team. Normally, the person presenting a section is the logical person to field questions about that section. You can refer questions to team members who are more knowledgeable, but avoid pleading looks for someone else to rescue you. Rather, check visually to see if the person wants to respond, and ask if he or she would like to add information. Tactfully contradict other presenters *only* when the presenter makes a mistake that will cause misunderstanding or confusion. Although you should be ready to help presenters having difficulty, resist the urge to tack on your response to a presenter's response when the question has already been answered adequately.

12-5c Distance Presentations

Videoconferencing has been used for some time for large, high-exposure activities, such as quarterly executive staff presentations, company-wide addresses, new product launches, and crisis management. The technology's lower cost, improved quality, and increased ease of use have opened videoconferencing to many settings.

Substantial cost savings from reduced travel is a compelling reason for companies to use videoconferencing. Threats of terrorism and contagious disease provide more reasons for companies to restrict business travel and look for alternative delivery methods. In addition, important communication benefits, such as the following, can be achieved with videoconferencing:[20]

- improving employee productivity by calling impromptu videoconferences to clear up issues

- involving more people in key decisions rather than limiting important discussions to those who are allowed to travel

- involving expertise critical to the mission, regardless of geographic boundaries

- creating a consistent corporate culture rather than depending on memos to describe company policy

- improving employees' quality of life by reducing travel time that often cuts into personal time (e.g., Saturday night layovers for a reasonable airfare)

Internet conferencing, or *webcasting*, allows a company to conduct a presentation in real time over the Internet simultaneously with a conference telephone call. Because it runs on each participant's Internet browser, a presentation can reach hundreds of locations at once. While listening to the call, participants can go to a designated website and view slides or a PowerPoint presentation that is displayed in sync with the speaker's statements being heard on the phone. Participants key comments and questions in chat boxes or press a keypad system to respond to an audience

Internet conferencing a method of real-time conferencing that allows a company to conduct a presentation in real time over the Internet simultaneously with a conference telephone call; also called *webcasting*

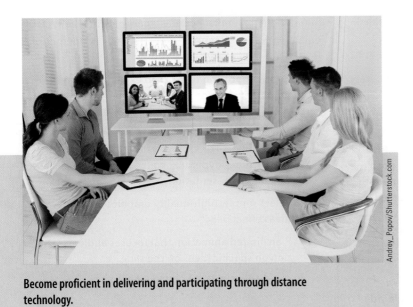

Become proficient in delivering and participating through distance technology.

poll, thus giving valuable feedback without interrupting the speaker.

Companies deliver live Web presentations on issues ranging from internal briefings on new developments and organizational and procedural changes to product strategy and training presentations. Ernst & Young uses Web presentations to announce organizational changes and has found it to be an effective alternative to memos and emails that weren't always remembered or understood. People most affected by an organizational change are able to interact with leaders announcing the change.

Follow these guidelines for adapting your presentation skills to videoconferences and Web presentations:

- **Determine whether a distance delivery method is appropriate for the presentation.** Is the presentation purpose suited to the technology? Can costs in time, money, and human energy be justified? Are key people willing and able to participate? For example, a videoconference for a formal presentation such as an important speech by the CEO to a number of locations justifies the major expense and brings attention to the importance of the message. Distance delivery formats are inappropriate for presentations that cover highly sensitive or confidential issues, for persuasive or problem-solving meetings where no relationship has been established among the participants, and whenever participants are unfamiliar with and perhaps unsupportive of the technology.

- **Establish rapport with the participants prior to the distance presentation.** If possible, meet with or phone participants beforehand to get to know

them and gain insights about their attitudes. This rapport will enhance your ability to interpret subtle nonverbal cues and to cultivate the relationship further through the distance format. Emailing or faxing a short questionnaire or posting presentation slides with a request for questions is an excellent way to establish a connection with participants and to ensure that the presentation is tailored to audience needs. Some enterprising distance presenters engage participants in email discussions before the presentation and then use this dialogue to develop positive interaction during the presentation.

- **Become proficient in delivering and participating through distance technology.** Begin by becoming familiar with the equipment and the surroundings. Although technical support staff might be available to manage equipment and transmission tasks, your goal is to concentrate on the contribution you are to make and not your intimidation with the delivery method.

- **Concentrate on projecting positive nonverbal messages.** Keep a natural, friendly expression; relax and smile. Avoid the tendency to stare into the camera. Instead, look naturally at the entire audience as you would in a live presentation. Speak clearly with as much energy as you can. If a lag occurs between the video and audio transmission, adjust your timing to avoid interrupting other speakers. Use gestures to reinforce points, but avoid fast or excessive motion that will appear blurry. Avoid side conversations, coughing, and clearing your throat, which could trigger voice-activated microphones. Pay close attention to other presenters to guard against easy distraction in a distance environment and to capture subtle nonverbal cues. You will need to judge the vocal tone of the person asking a question, because you might not see faces.

- **Adjust camera settings to enhance communication.** Generally, adjust the camera so that all participants can be seen, but zoom in more closely on participants when you wish to clearly observe nonverbal language. Project a wide-angle shot of yourself during rapport-building comments at the presentation's beginning and zoom in to signal the start of the agenda or to emphasize an important point during the presentation. Some systems accommodate a split screen, but others allow participants to view either you or your presentation visuals only. You will want to switch the camera between a view of you and your visuals, depending on what is needed at the time.

- **Develop high-quality graphics appropriate for the particular distance format.** Even more than in a live presentation, you will need graphics to engage and maintain participants' attention. Graphics are a welcome variation to the "talking head"—you—displayed on the screen for long periods. Some companies provide assistance from a webmaster or graphics support staff in preparing slide shows specifically for distance presentations. Also, e-conferencing companies will develop and post presentation slides and host live Web presentations, including managing email messages and audience polling. Regardless of the support you receive, you should understand basic guidelines for preparing effective visuals for videoconferencing and Web presentations.

- **Videoconferences.** Readability of text will be a critical issue when displaying visuals during a videoconference because text becomes fuzzy when transmitted through compressed video. Select large, sturdy fonts, and choose a color scheme that provides high contrast between the background and the text. Stay with a tested color scheme such as dark blue background, yellow title text, and white bulleted list text to ensure readability. Projecting your visuals ahead of time so you can adjust the color scheme, font selections, and other design elements is an especially good idea.

- **Web presentations.** In addition to considering overall appeal, clarity, and readability, Web presentations must be designed for minimal load time and compatibility with various computers. For your first presentation, consider using a Web template in your electronic presentations software, and experiment with the appropriateness of other designs as you gain experience.

Stand-alone presentations designed specifically for Web delivery require unique design strategies to compensate for the absence of a speaker.[21]

- **Consider posting text-based explanations in the notes view area or adding vocal narration.**

- **Develop interactive slide formats that allow viewers to navigate to the most useful information in your presentation.** For example, design an agenda slide that includes hyperlinks to the first slide in each section of the presentation.

- **Select simple, high-quality graphics that convey ideas effectively.**

- **Plan limited animation that focuses audience attention on specific ideas on the slide.**

- **Consider adding video if bandwidth is not an issue.**

12-5d Crisis Communication

Crisis communication requires management in situations that affect an organization's relationships with its stakeholders, particularly those that draw media attention. Discussions of crisis management typically focus on three issues: (1) planning and preparing for crisis events, (2) behavior of the organization during a crisis, and (3) communicating with important publics during the crisis.

The types of disasters that an organization might face can be divided into three categories: natural disasters, normal accidents, and abnormal or intentional accidents. Natural disasters include fires, earthquakes, or hurricanes. Normal accident is a term to describe industrial disasters such as those that occurred at Three Mile Island, Chernobyl, Bhopal, Alaska due to the Exxon Valdez spill, and Louisiana because of the BP oil spill. Abnormal accidents occur because of deliberate action, such as bombings, kidnappings, cyber attacks, and other types of sabotage.

The communication objective in any crisis management strategy should depend upon the stage of the crisis. In cases when communication programs can begin before a crisis occurs, messages should provide internalizing information to build a positive public opinion toward the organization. When it appears a crisis is imminent, the strategy should shift from internalizing messages to instructing messages that tell the public how to respond to the crisis. During the breakout stage of

Andrey_Popov/Shutterstock.com

and to do so promptly. It is also important to communicate directly with others who are affected, such as employees, customers, shareholders, and communities.

An organization should not wait for a crisis to develop relationships with members of the media if it wants to take advantage of the media's image-building capabilities. It is important that someone in the organization takes time to cultivate these relationships. Building relationships with the media is a generally considered a better method than sending out mass-produced public releases that may average a response rate of only 2%.[22]

Preparing to deliver a crisis briefing requires special attention to maintaining credibility, particularly composure. At the time of the briefing, make sure that you arrive on time and look professional. It might be helpful to take a page from presidential candidates and consider whether loosening your tie or taking off your jacket will help you to better establish common ground with an audience of people who don't wear a suit to work. During the briefing, practice the following points:

- **Anticipate questions and determine who will answer them.** Ideally, question-and-answer sheets should be prepared for management personnel who may be asked questions by the news media. During a briefing, anticipate which questions might be asked and who should best respond.

- **Prepare and deliver a brief statement.** After introducing yourself and others representing your company, deliver a brief statement (less than two minutes in length) that focuses only on the facts that can be confirmed at that time.

- **Outline your organization's current response effort and action plan.**

- **Express your key points from the public's point of view.** Telling the audience how the company's actions will contribute to better health or preserve jobs in the community may help it to better appreciate your points.

- **Use plain language.** Avoid language with which only those in your industry, company, or professional specialization are familiar.

- **Maintain control.** Focus on your goals for the interview, and offer responses aimed at achieving those goals.

the crisis, instructing communication should intensify so that the affected publics know what to do. As the crisis subsides, communication may shift to adjusting messages intended to help people cope with the effects of the crisis. When the crisis is over, the organization can shift back to an internalizing message strategy.

Any crisis communication plan should provide training for dealing with the media regarding crisis management; identify communication lines with local communities and intervening agencies, such as the police; and provide a strategy for communicating with employees.

During a crisis, an organization should follow the steps outlined below:

1. **Get control of the situation.** This involves defining the problem and setting measurable communication objectives. In addition, it is important to communicate to employees how and where to get information.

2. **Gather information about the situation.** It is important that an organization has a means to stay up to date with the situation as it is happening so that it can respond quickly and appropriately. One way to accomplish this task is to create a crisis center that creates crisis response plans, monitors potential crises, and develops crisis response capabilities.

3. **Communicate early and often.** It will benefit the organization's credibility to be prepared and to explain what is happening and what the company is doing about it, and to provide information about resources available to affected parties to deal with the situation.

4. **Communicate directly with affected parties.** It is important to be prepared to communicate with the media

- **Be honest.** Unless the corporate attorney has advised you against it, tell the truth. If there is a problem, then focus the bulk of your discussion on the steps you are taking to avoid the problem in the future. Don't guess at the answer. If you don't know something, say so.

- **Take responsibility.** Again, unless the corporate attorney has advised otherwise, take responsibility for problems rather than blaming others.

- **Remain calm and avoid arguments.** Becoming emotional can undermine your credibility and make you look as if you have lost control and composure.

- **Rephrase the question.** You don't need to accept a questioner's premise. If a reporter uses words you wouldn't, don't repeat them. Correct them if necessary.

- **Try to be friendly, helpful, and patient.** Shake hands with attendees, and call them by name. Be enthusiastic about your company and your job, if appropriate for the occasion. Avoid becoming impatient with attendees or acting as if they or their questions are stupid.

- **Limit the question-and-answer session to no more than 10 minutes.**

- **Don't speculate or make predictions.**

- **Don't make any remarks "off the record."** Such comments might lead reporters to believe there is more to the story that they can pursue.

As with many other types of professional communication situations, adequate preparation is often the key to a successful crisis briefing.

STUDY TOOLS 12

LOCATED AT BACK OF THE TEXTBOOK
☐ Tear-Out Chapter Review Card

LOCATED AT WWW.CENGAGEBRAIN.COM
☐ Review Key Term flashcards and create your own cards

☐ Track your knowledge and understanding of key concepts in business communication

☐ Complete practice and graded quizzes to prepare for tests

☐ Complete interactive content within BCOM8 Online

☐ View the chapter highlight boxes for BCOM8 Online

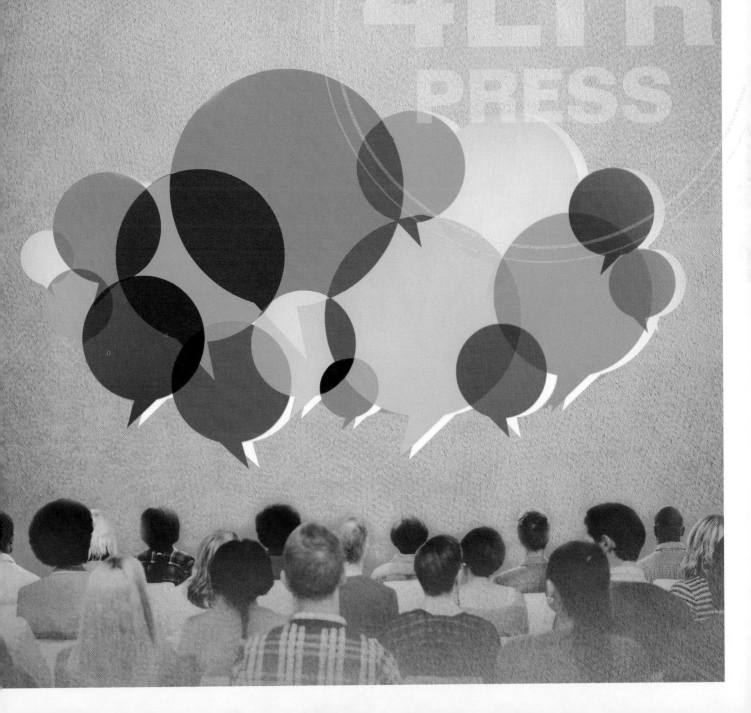

13 Preparing Résumés and Application Messages

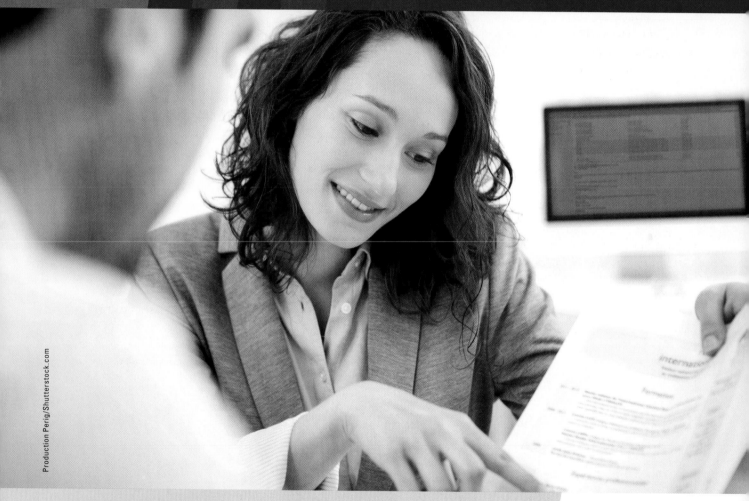

Production Perig/Shutterstock.com

LEARNING OBJECTIVES

After studying this chapter, you will be able to …

13-1 Prepare for employment by considering relevant information about yourself as it relates to job requirements.

13-2 Identify career opportunities using traditional and electronic methods.

13-3 Prepare an organized, persuasive résumé that is adapted for print and electronic postings.

13-4 Use employment tools other than the résumé that can enhance employability.

13-5 Write an application message that effectively introduces an accompanying print (designed) or electronic résumé.

After finishing this chapter, go to **PAGE 254** for **STUDY TOOLS.**

13-1 PREPARING FOR THE JOB SEARCH

Managing your career begins with recognizing that securing a new job is less important than assessing the impact of that job on your life. Work isn't something that happens from 8 a.m. to 5 p.m., with life happening after 5 p.m. Life and work are interconnected, and true satisfaction comes from being able to fully express yourself in what you do. This means merging who you are—your values, emotions, capabilities, and desires—with the activities you perform on the job.[1]

An ideal job provides satisfaction at all of Maslow's need levels, from basic economic to self-actualizing needs. The right job for you will not be drudgery; the work itself will be satisfying and give you a sense of well-being. Synchronizing your work with your core beliefs and talents leads to enthusiasm and fulfillment. You will probably work 10,000 days of your life, not including time spent commuting and on other related activities. Why spend all this time doing something unfulfilling when you could just as easily spend it doing what you enjoy?

> You will probably work 10,000 days of your life, not including time spent commuting and on other related activities.

Your **résumé** is a vital communication tool that provides a basis for judgment about your capabilities on the job. In preparing this document, your major tasks will be gathering essential information about yourself and the job, using traditional and electronic resources, planning and organizing the résumé to showcase your key qualifications, and adapting the résumé for various types of delivery. You will need to supplement your résumé with examples of your accomplishments and abilities. Finally, you'll prepare persuasive application messages appropriate for the delivery of your résumé.

13-1a Gathering Essential Information

The job search begins with research—collecting, compiling, and analyzing information—in order to assess your marketability. The research phase of the job search involves the steps shown in Figure 13.1 on the next page and are summarized as follows:

1. **Gather relevant information for decision making.** Complete a self-assessment to identify your own job-related qualifications, and an analysis of the career field that interests you and of a specific job in that field. Follow-up in an interview with a career person in your field to acquire additional information.

2. **Prepare a company/job profile.** Compile the information you gathered into a format that allows you to compare your qualifications with the company and job requirements. This organized information will help you determine a possible match between you and the potential job.

3. **Identify unique selling points and specific support.** Determine several key qualifications and accomplishments that enhance your marketability. These are the key selling points you'll target in your résumé and later in a job interview.

13-1b Identifying Potential Career Opportunities

Plan to begin your job search for prospective employers months in advance. Waiting too long to begin and then hurrying through the job search process could affect your ability to land a satisfying job.

Before you begin, take the time to develop an organized strategy for your search efforts. You might download a template such as Microsoft's job search log (**http://office.microsoft.com/en-us/templates/results.aspx?qu=job%20search%20log**) or invest in software such as Winway Résumé and Résumé Maker Deluxe to simplify the task of tracking your contacts. You'll need a record of the name, address, email address, and telephone number of each potential employer. Later, record the date of each job contact you make and receive (along with what you learned from the contact), the name of the contact person, the date you sent a résumé, and so on. Your search for potential career opportunities likely will involve traditional and electronic job search sources.

USING TRADITIONAL SOURCES

Traditional means of locating a job include printed sources, networks, career services centers, employers' offices, employment agencies and contractors, and professional organizations.

PRINTED SOURCES

Numerous printed sources are useful in identifying firms in need of employees. Responses to advertised positions in the employment sections of newspapers should be made as quickly as possible after the ad is circulated. If your résumé is

> **résumé** a vital communication tool that provides a basis for judgment about a person's capabilities on the job

FIGURE 13.1 | PROCESS OF APPLYING FOR A JOB

STEP 1	STEP 2	STEP 3	STEP 4	STEP 5
Conduct research and analysis of self, career, and job	Identify a job listing, using traditional and electronic sources	Prepare targeted résumé and application message in required formats	Consider supplementing the résumé: portfolio (print or electronic) or video recording	Interview with companies

{ self career job }

RÉSUMÉ

RÉSUMÉ PRESENTATION AND DELIVERY OPTIONS

Print (Designed)
- Mail to company accompanied by application letter
- Mail as follow-up to electronic submission

Scannable
- Print résumé formatted for computer scanning

Electronic Postings
- Email to network contacts, career and corporate sites, and career services centers
- Online form
- Electronic portfolio at personal website
- Beamer to PDA or cell phone

Cengage Learning

received early and is impressive, you could get a favorable response before other applications are received. If an ad requests that responses be sent to a box number without giving a name, be cautious. The employer could be legitimate but does not want present employees to know about the ad or does not want applicants to phone or drop by. However, you have a right to be suspicious of someone who wants to remain obscure while learning everything you reveal in your résumé. Print job listings can also be found in company newsletters, industry directories, and trade and professional publications, which often are available on the Internet.

NETWORKS

The majority of job openings are never advertised. Therefore, developing a network of contacts is often the most valuable source of information about jobs. A number of professional networking sites exist online. Today, LinkedIn is the most popular networking website for business professionals. Facebook plays the dual role

©Gil C/Shutterstock.com

of enabling personal as well as professional networking. Many entrepreneurs actively exploit social media, such as Facebook and Twitter, to promote their businesses and services. These are just a few of the social networking opportunities available.

Your network could include current and past employers, guest speakers in your classes or at student organization meetings, business contacts you met while interning or participating in shadowing or over-the-shoulder experiences, professors, and so on. Let these individuals know the type of job you are seeking, and ask their advice for finding employment in today's competitive market.

CAREER SERVICES CENTERS

You will want to register with your college's career services center at least three semesters before you graduate. Typically, the center has a website and a browsing room loaded with career information and job announcement bulletins. Career counseling is available at most career services centers, including workshops on résumé writing, interviewing, etiquette, mock interviews, "mocktail" parties for learning to mingle at pre-interview social events, and more. Through the center, you can learn about job fairs at which you can meet prospective employers and schedule on-campus, phone, and video interviews with company recruiters.

Most career services centers use electronic tracking systems. Rather than submitting printed résumés, students input their résumés into a computer file, following the specific requirements of the tracking system used by the college or university. A search of the résumé database generates an interview roster of the top applicants for a campus recruiter's needs. Some centers assist students in preparing electronic portfolios to supplement their résumés.

EMPLOYERS' WEBSITES AND OFFICE LOCATIONS

Most organizations post job openings on their website. For local businesses, it might be useful to schedule an informational interview to learn more about the employer and the type of skills that it looks for in new employees. Although you should not ask for a job during an informational interview, the contact you have made may pay off in the future as part of your professional network.

EMPLOYMENT AGENCIES AND CONTRACTORS

City, county, state, and federal employment agencies provide free or inexpensive services. Some agencies offer online listings or phone recordings so that applicants can get information about job opportunities and procedures for using their services. The fee charged by private agencies is paid by either the employee or the employer and usually is based on the first month's salary and due within a few months. Some agencies specialize in finding high-level executives or specialists for major firms. Employment contractors specialize in providing temporary employees and might be able to place you in a position on a temporary basis until you find a full-time job.

PROFESSIONAL ORGANIZATIONS

Officers of professional organizations, through their contacts with members, can be good sources of information about job opportunities. Much job information is exchanged at meetings of professional associations. In addition to job listings in journals or organization websites, interviews are sometimes conducted at conference locations.

In addition to the professional growth that comes from membership in professional organizations, active participation is a good way to learn about jobs. Guest speakers share valuable information about the industry and its career and job opportunities. Employers are often favorably impressed when membership and experiences gained are included on the résumé and discussed during an interview. They are even more impressed if the applicant has been an officer in the organization, as it indicates leadership, community commitment, and willingness to serve without tangible reward, social acceptance, or high level of aspiration. By joining and actively participating in professional, social, and honorary organizations, you increase your opportunities to develop rapport with peers and professors and gain an edge over less-involved applicants.

USING ELECTRONIC EMPLOYMENT RESOURCES

An increasing number of companies and job hunters are using the Internet to assist in various stages of the job search process. As part of this trend, a number of job sites have been established that provide a variety of services to both job applicants and employers. Figure 13.2 provides a list of the top 10 job websites as calculated by eBizMBA.[2]

The job sites include jobs of all levels, occupations, and locations. Others specialize in certain kinds of jobs. Most job sites provide these features and information:

- **Search and apply for job openings.** There are thousands of online job banks. Most work in the same basic way: employers pay to post job openings; job seekers search the openings and apply for those that interest them. Most sites allow you to search by occupation, location, industry, and other characteristics.

- **Post your résumé.** Sometimes you can post your résumé without applying for a specific job. On some job sites, employers can then review your résumé for positions they haven't even posted.

- **Get a feel for job requirements and pay.** Job websites can be a good research tool. They can help you learn what kinds of workers employers want, the skills they expect, and the pay and benefits they offer.

When using job sites, as with other online resources, be aware of possible fraudulent activities. For example, you should not have to pay to post your résumé or search job openings. However, you may have to register to use all the features of a job website. Likewise, some job postings are scams. Be wary of any that ask you for an "up-front" investment of money for products or instructions. Also, be wary of those that offer commissions or pay thousands of dollars for job duties such as processing checks on behalf of foreign nationals or reshipping goods from your home. Finally, never give out personal information. A legitimate company won't ask you for your social security number, credit card numbers, bank account information, or any other personal details.

LOCATING CAREER GUIDANCE INFORMATION

According to one career consultant, "Most people in the old days could go into an organization [during a job interview] and not really know about it and hope for the best. Now, people can understand the organization before they even apply."[3] The Internet places at your fingertips a wealth of information that will prepare you for the job interview if you use it as a research tool. Suggestions follow for effectively using the career guidance information you can locate on the Internet:

- **Visit career sites for information related to various phases of the job search.** You'll find a wide range of timely discussions at career sites: planning a job search, finding a job you love, researching employers, working a career fair, crafting winning résumés and cover letters, negotiating a salary, and so on.

- **Visit corporate websites to learn about companies.** You can locate information online for targeting your résumé appropriately and to prepare for the job interview. Read mission statements or descriptions of services to see how the organization describes itself, and review the annual report and strategic plan to learn about the financial condition and predicted growth rates. Search for "What's New" or "News" sections promoting new developments, as well as career opportunities and job postings. Evaluating the development and professional nature of the website will give you an impression of the organization. Supplement this information with independent sources to confirm the company's stability and status, as negative news likely will not be posted on the website.

- **Identify specific skills companies are seeking.** Study the job descriptions provided on corporate home pages and job sites to identify the skills required for the job and the latest industry buzzwords. Use this information to target your résumé to a specific job listing and to generate keywords for an electronic résumé.

- **Network with prospective employers.** It's easy to network online by attending electronic job fairs, chatting with career counselors, participating in news groups and LISTSERVs applicable to your field, and corresponding by email with contacts in companies. The value of these electronic networking experiences is to learn about an industry and career, seek valued opinions, and uncover potential job opportunities. By applying effective communication strategies for an online community, you can make a good impression, create rapport with employment contacts online, and polish your interviewing skills.

USING THE INTERNET TO IDENTIFY JOB LISTINGS

When using the Internet or online databases to search for specific job openings, follow these general suggestions to get started:

- Input words and phrases that describe your skills rather than job titles because job titles vary by company.

FIGURE 13.2   TEN MOST POPULAR JOB WEBSITES*

 36,000,000—Estimated Unique Monthly Visitors

 23,000,000—Estimated Unique Monthly Visitors

 22,400,000—Estimated Unique Monthly Visitors

 15,000,000—Estimated Unique Monthly Visitors

 11,000,000—Estimated Unique Monthly Visitors

 10,000,000—Estimated Unique Monthly Visitors

 8,000,000—Estimated Unique Monthly Visitors

 4,750,000—Estimated Unique Monthly Visitors

 4,500,000—Estimated Unique Monthly Visitors

 3,500,000—Estimated Unique Monthly Visitors

*The 10 Most Popular Job Sites were derived from the *eBizMBA Rank*, which is a constantly updated average of each website's *Alexa* Global Traffic Rank and U.S. Traffic Rank from both *Compete* and *Quantcast*.

Source: Top 15 Most Popular Job Websites (2014, May). Retrieved May 26, 2014, from http://www .ebizmba.com/articles/job-websites.

- Use specific phrases such as "entry-level job" or "job in advertising" rather than "job search."

- Start with a wider job description term, such as "pharmaceutical sales jobs"; then narrow down to the specific subject, geographic region, state, and so forth.

- Don't limit yourself to one search engine or online job site; try several, and bookmark interesting sites.

- Stay focused on your goal, and don't get distracted as you go.

PLANNING A TARGETED RÉSUMÉ

In order to match your interests and qualifications with available jobs, you'll need an effective résumé. To win a job interview in today's tight market where job seekers outnumber positions, you need more than a general résumé that documents your education and work history. The powerful wording of a **targeted résumé** reflects the requirements of a specific job listing that you have identified through traditional and electronic job search methods.

An employer typically scans résumés quickly, looking for reasons to reject the applicant, schedule an interview, or place it in a stack for rereading. This initial scan and a second brief look for those who make the cut give little time to explain why you are the best person for the job. To grab an employer's attention, you must selectively choose *what to say*, *how to say it*, and *how to arrange it* on the page so that it can be read quickly but thoroughly. A concise, informative, easy-to-read summary of your relevant qualifications will demonstrate that you possess the straightforward communication skills demanded in today's information-intensive society.

The goal of the résumé is to get an interview, so your résumé must show that you are, at least on the surface, qualified for the job for which you are applying. The best way to do this is to match your skills to those the employer is seeking. Hopefully, you have already done your homework and familiarized yourself with the type of skills, experience, and qualifications for which employers in your field are looking by finding and analyzing job advertisements for the position you desire. If you have performed this task well, you should have a solid understanding of the skills and qualifications you will need and will have also spent some time reviewing your own life history to identify situations in which you have demonstrated those skills and abilities.

If you have done both of these tasks effectively, you should be well prepared to write a résumé that matches your skills with those an employer is seeking. These are the skills and qualifications that should be easily gleaned from a quick scan of your completed résumé. Other irrelevant, yet perhaps valuable, skills and experiences should be omitted so that your résumé is well targeted to the specific position you are seeking and this fact should be almost immediately obvious to the employer reviewing your materials.

It is also important to remember that your

targeted résumé a résumé that reflects the requirements of a specific job listing

Another name for résumé is "*curriculum vitae*" or "CV," which is Latin for "course of one's life."

résumé is not being reviewed in a vacuum. It is likely that the employer also is reviewing dozens of other résumés at the same time he or she is reading yours. For this reason, you should also have a solid knowledge of what your competitors bring to the table and how well you compare. A strategic job seeker will have a clear idea of his or her strongest selling points as compared with others and will have considered how to best showcase these favorably.

13-2a Standard Parts of a Résumé

A winning résumé contains standard parts that are adapted to highlight key qualifications for a specific job. The sample résumés and in-depth explanation of each standard part provided in Figures 13.3 to 13.6 (see pages 239–244) will prepare you for creating a résumé that describes your qualifications best.

IDENTIFICATION

Your objective is to provide information that will allow the interviewer to reach you. Include your name, current address, phone number, and email address. Provide a clear, benign email address that reflects a positive impression (e.g., no "mustangsally"). You should also include your website address or professional networking page to provide access to more detailed information.

To ensure that the interviewer can quickly locate the identification information, center it on the page or use graphic design elements to call attention to your name. You should include a permanent address (parent's or other relative's address) if you are interviewing when classes are not in session. In addition, leave a clear, straightforward greeting on your phone that portrays you as a person serious about securing a job. Eliminate music, clever sayings, or background noise.

JOB AND/OR CAREER OBJECTIVE

Following the "Identification" section, state your job/career objective—the job you want. Interviewers can see quickly whether the job you seek matches the one they have to offer. A good job/career objective must be specific enough to be meaningful yet general enough to apply to a variety of jobs. The following example illustrates a general objective that has been revised to describe a specific job:

General Objective	Specific Objective
A challenging position that enables me to contribute to an organization's success.	Position where my creative Web design skills and ability to work under pressure will enable me to contribute to organizational success.
A position with a stable organization that provides an opportunity for development and career advancement.	Position where my accounting knowledge, attention to detail, and strong work ethic will enable me to contribute to a firm's financial success.

In addition to addressing your skills, values, and goals, a useful objective statement is positioned so as to show how these abilities will contribute to an organization. Some employment specialists have criticized objective statements as being generally too self-centered and thus not particularly useful. Other experts argue that a statement of your job or career objective can limit your job opportunities; your objective should be obvious from your qualifications. A strategic job applicant will consider the usefulness of including an objective statement when taken into consideration with other aspects of his or her résumé and how well he or she can best compete for a position.

CAREER SUMMARY

To survive the interviewer's 40-second scan, you must provide a compelling reason for a more thorough review of your résumé. To accomplish this goal, another strategy is to craft a persuasive introductory statement that quickly synthesizes your most transferable skills, accomplishments, and attributes, and place it in a section labeled "Summary" or "Professional Profile." As stated earlier, be aware that you are competing with others, so you want to position yourself favorably in comparison by highlighting your personal strengths as they relate to the desired skills or abilities.

In other words, the synopsis of your key qualifications should communicate why you should be hired. Your answer should evolve naturally from the career objective and focus on your ability to meet the needs of the company you have identified from your extensive research.

A high-impact career summary should be developed for your profile on job websites or professional networking sites. A version of this summary can be provided on your résumé as well. Compose a career summary that will interest any interviewer so he or she will instantly see you as an applicant with exactly the skills needed for the job, as in the following example:

Hardworking banking professional with two years of experience processing residential and commercial real-estate loans. Very active in professional organizations locally, resulting in a large network of potential clients. Named "Most Promising Young Banker" by the Iowa Banking Association in 2014.

SEPARATE OBJECTIVE AND CAREER SUMMARY

Objective: Position where my proven customer service skills and strong work habits will enable me to contribute to a growing company.

Career Summary: Six years of experience in telephone service center; promoted to team leader after two years and supervisor after four.

COMBINED OBJECTIVE WITH CAREER SUMMARY

Professional Profile: Entry-level position in investment banking or finance. Internship experience with two investment banking firms, where I prepared and delivered multiple sales presentations to potential high-volume clients.

LINKED OBJECTIVE AND CAREER SUMMARY

Profile: Position as sales representative in which demonstrated commission selling and hard work bring rewards.

Accomplishments:

▶ Three years' straight commission sales.

▶ Average of $35,000–$55,000 a year in commissioned earnings.

▶ Consistent success in development and growth of territories.

This example combines the applicant's career objective—loan officer at a bank—with her unique selling points: her involvement in the local business community and acknowledgment of her promise by a recognized and relevant professional organization.

QUALIFICATIONS

The "Qualifications" section varies depending on the information identified in the analysis of self, career, and job. This information is used to divide your qualifications into appropriate parts, label them appropriately, and arrange them in the best sequence. Usually, qualifications stem from your education and work experience (words that appear as headings in the résumé). Order these categories according to which you perceive as more impressive to the employer, with the more impressive category appearing first. For example, education is usually the chief qualification of a recent college graduate. However, a sales representative with related work experience might list experience first, particularly if the educational background is inadequate for the job sought.

EDUCATION

Beginning with the most recent, list the degree, major, school, and graduation date. Include a blank line between schools for easy reading. The interviewer will probably want to know first whether you have the appropriate degree, then the institution, and then other details. Recent or near college graduates should omit high school activities because that information is "old news." However, include high school activities if they provide a pertinent dimension to your qualifications. For example, having attended high school abroad is a definite advantage to an applicant seeking employment in an international firm. In addition, high school accomplishments could be relevant for freshmen or sophomores seeking cooperative education assignments, scholarships, or part-time jobs. Of course, this information will be replaced with college activities when the résumé is revised for subsequent jobs or other uses.

Include overall and major grade point averages if they are B or better—but be prepared to discuss any omissions during an interview. Some recruiters recommend that every candidate include his or her grade point average because an omission might lead the reader to assume the worst. Honors and achievements that relate directly to education can be incorporated in this section or included in a separate section. Listing scholarships, appearances on academic lists,

Your résumé should include educational experiences that are beyond requirements, such as study abroad.

and initiations into honor societies is common; but consider also including business-relevant skills you've developed, including client projects, team building, and field experiences. If honors and achievements are included in the "Education" section, be sure to include plenty of white space or use bullets to highlight these points (see Figure 13.3 on page 239 and Figure 13.5 on page 241).

The "Education" section could also include a list of special skills and abilities such as foreign language and computer competency. A list of courses typically required in your field is unnecessary and occupies valuable space. However, you should include any courses, workshops, or educational experiences that are not usual requirements, such as internships, cooperative education semesters, "shadowing," and study abroad.

WORK EXPERIENCE

The "Work Experience" section provides information about your employment history. For each job held, list the job title, company name, dates of employment, primary responsibilities, and key accomplishments. The jobs can be listed in reverse chronological order (beginning with the most recent) or in order of job relatedness. Begin with the job that most obviously relates to the job being sought if you have gaps in your work history, if the job you are seeking is very different from the job you currently hold, or if you are just entering the job market and have little, if any, related work experience.

Arrange the order and format of information about each job (dates, job title, company, description, and accomplishments) so that the most important information is emphasized—but format all job information consistently. If you have held numerous jobs in a short time, embed dates of employment within the text rather than surround them with white space. Give related job experience added emphasis by listing it first or surrounding it with white space.

Employers are interested in how you can contribute to their bottom line, so a winning strategy involves concentrating on accomplishments and achievements. Begin with the job title and company name that provides basic information about your duties, and then craft powerful descriptions of the quality and scope of your performance. These bullet points will provide deeper insight into your capability, ambition, and personality and set you apart from other applicants who take the easy route of providing only a work history.

Return to the in-depth analysis you completed at the beginning of the job search process to recall insights as to how you can add immediate value to this company. Consider the following questions to spur your recognition of marketable skills from your education, work, and community experiences.[4]

My Marketable Skills

- How does my potential employer define success in the job for which I'm applying? How do I measure up?

- What is my potential employer's bottom line (money, attendance, sales, etc.)? When have I shown that I know how to address that bottom line?

- What project am I proud of that demonstrates I have the skill for my job objective?

- What technical or management skills do I have that indicate the level at which I perform?

- What problem did I solve, how did I solve it, and what were the results?

Because interviewers spend such a short time reading résumés, the style must be direct and simple. Therefore, a résumé should use crisp phrases to help employers see the value of the applicant's education and experiences. To save space and to emphasize what you have accomplished, use these stylistic techniques:

1. Omit pronouns referring to yourself (*I, me, my*).

2. Use subject-understood sentences.

3. Begin sentences with action verbs as shown in the following examples:

Instead of	Use
I had responsibility for developing sales materials.	Developed sales materials, including brochures and website promotions.
My duties included meeting with potential clients to review financial products.	Met with potential clients and used interpersonal communication skills to sell a wide range of financial products.
I was the treasurer of my fraternity and managed a charitable fund-raising event.	Managed a $200,000-plus budget and organized a charitable fund-raising event that garnered $15,000, a 25% increase over previous year.
I worked in retail sales, selling fashions and accessories.	Named salesperson of the year for sales of more than $50,000.
I was the president of the Student Marketing Association and a member of a winning case-competition team.	Demonstrated excellent leadership skills as president of Student Marketing Association and collaborative teamwork skills as member of winning case-competition group.

Action verbs are especially appropriate for résumés because employers are looking for people who will work. Note the subject-understood sentences in the right column of the previous example: action words used as first words provide emphasis. One of the best places to find action words is in the advertisements for the jobs for which you are applying. Using key phrases from the job advertisement can help the applicant in two ways: (1) you look like a good fit with the company because you use the same language, and (2) your résumé will more likely be identified by the search software used to select the best qualified applicants for interviews. The following list provides examples of action verbs that are useful in résumés:

achieved	drafted	participated
analyzed	increased	planned
assigned	initiated	recruited
assisted	interpreted	researched
boosted	managed	streamlined
compiled	monitored	supervised
developed	organized	wrote

A quick Web search will result in additional action verbs from which to select.

To avoid a tone of egotism, do not use too many adjectives or adverbs that seem overly strong. Plan to do some careful editing after writing your first draft.

HONORS AND ACTIVITIES

Make a trial list of any other information that qualifies you for the job. Divide the list into appropriate divisions and then select an appropriate label. Your heading might be "Honors and Activities." You might include a section for "Activities," "Leadership Activities," or "Memberships," depending on the items listed. You might also include a separate section on "Military Service," "Civic Activities," "Volunteer Work," or "Interests." If you have only a few items under each category, use a more general term and combine the lists. If your list is lengthy, divide it into more than one category as interviewers prefer "bite-size" pieces that are easy to read and remember.

Resist the urge to include everything you have ever done; keep in mind that every item you add distracts from other information. Consider summarizing information that is relevant but does not merit several separate lines—for example, "Involved in art, drama, and choral groups." To decide whether to include certain information, ask these questions: How closely related is it to the job being sought? Does it provide job-related information that has not been presented elsewhere?

PERSONAL INFORMATION

Because a résumé should primarily contain information that is relevant to an applicant's experience and qualifications, you must be selective when including personal information that is not related to the job you are seeking. The space could be used more effectively to include more about your qualifications or to add more white space. Personal information is commonly placed at the end of the résumé just above the "References" section because it is less important than qualifications (education, experience, and activities).

Under the 1964 Civil Rights Act (and subsequent amendments) and the Americans with Disabilities Act (ADA), employers cannot make hiring decisions based on gender, age, marital status, religion, national origin, or disability. Employers prefer not to receive information about these protected areas because questions could be raised about whether the information was used in the hiring decision.

Follow these guidelines related to personal information:

- **Do not include personal information that could lead to discriminatory hiring.** Exclude height, weight, color of hair and eyes, and a personal photograph on the résumé.

- **Reveal ethnic background (and other personal information) only if it is job related.** For example, certain businesses might be actively seeking employees in certain ethnic groups because the ethnic background is a legitimate part of the job description. For such a business, ethnic information is useful and appreciated.

- **Include personal information (other than information covered by employment legislation) that will strengthen your résumé.** Select information that is related to the job you are seeking or that portrays you as a well-rounded, happy individual off the job. Include interests, hobbies, favorite sports, and willingness to relocate. You can also include the following topics if you have not covered them elsewhere in the résumé: spoken and written communication skills, computer competency, foreign language or computer skills, military service, community service, scholastic honors, job-related hobbies, and professional association memberships.

- **Consider whether personal information might be controversial.** For example, listing a sport that an interviewer might perceive to be overly time consuming or dangerous would be questionable. An applicant seeking a position with a religious or political organization could benefit from revealing a related affiliation.

REFERENCES

Providing potential employers a list of references (people who have agreed to supply information about you when requested) complements your employment credentials. Listing names, addresses, phone numbers, and email addresses of people who can provide information about you adds credibility to the résumé. Employers, former employers, and college instructors are good possibilities. Friends, relatives, and neighbors are not (because of their perceived bias in your favor). Some career experts recommend including a peer to document your ability

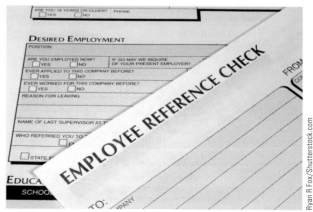

Your Facebook or myspace profile, photos, and "innermost" thoughts create a "shadow" résumé that may hurt your employment opportunities far into the future.

A recent employer survey indicated that 44% of employers use social networking sites to examine the profiles of job candidates, and 39% have looked up the profile of a current employee.[6]

to work as a member of a team, an important job skill in today's team-oriented environment.[5] According to Bob Daugherty, who heads U.S. recruiting for PricewaterhouseCoopers, the best references are people who work for the organization you are looking to join.[7] You'll gain these employee referrals by developing strong relationships through proactive and professional networking via traditional and electronic means. Update your reference list often to be certain that your choices remain relevant and credible (e.g., none are deceased or dismissed for embezzlement).

References can be handled on the résumé in several ways. As the closing section of your résumé, you can provide a list of references; include a brief statement that references are available on request or from a career services center; or omit any statement regarding references, assuming that references are not needed until after an interview. You can list references directly on the résumé if you have limited qualifications to include, if you know that a company interviews applicants *after* references are contacted, or when you believe the names of your references will be recognizable in your career field. You could include a statement such as "For references ... ," or "For additional information ... ," and give the address of the career services center of your college or university, the job bank posting your credentials, or the URL of your electronic portfolio.

Withholding the names of references until they are requested prevents unnecessary or untimely requests going to your present employer. This action also conveys genuine courtesy to the references. Even the most enthusiastic references could become apathetic if

required to provide recommendations to endless interviewers. For this same reason, be sure to communicate with your references regularly if your job search continues longer than expected. Suggestions for communicating with references are discussed in Chapter 14.

When preparing a separate list of references to be given after a successful interview, place the word *References* and your name in a visible position as shown in Figure 13.4 on page 240. Balance the list (name, address, phone number, and relationship of reference to applicant) attractively on the page, and use the same paper used for printing the résumé. Whether it is handed to the interviewer personally or mailed, the references page professionally complements your résumé. Confident that you have a good message, you are now ready to put it in writing—to construct a résumé that will impress an employer favorably.

13-2b Types of Résumés

The general organization of all résumés is fairly standard: identification (name, address, phone number, and email address), job objective, qualifications, personal information, and references. The primary organizational challenge is in dividing the qualifications section into parts, choosing labels for them, and arranging them in the best sequence. When you review your self-, career, and job analyses data and your career/job profile, you will recognize that your qualifications stem mainly from your education and your experience. Your task is to decide how to present these two categories of qualifications. Résumés usually are organized in one of three ways: reverse chronological order (most recent activity listed first), functional order (most important activity listed first), or a chrono-functional order, which combines the chronological and functional orders, as the name implies. To determine which organizational plan to use, draft your résumé in each.

CHRONOLOGICAL RÉSUMÉ

The **chronological résumé** is the traditional organizational format for résumés. Two headings normally appear in the portion that presents qualifications: "Education" and "Experience." Which one should appear first? Decide which one you think is more impressive to the employer, and put that one first. Within each section, the most recent information is presented first. Reverse chronological order is easier to use and is more common than functional order; however, it is not always more effective.

The chronological résumé is an especially effective format for applicants who have progressed up a clearly defined career ladder and want to move up another rung. Because the format emphasizes dates and job titles, the chronological résumé is less effective for applicants who have gaps in their work histories, are seeking jobs different from the job currently held, or are just entering the job market with little or no experience.[8]

If you choose the chronological format, look at the two headings from the employer's point of view, and reverse their positions if doing so is to your advantage. In the "Experience" section, jobs are listed in reverse-chronological order. Assuming you have progressed typically, your latest job is likely to be more closely related to the job being sought than the first job held. Placing the latest or current job first will give it the emphasis it deserves. Include beginning and ending dates for each job.

FUNCTIONAL RÉSUMÉ

In a **functional résumé**, points of primary interest to employers—transferable skills—appear in major headings. These headings highlight what an applicant can *do* for the employer—functions that the applicant can perform well. Under each heading, an applicant could draw from educational and/or work-related experience to provide supporting evidence.

A functional résumé requires a complete analysis of self, career, and the job sought. Suppose, for example, that a person seeking a job as an assistant hospital administrator wants to emphasize qualifications by placing them in major headings. From the hospital's advertisement of the job and from accumulated job appraisal information, an applicant sees this job as both an administrative and a public-relations job. The job requires skill in communicating and knowledge of accounting and finance. Thus, headings in the "Qualifications" section of the résumé could be "Administration," "Public Relations," "Communication," and "Budgeting." Under "Public Relations," for example, an applicant could reveal that a public relations course was taken at a state university, from which a degree is to be conferred in May, and that a sales job at ABC Store provided abundant opportunity to apply principles learned. With other headings receiving similar treatment, the qualifications portion reveals the significant aspects of education and experience.

Order of importance is the best sequence for functional headings. If you have prepared an accurate self- and job analysis, the selected headings will highlight points of special interest to the employer. Glancing at headings only, an employer can see that you understand the job's requirements and have the qualities needed for success.

Having done the thinking required for preparing a functional résumé, you are well prepared for a question that is commonly asked in interviews: "What can you do for us?" The answer is revealed in your major headings. They emphasize the functions you can perform and the special qualifications you have to offer.

If you consider yourself well qualified, a functional résumé is worth considering. If your education or experience is scant, a functional résumé could be best for you. Using "Education" and "Experience" as headings (as in a chronological résumé) works against your purpose if you have little to report under the headings; the format would emphasize the absence of education or experience.

CHRONO-FUNCTIONAL RÉSUMÉ

The **chrono-functional résumé** combines features of chronological and functional résumés. This format can give quick assurance that educational and experience requirements are met and still use other headings that emphasize qualifications.

chronological résumé the traditional organizational format for résumés, with headings that spotlight an applicant's education and experience

functional résumé the organizational format for résumés that highlights an applicant's transferable skills

chrono-functional résumé a résumé that combines features of chronological and functional résumés

13-3 PREPARING RÉSUMÉS FOR PRINT AND ELECTRONIC DELIVERY

Most employers prefer to receive résumés in standard format through electronic media. Whether presented on paper or electronically, the arrangement of a résumé is just as important as the content. If the arrangement is unattractive, unappealing, or in poor taste, the message might never be read. Errors in keyboarding, spelling, and punctuation could be taken as evidence of a poor academic background, lack of respect for the employer, or carelessness. Recognize that résumés serve as your introduction to employers and indicate the quality of work you'll produce.

As in preparing other difficult documents, prepare a rough draft as quickly as you can and then revise as many times as needed to prepare an effective résumé that sells you. After you are confident with the résumé, ask at least two other people to check it for you. Carefully select people who are knowledgeable about résumé preparation and the job you are seeking and who can suggest ways to present your qualifications more effectively. After you have incorporated those changes, ask a skillful proofreader to review the document.

To accommodate employers' preferences for the presentation and delivery of résumés, you should be aware of three versions of résumés, as shown in Figures 13.3, 13.5, and 13.6—a designed résumé printed on paper, a scannable résumé to be read by a computer, and a designed résumé accessible through email and websites.

iStockphoto.com/Tashatuvango

13-3a Preparing a Print (Designed) Résumé

Your print (designed) résumé is considered your primary marketing document, and appearance is critical. To win out among hundreds of competing résumés, it must look professional and reflect current formatting and production standards while maintaining a distinctive conservative tone. Follow these guidelines for designing and producing a highly professional résumé:

- **Develop an appealing résumé format that highlights your key qualifications and distinguishes your résumé.** Use the power of your word processing software for style enhancements rather than settle for overused, inflexible templates. Study the example résumés in this chapter and models from other sources for ideas for enhancing the style, readability, and overall impact of the document. Then, create a custom design that best highlights your key qualifications.

- **Format information for quick, easy reading.** To format your résumé so that it can be read at a glance, follow these guidelines:

  - Use attention-getting headings to partition major divisions, and add graphic lines and borders to separate sections of text.

  - Use an outline format when possible to list activities and events on separate lines, and include bullets to emphasize multiple points.

  - Use 10-point fonts or larger to avoid reader eye strain.

  - Use type styles and print attributes to emphasize key points. For example, to draw attention to the identification and headings, select a bold sans serif font (e.g., Calibri or Arial) slightly larger than the serif font (e.g., Cambria or Times New Roman) used for the remaining text. Capitalization, indention, and print enhancements (underline, italics, bold) are useful for adding emphasis. Limit the number of type styles and enhancements, however, so the page is clean and simple to read.

  - Include identification on each page of a multiple-page résumé. Place your name and a page number at the top of the second and successive pages, with "Continued" at the bottom of the first page. The interviewer is re-exposed to your name, and pages can be reassembled if separated.

- **Create an appealing output to produce top professional quality.**

  - Check for consistency throughout the résumé. Consistency in spacing, end punctuation, capitalization, appearance of headings, and sequencing of details within sections will communicate your eye for detail and commitment to high standards.

- Balance the résumé attractively on the page, with approximately equal margins. Allow generous white space so the résumé looks uncluttered and easy to read.

- **Consider adding a statement of your creativity and originality.** Be certain that your creativity will not be construed as gimmickry and distract from the content of the résumé. Demonstrating creativity is particularly useful for fields such as advertising, public relations, graphic design, and those requiring computer proficiency.

  - Select paper of a standard size (8-1/2" by 11"), neutral color (white, buff, or gray), and high quality (preferably 24-pound, 100% cotton fiber). Consider using a mailing envelope large enough to accommodate the résumé without folding. The unfolded documents on the reader's desk will get favorable attention and will scan correctly if posted to an electronic database.

  - Print with a laser printer that produces high-quality output. Position paper so the watermark is read across the sheet in the same direction as the printing.

Some employers insist that the "best" length for a résumé is one page, stating that long résumés are often ignored. However, general rules about length are more flexible. Most students and recent graduates can present all relevant résumé information on one page. However, as you gain experience, you might need two or more pages to format an informative, easy-to-read résumé. A résumé forced on one page will likely have narrow margins and large blocks of run-on text (multiple lines with no space to break them). This dense format is unappealing and complicates the interviewer's task of skimming quickly for key information.

The rule about length is simple: Be certain your résumé contains only relevant information presented as concisely as possible. A one-page résumé that includes irrelevant information is too long. A two-page résumé that omits relevant information is too short.

The résumés illustrated in Figures 13.3 and 13.5 (see pages 239 and 241) demonstrate the organizational principles for the chronological and functional résumés. A references page is illustrated in Figure 13.4 on page 240. Study the various layouts to decide on one that will highlight your key qualifications most effectively.

13-3b Preparing Electronic Résumé Submissions

To this point you have focused on the preparation of a print résumé. However, in the digital age of instant information, you'll use various online methods to apply for a job and present your qualifications to prospective employers.

The easiest and most common method of putting your résumé online is through emailing a résumé to a job bank for posting or to a networking contact who asked you to send a résumé. Many job banks, corporate sites, and career services centers require you to respond to specific openings by completing an online form or pasting your résumé into a designated section of the form. Frequently, you can input information directly on the website or download the form to be submitted by email, fax, or mail. You might also choose to post your résumé on your personal website as part of an electronic portfolio that showcases evidence of your qualifications. You could also develop a **beamer**, or *beamable résumé*, a quick version of your résumé designed in a format suitable for broadcasting on smartphones. Recruiting professionals predict that millions of these electronic résumés will be exchanged silently at conferences, business meetings, and power lunches, similar to exchanging business cards.[9]

Electronic submissions are quick and easy but present new challenges and many opportunities to jeopardize your employment chances and compromise your privacy.

beamer a quick version of a résumé designed in a format suitable for broadcasting on smartphones; also called a *beamable résumé*

Rawpixel/Shutterstock.com

FIGURE 13.3 **CHRONOLOGICAL RÉSUMÉ**

NED AVERS
45 Chester Street
Watertown, IA 62205
(530) 443-1565
na@gmail.com

MORTGAGE LOAN PROCESSOR

- Mortgage industry professional with loan-processing experience and a comprehensive knowledge of conventional and government loan programs.

- Thorough in gathering borrower information, verifying loan documents and reviewing file documentation to guide each loan from preapproval to closing.

- Computer savvy in MS Office Suite and proprietary mortgage-processing software.

Loan Processing Expertise

Conforming & Nonconforming Loans, FRMs, ARMs, GPMs, Jumbo Loans, Fannie Mae & Freddie Mac Guidelines, FHA, VA, USDA Rural Development Loans

Professional Experience

WATERTOWN FIRST FEDERAL BANK—Watertown, IA
Loan Processor, 2013 to Present

- Regarded as one of the bank's most productive loan processors, handling an average of 22 files monthly.

- Outperformed company average in achieving loan-processing turn-around time of 12 days or less (compared to typical 15 to 20 days).

- Provided expedient service cited as key to consistently high customer satisfaction and a 10% increase in referrals in 2013.

- Ensured all files were complete prior to underwriting hand-off and coordinated effectively with title companies to ensure smooth closings.

- Successfully processed some of the most challenging loan applications (e.g., first-time borrowers, self-employed applicants, and borrowers with problematic credit histories).

BANK OF IOWA—Watertown, IA
Teller, 2011 to 2013
Provided friendly service to individual and commercial bank customers within regional financial institution.

Education

WATERTOWN COMMUNITY COLLEGE—Watertown, IA
Associate of Science in Business, 2013
Overall GPA: 3.95

- Includes email address that reflects professional image.

- Reveals position sought and powerful summary of qualifications.

- Positions education as top qualification for recent graduate. Includes high GPA.

- Edges out competition by expanding on related experience and work achievements.

- Lists academic recognitions and highlights relevant skills.

Format Pointers
Places name at top center for easy viewing (top right is also acceptable).

Uses bold font to distinguish identification section and headings from remaining text.

Creates visual appeal through custom format rather than commonly used template, short readable sections focusing on targeted qualifications, and streamlined bulleted lists.

Diversity Considerations
Follows standard format and rules for résumés for application with U.S. company. Specific formats vary for specific countries and federal government.

Cengage Learning

FIGURE 13.4 **REFERENCES PAGE**

NED AVERS
45 Chester Street
Watertown, IA 62205
(530) 443-1565
na@gmail.com

REFERENCES

Leona Harden
Manager of Teller Services
Bank of Iowa
345 Main Street
Watertown, IA 65009
530-555-3209
lharden@bankofiowa.com
Relationship: Immediate supervisor, 2011 to 2013

Fred Murray, Instructor
Accounting Department
Watertown Community College
Postal Drop ACC 201
Watertown, IA 65009
530-855-8956
fmurray@wcc.edu
Relationship: Academic adviser and instructor for accounting courses

Linda Larsen, Manager
Watertown Boys and Girls Club
437 Oak Street
Watertown, IA 65009
530-855-3232
llarsen@wbgc.org

Relationship: Supervisor for volunteer activities

● Includes professor and immediate supervisors as references, but excludes friends, relatives, or clergy to avoid potential bias.

● Includes for each reference full contact information, including email address if available and relationship to job applicant.

Format Pointers
Prepares reference page at same time as résumé and makes available immediately after successful interview. Paper (color, texture, and size) and print type match résumé.

Balances references attractively.

Cengage Learning

Just consider recent struggles you might have faced in dealing with viruses and unwelcomed emails, attempting to access nonworking links, and more. Before sending your résumé into cyberspace, follow these suggestions to ensure that your electronic submission is both professional and technically effective:

- **Choose postings for your résumé with purpose.** Online résumé postings are not confidential. Once your résumé is online, anyone can read it, including your current employer. You might also begin to receive junk mail and cold calls from companies who see your résumé online; even more seriously, you could become a victim of identity theft. To protect your privacy online, limit personal information disclosed in the résumé and post only to sites with password protection allowing you to approve the release of your résumé to specific employers. Dating your electronic résumé will also prevent embarrassment should your employer find an old version of your résumé, which could occur as result of exchange of résumés between career sites and delays in updating postings.

Protect your references' privacy by omitting their names when posting online. Withholding this information will prevent unwelcomed calls by recruiters and other inappropriate contacts and threats to privacy. Because technology allows broadcast of your résumé to all available positions on a career site, read postings

FIGURE 13.5 **FUNCTIONAL RÉSUMÉ**

SAMUEL WINSTON
123 Franklin Street #12
Bakersfield, CA 92345
213-505-1234
swinston@aol.com

OBJECTIVE

A position in Medical/Pharmaceutical Sales

PROFILE

- Energetic sales professional with a knack for matching customers with optimal products and services to meet their specific needs. Consistently received excellent feedback from customers.

- More than two years as a medical doctor in hospitals and clinics in the U.S. and Europe.

- Lived and traveled abroad, developing a keen sensitivity to people from diverse cultural backgrounds. Fluent in Spanish and Italian; presently studying French.

- Computer skills include MS Word, Excel, and Internet applications.

SELECTED ACCOMPLISHMENTS

Sales & Customer Relations

- Generated the highest sales volume in department within the first two months of hire, resulting in an unprecedented salary promotion.

- Transferred to highest paid commission area in the store after only four months.

- Cultivated excellent relations with customers and significant repeat business.

- Consistently maintained professional demeanor, treating customers and coworkers with friendliness, patience and respect. Particularly known for success with "challenging" customers.

Medical Expertise

- Collaborated with research team at Bakersfield Hospital in the study of Pre-Arrest Scoring & Outcome of CPR Cardiac Markers in Rapid Evaluation of Acute Myocardial Infarction.

- Worked as Emergency Medical Technician for the Bakersfield Fire Department, providing emergency medical care to patients in transit to hospital, including accident, stroke, and cardiac cases.

- Volunteered at Bakersfield Community Clinic, treating immigrants with medical and social needs.

WORK HISTORY

2014–present, Retail Sales Associate, MARSHALL'S, Bakersfield, CA

2010–2014, Emergency Medical Technician, Bakersfield Fire Department, Bakersfield, CA

2012–2014, Volunteer, Bakersfield Community Clinic, Bakersfield, CA

EDUCATION & TRAINING

B.S. in Business Administration, 2014, California State University, Bakersfield, CA
CPR and EKG Training, 2010
Associate's Degree, Emergency Medical Technician, Bakersfield Communication College, Bakersfield, CA

- Includes clear objective and descriptive summary statements to grab attention and invite close reading.

- Arranges qualifications into sections that emphasize applicant's relevant skills and accomplishments. Uses headings that show applicant knows what skills are needed to succeed in sales.

- Uses employers' names and dates to match skills with work history.

- Limits education and work history to quick overview of basic qualifications and accommodates employers' preference for chronological format.

- Lists references for employer convenience and to strengthen résumé.

Format Pointers

Places name at top center, where it can be easily seen.

Uses bold font to distinguish identification section and headings from remaining text.

Creates visual appeal with easy-to-read columnar format and balanced page arrangement.

Cengage Learning

carefully, and apply only to those that match your qualifications. This action improves the efficiency of the job selection process for the company and the applicant, and depicts fair, ethical behavior.

- **Don't hurry.** The speed, convenience, and informality of filling in online boxes or composing an email cover letter for an attached résumé can lead to sloppiness that reflects negatively on your abilities and attitude. Make sure every aspect of your electronic submission is top-notch just as you would for a print résumé. Provide all information exactly as requested; write concise, clear statements relevant to the job sought, and proofread carefully for grammatical and spelling errors. If you direct an employer to an electronic portfolio, devote necessary time to make it attractive, informative, and technically sound. Double-check your files to ensure they can be opened and retain an appealing format. Finally, read the posting carefully to learn how long your résumé will remain active, how to update it, and how to delete it from the site.

- **Include your résumé in the format requested by the employer or job bank.** You could be instructed to send the résumé as an attachment to the message or include it in the body of an email message, known as an **inline résumé**. The inline résumé is becoming the preferred choice as fear of computer viruses and daily email overload prevent employers from opening attachments. Unless instructed to send your attachment in a specific format such as Word, save your résumé and cover letter in one file, beginning with the cover letter as an ASCII or Rich Text Format file with line length limited to 65 characters and spacing. This plain text version, referred to as a **text résumé**, removes formatting and lacks the appeal of your designed résumé; however, you can be confident that an employer can open the file and won't have to spend time "cleaning up" your résumé if it doesn't transmit correctly. For this reason, you'll also paste the text version of your résumé below your email message when sending an inline résumé.

As an added safeguard, send yourself and a couple of friends a copy of the résumé and see how it looks on different computers before sending it out to an employer. If you wish, follow-up with a print résumé and cover letter on high-quality paper.

- **Include a keyword summary after the identification section.** You'll want to grab the employer's attention by placing the keywords on the first screen (within the first 24 lines of text). Providing this relevant information will motivate the employer to keep scrolling down to see how the keywords are supported rather than click to the next résumé.

- **Email a cover message to accompany an online résumé.** Some companies consider this cover email message to be prescreening for a job interview. Write a formal, grammatically correct message just as you would if you were sending an application letter in the mail.

Some print résumés become electronic files when they are scanned by the employer into an electronic database where they can be read and sorted by a computer. Companies of all sizes are using **electronic applicant-tracking systems** to increase efficiency of processing the volume of résumés received in a competitive market. Such systems store scanned résumés in an electronic database where they can be sorted by keywords, with a resulting ranking of applicants. The system can also automatically prepare letters of rejection and interview offers and store the résumés of hired applicants for future promotion consideration.

When seeking a job with a company that scans résumés into an electronic database, you will need to submit a **scannable résumé** as well as a print résumé that will be read by a person. If you are unsure whether a company scans résumés, call and ask. If still in doubt, take the safe route and submit your résumé in both formats.

FORMATTING A SCANNABLE RÉSUMÉ

To ensure that the scanner can read your résumé accurately and clearly, you must prepare a plain résumé with no special formatting. Follow these guidelines to prepare an electronic résumé that can be scanned accurately:

- **Use popular, nondecorative typefaces.** Typefaces such as Cambria and Times New Roman are clear and distinct and will not lose clarity in scanning.

- **Use 10- to 14-point font.** Computers cannot read small, tight print well. With a larger font, your résumé may extend to two pages, but page length is not an issue because a computer is reading the résumé.

- **Do not include italics, underlining, open bullets, or graphic lines and boxes.** Use boldface or all capitals

---

inline résumé a résumé included in the body of an email message

text résumé a plain text (unformatted) version of a résumé

electronic applicant-tracking systems systems that increase the efficiency of processing résumés by storing scanned résumés in an electronic database where they can be sorted by keywords, with a resulting ranking of applicants

scannable résumé a résumé formatted to ensure a scanner can accurately read and convert it into a digital format for emphasis. Italicized letters that touch and underlining that runs into the text result in a garbled scanned image. Design elements such as graphic lines, shading, and shadowing effects can confuse equipment. Use solid bullets (•) because an open bullet (◦) could be read as an "o".

- **Use ample white space.** Use at least one-inch margins. Leave plenty of white space between the sections of a résumé so the computer recognizes the partitions.

- **Print on one side of white, standard-size paper with sharp laser print.** Colored and textured paper scans poorly, and the scanner can pick up dirty specks on a photocopy.

- **Use a traditional résumé format.** Complex layouts that simulate catalogs or newspaper columns can confuse scanners.

- **Do not fold or staple your résumé.** If you must fold it, do not do so on a line of text.

MAKING A SCANNABLE RÉSUMÉ SEARCHABLE

You have two concerns in preparing a scannable résumé. You want to (1) be certain information is presented in a manner the computer can read, and (2) maximize the number of "hits" your résumé receives in a computerized résumé search. Follow these guidelines for making your print résumé searchable:

- **Position your name as the first readable item on the page.** Follow with your address, phone number, fax number, and email below your name on separate lines.

- **Add powerful keywords in a separate section called "Keywords" or "Keyword Summary" that follows the identification.** To identify keywords, ask yourself what words best describe your qualifications. Make maximum use of industry jargon and standard, easily recognizable abbreviations (e.g., B.A., M.S.) in the keyword summary and the body of the résumé, as these buzzwords will likely be matches with the computer's keywords.

- **Format the keyword summary to maximize hits.** Capitalize the first letter of each word, and separate each keyword with a period. Position keywords describing your most important qualifications first, and then move to the least important ones. Order is important because some systems stop scanning after the first 80 keywords. The usual order is (a) job

Gustavo Frazao/Shutterstock.com

THE POWER OF KEYWORDS

title, occupation, or career field; (b) education; and (c) essential skills for a specific position. Be certain to include keywords that describe interpersonal traits, such as *adaptable, flexible, sensitive, team player, willing to travel, ethical, industrious, innovative, open minded,* and *detail oriented.*

- **Support your keywords with specific facts in the body of the résumé.** Use synonyms of your keywords in the body in the event the computer does not recognize the keyword (e.g., use *M.B.A.* in the keyword summary and *Master of Business Administration* in the body; use *presentation graphics software* in the keyword summary and a specific program in the body). One unfortunate applicant reported using "computer-assisted design" consistently throughout his résumé when the computer was searching for "CAD." Also, use a specific date of graduation in the education section. Some computer programs read two dates beside an institution to mean the applicant did not earn the degree (e.g., 2007–2011).

The scannable résumé Sara Barton prepared when seeking an entry-level computer Web development position appears in Figure 13.6. Note how she presents qualifications that correspond to the company/job profile posted at your companion website at **www.cengagebrain.com**. The scannable résumé is formatted for scanning into an electronic database to be matched with employer requirements.

13-4 SUPPLEMENTING A RÉSUMÉ

Some candidates feel their career accomplishments are not appropriately captured in a standard résumé. Two additional tools for communicating your qualifications and abilities are the portfolio and the employment video.

FIGURE 13.6 **SCANNABLE RÉSUMÉ**

SAMUEL WINSTON
123 Franklin Street #12
Bakersfield, CA 92345
213-505-1234
swinston@aol.com

OBJECTIVE

A position in Medical/Pharmaceutical Sales.

PROFILE

- Energetic sales professional with a knack for matching customers with optimal products and services to meet their specific needs. Consistently received excellent feedback from customers.

- More than two years as a medical doctor in hospitals and clinics in the U.S. and Europe.

- Lived and traveled abroad, developing a keen sensitivity to people from diverse cultural backgrounds. Fluent in Spanish and Italian; presently studying French.

- Computer skills include MS Word, Excel, and Internet applications.

SELECTED ACCOMPLISHMENTS

Sales & Customer Relations

- Generated the highest sales volume in department within the first two months of hire, resulting in an unprecedented salary promotion.

- Transferred to highest paid commission area in the store after only four months.

- Cultivated excellent relations with customers and significant repeat business.

- Consistently maintained professional demeanor, treating customers and coworkers with friendliness, patience and respect. Particularly known for success with "challenging" customers.

Medical Expertise

- Collaborated with research team at Bakersfield Hospital in the study of Pre-Arrest Scoring & Outcome of CPR Cardiac Markers in Rapid Evaluation of Acute Myocardial Infarction.

- Worked as Emergency Medical Technician for the Bakersfield Fire Department, providing emergency medical care to patients in transit to hospital, including accident, stroke, and cardiac cases.

- Volunteered at Bakersfield Community Clinic, treating immigrants with medical and social needs.

WORK HISTORY

2014–present, Retail Sales Associate, MARSHALL'S, Bakersfield, CA

2010–2014, Emergency Medical Technician, Bakersfield Fire Department, Bakersfield, CA

2012–2014, Volunteer, Bakersfield Community Clinic, Bakersfield, CA

EDUCATION & TRAINING

B.S. in Business Administration, 2014, California State University, Bakersfield, CA CPR and EKG Training, 2010
Associate's Degree, Emergency Medical Technician, Bakersfield Communication College, Bakersfield, CA

- Positions name as first readable item.

- Includes position sought and reason to hire in separate section.

- Includes "Keyword Summary" section listing qualifications that match job description.

- Edges out competition by expanding on related experience and work achievements.

- Omits references to use space for additional qualifications; references furnished when requested.

- Includes date of last revision to avoid confusion or embarrassment if résumé is accessed after hiring.

Format Pointers
Keeps résumé simple and readable by computer: easy-to-read font of 10 to 14 points; solid bullets; and no italics, underlining, or graphic lines or borders.

Mails cover letter and print résumé unfolded and unstapled in large envelope.

Cengage Learning

13-4a Professional Portfolios

The **professional portfolio** (also called the *electronic portfolio* or *e-portfolio* when presented in a digital format) can be used to illustrate past activities, projects, and accomplishments. It is a collection of artifacts that demonstrate your communication, people, and technical skills. Although portfolios were once thought of as only for writers, artists, or photographers, they are now seen as appropriate for other fields of work when the applicant wants to showcase abilities.

Many portfolios are now presented in digital format, making the portfolio easier to organize and distribute to prospective employers via a website or burned to a CD or other media. With the availability of user-friendly software, college campuses are offering e-portfolio systems that aid students in reflecting on their experiences and producing e-portfolios. Just as students currently are not asked if they have an email account, predictions are that soon they will also be expected to have "a Web space that represents their learning and their assessment."[10]

A clear understanding of your audience's needs and your qualifications will allow you to develop a logical organizational structure for your portfolio. Some possible items to include are

- **sample speeches with digitized audio or video clips of the delivery,**
- **performance appraisals,**
- **awards,**
- **certificates of completion,**
- **reports, proposals, or written documents prepared for classes or on the job,**
- **brochures or programs describing workshops attended, and**
- **commendation messages, records, or surveys showing client or customer satisfaction with service.**

After selecting the items for inclusion in your portfolio, select the appropriate software or binder you will use to showcase your accomplishments. Once you're organized, you can add items that demonstrate you have the characteristics the employer is seeking. Maintain your portfolio even after you are hired because it can demonstrate your eligibility for promotion, salary increase, or advanced training, or even justify why you should not be laid off.

For illustration purposes, take a look at Samuel Barkley's electronic portfolio shown in Figure 13.7 on the next page that was created using a Microsoft Web template and posted to her personal website.

13-4b Employment Videos

A video recording can be used to extend the impact of the printed résumé visually. A video can capture your stage presence and ability to speak effectively and add a human dimension to the written process. Current technology enables applicants to embed video segments into **multimedia résumés** created with presentation software such as Camtasia Studio and sent to prospective employers on CD or DVD or posted on the applicant's personal website.

Video résumés, which job seekers post on sites such as YouTube, are the latest trend in developing creative job qualifications. You can learn some important lessons for your video project by taking a look at the abundance of good and bad examples already posted. If possible, solicit

professional portfolio
a portfolio presented in digital format and distributed to prospective employers via a website, CD/DVD, or other media; also called an *electronic portfolio* or *e-portfolio*

multimedia résumé a résumé created with presentation software such as Camtasia Studio and sent to prospective employers on CD/DVD or posted on the applicant's personal website

video résumé a résumé created as a video for posting on the Web on sites such as YouTube

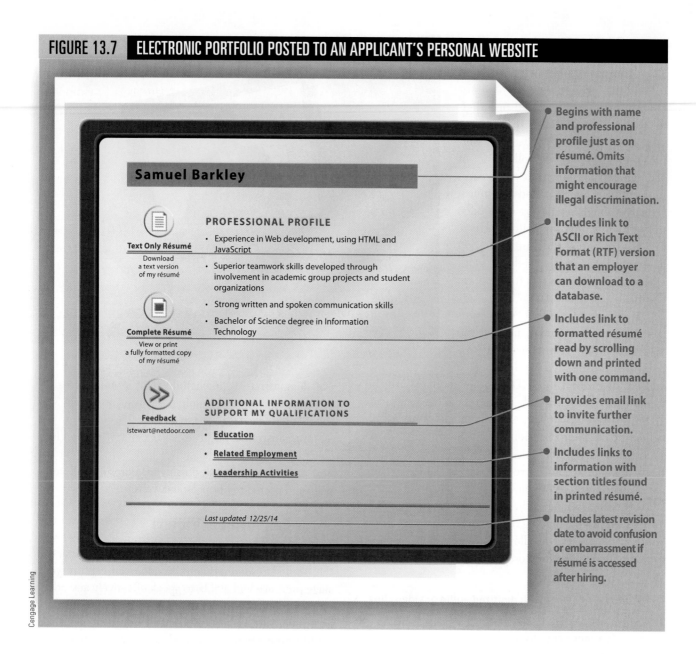

Samuel Barkley

Text Only Résumé
Download
a text version
of my résumé

Complete Résumé
View or print
a fully formatted copy
of my résumé

Feedback
istewart@netdoor.com

PROFESSIONAL PROFILE

- Experience in Web development, using HTML and JavaScript

- Superior teamwork skills developed through involvement in academic group projects and student organizations

- Strong written and spoken communication skills

- Bachelor of Science degree in Information Technology

ADDITIONAL INFORMATION TO SUPPORT MY QUALIFICATIONS

- **Education**

- **Related Employment**

- **Leadership Activities**

Last updated 12/25/14

Callouts:
- Begins with name and professional profile just as on résumé. Omits information that might encourage illegal discrimination.
- Includes link to ASCII or Rich Text Format (RTF) version that an employer can download to a database.
- Includes link to formatted résumé read by scrolling down and printed with one command.
- Provides email link to invite further communication.
- Includes links to information with section titles found in printed résumé.
- Includes latest revision date to avoid confusion or embarrassment if résumé is accessed after hiring.

Cengage Learning

---

the help of someone with film experience and follow these simple suggestions for creating a visually enhanced résumé that is brief, showcases your key qualifications, and reflects your personality:[11]

- Keep your video simple with one stationary shot using a good camera and tripod. Avoid gimmicky effects and excessive panning that distract from the message.

- Use proper lighting, making sure that the employer can see your face. Avoid light behind you that casts shadows.

- Invest in a good-quality microphone, and speak clearly and at an appropriate pace for easy listening.

- Choose clothing appropriate for the job you are seeking. Video yourself wearing different clothing, and watch the video to select the ideal choice. Avoid clothing that gaps and bunches when you sit, as well as bright colors and close patterns that tend to vibrate when filmed.

- Edit your video to eliminate dead air and other imperfections that detract from a professional image.

Employment videos are more commonly used to obtain employment in career fields for which verbal delivery or visual performance is a key element. These fields include broadcasting and the visual and performing arts. The following guidelines apply when preparing an employment video:

- **Be sure the video makes a professional appearance and is complimentary to you. A "home movie" quality recording will be a liability instead of an asset to your application.**
- **Avoid long "talking head" segments. Include segments that reflect you in a variety of activities; shots that include samples of your work are also desirable.**
- **Remember that visual media (such as photographs and videos) encourage the potential employer to focus on your physical characteristics and attributes, which might lead to undesired stereotyping and discrimination.**

Be sure to advertise the availability of your portfolio and employment video to maximize its exposure. List your URL address in the identification section of your résumé. In your application letter, motivate the prospective employer to view your portfolio or video by describing the types of information included. Talk enthusiastically about the detailed supplementary information available during your job interview, and encourage the interviewer to view it when convenient. Note Marin Jossey's promotion of her work in website development when you read her application letter later in this chapter (see Figure 13.8).

13-5 COMPOSING APPLICATION MESSAGES

When employers invite you to send either a print or electronic résumé, they may expect you to include an **application message** (also known as a *cover message*). Because most applications are now made online, fewer employers ask for application letters. However, you should be knowledgeable about composing an application message for those situations in which they are expected.

As you have learned, a résumé summarizes information related to the job's requirements and the applicant's qualifications. An application message complements a résumé by speaking more directly to a specific job posting by (1) introducing the applicant, (2) attracting interest to the résumé, and (3) interpreting the résumé in terms of employer benefits.

Because it creates interest and points out employer benefits, the application message is persuasive and thus written inductively. It is designed to convince an employer that qualifications are adequate just as a sales message is designed to convince a buyer that a product will satisfy a need. Like sales messages, application messages can be either solicited or unsolicited. Job advertisements *solicit* applications. Unsolicited application messages have greater need for attention-getters; otherwise, solicited and unsolicited application messages are based on the same principles.

Unsolicited application messages are the same basic message (perhaps with slight modifications) sent to many prospective employers. By sending unsolicited messages, you increase your chances of locating potential openings and possibly alert employers to needs they had not previously identified for someone of your abilities. However, sending unsolicited messages has some disadvantages. Because the employer's specific needs are not known, the opening paragraph will likely be more general (less targeted to a specific position) than the opening paragraph in solicited messages. The process could also be time consuming.

Marin Jossey wrote the letter in Figure 13.8 to accompany a chronological résumé she prepared after completing the company/job profile of a marketing manager. The time Marin devoted to analyzing the job, the company, and her qualifications was well spent.

13-5a Persuasive Organization

A persuasive message is designed to convince the reader to take action, which in this case is to read the résumé and invite you to an interview. Because an application message is persuasive, organize it as you would a sales message:

Sales Message	Application Message
Gets attention	Gets attention
Introduces product	Introduces qualifications
Presents evidence	Presents evidence
Encourages action	Encourages action
=	=
(sells a product, service, or idea)	(results in an interview)

Like a well-written sales message, a well-written application message uses a central selling feature as a theme. The central selling feature is introduced in the first or second paragraph and stressed in paragraphs that

application message a message placed on top of the résumé so it can be read first by the employer; also called a *cover message*

unsolicited application message an unrequested message sent to many prospective employers that contains the same basic message

FIGURE 13.8 — EXAMPLE OF AN APPLICATION LETTER

MARIN JOSSEY
215 Clark Way, Apartment 5
Boise, ID 85555
Home: 208-355-1122 | Cell: 208-434-2484
mjossey@gmail.com

May 8, 2016

Joseph Jimenez
VP Marketing
Turrell's, Inc.
1515 Market Street
Seattle, WA 80025

Re: Marketing manager position advertised on Monster.com

Dear Ms. Ramos:

I read your advertisement for a marketing manager with great interest. If you are seeking to augment your leadership team with an experienced and accomplished marketing professional known for breakthrough results, please call me for an interview.

As FashionXpress's marketing manager since 2013, I direct all phases of both the creative and technical elements of marketing initiatives, including data mining, brand creation, print/Web collateral development, lead generation, channel partner cultivation, and customer segmentation/profiling as well as CRM and acquisition strategies.

Perhaps most importantly, I offer a history of proven results, as evidenced by the following marketing accomplishments for my current employer:

- **Captured a 28% expansion in customer base since 2013,** achieved during a period of overall decline in the retail industry.

- **Led national marketing campaign** (comprised of trade show, media, and PR initiatives) of company's newly launched technology services division.

- **Developed and executed SEO strategy** that achieved and sustained top 3 rankings on Google and Yahoo! (organic, nonpaid results) for key product search terms.

- **Oversaw creation of new company logo** and rebranded 100+ products to cement a cohesive corporate identity and support new company direction.

Given the opportunity, I'm confident in my ability to achieve similar groundbreaking marketing results for Turrell's, Inc.

Mr. Jimenez, I would welcome the chance to discuss your marketing objectives and ways I can help you attain them. Feel free to call me at 208-355-1122 to arrange a meeting. I look forward to speaking with you.

Sincerely,

Marin Jossey
Marin Jossey

Addresses letter to specific person, using correct name and job title.

Identifies how applicant learned of position, specific position sought, and background.

Discusses how education relates to job requirements.

Uses bulleted list to highlight qualifications corresponding to job requirements.

Introduces résumé and website for additional information.

Encourages employer to take action without sounding pushy or apologetic.

Format Pointers
Formats as formal business letter because message is accompanying print résumé.

Abbreviated email message including online résumé in ASCII or RTF format would be appropriate for electronic submission.

Uses same high-quality, standard size paper as for résumé in neutral color.

Includes writer's address and contact information.

follow. Two to four paragraphs are normally sufficient for supporting evidence. Consider order of importance as a basis for their sequence, with the most significant aspects of your preparation coming first.

GAIN THE RECEIVER'S ATTENTION

To gain attention, begin the message by identifying the job sought and describing how your qualifications fit the job requirements. This information will provide instant confirmation that you are a qualified applicant for an open position. An employer who reads hundreds of application letters and résumés will appreciate this direct, concise approach.

For an announced job, you should indicate in the first paragraph how you learned of the position—for example, employee referral, customer referral, executive referral, newspaper advertising, or job fair. Your disclosure will confirm you are seeking an open job as well as facilitate evaluation of the company's recruiting practices. Note that the opening of the letter in Figure 13.8 indicates the applicant learned of the position through a referral from a company employee.

An opening for an unsolicited message must be more persuasive: you must convince the interviewer to continue to read your qualifications even though a job might not exist. As in the opening of a solicited message, indicate the type of position sought and your qualifications, but be more creative in gaining attention. The following paragraph uses the applicant's knowledge of recent company developments and an intense interest in the company's future to gain receiver attention.

> **In the past three years, OfficeWorx has experienced phenomenal growth through various acquisitions, mergers, and market expansion. With this growth comes new opportunities, new customers, and the need for new team players to work in store management. While following the growth of OfficeWorx, I have become determined to join this exciting team and am eager to show you that my educational background, leadership abilities, and internship experience qualify me for the job.**

PROVIDE EVIDENCE OF QUALIFICATIONS

For graduates entering the world of full-time work for the first time, educational backgrounds are usually more impressive than work histories. They can benefit from

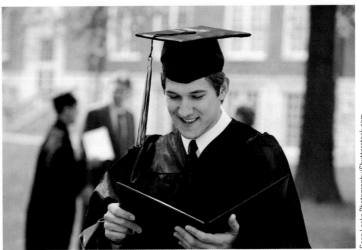

Sean Locke Photography/Shutterstock.com

interpreting their educational experiences as meaningful, job-related experiences. An applicant for a human resources position should do more than merely report having taken courses in organizational behavior.

> **In my business communication class, I could see specific application of principles encountered in my organizational behavior and marketing classes. Questions about leadership and motivation seemed to recur throughout the course: What really motivates people? Why do people fear change? How can those fears be overcome? What communication practices can be used to motivate people and help them accept change? The importance of the communication was a focus of many courses and my research report, "How to Get the Most from Others."**

Your application message will not necessarily refer to information learned in a class. Recognizing that managers must be tactful (a point on which the person reading the message will surely agree), the applicant included some details of a class. That technique is basic in persuasion: Do not just say a product or idea is good; say what makes it good. Do not just say that an educational or work experience was beneficial; say what made it so.

By making paragraphs long enough to include interpretation of experiences on the present or previous job, you show an employer that you are well prepared for your next job. For example, the following excerpt from an applicant whose only work experience was at a retail outlet is short and general:

> **I have been the assistant manager at Fashion Flash for the past year and have helped supervise a team of five associates. I received high performance evaluations for my work as a leader.**

Added details and interpretation could make the value of the work experience more convincing:

> **As assistant manager at Fashion Flash, I have learned to listen to associates' concerns and make them feel valued by acting on their suggestions. I have trained associates in policies and procedures, and learned to reinforce those procedures for existing employees. I am able to preserve a good working relationship with my team even in sometimes difficult conversations.**

The applicant has called attention to qualities that managers like to see in employees: willingness to listen, speed, accuracy, concern for clients or customers, a positive attitude, fairness, and tact. As a learning experience, the Fashion Flash job has taught or reinforced principles that the employer sees can be transferred to the job being sought.

In this section, you can discuss qualifications you have developed by participating in student organizations, student government, athletics, or community organizations. Be specific in describing gained skills that can be applied directly on the job—for example, organizational, leadership, spoken and written communication skills, and budgeting and financial management. You can also use your involvement as a channel for discussing important personal traits vital to the success of a business, such as interpersonal skills, motivation, imagination, responsibility, and team orientation.

> **For the past year, I have served as treasurer for Alpha Chi Epsilon. In that duty, I have managed a $200,000 annual budget. By coordinating our yearly charitable fund-raising event, I have exercised leadership and organizational and communication skills.**

Finally, end this section with an indirect reference to the résumé. If you refer to it in the first or second paragraph, readers might turn from the message at that point and look at the résumé. Avoid the obvious statement "Enclosed please find my résumé" or "A résumé is enclosed." Instead, refer indirectly to the résumé while restating your qualifications. The following sentence emphasizes that references can confirm the applicant's qualifications:

> **References listed on the enclosed résumé would be glad to comment on my marketing education and experience.**

ENCOURAGE ACTION

Once you have presented your qualifications and referred to your enclosed résumé, the next move is to encourage the receiver to extend an invitation for an interview. The goal is to introduce the idea of action without apologizing for doing so and without being demanding or "pushy." If the final paragraph (action closing) of your message is preceded by impressive paragraphs, you need not press hard for a response. Just mentioning the idea of a future discussion is probably sufficient. If you have significant related experience that you have developed as a central selling feature, mentioning this experience in the action closing adds unity and stresses your strongest qualification one last time. Forceful statements about *when* and *how* to respond are unnecessary and irritating. Avoid these frequently made errors:

- **Setting a date.** "May I have an appointment with you on January 15?" The date you name could be inconvenient; or even if it is convenient for the employer, your forwardness in setting it could be resented.

- **Expressing doubt.** "If you agree," "I hope you will," and "Should you decide" use subjunctive words that indicate lack of confidence.

- **Sounding apologetic.** "May I take some of your time" or "I know how busy you are" might seem considerate, but an apology is inappropriate when discussing ways you can contribute to a company.

- **Sounding overconfident.** "I will call you next week to set an appointment time that works for both of us." This statement is presumptuous and egotistical.

- **Giving permission to call.** "You may call me at 555-6543." By making the call sound like a privilege ("may call") you could alienate the reader. Implied meaning: You are very selective about the calls you take, but the employer does qualify.

The following sentences are possible closing sentences that refer to an invitation to interview. They are not intended as model sentences that should appear in your message. Because finding the right job is so important, you will be well rewarded for the time and thought you invest in original wording.

- **"When a date and time can be arranged, I would like to talk with you."** The statement does not indicate who will do the arranging, and the meeting place and the subject of the conversation are understood.

- "I would appreciate an opportunity to discuss the marketing assistant's job with you." The indirect reference to action is not forceful. However, if the applicant has impressive qualifications, the reader will want an interview and will not need to be pushed.

- "I look forward to talking with you about how my skills and experiences can benefit Beck Restaurant Group." The statement asks for the interview and re-emphasizes the applicant's strong qualifications.

> ~~I hope you will ...~~
>
> ~~I know how busy you are ...~~
>
> ~~You may call me at 555-6543 ...~~
>
> When a date and time can be arranged, I would like to talk with you.

13-5b General Writing Guidelines

An excellent application message might be the most difficult message you ever attempt to write. It's natural to feel uncomfortable writing about yourself; however, your confidence will increase as you study the wealth of model documents available through your career services center and other sources. The writing principles you've been introduced to in this chapter should help you write a thoughtful, original message that impresses the interviewer. Instead of standard verbiage included in dozens of models, your self-marketing connects *your* experiences to your future with a specific company and reflects *your* personality and values. The following writing techniques will help distinguish your application message from the competition:

- **Substitute fresh, original expressions that reflect contemporary language.** Overly casual expressions and overused statements will give your message a dull, unimaginative tone. Obvious ideas such as "This is an application," "I read your ad," and "I am writing to apply for" are sufficiently understood without making direct statements. With the application message *and* résumé in hand, a reader learns nothing from "I am enclosing my résumé for your review." Observe caution in choosing overused words such as *applicant*, *application*, *opening*, *position*, *vacancy*, and *interview*.

- **Avoid overuse of I and writer-focused statements.** Because the message is designed to sell your services, some use of *I* is natural and expected; but restrict the number of times *I* is used, especially as the first word in a paragraph. Focus on providing specific evidence that you can meet the company's needs. The employer is not interested in reading about your need to earn more income, to be closer to your work, to have more pleasant surroundings, or to gain greater advancement opportunities.

- **Avoid unconvincing generalizations that could sound boastful.** Self-confidence is commendable, but overconfidence (or worse still, just plain bragging) is objectionable. Overly strong adjectives, self-judgmental terms, and unsupported generalizations damage your credibility. Instead of labeling your performance as "superior" or "excellent," or describing yourself as "an efficient, technically skilled team player," give supporting facts that show the interviewer you can deliver on what you're selling.

- **Tailor the message to the employer's need.** To impress the interviewer that your message is not a generic one sent to everyone, provide requested information, and communicate an understanding of the particular company, job requirements, and field.

  - **Provide requested information.** Job listings often request certain information: "Must provide own transportation and be willing to travel. Give educational background, work experience, and salary expected." Discuss these points in your application message. Preferably, the question of salary is left until the interview, allowing you to focus your message on your contributions to the company—not what you want from the company (money). Discussion of salary isn't meaningful until after a mutually successful interview; however, if an ad requests a statement about it, the message should address it. You may give a minimum figure or range, indicate

Vasiliy Koval/Shutterstock.com

willingness to accept a figure that is customary for work of that type, or indicate a preference for discussing salary at the interview.

- **Communicate knowledge of the company, job requirements, and language of the field.** Your statements about a company's rapid expansion or competitive advantage show you really are interested in the company, read widely, do more than you are required to do, and gather information before making decisions. However, phrase these statements carefully to avoid the perception of insincere flattery. For example, referring to the employer as "*the* leader in the field," "*the* best in the business," or "a great company" could appear as an attempt to get a favorable decision as a reward for making a complimentary statement. To reflect your understanding of the job requirements, use indirect statements that are informative and tactful. Direct statements such as "The requirements of this job are ..." presents information the employer presumes you already know; "An auditor should be able to ..." and "Sales personnel should avoid ..." sound like a lecture and could be perceived as condescending. Discussing experiences related to a specific job requirement or your preference for work that requires this skill reveals your understanding without a direct statement. Including terminology commonly used by the profession allows you to communicate clearly in terms the reader understands; it also saves space and implies your background in the field.

- **Focus on strengths and portray a positive attitude.** Concentrate on the positive aspects of your education or experience that have prepared you for the particular job. Apologizing for a shortcoming or admitting failure only weakens your case and raises questions about your self-esteem. Do not discuss your current employer's shortcomings. Regardless of how negatively you perceive your present employer, that perception has little to do with your prospective employer's needs. Also, if you speak negatively of your present employer, you could be perceived as someone who would do the same to the next employer.

13-5c Finishing Touches

The importance of professional formatting and careful proofreading of job application messages is generally understood. Still, employers frequently voice concern with the sloppiness and unprofessional appearance and content of electronic submissions. To survive the skeptical eye of an interviewer scanning for ways to reject an applicant, allow yourself time to produce a professional-looking document regardless of the presentation or delivery option you've chosen.

In regard to preparing an application message for email submission, career experts recommend formatting it as a business letter with the complete address of the company exactly as presented in a letter sent by mail and a formal closing such as "Sincerely." To help people reach you, include a full signature block with your mailing and email addresses, and phone number(s). The recipient can easily contact you without opening your attachments. Although seemingly unnecessary, the email address is useful when a recipient forwards your email to someone else who might want to reply to you but cannot see your email address. Exclude quotes from your signature block that could be misunderstood or offensive. Add an enclosure notation drawing attention to your résumé attachment provided as requested by the employer, such as "Résumé attached as Word document."

To compete with the high volumes of junk mail, daily messages, and fear of computer viruses, you must provide a motive for an interviewer to open an unexpected message from an unknown person. Messages with missing or vague subject lines might be ignored or deleted immediately. To bring attention to your message, include the name of the person referring you to the position directly in the subject line or mention your email is a follow-up to a conversation, for example, "RE: Follow-up: Résumé for ...." If the message is unsolicited, describe the specific value you can add to the company, for example, "Résumé for Forensics Accountant with Extensive ACL Skills." Stay away from tricks such as marking an email "urgent" or adding "re" to pass your message off as a reply to an earlier message.

Check any instructions provided by the prospective employer, and follow them precisely. Typically, however, you will want to send a complete letter and copy of your résumé by regular mail as a follow-up to the email submission. Figure 13.9 shows a sample application email an applicant sent after talking with a prospective employer at a career fair.

FIGURE 13.9 | **EXAMPLE OF APPLICATION MESSAGE SENT BY EMAIL**

New Message

To: [cwalters@idahostatebank.com]
From: rortiz@hotmail.com
Subject: Career Fair Follow-up: Résumé for Roberto Ortiz

Attachment: roberto_ortiz_resume.docx

Dear Ms. Walters:

It was a pleasure meeting you at the career fair this morning. The opportunities offered in commercial lending identify your company as a leader in today's financial products marketplace.
My experience and knowledge of banking and commercial lending enable me to be a valuable asset to your company:

- Knowledge of banking and commercial lending practices, necessary documentation, and consumer laws.
- Demonstrated commitment to delivering excellent customer service to customers and clients.
- Hardworking and achievement oriented, as demonstrated by part-time employment throughout college, leadership, and maintenance of a 3.6 GPA.

After you have reviewed the attached résumé that you requested for additional information about my education and related work experience, please message me so we can discuss my joining Idaho State Bank.

Best Regards,

Roberto Ortiz
Cell: 208-556-8899
Email: rortiz@hotmail.com
Online Résumé: linkedin.com/in/robertoortiz
LinkedIn Profile: sites.google.com/site/robertoortiz
Résumé text included in email below and attached as MS Word attachment.

- Provides specific subject line that ensures message will be opened.
- Email program automatically shows attached file containing résumé.
- Reveals how applicant learned of position and confirms knowledge of and interest in company.
- Condenses persuasive application message to one screen. Avoids tendency to send impersonal message stating résumé is attached.
- Introduces résumé and reminds interviewer that submission was requested.
- Encourages employer to take action without sounding pushy or apologetic.
- Includes email address in .sig file to simplify access to all contact information without opening attached résumé.
- Includes enclosure notation pointing out that résumé is sent as required by the company.

Format Pointers
Formats as formal business letter with complete address exactly as done when job credentials are sent by mail. Complete letter and printed copy of résumé will be sent as follow-up to email.

Cengage Learning

Include these steps in your finishing phase:

- Regardless of your delivery option, address your application letter or email message to the specific individual who is responsible for hiring for the position you are seeking, rather than sending the document to the "Human Resources Department" or "To Whom It May Concern." If necessary, consult the company's annual report or website, or call the company to locate this information.

- Verify the correct spelling, job title, and address, and send a personalized message to the appropriate individual.

- Keep the message short and easy to read. A one-page letter is sufficient for most applications from students and graduates entering the job market.

- Apply visual enhancements learned previously to enhance the appeal and readability of the message and to draw attention to your strengths.

- Definitely keep the paragraphs short, and consider listing your top four or five achievements or other important ideas in a bulleted list.

- In print documents, include "Enclosure" below the signature block to alert the employer that a résumé is enclosed. The proper letter format is shown in the example in Figure 13.8.

- Get opinions from qualified individuals, and make revisions where necessary.

STUDY TOOLS 13

LOCATED AT BACK OF THE TEXTBOOK

☐ Tear-Out Chapter Review Card

LOCATED AT WWW.CENGAGEBRAIN.COM

☐ Review Key Term flashcards and create your own cards

☐ Track your knowledge and understanding of key concepts in business communication

☐ Complete practice and graded quizzes to prepare for tests

☐ Complete interactive content within BCOM8 Online

☐ View the chapter highlight boxes for BCOM8 Online

14 Interviewing for a Job and Preparing Employment Messages

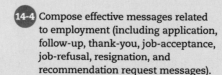

PeopleImages.com/Getty Images

LEARNING OBJECTIVES

After studying this chapter, you will be able to …

14-1 Explain the nature of structured, unstructured, stress, group, phone, and virtual interviews.

14-2 Explain the steps in the interview process.

14-3 Prepare effective answers to questions often asked in job interviews, including illegal interview questions.

14-4 Compose effective messages related to employment (including application, follow-up, thank-you, job-acceptance, job-refusal, resignation, and recommendation request messages).

After finishing this chapter, go to **PAGE 272** for **STUDY TOOLS**.

14-1 UNDERSTANDING TYPES OF EMPLOYMENT INTERVIEWS

Most companies conduct various types of interviews before hiring a new employee. Although the number and type of interviews vary among companies, applicants typically begin with a screening interview often completed by phone or videoconferencing, an in-depth interview, an on-site interview with multiple interviewers, and sometimes a stress interview. Depending on the goals of the interviewer, interviews follow a structured or an unstructured approach.

14-1a Structured Interviews

In a **structured interview**, the interviewer follows a predetermined agenda, including a checklist of questions and statements designed to elicit necessary information and reactions from the interviewee. Because each applicant answers the same questions, the interviewer has comparable data to evaluate. A particular type of structured interview is the behavior-based interview, in which you are asked to give specific examples of occasions in which you demonstrated particular behaviors or skills. The interviewer already knows what skills, knowledge, and qualities successful candidates must possess. The examples you provide will indicate whether you possess them.[1]

Many companies are finding computer-assisted interviews to be a reliable and effective way to conduct screening interviews. Applicants use a computer to provide answers to a list of carefully selected questions. A computer-generated report provides standard, reliable information about each applicant that enables an interviewer to decide whether to invite the applicant for a second interview. The report flags any contradictory responses (e.g., an applicant indicated he was terminated for absenteeism but later indicated that he thought his former employer would give him an outstanding recommendation), highlights any potential problem areas (e.g., an applicant responded that she would remain on the job less than a year), and generates a list of structured interview questions for the interviewer to ask (e.g., "Todd, you said you feel your former employer would rate you average. Why don't you feel it would be higher?").

> Many companies are finding computer-assisted interviews to be a reliable and effective way to conduct screening interviews.

Research has shown that applicants prefer computer interviews to human interviews and that they respond more honestly to a computer, feeling less need to give polite, socially acceptable responses. Because expert computer systems can overcome some of the inherent problems with traditional face-to-face interviews, the overall quality of the selection process improves. Typical interviewer errors include talking too much, forgetting to ask important questions, being reluctant to ask sensitive or tough questions, forming unjustified negative first impressions, obtaining unreliable and illegal information that makes an applicant feel judged, and using interview data ineffectively.[2] Regardless of whether the interview is face-to-face or computer assisted, you will need to provide objective, truthful evidence of your qualifications as they relate to specific job requirements.

14-1b Unstructured Interviews

An **unstructured interview** is a freewheeling exchange and can shift from one subject to another, depending on the interests of the participants. Some experienced interviewers are able to make a structured interview seem unstructured. The goal of many unstructured interviews is to explore unknown areas to determine the applicant's ability to speak comfortably about a wide range of topics.

14-1c Stress Interviews

A **stress interview** is designed to place the interviewee in an anxiety-producing situation so an evaluation can be made of the interviewee's performance under stress. In all cases, interviewees should attempt to assess the nature of the interview quickly and adjust behavior accordingly. Understanding that interviewers sometimes deliberately create anxiety to assess your ability to perform under stress should help

structured interview interview format generally used in the screening process, in which the interviewer follows a predetermined agenda, including a checklist of items or a series of questions and statements designed to elicit the necessary information or interviewee reaction

unstructured interview a freewheeling exchange that may shift from one subject to another, depending on the interests of the participants

stress interview interview format designed to place the interviewee in an anxiety-producing situation so an evaluation of the interviewee's performance under stress may be made

© Monkey Business Images /shutterstock.com

Phone interviews are often used to screen candidates in order to narrow the pool of applicants who will be invited for in-person interviews. They are also used as a way to minimize the expenses involved in interviewing out-of-town candidates.

While you're actively job searching, it's important to be prepared for a phone interview on a moment's notice. You never know when a recruiter or a networking contact might call and ask if you have a few minutes to talk.

Prepare for a phone interview just as you would for a regular interview. Compile a list of your

you handle such interviews more effectively. As the following discussion of different interviewer styles reveals, you can perform much better when you understand the interviewer's purpose.

strengths and weaknesses, as well as a list of answers to typical phone interview questions. In addition, plan on being prepared for a phone conversation about your background and skills. Other considerations to make when preparing for a phone interview include:

14-1d Series Interviews

As organizations have increased emphasis on the team approach to management and problem solving, selecting employees who best fit their cultures and styles has become especially important. Involving key people in the organization in the candidate selection process has led to new interview styles. In a series interview, the candidate meets individually with a number of different interviewers. Each interviewer will likely ask questions from a differing perspective; for instance, a line manager might ask questions related to the applicant's knowledge of specific job tasks, while the vice president of operations might ask questions related to the applicant's career goals. Some questions will likely be asked more than once in the process. A popular trend in organizations that desire a broad range of input in the hiring decision but want to avoid the drawn-out nature of series interviews is to conduct group interviews.

- **keeping your résumé in clear view, on the top of your desk, or taping it to the wall near the phone, so it's at your fingertips when you need to answer questions;**
- **having a short list of your accomplishments available to review;**
- **having a pen and paper handy for note taking; and**
- **turning call-waiting off so your call isn't interrupted.**

Unless you're sure your cellphone service is going to be perfect, you might consider using a landline rather than your cellphone to avoid a dropped call or static on the line.

14-1f Virtual Interviews

Technology is allowing much business activity, including job interviews, to be conducted virtually. Companies such as IBM, Microsoft, Nike, and Hallmark Cards save money and time by screening candidates through video interviews from remote locations. **Virtual interviews** help widen the applicant pool and decrease the cost of travel (because they can be conducted regardless of geography) and fill the position more quickly. The consensus is that the video interview is excellent for screening applicants, but a face-to-face interview is appropriate whenever possible for the important final interview.

14-1e Phone Interviews

virtual interview
interview conducted using videoconferencing technology

Employers use telephone interviews as a way of identifying and recruiting candidates for employment.

Various companies have direct hookups with the career services centers of colleges and universities to interview students. These virtual interviews allow students to meet large companies whose representatives typically would not visit colleges with small applicant pools and to interview with companies whose representatives could not travel because of financial constraints or other reasons. Students simply sit in front of a camera, dial in, and interview with multiple interviewers; in some cases, several applicants are interviewed simultaneously. As you would imagine, some candidates who interview well in person can fail on camera or in a group conference call. Virtual interviewing is an excellent method for screening out candidates who are unable to communicate their competence, enthusiasm, and conviction in a technology-rich environment.

You should prepare for a virtual interview differently than you would for a traditional interview. First, suggest a preliminary telephone conversation with the interviewer to establish rapport. Arrive early and acquaint yourself with the equipment; know how to adjust the volume and other camera functions for optimal performance after the interview begins. Second, concentrate on projecting strong nonverbal skills: speak clearly, but do not slow down; be certain you are centered in the frame; sit straight; look up, not down; and use gestures and an enthusiastic voice to communicate energy and reinforce points while avoiding excessive motion that will appear blurry. Third, realize voices can be out of step with the pictures if there is a lag between the video and audio transmissions. You will need to adjust to the timing (e.g., slow down your voice) to avoid interrupting the interviewer.

14-2 PREPARING FOR AN INTERVIEW

College students frequently schedule on-campus interviews with representatives from various business organizations. Following the on-campus interviews, successful candidates often are invited for further interviews at the company location. The purpose of the second interview is to give executives and administrators other than the human resources interviewer an opportunity to appraise the candidate. Whether on campus or at the company location, interview methods and practices vary with the situation.

Pre-interview planning involves learning something about the company or organization, studying yourself,

and making sure your appearance and mannerisms will not detract from the impression you hope to make.

14-2a Research the Company

Nothing can hurt a job candidate more than knowing little about the organization. Preparation will also arm candidates with information needed to develop pertinent qualifications and point their stories to solve an employer's specific problems.

> No knowledge indicates insincerity, and the interviewer does not want to waste precious interview time providing candidates with information they should have considered long before.

Companies that have publicly traded stock are required to publish annual reports that are available in school libraries or online. Be sure to read news items and blog posts, and sign up to receive news alerts from the prospective company for current company information up until the day of the interview. Use social networking utilities such as LinkedIn and Hoovers.com to find profiles of company leaders and gain insights into the types of managers this company employs.

Employees of the company or other applicants who have interviewed might be of help to the interviewee. Employee reviews of selected companies, salaries, and sample interview questions are available online, and some universities share taped interviews with various company recruiters. Information about the company and the job sought pertinent in an interview includes the following:

COMPANY INFORMATION

Be sure to research the following on the companies with which you interview:

▶ **Name.** Know, for example, that the publishing company Cengage Learning was so named to reflect the company's mission to be a "center of engagement" for its global customers.[3]

▶ **Status in the industry.** Know the company's share of the market, its *Fortune* 500 standing (if any), its sales, and its number of employees.

▶ **Latest stock market quote.** Be familiar with current market deviations and trends.

▶ **Recent news and developments.** Read current business periodicals, news, and blogs for special feature articles on the company, its new products, and its corporate leadership.

▶ **Scope of the company.** Is it local, national, or international?

▶ **Corporate officers.** Know the names of the chairperson, president, and chief executive officer.

▶ **Products and services.** Study the company's offerings, target markets, and innovative strategies.

JOB INFORMATION

Be sure to know the following about the job you are seeking:

▶ **Job title.** Know the job titles of typical entry-level positions.

▶ **Job qualifications.** Understand the specific knowledge and skills desired.

▶ **Probable salary range.** Study salaries in comparable firms, as well as regional averages.

▶ **Career path of the job.** What opportunities for advancement are available?

14-2b Study Yourself

When you know something about the company, you will also know something about the kinds of jobs or training programs the company has to offer. Next, compare your qualifications to the company/job profile. This systematic comparison of your qualifications and job requirements helps you identify pertinent information (strengths or special abilities) to be included in your résumé. If you cannot see a relationship between you and the job or company, you might have difficulty demonstrating the interest or sincerity needed to sell yourself.

14-2c Plan Your Appearance

An employment interviewer once said she would not hire a job applicant who did not meet her *extremities* test: fingernails, shoes, and hair must be clean and well kept. This interviewer felt that if the candidate did not take care of those details, the candidate could not really be serious about, or fit into, her organization. Other important guidelines include avoiding heavy makeup and large, excessive jewelry. Select conservative clothes, and be certain clothing is clean, unwrinkled, and properly fitted. Additionally, avoid smoking, drinking, or wearing heavy fragrance.

You can locate a wealth of information on appropriate interview dress from numerous electronic and printed sources. Also, talk with professors in your field,

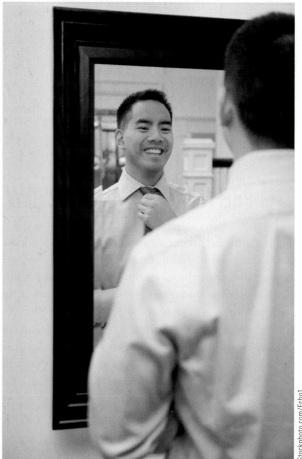

iStockphoto.com/Echo1

professors of business etiquette and professional protocol, personnel at your career services center, and graduates who have recently acquired jobs in your field. Research the company dress code—real or implied—ahead of time. If you *look* and *dress* like the people who already work for the company, the interviewer will be able to visualize you working there.

14-2d Plan Your Time and Materials

One of the worst things you can do is be late for an interview. If something should happen to prevent your arriving on time, phone an apology. Another mistake is to miss the interview entirely. Plan your time so that you will arrive early and can unwind and review mentally the things you plan to accomplish. Be sure to bring a professional briefcase or notebook that contains everything you will need during the interview. These items might include copies of your résumé, a list of references and/or recommendations, a professional-looking pen, paper for taking notes, highlights of what you know about the company, a list of questions you plan to ask, and previous correspondence with the company.

14-2e Practice

The job interview could be the most important face-to-face interaction you ever have. You will be selling yourself in competition with others. How you listen and how you talk are characteristics the interviewer will be able to measure. Your actions, your mannerisms, and your appearance will combine to give the total picture of how you are perceived. Added to the marketable skills you have acquired from your education, experience, and activities, your interview performance can give a skilled interviewer an excellent picture of you. Practicing for an interview will prepare you to handle the nervousness that is natural when interviewing. However, do not memorize answers, as it will sound rehearsed and insincere. Instead, think carefully about how your accomplishments match the job requirements and practice communicating these ideas smoothly, confidently, and professionally.

Prepare for standard interview questions and other interview issues by following suggestions provided later in this chapter. Once you are satisfied you have identified your key selling points, have a friend ask you interview questions you have developed and surprise you with others. Participate in mock interviews with someone in your career services center or with a friend, alternating roles as interviewer and interviewee. Then, follow each practice interview with a constructive critique of your performance.

14-3 CONDUCTING A SUCCESSFUL INTERVIEW

The way you handle an interview will vary somewhat depending on your stage in the hiring process. Regardless of whether you are being screened by a campus recruiter in person, by phone, or by videoconference, or have progressed to an on-site visit, an interview will have three parts: the opening formalities, an information exchange, and the closing.

14-3a The Opening Formalities

According to management consultant Dan Burns, most candidates don't realize that in the first 60 seconds, interviewers typically decide whether the candidate will be moved to the top of the list or dropped from consideration. Burns emphasizes that skills missing during the interview are important because he assumes these same deficiencies will carry over during employment.[4] Clearly, because the impression created during the first few seconds of an interview often determines the outcome, you cannot afford to take time to warm up in an interview. You must enter the door selling yourself!

Common courtesies and confident body language can contribute to a favorable first impression in the early moments when you have not yet had an opportunity to talk about your qualifications:

- **Use the interviewer's name, and pronounce it correctly.** Even if the interviewer calls you by your first name, always use the interviewer's surname unless specifically invited to do otherwise.

Ed Samuel/Shutterstock.com

- **Apply a firm handshake.** Usually, the interviewer will initiate the handshake, although you may do so. In either case, apply a firm handshake. You do not want to leave the impression that you are weak or timid. At the same time, you do not want to overdo the firm grip and leave an impression of being overbearing.

- **Wait for the interviewer to ask you to be seated.** If you aren't invited to sit, choose a chair across from or beside the interviewer's desk.

- **Maintain appropriate eye contact, and use your body language to convey confidence.** Sit erect and lean forward slightly to express interest. For a professional image, avoid slouching, chewing gum, and fidgeting.

- **Be conscious of nonverbal messages.** If the interviewer's eyes are glazing over, end your answer, but expand it if eyes are bright and the head is nodding vigorously. If the interviewer is from a different culture, be conscious of subtle differences in nonverbal communication that could affect the interviewer's perception of you. For example, a North American interviewer who sees eye contact as a sign of trust might perceive an Asian female who keeps her eyes lowered as a sign of respect to be uninterested or not listening.[5] Women should also be aware of typical "feminine behavior" during the interview. For instance, women nod more often than men when an interviewer speaks. Women are also likely to smile more and have a rising intonation at the end of sentences; such behaviors can convey a subservient attitude.[6]

Following the introductions, many interviewers will begin the conversation with nonbusiness talk to help you relax and to set the stage for the information exchange portion of the interview. Other interviewers bypass these casual remarks and move directly into the interview.

14-3b The Information Exchange

Much of the information about you will appear on your résumé or application form and is already available to the interviewer. Thus, the interviewer most likely will seek to go beyond such facts as your education, work experience, and extracurricular activities. He or she will attempt to assess your general attitude toward work and the probability of your fitting successfully into the organization.

©Keith Bell/Shutterstock.com

PRESENTING YOUR QUALIFICATIONS

Your preparation pays off during the interview. Like a defense attorney ready to win a case, you are ready to present evidence that you should be hired. According to Joyce Kennedy and Thomas Morrow, leading career consultants, your case will have three major points: you must convince the interviewer that you (1) can do the job, (2) will do the job, and (3) will not stress out everyone else while doing the job.[7] That's an overwhelming task. Where do you begin? You learned during your study of persuasive writing that saying you're the best at what you do is not convincing. To convince an interviewer to allow you to continue to the next interview or to extend you a job offer, you must provide specific, concrete evidence that your qualifications match the job description and equip you to add immediate value to the company. Use the following guidelines to help you relate your skills and knowledge to the job:

- **List five or six key points that you want to emphasize.** You will probably want to present your education as a major asset. You should point out its relationship to the job sought. Even more important, the fact that you have succeeded in academics indicates that you have the ability and self-discipline to learn. Because most companies expect you to learn something on the job, your ability to learn and thus quickly become productive will be your greatest asset. Even lack of work experience can be an asset: you have acquired no bad work habits that you will have to unlearn.

- **Additionally, be sure to provide evidence of your interpersonal skills.** Communicate that you can get along with others and are sensitive to diversity.

  - What did you do in college that helped you get along with others?

  - Were you a member, an officer, or president of an organization? What did you accomplish? How did others perceive you? Were you a leader? How did your followers respond to your leadership style? To your commitment to ethical standards?

  - Can you organize projects, motivate people to complete important goals, and deal with difficult people?

The extracurricular activities listed on your résumé give an indication of these traits, but how you talk about them

FIGURE 14.1

SKILLS NEEDED: BALANCE OF SOFT AND HARD SKILLS

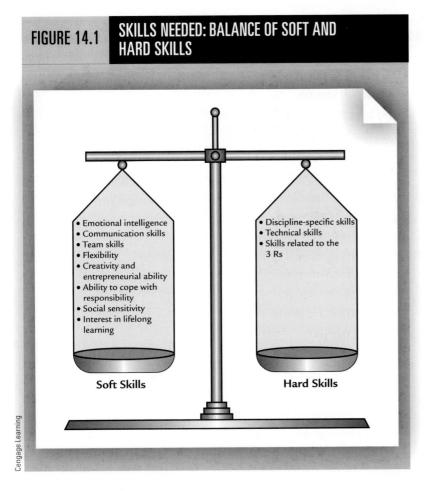

Soft Skills

- Emotional intelligence
- Communication skills
- Team skills
- Flexibility
- Creativity and entrepreneurial ability
- Ability to cope with responsibility
- Social sensitivity
- Interest in lifelong learning

Hard Skills

- Discipline-specific skills
- Technical skills
- Skills related to the 3 Rs

Cengage Learning

element of a winning argument: you are able and willing to become a contributing part of a high-performance team that will enhance the company's performance.

- **Be prepared to answer standard interview questions.** These questions are designed to show (a) why you want the job, (b) why you want to work for this organization, and (c) why the company should want you. Practice concise but fully developed answers that reflect your personality and your communication power. Although one-word answers aren't adequate, long-winded answers can prevent interviewers from asking you other planned questions critical to making an informed decision.

- **Be prepared to answer behavioral questions.** These questions are designed to challenge you to provide evidence of your skills or the behaviors required to perform the job. Rather than asking applicants how they feel about certain things, interviewers are finding that asking potential employees for specific examples to illustrate their answers is a more objective way to evaluate applicants' skills. A sample list of behavioral interviewing questions by skill can be found in Figure 14.2.

in your interview helps demonstrate them. "I started as public relations vice president and was subsequently elected to higher office for four semesters, eventually becoming president" is a statement that proves your leadership qualities. If you can show your organization moved to greater heights, you will appear successful as well. You can also use questions about your extracurricular activities to show that you have broad, balanced interests rather than a single, time-consuming avocation that could lead to burnout and stress if carried to the job.

What are other skills that graduating students need to succeed in a cross-cultural, interdependent workforce? While academic performance is weighted more heavily for some types of jobs than others, the ability to juggle a complicated schedule is weighed heavily by many employers as an important job-success factor. Additionally, a UNESCO report of employer views revealed certain skills to be essential for workers in today's business climate, as shown in Figure 14.1.[8]

Consider these general job-success traits, and then use your knowledge of the job requirements and your own strengths to develop your "central selling features." These key points targeted to your audience are the central

Other behavioral questions include the following:

- Describe a time when you worked well under pressure, worked effectively with others, organized a major project, motivated and led others, solved a difficult problem, or used persuasion to convince someone to accept your idea.

- What was the most difficult problem you had to overcome in your last job (or an academic or extracurricular activity)? How did you cope with it? What lesson did you learn from the situation? Share a time you applied the lesson learned.

- Tell me about a time you had difficulty working with a supervisor or coworker (or professor or peer in a team in a class setting). How did you handle the situation?

- Describe something you have done that shows initiative and willingness to work or required you to think on your feet to solve a problem.

- How have your extracurricular activities, part-time work experience, or volunteer work prepared you for work in our company?

- Tell me about a time you hit a wall trying to push forward a great idea.

FIGURE 14.2   BEHAVIORAL INTERVIEW QUESTIONS BY SKILL

ADAPTABILITY

- Tell me about a situation when you had to be tolerant of an opinion that was different from your own.
- Tell me about a time when you had to adjust to changes over which you had no control.

COMMUNICATION

- Tell me about a time when you were able to use persuasion to convince someone to see things your way.
- Tell me about a time when you dealt with an irate customer.

GOAL SETTING

- Describe a goal you set for yourself and how you reached it.
- Tell me about a goal that you set and did not reach.

PROBLEM SOLVING

- Tell me about a situation where you had to solve a difficult problem.
- Tell me about a time when you had to analyze information and provide a recommendation.

TEAMWORK

- Tell me about a time when you worked on a team and a member was not doing his or her share.
- Tell me about a time when you were working in a team in which the members did not get along.

TIME MANAGEMENT

- Describe a situation in which you had to do a number of things at the same time.
- Tell me about a time when you were unable to complete a project on time.

Cengage Learning

To prepare for answering behavioral questions, brainstorm to identify stories that illustrate how your qualifications fit the job requirements. These stories should show you applying the skills needed on the job. Career counselors recommend using the STAR method (Situation or Task/Action/Result) as a consistent format to help you present a complete answer to these open-ended questions. You first describe a situation or task you were involved in, the action you took, and finally the result of your effort.[9]

- **Be prepared to demonstrate logical thinking and creativity.** Many interviewers ask applicants to solve brain teasers and riddles, create art out of paper bags, and solve complex business problems. Some are asked to "do the job before we give it to you," for example, write a press release on the spot or field a tech-support call.[10] These techniques are used to gauge an applicant's ability to think quickly and creatively and observe an emotional response to an awkward situation. You cannot anticipate this type of interview question, but you can familiarize yourself with mind teasers that have been used. Most important, however, recognize the interviewer's purpose; relax, and do your best to showcase your logical reasoning, creativity, or your courage to even try.

- **Display a professional attitude.** First, communicate your sincere interest in the company; show that you are strongly interested in the company and not just taking an interview for practice. Reveal your knowledge of the company gained through reading published information, and refer to the people you have talked with about the working conditions, company achievements, and career paths.

  Second, focus on the satisfaction gained from contributing to a company rather than the benefits you will receive. What's important in a job goes beyond financial reward. All applicants are interested in a paycheck; any job satisfies that need—some will pay more, some less. Recognize that the paycheck is a part of the job and should not be your primary concern. Intrinsic rewards such as personal job satisfaction, the feeling of accomplishment, and making a contribution to society are ideas to discuss in the interview. You should like what you are doing and find a challenging job that will satisfy these needs.

- **Be prepared to discuss salary and benefits.** For most entry-level positions, the beginning salary is fixed. However, if you have work experience, excellent scholarship records, or added maturity, you might be able to obtain a higher salary. The interviewer should initiate the salary topic. What you should know is the general range for candidates with your qualifications so that your response to a question about how much you would expect is reasonable.

  If you have other job offers, you are in a position to compare salaries, jobs, and companies. In this case, you might suggest to the interviewer that you would expect a competitive salary and that you have been offered X dollars by another firm. If salary has not been mentioned, and you really want to know about it, simply ask courteously how much the salary would be for someone with your qualifications. In any case, if you really believe the job offers the non-monetary benefits you seek, do not attempt to make salary a major issue.

- **Typically, an interviewer will introduce the subject of benefits without your asking about them.** In some cases, a discussion of total salary and "perks" is reserved for a follow-up interview. If nothing has been said about certain benefits, you should take the liberty of asking, particularly when an item is especially important to you.

- **Be knowledgeable of interview questions and information on your social networking sites that might lead to discriminatory hiring practices.** The Equal Employment Opportunity Commission (EEOC) and Fair Employment Practices Guidelines make

PEOPLE ANALYTICS

More and more companies are using personality testing to screen job applicants. In fact, some 35 percent of Human Resource professionals worldwide said they had used personality inventories in 2012, up nearly 20 percent from 2005. Josh Bersin, a researcher at Deloitte, says his surveys claim that 15 to 20 percent of jobs involve some sort of prehire assessment, such as a personality test. JetBlue, for example, uses personality tests to separate applicants into colors: Greens are a good fit, Yellows will do in a pinch, and Reds are a no go.

This trend is being driven by two of the business world's latest buzzwords, Big Data and analytics. Big Data involves collecting as much information as possible about almost anything so that it can be mined to make predictions, while analytics describes looking for patterns in data that can be used to optimize performance. The collision of these two trends as led to what is called "people analytics," which involves looking at everything from the correlation between compensation and attrition to analyzing employees' email and calendars to see if they are using their time effectively. One company, Bridgewater Associates of Westport, Conn., uses this information to create digital "baseball cards" of each employee, which are made available to everyone at the company so that he or she might get a sense of what it is like to work with others.[11]

it clear that an employer cannot legally discriminate against a job applicant on the basis of race, color, gender, age, religion, national origin, or disability. Interviewers must restrict questions to an applicant's ability to perform specific job-related functions essential to the job sought. Generally, the following topics should not be introduced:

- *National origin and religion.* "You have an unusual accent; where were you born?" "What religious holidays will require you to miss work?"

- *Age.* "I see you attended Central High School; what year did you graduate?" "Could you provide a copy of your birth certificate?"

- *Disabilities, health conditions, and physical characteristics not reasonably related to the job.* "Do you have a disability that would interfere with your ability to perform the job?" "Have you ever been injured on the job?" "Have you ever been treated by a psychiatrist?" "How much alcohol do you consume each week?" "What prescription drugs are you currently taking?"

▶ How would you describe the ideal employee, or what's the best background for this job?

▶ What is a typical day like in this job?

▶ What type of people would I be working with (peers) and for (supervisors)?

▶ Why do you need someone for this job (why can this job not be done by a current employee)?

▶ What circumstances led to the departure of the person I would be replacing? What is the turnover rate of people in this job? (Or, how many people have held this job in the past five years?)

▶ Why do you continue to work for this company (to an interviewer with several years' tenure with the company)?

▶ Would you describe the initial training program for people in this position?

▶ What types of ongoing employee in-service training programs are provided?

▶ How much value does your firm place on a master's degree?

▶ How do you feel this field has changed in the past 10 years? How do you feel it will change in the next 10 years?

▶ What advice do you wish you had been given when you were starting out?

▶ When do you expect to make your decision about the position?

○ *Marital status, spouse's employment, or dependents.* "Are you married?" "Who is going to care for your children if you work for us?" "Do you plan to have children?" "Is your spouse employed?" Additionally, employers may not ask the names or relationships of people with whom you live.

○ *Arrests or criminal convictions that are not related to the job.* "Have you ever been arrested other than for traffic violations? If so, explain." Keep in mind that the arrest/conviction record of a person applying for a job as a law enforcement officer or a teacher could be highly relevant to the job, but the same information could be illegal for a person applying for a job as an engineer.

As interviewers may ask illegal questions because of lack of training or an accidental slip, you must decide how to respond. You can refuse to answer and state that the question is improper, though you risk offending the interviewer. A second option is to answer the inappropriate question, knowing it is illegal and unrelated to job requirements. A third approach is to provide a low-key response such as "How does this question relate to how I will do my job?" or to answer the legitimate concern that likely prompted the question. For example, an interviewer who asks, "Do you plan to have children?" is probably concerned about how long you might remain on the job. An answer to this concern would be, "I plan to pursue a career regardless of whether I decide to raise a family." If you can see no legitimate concern in a question, such as "Do you own your home, rent, or live with parents?" answer, "I'm not sure how that question relates to the job. Can you explain?"[12]

ASKING QUESTIONS OF THE INTERVIEWER

Both the interviewer and interviewee want to know as much as possible about each other before making a commitment to hire. A good way to determine whether the job is right for you is to ask pertinent questions.

Good questions show the interviewer that you have initiative and are interested in making a well-informed decision. Responses can provide insight to job requirements that you can then show you possess. Therefore, be sure not to say, "I don't have any questions." Focus on questions that help you gain information about the company and the job that you could not learn from published sources or persons other than the interviewer. Respect the interviewer's time by avoiding questions that indicate you are unprepared (for example, questions about the company's scope, products or services, job requirements, or new developments). Avoid questions about salary, required overtime, and benefits that imply you are interested more in money and the effort required than in the contribution you can make.

14-3c The Closing

The interviewer will provide cues indicating that the interview is completed by rising or making a comment about the next step to be taken. At that point, do not prolong the interview needlessly. Simply rise, accept the handshake, thank the interviewer for the opportunity to meet, and close by saying you look forward to hearing from the company. The tact with which you close the interview can be almost as important as the first impression you made. Be enthusiastic. If you really want the job, you must ask for it.

Your ability to speak confidently and intelligently about your abilities will help you secure a desirable job. Effective interviewing skills will be just as valuable once you begin work. You will be involved in interviews with your supervisor for various reasons: to seek advice or information about your work and working conditions, to receive informal feedback about your progress, to receive a deserved promotion, and to discuss other personnel matters. In addition, your supervisor will likely conduct a performance appraisal interview to evaluate your performance. This formal interview typically occurs annually on the anniversary of your start of employment.

14-3d **Additional Considerations for Phone Interviews**

Although many of the guidelines for interviewing also apply to phone interviews, some additional considerations are useful. For example, you will need to make sure that you are located in a quiet place, so that no distracting noises can be heard in the background. Other persons should be asked to leave, and pets should be put in another room or outside.

If you receive an unexpected call from an interviewer and the time isn't convenient, ask if you could talk at another time, and suggest some alternatives.

During the interview, you should

- avoid smoking, chewing gum, eating, or drinking;
- keep a glass of water handy, in case you need to wet your mouth;
- smile—smiling will add enthusiasm to your voice and help to project a positive image to the listener;
- speak slowly and enunciate clearly;
- use the person's title (Mr. or Ms. and their last name) and only use a first name if he or she asks you to;
- avoid interrupting the interviewer;
- pause if you need to collect your thoughts; and
- give short answers.

Remember, your goal is to set up a face-to-face interview. After you thank the interviewer, ask if it would be possible to meet in person.

14-4 PREPARING OTHER EMPLOYMENT MESSAGES

Preparing a winning résumé and application letter is an important first step in a job search. To expedite your job search, you will need to prepare other employment messages. For example, you might complete an application form, send a follow-up message to a company that does not respond to your résumé, send a thank-you message after an interview, accept a job offer, reject other job offers, and communicate with references. A career change will require a carefully written resignation letter.

14-4a **Application Forms**

Before beginning a new job, you will almost certainly complete the employer's application and employment forms. Some application forms, especially for applicants who apply for jobs with a high level of responsibility, are very long. They can actually appear to be tests in which applicants give their answers to hypothetical questions and write defenses for their answers. Application forms also ensure consistency in the information received from each candidate and can prevent decisions based on illegal topics which might be presented in a résumé.

> Increasing numbers of companies are designing employment forms as mechanisms for acquiring information about a candidate that often is not included in the résumé.

14-4b **Follow-Up Messages**

When an application message and résumé do not elicit a response, a follow-up message might bring results. Sent a few weeks after the original message, it includes a reminder that an application for a certain job is on file, presents additional education or experience accumulated and its relationship to the job, and closes with a reference to desired action. In addition to conveying new information, follow-up messages indicate persistence (a quality that impresses some employers). Figure 14.3 shows a good example of a follow-up message.

FIGURE 14.3 **EXAMPLE OF A FOLLOW-UP MESSAGE** Good

Dear Ms. Nelson:

Recently I applied for an auditing position with Frederick Associates and now have additional qualifications to report.

The enclosed, updated résumé shows that I attended the annual Fraud Conference and Exhibition sponsored by the Association of Certified Fraud Examiners. I attended sessions in the technology track and learned about a variety of tools used to detect fraudulent financial transactions. In a post-conference session, I was introduced to interrogation techniques.

Ms. Nelson, I would welcome the opportunity to visit your office and talk more about the contributions I could make as an auditor with Frederick Associates. Please write or call me at (812) 455-9803.

● *States main idea and clearly identifies position being sought.*

● *Refers to enclosed résumé; summarizes additional qualifications.*

● *Assures employer that applicant is still interested in job.*

Format Pointers
Format as formal business letter, but could send message electronically if previous communication with employer had been by email.

Print letter and envelope with laser printer on paper that matches résumé and application letter.

Cengage Learning

14-4c **Thank-You Messages**

What purposes are served in sending a thank-you message, even though you expressed thanks in person after the interview or a discussion with a special employer at a career fair? After a job interview, a written message of appreciation is a professional courtesy and enhances your image within the organization. To be effective, it must be sent promptly. For maximum impact, send a thank-you message the day of the interview or the following day. Even if during the interview you decided you do not want the job, or you and the interviewer mutually agreed that the job is not for you, a thank-you message is appropriate. As a matter of fact, if you've made a positive impression, interviewers might forward your résumé to others who are seeking qualified applicants.

The medium you choose for sending this message depends on the intended audience. If the company you've interviewed with prefers a traditional style, send a letter in complete business format on high-quality paper that matches your résumé and application letter. If the company has communicated with you extensively by email, follow the pattern and send a professional email that can be read in a timely manner. Choosing to send an email rather than using slower mail delivery can give you a competitive edge over other candidates whose mailed letters arrive several days later than yours.

After an interview has gone well and you think a job offer is a possibility, include these ideas in the message of appreciation: express gratitude, identify the specific job applied for, refer to some point discussed in the interview (the strength of the interview), and close by making some reference to the expected call or message that conveys the employer's decision. The tone of this business message should remain professional

Tashatuvango/Shutterstock.com

FIGURE 14.4 | **EXAMPLE OF A THANK-YOU MESSAGE**

NEW MESSAGE

To: Carl Chander [cchandler@srwp.org]
From: Ely Sorenson [esorenson@bsu.edu]
Subject: Appreciation for yesterday's interview opportunity

Dear Mr. Chandler:

Thank you for the opportunity to visit the Snake River Wildlife Preserve for an interview yesterday. I enjoyed meeting you and your staff and the opportunity to learn about the important programs sponsored by the SRWP.

Having lived in Boise for more than seven years, I often read reports about how the SRWP has influenced the development in the area. The office visit allowed me to learn more about mission of the SRWP, from monitoring wildlife numbers and environmental trends, educating residents, and promoting legislative initiatives, to writing state and federal grants to fund preservation activities.

After visiting your office on Thursday, I am confident that my interest and previous experience working at the Nampa Bird Refuge Area will allow me to contribute immediately to the SRWP's important role as an environmental steward for the region. I would also gain valuable real-world experience needed to enhance my public policy degree at the university.

Mr. Chandler, I am eager to receive an offer from the SRWP for the planning position. If you need additional information in the meantime, please contact me.

Thanks,

Ely Sorenson

• *States main idea of appreciation for interview and information gained.*

• *Includes specific points discussed during interview, increasing sincerity and recall of applicant.*

• *Assures employer of applicant's continued interest in position.*

• *Politely reminds employer that applicant is awaiting reply.*

Format Pointers
Prepare as email message because previous communication with the organization has been by email.

Cengage Learning

---

regardless of the personal relationship you might have developed with the interviewer and the informality encouraged by email. The message could be read by many others once it is placed in your personnel file as you complete annual appraisals and compete for promotions. Specific points to cover are illustrated in Figure 14.4.

The résumé, application letter, and thank-you message should be stored in a computer file and adapted for submission to other firms when needed. Develop a database for keeping a record of the dates on which documents and résumés were sent to certain firms and answers were received, names of people talked with, facts conveyed, and so on. When an interviewer calls,

you can retrieve and view that company's record while you are talking with the interviewer.

14-4d Job-Acceptance Messages

A job offer may be extended either by phone or in writing. If a job offer is extended over the phone, request that the company send a written confirmation of the job offer. The confirmation should include the job title, salary, benefits, starting date, and anything else negotiated.

Often, companies require a written acceptance of a job offer. Note the deductive sequence of the message shown in Figure 14.5: acceptance, details, and closing (confirms the report-for-work date).

FIGURE 14.5   EXAMPLE OF A JOB-ACCEPTANCE MESSAGE

Good

I accept your employment offer as a management trainee. Thank you for responding so quickly after our discussion last week.

As you requested, I have signed the agreement outlining the specific details of my employment. Your copy is enclosed, and I have kept a copy for my records.

If you should need to communicate with me before I report to work on May 15, please call me at 777-2323.

- States main idea of the job acceptance.
- Continues with any necessary details.
- Confirms beginning employment date.

Cengage Learning

14-4e Job-Refusal Messages

Like other messages that convey unpleasant news, job-refusal messages are written inductively—with a beginning that reveals the nature of the subject, explanations that lead to a refusal, the refusal, and a pleasant ending. Of course, certain reasons (even though valid in your mind) are better left unsaid, such as questionable company goals or methods of operation, negative attitude of present employees, possible bankruptcy, unsatisfactory working conditions, and so on. The applicant who prefers not to be specific about the reason for turning down a job might write this explanation: *After thoughtfully considering job offers received this week, I have decided to accept a job in the finance department of a commercial bank.*

You might want to be more specific about your reasons for refusal when you have a positive attitude toward the company or believe you will want to reapply at some later date. The letter excerpt in Figure 14.6 includes the reasons for refusal.

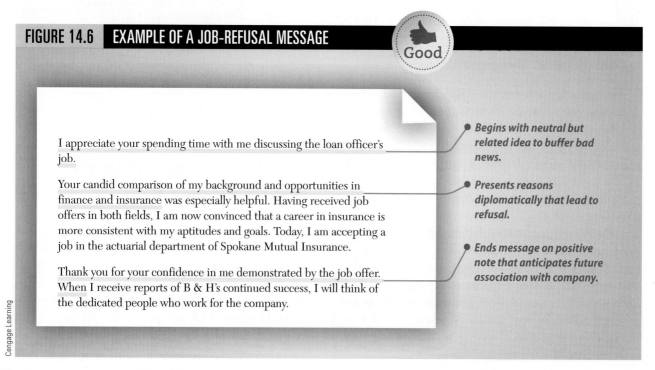

FIGURE 14.6   EXAMPLE OF A JOB-REFUSAL MESSAGE

Good

I appreciate your spending time with me discussing the loan officer's job.

Your candid comparison of my background and opportunities in finance and insurance was especially helpful. Having received job offers in both fields, I am now convinced that a career in insurance is more consistent with my aptitudes and goals. Today, I am accepting a job in the actuarial department of Spokane Mutual Insurance.

Thank you for your confidence in me demonstrated by the job offer. When I receive reports of B & H's continued success, I will think of the dedicated people who work for the company.

- Begins with neutral but related idea to buffer bad news.
- Presents reasons diplomatically that lead to refusal.
- Ends message on positive note that anticipates future association with company.

Cengage Learning

14-4f Resignation Messages

Resigning from a job requires effective communication skills. You might be allowed to give your notice in person or be required to write a formal resignation. Your supervisor will inform you of the company's policy. Regardless of whether the resignation is given orally or in writing, show empathy for your employer by giving enough time to allow the employer to find a replacement. Because your employer has had confidence in you, has benefited from your services, and will have to seek a replacement, your impending departure *is* bad news. As such, the message is written inductively. It calls attention to your job, gives your reasons for leaving it, conveys the resignation, and closes on a positive note. A written resignation is shown in Figure 14.7.

A resignation is not an appropriate instrument for telling managers how a business should be operated. Harshly worded statements could result in immediate termination or cause human relations problems during your remaining working days. If you can do so sincerely, recall positive experiences you had with the company. Doing so will leave a lasting record of your goodwill, making it likely that your supervisor will give you a good recommendation in the future.

14-4g Recommendation Requests

Companies seek information from references at various stages. Some prefer talking with references prior to an interview, and others, after a successful interview. Specific actions on your part will ensure that your references are treated with common courtesy and that references are prepared for the employer's call.

- **Remind the reference that he or she had previously agreed to supply information about you.** Identify the job for which you are applying, give a complete address to which the message is to be sent, and indicate a date by which the prospective employer needs the message. By sharing information about job requirements and reporting recent job-related experiences, you can assist the reference in writing an effective message. Indicate your gratitude, but do not apologize for making the request. The reference has already agreed to write on your behalf and will likely take pleasure in assisting a deserving person.

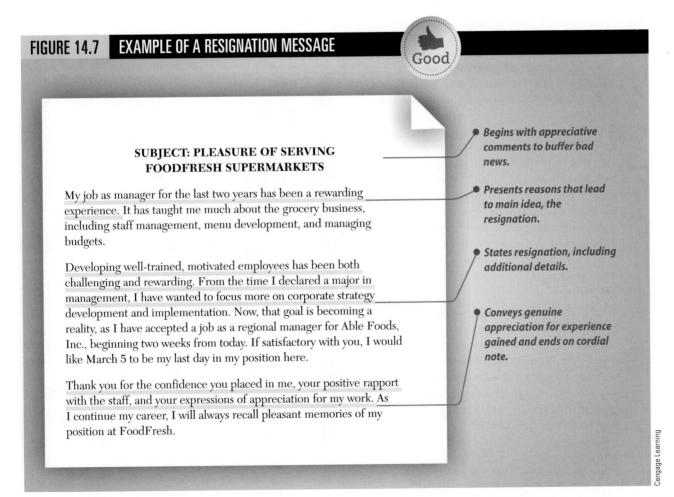

FIGURE 14.7   EXAMPLE OF A RESIGNATION MESSAGE   Good

SUBJECT: PLEASURE OF SERVING FOODFRESH SUPERMARKETS

My job as manager for the last two years has been a rewarding experience. It has taught me much about the grocery business, including staff management, menu development, and managing budgets.

Developing well-trained, motivated employees has been both challenging and rewarding. From the time I declared a major in management, I have wanted to focus more on corporate strategy development and implementation. Now, that goal is becoming a reality, as I have accepted a job as a regional manager for Able Foods, Inc., beginning two weeks from today. If satisfactory with you, I would like March 5 to be my last day in my position here.

Thank you for the confidence you placed in me, your positive rapport with the staff, and your expressions of appreciation for my work. As I continue my career, I will always recall pleasant memories of my position at FoodFresh.

- Begins with appreciative comments to buffer bad news.
- Presents reasons that lead to main idea, the resignation.
- States resignation, including additional details.
- Conveys genuine appreciation for experience gained and ends on cordial note.

Cengage Learning

FIGURE 14.8 | EXAMPLE OF A THANK-YOU MESSAGE TO A REFERENCE

Good

Thank you so much for the letter of recommendation you prepared for my application to ComNet Associates. I learned today that I have been hired and will begin work in June.

Because the position is in public relations, I believe your comments about my performance in your communication classes carried a great deal of weight. Mr. Miller commented he was impressed with the wealth of evidence and examples you provided to support your statements, unlike the general recommendations he frequently receives.

Dr. Watson, I appreciate your helping me secure an excellent position in a highly competitive job market. Thanks for the recommendation and your outstanding instruction. I look forward to talking with you about how I am faring in the real world when I return to campus for fall homecoming.

- States main idea of appreciation for recommendation. Informs reference of success in locating job.

- Communicates sincere appreciation for assistance; uses specific examples and avoids exaggeration, unlike the general recommendations he frequently receives.

- Restates main idea and anticipates continued relationship; is original and sincere.

Cengage Learning

- **Alert the reference of imminent requests for information, especially if considerable time has elapsed since the applicant and reference have last seen each other.** Enclosing a recent résumé and providing any other pertinent information (e.g., name change) will enable the reference to write a message that is specific and convincing. To ensure on-target job references, politely explain the types of information you perceive relevant to the job sought: specific job skills, work ethic, attitude and demeanor toward work, leadership style, and so on. If the job search becomes longer than anticipated, a follow-up message to references explaining the delay and expressing gratitude for their efforts is appropriate.

- **Send a sincere, original thank-you message after a position has been accepted.** This thoughtful gesture will build a positive relationship with a person who might continue to be important to your career. The message in Figure 14.8 is brief and avoids clichés and exaggerated expressions of praise, but instead gives specific examples of the importance of the reference's recommendation.

STUDY TOOLS 14

LOCATED AT BACK OF THE TEXTBOOK
☐ Tear-Out Chapter Review Card

LOCATED AT WWW.CENGAGEBRAIN.COM
☐ Review Key Term flashcards and create your own cards

☐ Track your knowledge and understanding of key concepts in business communication

☐ Complete practice and graded quizzes to prepare for tests

☐ Complete interactive content within BCOM8 Online

☐ View the chapter highlight boxes for BCOM8 Online

GRAMMAR & USAGE APPENDIX

Polishing your language skills will aid you in preparing error-free documents that reflect positively on you and your company. This text appendix is an abbreviated review that focuses on common problems frequently encountered by business writers and offers a quick "refreshing" of key skills.

GRAMMAR

Sentence Structure

1. **Rely mainly on sentences that follow the normal subject-verb-complement sequence for clarity and easy reading.**

   Jennifer and I withdrew for two reasons.
   (subject)　　　(verb)　　　(complement)

Original	Better
There are two reasons for our withdrawal.	Two reasons for our withdrawal are ….
	Jennifer and I withdrew for two reasons.
It is necessary that we withdraw.	We must withdraw.
Here is a copy of my résumé.	The enclosed résumé outlines ….

   There, it, and *here* are *expletives*—filler words that have no real meaning in the sentence.

2. **Put pronouns, adverbs, phrases, and clauses near the words they modify.**

Incorrect	Correct
Angie put a new type of gel in her hair, which she had just purchased.	Angie put a new type of gel, which she had just purchased, in her hair.
He works only in the call center during peak periods.	He works in the call center only during peak periods.
The clerk stood near the fax machine wearing a denim skirt.	The clerk wearing a denim skirt stood near the fax machine.

3. **Do not separate subject and predicate unnecessarily.**

Incorrect	Clear
She, hoping to receive a bonus, worked rapidly.	Hoping to receive a bonus, she worked rapidly.

4. **Place an introductory phrase near the subject of the independent clause it modifies.** Otherwise, the phrase dangles. To correct the dangling phrase, change the subject of the independent clause, or make the phrase into a dependent clause by assigning it a subject.

Incorrect	Correct
When a young boy, my mother insisted I learn a second language.	When I was a young boy, my mother insisted I learn a second language.
[Implies that the mother was once a young boy]	
Working at full speed every morning, fatigue overtakes me in the afternoon.	Working at full speed every morning, I become tired in the afternoon.
[Implies that "fatigue" was working at full speed]	Because I work at full speed every morning, fatigue overtakes me in the afternoon.
To function properly, you must oil the machine every hour.	If the equipment is to function properly, you must oil it every hour.
[Implies that if "you" are "to function properly," the machine must be oiled hourly]	To function properly, the equipment must be oiled every hour.

5. **Express related ideas in similar grammatical form (use parallel construction).**

Incorrect	Correct
The machine operator made three resolutions: (1) to be punctual, (2) following instructions carefully, and third, the reduction of waste.	The machine operator made three resolutions: to be punctual, to follow instructions carefully, and to reduce waste.
The human resources manager is concerned with the selection of the right worker, providing appropriate orientation and the worker's progress.	The human resources manager is concerned with selecting the right worker, providing appropriate orientation, and evaluating the worker's progress.

6. Do not end a sentence with a needless preposition.

Where is the new sushi bar to be <u>located</u> (not *located at*)?

The applicant did not tell us where he was <u>going</u> (not *going to*).

End a sentence with a preposition if for some reason the preposition needs emphasis.

I am not concerned with what he is paying <u>for</u>. I am concerned with what he is paying <u>with</u>.

The prospect has everything—a goal to work <u>toward</u>, a house to live <u>in</u>, and an income to live <u>on</u>.

7. Avoid split infinitives.
Two words are required to express an infinitive: *to* plus a *verb*. The two words belong together. An infinitive is split when another word is placed between the two.

Incorrect	Correct
The superintendent used <u>to</u> occasionally <u>visit</u> the offices.	**The superintendent used <u>to visit</u> the offices occasionally.**
I plan <u>to</u> briefly <u>summarize</u> the report.	**I plan <u>to summarize</u> the report briefly.**

EXERCISE 1
Identify the weakness in each sentence, and write an improved version.

1. It is essential that you learn to design spreadsheets that make financial information meaningful to users.
2. There are many online tools available that build relationships with customers.
3. I am submitting an employee testimonial to the company website, which I first posted to a presentation blog.
4. More companies are videoconferencing because of the need to significantly reduce travel costs.
5. To operate efficiently, you must perform periodic maintenance on your computer.
6. Planned store improvements include widening the aisles, improved lighting, and lower shelves for a sophisticated feel.

Pronoun Reference

1. Make a pronoun agree in number with its antecedent (the specific noun for which a pronoun stands).

a. Use a plural pronoun when it represents two or more singular antecedents connected by *and*.

The <u>secretary</u> <u>and</u> the <u>treasurer</u> will take <u>their</u> vacations.

["The" before "treasurer" indicates that the sentence is about two people.]

The <u>secretary</u> and <u>treasurer</u> will take <u>his</u> vacation.

[Omitting "the" before "treasurer" indicates that the sentence is about one person who has two sets of responsibilities.]

b. Parenthetical remarks (remarks that can be omitted without destroying the basic meaning of the sentence) that appear between the pronoun and its antecedent have no effect on the form of the pronoun.

President Ritter, <u>not the managers</u>, is responsible for his strategic goals.

[Because "his" refers to President Ritter and not to "managers," "his" is used instead of "their."]

c. Use a singular pronoun with *each*, *everyone*, *no*, and their variations.

<u>Each</u> student and <u>each</u> team member will perform <u>his or her</u> own data collection.

<u>Everyone</u> is responsible for <u>her or his</u> work.

d. Use a singular pronoun when two or more singular antecedents are connected by *or* or *nor*.

<u>Neither</u> Brandon <u>nor</u> Will can complete <u>his</u> work.

Ask <u>either</u> Mallory <u>or</u> Suzanne about <u>her</u> in-service training.

e. Use pronouns that agree in number with the intended meaning of collective nouns.

The <u>team</u> has been asked for <u>its</u> contributions. ["Team" is thought of as a unit; the singular "its" is appropriate.]

The <u>team</u> have been asked for <u>their</u> contributions. ["Team" is thought of as more than one individual; the plural "their" is appropriate.]

2. Place relative pronouns as near their antecedents as possible for clear understanding.
A relative pronoun joins a dependent clause to its antecedent.

Ambiguous	Clear
The <u>members</u> were given receipts <u>who</u> have paid.	**The <u>members</u> <u>who</u> have paid were given receipts.**
The agreement will enable you to pay <u>whichever</u> is lower, 6 percent or $50.	**The agreement will enable you to pay 6 percent or $50, <u>whichever</u> is lower.**

Restate a noun instead of risking a *vague* pronoun reference.

Vague

The officer captured the suspect even though <u>he</u> was unarmed.

Clear

The officer captured the suspect even though <u>the officer</u> was unarmed.

3. **Do not use a pronoun by itself to refer to a phrase, clause, sentence, or paragraph.** A pronoun should stand for a noun, and that noun should appear in the writing.

Incorrect

He expects to take all available accounting courses and obtain a position in a public accounting firm. <u>This</u> appeals to him.

Correct

He expects to take all available accounting courses and obtain a position in a public accounting firm. <u>This plan</u> appeals to him.

EXERCISE 2

In each of the sentences below, choose the correct word in parentheses.

1. Conversation skills and good listening (affect, affects) a leader's effectiveness.

2. Each sales rep (was, were) trained to encourage customers to buy more than one size or color since shipping is free.

3. The production manager, not the controller, presented (her, their) strongly opposing views.

4. Neither Stephen nor Lydia (was, were) recognized for their contribution.

5. The company restructured (its, their) recreation event to avoid a frivolous perception.

6. The committee will present (its, their) recommendation at the next staff meeting.

7. Jenna forgot to retain her receipts; (this, this oversight) caused a delay in reimbursement.

Pronoun Case

1. **Use the correct case of pronouns.** *Case* tells whether a pronoun is used as the subject of a sentence or as an object in it.

   a. Use nominative-case pronouns (also known as subjective-case pronouns) (*I, he, she, they, we, you, it, who*) as subjects of a sentence or clause.

      <u>You</u> and <u>I</u> must collaborate. ["You" and "I" are subjects of the verb "collaborate."]

      Those <u>who</u> work will be paid. ["Who" is the subject of the dependent clause "who work."]

   b. Use objective-case pronouns (*me, him, her, them, us, you, it, whom*) as objects of verbs and prepositions.

      His mother texted <u>him</u> about the family emergency. ["Him" is the object of the verb "texted."]

      The customer feedback survey was sent to the project manager and <u>them</u>. ["Them" is the object of the preposition "to."]

      To <u>whom</u> should we send the analysis? ["Whom" is the object of the preposition "to."]

      TIP: Restate a subordinate clause introduced by *who* or *whom* to determine the appropriate pronoun.

      She is the type of manager <u>whom</u> we can promote. [Restating "whom we can promote" as "We can promote her (whom)" clarifies that "whom" is the object.]

      She is the type of manager <u>who</u> can be promoted. [Restating "who can be promoted" as "She (who) can be promoted" clarifies that "who" is the subject.]

      TIP: Change a question to a statement to determine the correct form of a pronoun.

      <u>Whom</u> did you call? [You did call *whom*.]

      <u>Whom</u> did you select for the position? [You did select *whom* for the position.]

   c. Use the nominative case when forms of the linking verb *be* require a pronoun to complete the meaning.

      It was <u>he</u> who received credit for the sale.

      It is <u>she</u> who deserves the award.

      ["It was he" may to some people sound just as distracting as the incorrect "It was him." Express the ideas in a different way to avoid the error and an expletive beginning.]

      He was the one who received credit for the sale.

      She deserves the award.

   d. Use the possessive form of a pronoun before a gerund (a verb used as a noun).

      We were delighted at <u>his</u> (not *him*) assuming a leadership role.

      ["Assuming a leadership role" is used here as a noun. "His" in this sentence serves the same purpose it serves in "We are delighted at his initiative."]

Verb Agreement

1. **Make subjects agree with verbs.**

   a. Ignore intervening phrases that have no effect on the verb used.

      Good material and fast delivery are (not is) essential.

      You, not the carrier, are (not is) responsible for the damage. [Intervening phrase, "not the carrier," does not affect the verb used.]

      The attitude of these investors is (not are) a deep concern. [The subject is "attitude"; "of these investors" is a phrase coming between the subject and the verb.]

   b. Use a verb that agrees with the noun closer to the verb when *or* or *nor* connects two subjects.

      Only one or two questions are (not is) necessary.

      Several paint brushes or one paint roller is (not are) necessary.

   c. Use singular verbs with plural nouns that have a singular meaning or are thought of as singular units.

The news is good.	**Economics is a required course.**
Twenty dollars is too much.	**Ten minutes is sufficient time.**

   d. Use a singular verb for titles of articles, firm names, and slogans.

      "Etiquette in the Age of Social Media" is an interesting article.

      Forestieri and Chaudrue is the oldest firm in the city.

      "Eat Smart for Hearts" is a campaign slogan directed at better nutrition for senior adults.

2. **Choose verbs that agree in person with their subjects.** *Person* indicates whether the subject is (1) speaking, (2) being spoken to, or (3) being spoken about.

First person:	**I am, we are.** [Writer or speaker]
Second person:	**You are.** [Receiver of message]
Third person:	**He is, she is, they are.** [Person being discussed]

   She doesn't (not *don't*) eat well or exercise regularly.

   They don't recognize the value of strong networking skills.

Verb Tense and Mood

1. **Use the appropriate verb tense.** *Tense* indicates time. Tense can be either simple or compound.

   Simple tenses:

Present:	**I see you.** [Tells what is happening now]
Past:	I **saw** you. [Tells what has already happened]
Future:	I **will see** you. [Tells what is yet to happen]

   Compound tenses:

Present perfect:	**I have seen you.** [Tells of past action that extends to the present]
Past perfect:	I **had seen** you. [Tells of past action that was finished before another past action]
Future perfect:	I **will have seen** you. [Tells of action that will be finished before a future time]

   a. Use present tense when something was and still is true.

      The speaker reminded us that Rhode Island is (not *was*) smaller than Wisconsin.

      The consultant's name is (not *was*) Ryan Abrams.

   b. Avoid unnecessary shifts in tense.

      The carrier brought (not *brings*) my package but left without asking me to sign for it.

      Verbs that appear in the same sentence are not required to be in the same tense.

      The contract that was prepared yesterday will be signed tomorrow.

2. **Use subjunctive mood to express situations that are untrue or highly unlikely.** Be sure to use *were* for the present tense of to *be* to indicate the subjunctive mood. Use *was* when the statement could be true.

   I wish the story <u>were</u> (not *was*) true.

   If I <u>were</u> (not *was*) you, I would try again.

EXERCISE 4

In each of the sentences below, choose the correct verb in parentheses.

1. Only one of the free smartphone applications (has, have) value to me.

2. Taxpayers, not the government, (are, is) held accountable for paying the national debt.

3. Neither the manager nor the employees (was, were) aware of the policy change.

4. Both Josh and Krystal (was, were) notified of the impending layoffs.

5. The news from the rescue mission (is, are) encouraging.

6. *Good to Great* (has, have) been placed in the company library.

7. The sales manager announced that Portsmouth, South Carolina, (is, was) the site for the annual sales meeting.

8. Tylor (don't, doesn't) expect preferential treatment.

9. The client studied the financial analysis for a minute and (starts, started) asking questions.

10. If the applicant (was, were) experienced with databases, she would have been hired.

Adjectives and Adverbs

1. **Use an adjective to modify a noun or pronoun and an adverb to modify a verb, an adjective, or another adverb.**

Adjective:	**Bryan gave an <u>impressive</u> sales pitch.**
Adverb:	The new employee looked **<u>enthusiastically</u> at the sales prospect.** [The adverb "enthusiastically" modifies the verb "looked."]
	The team leader was **really visionary.** [The adverb "really" modifies the adjective "visionary."]
	Worker A progressed **relatively faster than did Worker B.** [The adverb "relatively" modifies the adverb "faster."]

2. **Use an adjective after a linking verb when the modifier refers to the subject instead of to the verb.** [A linking verb connects a subject to the rest of the sentence. "He is old." "She seems sincere."]

   The man entering the building looked <u>suspicious</u>. [The adjective "suspicious" refers to "man," not to "looked."]

3. **Use comparatives (to compare two) and superlatives (to compare three or more) carefully.**

   She is the <u>faster</u> (not *fastest*) of the two workers.

   Edwin is the <u>better</u> (not *best*) writer of the two team members.

   Exclude a person or thing from a group with which that person or thing is being compared.

   He is more observant than <u>anyone else</u> (not *anyone*) in his department. [As a member of his department, he cannot be more observant than himself.]

   "The X-60 is newer than <u>any other machine</u> (not *any machine*) in the plant." [The X-60 cannot be newer than itself.]

EXERCISE 5

Select the correct word in parentheses.

1. Despite the dangers, employees change their computer passwords (infrequent, infrequently).

2. Daniel looked (impatient, impatiently) at the new production assistant.

3. The server moved (quick, quickly) from table to table.

4. Of the several people I met during the recent speed networking event, Olivia made the (better, best) impression.

5. The Chicago plant has a higher safety record than (any, any other) plant.

PUNCTUATION

Commas

1. **Use a comma**

   a. Between coordinate clauses joined by *and, but, for, or,* and *nor.*

      He wanted to pay his bills on time, <u>but</u> he did not have the money.

   b. To separate introductory clauses and certain phrases from independent clauses. Sentences that begin with dependent clauses (often with words such as *if, as, since, because, although,* and *when*) almost always need a comma.

Prepositional phrases and verbal phrases with five or more words require commas.

Dependent clause:	**If you can postpone your departure, the research team will be able to finalize its proposal submission.** [The comma separates the introductory dependent clause from the independent clause.]
Infinitive:	**To get the full benefit of our insurance plan, complete and return the enclosed card.** [A verb preceded by "to" ("to get")]
Participial:	**Believing that her earnings would continue to increase, she requested a higher credit card limit.** [A verb form used as an adjective: "believing" modifies the dependent clause "she requested"]
Prepositional phrase:	**Within the next few days, you will receive written confirmation of this transaction.** [Comma needed because the phrase contains five words] **Under the circumstances we think you are justified.** [Comma omitted because the phrase contains fewer than five words and the sentence is clear without the comma]

c. To separate three or more words in a series.

You must choose between gray, green, purple, and white. [Without the comma after "purple," no one can tell for sure whether four choices are available, the last of which is "white," or whether three choices are available, the last of which is "purple and white."]

You must choose between purple and white, gray, and green. [Choice is restricted to three, the first of which is "purple and white."]

d. Between two or more independent adjectives that modify the same noun.

New employees are given a long, difficult examination. [Both "long" and "difficult" modify "examination."]

We want quick, factual news. [Both "quick" and "factual" modify "news."]

Do not place a comma between two adjectives when the second adjective modifies the adjective and noun as a unit.

The supervisor is an excellent team player. ["Excellent" modifies the noun phrase "team player."]

e. To separate a nonrestrictive clause (a clause that is not essential to the basic meaning of the sentence) from the rest of the sentence.

Kent Murray, who is head of customer resource management, has selected Century Consulting to oversee the product launch. [The parenthetical remark is not essential to the meaning of the sentence.]

The man who is head of customer resource management has selected Century Consulting to oversee the product launch. [Commas are not needed, because "who is head of customer resource management" is essential to the meaning of the sentence.]

f. To set off or separate dates, addresses, geographical names, degrees, and long numbers:

On July 2, 2013, Jason Kennedy made the final payment. [Before and after the year in month-day-year format]

I saw him in Tahoe City, California, on the 12th of October. [Before and after the name of a state when the name of a city precedes it]

Jesse Marler, President [Between the printed name and the title on the same line beneath a signature or in a letter address]

Tristan A. Highfield
President of Academic Affairs [No comma is used if the title is on a separate line.]

g. To separate parenthetical expressions or other elements interrupting the flow from the rest of the sentence.

Ms. Watson, speaking on behalf of the entire department, accepted the proposal. [To set off a parenthetical expression]

Cole, I believe you have earned a vacation. [After a direct address]

Yes, you can count on me. [After the words *No* and *Yes* when they introduce a statement]

Arun Ramage, former president of the Jackson Institute, spoke to the group. [To set off appositives when neutral emphasis is desired]

The job requires experience, not formal education. [Between contrasted elements]

Semicolons and Colons

1. Use a semicolon

a. To join the independent clauses in a compound sentence when a conjunction is omitted.

> **Your voice counts; email us with your ideas and concerns.**

b. To join the independent clauses in a compound-complex sentence.

> **As indicated earlier, we prefer delivery on Saturday morning at four o'clock; but Friday night at ten o'clock will be satisfactory.**

> **We prefer delivery on Saturday morning at four o'clock; but, if the arrangement is more convenient for you, Friday night at ten o'clock will be satisfactory.**

c. Before an adverbial conjunction. Use a comma after the adverbial conjunction.

Adverbial conjunction:	**The shipment arrived too late for our weekend sale; therefore, we are returning the shipment to you.**

Other frequently used adverbial conjunctions are *however, otherwise, consequently,* and *nevertheless.*

d. Before words used to introduce enumerations or explanations that follow an independent clause.

Enumeration with commas:	**Many factors affect the direction of the stock market; namely, interest rates, economic growth, and employment rates.**
Explanation forming a complete thought:	**We have plans for improvement; for example, we intend .... The engine has been "knocking"; that is, the gas in the cylinders explodes before the pistons complete their upward strokes.**

NOTE: The following exceptions require a comma to introduce the enumeration or explanation:

Enumeration without commas:	**Several Web 2.0 tools are available, for example, blogs and wikis.** [A comma, not a semicolon, is used because the enumeration contains no commas.]
Explanation forming an incomplete thought:	**A trend is to replace expensive employee networking events with purposeful recreation, for instance, community service events.** [A comma, not a semicolon, is used because the explanation is not a complete thought.]

e. In a series that contains commas.

> **Some of our workers have worked overtime this week: Smith, 6 hours; Hardin, 3; Cantrell, 10; and McGowan, 11.**

2. Use a colon

a. After a complete thought that introduces a list of items. Use a colon following both direct and indirect introductions of lists.

| Direct introduction: | **The following three factors influenced our decision: an expanded market, an inexpensive source of raw materials, and a ready source of labor.** [The word "following" clearly introduces a list.] |
| Indirect introduction: | **The carpet is available in three colors: green, burgundy, and blue.** |

Do not use a colon after an introductory statement that ends with a preposition or a verb (*are, is, were, include*). The list that follows the preposition or verb finishes the sentence.

| Incomplete sentence: | **We need to (1) expand our market, (2) locate an inexpensive source of materials, and (3) find a ready source of labor.** [A colon does not follow "to", because the words preceding the list are not a complete sentence.] |

b. To stress an appositive (a noun that renames the preceding noun) at the end of a sentence.

A majority of white collar criminals report that a single factor led to their crimes: pressure to achieve revenue targets.

Our progress is due to the efforts of one person: Brooke Keating.

EXERCISE 7

Insert semicolons, colons, and commas where needed, and delete them where they are unnecessary. Write "correct" if you find no errors.

1. Some privacy concerns have become less important in recent years, however, most people feel extremely vulnerable to privacy invasion.
2. The following agents received bonuses Barnes, $750, Shelley, $800, and Jackson, $950.
3. Employees were notified today of the plant closing they received two weeks' severance pay.
4. This paint does have some disadvantages for example a lengthy drying time.
5. Soon after the applications are received, a team of judges will evaluate them, but the award recipients will not be announced until January 15.
6. The program has one shortcoming: flexibility.
7. The new bakery will offer: frozen yogurt, candies, and baked goods.
8. We are enthusiastic about the plan because: (1) it is least expensive, (2) its legality is unquestioned, and (3) it can be implemented quickly.

Apostrophes

1. **Use an apostrophe to form possessives.**

   a. Add an apostrophe and *s* (*'s*) to form the possessive case of a singular noun or a plural noun that does not end with a pronounced *s*.

Singular noun:	**Jenna's** position
	firm's assets
	employee's benefits

Plural noun without a pronounced *s*:	**men's** clothing
	children's games
	deer's antlers

   b. Add only an apostrophe to form the possessive of a singular or plural noun that ends with a pronounced *s*.

   | Singular noun with pronounced *s*: | **Niagara Falls'** site |
   | | **Ms. Jenkins's** interview |

   | Plural noun with pronounced *s*: | **two managers'** decision |
   | | **six months'** wages |

   Exception: An apostrophe and *s* (*'s*) can be added to singular nouns ending in a pronounced *s* if an additional *s* sound is pronounced easily.

Singular noun with additional *s* sound:	**boss's** decision
	class's party
	Jones's invitation

   c. Use an apostrophe with the possessives of nouns that refer to time (minutes, hours, days, weeks, months, and years) or distance in a possessive manner.

eight **hours'** pay	two **weeks'** notice
today's global economy	ten **years'** experience
a **stone's** throw	a **yard's** length

EXERCISE 8

Correct the possessives.

1. The new hires confidence was crushed by the managers harsh tone.
2. This companies mission statement has been revised since it's recent merger.
3. Employees who are retained may be asked to accept a reduction of one weeks pay.
4. Vendors' have submitted sealed bids for the construction contract that will be opened in two week's.
5. Younger workers must appreciate older employees extensive company knowledge.

Hyphens

1. Use a hyphen

a. Between the words in a compound adjective. (A *compound adjective* is a group of adjectives appearing together and used as a single word to describe a noun.)

An <u>eye-catching</u> device   A <u>two-thirds</u> interest

Do not hyphenate a compound adjective in the following cases:

(1) When the compound adjective follows a noun.

A design that is <u>eye catching</u>.

Today's consumers are <u>convenience driven</u>.

NOTE: Some compound adjectives that are familiar hyphenated words or phrases remain hyphenated when they follow a noun.

The news release was <u>up-to-date</u>.

For jobs that are <u>part-time</u>, ...

(2) An expression made up of an adverb that ends in *ly* and an adjective is not a compound adjective and does not require a hyphen.

<u>commonly accepted</u> principle

<u>widely quoted</u> authority

(3) A simple fraction and a percentage.

Simple fraction: <u>Two thirds</u> of the respondents

Percentage: <u>15 percent</u> sales increase

b. To prevent misinterpretation.

<u>Recover</u> a chair [To obtain possession of a chair once more]

<u>Re-cover</u> a chair [To cover a chair again]

<u>Eight inch</u> blades [Eight blades, each of which is an inch long]

<u>Eight-inch</u> blades [Blades eight inches long]

EXERCISE 9

Add necessary hyphens and delete those that are unnecessary. Write "correct" if you find no errors.

1. The Web based application was unavailable because of a denial of service attack.

2. State of the art computers provide quick access to timely-business information.

3. A large portion of holiday orders are time sensitive.

4. A two thirds majority is needed to pass the 5-percent increase in employee wages.

5. Nearly one-half of the respondents were highly-educated professionals.

Quotation Marks and Italics

1. Use quotation marks

a. To enclose direct quotations.

Single-sentence quotation:	The supervisor said, "We will make progress."
Interrupted quotation:	"We will make progress," the supervisor said, "even though we have to work overtime."
Multiple-sentence quotation:	The manager said, "Have a seat, Seth. Please wait a moment while I complete this email." [Place quotation marks before the first word and after the last word of a multiple-sentence quotation.]
Quotation within quotation:	The budget director said, "Believe me when I say 'A penny saved is a penny earned' is the best advice I ever had." [Use single quotation marks to enclose a quotation that appears within a quotation.]

b. To enclose titles of songs, magazine and newspaper articles, lecture titles, and themes within text.

"Candle in the Wind"   "Making an Impact"

The chapter, "Online Presence," ....

c. To enclose a definition of a defined term. Italicize the defined word.

The term *downsizing* is used to refer to "the planned reduction in the number of employees."

d. To enclose words used in humor, a word used when a different word would be more appropriate, slang expressions that need to be emphasized or clarified for the reader, or nicknames. These words can also be shown in italics.

Humor/ different word:	**Our "football" team ....** [Hints that the team appears to be playing something other than football]
	Our football "team" .... [Hints that "collection of individual players" would be more descriptive than "team"]
	... out for "lunch." [Hints that the reason for being out is something other than lunch]
Slang:	**The "tipping point" in the planned reorganization is securing support of union management.**
Nicknames:	**And now for some comments by Robert "Bob" Johnson**.

2. **Use italics**

a. To mention words, letters, numbers, and phrases within a sentence.

He had difficulty learning to spell *recommendation*.

b. To emphasize a word that is not sufficiently emphasized by other means.

Our goal is to hire the *right* person, not necessarily the most experienced candidate.

c. To indicate the titles of books, magazines, and newspapers.

Creating a Culture of Excellence

The New York Times

Reader's Digest

Dashes, Parentheses, and Periods

1. **Use a dash**

a. To place emphasis on appositives.

His answer—the correct answer—was based on years of experience.

Compare the price—$125—with the cost of a single repair job.

b. When appositives contain commas.

Their scores—Chloe, 21; Tairus, 20; and Drew, 19—were the highest in a group of 300.

c. When a parenthetical remark consists of an abrupt change in thought.

The committee decided—you may think it's a joke, but it isn't—that the resolution should be adopted.

NOTE: Use an em dash (not two hyphens) to form a dash in computer-generated copy.

2. **Use parentheses for explanatory material that could be left out.**

Three of our employees (Kristen Hubbard, Alex Russo, and Mark Coghlan) took their vacations in August.

All our employees (believe it or not) have perfect attendance records.

3. **Use a period after declarative and imperative sentences and courteous requests.**

   We will attend. [Declarative sentence]

   Complete this report. [Imperative sentence]

   Will you please complete the report today. [Courteous request is a question but does not require a verbal answer with requested action.]

EXERCISE 11

Add necessary dashes, parentheses, or periods.

1. Additional consultants, programmers and analysts, were hired to complete the computer conversion. [Emphasize the appositive.]

2. The dividend will be raised to 15 cents a share approved by the Board of Directors on December 1, 2013. [De-emphasize the approval.]

3. Would you link this YouTube video to my slide show?

Number Usage

1. Use figures

   a. In most business writing because figures provide deserved emphasis and are easy for readers to locate if they need to reread for critical points. Regardless of whether a number has one digit or many, use figures to express dates, sums of money, mixed numbers and decimals, distance, dimension, cubic capacity, percentage, weights, temperatures, and chapter and page numbers.

May 10, 2013	**165 pounds**
$9 million	**Chapter 3, page 29**
5 percent (use % in a table)	

   more than 200 applicants (or two hundred) [An approximation]

   b. With ordinals (*th, st, rd, nd*) only when the number precedes the month.

   The meeting is to be held on June 21.

   The meeting is to be held on the 21st of June.

   c. With ciphers but without decimals when presenting even-dollar figures, even if the figure appears in a sentence with another figure that includes dollars and cents.

   Miranda paid $70 for the cabinet.

   Miranda paid $99.95 for the table and $70 for the cabinet.

   d. Numbers that represent time when a.m. or p.m. is used. Words or figures may be used with o'clock.

   Please meet me at 10:15 p.m.

   Please be there at ten o'clock (or 10 o'clock).

   Omit the colon when expressing times of day that include hours but not minutes, even if the time appears in a sentence with another time that includes minutes.

   The award program began at 6:30 p.m. with a reception at 7 p.m.

2. Spell out

   a. Numbers if they are used as the first word of a sentence.

   Thirty-two people attended.

   b. Numbers one through nine if no larger number appears in the same sentence.

   Only three auditors worked at the client's office.

   Send 5 officers and 37 members.

   c. The first number in two consecutive numbers that act as adjectives modifying the same noun; write the second number in figures. If the first number cannot be expressed in one or two words, place it in figures also.

   The package required four 44-cent stamps. [A hyphen joins the second number with the word that follows it, thus forming a compound adjective that describes the noun "stamps."]

   We shipped 250 180-horsepower engines today. [Figures are used because neither number can be expressed in one or two words.]

EXERCISE 12

Correct the number usage in the following sentences taken from a letter or a report.

1. The question was answered by sixty-one percent of the respondents.

2. The meeting is scheduled for 10:00 a.m. on February 3rd.

3. These 3 figures appeared on the expense account: $21.95, $30.00, and $35.14.

4. The purchasing manager ordered 50 4-GB hard drives.

5. 21 members voted in favor of the $2,000,000 proposal.

6. Approximately one hundred respondents requested a copy of the results.

7. Mix two quarts of white with 13 quarts of brown.

8. Examine the cost projections on page eight.

CAPITALIZATION

Capitalize

1. **Proper nouns (words that name a particular person, place, or thing) and adjectives derived from proper nouns.** Capitalize the names of persons, places, geographic areas, days of the week, months of the year, holidays, deities, specific events, and other specific names.

Proper nouns	Common nouns
Jessica Moore	An applicant for the management position
Bonita Lakes	A land development
Centre Park Mall	A new shopping center
Veteran's Day	A federal holiday
Information Age	A period of time
Proper adjectives:	Irish potatoes, Roman shades, Swiss army knife, Chinese executives, British accent, Southern dialect

Do not capitalize the name of the seasons unless they are personified.

Old Man Winter

2. **The principal words in the titles of books, magazines, newspapers, articles, compact discs, movies, plays, television series, songs, and poems.**

The Carrot Principle [Book]

"Smart Moves for New Leaders" [Article]

Time [Magazine]

The White Album [Compact disc]

3. **The names of academic courses that are numbered, are specific course titles, or contain proper nouns.** Capitalize degrees used after a person's name and specific academic sessions.

Addison Malone is enrolled in classes in French, mathematics, science, and English.

Students entering the MBA program must complete Accounting 6093 and Finance 5133.

Allison Ward, M.S., will teach International Marketing during Spring Semester 2013.

Professor O'Donnell earned a master's degree in business from Harvard.

4. **Titles that precede a name.**

Mr. Ronald Moxley	Editor Deeden
Dr. Lauren Zolna	President Lopez
Uncle Ian	Professor Copley

Do not capitalize titles appearing alone or following a name unless they appear in addresses.

The manager approved the proposal submitted by the editorial assistant.

Jon Sharma, executive vice president, is responsible for that account.

Clint has taken the position formerly held by his father.

Address all correspondence to Colonel Michael Anderson, Department Head, 109 Crescent Avenue, Baltimore, MD 21208.

5. **The main words in a division or department name if the official or specific name is known or the name is used in a return address, a letter address, or a signature block.**

Official or specific name known:	Return the completed questionnaire to the Public Relations Department by March 15.
Official or specific name unknown:	Employees in your information systems division are invited ....
Return or letter address, signature block:	Mr. Blake Cain, Manager, Public Relations Department

6. **Most nouns followed by numbers (except in page, paragraph, line, size, and verse references).**

Policy No. 8746826	Exhibit A	Chapter 7
page 97, paragraph 2	Figure 3-5	Model L-379
Flight 340, Gate 22	size 8, Style 319 jacket	

7. **The first word of a direct quotation.**

The placement officer warned, "Those with offensive email habits may be the first to lose their jobs during layoffs."

Do not capitalize the first word in the last part of an interrupted quotation or the first word in an indirect quotation.

"We will proceed," he said, "with the utmost caution." [Interrupted quotation]

He said that the report must be submitted by the end of the week. [Indirect quotation]

8. **The first word following a colon when a formal statement or question follows.**

Here is an important rule for report writers: Plan your work and work your plan.

Each sales staff should ask this question: Do I really look like a representative of my firm?

EXERCISE 13

Copy each of the following sentences, making essential changes in capitalization.

1. The first question professor Burney asked me during interviewing 101 was "why do you want to work for us?"

2. The remodeling will give the store a more sophisticated feel according to the Public Relations Director.

3. As the Summer Season arrives, gas prices are expected to rise.

4. We recently purchased digital juice, an excellent source of copyright-free animated images.

5. Thomas Frieden, Director of the Centers for Disease Control, is the agency's key communicator.

WORDS FREQUENTLY MISUSED

These words are frequently misused. If you're not certain of meaning or usage, check a dictionary or style guide.

1. Accept, except
2. Advice, advise
3. Affect, effect
4. Among, between
5. Amount, number
6. Capital, capitol
7. Cite, sight, site
8. Complement, compliment
9. Continual, continuous
10. Credible, creditable
11. Council, counsel
12. Different from, different than
13. Each other, one another
14. Eminent, imminent
15. Envelop, envelope
16. Farther, further
17. Fewer, less
18. Formally, formerly
19. Infer, imply
20. Its, it's
21. Lead, led
22. Lose, loose
23. Media, medium
24. Personal, personnel
25. Principal, principle
26. Reason is, because
27. Stationary, stationery
28. That, which
29. Their, there, they're
30. To, too, two

EXERCISE 14

Select the correct word or phrase in parentheses.

1. What (affect, effect) will the change have on us?

2. The consultant plans to (advice, advise) the company to eliminate the fourth shift for at least three months.

3. The (amount, number) of complaints from customers declined with the addition of online chat.

4. The (cite, sight, site) of the new 24/7 fitness center is being debated.

5. I consider your remark a (compliment, complement); I agree that the granite countertops (compliment, complement) the deep, earthy tones in the room.

6. The three panelists were constantly interrupting (each other, one another).

7. Generally staple merchandise is placed (farther, further) from the cashier than impulse items.

8. Limit your discussion to five or (fewer, less) points.

9. I (infer, imply) from Avanti's comments to the press that the merger will occur.

10. The hurricane seems to be (losing loosing) (its, it's) force, which is (different from, different than) predictions.

11. The chemical engineer (lead, led) the research team's investigation to eliminate (lead, led) from gas emissions.

12. Employees may handle (personal, personnel) business during e-breaks beginning next week.

13. Customer perception is the (principal, principle) reason for the change.

14. (Their, There, They're) planning to complete (their, there, they're) strategic plan this week.

15. The (to, too, two) external auditors expect us (to, too, two) complete (to, too, two) many unnecessary reports.

SOLUTIONS TO EXERCISES

Exercise 1—Sentence Structure

1. You must learn to design spreadsheets that make financial information meaningful to users.

2. Many online tools are available that build relationships with customers.

3. I am submitting an employee testimonial, which I first posted to a presentations blog, to the company website.

4. More companies are videoconferencing because of the need to reduce travel costs significantly.

5. You must perform periodic maintenance on your computer to keep it operating efficiently. [The introductory phrase dangles.]

6. Planned store improvements include widening the aisles, improving lighting, and lowering shelves for a sophisticated feel.

   Planned store improvements include widened aisles, improved lighting, and lowered shelves for a sophisticated feel.

Exercise 2—Pronoun Reference

1. affect
2. was
3. her
4. was
5. its
6. its
7. this oversight

Exercise 3—Pronoun Case

1. us
2. her
3. she; who
4. his
5. whom

Exercise 4—Verb Agreement, Tense, and Mood

1. has
2. are
3. were
4. were
5. is
6. has
7. is
8. doesn't
9. started
10. were

Exercise 5—Adjectives and Adverbs

1. infrequently
2. impatiently
3. quickly
4. best
5. any other

Exercise 6—Commas

1. Correct

2. Emoticons, which are created by keying combinations of symbols to produce "sideway faces," communicate emotion in electronic messages.

3. Sean Cohen, a new member of the board, remained silent during the long, bitter debate.

4. Top social networking sites include Facebook, MySpace, and Flickr.

5. The entire population was surveyed, but three responses were unusable.

6. If you tag websites in a social bookmarking site, you can locate them easily for later use.

7. To qualify for the position, applicants must have technology certification.

8. We should be spending less money, not more.

9. On May 9, 2013, the company's Twitter site was launched.

10. Yes, the president approved a team building event to replace our annual golf outing.

Exercise 7—Semicolons and Colons

1. Some privacy concerns have become less important in recent years; however, most people feel extremely vulnerable to privacy invasion.

2. The following agents received bonuses: Barnes, $750; Shelley, $800; and Jackson, $950.

3. Employees were notified today of the plant closing; they received two weeks' severance pay.

4. This paint does have some disadvantages, for example, a lengthy drying time.

5. Soon after the applications are received, a team of judges will evaluate them; but the award recipients will not be announced until January 15.

6. Correct

7. The new bakery will offer frozen yogurt, candies, and baked goods.

8. We are enthusiastic about the plan because (1) it is least expensive, (2) its legality is unquestioned, and (3) it can be implemented quickly.

Exercise 8—Apostrophes

1. hire's; manager's
2. company's; its
3. week's
4. Vendors; weeks
5. employees'

Exercise 9—Hyphens

1. Web-based; denial-of-service attack

2. State-of-the-art; timely business

3. Correct

4. two-thirds; 5 percent

5. one half; highly educated

Exercise 10—Quotation Marks and Italics

1. Cynthia Cooper's *Extraordinary Circumstances* is required reading in some forensic accounting classes. [Italicizes a book title]

2. The article "How to Persuade People to Say Yes" appeared in the May 2009 issue of *Training Journal.* [Encloses the name of an article in quotation marks and italicizes the title of a journal]

3. The consultant's "accomplishments" are summarized on her opening blog page. [Uses quotation marks to introduce doubt about whether *accomplishments* is the right label; her undertakings may have been of little significance]

4. Connie said, "I want to participate in a volunteer program that serves such a worthy cause." [Uses quotations marks in a direct quotation]

5. The term *flame* is online jargon for "a heated, sarcastic, sometimes abusive message or posting to a discussion group." [Italicizes a defined term and encloses the definition in quotes]

6. Limit random "tweets," but focus on ideas and issues that are interesting and relevant. [Uses quotation marks to emphasize or clarify a word for the reader]

Exercise 11—Dashes, Parentheses, and Periods

1. Additional consultants—programmers and analysts—were hired to complete the computer conversion.

2. The dividend will be raised to 15 cents a share (approved by the Board of Directors on December 1, 2013).

3. Would you link this YouTube video to my slide show. [Uses a period to follow courteous request that requires no verbal response]

Exercise 12—Number Usage

1. The question was answered by 61 percent of the respondents.

2. The meeting is scheduled for 10 a.m. on February 3.

3. These three figures appeared on the expense account: $21.95, $30, and $35.14.

4. The purchasing manager ordered fifty 4-GB Flash drives.

5. Twenty-one members voted in favor of the $2 million proposal.

6. Approximately 100 respondents requested a copy of the results. [Approximations above nine that can be expressed in one or two words may be written in either figures or words, but figures are more emphatic.]

7. Mix 2 quarts of white with 13 quarts of brown.

8. Examine the cost projections on page 8.

Exercise 13—Capitalization

1. The first question Professor Burney asked me during Interviewing 101 was "Why do you want to work for us?"

2. The remodeling will give the store a more sophisticated feel according to the public relations director.

3. As the summer season arrives, gas prices are expected to rise.

4. We recently purchased Digital Juice, an excellent source of copyright-free animated images.

5. Thomas Frieden, director of the Centers for Disease Control, is the agency's key communicator.

Exercise 14—Words Frequently Misused

1. effect
2. advise
3. number
4. site
5. compliment; complement
6. one another
7. farther
8. fewer
9. infer
10. losing; its; different from
11. led; lead
12. personal
13. principal
14. they're; their
15. two; to; too

REFERENCES

1

1. Koncz, A. (2007, March 15). Employers cite communication skills, honesty/integrity as key for job candidates. National Association of Colleges and Employers. Retrieved from www.naceweb.org/press/display.asp?year=2007&prid+254.

2. *Huffington Post* (2013). What big businesses can teach you about building company culture. Retrieved May 13, 2014 from http://www.huffingtonpost.com/2013/12/10/what-big-business-can-tea_n_4194514.html.

3. Tapscott, D. (2008, December 8). Supervising Net Gen. Business Week Online, 5. Retrieved from Business Source Complete Database.

4. Slayton, M. (1980). *Common sense and everyday ethics*. Washington, D.C.: Ethics Resource Center.

5. Brzezinski, N. (2014). Diversity and ethics, keys to corporate success: Interview with Global CEO Skanska. *Huffington Post*. Retrieved May 13, 2014 from http://www.huffingtonpost.com/natalia-lopatniuk-brzezinski/diversity-ethics-keys-to-_b_4901755.html.

6. A gift or a bribe? (2002, September). *State Legislatures*, 2 (8), 9.

7. Mathison, D. L. (1988). Business ethics cases and decision models: A call for relevancy in the classroom. *Journal of Business Ethics*, 10, 781.

8. Wile, R. (2014). France didn't actually ban work email after 6 PM—But what did happen is still really funny. *Business Insider*. Retrieved May 13, 2014 from http://www.businessinsider.com/the-truth-about-frances-work-email-ban-2014-4#ixzz31dgeCZqP.

9. Mayer, M. (2014). The most hilarious responses to Marie Claire's cornrow Twitter drama. *The Huffington Post*. Retrieved May 13, 2014 from http://www.huffingtonpost.com/2014/04/05/marie-claire-cornrows-twitter-reactions_n_5093125.html.

10. Earley, P. C. and Ang, S. (2003). *Cultural Intelligence: Individual Interactions Across Cultures*. Stanford: Stanford Business Books.

11. Kaplan A. M. & Haenlein M. (2010). Users of the world, unite! The challenges and opportunities of social media. *Business Horizons*, 53 (1), 61.

12. Felts, C. (1995). Taking the mystery out of self-directed work teams. *Industrial Management*, 37 (2), 21–26.

13. Miller, B. K., & Butler, J. B. (1996, November/December). Teams in the workplace. *New Accountant*, 18–24.

14. Ray, D., & Bronstein, H. (1995). *Teaming Up*. New York: McGraw-Hill.

15. The trouble with teams. (1995, January 4). *Economist*, 61.

16. Frohman, M. A. (1995, April 3). Do teams … but do them right. *Industry Week*, 21–24.

17. Zuidema, K. R., & Kleiner, B. H. (1994). New developments in developing self-directed work groups. *Management Decision*, 32 (8), 57–63.

18. Barry, D. (1991). Managing the baseless team: Lessons in distributed leadership. *Organizational Dynamics*, 20 (1), 31–47.

19. Powell, A., Piccoli, G. & Ives. B. (2004). Virtual teams: A review of current literature and directions for future research. *The DATABASE for Advances in Information Systems*, 35 (1).

2

1. Interpersonal intelligence. (2009). My Personality. Retrieved from www.mypersonality.info/multiple -intelligences/interpersonal/.

2. Galpin, T. (1995, April). Pruning the grapevine. *Training & Development*, 49 (4), 28+.

3. Hershey, P., & Blanchard, K. H. (1982). *Management of Organizational Behavior: Utilizing Human Resources* (4th Ed.). Englewood Cliffs, NJ: Prentice-Hall.

4. Felts, C. (1995). Taking the mystery out of self-directed work teams. *Industrial Management*, 37 (2), 21–26.

5. Mehrabian, A. (1971). *Silent Messages*. Belmont, CA: Wadsworth.

6. Andrew D. Wolvin and Carolyn G. Coakley, Listening, 5th ed. (Madison, WI: Brown and Benchmark, 1996), p. 15.

7. Michael Purdy, "The Listener Wins," http://featuredreports.monster.com/listen/overview.

8. Costa, J. (2013). 3 ways listening can make you a better leader. *The Huffington Post*. Retrieved May 15, 2014 from http://www.huffingtonpost.com/jose-costa/leadership-skills-advice_b_3796177.html.

9. Drucker, Peter. (1990). The Fifth Discipline. The art and practice of the learning organization. London: Random House.

10. Gratton, L. (2007, June 6). Working together … When apart. *Wall Street Journal*. Retrieved from http://online.wsj.com/news/articles/SB118165895540732559.

11. Zuidema, K. R., & Kleiner, B. H. (1994, October). Self-directed work groups gain popularity. *Business Credit*, 21–26.

12. Hunt, V. D. (1993). *Managing for quality: Integrating quality and business strategy* (121). Homewood, IL: Business One Irwin.

13. Munter, M. (1998, June). Meeting technology: From low-tech to high-tech. *Business Communication Quarterly*, 61 (2), 80–87.

3

1. Canavor, N., & Meirowitz, C. (2005). Good corporate writing: Why it matters, and what to do; Poor corporate writing—in press releases, ads, brochures, web sites and more—is costing companies credibility and reviews. Here's how to put the focus back on clear communication. *Communication World*, 22 (4), 30–34.

2. Schein, E. H. (1992). *Educational Culture and Leadership*. New York: Jossey-Bass, 12.

3. Stallard, M. L. (2011, January 21). Has SAS Institute's goodnight cracked the code on corporate culture? Insights on Leadership and Employee Engagement. Retrieved from http://www.michaelleestallard.com/has-sasinstitutes-goodnight-cracked-the-code-oncorporate-culture.

4. Cameron, K. S. & Quinn, R. E. (2011). *Diagnosing and Changing Organizational Culture: Based on the Competing Values Framework*. New York: John Wiley & Sons.

5. Bradford, J. (2013). 5-Hour Energy accused of false advertising over "no crash" claim. *The Huffington Post*. Retrieved May 15, 2014 from http://www.huffingtonpost.com/2013/01/03/5-hour-energy-no-crash-false-advertising_n_2403015.html.

6. Karoub, J. (2013). McDonald's to pay $700,000 to settle allegations franchise falsely claimed food complied with halal. *The Huffington Post*. Retrieved May 15, 2014 from http://www.huffingtonpost.com/2013/01/21/mcdonalds-halal_n_2522254.html.

7. Thomas, E. (2014). Vibram, "barefoot running shoe" company, settles multi-million dollar lawsuit. *The Huffington Post*. Retrieved May 15, 2014 from http://www.huffingtonpost.com/2014/05/10/_n_5302213.html.

8. Mackay, M. (2012). Ex-Yahoo CEO Scott Thompson and seven other cases of resume fraud. *The Huffington Post*. Retrieved May 15, 2014 from http://www.huffingtonpost.com/2012/05/15/yahoo-ceo-scott-thompsons-resume-fraud_n_1516061.html.

9. Telushkin, J. (1997). Avoid words that hurt. *USA Today*, 74.

10. Choi, Candace (2012). Odd Snack Flavors Prove Successful for International Food Companies. Retrieved June 13, 2015 from http://www.huffingtonpost.com/2012/05/06/odd-snack-flavors_n_1489639.html

4

1. Charlton, J. (Ed.). (1995). *The Writer's Quotation Book*. Stamford, CT: Ray Freeman.

2. Is email making bosses ruder? (2005). *European Business Forum*, 21, 72.

3. Rindegard, J. (1999). Use clear writing to show you mean business. *InfoWorld*, 21 (47), 78.

4. Dyrud, M. A. (1996). Teaching by example: Suggestions for assignment design. *Business Communication Quarterly*, 59 (3), 67–70.

5. Redish, J. C. (1993). Understanding readers. In C. M. Barnum & S. Carliner (Eds.), *Techniques for Technical Communicators*. New York: Prentice-Hall.

6. Ibid.

7. Good, C. (2009, March 20). Quote of the Day: Special Olympics Chairman Tim Shriver on Obama's Special Olympics Joke. Retrieved from http://www.theatlantic.com/politics/archive/2009/03/quote-of-the-day-special-olympics-chairman-tim-shriver-on-obamas-special-olympics-joke/1689/.

8. Neuwirth, R. (1998). Error message: To err is human, but darn expensive. *Editor & Publisher*, 131 (29), 4.

9. UCSD sends acceptance email to wrong list. (2009, April 2). *Eschool News*. Retrieved from http://www.eschoolnews.com/news/around-the-web/index.cfm?i=58045.

5

1. Hear no evil, see no evil: Business e-mail overtakes the telephone. (2007, August 20). *Network*. Retrieved from www.networkworld.com/community/node/18555.

2. Silverman, D. (2009, April 14). Words at work: How to revise an email so that people will read it. Retrieved from http://blogs.harvardbusiness.org/silverman/2009/04/how-to-revise-an -email-so-that.html.

3. Silverman, D. (2009, April 14). Words at work: Is your email businesslike—or brusque? Retrieved from http://blogs.harvardbusiness.org/silverman/2009/04/is-your-email-businesslike-or.html.

4. New technology makes work harder. (1999, June 1). *BBC News*. Retrieved from http://news.bbc.co.uk/2/hi/science/nature/357993.stm.

5. Lacy, S. (2006, January 6). IM security one tough sell. *Business Week Online*, 11.

6. Knapp, L. (2007, January 20). Switching to texting has pluses, minuses: Getting started. *Seattle Times*, E6. Retrieved from General Business File database.

7. McGrath, C. (2006, January 22). The pleasures of the text. *The New York Times*, 15.

8. Knapp, L. (2007, January 20). Switching to texting has pluses, minuses: Getting started. *Seattle Times*, E6. Retrieved from General Business File database.

9. Electronic Privacy Information Center. (2008, September 15). Public opinion on privacy. Retrieved from www.epic.org/privacy/survey.

10. 9th circuit court rules on text-messaging privacy. (2008, July 15). Law.com. Retrieved from www.law.com/jsp/legaltechnology/pubArticleLT-jsp?id=1202422970200.

11. Brown, P. B. (2005, December 31). Resolved: I will take good advice. *The New York Times*. Retrieved from http://www.nytimes.com/2005/12/31/business/31offline.html.

12. Mabrey, V., Scott, D. W., & Foster, M. (2008, March 24). Charges filed in Detroit mayor scandal. *ABC News*. Retrieved from http://abcnews.go.com/print?id=4355795.

13. Varchaver, N. (2003). The perils of e-mail. *Fortune*, 147 (3), 96+.

14. Ibid.

15. Downer, K. (2008). A great website in five steps. *Third Sector*, 9.

16. Tierney, J. (2007, April). Ignore universal web design at your own peril. *Multi-channel Merchant*, 8.

17. Fichter, D. (2001, November/December). Zooming in: Writing content for intranets. *Online*, 25(6), 80+.

18. McAlpine, R. (2001). *Web Word Wizardry: A Guide to Writing for the Web and Intranet*. Berkeley, CA: Ten Speed Press.

19. Seventy-nine percent of large international companies are using (2010, February 23). *Bloomberg*. Retrieved from http://www.bloomberg.com/apps/news?pid=newsarchive&sid=a_M.jlgajlbw.

20. Weblog. (2005). Loosely coupled. Retrieved from www.looselycoupled.com/glossary/weblog.

21. Quible, Z. K. (2005). Blogs and written business communication courses: A perfect union. *Journal of Education for Business*, 80 (6), 327–332.

22. Jones, D. (2005, May 10). CEOs refuse to get tangled up in messy blogs. *USA Today*. Retrieved from Academic Search Premier database.

23. DeBare, I. (2005, May 5). Tips for effective use of blogs in business. *San Francisco Chronicle*, C6.

24. Hutchins, J. P. (2005, November 14). Beyond the water cooler. *ComputerWorld*, 39 (46), 45–46.

25. How to write for the web. (2008, March 26). *The Online Journalism Review*. Retrieved from www.ojr.org/ojr/wiki/writing.

26. Goodnoe, E. (2005, August 8). How to use wikis for business. *Information Week*. Retrieved from www.informationweek.com/news/management/showArticle.jhtml?articleID=16760331&pgno=3&queryText=&isPrev=.

27. Johnson, C. Y. (2008, July 7). Hurry up, the customer has a complaint: As blogs expand the reach of a single voice, firms monitor the Internet looking for the dissatisfied. *The Boston Globe*. Retrieved from www.Boston.com.

28. How to get the most out of voice mail. (2000, February). *The CPA Journal*, 70 (2), 11.

29. Leland, K., & Bailey, K. (1999). *Customer Service for Dummies* (2nd Ed.). New York: Wiley.

30. Berkley, S. (2003, July). Help stamp out bad voicemail! *The Voice Coach Newsletter*. Retrieved from www.greatvoice.com/archive_vc/archiveindex_vc.html.

31. McCarthy, M. L. (1999, October). Email, voicemail and the Internet: How employers can avoid getting cut by the double-edged sword of technology. *Business Credit*, 100 (9), 44+.

32. Norris, D. (2007). Sales communications in a mobile world: Using the latest technology and retaining the personal touch. *Business Communication Quarterly*, 70, 492–498.

33. Au: Please provide complete reference as per first pass page.

34. Krotz, J. L. (2008). Cell phone etiquette: 10 dos and don'ts. *Microsoft Business*. Retrieved from www.microsoft.com/smallbusiness/resources/technology/communications/cell-phone-etiquette-10-dos-and-donts.aspx#Cellphoneetiquettedosanddonts.

35. Cell phone etiquette. (2001, March). *Office Solutions*, 18 (3), 13.

36. Coustan, D., & Strickland, J. (n.d.). How smartphones work: The future of smartphones. Retrieved from http://communication.howstuffworks.com/smartphone5.htm.

37. Stebben, G. (2013). Tech Q&A: How secure is the cloud? What you need to know about your personal data being stored everywhere. *Men's Health*. Retrieved May 16, 2014 from http://www.menshealth.com/techlust/tech-qa-how-secure-cloud.

6

1. Williamson, M. (2008, June 11). Twittering the Internet. *TechnologyStory.com*. Retrieved from http://www.technologystory.com/2008/06/11/twittering-the-internet.

7

1. Swisher, K. (2007, October 15). AOL layoffs letter from CEO Randy Falco. *All Things Digital*. Retrieved from http://allthingsd.com/20071015/aol-layoffs-letter-from-randy-falco/.

2. Ethical workforce reflects honest management. (2008, June). *Internal Auditor*, 18–19.

3. Advice from the pros on the best way to deliver bad news. (2003, February). *IOMA's Report on Customer Relationship Management*, 5–6.

4. Purina on pet food recall 4-26-07. (2007). American Kennel Club. Retrieved from http://clubs.akc.org/brit/NEWS/07 .PurinaPetFoodRecall.htm.

5. Workers get better at bearing bad news. (2005, October 11). *Personnel Today*, 46.

6. Expert offers advice about how to lay off employees. (2008, October 9). *Immediate Care Business*. Retrieved from http:// www.immediatecarebusiness.com/hotnews/ layingoff-employees.html.

7. Coombs, W. T. (2007). Protecting organization reputations during a crisis: The development and application of situational crisis communication theory. *Corporate Reputation Review 10* (3), 163–176; Coombs, W. T. (2004). Impact of past crisis on current crisis communications: Insights from situational crisis communication theory. *Journal of Business Communication 41* (3), 265–289; Coombs, W. T. & Holladay, S. J. (2002). Helping crisis managers protect reputational assets: Initial tests of the situational crisis communication theory. *Management Communication Quarterly 16* (2), 165–186.

8. Coombs, W. T. (2007). Protecting organization reputations during a crisis: The development and application of situational crisis communication theory. *Corporate Reputation Review 10* (3), 163–176; Coombs, W. T. (2004). Impact of past crisis on current crisis communications: Insights from situational crisis communication theory. *Journal of Business Communication 41* (3), 265–289; Coombs, W. T. & Holladay, S. J. (2002). Helping crisis managers protect reputational assets: Initial tests of the situational crisis communication theory. *Management Communication Quarterly 16* (2), 165–186.

8

1. Cody, S. (1906). *Success in letter writing: Business and social* (pp. 122–126). Chicago: A. C. McClurg.

2. Lotus Cars. Retrieved July 28, 2013, from www.lotuscars.com/gb/our-cars/current-range/elise-range.

3. Apple. Retrieved July 28, 2013, from www.apple.com/ipad/why-ipad-retina/.

4. http://home.mcafee.com/Store/Package-Detail.aspx?pkgid=275.

5. Sinclair, B. (2003, July 20). Handle client complaints. *The Web design business kit*. Retrieved from http:// www.sitepoint.com/ article/handle -client-complaints/.

9

1. Grimes, B. (2003, May 6). Fooling Google. *PC Magazine*, 22(8), 74.

2. McIntyre, Douglas A., Ashley C. Allen, Samuel Weigley, and Michael B. Sauter. (October 17, 2012). The worst business decisions of all time. *24/7 Wall St*. Retrieved from http://247wallst.com/specialreport/2012/10/17/the-worst-businessdecisions-of-all-time/3/.

10

1. Gallo, C. (2008, December 10). Making YouTube work for your business. *Business Week Online*. Retrieved from www.businessweek.com/stories/ 2008-12-09/making-youtube-work-for-yourbusinessbusinessweek-business-news-stockmarket-and-financial-advice.

2. Martin, M. H. (1997, November 27). The man who makes sense of numbers. *Fortune*, 273–275.

3. Simons, T. (2004). The multimedia paradox. *Presentations*, 18(9), 24–25.

11

No endnotes.

12

1. Kalytiak, T. (2008, October). Overcoming speaking anxiety: Toastmasters sculpt shy speakers into outstanding orators. *Alaska Business Monthly*. Retrieved from http:// www.akbizmag.com.

2. Axtell, R. E. (1992). *Do's and Taboos of Public Speaking: How to Get Those Butterflies Flying in Formation*. New York: John Wiley.

3. National Center for Biotechnology Information, U.S. National Library of Medicine, *The Associated Press*, (2014). Retrieved May 25, 2014 from http://statisticbrain.com/ attention-span-statistics/.

4. Britz, J. D. (1999, October). You can't catch a marlin with a meatball. *Presentations*, 13 (10), A1–22.

5. Hughes, M. (1990). Tricks of the speechwriter's trade. *Management Review*, 9 (11), 56–58.

6. Somerville, J. (2003). Presentation tip: Stop the verbal spam. About. com:Entrepreneurs. Retrieved from http:// entrepreneurs.about.com/cs/marketing/a/ infodumping.htm.

7. Simmons, A. (2007). *Whoever Tells the Best Story Wins: How to Use Your Own Stories to Communicate with Power and Impact*. New York: Amacon.

8. Gallo, C. (2009, April 8). Making your presentations relevant. *Business Week Online*, 15.

9. Axtell, R. E. (1992). *Do's and Taboos of Public Speaking: How to Get Those Butterflies Flying in Formation*. New York: John Wiley.

10. Decker, B. (1992). *You've Got to Be Believed to Be Heard*. New York: St. Martin's Press.

11. Hillary Clinton's campaign sends "docu-points" to House Dems. (2008, May 10). *Presentation Zen*. Retrieved from http://www.presentationzen.com/presentationzen/2008/05/hillary-campaig.html.

12. Earnest, W. (2007). *Save Our Slides: PowerPoint Design That Works*. Dubuque, IA: Kendall/Hunt.

13. CNN Staff (2008, April 5). Jonathan Knight exits New Kids on the Block show mid-concert. *CNN Entertainment*. Retrieved from http://www.cnn.com/2013/04/05/ showbiz/music/jonathan-knight-walks-off-concert/index.html.

14. Decker, B. (1992). *You've Got to Be Believed to Be Heard*. New York: St. Martin's Press

15. Hanke, J. (1998, January). Presenting as a team. *Presentations*, 12 (1), 74–82.

16. Ibid.

17. Ibid.

18. Davids, M. (1999). Smiling for the camera. *Journal of Business Strategy*, 20 (3), 20–24.

19. Turner, C. (1998, February). Become a web presenter? (Really it's not that hard). *Presentations*, 12 (2), 26–27.

20. Sturges, D. L. (1994). Communicating through crisis: A strategy for organizational survival. *Management Communication Quarterly*, 7, 297–316.

21. Mitroff, I.I. & Alpasian, M. C. (2004, Spring). A toolkit for managing crises and preparing for the unthinkable. *The Mitroff Report*, 1, 81–88.

22. Argenti, P. (1998). *Corporate Communication* (2nd Ed.). Boston, MA: Irwin/McGraw-Hill.

13

1. Jackson, T. (2003). Find a job you love and success will follow. Career Journal (*The Wall Street Journal*). Retrieved from http://www.careerjournal.com/jobhunting/ strategies/20030415-jackson.html.

2. Top 15 Most Popular Job Websites (2014, May). Retrieved May 26, 2014 from http:// www.ebizmba.com/articles/job-websites.

3. Riley, M. F. (2009). The Riley guide: Employment opportunities and job resources on the Internet. Retrieved from http://www .rileyguide.com.

4. Ireland, S. (2002, July–August). A resume that works. *Searcher*, 10 (7), 98–110.

5. Harshbarger, C. (2003). You're out! *Strategic Finance*, 84 (11), 46–50.

6. Elefant, C. (2008, March 11). Do employers using Facebook for background checks face legal risks? Legal Blog Watch. Retrieved from http://legalblogwatch. typepad.com/legal_blog_watch/2008/03/do-employers-us.html.

7. Garone, E. (2009, March 18). Do references really matter? WSJ.com: Careers Q&A. Retrieved from http://online.wsj.com/article/SB123672074032087901.html.

8. Are you using the wrong resume? (2009). Careerbuilder.com. Retrieved from http://www.careerbuilder.com/Article/CB-998-Cover-Letters-and-Resumes-Are-You-Using-the-Wrong-R%C3%A9sum5C3%A9/.

9. Resumes you don't see everyday. (2006). Retrieved from http://www.dummies.com/WileyCDA/DummiesArticle/id-1610.html.

10. Young, J. (2002). "E-portfolios" could give students a new sense of their accomplishments. *Chronicle of Higher Education*, 48 (26), 31–32.

11. Sipper, R. A. (2007, October 15). Tips for creating a YouTube video resume. Retrieved from http://www.associatedcontent.com/article/414702/tips_for_creating_a_youtube_video_resume.html?cat=3.

14

1. Vogt, P. (2006). Acing behavioral interviews. *Career Journal.com*. Retrieved from www.careerjournaleurope.com/jobhunting/interviewing/19980129-vogt.html

2. Marion, L. C. (1997, January 11). Companies tap keyboards to interview applicants. *The News and Observer*, p. B5.

3. Thomson Learning announces name change to Cengage Learning. (2007, October). High Beam Research. Retrieved from www.highbeam.com/doc/1G1-168632242.html (pay to view)

4. Burns, D. (2009). *The first 60 seconds: Win the job interview before it begins*. Naperville, IL: Sourcebooks.

5. Lai, P., & Wong, I. (2000). The clash of cultures in the job interview. *Journal of Language for International Business*, 11 (1), 31–40.

6. Austin, N. K. (1996, March). The new job interview. *Working Woman*, 23–24.

7. Kennedy, J. L., & Morrow, T. J. (1994). *Electronic résumé revolution: Create a winning résumé for the new world of job seeking*. New York: John Wiley.

8. Kleiman, P. (2003, May). Armed for a multitude of tasks. *The Times Higher Education Supplement*, p. 4.

9. MIT Career Development Center (2008, September 16). STAR method: *Behavioral interviewing*. Retrieved from www.lpnet.org/site/programs/docs/STAR%20MethodHandout.pdf.

10. Stern, L. (2005, January 17). The tough new job hunt. *Newsweek*, 73–74.

11. Gray. E. (2015, June 22). Do you understand why stars twinkle? Would you rather read than watch TV? Do you trust data more than your instincts? And other strange questions you need to get a job in the era of optimized hiring. *Time*, 40–47.

12. Interviews: Handling illegal interview questions. *JobWeb*. Retrieved from http://www.jobweb.org/interviews.aspx?id=1343.

BCOM ONLINE

STUDY YOUR WAY
WITH STUDYBITS!

INDEX

A

ABI Inform First Search, 153
abstract, 180
Academic Search Elite, 153
accents, 211
accident crisis, 125
acknowledgment messages, 99–100
active voice, 51–52
  formal reports, 186
  readability, 62–64
addenda
  formal reports, 179, 182–183
  proposals, 196
adhocracy culture, 38
adjustment messages, 93
age bias, 68
agenda, 34
aggressive interpersonal communication, 29
AIDA (attention, interest, desire, action), 130
Allen, Sharon, 121
Alpha Chi Epsilon, 250
American Broadcast English, 211
analogies, 60
analysis, 182
analytical reports, 147, 182
analytics, 265
antivirus software program, 76
AOL, 153
APA Publication, 161
appendix, 182–183
Apple Keynote, 207
application forms, 267
application messages, 247
  encouraging action, 250–251
  evidence of qualifications, 249–250
  formatting, 252
  gaining receiver's attention, 249
  persuasive organization, 247, 249
  proofreading, 252
  unsolicited, 247
  writing, 251–252
appreciation messages, 90–92
The Apprentice, 107
area charts, 173
Arthur Andersen, 80
articulation, 211
Ashley, 134
Ask, 153
assertive interpersonal communication, 29
AT&T, 68
audience
  adapting message to needs and concerns of, 44–46
  age of, 42
  compliments, 45
  culturally diverse audiences, 215–216
  culture, 42–43
  economic level, 42
  education/occupational background, 42
  envisioning, 41–44
  expectations, 43
  mental picture of, 44
  needs and concerns of, 42
  outlining message benefits to, 47

persuasive messages, 129–130
presentations, 202–203
rapport, 43
reaction to message, 48
relationship with product, service, or idea, 132
revising messages to grab attention, 56–60
viewpoint of, 44–45
audience handouts, 208
awareness, 16
Axtell, Roger E., 201

B

bad-news messages
  channels of communication, 107
  closing positively, 112–113
  constructive criticism, 119–120
  counterproposal, 112
  denying claim, 115–117
  denying credit, 118–119
  developing, 109–113
  exceptions to inductive approach, 109
  facts, analysis, and reasons, 110
  inductive approach, 107–108
  introductory paragraph, 109–110
  negative organizational news, 120–126
  passive voice, 111
  refusing request, 113–114
  refuting supporting details, 107
  silver-lining idea, 112
  writing, 110–112
bar charts, 171–173
Barkley, Samuel, 245
barriers to effective communication, 4
  cultures, 13–14
  perception, 41–42
Bay College, 145
beamable résumés, 238
beamer, 238
behavioral adaptability, 14
behavioral theories of communication
  contrasting management styles, 22–23
  interpersonal intelligence, 21
  Johari Window, 21–22
  recognizing human needs, 21
  strokes, 21
behavior-based interviews, 257
Bersin, Josh, 265
bias-free language, 67–68
bibliography, 161, 182
Big Data, 25, 265
Bilstein, 133
Bing, 153
Blanchard, Kenneth, 22
blogs, 81–82
body
  formal reports, 179, 182
  presentations, 204–206
body language, 14
borders, 58
Boxcar, 82
brainstorming, 34
breaking bad news message, 122
Bridgewater Associates, 265

bulleted lists, 57–58
bureaucracy, 5
Burns, Dan, 261
business activities and laws, 9
Business and Company Resource Center, 153
business communication
  contextual forces influencing, 9–19
  effective, 3
Business Source Premier, 153, 155

C

career guidance information, 228
career services centers, 227
career summary, 231–232
Carillo, Frank, 216
casual listening, 26
cellphones
  communication, 84
  text messaging, 77–78
central selling point, 130
channels of communication, 40–41
  choosing, 107
  presentations, 201–202
chartjunk, 168–169
chronemics, 13–14
chrono-functional résumés, 236
chronological context, 39
chronological résumés, 236
chunking, 57–58
citations, 161
claim messages, 138–141
  persuasive claims, 92
  routine claims, 92–94
claims, 92
clan culture, 38
clichés, 60–61, 62
clip art, 58
clustered bar charts, 171
code of ethics, 12
cognitive knowledge, 14
coherence, 54–55
common language, 167
communicating
  within organizations, 4–8
  persuasively, 46
  quantitative data, 167
communication, 3
  barriers to effective, 4
  behavioral theories, 21–23
  cellphones, 84
  channels of, 40–41
  context, 9–19
  diversity opportunities and challenges, 13
  email, 73–77
  face-to-face, 4
  horizontal communication, 8
  listening skills, 25–27
  organizational culture, 38
  strokes, 21
  teams, 31
  transactional process model of, 3–4
  voice mail, 83–84
  web sites, 80–81
communication flows
  downward communication, 6
  formal communication network, 4–5

informal communication network, 5–6
  upward communication, 6–7
communication levels, 8
  global communication competence, 16
communication media, 42
communication process, 3–4
companies
  code of ethics, 12
  promoting products, services, and image, 3
  researching before interview, 259–260
Competing Values Framework, 38
compliments, 45
computer-assisted interviews, 257
computer hoaxes, 76
concise communication, 61–63
conclusions, 164, 182
condescending expressions, 65–66
connotative meaning, 66
consensus, 35
constructive criticism message, 119–120
context
  dimensions of, 38–39
  organizational culture, 38
  presentations, 202–203
contextual forces
  changing technology, 14–17
  diversity challenges, 12–13
  legal and ethical constraints, 9–12
  messages, 37–39
  team environment, 17–19
contrasting management styles, 22–23
cooperation, 28–29
Corning, 17
corporate speak, 65
corporate websites, 228
corporations
  misplaced loyalty, 10
correlation analysis, 162
counterproposal, 112
cover messages, 247
Creative Diversions Software, 132
credit information messages, 100–101
credo, 12
crisis communication, 220–222
cross-functional team, 31
cultural context, 39
cultural differences, 12
cultural intelligence, 14
cultures
  assertiveness, 43
  audience, 42–43
  body language, 14
  communicating with different, 12, 13–14
  cultural intelligence, 14
  culturally diverse audiences, 215–216
  ethnocentrism, 13
  interpretation of time, 13–14
  nonverbal messages, 24
  personal space requirements, 14
  power distance, 43
  stereotypes, 13
  translation limitations, 14
cumulative line charts, 173

inductive approach in persuasive
    messages, 130
inductive paragraphs, 53–54
informal communication network,
    5–6
informal reports, 147
    versus formal reports, 179
information, documenting sources,
    159, 161
informational reports, 147
in-group collectivism, 43
inline résumés, 242
instant messaging (IM), 77
institutional collectivism, 43
Intel Corp., 82
intensive listening, 26
intentional accidents, 220
intercultural communication barri-
    ers, 13–14
interferences, 4
internal messages, 8
internal proposals, 193–194
internal reports, 148
internationalization, 16
Internet
    career guidance information,
        228
    identifying job listings, 228–229
    job search, 228
    netiquette, 75
    secondary research, 153
Internet conferencing, 218–220
interpersonal communication, 8, 29
interpersonal intelligence, 21
interpersonal skills, 262–263
interviews
    appearance, 260–261
    asking questions of interviewer,
        267
    behavioral questions, 263–264
    behavior-based interviews, 257
    closing, 267–268
    comparing qualifications to
        company/job profile, 260
    computer-assisted interviews,
        257
    conducting successful, 261–267
    discriminatory hiring practices,
        265–266
    extracurricular activities,
        262–263
    face-to-face interviews, 257
    first impressions, 261–262
    information exchange, 262–266
    interpersonal skills, 262–263
    key points to emphasize, 262
    logical thinking and creativity,
        264
    nonverbal messages, 262
    opening formalities, 261–262
    personality testing, 265
    phone interviews, 258
    practicing for, 261
    preparing for, 259–261
    professional attitude, 264–265
    researching company, 259–260
    salary and benefits, 265
    series interviews, 258
    standard questions, 263
    STAR method (Situation or Task/
        Action/Result), 264
    stress interviews, 257–258
    structured interviews, 257
    time and materials, 261
    unstructured interviews, 257
    virtual interviews, 258–259
in-text parenthetical citations, 161
intranets, 15–16
intrapersonal communication, 8
introduction
    formal reports, 182
    presentations, 203–204

iPad, 133
iPhone, 82

J

jargon, 61
    email, 74
    presentations, 205
Jenner, Kendall, 13
JetBlue, 265
job-acceptance messages, 269
job and/or career objective, 231
job-refusal messages, 270
job search
    career services centers, 227
    electronic employment
        resources, 228
    employers' websites and office
        locations, 227
    employment agencies and
        contractors, 227
    gathering essential informa-
        tion, 225
    identifying job listings, 228–229
    identifying potential career
        opportunities, 225–230
    Internet, 228
    locating career guidance infor-
        mation, 228
    networks, 226–227
    printed sources, 225–226
    professional organizations, 227
    social media, 227
    traditional sources, 225
Johari Window, 21–22
*Jones' Parliamentary Procedure at a
    Glance*, 34
Jossey, Marin, 247
justification reports, 148, 183–184

K

Karlstrom, Johan, 10
Kennedy, Joyce, 262
Kilpatrick, Kwame, 79
Kimi Räikkönen, 133
kinesic messages, 24
kinesics, 14
Knight, Jonathan, 212
Kraft Foods, Inc., 17

L

laptops, 15
lateral communication, 8
lateral reports, 148
law and electronic messaging, 79–80
leadership
    groups, 30
    social constructionist view of, 23
legal behavior, 10, 12
legal constraints, 9–12
letters, 87
    short reports, 187
    unified, 55
LexisNexis Academic Universe, 153
Library of Congress classification
    system, 152
Likert scales, 158
Lincoln, Abraham, 61
Lincoln Business Data, Inc., 135
line charts, 173
lines, 58
LinkedIn, 82, 226, 259
listening, 25–27
Living Essentials, 45
Loeb, Daniel S., 46
LogicTech, 132
Lombardi, Vince, 132

longitudinal studies, 151
long reports, 147
Lotus Dynamic Performance Man-
    agement (DPM), 133

M

management
    contrasting styles, 22–23
    explaining and clarifying pro-
        cedures and work assign-
        ments, 3
    social constructionist view of
        leadership, 23
    Theory X style, 22
    Theory Y style, 22
    unethical tone set by, 10
managers
    communication, 3
    empowering employees, 23
    organizational development
        (OD), 22
manuscript presentations, 209
maps, 174
Marie Claire, 12–13
market culture, 38
Maslow, Abraham, 21, 129
McAfee Total Protection technol-
    ogy, 134
McDonald's, 45
McGregor, Douglas, 22
measures of central tendency, 162
me attitude, 44–45
meetings, 32–35
    consensus, 35
    distributing agenda in advance, 34
    effective, 33–35
    electronic meetings, 33
    encouraging participation, 34
    face-to-face meetings, 32–33
    generic agenda, 34
    identifying purpose of, 33
    maintaining order, 34
    managing conflict, 35
    minutes, 35
    negative attitudes of workers
        toward, 32
    satisfactory arrangements for, 34
memorized presentations, 209
memos, 87, 101–104, 187
    unified, 55
messages
    adapting to audience needs and
        concerns, 44–46
    adjustment messages, 93
    audience reaction to, 48
    central idea, 48
    chunking, 57–58
    claim messages, 92–94
    clear and understandable ideas,
        46
    clichés, 60–61, 62
    communicating ethically and
        responsibly, 45–46
    concise communication, 61–63
    contextual forces, 37–39
    deductive sequence, 87
    direct sequence, 87
    diverse audience, 49
    effective sentences and coherent
        paragraphs, 51–56
    envisioning audience, 41–44
    evaluating effectiveness, 57
    good-news messages, 87,
        88–92
    grabbing audience's attention,
        56–60
    graphics, 46
    headings, 58
    honor, honesty, and credibility,
        45–46

informing and persuading oth-
    ers, 3
misunderstanding, 3
neutral-news messages, 87
organizational culture, 37–38
organizing, 46–49
outdated expressions, 60
persuasive requests, 94
planning and preparing, 37
positive tone, 63–65
procedural messages, 101–104
profanity, 61
proofreading, 56–57
purpose, 39–41, 73
readability and appeal of text, 55
receiver-centered statements, 45
redundancies, 62
routine messages, 99–101
routine requests, 94–99
sender-centered statements, 45
style and tone, 60–68
topics, 55
viewpoint supported with objec-
    tive facts, 46
visual enhancements, 57–59
white space, 57–58
metacommunication, 23–24
metaphors, 60
methodology, 151
MicroDenier Polyester Suede, 134
Microsoft, 82, 258
Microsoft job search log, 225
Microsoft Word, 59
Mindvalley, 38
*MLA Handbook for Writers of
    Research Papers,* 161
Mobile Web Accessibility Guide-
    lines, 81
Morrow, Thomas, 262
motivation, 14
Motorola, 17
multimedia résumés, 245
MySpace, 76
MyWebSearch, 153

N

National Advertising Division, 45
National Commission on Writing, 37
National Federation of the Blind, 81
natural disasters, 220
negative group roles, 30
negative organizational news messages
    breaking bad news, 122
    responding to crisis situations,
        122–126
netiquette, 75
networks, 226–227
neutral-news messages, 87
New Kids on the Block, 212
New York Times, 85
Nike, 258
nonverbal communication, 40
    face-to-face communication, 4
    kinesic messages, 24
    metacommunication, 23–24
nonverbal messages, 24–25
    interviews, 262
non-words, 210
normal accidents, 220
normative survey research, 154
norming, 31, 32
norms, 30
notes pages, 208
null hypothesis, 150

O

Obama, Barack, 66
observational studies, 154

Rough Draft of a Letter (excerpt)

April 1, 2016

Fax Transmission

Louisa Fox, Marketing Manager
Learner Consumer Products Group
2304 Pike Market Street
Seattle, Washington 90322 *(WA)*

Dear Ms. Fochs:

Are you looking for help developing your organization's social media platform? . . . improve your retail marketing? . . . plan your external communication program? . . . enhance your mass advertising strategy? **Then you need the services of the full-service brand engagement firm Souther and Associates to develop an integrated media plan that ensures your company's continued success.**

With Souther and Associates full-service capabilities, you will receive support in all of the following areas:

- Social media. Leverage the millions of conversations taking place through the use of social media by taking advantage of our four-step approach, which tracks conversations and dialogue; extracts insights from consumer conversations; interacts with key influences, brand advocates, and detractors; and measures consumer sentiment, advocacy, and engagement.
- Retail marketing. Engage consumers away from the noise and competing advertising, and reach them on an intimate, meaningful, and locally relevant level that will help you to drive trial, traffic, and sales.
- Communication planning. Build preference for your brand by translating emotional insights into high-impact brand strategy and innovation. Our experts bypass consumers' rational thinking with tools and techniques that are reactive and observational. Then, we integrate these emotional insights with your brand's functional benefits to create the foundation for lasting behavior change.
- Influence marketing. Mass advertising still plays an important role in branding, but these days, credibility is especially important, and who is more credible than a trusted professional? We identify professionals to give your products that powerful endorsement.

~~Interested customers can~~ Visit www.souther.com today and check out the list of consulting services we provide and read real-life stories from past clients about how we increased brand awareness for them. If you contact us before May 15, you will also receive a free assessment of your current marketing program from our proprietary MarketLab analysis tool. Our team is ready to assist you in improving the impact of your marketing programs today. Please call me at 509-788-1302 to make an appointment with a consultant.

Sincerely,

Frank Forester

Frank Forester
Engagement Director

Enclosure

- Adds mailing notation.
- Uses two-letter state abbreviation.
- Corrects spelling of name.
- Adds smooth transition to next paragraph.
- Bullet list for emphasis and conciseness.
- Divides into two sentences to enhance readability.
- Recasts from receiver's viewpoint.
- Includes specific action ending.

Errors Undetectable by Spell-Check

Verify spelling of names.

Correct proofreading grammatical error.

Check correctness of word substitutions, such as "to" for "too" and "your" for "you."

MODEL DOCS

Improving Readability Through Cautious Use of a Grammar and Style Checker

Step 1: Evaluate and respond to advice given for grammar and style errors detected.

Step 2: Use counts, averages, and readability indexes as guides for adjusting writing level appropriately.

IMPROVING YOUR WRITING WITH THE COMPUTER

Hone your computer skills to spend more time writing and less time formatting.

☑ Draft in a font style and size easily read on-screen; postpone formatting until the revision is done.

☑ Use the *Find* and *Go To* commands to search and make changes.

☑ Learn time-saving keyboard shortcuts for frequently used commands such as *Copy* and *Cut*. Customize software so that you can access these commands easily.

☑ Use automatic numbering to arrange numerical or alphabetical lists and to ensure accuracy.

☑ Save time by using built-in styles such as cover pages, headers/footers, list and table formats, text boxes, and graphical effects.

☑ Save frequently used text such as a letterhead or your signature line so you can insert it with a single click.

☑ Use the *Citations and Bibliography* command to format references and the *Document Styles* feature to automatically generate a content page and index.

Use formatting features to create an organized and polished appearance.

☑ Add spacing between lines and paragraphs, and use crisp, open fonts such as Calibri for a contemporary look that is easy to read on-screen.

☑ Apply color-infused document themes and built-in styles to reflect a consistent brand identity.

Use proofing features to locate errors.

☑ Use the spell-checker frequently as you draft and revise. Be aware that the spell-checker will not identify miskeyings (*than* for *then*), commonly misused words, homophones (*principle, principal*), omitted words, missing or out-of-order enumerations, and content errors.

☑ Use grammar check to provide feedback on usage, reading level, comprehension factors, and other errors and weaknesses that cannot be detected electronically.

☑ Use a thesaurus only when you can recognize the precise meaning needed.

Email Format

New Message

To: Pablo Gonzales [pgonzales@computersolutions.com]
From: Jennifer Reagan [jreagan@lauder.com]
Subject: <u>Laptop Repair or Replacement Needed</u> ●————— **Includes descriptive subject line.**

Mr. Gonzales,

Please repair or send us a replacement for the laptop computer listed on the attached sales agreement. It has a faulty cooling fan. You should receive the computer tomorrow via overnight freight.

The computer was purchased six months ago under our agreement with your company to provide our salespeople with laptops. The computers are covered by a 12-month warranty for faulty parts replacement. I spoke with your sales manager, Tom Wilkins, this morning, and he instructed me to contact you for extradited service.

Our salesperson Maria Rodriguez eagerly awaits the return of her laptop. Our salespeople are highly dependent on their computers because they spend so much time on the road.

Thanks,

Jennifer Reagan

●————— **Includes signature file that identifies writer.**

Format Pointers

Includes single-spaced, unindented paragraphs and short lines for complete screen display.

Uses mixed case for easy reading.

Keeps format simple for quick download and compatibility.

• Email Format

While certain email formats are standard, some degree of flexibility exists in formatting email messages. Primarily, be certain your message is easy to read and represents the standards of formality that your company has set. The following guidelines and the model email illustrated above will assist you in formatting professional email messages:

- *Include an appropriate salutation and closing.* You might write "Dear" and the person's name or simply the person's first name when messaging someone for the first time. Casual expressions such as "Hi" and "Later" are appropriate for personal messages, but not serious business email. A closing of "Sincerely" or "Regards" is considered quite formal for email messages; instead, a simple closing such as "Best wishes" or "Thank you" provides a courteous end to your message.

- *Include a signature file at the end of the message.* The signature file (known as a .sig file) contains a few lines of text that include your full name and title, mailing address, telephone number, and any other information you want people to know about you. You might include a clever quote that you update frequently.

- *Format for easy readability.* Follow these suggestions:
  - Limit each message to one screen to minimize scrolling. If you need more space, consider a short email message with a lengthier message attached as a word-processing file. Be certain the recipient can receive and read the attachment.

MODEL DOCS

- Limit the line length to 60 characters so that the entire line is displayed on the monitor without scrolling.

- Use short, unindented paragraphs. Separate paragraphs with an extra space.

- Use mixed case for easy reading. Typing in all capital letters is perceived as shouting in email and considered rude online behavior.

- Emphasize a word or phrase by surrounding it with quotation marks or keying in uppercase letters.

- **Use emoticons or email abbreviations in moderation when you believe the receiver will understand and approve. Emoticons,** created by keying combinations of symbols to produce "sideways" faces, are a shorthand way of lightening the mood, adding emotion to email messages, and attempting to compensate for nonverbal cues lost in one-way communication:

:-)	smiling, indicates humor or sarcasm	%-(	confused
:-(	frowning, indicates sadness or anger	:-0	surprised

Alternately, you might put a "g" (for grin) or "smile" in parentheses after something that is obviously meant as tongue-in-cheek to help carry the intended message to the receiver. Abbreviations for commonly used phrases save space and avoid unnecessary keying. Popular ones include BCNU (be seeing you), BTW (by the way), FYI (for your information), FWIW (for what it's worth), HTH (hope this helps), IMHO (in my humble opinion, AFAIK (as far as I know), F2F (face-to-face), IOW (in other words), and LOL (laugh out loud).

Some email users feel strongly that emoticons and abbreviations are childish or inappropriate for serious email and decrease productivity when the receiver must take time for deciphering. Before using them, be certain the receiver will understand them and that the formality of the message and your relationship with the receiver justify this type of informal exchange. Then use only in moderation to punctuate your message.

 Good Example of an Email Message

> **New Message**
>
> **To:** Linda Roberts, Loan Officer
> **From:** Juan Alvarez, Director of Loan Compliance
> **Subject:** New Policies Affect Loans to Real-Estate Investors
>
> Linda,
>
> Please be aware of the new policies regarding mortgages to real-estate investors.
>
> Loans can no longer be made to mortgage applicants who already have four or more outstanding mortgages. Because of the problems caused by the sub-prime lending situation, we are required to limit our exposure to mortgage debt. Applicants who have four or more active mortgages are now considered too risky because of a potential lack of liquidity in their current asset portfolio.
>
> You will find this latest policy change attached to this message. Please come by my office if you have additional questions after reading the attached policy statement.
>
> Regards,
>
> Juan

Provides subject line that is meaningful to reader and writer.

Includes salutation and closing to personalize message.

Format Pointer

Composes short, concise message limited to one idea and one screen.

Good Example of an Apology

New Message

To: Allen Melton [amelton@meltonpr.com]

cc:

Subject: Yesterday's Advertising Presentation

Allen:

Please accept my apology for the inconvenience you experienced yesterday because of the unavailability of computer equipment. Fortunately, you saved the day with your backup transparencies and gave an effective presentation on the new advertising campaign.

The next time you make a presentation at our company, I'll be sure to schedule the LGI room. This room has the latest technology to support multimedia presentations. Just call and let me know the date.

Later,

Thomas Lee Raferty
Administrative Assistant

• States the apology briefly without providing an overly specific description of the error.

• Reports measures taken to avoid repetition of such incidents, which strengthens the credibility of the apology.

• Closes with a positive statement.

Format Pointers

Limits the message to a single idea—the apology.

Composes a short, concise message that fits on one screen.

Includes a salutation and closing to personalize the message.

MODEL DOCS

Good Good Example of an Appreciation Message

New Message

To: Ellen Meyer [emeyer@techno.com]
cc: Martha Riggins [mriggins@techno.com]
Subject: Appreciation for Outstanding Contribution

Ellen,

Thank you for spearheading the initiative to improve interpersonal communication within the office and for arranging for the training sessions to achieve that goal. It was a big commitment on your part in addition to your regular duties.

Your efforts are already paying off. I have observed the techniques we learned in the training sessions being used in the department on several occasions already. In times of uncertainty, anxiety can often spill over into people's professional lives, so the seminar was very timely in helping to ensure a collaborative and civil workplace where everyone is treated respectfully.

You have proven yourself a dedicated and insightful employee, a true asset to the continued success of our organization.

Best regards,
Martha

• Extends appreciation for employee's efforts to improve departmental communication.

• Provides specific evidence of worth of experience without exaggerating or using overly strong language or mechanical statements.

• Assures writer of tangible benefits to be gained from the training session.

Format Pointer

Uses short lines, mixed case; omits special formatting such as emoticons and email abbreviations for improved readability.

Developing the Components of a Bad-News Message

The current sub-prime mortgage situation and its subsequent effects on the economy have provided an opportunity to better educate loan seekers about the types of financial risk they might safely assume. For this reason, mortgage seekers may be restricted in the number of mortgage loans they might hold.

- Begins with statement with which both can agree. Sets stage for reasons for bad news.
- Reveals subject of message and transitions into reasons.

As part of the effort to help loan seekers reduce their financial risk, banks now limit the number of mortgages a person might judiciously hold to no more than four. Because of current sluggishness in the housing market, house sellers now have more difficulty selling homes in a timely manner, making such assets much less liquid. If a mortgage holder gets into trouble, he/she will have less ability to resell the property and recover the loan amount. This puts the mortgage holder and the lender at greater financial risk.

- Provides rule and clearly applies rule to situation.
- States refusal positively and clearly using complex sentence and positive language.

In order to secure an additional mortgage, you must first pay off one of your current mortgages. Alternately, our affiliated real-estate brokers are available to help you sell one of your properties so that you might secure another. Please call me at 213-555-3400 to discuss these services.

- Includes counterproposal as alternative.
- Closes with sales promotion for other services, inferring a continuing business relationship.

Note the closing paragraph is a positive, forward-looking statement that includes sales promotion of other services the mortgage firm and its affiliated real-estate brokers can offer.

Aleksandr Bryliaev/Shutterstock.com

Good Good Example of a Claim Denial

June 14, 2016

Meera Biswas
Snowcap Limited
1905 Southhaven Street
Santa Fe, NM 87501-7313

Dear Ms. Biswas:

Restocking of Returned Merchandise

The HighFly skis you stocked this past season are skillfully crafted and made from the most innovative materials available. Maintaining a wide selection of quality skiing products is an excellent strategy for developing customer loyalty and maximizing your sales.

Our refund policies provide you the opportunity to keep a fully stocked inventory at the lowest possible cost. You receive full refunds for merchandise returned within 10 days of receipt. For unsold merchandise returned after the primary selling season, a modest 15 percent restocking fee is charged to cover our costs of holding this merchandise until next season. The credit applied to your account for $2,069.75 covers merchandise you returned at the end of February.

While relaxing from another great skiing season, take a look at our new HighFly skis and other items available in the enclosed catalog for the 2016 season. You can save 10 percent by ordering premium ski products before May 10.

Sincerely,

Galen Fondren

Galen Fondren
Credit Manager
Enclosure: Catalog

• Begins with a statement with which the reader can agree to get the message off to a good start.

• Presents a clear explanation for the additional charge.

• Shifts emphasis away from the refusal by presenting sales promotion on other services.

Format Pointer
Illustrates block format—all lines begin at the left margin.

Good Good Example of a Persuasive Claim

Palmdale Galleria
3109 Overlook Drive / Palmdale, CA 93550
P: (661) 555-2130 \ F: (661) 555-3129

October 27, 2016

Samantha Reynolds
Senior Architect
Primera Design
3400 Wilshire Boulevard
Los Angeles, CA 90052-3674

Dear Samantha:

When Palmdale Galleria selected your firm to redesign our retail space, we were impressed by the work that you had done in a number of hotels and mall properties in Las Vegas and other upscale developments throughout the country. We were most impressed with the fantasy world that you created for the Insight Hotel's shopping galleria, a space that attended to every aspect of the consumer's shopping experience, including sight, sound, smell, taste, and sensation, through the implementation of the latest technological and design advances.

> Seeks attention by giving sincere compliment that reveals subject of message.

In our meeting with your creative team, we asked for attention to the visual design, the entertainment elements, and the creation of an ambiance that addressed all aspects of the consumers' sensual experience. After reviewing the initial plan for our redesign, we find the degree of incorporation of entertainment and sensual experiences for consumers to be disappointing. The redesign incorporates the latest trends in architectural design but needs more attention to entertainment features, including spaces for "street" entertainers, mini-concerts, and amusement park rides, including bungee jumping, etc. We also expected a more complete integration of water features, such as fountains, waterfalls, and streams, with the associated opportunities for entertainment, such as a simulated river rafting experience. In the tropical forest region of the mall, we hoped to have a better integration of spaces for zoo animals and an apparatus to create the "smells" and "sounds" of the jungle. Consumers no longer go to malls to simply shop, but want to be transported to a world of leisure, pampering, and entertainment, one that appeals to all of their senses.

> Continues central appeal—commitment to creative redesign—while providing needed details.

> Presents reasoning that leads to request and subtle reminder of central appeal.

> Connects specific request with firm's commitment to develop a creative redesign.

With Primera Design's reputation for creative productions, we are confident the redesign plan for the Palmdale Galleria will be revised to incorporate these elements. Please let us know if you would like to meet to discuss and clarify any of the design issues raised here. Because of the importance of this project, I am at your disposal. Please call me at 444-1920 to schedule a meeting.

> **Legal and Ethical Consideration**
> Uses letter rather than less formal email format to emphasize importance of these differences regarding contractual agreement.

Sincerely,

Martinique Cole

Martinique Cole
General Manager
Palmdale Galleria

MODEL DOCS

Down-Home Restaurants

83 South Pass Road • Chattanooga TN 37426-2723 • (423) 555-5320

March 15, 2016

Mrs. Joyce Smith
976 Thompson Road
Crossville, TN 38555-0976

Dear Mrs. Smith:

Meeting you and touring the building on your property last week was a pleasure. That little building provided me with a fascinating glimpse of the past. You must have found it convenient using the building as a big "attic," storing all your canned goods and old farm implements over the years.

As the manager of the Down-Home Barbeque in Mena, I am constantly looking for items to build and display in our restaurants. Our restaurants are constructed of weathered wood to create a genuine rustic atmosphere, which we think complements our "down-home" menu.

As I toured your building, I couldn't help but notice some of the unique items inside and the old weathered boards hanging outside. The wood from the building and its contents would enable us to build and furnish a new restaurant in Clarksville and refurbish our Jackson location. Marc Lane, owner of Down-Home Restaurants, has asked me to extend you the offer explained in the enclosed proposal.

Naturally, no amount of money can compensate you for a building that holds so many memories for you. However, we would be happy to purchase the entire contents of the building, excluding any special items of sentimental value that you may want to keep.

Although the thought of selling the building may sadden you, think of the "second life" that the old farm equipment, dishes, washboards, seed bags, and weathered boards would have in our restaurants. People who would otherwise never see such Americana will have the opportunity to learn a little about its rich past.

After you have reviewed the proposal, please call me at 555-3253 to discuss our offer to display your treasures in our restaurants.

Sincerely,

Karla Ash

Karla Ash, Manager
Chattanooga Store
Enclosure

Opens with a compliment that introduces an appeal to the owner's pride in the old property.

Introduces the writer's interest in acquiring property and continues the primary appeal (desire to preserve the past).

Offsets reluctance to sell by acknowledging the sentimental value and suggesting options.

Stresses benefits of selling property in terms of the primary appeal.

Connects the specific request for action with the reward for saying "Yes."

Format Pointers
Illustrates modified block format—the date and closing lines (complimentary close and signature block) begin at the horizontal center.

Uses mixed punctuation—a colon follows the salutation, and a comma follows the complimentary close.

Uses an enclosure notation to alert the reader that something is included.

Example of an Effective Questionnaire

- Uses variety of items to elicit different types of responses.

- Uses clear, concise language to minimize confusion.

- Provides clear instructions for answering each item.

- Provides additional lines to allow for individual opinions.

- Provides even number of rating choices to eliminate "fence" responses.

- Asks for easily recalled information.

- Provides non-overlapping categories of response and open-ended final category.

Format Pointers

Provides adequate space for answering open-ended item.

Keeps length as short as possible while meeting survey objectives.

Includes instructions for submitting completed questionnaire.

1. Rank the following new vehicle purchase factors in order of their importance to you.

		1	2	3	4	5	6
a.	Price	○	○	○	○	○	○
b.	Overall performance	○	○	○	○	○	○
c.	Reliability	○	○	○	○	○	○
d.	Comfort	○	○	○	○	○	○
e.	Driving enjoyment	○	○	○	○	○	○
f.	Safety record	○	○	○	○	○	○
g.	Fuel economy	○	○	○	○	○	○
h.	Other (specify) [▼]	○	○	○	○	○	○

2. Which of the following is the single most important purchase factor that you feel needs more attention by today's car makers? (Please select only one.)

- ○ Price
- ○ Overall performance
- ○ Reliability
- ○ Comfort
- ○ Safety record
- ○ Fuel economy
- ○ Other (specify) [▼]

3. Would you purchase this vehicle again?

Definitely not	Probably not	I'm not sure	Only if improved	Probably would	Definitely yes
1	2	3	4	5	6
○	○	○	○	○	○

4. How would you rate your overall purchase satisfaction?

Very unsatisfied	Somewhat dissatisfied	Neutral	Somewhat satisfied	Satisfied	Very satisfied
1	2	3	4	5	6
○	○	○	○	○	○

5. Indicate your age group:

- ○ 20–29
- ○ 30–39
- ○ 40–49
- ○ 50–59
- ○ 60–69
- ○ 70 years and over

6. Indicate how many vehicles you have previously purchased.

- ○ None
- ○ 1–3
- ○ 4–6
- ○ 7–10
- ○ More than 10

7. What could the car maker do to enhance your satisfaction with your new car purchase?

[   ]

Thanks for your participation. Click to submit your questionnaire.

[Submit]

MODEL DOCS
• Sample Report and References Pages in APA (6th Edition) Style

Culturally diverse virtual teams do have a greater potential for conflict than do teams that are homogeneous and are able to meet face to face ("Collaborative Teams," 2008). While variations in beliefs, behaviors, and expectations occur within all cultural groups, certain generalities about one based on his or her cultural group can be useful for others seeking better understanding. "Given little or no other information about an individual's values and behaviours, culture provides a good first impression of that person" (Maznevski & Peterson, 1997, p. 37).

Neyer and Harzing (2008) found that experiences in cross-cultural interactions do serve to improve one's abilities to adapt in such situations. One advantage gained through experience is the overcoming of cultural stereotypes which often stand in the way of effective communication (Williams & O'Reilly, 1998). Cross-cultural experience also leads to the establishment of norms that support interaction among individuals and to the development of mutual consideration for others (Neyer & Harzing, 2008). Studies have established that individuals who learn a foreign language also gain appropriate culturally determined behavior and are thus better able to adapt to specific characteristics of the other culture (Harzing & Feely, 2008).

In addition to possessing strong technical skills, qualities that are important to successful membership on cross-cultural virtual teams include the following (Adler, 1991; Hurn & Jenkins, 2000):

- Flexibility and adaptability
- Strong interpersonal skills
- Ability to think both globally and locally
- Linguistic skills

References

Adler, N. J. (1991). *International dimensions of organizational behavior*. Boston: PWS Kent.

Collaborative teams. (2008, June). *Bulletpoint 152*, 3–5.

Hurn, B. F., & Jenkins, M. (2000). International peer group development. *Industrial and Commercial Training, 32*(4), 128–131. doi: 10.1108/00197850010372205

Maznevski, M. L., & Peterson, M. F. (1997). Societal values, social interpretation, and multinational teams. In C. Granrose (Ed.), *Cross-Cultural Workgroups* (pp. 27–29). Thousand Oaks, CA: Sage.

Neyer, A., & Harzine, A. (2008). The impact of culture on interactions: Five lessons learned from the European Commission. *European Management Journal 26*(5), 325–334. doi: 10.1016/j.emj .2008.05.005

Williams, K. Y., & O'Reilly, C. A. (1998). Demography and diversity in organizations. In B. M. Staw & R. M. Sutton (Eds.), *Research in Organizational Behavior* (pp. 77–140). Stamford, CT: JAI.

Choosing the Appropriate Graphic to Fit Your Objective

KoffeeKup Corporation
Market Price of Common Stock

Quarter	October 2, 2013		October 2, 2014	
	High	Low	High	Low
Fourth	$23.94	$21.29	$26.35	$23.08
Third	22.09	18.62	28.13	22.78
Second	19.48	16.15	30.80	24.79
First	16.50	14.40	31.94	23.53

Source: KoffeeKup Corporation, Annual Report, 2013

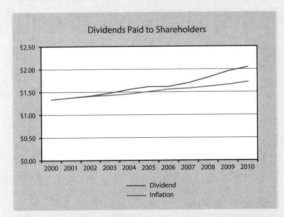

BigBurger Achieves Consistent Revenue Growth in Primary International Markets

Legend: US, Europe, APMEA, Latin America, Canada, Other

Dividends Paid to Shareholders

Legend: Dividend, Inflation

Composition of Mmm! Brands, Inc. System Units as of December 31, 2013

- Yummmly Fried Chicken US 17%
- International 42%
- Mmm!Taco US 18%
- Hammm!burger US 23%

Graphic Type and Objective

Table—To show exact figures

Bar chart—To compare one quantity with another

Line Chart—To illustrate changes in quantities over time

Pie Chart—To show how the parts of a whole are distributed

MODEL DOCS

Graphic Type and Objective

Gantt chart—To track progress toward completing a project

Map—To show geographic relationships

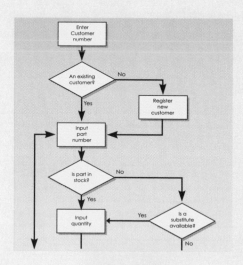

US SUSPECTED SARS

Flowchart—To illustrate a process or procedure

Photograph—To provide a realistic view of a specific item or place

Robootb/Shutterstock.com

Good Short, Periodic Report in Memorandum Format

ETO Industries

233 State Boulvard
Kansas City, MO 64123-7600

TO: Candice Russell, Director, Human Resources
FROM: Tim Johnson, Manager, In-House Exercise Program
DATE: January 1, 2016
SUBJECT: Annual Report on In-House Exercise Program

The in-house exercise center has made significant gains in the past year. Data related to participation in our programs and current staffing follow:

Enrollment: 506 employees, up from 384 at end of 2014
Staff: One full-time trainer/manager and two part-time trainers

Our goal for the coming year is to increase our enrollment in the in-house exercise programs another 10 percent. We also have plans to create a nutrition program that will be rolled out next month. If that program is successful initially, we may need to hire a certified nutritionist. This person might also be used part-time in the company cafeteria to improve the nutritional value of the lunches and snacks provided there.

Employees report overall satisfaction with the quality of the current program. At the end of 2014, we asked program participants to complete a questionnaire. Eighty-eight percent indicated that they were very satisfied or extremely satisfied with our program. The most frequently mentioned suggestion for improvement was the extension of hours until 7 p.m. This change would allow employees to work late and still take advantage of the exercise facility. A copy of the questionnaire is provided for your review.

Call me should you wish to discuss the nutritional program, extended service hours, or any other aspects of this report.

Attachment

- **Includes header to serve formal report functions of transmittal and title page.**

- **Includes horizontal line to add interest and separate transmittal from body of memo.**

- **Uses deductive approach to present this periodic report requested by management on an annual basis.**

- **Uses headings to highlight standard information; allows for easy update when preparing subsequent report.**

- **Includes primary data from survey completed by program participants.**

- **Attaches material to memorandum, which would be an appendix item in formal report.**

Format Pointer
Uses memorandum format for brief periodic report prepared for personnel within company.

Good

Audit Report in Letter Format

CommPlus Consultants, Inc.
101 MAIN STREET, SUITE 203
ST. LOUIS, MO 54011
800-555-3000

January 10, 2016

John Simpson
Franklin Associates
345 Plum Street
St. Louis, MO 54002

Dear Mr. Simpson:

The communication audit of Franklin Associates' external communication program has been completed. You will find a brief summary of our findings and conclusions and recommendations below.

FINDINGS

Findings from our audit can be found below:

1. Franklin Associates is a consultant to the oil and gas industry. It is a well-established business with a 100-year history. Its branding is well recognized, but in recent years, it has been surpassed by several new entrants who have marketed themselves as innovative and using the latest technologies. This has created a challenge for Franklin Associates in terms of its external branding.
2. Franklin's major external stakeholders include its clients, the media, investors, government agencies, competitors, and the public. In terms of its clients, Franklin has focused its marketing efforts on the largest oil and gas producers. Because there are so few, this has created some competitive challenges for Franklin.
3. Franklin's most common methods for communicating its corporate message includes press releases; a company website; and personal communications with its clients through use of written, oral and electronic media.

CONCLUSIONS AND RECOMMENDATIONS

The following recommendations are made:

1. Continue advertising and service promotion at current levels but with some changes that help you better reach mid-sized clients and increase your market share.
2. Update the design for your company logo, and roll out a campaign that introduces this new image to current and prospective customers.
3. Develop a plan for shaping public opinion on issues important to Franklin Associates. As a consultant for the oil industry, it is important to show that your organization is interested in addressing global climate issues.

Thank you for the opportunity to assist you in reviewing your external communication program. We are also available to help you in completing the final step in the audit process: Create, refine, and test new messages with the appropriate stakeholders. If you are interested in continuing our consulting relationship in order to develop an implementation plan, please call me at 415-640-9001.

Sincerely,

Louise Parker

Louise Parker
Chief Auditor

Letterhead and letter address function as title page and transmittal.

Introduces overall topic and leads into procedures and findings.

Uses side heading to denote beginning of body.

Closes with appreciation for business and offer to answer questions.

Format Pointers
Uses letter format for short report prepared by outside consultant.

Includes reference initials of typist, who did not write message.

MODEL DOCS

Designing and Delivering Business Presentations

Selecting an Appropriate Presentation Visual

VISUAL	ADVANTAGES	LIMITATIONS
HANDOUTS	• Provide detailed information that audience can examine closely • Extend a presentation by providing resources for later use • Reduce the need for note taking and aid in audience retention	• Can divert audience's attention from the speaker • Can be expensive
BOARDS AND FLIPCHARTS	• Facilitate interaction • Are easy to use • Are inexpensive if traditional units are used	• Require turning speaker's back to audience • Are cumbersome to transport, can be messy and not professional looking • Provide no hard copy and must be developed on-site if traditional units are used
ELECTRONIC PRESENTATIONS	• Meet audience expectations of visual standards • Enhance professionalism and credibility of the speaker • Provide special effects to enhance retention, appeal, flexibility, and reuse	• Can lead to poor delivery if misused • Can be time-consuming to create • Pose technology failure and transportability challenges
MODELS OR PHYSICAL OBJECTS	• Are useful to demonstrate an idea	• Can compete with the speaker for attention

MODEL DOCS

Writing Effective Slide Content: Poor (left) and Good (right) Examples

Humor

- Important element in any presentation
- Easy connection with the audience
- Gets attention
- Alleviates boredom
- Reduces mental tension
- Discourages conflict
- Enhances comprehension
- Shouldn't embarrass people
  - Ethnic jokes are inappropriate
  - Profane language is definitely not recommended

Bad

Value of Humor in a Presentation

- Establishes a connection with the audience
- Increases audience's willingness to listen
- Makes message more understandable and memorable
- Alleviates negativity associated with sensitive subjects

Good

The revised slide

- Includes a descriptive title that captures major idea of slide, in this case, the value of humor.

- Omits items unrelated to value of humor. Specifically, "important element in any presentation" is a verbal transition and not needed on a slide; "shouldn't embarrass people" and related subpoints will appear on a separate slide focusing on tips for using humor.

- Collapses remaining content into a few memorable points that use parallel structure for clarity and grammatical accuracy (singular action verbs).

- Proofreads carefully to avoid misspellings that damage credibility, such as "conflect" in original slide.

Engaging Conceptual Slide Design: Poor (left) and Good (right) Examples

Business Presentations

- Rated boring and unbearable in a survey of 200 US corporate vice presidents

Bad

Iconic Bestiary/Shutterstock.com

How Well Do Business Presentations Measure Up?

Boring. Unbearable.

Survey of 200 corporate vice presidents, 2015

Good

Monkey Business Images/Used under license from Shutterstock.com

The revised slide

- Uses descriptive title that captures central idea of dissatisfaction with typical business presentation.

- Selects images that imply intended message—ineffectiveness of business presenters; enlarges images for slide appeal and balance.

- Trims text to emphasize central idea and eliminates bullet, as bulleted list should have at least two items.

- Moves source to less prominent slide position to add credibility to research data while keeping focus on central idea.

Good

Chronological Résumé

Includes email address that reflects professional image.

Highlights professional skills.

Positions education as top qualification for recent graduate. Includes high GPA (B or better).

Edges out competition reflecting related experience and work achievements.

Uses separate section to emphasize language proficiencies listed in job requirements.

Emphasizes activities that reflect service attitude, high level of responsibility, and people-oriented experiences.

Format Pointers

Places name at top center, where it can be easily seen when employers place it in file drawer (top right is also acceptable).

Creates visual appeal through custom format rather than commonly used template, short readable sections focusing on targeted qualifications, and streamlined bulleted lists.

JOSEPH PRIESTLEY
89 Lincoln Street
Santa Fe, NM 78285-9063
512 555-9823
jpriestley@hotmail.com

Professional Profile
- Technical proficiency in ERP systems, ACL, database, and spreadsheet software.
- Hands-on experience in accounting gained through internship with well-regarded local firm.
- Excellent interpersonal communication and teamwork skills developed through course projects and active involvement in student organizations.
- Ability to manage time effectively, excellent work ethic, and dedication to high-quality work as demonstrated by 3.87 GPA and part-time work to finance my education.

EDUCATION
B.B.A., Accounting,
University of New Mexico, May 2014, GPA 3.87
- Dean's List, 2010–2014
- Deanna D. Darling Academic Scholarship

RELATED EXPERIENCE
Intern, Gerald and Associates, CPAs, Santa Fe, NM
June–August 2013
- Shadowed auditor and helped write numerous auditing reports for corporate clients.
- Created and maintained spreadsheets and databases, containing client audit information.
- Worked with audit teams to hone communication skills and developed phone skills necessary to effectively interact with professional clientele.

OTHER EXPERIENCE
- Server, Bubba's BBQ, Santa Fe, NM 2011–2013
- Stockperson, University of New Mexico Bookstore, Santa Fe, NM 2010–2011

LANGUAGES
- **Fluent in English**
- **Conversational Spanish**

LEADERSHIP ACTIVITIES
Beta Alpha Psi, honorary accounting society, 2012–2014,
Chapter president, 2012–2013
Chess Team, 2010–2014; president, 2013–2014

Good Functional Résumé

Clarence Foster
715 Armadillo Circle
San Antonio, TX 78710-0715
(512) 555-1396
cfoster@hotmail.com

Position in retail clothing sales with advancement to sales   OBJECTIVE
management.

CUSTOMER SERVICE
- Processed customer financial transactions within assigned limits and established guidelines.
- Provided excellent customer service in completing transactions efficiently and in a friendly, professional manner.
- Met sales and referral goals by identifying and selling financial products and services beneficial to the customer needs.
- Identified fraudulent activity to prevent potential losses to the bank.

SALES
- Provided quality customer service to store patrons.
- Handled cash transactions and daily receipt balances.
- Usually surpassed weekly goal of opening new credit accounts.
- Employee of the month.

COMMUNICATION SKILLS AND WORK ETHIC
- Ability to communicate effectively over the phone and in person.
- Ability to work well unsupervised.
- Experience working on team projects both at work and in courses.
- Report consistently and promptly when scheduled for work.

COMPUTER SKILLS
Proficient in spreadsheet and word-processing software.

Sales Associate, Claremont Department Store, 2012–Present   EMPLOYMENT
HISTORY
Customer Service Associate, Union Bank, 2011–2012

B.S., Marketing, Claremont State College, Expected   EDUCATION
graduation, May 2013

Clare Randall, Sales Manager, Claremont Department Store,   REFERENCES
435 Main Street, Claremont, TX 78009, (818) 555-2345

Daniel Shore, Professor, Marketing Department, Claremont State College, 890 Alamo Street, San Antonio, TX 87003, (803) 555-8907

Lisa Cox, Senior Teller, Union Bank, 900 Main Street, Claremont, TX 87303, (818) 555-1234

- **Includes clear objective statement to grab attention and invite close reading.**

- **Uses headings that show applicant knows what skills are needed to succeed in sales.**

- **Arranges qualifications into sections that emphasize applicant's relevant skills and accomplishments.**

- **Uses employers' names and dates to match skills with work history.**

- **Lists references for employer convenience and to strengthen résumé.**

Format Pointers
Creates visual appeal with easy-to-read columnar format and balanced page arrangement.

Places name at top center, where it can be easily seen.

Uses bold font to distinguish identification section and headings from remaining text.

Lists education and work history as quick overview of basic qualifications and to accommodate employers' preference for chronological format.

Good   Example of a Follow-Up Letter

Dear Mr. Wagner:

Thank you for taking the time to meet with me today to discuss the position of Financial Planning Analyst with Carson Fine Foods.

During our discussion, you stated that you're looking for an organized and outgoing candidate to join your team. Through my previous work and life experience, I gained organizational and customer development skills and learned how to meet goals through teamwork. In my position with Biotech Inc., I communicated with internal and external customers and assisted in efficiency and customer relations for the Fraud Detection program. I am confident that my skills and background will make me an asset as a Financial Planning Analyst with Carson Fine Foods.

I am eager to discuss this opportunity with you further. Please let me know what additional information I can provide you and your colleagues in order to secure this position and begin working for your organization.

- **States main idea and clearly identifies position being sought.**
- **Assures employer that applicant is still interested in job.**

Format Pointers
Formats as formal business letter but could have sent message electronically if previous communication with employer had been by email.

Prints letter and envelope with laser printer on paper that matches résumé and application letter.

 Good   Example of a Thank-You Message to a Reference

Thank you so much for the letter of recommendation you prepared for my application to law school. I learned today that I have been accepted by Cleveland University for the fall semester.

Because of the rigor of that law program, I believe your comments about my work ethic, dedication to high-quality work, and willingness to seek out feedback for improvement carried a great deal of weight. The dean commented that she was impressed with the detailed evidence and examples you provided to support your statements, unlike the general recommendations she often receives.

Dr. Kenney, I appreciate your helping me secure a seat in a highly competitive academic discipline with such a well-regarded law program. Thanks for the recommendation and your outstanding instruction. I will keep you informed about my law school experience and hope to stop by your office next time I am in town to catch up.

- **States main idea of appreciation for recommendation. Informs reference of success in acceptance to academic program.**
- **Communicates sincere appreciation for assistance; uses specific examples and avoids exaggeration.**
- **Restates main idea and anticipates continued relationship; is original and sincere.**

MODEL DOCS

 Good — Example of a Thank-You Message

New Message

To: wrfann@viking.com
From: mperkins@hotmail.com
Subject: Appreciation for Plant Interview

Dear Mr. Fann:

Thank you for the opportunity to visit Viking Range for a plant interview yesterday. I enjoyed meeting you and appreciated the complete tour of the operation and the opportunity to learn about the exciting research efforts underway at Viking.

Viking's success in developing higher quality products than its competitors after such a short time in the refrigeration market is impressive. Additionally, I was impressed with the many friendly, enthusiastic employees who were willing to share with me their knowledge and commitment to Viking.

After visiting your plant on Thursday, I am confident that my interest and previous experience in research and development at the DIAL labs in Starkville would allow me to contribute to Viking's important research efforts in the refrigeration area. I would also gain valuable real-world experience needed to enhance the mechanical engineering degree I'm pursuing at Mississippi State.

Mr. Fann, I am eager to receive an offer from Viking for the co-op position. If you need additional information in the meantime, please contact me.

Thanks,

Matt Perkins

- **States main idea of appreciation for interview and information gained.**

- **Includes specific points discussed during interview, increasing sincerity and recall of applicant.**

- **Assures employer of continued interest in position.**

- **Politely reminds employer that applicant is awaiting reply.**

Format Pointer
Prepared as email message because previous communication with the company has been by email.

 Good — Example of a Job-Refusal Message

I appreciate your spending time with me discussing the sales associate position.

Your feedback regarding my fit for your organization and the opportunities available to me were particularly valuable. Having received offers in both sales and marketing, I feel that a career in the latter field better suits my personality and long-term career goals. Today, I am accepting an entry-level marketing position with Fashion Trends, Inc.

Thank you for your confidence demonstrated by the job offer. When I hear about Marasol's continued success, I will think of the dedicated people who work for the company.

- **Begins with neutral but related idea to buffer bad news.**

- **Presents reasons diplomatically that lead to refusal.**

- **Ends message on positive note that anticipates future association with company.**

CHAPTER PREP 1

Establishing a Framework for Business Communication

KEY CONCEPTS

Understanding what communication is and how it occurs is central to successful transactions in the workplace. Business communication does not take place in a vacuum, but is impacted by various external forces, including legal and ethical constraints, diversity challenges, changing technology, and team environment.

LEARNING OBJECTIVES

1-1 Define communication and describe the value of communication in business.

1-2 Explain the communication pro___ model and the ultimate objective of the communication p___

1-3 Discuss how informatio___

1-4 Explain how legal and e___ changing technology, an___ that influence the process of business communication.

> For quick reference, this column lists the Learning Objectives that will be met in the chapter and presents a chapter outline with page references.

CHAPTER OUTLINE

KEY TERMS

> Key terms from the chapter are listed here in alphabetical order for quick reference.

CONCEPTUAL FIGURES AND TABLES

Figure 1.1 The Transactional Process Model of Communication

Figure 1.2 Flow of Information Within ___ ___

> This column lists the figures and tables in the chapter as well as a number of key lecture slides from the PowerPoint slide set.

Figure ___

Figure ___

Figure ___ ___ Behavior

Figure 1.6 Global Leadership Competency Model

Figure 1.7 Levels of Global Communication Competence

Figure 1.8 Characteristics of Defensive and Supportive Communication Climates

POWERPOINT HIGHLIGHTS

LECTURE PRESENTATION

Communication Channels

Contextual Forces Influencing Business Communication

Four Dimensions of Business Behavior

Diversity Challenges

Impacts of Technology

BCOM 8 ONLINE

New BCOM Online includes exposition assessment for students and chapter highlight boxes that supplement text material.

ASSIGNMENTS AND ACTIVITIES

READ

1. Ask students to read the following arti___ about predicted

> To push your students to think critically about the material, or to add an experiential, applied element to your course, each card offers a variety of in-class or homework assignments organized according to essential business communication skills: reading, writing, thinking, speaking, and collaborating.

CHAPTER PREP 1

NEW IN BCOM8

Chapter 1
– Added discussion of communication climates and related Figure 1.9

c. How do the predicted trends relate to the four strategic forces presented in this chapter?

d. Select one of the communication means discussed in the article. Share your findings in a short class presentation. **(Obj. 1–4)**

WRITE

2. Direct students to take the team player quiz at **www.quintcareers .com /team_player_quiz.html** and to write a brief paper about their team orientation and how being a team player may affect their career success. **(Obj. 4)**

THINK

3. Have students research a scandal in the business or popular press, using campus resources. Assign students to read the article and respond to questions a–c. **(Obj. 4)**

   a. Who are the stakeholders in the case? What does each stand to gain or lose, depending on your decision?

   b. How does the situation described in the case relate to the four-dimension model shown in Figure 1-4?

   c. What factors might influence your decision as the manager in the case?

SPEAK

4. Have students assemble in groups of three, interview an international student at your institution, and generate a list of English words that have no equivalents in his or her language. Your students should also find out about nonverbal communication that may differ

from that used in American culture. Students can share their findings in a short presentation to the class. **(Obj. 4)**

COLLABORATE

5. Assign students to get into groups and discuss experiences in which "communication failure" was blamed for problems that occurred in their work, academic, or personal interactions. Instruct students to generate three to five additional ways communication can fail and to give suggestions for correcting them. Groups can share their results with the case in a short presentation. **(Obj. 1 & 2)**

DIGGING DEEPER

Ask students to respond to the following discussion questions.

1. What aspect of cultural diversity do you feel will impact you most in your career: international, intercultural, intergenerational, or gender? Explain your answer, including how you plan to deal with the challenge.

2. Lack of Internet access is causing some nations to be classified as information "have nots." What international communication problems could result?

3. Considering the four strategic forces discussed, how is business communication today different from that of 30 years ago? In what ways is it easier? In what ways is it more difficult?

Establishing a Framework for Business Communication

KEY CONCEPTS

Understanding what communication is and how it occurs is central to successful transactions in the workplace. Business communication does not take place in a vacuum, but is impacted by various external forces, including legal and ethical constraints, diversity challenges, changing technology, and team environment.

CHAPTER OUTLINE

KEY TERMS

LEARNING OBJECTIVES

1-1 Define communication and describe the value of communication in business.

1-2 Explain the communication process model and the ultimate objective of the communication process.

1-3 Discuss how information flows in an organization.

1-4 Explain how legal and ethical constraints, diversity challenges, changing technology, and team environment act as contextual forces that influence the process of business communication.

CONCEPTUAL FIGURES AND TABLES

Four Dimensions of Business Behavior

Diversity Challenges

Impacts of Technology

BCOM 8 ONLINE

New BCOM Online includes exposition assessment for students and chapter highlight boxes that supplement text material.

ASSIGNMENTS AND ACTIVITIES

READ

1. Ask students to read the following article about predicted communication trends: Future Work Skills (2011). Available at **http://www.iftf.org/futureworkskills/**. Have students break into small groups and discuss the following:

   a. What communication trends are predicted in the workplace? Are any of these surprising? Why?

   b. Which trends are likely to impact your chosen career field most significantly? In what ways?

POWERPOINT HIGHLIGHTS

LECTURE PRESENTATION

Communication Channels

Contextual Forces Influencing Business Communication

CHAPTER PREP 1

NEW IN BCOM8

Chapter 1

– Added discussion of communication climates and related Figure 1.9

---

c. How do the predicted trends relate to the four strategic forces presented in this chapter?

d. Select one of the communication means discussed in the article. Share your findings in a short class presentation. **(Obj. 1–4)**

WRITE

2. Direct students to take the team player quiz at **www.quintcareers .com /team_player_quiz.html** and to write a brief paper about their team orientation and how being a team player may affect their career success. **(Obj. 4)**

THINK

3. Have students research a scandal in the business or popular press, using campus resources. Assign students to read the article and respond to questions a–c. **(Obj. 4)**

a. Who are the stakeholders in the case? What does each stand to gain or lose, depending on your decision?

b. How does the situation described in the case relate to the four-dimension model shown in Figure 1-4?

c. What factors might influence your decision as the manager in the case?

SPEAK

4. Have students assemble in groups of three, interview an international student at your institution, and generate a list of English words that have no equivalents in his or her language. Your students should also find out about nonverbal communication that may differ

---

from that used in American culture. Students can share their findings in a short presentation to the class. **(Obj. 4)**

COLLABORATE

5. Assign students to get into groups and discuss experiences in which "communication failure" was blamed for problems that occurred in their work, academic, or personal interactions. Instruct students to generate three to five additional ways communication can fail and to give suggestions for correcting them. Groups can share their results with the case in a short presentation. **(Obj. 1 & 2)**

DIGGING DEEPER

Ask students to respond to the following discussion questions.

1. What aspect of cultural diversity do you feel will impact you most in your career: international, intercultural, intergenerational, or gender? Explain your answer, including how you plan to deal with the challenge.

2. Lack of Internet access is causing some nations to be classified as information "have nots." What international communication problems could result?

3. Considering the four strategic forces discussed, how is business communication today different from that of 30 years ago? In what ways is it easier? In what ways is it more difficult?

KEY CONCEPTS

Behavioral theories form the conceptual basis for business communication. Nonverbal communication, listening, and group communication are essential interpersonal skills for success in today's organizations. A team is a group with a clear identity and a high level of member commitment. Groups and teams communicate via both traditional and electronic meetings, which must be managed successfully to ensure that organizational goals are met.

LEARNING OBJECTIVES

2-1 Explain how behavioral theories about human needs, trust and disclosure, and motivation relate to business communication.

2-2 Describe the role of nonverbal messages in communication.

2-3 Identify aspects of effective listening.

2-4 Identify factors affecting group and team communication.

2-5 Discuss aspects of effective meeting management.

CHAPTER OUTLINE

CONCEPTUAL FIGURES AND TABLES

POWERPOINT HIGHLIGHTS

LECTURE PRESENTATION

Nonverbal Communication Conveys Added Meaning

Understanding Nonverbal Messages

Effective Listeners …

Characteristics of Effective Groups

Suggestions for Effective Meetings

BCOM 8 ONLINE

New BCOM Online includes exposition assessment for students and chapter highlight boxes that supplement text material.

ASSIGNMENTS AND ACTIVITIES

READ

1. Have students read the following article, which describes the importance of team development activities: Linley, A. (2008, January 29). Our top 10 team building exercises. *Ezine*. Available at **http://ezinearticles.com/?Our-Top-Ten-Team-Building-Exercises&id=955336**.

Ask students to form small groups in which they should discuss the shift in corporate team building over the past two or more years and the value gained from various types of team-building activities. Students should brainstorm ways that they believe these approaches could be used to boost the effectiveness of teams in an academic setting and the projected results. Afterward, they should share their ideas with the class in a short presentation. **(Obj. 1 & 4)**

2. Have students read the following article, which gives useful suggestions ensuring that nonverbal behavior communicates the intended message: Shephard, L. C. (2007, May 1). Reading body language can offer insight to HR pros. *Employee Benefit News*. Available from Business Source Complete database.

Instruct students to expand the list of recommended and nonverbal messages and the

CHAPTER PREP 2

KEY TERMS

NEW IN BCOM8

Chapter 2

– Enhanced discussion of listening
– Figure 2.2 with a discussion of interpersonal communication style
– Figure 2.3, which provides additional information on virtual team formation
– Enhanced discussion of meeting management

interpretations mentioned in the article. They should then share their list with the class, complete with demonstrations, in an informal presentation. **(Obj. 2)**

WRITE

3. Assign students to keep a journal over a period of two to five days that records events involving metacommunication. Describe how each incident influences the understanding of the verbal message involved. **(Obj. 4)**

THINK

4. Ask students to consider a distance learning conference or course in which they have participated. How were nonverbal communication, listening, and other factors different from what they have experienced in traditional class settings? How do their experiences relate to the conducting of electronic meetings? **(Obj. 2, 3, & 5)**

SPEAK

5. Have students locate one or more articles from a database or the Internet that discuss nonverbal communication in various cultures. Assign them to create a list of examples of body language and behaviors that have different meanings among cultures. Then lead the class in a discussion of how ignorance of these differences might affect interpersonal communication. **(Obj. 2)**

COLLABORATE

6. Assign students to groups of three to five, and have each team visit the website of the Institute for Performance Culture at **http://teaming-up.com**. The groups should take the survey that can be found in the Free Resources menu tab, under "Your team's performance blind spots?" Some of the items may not relate to the short-term project team but will provide students with ideas of issues faced in real-world work teams. After taking the survey, each group should discuss the evaluation report produced from the survey. Have each group send the instructor an email summarizing what the team survey revealed and how they will use the information to improve team performance. **(Obj. 4)**

DIGGING DEEPER

Ask students to respond to the following discussion questions.

1. How can managers use Maslow's need levels, the Johari Window, and the management theories of McGregor and Hersey and Blanchard to improve communication with employees?

2. How do effective conversation and listening impact a business's overall success?

3. Why do some teams never reach the highest stage of team development? What can be done to overcome the obstacles to peak team performance?

KEY CONCEPTS

Effective spoken and written communication involves a process of careful analysis, planning, adaptation, and organization that precedes the actual creation of the message. Chapter 3 focuses on these essential steps of preparation: Step 1: Consider the Applicable Contextual Forces, Step 2: Determine the Purpose and Select an Appropriate Channel and Medium, Step 3: Envision the Audience, Step 4: Adapt the Message to the Audience's Needs and Concerns, and Step 5: Organize the Message.

LEARNING OBJECTIVES

3-1 Consider contextual forces that may affect whether, how, to whom, and when a message is sent.

3-2 Identify the purpose of the message and the appropriate channel and medium.

3-3 Develop clear perceptions of the audience to enhance the impact and persuasiveness of the message, improve goodwill, and establish and maintain the credibility of the communicator.

3-4 Apply tactics for adapting messages to the audience, including those for communicating ethically and responsibly.

3-5 Recognize the importance of organization when planning the first draft.

CHAPTER OUTLINE

CONCEPTUAL FIGURES AND TABLES

POWERPOINT HIGHLIGHTS

LECTURE PRESENTATION

Step 1: Consider the Applicable Contextual Forces

Step 2: Determine the Purpose and Select an Appropriate Channel and Medium

Step 3: Envision the Audience

Step 4: Adapt the Message to the Audience's Needs and Concerns

Step 5: Organize the Message

BCOM 8 ONLINE

New BCOM Online includes exposition assessment for students and chapter highlight boxes that supplement text material.

ASSIGNMENTS AND ACTIVITIES

READ

1. Ask students to conduct an online search to identify strategies companies have adopted to raise their employees' awareness of diversity in the workplace. The students should, in chart form, summarize the indexes they used to locate articles, the companies they read about, and the successful strategies that companies used to promote diversity. **(Obj. 2 & 3)**

CHAPTER PREP 3

KEY TERMS

deductive 48

inductive 48

libel 46

organizational culture 37

outlining 47

slander 46

NEW IN BCOM8

Chapter 3

– New Figure 3.3 on Cultural Dimensions
– New content for "Meeting Diverse Audience Needs"
– Updated examples

WRITE

2. Assign students to conduct research on social networking sites such as Twitter. They can begin with the following article: Graham, J. (2008, July 21). Twitter took off from simple "tweet" success. *USA Today*. Available from LexisNexis Academic database.

   Once students complete their research, assign the following activities:

   a. Compile a list of advantages and disadvantages of this communication medium, including examples of how two businesses have used this social networking site.

   b. Register at Twitter (or use your existing account) and exchange messages with a small group of students in the class. Prepare an engaging flyer describing efficient use of Twitter that will be distributed to staff as an attachment to an email.
   (Obj. 1 & 2)

THINK

3. Ask students to compile a list of the advantages and disadvantages of email, as well as recommended uses and precautions for its use, after reading the following article: Seckler S., & Toomey, R. (2005, December 18). Commentary: E-mail: Career opportunities and pitfalls in workplace communication. *The Daily Record* (Kansas City, MO). Available from LexisNexis Academic database. **(Obj. 1)**

4. Divide the class into a number of small groups in which they should discuss a specific situation in work or educational experience that illustrates the negative effects of an individual who did not consider the impact of his or her message on the receiver.

SPEAK

5. Have students generate a list of phrases and nonverbal expressions peculiar to their culture that groups from another culture might not understand. Ask them to identify any conflict situations that could arise from the misinterpretation of the collectively understood terms. Have them also consider how group norms play a part in the understanding of collective culture. If time allows, assign each student to select one item from his or her list as the topic for a five-minute presentation to the class. **(Obj. 2)**

COLLABORATE

6. Explain to students that however experienced businesses are at writing formal business documents, such as press releases, advertising, and financial reports, creating an online brand or authentic voice through an online blog provides a new challenge for many business

communicators. To learn more, have students locate the following articles:

Five Awesome Benefits of Blogging for Business (June 2014), **http://blog.canva.com/five-benefits-blogging-business/**

15 Excellent Corporate Blogs to Learn From (Aug. 13, 2010), **www.mashable.com/**

How to Create a Business Blogging Plan. (May 2014), **http://www.socialmediaexaminer.com/business-blogging-plan/**

After reading the articles, students should work in small teams to prepare an engaging flier describing efficient blog communication that will be distributed to staff as an attachment to an email message. **(Obj. 1 & 2)**

DIGGING DEEPER

Ask students to respond to the following discussion questions.

1. What is empathy and how does it affect business communication? How are empathy and sympathy different?

2. Explain what is meant by writing to *express* and not to *impress*.

3. How can you ensure quality in a collaboratively written document? Perhaps someone on your team makes unnecessary additions or questionable edits such as revising to make the document "sound more professional" while sacrificing clarity. What would you do?

KEY CONCEPTS

Chapter 4 focuses on preparing a first draft and on revising and proofreading for accuracy and desired impact. Such communication is carefully drafted and proofread for correct sentence structure, emphasis on important ideas, coherent paragraphs, and easy readability. After a review of the writing process in Chapters 3 and 4 (and the Grammar and Usage Appendix), students will prepare letters, memos, and a variety of electronic messages (email, instant and text messages, blogs, and other web communications) and business reports and presentations.

LEARNING OBJECTIVES

4-1 Apply techniques for developing effective sentences and unified and coherent paragraphs.

4-2 Prepare visually appealing documents that grab the audience's attention and increase comprehension.

4-3 Identify factors affecting readability and revise messages to improve readability.

4-4 Revise and proofread a message for content, organization, style, and tone; mechanics; and format and layout.

CHAPTER OUTLINE

CONCEPTUAL FIGURES AND TABLES

POWERPOINT HIGHLIGHTS

LECTURE PRESENTATION

Process for Planning and Preparing Spoken and Written Messages

Step 6: Prepare the First Draft

Factors Affecting Readability

Step 7: Revise for Style and Tone

Proofreading Procedures

BCOM 8 ONLINE

New BCOM Online includes exposition assessment for students and chapter highlight boxes that supplement text material.

ASSIGNMENTS AND ACTIVITIES

READ

1. Have students locate the following article that offers tips on writing powerful business messages: Jolley, D. A. (2009). Clear and compelling messages: The foundation for effective communication. *Public Relations Tactics*. Available from Business Source Complete database. After they've read the article, ask students to respond to the following questions:

   a. What are the "Master P's"?

   b. Explain what the writer means by a "memorable quote." Could you foresee exceptions to the use

CHAPTER PREP 4

KEY TERMS

NEW IN BCOM8

Chapter 4
– Revised examples

of this approach for all business messages? Provide examples.

c. What is the role of rehearsing in ensuring clear and compelling messages? **(Obj. 1–4)**

WRITE

2. Have students conduct an online search related to recent developments in speech (voice-recognition) technology. Students should prepare a brief written report providing information such as (a) current status of speech technology as a viable business application, including (a) challenges that have hampered past developments; (b) examples of leading speech technology applications with related results; and (c) projections for future development of this technology. **(Obj. 1)**

THINK

3. Ask students to complete the business usage quiz at **http://businesswriting.com/tests/commonusage.html**. Then have students assess their understanding of 26 common business writing problems. Once they have reviewed the feedback provided for each question, students should compile a list of areas in which they need improvement. **(Obj. 1–4)**

4. Have students access the Plain Language website at **www.plainlanguage.gov/examples/index.cfm**, view a variety of documents revised for easy reading following Plain English principles, and then select the "Before and After Comparisons" link. Once students have reviewed the examples posted under the "Using Visual Explanations to Convey Information More Clearly" section, they should complete the following activity

a. Have students prepare a brief paper explaining how applying Plain English principles improved the readability of these documents. Ask them to suggest revisions to further improve the documents.

SPEAK

5. Jon Warshawsky, coauthor of *Why Business People Speak Like Idiots*, was interviewed by Martha Barnette, who is host of *A Way with Words*, a program that airs on National Public Radio. In the interview, Jon says that many executives might feel "it's dangerous to have an original thought," which often leads to the use of a series of words they think they have to use to be seen as smart. Martha refers to this tendency as *corporate speak*. Please refer to **http://www.mcmcse.com/articles/corporatespeak.html** to see a glossary of terms and phrases used in corporate America. Assign the following activities:

a. Ask students to conduct an interview in person, by phone, or online with an executive in the student's chosen career field. Students should ask the executive whether corporate speak is a noticeable problem in the work environment, to identify common examples of corporate speak, and for advice related to communicating effectively in their career field.

DIGGING DEEPER

Ask students to respond to the following discussion questions.

1. What habits hinder your success or enjoyment of writing? Identify ways to overcome them.

2. How does online writing challenge a writer's effort to develop a seamless, coherent document?

3. Why do some writers rush through the proofreading phase of message development?

CHAPTER PREP

Communicating Electronically

5

KEY CONCEPTS

A full chapter is devoted to the preparation of electronic communications—not only because of popular use in organizations but also because of their particular characteristics as informal but powerful forms of communication. Emphasis is given to email, instant and text messaging, Web communications, and voice and wireless communication. Legal and ethical issues related to the use of technology are also discussed.

LEARNING OBJECTIVES

5-1 Discuss the effective use of email, instant messaging, and text messaging in business communication.

5-2 Explain principles for writing effectively for the Web.

5-3 Discuss the effective use of voice and wireless technologies in business communication.

5-4 Consider legal and ethical implications associated with the use of communication technology.

CHAPTER OUTLINE

CONCEPTUAL FIGURES AND TABLES

Figure 5.1 Good Example of an Email Message

Figure 5.2 Good Example of an Instant Message

Figure 5.3 Levels of Formality Required by Various Technologies

POWERPOINT HIGHLIGHTS

LECTURE PRESENTATION

Guidelines for Preparing Email Messages

Email Fundamentals

Instant Messaging

Electronic Messages and the Law

Making a Professional Impression with Voice Mail

Cellphone Communication

BCOM 8 ONLINE

New BCOM Online includes exposition assessment for students and chapter highlight boxes that supplement text material.

ASSIGNMENTS AND ACTIVITIES

READ

1. Have students conduct an electronic search to locate an article that deals with the successful use of electronic communication in a company or organization. They should prepare an abstract of the article that includes the following parts: (1) article citation, (2) name of organization/company, (3) brief description of the communication technique and situation, and (4) outcome(s) of the successful communication. As an alternative to locating an article, propose that

CHAPTER PREP 5

KEY TERMS

instant messaging (IM) 77

netiquette 75

social networking sites 76

text messaging 77

weblog (or blog) 81

NEW IN BCOM8

Chapter 5
- Reorganized sections; 5–4 now begins the chapter
- New and revised writing examples throughout

students write about a successful communication situation in the organization/company for which they work. **(Obj. 1–4)**

WRITE

2. For the first part of this activity, have students read the following article, which discusses strategies for making Web information accessible to those who cannot access information in various ways: Tierney J. (2007, April 1). Ignore universal Web design at your peril. *Multichannel Merchant*, p. 8. Available at **http://multichannelmerchant.com/ecommerce/ignore_universal_web/**. After reading the article, ask students to visit a corporate website of their choice. Assign them to evaluate the accessibility of information on that site to viewers who are physically challenged. Students should imagine that they are an employee of that company and send an email to the instructor with recommendations for making the information on the site more accessible. **(Obj. 2)**

THINK

3. Ask students to locate a company example of both a well-written and a poorly written email message. Students should analyze the strengths and weaknesses of each document and be prepared to discuss their analyses in class. **(Obj. 1)**

SPEAK

4. In today's world, initial contact with a person is often via the telephone, so those important first impressions are dependent on practicing proper telephone etiquette. Ask students

to make a list of ideas for increasing levels of telephone courtesy to build image and trust. Have them prepare a brief presentation providing suggestions for placing calls, answering calls, and taking telephone messages. **(Obj. 3)**

COLLABORATE

5. Assign students to small groups and ask them to share incidents of inappropriate cellphone behavior they have experienced in a school, work, or public setting. Ask them to explain how each incident affected the individuals involved. They should also discuss etiquette rules they believe are critical for courteous, productive cellphone use. Are some etiquette rules appropriate for business calls, but not for personal calls, or vice versa? Finally, each group should prepare a brief presentation on the dos and don'ts of cellphone usage. **(Obj. 3)**

DIGGING DEEPER

Ask students to respond to the following discussion questions.

1. Describe three business communication situations in which a technology channel would be inappropriate for exchanging information. Explain your choices.

2. How does a communicator balance the equally important goals of communicating efficiently and building team camaraderie?

3. How is Web communication different from other forms of business communication? How is it similar?

KEY CONCEPTS

Good-news and neutral-news messages are included together in this chapter because the outlines for these communications are both deductive. Strategies and examples are presented for the creation of good-news messages, appreciation messages, routine claims and requests, routine messages about orders and credit, and procedural messages. Strategies for the use of form documents and for adapting messages sent to international audiences are also presented.

LEARNING OBJECTIVES

6-1 Describe the deductive outline for good and neutral news and its adaptations for specific situations and for international audiences.

6-2 Prepare messages that convey good news, including thank-you and appreciation messages.

6-3 Write messages presenting routine claims and requests and favorable responses to them.

6-4 Write messages acknowledging customer orders, providing credit information, and extending credit.

6-5 Prepare procedural messages that ensure clear and consistent application.

CHAPTER OUTLINE

CONCEPTUAL FIGURES AND TABLES

POWERPOINT HIGHLIGHTS

LECTURE PRESENTATION

Advantages of the Deductive Outline

Types of Good-News Messages

Making the Most of Appreciation
  Messages

Extending Credit: Write Deductively

Guidelines for Procedural Messages

CHAPTER PREP 6

NEW IN BCOM8

Chapter 6
– Revised examples

ASSIGNMENTS AND ACTIVITIES

READ

1. Assign students to conduct an electronic search to locate an article that deals with successful communication in a company or organization. Have them prepare an abstract of the article that includes the following parts: (1) article citation, (2) name of organization/company, (3) brief description of communication technique/situation, and (4) outcome(s) of the successful communication. **(Obj. 1–5)**

WRITE

2. Give students the following scenario and have them prepare the exercise listed. As the marketing manager for Pacific Golf Supply Co. (PGS), you have just approved a credit account for Highland Lake Golf Club, a new golf course in northern California. Send Jordan Martin, the golf pro at the club, a letter stating that you have approved a $25,000 initial credit line. PGS offers its customers 2/10, n/30 payment terms and charges interest at an 18% annual rate on overdue accounts. Each quarter, PGS reviews its outstanding accounts and offers an increase in its credit line to any customer with a current account. The letter should confirm that the initial order of golf balls, clubs, and accessories has been shipped via UPS ground, with an expected delivery time of 10 days. Encourage Kevin to use his remaining $12,400 credit line to invest in quality display units. Explain that experience demonstrates that sales increase by 25% when the product is displayed using your display units.

Exercise

Write the credit approval/order acknowledgment letter to Jordan at 2500 Country Club Drive, Klamath, CA 95548-1200. **(Obj. 1 & 4)**

THINK

3. Have students find an example of both a well-written and a poorly written good-news or routine memo, email message, or letter; analyze the strengths and weaknesses of each document; and prepare to discuss them in class. **(Obj. 1–5)**

SPEAK

4. Assign students to obtain a copy of a business letter written by someone from another culture and to identify the major differences between this letter and a traditional US letter. Their report should include information about cultural differences that might be reflected in the message style. Ask students to create a visual of their letter and share their analysis with the class. **(Obj. 1)**

COLLABORATE

5. Many companies naively rely on a file of form letters composed to fit almost any conceivable situation in order to protect against potentially poor writing and to get messages out as quickly as possible. Although these form letters may form the basis for routine communication, they often miss the mark.

Have students read and discuss the form letter that the National Mentoring Partnership sent to organizations who mentor, at **www.theregister.co.uk/2008/03/15/apple_iphone_developer_form_letter/**. After reading the letter, divide the class into groups of three or four. Each group should identify an organization and a form letter that it might send to customers or clients. Using the team's knowledge and Internet resources to research the organization, the group should write the form letter and include an incentive for the reader to follow the letter's request. **(Obj. 1–5)**

DIGGING DEEPER

Ask students to respond to the following discussion questions.

1. What criteria should be used in determining whether a good- or neutral-news message would best be communicated on paper, electronically, or verbally?

2. What considerations should be given to a message recipient's culture when planning a good-news or neutral-news message?

3. What role does goodwill play in composing effective deductive messages?

KEY CONCEPTS

Bad-news messages typically require an inductive strategy. Situations covered include sharing bad news, refusing a request, denying a claim, refusing an order, denying credit, delivering constructive criticism, and communicating negative organizational news. The construction of bad-news messages involves more delicate human relations issues than good news and neutral messages.

LEARNING OBJECTIVES

7-1 Explain the steps in the inductive outline, and understand its use for specific situations.

7-2 Discuss strategies for developing the five components of a bad-news message.

7-3 Prepare messages refusing requests and claims.

7-4 Prepare messages handling problems with customers' orders and denying credit.

7-5 Prepare messages providing constructive criticism and communicating negative organizational news.

7-6 Prepare messages communicating negative organizational news.

7-7 Prepare messages responding to crises.

CHAPTER OUTLINE

CONCEPTUAL FIGURES AND TABLES

MODEL DOCUMENT FIGURES

POWERPOINT HIGHLIGHTS

LECTURE PRESENTATION

Advantages of the Inductive Outline

Techniques for Closing Positively

Sharing Negative Organizational News

CHAPTER PREP 7

ASSIGNMENTS AND ACTIVITIES

READ

1. Have students conduct an electronic search to locate an article that deals with successful negative communication in a company or organization. Assign them to prepare an abstract of the article that includes the following parts: (1) article citation, (2) name of organization/company, (3) brief description of communication technique/situation, and (4) outcome(s) of the successful communication. Students should present their abstract in a memo and give a short presentation in class. **(Obj. 1–5)**

THINK

2. Instruct students to refer to a recent political or business event in which bad news was shared and to prepare a written critique that includes (1) an assessment of the effectiveness of the message and the manner in which it was delivered, (2) an analysis of the results, and (3) a summary of what students learned from their analysis. **(Obj. 1, 2, & 5)**

WRITE

3. Give students the following scenario and have them complete the related exercises. **(Obj. 1, 2, & 4)**

   HGA Electronics is replacing its fleet of 100 automobiles used by its field representatives. As the regional corporate sales representative for the automobile manufacturer, you notice that HGA Electronics has not ordered sound system upgrades to accommodate MP3 players and smartphones that will enhance the employees' driving experience.

Exercises

1. Search the Internet to identify other options that you believe employers should consider for company vehicles.

2. Write an email to Joanny Gayle, the buyer at HGA Electronics, suggesting that she add these options to the automobiles that she's already ordered.

SPEAK

4. Give students the following scenario and have them complete the related exercise. **(Obj. 3)**

   Gulf South Communications Corporation has purchased a significant number of season tickets to the Riverside Community Theatre since its inaugural season in 1979. Gulf South distributes the tickets to special customers, vendors, and employees to foster goodwill and promote the company. Because of the financial crisis in the telecommunications industry, Gulf South's management has regrettably been forced to eliminate all noncritical expenditures. As a supervisor in the human resources department, you have been asked by management to inform Steve Cafferty, the business manager of the theatre, that Gulf South will not purchase season tickets this year. Because the loss of your long-time support will be a hard blow to the theatre, you decide to break the news to Steve over lunch at his favorite restaurant.

Exercise

Ask students to develop a script of the conversation they will have with Steve, conveying the company's disappointing decision.

COLLABORATE

5. Despite the benefits of online brainstorming, waves are being generated as companies and individuals become victims of negative postings. The widespread electronic distribution of unflattering and possibly slanderous comments, often posted anonymously, is a major concern to many. Ask students to learn more about the negative effects of being "zapped in cyberspace" by reading the following articles: **(Obj. 1–5)**

   Valiquette, L. (2006). The dangerous myth of online invulnerability. *Ottawa Business Journal*, 11(23), p. 6. Available from Business Source Complete database.
   McCormick, J. B., & Rudlin, D. A. (2002). Zapped in cyberspace; as use of the Internet increases, so does the risk that people will post defamatory statements on message boards and in chat rooms. Here's how defamation law, which originated in medieval times, can be used in the 21st century. *Trial Magazine*. Available at **http://www.highbeam.com/doc/1G1-84549980.html**.

   After they've completed the reading, assign students to prepare a presentation that (a) summarizes the advantages and disadvantages of online discussions and (b) provides a checklist for writing an effective reply to an online posting calling for constructive criticism of a company or individual.

DIGGING DEEPER

Ask students to respond to the following discussion questions.

1. Explain the rationale and significance of this statement: Saying "no" is not difficult; the challenge is to do so while protecting goodwill.

2. How might standard practices for internal and external communication change when a company is facing uncertain times (e.g., an economic recession, bankruptcy proceedings)?

KEY TERMS

counterproposal 112
Fair Credit Reporting Act 119

NEW IN BCOM8

Chapter 7
– Revised examples throughout
– Added crisis communication discussion and example
– Three new figures

CHAPTER PREP

Delivering Persuasive Messages

8

KEY CONCEPTS

The persuasive principles presented in Chapter 8 have applications in face-to-face business relationships as well as in written messages. The ability to persuade is useful to a variety of life circumstances in which students will need to motivate action, such as selling a product, a service, or their abilities; gaining acceptance of an idea; or collecting money. Various types of persuasive writing situations are covered.

LEARNING OBJECTIVES

8-1 Develop effective outlines and appeals for messages that persuade.

8-2 Write effective sales messages.

8-3 Write effective persuasive requests (making a claim or asking for a favor or information) and persuasion within an organization.

POWERPOINT HIGHLIGHTS

LECTURE PRESENTATION

Persuasive Message: Plan Before You Write

Inductive Outline Used for Persuasive Messages

Apply Sound Writing Principles

Ways to Convince Customers

Motivating Action

BCOM 8 ONLINE

New BCOM Online includes exposition assessment for students and chapter highlight boxes that supplement text material.

CHAPTER PREP 8

ASSIGNMENTS AND ACTIVITIES

READ

1. Assign students to conduct an electronic search to locate an article that deals with the successful use of persuasive communication in a company or organization. Ask them to prepare an abstract of the article that includes the following: (1) article citation, (2) name of the organization or company, (3) a brief description of the communication technique or situation, and (4) the outcome(s) of the successful communication. **(Obj. 1–3)**

WRITE

2. Provide students with the scenario below, and assign the accompanying exercise.

   You recently paid $250 to Keller & Jenkins for adding a provision in your will to establish a scholarship endowment at your alma mater. While eating lunch in a crowded restaurant, Abigail Kemp, a clerk at Keller & Jenkins, stopped by your table to commend you on your planned generosity. Although no harm was intended, you were placed in the uncomfortable position of explaining the clerk's comments to your lunch guests. Keller & Jenkins provides its clients with a bill of rights that clearly states that client information will be kept strictly confidential.

Exercise

Write a letter to H. Daniel Keller, the lawyer who performed the legal work for you. Inform him of the situation and seek a full refund for the legal services.

THINK

3. Wyndham Vacation Resorts is continually expanding the selection of resorts available to its FairShare Plus members. One expansion method is to establish an alliance with an existing, independent resort, enabling FairShare Plus members to use their points to vacation there. Wyndham Vacation Resorts has even extended the "resort" concept by establishing an alliance with Carnival Cruise Lines.

   Ask students to use the Internet or print resources to identify a potential association location. Students should assume that Wyndham Vacation Resorts has just established an alliance with the resort. Ask them to write the script of a voice mail message that Wyndham Vacation Resorts could leave for its FairShare Plus members, which invites them to visit the new location. **(Obj. 1 & 2)**

SPEAK

4. Have students form groups of two; then have each group select a tangible item from a collection that you have prepared beforehand (include items such as a cellphone, stapler, pen, backpack, T-shirt). After each group has selected an item, have students complete the following exercises. **(Obj. 1 & 2)**

Exercise

1. Designate one member of the team as the buyer and one as the seller. The seller will present a compelling sales pitch for the item to the buyer, focusing on an appropriate central appeal and convincing evidence. Following the sales pitch, the buyer will give friendly feedback for making the pitch more convincing. Next, have students reverse roles, but this time have the buyer sell himself/herself as a potential employee of the company that makes the item. Again, students should share friendly feedback for improving the presentation and in addition discuss differences they encountered in selling a product versus promoting themselves. Students should be prepared to share their experiences with the class.

COLLABORATE

5. Divide the class into groups of three to four students; then give them the following scenario and ask them to complete the related exercise. **(Obj. 1 & 3)**

   Despite having written what you consider an outstanding business proposal, you have not been successful in persuading any regional banks to finance the new venture. While attending a fund-raising dinner for a local charity, you had the good fortune to meet B. Stephen Richardson, a successful entrepreneur who you believed to be interested in your idea. He gave you his business card, stating, "Let me know if I can ever lend a helping hand." More important, you interpreted his nonverbal cues as clear interest in financing the project.

Exercises

1. In your groups, identify a retail business you believe would be successful in your community. Assuming you have written a business proposal, write a cover letter to B. Stephen Richardson, seeking his financial support of the project. The letter should include a brief summary of the proposed business and your justification for its potential success.

DIGGING DEEPER

Ask students to respond to the following.

1. Where does one cross the line between being persuasive and being coercive or overbearing?

CHAPTER PREP

9

Understanding the Report Process and Research Methods

KEY CONCEPTS

After having studied informal communications, including letters, memos, and electronic communication, students seem to understand the objective and formal nature of reports simply because of the contrast. Chapter 9 follows a sequence that begins with report characteristics and then covers the four steps in problem solving. Methods of research are presented, with considerable attention given to sampling and designing survey instruments used in normative surveys. Information is included for locating both printed and electronic sources of information.

LEARNING OBJECTIVES

9-1 Identify the characteristics of a report and the various classifications of business reports.

9-2 Apply steps in the problem-solving process and methods for solving a problem.

9-3 Use appropriate printed, electronic, and primary sources of information.

9-4 Demonstrate appropriate methods of collecting, organizing, and referencing information.

9-5 Explain techniques for the logical analysis and interpretation of data.

CHAPTER OUTLINE

CONCEPTUAL FIGURES AND TABLES

MODEL DOCUMENT FIGURES

POWERPOINT HIGHLIGHTS

LECTURE PRESENTATION

Formal–Informal Report Continuum

Types of Sources

Objectives of Secondary Research

Reasons for Accurate, Complete Documentation

Common Errors in Data Interpretation

ASSIGNMENTS AND ACTIVITIES

READ

1. Have students use an online database to locate and read an article related to challenges associated with experimental research. What legal and ethical challenges do researchers face when conducting experimental research with human subjects? How can they be managed? **(Obj. 4)**

CHAPTER PREP 9

KEY TERMS

NEW IN BCOM8

Chapter 9
– Updated hypotheses examples

BCOM 8 ONLINE

New BCOM Online includes exposition assessment for students and chapter highlight boxes that supplement text material.

WRITE

2. A focus group is a form of qualitative research in which a group of people are asked about their attitudes toward a product, service, concept, advertisement, idea, or packaging. Questions are asked in an interactive group setting where participants are free to talk with other group members. For marketers, focus groups are an important tool for acquiring feedback regarding product development, such as product name, features, and packaging. Information from the focus group can provide invaluable insight about the potential market acceptance of a product.

   Ask students to select an existing product that could be improved and to write five questions that could be asked of a focus group to elicit needed responses for the improvement of the product. Next, students should ask several people to serve as a focus group, selecting participants who are knowledgeable about the product you have selected. After conducting the focus group with the questions they have prepared, students are to prepare reports of their findings and present them to the class. **(Obj. 1–5)**

THINK

3. Have students prepare a one-page description of their plans to solve the problem for one of the following research studies. Use the following headings for the problem: (1) Statement of the Problem, (2) Research Method and Sources of Information, (3) Nature of Data to Be Gathered and Analyzed, (4) Hypothesis or Hypotheses to Be Proved or Disproved (if feasible). Here are some ideas to get students started:

   • Investigate a problem occurring on your campus (e.g., declining enrollment in some majors, increasing tuition, delayed financial aid payments, high cost of textbooks, or closed classes) or in a job or student organization position you hold.

   • Superior Foods, Inc., is considering adding organic versions of its frozen vegetables in an effort to establish itself as a leader in this fast-growing market. To increase its available supply of organic produce, management recognizes the need to assist local growers in adopting organic farming methods. The first step in this process is to recruit experts in organic farming to design and implement training.

SPEAK

4. Have students locate an article using either printed or electronic sources that addresses a problem that has occurred for some organization when it failed to realize that research findings that were true for one country or culture were not accurate for another. Ask each student to make a brief presentation to the class about his or her findings. **(Obj. 4 & 5)**

COLLABORATE

5. Organize students into groups of three or four, and have each group design a survey instrument for one of the scenarios in the Think section above. **(Obj. 4)**

DIGGING DEEPER

Ask students to respond to the following question.

1. How has the process of research changed in recent years? How have the changes been both beneficial and detrimental?

KEY CONCEPTS

To ensure that communication is effective, the elements of quantitative data must be classified, summarized, and condensed into a manageable size, then interpreted and written in common language. Readers remember information they gain from pictures or graphs longer than they remember the text they read. In this chapter, you will find tips for creating effective and ethical charts, descriptions of acceptable types of graphics, and methods for integrating graphics into text.

LEARNING OBJECTIVES

10-1 Communicate quantitative information effectively.

10-2 Apply principles of effectiveness and ethical responsibilities in the construction of graphic aids.

10-3 Select and design appropriate and meaningful graphics.

10-4 Integrate graphics within documents.

CHAPTER OUTLINE

KEY TERMS

CONCEPTUAL FIGURES AND TABLES

MODEL DOCUMENT FIGURES

POWERPOINT HIGHLIGHTS

LECTURE PRESENTATION

Communicating Quantitative Information

Using Graphics Effectively and Ethically

BCOM 8 ONLINE

New BCOM Online includes exposition assessment for students and chapter highlight boxes that supplement text material.

ASSIGNMENTS AND ACTIVITIES

READ

1. Business professionals are responsible for communicating quantitative information, but many are unfamiliar with the design practices that make them effective. Have students read the following articles that discuss design strategies for effective charts and graphs:

   Royston, R. A. (2007, November/December). Book review: Show me the numbers: Designing tables and graphs to enlighten. *The Value Examiner*, 11–14. Available from Business Source Complete database.

CHAPTER PREP 10

Jorge Cameos' Charts. (2008, October). 14 Misconceptions about charts and graphs. Available at **http:// www.excelcharts .com/blog/misconceptions -charts-graphs/**.

After reading the articles, ask students to select three design techniques from these readings that were not covered in this chapter. Students should be prepared to share their insights with the class. **(Obj. 1–3)**

WRITE

2. Have each student prepare a table that shows the total revenue Scottsdale Fitness earned from membership fees for a fiscal period. Fees were collected by type of membership: single, $25; double, $40; family, $50; corporate, $22.50; senior, $20. Scottsdale Fitness has 1,439 single memberships, 642 double, 543 family, 3,465 corporate, and 786 senior memberships. **(Obj. 2–4)**

3. Ask each student to prepare a pie chart that shows the percentage of operating income the Walt Disney Company generated in the following

NEW IN BCOM8

Chapter 10

– Revised text examples
– New Figures 10.2 and 10.7

categories during 2010: media networks (56.2%), parks and resorts (22.4%), studio entertainment (12.9%), and consumer products (8.5%). Each student should write a descriptive or talking title that interprets the data depicted in the chart and then write a sentence to introduce the graphic and emphasize its most important idea(s). **(Obj. 2–4)**

THINK

4. Have students clip a pictogram from *USA Today* and share it with groups in class. Ask them to discuss the effectiveness of the symbols used and the ethical presentation of the data. **(Obj. 1–3)**

5. Assign students to create graphics that would most effectively aid a human resources manager in identifying potential areas for employees' personal enrichment. Each student should write a descriptive or a talking title that interprets the data depicted in the table below, and each should also write a sentence that introduces the table and emphasizes its most important ideas. **(Obj. 2–4)**

SPEAK

6. Ask each student to locate a recent annual report of a company of his or her choice. They should prepare short summaries of effective graphic elements they observe; these could include photos, charts, and graphs as well as the use of color, fonts, positioning, and spacing. In their summaries, students should describe how the graphic elements reflect the message each company wishes to convey. In addition, have each student identify a graphic that violates design principles and revise

the graphic incorporating his or her suggestion. In their summaries, have students include the revised graphics and a list of their suggestions for improving it. **(Obj. 2–4)**

COLLABORATE

7. A movie theater must determine the genre of the films to show on each screen during its 7:00, 9:00, and midnight show times. A G-rated animated film historically sells 60% of the available seats at 7:00 and only 25% of the available seats at 9:00. Theaters usually consider 80% capacity to be sold out.

Ask students to play the role of a work group at a software company developing a management information system targeted specifically to movie theaters. Using hypothetical data, they should create the reports the system should generate to enable theaters to manage their screens efficiently. For example, given a limited number of screens, a theater may elect to show an animated film on two screens at 7:00 but switch one of the screens to an action film at 9:00. **(Obj. 1–3)**

DIGGING DEEPER

Ask students to respond to the following discussion questions.

1. A poorly designed electronic slideshow can detract from the effectiveness of your presentation. Compose a list of blunders to avoid in designing effective slideshows.

2. How much is "too much" when considering the use of graphics in a business document?

KEY CONCEPTS

The structure and the preparation of various types of reports are presented including formal reports, letter reports, memorandum reports, and proposals. The problem-solving, research-based orientation of reports is emphasized for each of the various types.

CHAPTER OUTLINE

BCOM 8 ONLINE

New BCOM Online includes exposition assessment for students and chapter highlight boxes that supplement text material.

LEARNING OBJECTIVES

11-1 Identify the parts of a formal report and the contribution each part makes to the report's overall effectiveness.

11-2 Organize report findings.

11-3 Prepare effective formal reports using an acceptable format and writing style.

11-4 Prepare effective short reports in memorandum, email, and letter formats.

11-5 Prepare effective proposals for a variety of purposes.

CONCEPTUAL FIGURES AND TABLES

Figure 11.1 Parts of a Formal Report: Preliminary Parts, Report Text, and Addenda

Figure 11.2 The Number of Addenda Parts Increases as the Length of a Report Increases

Figure 11.3 The Basic Outline Expands into a Contents Page

MODEL DOCUMENT FIGURES

Figure 11.4 Short, Periodic Report in Memorandum Format

Figure 11.5 Audit Report in Short Report Format

Figure 11.6 Short Report in Expanded Letter Format

Figure 11.7 Short Proposal

POWERPOINT HIGHLIGHTS

LECTURE PRESENTATION

Parts of a Formal Report

Developing a Report Outline

Choosing an Effective Writing Style

Structure of a Proposal

Process for Preparing Proposals

ASSIGNMENTS AND ACTIVITIES

READ

1. Have students use the selection of databases to which the campus library subscribes to find three articles on firewalls as a means to secure a company's intranet. Students should mark the main points of each article and create a bibliographic citation for each. **(Obj. 2 & 4)**

WRITE

2. Instruct students to visit a computer lab on your campus. Through observation and interviews, each student should prepare an audit report of the lab's offerings. They should include the following items

in their reports: (1) the types of equipment available (e.g., PCs, Macs, mainframe terminals), (2) the quantity of each type, and (3) the operating systems and applications software available (products, versions). Require students to attach a table that summarizes their analyses and submit their work as letter reports. **(Obj. 4)**

THINK

3. Assign students to attend a professional meeting of a campus or community organization and take notes on the program presented, the issues discussed, and so on. Students should submit a short report summarizing the events of the meeting and include a section that describes the benefits that might be derived from membership in that organization. **(Obj. 2 & 4)**

KEY TERMS

addenda 182

analytical report 182

executive summary 180

external proposal 194

form reports 188

internal proposals 193

justification report 183

preliminary parts 179

short reports 187

solicited proposals 194

unsolicited proposal 194

NEW IN BCOM8

Chapter 11
– Revised Figures 11.4–11.7

SPEAK

4. Ask each student to obtain a copy of a report prepared by an organization and analyze each of the following elements of the report:
   a. Purpose
   b. Intended audience
   c. Degree of formality
   d. Use of graphic support
   e. Parts included (see Figure 11.1)
   f. Referencing method

   Extend the research by having each student make a brief presentation to the class about his or her findings. **(Obj. 1 & 2)**

COLLABORATE

5. Divide the class into small groups of three or four students each. Present the scenario below and then give them the related exercise. **(Obj. 4 & 6)**

   Your team plans to open a business establishment in your city. Do you obtain a franchise or start your own independent restaurant? Select a franchise opportunity and research it. Include in your findings the initial investment cost, start-up expenses, franchise requirements and fees, and success and failure rate.

Exercise

Using the information on team writing, prepare a report that compares the options of franchising versus independent ownership. Make a recommendation as to the more desirable action to take.

6. Provide students with detailed instructions for completing a long or short report or proposal in teams.
   a. Ask students to send you weekly progress reports via email. The reports should contain the following information about each meeting held during the week: date, place, and duration of the meeting, members present; report of work accomplished since last meeting; brief description of work accomplished during the current meeting; and work allocated to be completed before the next meeting.
   b. About midway through the preparation of their reports, ask each student to send you an email message containing an evaluation of each member of his or her group. Students should assign a percentage indicating the contribution each member has made to the group. The total percentages awarded should equal 100%. Each student should also write a brief statement justifying the rating assigned to each member, along with specific, verifiable evidence.
   c. Once the reports are completed, have each student email you a debriefing memo that describes his or her perceptions about the team's performance.

DIGGING DEEPER

Ask students to respond to the following discussion questions.

1. How do diversity considerations impact the choices made in report style and format?

2. Considering general trends in society toward more informality in many situations, how might the style of reports be impacted?

KEY CONCEPTS

In today's environment, delivering a successful business report involves not only making an effective spoken presentation but incorporating appropriate visuals as well. Chapter 12 emphasizes timeless techniques of spoken delivery as well as visual and graphic design principles. Because the ability to give presentations using alternate delivery situations is important in today's workplace, the chapter covers strategies for responding to a culturally diverse audience and effective team and distance presentations.

LEARNING OBJECTIVES

12-1 Plan a business presentation that accomplishes the speaker's goals and meets the audience's needs.

12-2 Organize and develop the three parts of an effective presentation.

12-3 Select, design, and use presentation visuals effectively.

12-4 Deliver speeches with increasing confidence.

12-5 Discuss strategies for presenting in alternate delivery situations such as culturally diverse audiences, teams, and distance presentations.

CHAPTER OUTLINE

CONCEPTUAL FIGURES AND TABLES

Figure 12.1 Process for Planning, Preparing, and Rehearsing Presentations

Figure 12.2 Designing Compelling Slides

POWERPOINT HIGHLIGHTS

LECTURE PRESENTATION

Preparing an Effective Presentation

Organizing Your Presentation

An Effective Introduction …

Crafting an Effective Body

Crafting an Effective Closing

Speaking to Culturally Diverse Audiences

ASSIGNMENTS AND ACTIVITIES

READ

1. Assign students to read the following article, which offers suggestions for developing business presentations for an international audience: St. Amant, K. R. (2005, May). Presentations for international audiences. *Intercom*, 13–15. Available from Business Source Complete database.

   After they've read the article, have students prepare a grid that compares presentation practices appropriate for audiences of the same culture as compared to international audiences. They should research further as necessary to complete the informational comparison. **(Obj. 1–5)**

WRITE

2. Have students read the presentation code of ethics for

CHAPTER PREP 12

professional communicators: International Association of Business Communicators (IABC): IABC code of ethics for professional communicators. Available at **www.iabc.com/about /code.html**.

Ask students to consider the ethical challenges presenters face and the behavioral guideposts presented in these readings. Have them write a presenter's pledge to ensure honesty and integrity in their professional presentations. Students should also be prepared to explain to the rest of the class their rationale for the actions included. **(Obj. 1–5)**

THINK

3. Assign students to evaluate the speaking skill of a well-known television newscaster, political figure, or a recognized speaker on your campus. Propose students locate a webcast or podcast of their most admired CEO or company spokesperson at the company website or at the *Wall Street Journal* online or *BusinessWeek* online. What are the strengths and weaknesses? Students can use the "Check Your Communication" checklist on their Review Cards to direct their attention to the various components of effective speaking. Ask each student to draft a proposal offering with suggestions for improving the person's spoken communication skills, including paying special attention to vocal qualities, audience eye contact, audience rapport, and organization. **(Obj. 1–5)**

SPEAK

4. Provide students with specific instructions for presenting a proposal to management. Each student should select a topic from the following list of suggested proposals topics or use them as a springboard for other in-house presentations. **(Obj. 1–5)**

   a. Proposal to develop a policy that provides up to five paid days annually for volunteer work.

   b. Proposal to implement an in-house recycling program.

   c. Proposal to a local business to enhance the customer experience without increasing costs.

   d. Proposal to the board of directors to forge a strategic alliance with another company. Choose two likely companies and present the concept and the benefits that could be derived for each company.

   e. Proposal to extend your company's domestic retail market into an international market of your choice.

   f. Proposal to management for creating a joint venture with another company to offer a business-to-business (B2B) exchange for online commerce and supply-chain services.

   Choose two feasible companies that could take advantage of the benefits of supply-chain management (e.g., HomebuildersXchange links suppliers, distributors, and trade contractors and builders to bring efficiencies to every participant in the construction process).

COLLABORATE

5. Divide the class into small groups and ask each student to present a one- to two-minute presentation to his or her group explaining a key concept or new development in his or her career field. You should offer a brief period of time for preparation; however, the purpose of the activity is to prepare for impromptu spoken presentations. After all presentations are given, ask each group to briefly discuss the strengths and weaknesses of each presentation and provide each member with a few specific suggestions for improvement in delivering an impromptu presentation. **(Obj. 1, 2, 4, & 5)**

DIGGING DEEPER

Ask students to respond to the following discussion questions.

1. What is the single most important piece of advice you would give for making an effective business presentation?

2. With current advancements in technology, how has the business presenter's role been simplified? How has it become more difficult?

3. How does the advice "communicate a lot, using as little as possible" relate to the design of presentation visuals? Provide an example to support your point.

KEY TERMS

articulation 211

extemporaneous presentation 210

impromptu presentation 210

Internet conferencing 218

manuscript presentation 209

memorized presentation 209

oral briefings 201

phonation 210

pronunciation 212

NEW IN BCOM8

Chapter 12
– Revised text examples
– Revised Figure 12.2

KEY CONCEPTS

Chapter 13 aids students in seeing the need for career planning, gathering information for inclusion on a résumé, and arranging the information on paper or for electronic distribution. Additionally, students learn to use traditional and electronic means to identify career opportunities and prospective employers to whom the résumé might be sent. The chapter discusses principles for writing a persuasive résumé using appropriate organizational patterns, and it explores alternate delivery options for résumés, including text formats, scannable versions, electronic postings, and YouTube video résumés. The chapter also presents techniques for writing effective application messages.

CHAPTER OUTLINE

LEARNING OBJECTIVES

13-1 Prepare for employment by considering relevant information about yourself as it relates to job requirements.

13-2 Identify career opportunities using traditional and electronic methods.

13-3 Prepare an organized, persuasive résumé that is adapted for print and electronic postings.

13-4 Use employment tools other than the résumé that can enhance employability.

13-5 Write an application message that effectively introduces an accompanying print (designed) or electronic résumé.

CONCEPTUAL FIGURES AND TABLES

Figure 13.1 Process of Applying for a Job

Figure 13.2 Ten Most Popular Job
                   Websites

Standard Résumé Parts

Preparing a Print (Designed) Résumé

Preparing a Scannable Résumé

Making a Résumé Search Friendly

Preparing Effective Application
   Messages

MODEL DOCUMENT FIGURES

Figure 13.3 Chronological Résumé

Figure 13.4 References Page

Figure 13.5 Functional Résumé

Figure 13.6 Scannable Résumé

Figure 13.7 Electronic Portfolio Posted
                   to an Applicant's Personal
                   Website

Figure 13.8 Example of an Application
                   Letter

Figure 13.9 Example of Application
                   Message Sent by Email

POWERPOINT HIGHLIGHTS

LECTURE PRESENTATION

Process of Applying for a Job

BCOM 8 ONLINE

New BCOM Online includes exposition assessment for students and chapter highlight boxes that supplement text material.

ASSIGNMENTS AND ACTIVITIES

READ

1. Have students watch the YouTube video that provides résumé tips entitled "How to Write a Great Resume and Cover Letter" created by Harvard Extension. Available at **www.youtube.com/watch?v=PAthQKLhBTs**. Afterward, ask students to prepare their own

CHAPTER PREP 13

KEY TERMS

NEW IN BCOM8

Chapter 13
– Revised Figures 13.3–13.6 and 13.8

résumés for a job posting in their preferred career field. **(Obj. 3 & 4)**

WRITE

2. Tell students to imagine a networking contact asked them to email their résumés for a potential opening in his firm. Each student should prepare an abbreviated version of an application letter and email to you the application message with an inline résumé positioned below the letter. Remind students to use a subject line that stands out in an overloaded mailbox as an expected message from a known person. **(Obj. 5)**

THINK

3. Ask students to exchange résumés with another class member. Each should critique the document's effectiveness using the guidelines and examples provided in the chapter. Ask students to send their critiques to their partners via email. The emails should contain their overall impressions of the résumés and specific suggestions for improving them. **(Obj. 3)**

SPEAK

4. Have each student prepare a class presentation that will showcase his or her employment strengths. They may need to assemble a series of materials in a career portfolio. Suggest they emphasize preparation, experiences, and skills that have prepared them for their ideal career positions. **(Obj. 3–5)**

COLLABORATE

5. Divide the class into small groups, and ask each one to assume the role of a student organization that is initiating an online monthly recruiting newsletter for the organization's website. The vision is to create a fresh, personalized approach to career information specifically related to the needs of the members of the organization and the current competitive market. Each newsletter will include at least one article addressing specific job search skills, highlights of special recruiting events and previews of upcoming events, and an interview providing insights from an employer, returning co-op students, campus recruiters, and so on. Students should prepare a one-page issue of the newsletter, after which they should email a copy to you and distribute it to the rest of the class. **(Obj. 1–5)**

DIGGING DEEPER

Ask students to respond to the following discussion questions.

1. Explain the rise in popularity of the "Career Summary" section on résumés. How else have résumés changed in recent years?

2. Is it possible for a candidate to "try too hard" when preparing a résumé? Explain your answer.

KEY CONCEPTS

Because it is probably the type of interview most familiar and of most concern to students, the employment interview receives primary emphasis in Chapter 14. Additionally, employment interviews are a logical continuation of the résumé and application-message topics in Chapter 13. Students are exposed to traditional interviews, as well as more contemporary techniques including computer-assisted, stress, series, and virtual interviews. The chapter gives special attention to preparation for interviews, interview behavior and feedback techniques (paraphrasing and questioning), and dress and grooming.

LEARNING OBJECTIVES

14-1 Explain the nature of structured, unstructured, stress, group, and virtual interviews.

14-2 Explain the steps in the interview process.

14-3 Prepare effective answers to questions often asked in job interviews, including illegal interview questions.

14-4 Compose effective messages related to employment (including application, follow-up, thank-you, job-acceptance, job-refusal, resignation, and recommendation-request messages).

CHAPTER OUTLINE

CONCEPTUAL FIGURES AND TABLES

MODEL DOCUMENT FIGURES

POWERPOINT HIGHLIGHTS

LECTURE PRESENTATION

Preparing for an Interview

Exchanging Information

Standard Interview Questions

Sample Interviewee Questions

Other Employment Messages

BCOM 8 ONLINE

New BCOM Online includes exposition assessment for students and chapter highlight boxes that supplement text material.

CHAPTER PREP 14

KEY TERMS

NEW IN BCOM8

Chapter 14

– New text box on Personality Testing

– Revised Figures 14.3, 14.4, 14.6, 14.7, and 14.8

ASSIGNMENTS AND ACTIVITIES

READ

1. Each year, many workers from every career field find themselves out of work. The process of becoming re-employed can be stressful, to say the least. Have students locate the following article that presents strategies for surviving a job termination and successfully becoming re-employed: Lim, F. (2007, March 28). What to do after job termination. Ezine Articles. Available at **http://ezinearticles .com/?What-to-Do -After-Job -Termination&id=506760**.

   Using the information in the article, ask students to develop checklists of strategies for locating and landing a desirable job. They should also add additional strategies of their own and submit the checklists to you. **(Obj. 1–4)**

WRITE

2. Ask students to assume that they have each applied for a position earlier in the class term. They should assume one of the following about the position: (a) It is an immediate part-time job; (b) it is a full-time job for next summer; (c) it is a cooperative education assignment or internship; or (d) it is a full-time job that begins immediately after graduation. Students should write follow-up letters to their applications, with special mention of the courses they have completed this term. **(Obj. 4)**

THINK

3. Ask students, either in small groups or individually, to research a company of their choice. As a guide for their research, they should use the chapter information in the "Study the Company" section and the following article: "Why Finding the Right Job Fit Is So Important" posted on America's Job Exchange website. Available at **www .americasjobexchange.com/ career-advice/right-job-fit**. Or group should generate a list of 10 questions to ask an interviewer from the company. The questions should communicate initiative, intelligence, and genuine interest in the company and the job. Have each student or group submit a memo to you that summarizes important facts about the organization and shows the rationale for the selection of the questions. **(Obj. 2 & 3)**

SPEAK

4. Assign each student to interview a manager, preferably in his or her field, who conducts job interviews regularly. Instruct students to discuss techniques that will improve their interviewing techniques.

Students can prepare short presentations to share their findings with the class. Alternatively, you can require them to contribute to a blog related to job interview strategies. **(Obj. 2 & 3)**

COLLABORATE

5. Divide students into small groups and ask each group to organize an employer panel for a class session on successful interviewing. The following elements should be included in the panel activity:

   a. Contact employers who would be willing to serve on the panel and share their views about successful job interviewing.

   b. In advance of the panel presentation, prepare a list of questions to be asked of the panel.

   c. Select a team member to serve as moderator for the panel discussion.

   d. As part of the panel discussion, solicit questions from the class for response by the guest employers. **(Obj. 1–4)**

DIGGING DEEPER

Ask students to respond to the following discussion questions.

1. How can a job applicant maximize the likelihood of accepting the "right" job?

2. Explain why communication skills are the universal job requirement.

3. How relevant are references when information about an applicant can be easily located through an online search of blogs, social networking sites, and news sources?

Decisions about page format impact the effectiveness of the message. Many companies have policies that dictate the page layout, letter and punctuation style, and other formatting issues. In the absence of company policy, make your format choices from among standard acceptable options illustrated on this style card.

• Page Layout, Punctuation, and Letter Style

The default margins set by word-processing software typically reflect the standard line length to increase the efficiency of producing business correspondence. Letters are balanced on the page with approximately equal margins on all sides of the letter, a placement often referred to as fitting the letter into a picture frame. Short letters (one or two paragraphs) are centered on the page; all other letters begin 1 inch from the top of the page. Side margins may be adjusted to improve the appearance of extremely short letters.

Current word-processing software has increased the default line spacing and space between paragraphs for easier on-screen reading. If you prefer the tighter, traditional spacing, simply adjust the line spacing to 1.0. Also, to conserve space but keep the fresh, open look, try reducing the line spacing in the letter address but retaining the wider line and paragraph spacing in the body of the letter. Another new default is a crisp, open font such as Calibri (replacing the common Times New Roman) designed for easy reading on monitors.

NEW DOCUMENT LOOK

July 24, 2016   **Tap Enter 2 times**

Mr. Abbie S. Jackson

1938 South Welch Avenue

Northwood, NE 65432-1938   **Tap Enter 1 time**

Dear Mr. Jackson,   **Tap Enter 1 time**

Your recent article, "Are Appraisers Talking to Themselves?" has drawn many favorable comments from local real estate appraisers.
     Tap Enter 1 time

The Southeast Chapter of the Society of Real Estate Appraisers ...

TRADITIONAL SPACING

July 24, 2016   **Tap Enter 4 times (QS)**

Mr. Abbie S. Jackson

1938 South Welch Avenue

Northwood, NE 65432-1938   **Tap Enter 2 times (DS)**

Dear Mr. Jackson,   **Tap Enter 2 times (DS)**

Your recent article, "Are Appraisers Talking to Themselves?" has drawn many favorable comments from local real estate appraisers.
     Tap Enter 2 times (DS)

The Southeast Chapter of the Society of Real Estate Appraisers ...

STYLE CARD

PUNCTUATION STYLES. Two punctuation styles are customarily used in business letters: mixed and open. Letters using mixed punctuation style have a colon after the salutation and a comma after the complimentary close. Letters using open punctuation style omit a colon after the salutation and a comma after the complimentary close. Mixed punctuation is the traditional style; however, efficiency-conscious companies are increasingly adopting the open style (and other similar format changes), which is easier to remember.

LETTER STYLES. Business letters are typically formatted in either block or modified block letter styles. The Sample Letters card has examples of these two styles:

- **Block.** Companies striving to reduce the cost of producing business documents adopt the easy-to-learn, efficient block format. All lines (including paragraphs) begin at the left margin.
- **Modified Block.** Modified block is the traditional letter format still used in many companies. The dateline, complimentary close, and signature block begin at the horizontal center of the page. Paragraphs may be indented ½ inch if the writer prefers or the company policy requires it. However, the indention creates unnecessary keystrokes that increase the production cost. All other lines begin at the left margin.

• Standard Letter Parts

Professional business letters include seven standard parts. Other parts are optional and may be included when necessary.

1

DATELINE. When the letterhead shows the company name, address, telephone and/or fax number, and logo, the letter begins with the **dateline.** Use the month-day-year format (September 2, 2016) for most documents prepared for US audiences. When preparing government documents or writing to an international audience, use the day-month-year format (2 September 2016). Company policy may require another format.

2

LETTER ADDRESS. The **letter address** includes a personal or professional title (e.g., Mr., Ms., or Dr.), the name of the person and company receiving the letter, and the complete address.

3

SALUTATION. The **salutation** is the greeting that opens a letter. To show courtesy for the receiver, include a personal or professional title (for example, Mr., Ms., Dr., Senator). Refer to the first line of the letter address to determine an appropriate salutation. "Dear Ms. Henson" is an appropriate salutation for a letter addressed to Ms. Donna Henson (first line of letter address). "Ladies and Gentlemen" is an appropriate salutation for a letter addressed to "Wyatt Enterprises," where the company name is keyed as the first line of the letter address.

4

BODY. The **body** contains the message of the letter. Because extra space separates the paragraphs, paragraph indention, which requires extra setup time, is not necessary. However, for organizations that require paragraph indention as company policy, the modified block format with indented paragraphs is the appropriate choice.

5

COMPLIMENTARY CLOSE. The **complimentary close** is a phrase used to close a letter in the same way that you say good-bye at the end of a conversation. To create goodwill, choose a complimentary close that reflects the formality of your relationship with the receiver. Typical examples are "Sincerely," "Regards," "Cordially," and "Respectfully." Using "yours" in the close has fallen out of popularity (as in "Sincerely yours" and "Very truly yours"). "Sincerely" is considered neutral and is thus appropriate in a majority of business situations. "Cordially" can be used for friendly messages, and "Respectfully" is appropriate when you are submitting information for the approval of another.

6

SIGNATURE BLOCK. The *signature block* consists of the writer's name keyed below the complimentary close, allowing space for the writer to sign legibly. A woman may include a courtesy title to indicate her preference (e.g., Miss, Ms., Mrs.), and a woman or man may use a title to distinguish a name used by both men and women (e.g., Shane, Leslie, or Stacy) or initials (E. M. Goodman). A business or professional title may be placed on the same line with the writer's name or directly below it as appropriate to achieve balance.

Title on the Same Line	Title on the Next Line
Ms. Leslie Tatum, President	Ms. E. M. Goodman
Perry Watson, Manager	Assistant Manager
Quality Control Division Head	Richard S. Templeton
	Human Resources Director

7

REFERENCE INITIALS. The *reference initials* consist of the keyboard operator's initials keyed in lowercase below the signature block. The reference initials and the signature block identify the persons involved in preparing a letter in the event of later questions. Reference initials are frequently omitted when a letter is keyed by the writer. However, company policy may require that the initials of all people involved in preparing a letter be placed in the reference initials line to identify accountability in the case of litigation. For example, the following reference initials show the indicated level of responsibility. The reference line might also include department identification or other information as required by the organization.

SF:lm:cd

Person who signed document   Person who wrote document   Person who keyed document

• Optional Letter Parts

DELIVERY AND ADDRESSEE NOTATIONS. A *delivery notation* provides a record of how a letter was sent. Examples include air mail, certified mail, Federal Express, registered mail, and fax transmission. Addressee notations such as "Confidential" or "Personal" give instructions on how a letter should be handled.

ATTENTION LINE. An *attention line* is used for directing correspondence to an individual or department within an organization while still officially addressing the letter to the organization. The attention line directs a letter to a specific person (Attention Ms. Laura Ritter), position within a company (Attention Human Resources Director), or department (Attention Purchasing Department). Current practice is to place the attention line in the letter address on the line directly below the company name and use the same format for the envelope address. The appropriate salutation in a letter with an attention line is "Ladies and Gentlemen."

REFERENCE LINE. A *reference line* (Re: Contract No. 983–9873) directs the receiver to source documents or to files.

SUBJECT LINE. A *subject line* tells the receiver what a letter is about and sets the stage for the receiver to understand the message. For added emphasis, use initial capitals or all capitals, or center the subject line if modified block style is used. Omit the word *subject* because its position above the body clearly identifies its function.

STYLE CARD

SECOND-PAGE HEADING. The second and succeeding pages of multiple-page letters and memorandums are keyed on plain paper of the same quality as the letterhead. Identify the second and succeeding pages with a ***second-page heading*** including the name of the addressee, page number, and the date. Place the heading 1 inch from the top edge of the paper, using either a vertical or horizontal format as illustrated. The horizontal format is more time-consuming to format but looks attractive with the modified block format and may prevent the document from requiring additional pages.

Vertical Format
Communication Systems, Inc.
Page 2
January 19, 2016
Horizontal Format
Communication Systems, Inc.　　　2　　　January 19, 2016

COMPANY NAME IN SIGNATURE BLOCK. Some companies prefer to include the ***company name*** in the signature block, but often it is excluded because it appears in the letterhead. The company name is beneficial when the letter is prepared on plain paper or is more than one page (the second page of the letter is printed on plain paper). Including the company name also may be useful to the writer wishing to emphasize that the document is written on behalf of the company (e.g., a letter establishing an initial customer contact).

ENCLOSURE NOTATION. An ***enclosure notation*** indicates that additional items (brochure, price list, résumé) are included in the same envelope. Key the plural form (Enclosures) if more than one item is enclosed. You may identify the number of enclosures (Enclosures: 3) or the specific item enclosed (Enclosure: Bid Proposal). Avoid abbreviations (Enc.) that may give the impression that your work is hurried and careless and may show disrespect for the recipient. Some companies use the word *Attachment* on memorandums when the accompanying items may be stapled or clipped and not placed in an envelope.

COPY NOTATION. A ***copy notation*** indicates that a courtesy copy of the document was sent to the person(s) listed. Include the person's personal or professional title and full name after keying "c" for *copy* or "cc" for *courtesy copy*. Key the copy notation below the enclosure notation, reference initials, or signature block (depending on the optional letter parts used).

POSTSCRIPT. A ***postscript***, appearing as the last item in a letter, is commonly used to emphasize information. A postscript in a sales letter, for example, is often used to restate the central selling point; for added emphasis, it may be handwritten or printed in a different color. Often handwritten postscripts of a personal nature are added to personalize the printed document. Postscripts should not be used to add information inadvertently omitted from the letter. Because its position clearly labels this paragraph as a postscript, do not begin with "PS."

COMPUTER FILE NOTATION. A ***computer file notation*** provides the path and file name of the letter. Some companies require this documentation on the file copy to facilitate revision. Place the computer file notation a single space below the last keyed line of the letter.

Block Letter Style with Open Punctuation

Pots and Pantries, Inc.
123 Colville Avenue Spokane, WA 89001

Begin 2" from top or 1/2" below letterhead

- **Dateline**

July 24, 2016

- **Letter address**

José Navarro
Purchasing Department
Pots and Pantries, Inc.
123 Colville Avenue
Spokane, WA 89001

- **Salutation**

Dear Mr. Navarro

- **Body**

Welcome to the most unique designs in glassware available in the United States. Our expert buyers tour every region of the world to find the most innovative creations in kitchen and dining glassware.

Because of your current favorable credit rating, we are pleased to provide you with a $15,000 credit line subject to our standard 2/10, n/30 terms. By paying your invoice within 10 days, you can save 2 percent on your glassware purchases.

You can use our convenient online ordering system to search our extensive line of glassware products and to place your orders. If you need additional assistance, please call our 24-hour service line, where you will be assisted by our number one–rated customer service personnel.

The most innovative glassware designs are now available to you and your customers, so please take some time to familiarize yourself with our extensive line.

Sincerely

Luther Crosby

- **Complimentary close**
- **Signature block**

Luther Crosby
Credit Manager

- **Reference initials**

JM:tw

Right-side callouts:

- Begins all lines at left margin; uses easy-to-read jagged right margin and single-spaced, unindented paragraphs.
- Omits colon after salutation and comma after complimentary close in open punctuation style.
- Signs legibly in available space and identifies writer.
- Identifies person keying document.

The document illustrates contemporary spacing with 1.15 spaces between lines. If using traditional single spacing (1.0), tap Enter 2 times to double-space between paragraphs and 4 times to quadruple space after the dateline and the complimentary close.

STYLE CARD

Modified Block Letter Style with Mixed Punctuation

● **Dateline**

Begin 2" from top or 1/2" below letterhead

October 15, 2016   **Tap Enter 2 times**

● Begins dateline, complimentary close, and signature block at horizontal center.

● **Letter address**

Mr. Ricky Sanchez, Manager

Tropical Importers, Inc.

1240 Coastal Lane

Miami, FL 33140-1000   **Tap Enter 1 time**

● **Salutation**

Dear Mr. Sanchez: **Tap Enter 1 time**

● Includes colon after salutation in mixed punctuation style.

It was a pleasure meeting you at the career fair this morning. The opportunities offered in logistics management identifies your company as being a leader in today's international marketplace.   **Tap Enter 1 time**

My experience and knowledge of logistics management enable me to be a valuable asset to your company:

● **Body**

- Realistic international experience with a delivery company

- Demonstrated commitment to developing an appreciation for international cultures and business practices

- Excellent performance evaluations, including special recognition for troubleshooting transportation problems to remote locations

Tap Enter 1 time

● Uses single-spaced, unindented paragraphs, but indentions are acceptable with modified block style.

Please contact me so we can discuss my joining Tropical Importers.

Tap Enter 1 time

Sincerely,   **Tap Enter 2 times**
leaving space for signature

● **Complimentary close**

Brandon Shaw

● Includes comma after complimentary close in mixed punctuation style.

Brandon Shaw

● **Signature block**

● Signs legibly in available space and identifies writer.

● Omits reference initials since writer keyed document

Document illustrates contemporary spacing. If using traditional spacing (1.0) between lines, tap Enter 2 times to double-space between paragraphs and 4 times to quadruple space after the dateline and the complimentary close.

• Envelopes

An envelope should be printed on the same quality and color of paper as the letter and generated using the convenient envelope feature of your word-processing program. Adjust defaults as needed to adhere to the recommendations of the United States Postal Service (USPS). To increase the efficiency of mail handling, use the two-letter abbreviations for states, territories, and Canadian provinces. USPS official state abbreviations are available at **www.USPS.gov**.

Most companies today do not follow the traditional USPS recommendation to key the letter address in all capital letters with no punctuation. The mixed case format matches the format used in the letter address, looks more professional, and allows the writer to generate the envelope automatically without rekeying text. No mail-handling efficiency is lost as today's optical character readers that sort mail can read both upper- and lowercase letters easily. Proper placement of the address on a large and a small envelope generated using an envelope template available with word-processing software is shown here:

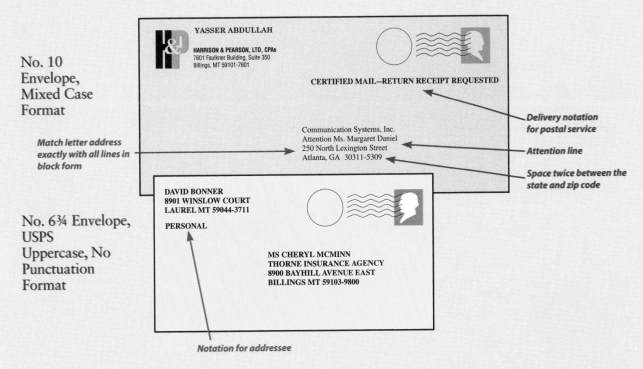

No. 10 Envelope, Mixed Case Format

Match letter address exactly with all lines in block form

YASSER ABDULLAH

HARRISON & PEARSON, LTD, CPAs
7601 Faulkner Building, Suite 350
Billings, MT 59101-7601

CERTIFIED MAIL—RETURN RECEIPT REQUESTED

Delivery notation for postal service

Communication Systems, Inc.
Attention Ms. Margaret Daniel
250 North Lexington Street
Atlanta, GA 30311-5309

Attention line

Space twice between the state and zip code

No. 6¾ Envelope, USPS Uppercase, No Punctuation Format

DAVID BONNER
8901 WINSLOW COURT
LAUREL MT 59044-3711

PERSONAL

MS CHERYL MCMINN
THORNE INSURANCE AGENCY
8900 BAYHILL AVENUE EAST
BILLINGS MT 59103-9800

Notation for addressee

Additionally, to create a highly professional image, business communicators should fold letters to produce the fewest number of creases. Here are the proper procedures for folding letters for large (No. 10) and small (6¾) envelopes:

Folding and Inserting Procedures for Large Envelopes

Step 1
With letter face up, fold slightly less than 1/3 of sheet up toward top.

Step 2
Fold down top of sheet to within 1/2 inch of bottom fold.

Step 3
Insert letter into envelope with last crease toward bottom of envelope.

Folding and Inserting Procedures for Small Envelopes

Step 1
With letter face up, fold bottom up to 1/2 inch from top.

Step 2
Fold right third to left.

Step 3
Fold left third to 1/2 inch from last crease.

Step 4
Insert last creased edge first.

STYLE CARD

• Memorandum Formats

To increase productivity of memorandums (memos), which are internal messages, companies use formats that are easy to input and that save time. Most companies use customized or standard memo templates found in most word-processing software that include the basic headings (TO, FROM, DATE, SUBJECT) to guide the writer in providing the needed transmittal information. Memos may be printed on memo forms, plain paper, or letterhead, depending on the preference of the company. Follow the guidelines for formatting a memo illustrated here.

Begin 2" from top of page or 1/2" below letterhead

TO: Sandra Linkletter, President

FROM: Donald Worthy, Sales Manager

DATE: April 1, 2016

SUBJECT: Monthly Sales Report, Appliance Department

Sales for the month remained at about the same level as previous months this year, at $23,819. Sales figures for the month by item are as follows:

Item	Quantity Sold	Total Revenue from Sales ($)
Washers	12	5,102
Dryers	11	6,543
Stoves	8	4,276
Refrigerators	10	5,899
Dish Washers	6	1,989

Marketing

This month, we continued to publish a circular, which was distributed each Thursday in the *News Tribune*. The cost of that circular is $2,400 per month. That was our only cost of advertising and marketing. Please see the attached file for a complete breakdown of the departments' costs and sales for the month.

Staffing

We continue to employ two full-time salespeople on the floor and two part-time salespersons to cover the weekend shift. Current staffing levels are sufficient for the current sales volume, but if the home construction sector improves, we expect appliance sales to increase along with that improvement. If this occurs, we will need to hire an additional full- and part-time salesperson to return to our 2008 employment numbers.

Future Plans

We are continuing to look at ways that we might increase our marketing presence in the local community. One suggestion offered by Dale, one of our full-time salespersons, is to have a weekly promotion that runs as a banner on our web page. We could institute this opportunity storewide and have banners for the other departments running randomly with ours throughout the week. The cost of such a promotional program storewide needs to be calculated; perhaps this is something that we might put on our agenda for next week's managers' meetings.

Attachment

• Formal Report Format

Page arrangement for reports varies somewhat, depending on the documentation style guide followed or individual company preferences. Take advantage of your software's automatic formatting features for efficient formatting and generating report parts. Portions of a sample report are shown below.

MARGINS. For formal reports, use 1-inch side margins. If the report is to be bound, increase the left margin by a ½ inch. Use a 2-inch top margin for the first page of each report part (table of contents, executive summary) and a 1-inch top margin for all other pages. Leave at least a 1-inch bottom margin on all pages.

SPACING. Although documentation style guides typically specify double-spacing of text, company practice is often to single-space reports. Double-spacing accommodates editorial comments and changes but results in a higher page count. Even if you choose to double-space the body of a report, you may opt to single-space some elements, such as the entries in your references page and information in tables or other graphic components.

HEADINGS. Several levels of headings can be used throughout the report and are typed in different ways to indicate level of importance. Suggested formatting guidelines for a report divided into three levels are illustrated in the document on the next page. Develop fourth- and fifth-level headings simply by using boldface, underline, and varying fonts.

Formal Report Parts

Title page

Transmittal document

Table of contents

Executive summary

First page of report

Page with graphic

References in APA style

Appendix

STYLE CARD

- Capitalizes all letters in report title.

- Places first- and second-level headings at left margin and capitalizes initial letters. Larger font size makes the first level stand out.

- Includes intervening text between first- and second-level headings.

- Uses default indentation and decreased spacing between enumerated and bulleted items.

- Places third-level subheadings at left margin and capitalizes first letter.

Format Pointers

This report document illustrates Word 2013 Style Set with style formats applied for the report title, the three heading levels, and the enumerated list. Creating a custom style set allows businesses to create a report style that is consistent with their company image and brand.

The increased spacing after each paragraph eliminates the need for indented paragraphs.

1" top margin

REPORT TITLE   Title style (26-point Cambria font)

Tap Enter 1 time

xxx xxxxxx xxxxxxx xxxxx xxxxxxxxx xxxx xxxxxx xxxxx xxxxxx xxxxx xx xxxxxx xxxx x xxxxx xxxxx xxxxxxxxx xxx xxxx xxxxx xxxxx.

Tap Enter 1 time

First-Level Heading   Heading 1 (14-point Cambria font)

Tap Enter 1 time

xxx xxxxxx xxxxxxx xxxxx xxxxxxxxx xxxx xxxxxx xxxxx xxxxxx xxxxx xx xxxxxx xxxx x xxxxx xxxxx xxxxxxxxx xxx xxxx xxxxx xxxxx.

Tap Enter 1 time

Second-Level Subheading   Heading 2 (13-point Cambria font)

Tap Enter 1 time

xxx xxxxxx xxxxxxx xxxxx xxxxxxxxx xxxx xxxxxx xxxxx xxxxxx xxxxx xx xxxxxx xxxx x xxxxx xxxxx xxxxxxxxx xxx xxxx xxxxx xxxxx.

Tap Enter 1 time

1. xxxx x xxxxxx xx xxxxxx xxxx xxx xxxxxxxxx xx xxxxx xxxxx xx. xx xxxx xxx.

   Space automatically reduced between enumerated items.

2. xxxx x xxxxxx xx xxxxxx xxxx xxx xxxxxxxxx xx xxxxx xxxxx xx. xx xxxx xxx xxxx xxxx xx x xxxxxxxxx.

Tap Enter 1 time

Second-Level Subheading

Tap Enter 1 time

xxx xxxxxx xxxxxxx xxxxx xxxxxxxxx xxxx xxxxxx xxxxx xxxxxx xxxxx xx xxxxxx xxxx x xxxxx xxxxx xxxxxxxxx xxx xxxx xxxxx xxxxx.

Tap Enter 1 time

Heading 3 (11-point Cambria font)

Third-Level Subheading. xxx xxxxxx xxxxxxx xxxxx xxxxxxxxx xxxx xxxxxx xxxxxx xxxxxxx xxxxx xx xxxxxx xxxx x xxxxx xxxxx xxxxxxxxx xxx xxxx xxxxx xxxxx.

Tap Enter 1 time

Third-Level Subheading. xxx xxxxxx xxxxxxx xxxxx xxxxxxxxx xxxx xxxxxx xxxxx xxxxxxx xxxxx xx xxxxxx xxxx x xxxxx xxxxx xxxxxxxxx xxx xxxx xxxxx xxxxx.

MLA Referencing

A number of widely used reference styles are available for documenting the sources of information used in report writing. Two of the more popular style manuals for business writing are as follows:

Publication Manual of the American Psychological Association, 6th ed., Washington, DC: American Psychological Association, 2001.

Joseph Gibaldi, *MLA Handbook for Writers of Research Papers*, 7th ed., New York: Modern Languages Association of America, 2003. The *MLA Handbook* is designed for high school and undergraduate college students; the *MLA Style Manual and Guide to Scholarly Publishing*, 3rd ed. (2008) is designed for graduate students, scholars, and professional writers.

These sources, commonly referred to as the APA and MLA styles, provide general rules for referencing and give examples of the citation formats for various types of source materials. This style card reflects the rules along with examples for the MLA style. Whenever you are not required to use a particular documentation style, choose a recognized one and follow it consistently. Occasionally, you may need to reference something for which no general example applies. Choose the example that is most like your source, and follow that format. When in doubt, provide more information, not less. Remember that a major purpose for listing references is to enable readers to retrieve and use the sources. This style card illustrates citation formats for some common types of information sources and refers you to various electronic sites that provide further detailed guidelines for preparing electronic citations.

• In-Text Parenthetical Citations

The *MLA Handbook* supports the use of **in-text citations**. Abbreviated information within parentheses in the text directs the reader to a list of sources at the end of a report. The list of sources at the end contains all bibliographic information on each source cited in a report. This list is arranged alphabetically by the author's last name or, if no author is provided, by the first word of the title.

The in-text citations contain minimal information needed to locate the source in the complete list. The *MLA* style includes the author's last name and the page number for both quotes and paraphrases, but not the date of publication. Note the format of the in-text parenthetical citations shown below.

One author not named in the text, direct quotation

"A recent survey … shows that more and more companies plan to publish their annual reports on the Internet" (Prinn 13).

Direct quotation, no page number on source

According to James, "traditional college students have a perspective that is quite different from adult consumers" (par. 2).

Use par. 2 *in place of missing page number only if paragraphs are numbered in original text.*

Multiple authors for sources not named in the text wording

Globalization is becoming a continuous challenge for managers … (Tang and Crofford 29).

"For all its difficulty, teamwork is still essential … " (Nunamaker et al. 163).

For sources by more than three authors, use et al. *after the last name of the first author or include all last names. Do not underline or italicize* et al.

More than one source documenting the same idea

… companies are turning to micromarketing (Heath 48; Roach 54).

More than one source by the same author documenting the same idea

Past research (Taylor, "Performance Appraisal" 6, "Frequent Absenteeism" 89) shows …

Reference to author(s) or date in the text wording

Kent Spalding and Brian Price documented the results …

In 2006, West concluded … (E2).

Omit a page number when citing a one-page article or nonprint source.

STYLE CARD

No author provided

… virtues of teamwork look obvious ("Teams Triumph in Creative Solutions" 61).

Include full title or shortened version of it.

• Works Cited

The ***works cited*** page located at the end of your document contains an alphabetized list of the sources used in preparing a report, with each entry containing publication information necessary for locating the source. A researcher often uses sources that provide information but do not result in citations. If you want to acknowledge that you have consulted these works and provide the reader with a comprehensive reading list, include these sources in the list of works cited and refer to list as Works Consulted. Your company guidelines may specify whether to list works cited only or works consulted. If you receive no definitive guidelines, use your own judgment. If in doubt, include all literature cited and read, and label the page with the appropriate title so that the reader clearly understands the nature of the list.

To aid the reader in locating sources in lengthy bibliographies, you may include several subheadings denoting the types of publications documented, for example, books, articles, unpublished documents and papers, government publications, and nonprint media. Check your reference manual to determine if subheadings are allowed.

• Formats for Print and Recorded References

Reference styles for a variety of print and recorded sources prepared using the MLA style are shown in Figure 3. Note that the following rules apply for MLA works cited.

Indention and spacing	Begin first line of each entry at left margin and indent subsequent lines ½ inch. Although the MLA style manual specifies double-spacing within and between entries, common practice in preparing reports is to single-space each entry and double-space between entries.
Author names	List last name first for first author only. Use "and" before final author's name.
Date	Place date at end of citation for books and after periodical title and volume for articles. Months are abbreviated.
Capitalization	In titles of books, periodicals, and article titles, capitalize all main words.
Italicizing and quotation marks	Italicize titles of books, journals, and periodicals (or underline if directed). Place titles of articles within quotation marks.
Page notations	Omit the use of *p.* or *pp.* on all citations.

MLA (7th Edition Style)

Works Cited

Centento, Antonio. "The Appropriate Men's Attire For Every Occasion." *businessinsider.com*. Business Insider, 12 September 2014. Web. 23 October 2014.

Freeburg, Beth Winfrey, & Arnett, Sally E. "The Impact of Appearance Management Training, Work Status, and Plans After High School on Opinions Regarding Appearance at Work and School." *Journal of Career and Technical Education* 25.2 (2010)

"Proper Business Attire and Etiquette." *tcbsolutions.net*. The Country's Best Solutions, n.d. Web. 23 October 2014.

"Dress Speak for Men." *ECG*. Executive Communications Group, n.d. Web. 23 October 2014.

"Dress Speak for Women." *ECG*. Executive Communications Group, n.d. Web. 23 October 2014.

Goman, Carol Kinsey. "What It Really Means to Dress for Success." *Forbes.com*. Forbes, 20 March 2012. Web. 23 October 2014.

Smith, Jacquelyn. "Here's What 'Business Casual' Really Means." *businessinsider.com*. Business Insider, 19 August 2014. Web. 23 October 2014.

Heathfield, Susan M. "Dress for Work Success: A Business Casual Dress Code." *About.com*. About, n.d. Web. 23 October 2014.

Jensen, Andrew . "How Does Workplace Attire Affect Productivity?" *Andrew Jensen*. Andrew Jensen, 27 June 2014. Web. 23 October 2014.

LeTrent, Sarah. "Decoding the workplace dress code." *CNN.com*. Cable News Network, 15 August 2012. Web. 23 October 2014.